CIVIL DISOBEDIENCE

A Practical Guide

Malcolm Coxall

Edited by Guy Caswell

"I prefer the tumult of liberty to the quiet of servitude"

Cornelio
Books

Published by M.Coxall - Cornelio Books
Copyright 2015 Malcolm Coxall
First Published in United Kingdom and Spain, 2015

Contents

4

Notes on Chapter 4

5. A History of Civil Disobedience

5.1 Social Influences on Human and Civil Rights, Technology and the Hierarchy of Needs

5.2 No Going Back: The Evolution of Human Freedom

5.3 Classical Ideas of Civil Disobedience in Europe

5.4 Christian Influences on Concepts of Civil Disobedience

5.5 Concepts of Civil Disobedience in Mediaeval Europe: Thomas Aquinas

5.6 The Peasants' Revolt

5.7 Religious Civil Disobedience in 16th Century Europe

5.8 The Diggers of 1649 - The First English Hippies

5.9 Pre-Revolutionary Ideas of Civil Responsibility and The Social Contract

5.10 The White Boys

5.11 The Enlightenment (I): The Utilitarians and Atheists

5.12 The Enlightenment (II): Kant and the Right to Revolution and Disobedience

5.13 Modern Times: Utilitarianism and Libertarianism

5.14 Anarchist Challenges to "Political Obligation"

5.15 Civil Disobedience in the Aftermath of the French Revolution

5.16 Shelly: The Masque of Anarchy, the Massacre at Peterloo and Nonviolence

5.17 Slavery in the United States, Thoreau and Civil Disobedience

5.18 The Luddite Rebels and Worker Disobedience

5.19 Daniel O'Connell, the Start of the Land League and the Monster Meetings.

5.20 Land Wars and the First Boycott

5.21 Marx, Engels and the Birth of Modern Socialism

5.22 Trade Unions and Worker Direct Action

5.23 Feminism and the Suffragette Struggle for Women's Equality

5.24 Pacifism and the Anti-War Movement

6. Strategic Considerations in Civil Disobedience and Protest

Preface

What do we think when we hear the words "Civil Disobedience"? Perhaps we imagine a passive, seated Mahatma Gandhi, surrounded by his supporters in an act of nonviolent protest against British rule in India. Or maybe we think of some huge student sit-in against yet another government incursion into civil liberties, or perhaps an unauthorised public demo outside parliament of citizens protesting against an unpopular political decision, such as a war, for example.

All of these are indeed manifestations of civil disobedience in action. But these images of grand, large-scale actions belie the fact that civil disobedience is much more subtle and widespread than we imagine. It is certainly not confined to big collective acts of revolt or protest. In fact, civil disobedience is actually a very pervasive form of human behaviour which is employed whenever a citizen is confronted by acts of unreasonable authority. Indeed, civil disobedience is by far the most popular, most direct and least violent means of bringing about social and political change. There are good reasons for this.

Firstly, civil disobedience is not just confined to use by organised political or social movements such as unions or political groups. It is a strategy that is available to all of us, as individuals, or in groups, acting alone or collaboratively. It is also often considered to carry a high personal risk but, in reality, there are many ways in which acts of civil disobedience can be carried out covertly without personal danger. Thus it is a technique of political change within everyone's grasp.

Secondly, civil disobedience is not just a tool of defiance or rebellion against government. It may be equally useful against any form of authority, including business and even public opinion. Civil disobedience is essentially a refusal to conform. This refusal to conform may be aimed at laws, regulations, orders, social norms, demands or expectations imposed on any individual or group by any other external individual or group. So we can widen our understanding of the targets of civil disobedience to be almost any member of society with authority, ranging from a primary school headmaster, through the board of directors of a multi-national corporation all the way to government or military powers.

Despite common preconceptions, civil disobedience need not involve large-scale actions. Indeed, much of the most effective civil disobedience consists of small-scale acts by relatively powerless individuals. One only needs to look at the history of resistance in Nazi-occupied Europe, or the last years of the occupation of Ireland by the British to see how corrosive many small protest actions can be on an authority's ability to govern. Indeed, Jonathan Swift's allegorical Lilliputian depiction of the power of many small people acting in unison is an old reminder of how a big, powerful institution (or person) can be effectively tied down by the little people when they work together.

Civil disobedience knows no political or social boundaries. It is not confined to our Western "liberal" democracies nor is it only used against obviously oppressive regimes elsewhere in the world. Certainly, the opportunity for large-scale civil disobedience is much greater in the "liberal" environments of Western society, but even in most totalitarian societies every citizen retains some scope for acts of civil disobedience to confound and challenge a repressive regime.

Finally, civil disobedience is not necessarily a passive or defensive act, a simple refusal to conform. Rather, it is very often an active response or revolt against authority. It may even be pro-active rather than reactive and it can employ methods which actively damage the interests of the authority against which it is aimed. It might resort to acts of political violence.

So, why is civil disobedience important, especially in the present day?

Ironically, despite the advances of the last centuries in human freedoms and the spread of humanism as a common moral basis, we can see that the powers of authoritarianism have certainly not waned with improved affluence. If anything, these authoritarian tendencies are more potent today than they have been at any time since the Industrial Revolution.

These days, in the Western world, authority is patently less brutish or obvious than it was in the past; the authoritarians have wrapped themselves in the cloak of public security, political stability and economic well-being to operate under the pseudo-democratic justification of protection of the public for the "greater good". The use of mass communication techniques, political manipulation and fear are the new tools of modern oppression rather than the rifle butt, the dungeon or the torture rack of former days. Nonetheless, we now know that Western governments still engage in kidnap and physical torture against their political adversaries, though normally they do this in some backward foreign land far from the stares of their cosy electorates.

Alongside the modernisation of authoritarian techniques of government there has also been a morphing of authoritarianism in Western society as capital and government merge into a single vector of power. Authorities such as government and big capital now collaborate in powerful coalitions of intertwined political and commercial self-interest. The infamous revolving door system makes a mockery of concepts of political integrity and public service. Our political leaders work for their capitalist clients and these same capitalist clients support our politicians with funds and well-paid jobs. And so, the relationship between business and government has made the two almost indistinguishable in terms of their objectives, which is, in a nutshell, the acquisition of money and power by powerful elites. It is a perfect storm of political, economic and social corruption that permeates virtually all established political parties and all corporate entities. It's not surprising the general public has become cynical about democratic politics.

Despite very real improvements in living conditions in the last century, our world has not become a more just or equitable place. We now inhabit societies in which huge sectors of our population are in some way dispossessed. Many of the world's citizens suffer racial, sexual, religious discrimination, even in the "liberal West". Billions live in or close to poverty whilst our governments wage wars which we, ordinary citizens, mostly don't want. We are taxed both to finance arms we don't need or want and to finance corrupt relationships with big business. We are forced into debt by our governments and corporate interests simply in order to have a roof over our heads. Our governments spy on us, exploit our labour and try to keep us and our children ignorant, whilst perpetuating a system of privilege and exclusion for themselves. The moneyed elites control the majority of land, capital, political power and the best job opportunities whilst the common folk are left with the crumbs, bound to a life of debt and tedium with few opportunities to escape.

Plainly, many of us in the Western world live sufficiently comfortable lives that we are rarely afflicted by many of the more extreme cases of poverty, discrimination or other forms of repression. However, even though we are encouraged to be politically apathetic by the authoritarian elements of our governments, in our more cosseted lives we are gradually becoming more and more controlled. Our freedoms are daily more curtailed as the moderate Western middle-classes are increasingly being confronted by a rising and alarmingly authoritarian political class. Simultaneously, the opportunities to escape poverty are being limited as our modern political and capitalist systems concentrate wealth in the hands of increasingly small numbers of super-rich elite.

Fault lines are clearly visible in the relationship between citizen and government and corporate authority even in our rich Western societies. For example, the rise of middle-class protest movements (such as Occupy) willing to take on big government and big corporations is a completely new phenomenon of the last decade and they have had some spectacular successes. Also, we see the voting patterns in Western democracies reflect a discontented populace with turnout numbers at unprecedented low levels, revealing an overall loss of public confidence in the democratic process and the conventional political parties. Once solid, two party democracies are now splintering as new political parties rise from popular protest movements and start to challenge the old monolithic political parties. Things are changing.

There are several tangible reasons for this increasingly general discontent. The public has become more demanding, and now has much higher expectations of political and government institutions and from public figures than ever before. The public has also become politically cynical and no longer automatically trusts political or business leaders as they would have done in the past. Alongside this public distrust the merging of political and commercial interests (aka corruption) has set off alarm bells. This further exacerbates the lack of trust, as the perception of politicians and businesses as self-serving, manipulative and devious schemers is reinforced in the public psyche. The public no longer see politicians as their protectors against the excesses of capitalism but rather as just another wing of the same dubious profiteering elite.

The concept of "liars, damn liars and politicians" has probably never been more widespread than it is now. Simultaneously the public is crying out for more political transparency and greater personal freedoms, yet our politicians seem hell-bent on removing more and more civil liberties and human rights using all kinds of fear-inducing stratagems against us. And so the public is becoming increasingly frustrated by what it sees as a power-hungry political class that cares nothing for the people. We are fed up of successive governments that will not listen to us, and that are incapable of telling the truth or sticking to a promise and we are angry with institutions that dehumanise and abuse us.

Throughout human history the frustration of a disenfranchised citizenry has always resulted in some kind of public reaction. In the best case this reaction takes the form of civil disobedience. In more extreme cases, it results in bloody revolution or what modern politicians prefer to call "terrorism". The two reactions are simply opposite ends of the same spectrum of the inevitable human reaction to unacceptable oppression. And this brings us directly to the subject of civil disobedience and its role in human society.

Civil disobedience is a potent weapon in the hands of those who understand how to use it. It has brought down governments, even empires, overturned despots, won great civil and human rights victories, driven the engine of human development and brought dignity and power to the peoples of the world. Equally, civil disobedience has been used in pursuit of quite modest ambitions, such as the defence of consumer rights or improving local government services. It is completely multi-purpose. But despite its long and honourable history, the technique of civil disobedience is still under-used and misunderstood by most of us. Many of us live under the illusion that it is "not for the likes of us", or that "we can't change things anyway", or "we are just ordinary people, powerless", or that it is "too dangerous to try". None of these preconceptions are actually true.

Carefully planned acts of civil disobedience can be fantastically direct and effective and can be carried out by virtually any citizen or group with a minimal amount of personal risk or cost and the maximum amount of benefit.

In the face of an increasingly disillusioned electorate, corrupt political classes and failing democratic system, civil disobedience is now beginning to replace the ballot as a means by which the ordinary citizen can bring about direct political change.

This book is going to explain just exactly how civil disobedience works and how it can and should be used to manage, control, frustrate and in some cases overturn authoritarian societies and the political elites that seek to control us.

---oOo---

1. The Relationship between Citizen, Authority and Civil Rebellion

The political systems which determine the relationship between citizen and authority vary enormously. In different times and places citizens have lived in egalitarian tribes, ancient and modern democracies, militaristic or totalitarian regimes, feudal fiefdoms and constitutional monarchies. For all kinds of geographical and economic reasons, the evolution of global political systems of government has shown an amazing diversity since the beginnings of civilisation. Despite this extraordinary variety, the problems of citizens in relation to their governing authorities have shown a remarkable similarity, namely the behaviour of their rulers when they gain power. It is as if the act of becoming part of a political authority transforms our leaders into conniving, brutal, self-serving autocrats, putting them into instant conflict with the interests of their citizens.

Neither the passage of time nor the invention of new political systems seems to have done anything to remedy this. The corrupting influence of power is alive and well and at work in every authority in the world. Within living memory, indeed at this very moment, we have regimes that support some of the very worst abuses of human and civil rights, that wage illegal wars, openly commit crimes against humanity and justify their own war crimes as being in the interests of "national security". We see governments that openly repress their own people with acts of arbitrary coercion and detention. We have so-called "modern" Western democracies that happily tolerate political corruption, discrimination, censorship, kidnap and torture in their own societies and that of any nation they care to declare war on or define as "terrorists". We now have government authorities expressly operating in the interests of large capital and against the interests of their own citizens and doing this for the personal monetary gain of a handful of political cronies.

The relationship between citizen and authority has never been without its problems, but it seems that, rather than evolving more refined and harmonious systems of government, our political evolution has stalled. Our political classes now seem more intent on using their power for personal gain than in protecting the interests of the greater good. The "Climate Change" debate is a case in point. We have wasted almost 20 years because the climate change deniers in the pay of big business have dragged down important CO_2-reduction initiatives. Why? They did this simply to prop up the interests of Big Oil and to line their own pockets.

This is just one of a long litany of appalling examples of the duplicity and lack of integrity of our political and corporate leaders.

Clearly, in some forms of regime, such as a one party state, one may argue that there is little room for choice in political leadership. But the problem is that these conflicts between the interest of the citizens and their governing authority also exist in sophisticated multi-party democracies. It could be argued that in a democracy these conflicts are even worse than those in a totalitarian regime because a citizen's expectations for good governance and consequent disappointment are so much greater in a democracy. In an authoritarian state such as Burma, the citizen doesn't expect much in terms of freedom and it's taken as read that the country's leaders are stealing from the state coffers. In a democracy we expect some honesty and transparency. The problem is that we aren't getting either.

In many modern democratic regimes it seems that the relationship between citizen and authority has degenerated into mutual disrespect and continuous conflict. The authority seems to be in a constant struggle to control and bully the citizen, who reacts by evading, ducking and weaving the authoritarian ambitions of the government. In such an atmosphere there is no place for consensus or productive dialogue, only wasteful political chicanery, mutual suspicion and distrust.

The citizens in both political structures, democratic and authoritarian, feel disenfranchised by lack of trustworthy politicians, a fair political landscape, by a sense that no-one is protecting their interests or cares about the "greater good". This creates a breakdown in the basic social contract between citizen and government, which further alienates both parties. It is at this point of realisation that the citizen becomes inventive and turns to nonviolent civil rebellion as a means of exerting political influence on an authority's decision-making. Civil disobedience and protest are aimed at authority as a counter-measure to state coercion imposed on the citizen by government. In the absence of persuasion or a properly functioning political system for dialogue, it is all that is left to the citizen, bar bloody insurrection.

In the following sections we will examine the basic mechanisms that cause conflicts between a civil population and an authority in terms of human needs and why peaceful civil rebellion is an important part of our relationship with authority.

1.1 Human Needs and our Relationship with Authority

When all human needs are entirely satisfied, it is most unlikely that a civil population will find itself in conflict with its authorities. This utopian scenario would involve our leaders creating a safe, comfortable environment where all are well-fed, respected, educated, creative, economically satisfied, all have friends, family, love and feel entirely content. Sadly, very few authorities in the world are even attempting to build such a world for their subjects and indeed, conflicts between authority and civil populations continue throughout the planet. Many of these disputes can be traced directly to the trampling of human needs by authorities.

1.1.1 What are Human Needs? An Introduction to Maslow

Maslow was a 20th century psychologist who proposed a theory of psychological health based on a hierarchy of human needs. His theory elaborated on the fulfilment of human needs according to priorities, beginning with basics such as food, water, and breathing, rising to needs such as physical security, self-esteem etc. and culminating in what he called "self-actualization". In Maslow's theory, a higher need such as "the respect of others" could not be satisfied unless more fundamental needs lower in the hierarchy had been satisfied first. Thus, a pressing need would have to be gratified before attention could be turned to needs higher in the hierarchy. The following diagram shows the relationship between these needs:

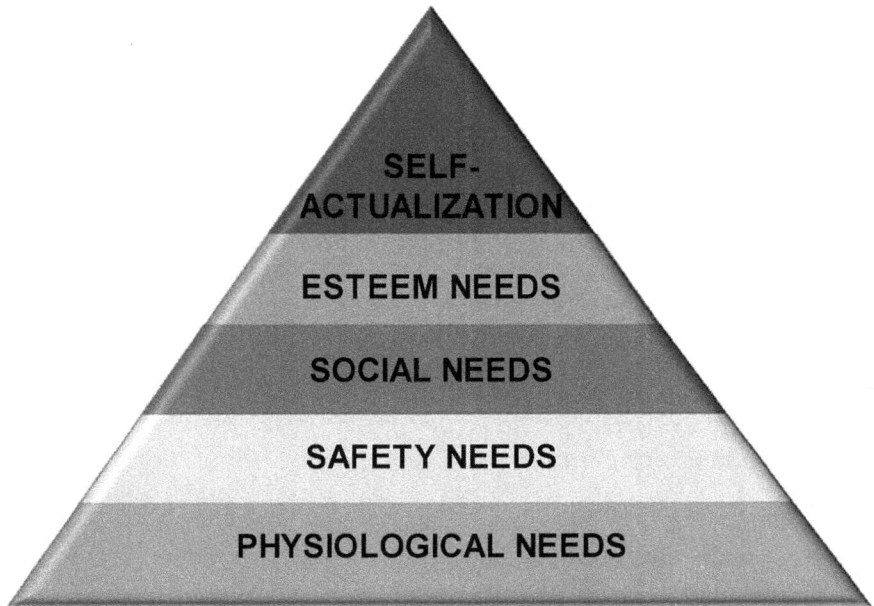

Level 1: Physiological Needs

Physiological needs are those required to sustain life, such as:

- Air
- Water
- Food
- Sleep

According to Maslow, if these fundamental needs are not fulfilled, then one will surely be motivated to satisfy them. Higher aspirations such as social needs and esteem are not recognized until one first satisfies those needs which are most basic to physical existence.

Level 2: Safety Needs

Once physiological needs are met, one's attention turns to safety and security in order to be free from the threat of physical and emotional harm. These two steps are important to the physical survival of the person. Once individuals have basic nutrition, shelter and safety, they can attempt to accomplish more.

Such needs might be fulfilled by:

- Living in a safe, permanent place
- Having medical insurance
- Having job security
- Having economic reserves

Level 3: Social Needs

Once a person has met the lower level physiological and safety needs, higher level motivators are awakened. The first of the higher level needs are social, i.e. related to our needs when interacting with others. This can be referred to as "Love and Belonging". These are psychological needs that become relevant when individuals have taken care of themselves physically and are then ready to share themselves with others, such as with family and friends. These needs may include:

- Friendship
- Belonging to a group
- Giving and receiving love

Level 4: Esteem Needs

After a person feels that they "belong", the urge to attain a degree of importance emerges. The fourth level is achieved when individuals feel comfortable with what they have accomplished. This is the "Esteem" level, the need to be competent and recognized, such as through status and a degree of success. Esteem needs can be categorized as external motivators and internal motivators. Internally motivating esteem needs are those such as self-esteem, accomplishment, and self-respect. External esteem needs are those such as reputation and recognition. Some examples of esteem needs are:

- Recognition by colleagues / friends / family
- Attention, i.e. being considered by others
- Social Status
- Accomplishment
- Self-respect

Level 5: Cognitive needs

Although not in the original theory, Maslow later improved his model to add a layer in between self-actualization and esteem needs: the need for aesthetics and knowledge: and he referred to these as "cognitive needs", where individuals need to intellectually stimulate themselves and explore. This is the "Aesthetic" level, which is the need for harmony, order, knowledge and beauty. These needs include:

- Knowledge
- Meaning
- Aesthetics
- Self-awareness

Level 6: Self-Actualization

Self-actualization is the summit of Maslow's motivation theory. It is about the goal of reaching one's full potential as a person. Unlike lower level needs, this need is never fully satisfied; as one grows psychologically there are always new opportunities to continue to develop. Self-actualized persons have frequent occurrences of "peak experiences", which are moments of profound happiness, understanding and harmony. According to Maslow, only a small percentage of the population reaches this level of self-actualization. Self-actualized people tend to have motivators such as:

- Truth
- Justice
- Wisdom
- Meaning

1.1.2 Human Needs and Civil Rebellion:

The first four (lowest) levels of the hierarchy of human needs are known as "Deficit needs" or D-needs. This means that if you do not sufficiently satisfy any one of those four levels of need, you will feel a compulsion to deal with whatever is stopping you from satisfying these needs, but, once achieved, you feel content. These needs alone are not motivators, but unless fulfilled, the person will feel discontented until they are met. Anything which threatens the fulfilment of these deficit needs may trigger dissatisfaction, fear and/or anger.

Maslow wrote that there are certain conditions that must be fulfilled in order for basic needs to be satisfied. For example, freedom of speech, freedom to express oneself, and freedom to seek new information are a few of the prerequisites. Prevention of any of these freedoms can result in the failure of gratification of one or more basic needs. It is in this respect that we can see the clear relationship between failures to satisfy human needs and the incidence and strength of civil rebellion. One way or another all civil rebellions stem from a society's failure to satisfy one or more human needs in one or more of its citizens. When an authority accidentally or deliberately blocks the satisfaction of human needs, the victim(s) will eventually target the authority and attempt to force an authority to step aside.

Reactions to threats: In general, we can say that the severity of reaction of a civil population to having some of its basic needs thwarted is dependent on how profound the need is. If level 1 needs are unsatisfied, such as when a group is deprived of physiological essentials like food or water, then this may well trigger a powerful and violent reaction, as it did in the case of the French and Russian Revolutions, where millions were on the brink of starvation. Less profound deprivations such as unsatisfied aesthetic needs are unlikely to lead to bloody revolution, but they may over time, for instance, turn into street demonstrations by students denied access to education. We can refer to the threat to satisfy a level 1 need as a "level 1 threat" and so on.

Threats to the future: The relationship between human needs and threats can also be projected into the future. For instance, environmental damage caused by an authority may be seen as endangering the future safety and security of our children or grandchildren, and so climate change, for instance, may be seen as level 1 or level 2 threats. GM technology and intensive agriculture may be perceived as a level 1 threat that will happen at some time in the near future. A planned development damaging the countryside offends our aesthetic senses and may be seen as a future level 6 threat.

Of course, not all threats to human needs are the same because the danger may not last very long and our basic needs may be only partially disrupted. For instance, a development may call for a forest to be felled. However, the forest may be replanted in an act of mitigation. In such a case the threat is later mitigated so that whilst an aesthetic need may be somewhat offended, it will be only temporary and the situation may become tolerable again after some time. Thus, not all threats to our basic needs end in civil rebellion. Most, in fact, do not.

1.2 Why is Peaceful Civil Rebellion Important?

We live in an imperfect world. Even modern democracy, whilst promising citizen participation in government, rarely delivers. Somewhere between the ideals of public consultation and the reality of public administration are insurmountable obstacles which make democracy an imperfect system of political representation. It may be the best we have, but it is riddled with weaknesses. Perhaps the Swiss system of continuous referenda offers a partial solution to some of the problems of citizen participation in government. But aside from the practical design faults in our democratic political systems, we are primarily stuck with the problem that power, however it is obtained, is corrupting. Good, decent politicians become corrupted, even whilst trying to do the "right thing" for their constituents. Meanwhile, bad politicians find democracies fertile places to line their pockets and manipulate the electoral system and their voters for personal gain.

This is the world of the "democratic deficit", where our politicians fall short of fulfilling the basic principles of democracy and integrity and where there exists a state of mutual distrust and antagonism between the ruler and the ruled.

In non-democratic systems the relationship between authority and its subjects is seen in even starker contrast. In authoritarian states, governments don't need to fret over problems such as the "democratic deficit". The distrust and antagonism between an authority and its people and vice-versa are just a part of the status quo. In either case, communication between a civil population and a ruling authority becomes awkward or impossible. In authoritarian states, protest thus becomes the last resort of a frustrated and voiceless population struggling to express its opinions, hoping that someone "out there" will hear and help them.

In democratic societies, the sad reality is that few citizens have much faith in their political classes or their governments. This is where civil rebellion becomes relevant as a means of communication (by megaphone) between the electorate and their elected representatives in government. In many Western democracies, the relationship between government and people is so poor that the only means of interaction between the electorate and their governing authority is either at the ballot box every few years or as a target of protest. Protest has become the nearest thing that modern Western democracy has to real dialogue or staging referenda as in Switzerland.

1.2.1 Civil rights and Responsibilities within a Social Contract

In the traditional model of the social contract the rights and responsibilities of the citizen and a governing authority are defined. The role of the civil population is to be law-abiding and supportive of their government. The role of the civil authority is to make and keep fair laws, using the forces of coercion and state violence in the best interests of the civil population.

Any breach of this symbiosis creates a breach of the social contract. It could be a minor infraction or maybe a major breach of trust between the government and the governed. All systems of government embody some sense of this social contract. Authoritarian governments, feudalism, tribalism and modern democracies all embody a social contract which is, to a greater or lesser degree, acceptable to its subjects. However, sometimes social contracts are seen as unfair or one-sided and they become unacceptable (usually to the civil population). This may trigger acts of civil rebellion.

1.2.2 Authoritarianism, Civil Order and Civil Rebellion

In the authoritarian model, the maintenance of civil order is carried out using a mixture of coercion and violence. Democratic states may also resort to authoritarian measures in a misguided attempt to maintain civil order and control. As we will discuss at a later stage, the usual response to this strategy by a disgruntled population is an escalation of civil rebellion. Thus, acts of civil rebellion may begin with civil disobedience, escalating into acts of direct action, and, at times, it may spill over into violent insurrection in cases where an authority becomes violently repressive.

1.2.3 Civil power: The Balance between Social Contract and Social Conflict

Breaches in the perceived social contract trigger social conflict. Small breaches trigger small conflicts. A large infraction may trigger a revolution. Between minor incidents and full scale insurrection there is the spectrum of civil rebellion.

When a civil population has decided to challenge an authority, there is a clear correlation between the level of authoritarian abuse and the severity of popular rebellion. As governments become more unreasonable, civil rebellion becomes more focused and radical. As governments react more emotionally to popular dissent, protest movements become more organised. As governments become more violent, dissenters become more militant.

Often (unfortunately) governments move seamlessly across the red line which turns a protesting civil population into an angry stone throwing mob, and onwards to a full-scaled armed insurgency. There are so many historical examples, where a simple dispute between a rebelling population and an authority could have been easily resolved, but where the authority, for reasons of "principle", felt the need to "make an example" of the rebels and ended up having a full-scale violent rebellion on their hands.

The balance between social contract and social conflict is a complex one. As we will discuss in the section on "Fight and Flight" and the catastrophic relationship between fear and anger, a population may well tolerate a great deal of social injustice and continuous breaches in the perceived social contract with an authority before it suddenly snaps and decides to attack the authority. At a certain moment a population's fear will suddenly and radically turn to aggression. At this point, it is very difficult for an authority to negotiate a way back to any form of stable social contract, because the population's relationship with authority has ruptured. Things have "gone too far".

The emotional transition through the "cusp" between fear and fight alters everything in the relationship between authority and subject. Oppressed populations cease feeling oppressed, they become combative. They cease to care about another beating, they are "punch drunk". Their fear of their oppressor is gone. They move into a mode which may be a fight to the death.

It's a natural enough reaction. Surely, all of us would fight for our very existence and that of our families if we were so badly oppressed. For instance, if we look at the history of the Palestinian people, in the last 50 years they have been successively ignored, abused, bombed, repressed, ghettoised, vilified as terrorists and exiled in their millions from their own country. Unsurprisingly, the Palestinians have moved beyond fear into aggressive self-defence because they have literally nothing to lose. They stand, as did European Jewry during WWII, on the brink of extinction. All they can do now is fight.

In less dramatic cases of civil conflict, groups of rational, moderate, middle-class citizens may feel obliged to take up more radical, politically-mobilised positions. They may even become disobedient demonstrators when an authority pushes them beyond the cusp of fear of authority into the new region of dissent and protest.

The social landscape which connects authoritarian oppression with bloody revolution is exactly the same one which connects political corruption, discrimination or deceit with popular civil rebellion. The connections resonate, only differentiated by the degree of misuse of power by an authority. Authorities that ignore this fact do so at their own peril.

Notes on Chapter 1

Note 1: Luttwak, Edward (1979). Coup d'état: A Practical Handbook. Cambridge, MA: Harvard University Press. ISBN 978-0-674-17547-1. OCLC 5171600.

---oOo---

2. Concepts of Civil Rebellion

2.1 Towards a Definition of Peaceful Civil Rebellion

There are few people in the world that actively seek violent rebellion if there is a peaceful alternative. It is a sad fact that crass, authoritarian governments that refuse to listen to their people, or vainglorious leaders who run their governments on the basis of some hubristic fantasies are the main incubators of violent rebellion and terrorism. Even US President Obama admitted as much, in 2015, with reference to the relationship between terrorism and misguided US foreign policy in Iraq and elsewhere [Note 36].

Aside from this world of global power games, most people really just want to lead a decent, peaceful life. Unfortunately, this highly reasonable ambition is not always possible, simply because someone else in government or business has a different agenda. That doesn't mean that most people want to launch a full-scale militarised revolution every time they don't get what they want. On the contrary, most people are extremely patient and will try to resolve a problem by themselves, with the minimum of fuss or force. But there are limits to this tolerance and at a certain moment a civil population will begin to rebel against a civil authority or corporate management. It may begin with small acts of civil disobedience by individuals and, if the causes are not addressed by the authority, it will escalate into more open and organised protest. Protesters will then attempt to intervene in the situation themselves and this will be followed by more aggressive direct actions.

A wise authority should see peaceful civil rebellion as a sign that preventive action and negotiations are needed to avoid escalation. It's not the time for sending out the riot police, the knee-jerk reaction by most governments when they feel challenged by a protest group. The same shrewd government should see peaceful protest as a safety valve and an indirect route to dialogue with the civil population. This is because, whilst some protests may be inconvenient or embarrassing to an authority, they are a great deal less inconvenient than a full-scale bloody insurrection. Sadly, the British government wasn't astute enough to see this on the morning of Bloody Sunday, when it opened fire on unarmed protesters and, by doing so, opened a Pandora's Box of 30 years of armed insurrection in Ireland.

So, what defines peaceful civil rebellion? What can it achieve? How successful is it? The political philosopher Gene Sharp defined it as follows: "Nonviolent resistance is a civilian-based method used to wage conflict through social, psychological, economic, and political means without the threat or use of violence. It includes acts of omission, acts of commission, or a combination of both" [Note 38].

Peaceful civil rebellion or nonviolent resistance are interchangeable terms for the same collection of strategies and techniques that can be used by a citizen or a group of citizens to challenge authority. The method of challenge has a wide application. It has been successfully employed in minor disputes between workers and their management, and all the way up to toppling a government or ejecting a colonial power.

The historical record indicates that nonviolent campaigns of civil rebellion have been more successful than armed campaigns in achieving the goals of political struggles, even when used against similar opponents and in the face of repression. Nonviolent campaigns are more likely to win legitimacy, attract widespread domestic and international support, neutralise the opponent's security forces, and compel loyalty shifts among erstwhile opponent supporters than are armed campaigns. Armed campaigns tend to attract the active support of a relatively small number of people. Violent protest also gives authorities a justification for violent counterattacks and violence is much less likely to prompt loyalty shifts and defections by other members of the public or those in an authority.

For all these reasons, peaceful civil rebellion is certainly the preferred route to achieving a successful end to a conflict with an authority. As Sun Tzu, the author of "The Art of War", noted: "A good general doesn't seek victory in battle, he seeks victory without battle". Nonetheless, the hint of a threat of violence may also act as a powerful persuasive catalyst in bringing a reluctant authority to the negotiating table. There are some people who believe that "Political power grows out of the barrel of a gun" and a threat of escalation may persuade authorities of the wisdom of seeking a peaceful solution. Sadly, if they ignore this, violent escalation may well follow.

2.2 Reasons for Civil Rebellion

There are many specific causes for civil rebellion, but they all fall into one of the following categories of maladministration by a government or corporate authority, causing the relationship between government and the governed to descend to the point where civil disobedience becomes inevitable:

• The abuse of power - the deliberate misuse of power by those in authority. The government (or management) becomes excessively oppressive towards its citizens or subordinates, to the point where this behaviour triggers one or more defiant and undesirable responses from the population, sometimes as part of a strategy of self-defence.

• Negligence and hubris of authority - the dereliction of duty by those in authority or a disconnection from reality by an authority. The government's (or management's) lack of concern for its citizens or subordinates inexorably leads to the point where the population feel obliged to use unorthodox means to attract their government's attention to their cause, or to unseat and replace their government or management.

• Lack of ethics in government - the exercise of authority without ethical considerations.

2.2.1 The Abuse of Power

One of the most common motivations for acts of civil disobedience is the "abuse of power" by those who have control over various aspects of our lives.

The abuse of power is the commission of immoral or unlawful acts by those holding political or administrative positions of authority. It ranges from a single abusive act by an individual official or politician right through to the institutionalised misuse of power by an entire government. The abuse may be minor, such as being partial to a particular sector of society, but it can range up to the active genocide of entire groups of citizens. It may be carried out for the personal gain of an individual, or it may be motivated by the political ambitions of a whole political party or other group, such as a religious faction.

Who are the main abusers of power? All organisations, large or small, are capable of impropriety in some way, but generally the sources of serious abuse and oppression come down to three basic groups:

- Governments and their agencies
- Corporate entities
- Organised religions

The phrase "abuse of power" is normally applied to malfeasance in government, but many forms of abuse of power are also found in corporations. Abuse of power may be aimed at a country's own citizens or it may be directed at others abroad. Equally in a corporate context, the abuses may hurt a company's employees or persons entirely outside the company, such as suppliers or customers.

Politically, the abuse of power is a characteristic of fascist political ideology. In this mindset, the powerful achieve their authoritarian goals by whatever means are necessary in order to dominate more vulnerable members of society. It is the logical extension of the concept that those with power are morally entitled to wield that power as they see fit over those that are weak.

The exercise of power and authority in the interests of the greater good is a socialist or communalist principle, and the complete antithesis of right-wing mentality, which exhorts the supremacy of powerful, authoritarian elites as their highest priority. This is not to suggest that abuses of power are confined to extreme right-wing regimes. This is not the case. What can be said is that power is a corrupting tendency of all authorities, whether left or right-wing. The prime difference is that the ethics of left-wing philosophy define the abuse of power as immoral and unjust, whereas right-wing politicians see it as an extension of their traditional "right to rule". To illustrate this, one only needs to look at any Western democracy and make a numeric comparison of corruption cases against right-wing as opposed to left-wing politicians. Right-wing governments and parties dominate the "race" to be the most corrupt and abusive by an order of magnitude over their fairly innocent left-wing colleagues.

The abuse of power and civil rebellion: All authorities are guilty of some abuse of power. The nature of power is that it tends to corrupt those who hold it, and the temptation to use authority as a means to satisfy another agenda can be irresistible. However, not all misuses of power trigger off civil rebellion and some misapplications of power can go largely ignored. There are two factors which determine whether a misappropriation of power will trigger off a civil rebellion:

- Severity of the abuse
- Impact of the abuse: Direct or Indirect

Severity of abuse: Minor acts of abuse of power, such as special privileges for politicians or directors, might be annoying, but rarely trigger off a strong reaction. However, rounding up all the young men in a particular district and keeping them in prison for several years without trial will certainly initiate a strong and probably violent backlash!

Impact of the abuse: Direct or Indirect: Some forms of exploitation of power directly impact and hurt people. Suppressing free speech or acts of collective punishment affront and, in some cases, physically hurt their victims. Political corruption which puts money in a politician's wallet hurts the public, but does so indirectly. The same can be said for illegal surveillance. However shocking it may be, it doesn't have any tangible or immediate effect on its victims.

Modes of abuse: Some important characteristics and styles of abuse are:

• Overt abuse: Blatant abuse of power that is plain for all to see.

• Covert (or controlling) abuse: An abusive authority seeks to maintain control without the abuse being recognised.

• Dehumanisation and objectification: This often involves strategies designed to dehumanise victims by referring to them as if they were objects. The intention is to limit public sympathy or support for the victims.

• Unpredictability: Unforeseeable abuses of power make it difficult for a victim to manage the abuser.

• Abuse of information: The authority's control of information means that it can use information for its own benefit.

• Control by proxy: Abusive authorities often act via a proxy. The police may get the blame for the brutality on the streets, but who actually ordered it?

• Ambient abuse (also known as gas lighting): This is the misuse of power to manipulate and deliberately twist and misrepresent a victim's words or position.

Who are the main targets of the abuse of power? The targets may be single individuals, small groups or entire populations. For example, many corporate entities abuse their customers, or target union members for persecution.

Governments or other authorities often zero in on minorities that they wish to demonise or marginalise, such as immigrants, the unemployed, people of particular sexual orientation, religious minorities, the poor, the disabled, the young, the old, even the fat and the thin! The range of targets for abuse is almost endless, limited only by the perversity of political agendas.

Trigger mechanisms and abuses of power: Mild indirect forms of abuse of power rarely trigger off civil rebellion. Such abuses are usually tolerated in order to keep the peace. Conversely, civil rebellion tends to be triggered by violent, intolerable direct assaults on individuals or groups.

However, once a civil rebellion begins, it becomes somewhat like a snowball rolling down a hill, gathering momentum and size as it hurtles downwards. It tends to "mop up" all other outstanding offences, however minor or indirect, that the authority has been guilty of in the past. In practice, once a victim has passed the point of tolerance, every little abusive act in the past, every unethical decision and every negligent action by an authority is cited as proof of their guilt.

The relationship between abuse and civil rebellion: History teaches us that human reactions to abuse or repression very much conform to the concepts of Newton's Third Law of Dynamics, which states that "For every action there is an equal and opposite reaction". The severity of civil rebellion tends to match the harshness of the abuse of power. This rule works all the way to violent insurgency when a civilian population has to defend itself against a severely abusive authority attempting to destroy it.

For instance, the Christian Reformation began as an act of fairly peaceful civil disobedience. The church's initial abuses of power resulted in certain peaceful protests to the Vatican by priests and monks. Luther began by criticising the relatively recent practice of selling indulgences, started by the Church to fund the construction of the St. Peter's Basilica. He attacked this profitable scam by insisting that the Pope had no authority over purgatory and that the doctrine of the "merits of the saints" had no foundation in the Christian gospel. It was all fairly ideological at this stage. The debate widened, until it touched on many of the doctrines and devotional practices at the heart of the Roman Catholic Church. This caused a violent suppression of the Reformation by the Vatican using all its secular and military influence. This in turn triggered 200 years of religious disobedience, sectarian wars and schisms.

This escalation from Luther's ideological objections to open religious war throughout large parts of the Christian world is a good example of how the abuse of power (in this case by the Catholic Church) triggered a minor rebellion, which the Church itself rapidly converted into a European conflagration. This happened because the authorities of the Roman Catholic Church were incapable of compromise and considered their powers to be unassailable. They continued in the same state of hubris until very recently. Meanwhile, the Reformation liberated much of Europe from the abusive military-ecclesiastical complex called the Roman Catholic Church and the remains of the Holy Roman Empire.

There seems to be a direct relationship between the degree of oppression or abuse and the intensity of the reaction by the victim(s). The centuries of slavery and oppression suffered by the French and Russian peasantry gave rise to a swift, unpredictable, vicious and bloody overthrow of these regimes. For the Romanovs and their aristocracy this meant almost total annihilation. Similarly, for the French aristocracy, a trigger event (a series of famines) set off a popular revolutionary reaction, which led to a period of bloody revenge.

The feudal repressions of France and Russia were long and wicked, and the resulting revolutions exacted a settling of accounts of similarly brutal magnitude, but condensed into a short act of bloody catharsis. It was as if the extent and duration of the oppression and abuse of power generated an equal and opposite reaction in the bloodletting that followed these revolutions.

Though we are not concerned with bloody revolution here, there is a salutary message in these comparisons and that is that whereas moderate abuses of power may generate moderate forms of civil rebellion, extreme forms of abuses of power may well herald the entry of the guillotine or the assassin's pistol. Every leader should realise the limits of their population's patience.

2.2.1.1 Forms of Abuse of Power

There are many forms of abuse of power which we will examine in detail:

- Spying on citizens
- Manipulation of public opinion
- Kidnapping and torture
- Political corruption
- Detention without trial
- Collective punishment
- Rigging of elections
- State terrorism
- Impoverishment
- Denial of justice
- Perversion of justice: Show trials
- State and corporate censorship
- Covering up misdeeds
- Suppression of dissent
- Pork barrel politics
- Misuse of police powers
- Discrimination against certain groups
- Blackmail by authority
- Theft of citizens' property
- Miscellaneous abuses of power

2.2.1.1.1 Spying on Citizens: This is not a new abuse of power; governments have been spying on their populations for centuries. What is alarming about the recent US NSA and UK GCHQ surveillance revelations is that our governments are now spying on us on an industrial scale.

They don't just spy on their military or commercial enemies anymore, they spy on everyone. This is because, in a sense, everyone is potentially the enemy of the authoritarian elites that run these governments. We can see, from the NSA revelations, that the US government to some extent considers its own population as hostile. In a sense it is at war with its own electorate.

Recent disclosures about the scope of government surveillance are staggering. We know now that the UK's Tempora program records huge amounts of private communications, including our emails (as standard), social networking activity, internet histories, and telephone calls. And this is just the tip of one iceberg. Much of this other data is then shared with the US National Security Agency (NSA), which operates its own (previously) clandestine surveillance operations. Similar programs operate in India, China, Russia, and throughout all European countries.

In the Western world, this surveillance culture by our governments has largely come about as a result of the infectious paranoia that originated in various US and UK intelligence organisations during the Cold War. Aware as they are that their organisations are riddled with moles and sleepers, and that the internet just blew the lid off global communications, these intelligence communities are engaged in a rearguard attempt to regain their supremacy over the world of information.

Counter-measures: Despite the shocking extent of these surveillance operations, it is also slightly absurd to watch rather inept government intelligence agencies trying to spy on everyone, whilst simultaneously every Tom, Dick and Harry is installing high quality, publicly available encryption software on their own laptops and mobile phones. Indeed, the public are now using more secure encryption systems than the military-grade encryption systems used by their own governments! Technology has been democratised in the last 20 years and is now largely uncontrollable by governments. The story is still playing out, but technological and strategic responses to government surveillance are rolling out by the day.

Unintended consequences: Nonetheless, this spying is invasive and annoying, as well as being illegal in most countries. Apart from being ineffective, it is also quite counterproductive. Why?

Universal surveillance has the effect of discrediting Western governments in the eyes of allies and citizens. People will trust an authority to the extent that it is seen to behave in their interests. Research suggests that people tolerate limited surveillance, provided they believe their security is being bought with someone else's liberty. When it becomes clear that they are in fact trading their own liberty, the social contract is broken. Violating this trust changes the definition of "them" and "us" in a way that can be dangerous to democratic authority because suddenly, most of the population stands in opposition to their own government [Note 1].

Research has shown that indiscriminate monitoring fosters distrust, mediocrity and conformity. No-one believes any more that government spying has anything to do with security or terrorism. It has become clear that it has a lot to do with state paranoia, a desire to control, and attempts to keep citizens under the thumb of authority, using fear of the terrorist bogeyman as a pretext for more surveillance. We are beginning to understand that governments are actually afraid of their own citizens and are inventing outside threats in an attempt to manipulate their people into allowing more public surveillance.

Not only is this "total surveillance" corrosive to trust in governments, but it has been proven that surveillance also impairs mental health and performance. For more than 15 years we've known that surveillance leads to higher levels of stress, anxiety and fatigue [Note 2]. In the workplace it reduces performance and our sense of personal control. A government that engages in mass surveillance cannot claim to value the wellbeing or productivity of its citizens because, on the contrary, mass surveillance is positively harmful to society in every sense.

Mass surveillance is also counterproductive to innovation and originality. For more than 50 years we've known that surveillance encourages conformity to social norms. In a series of experiments during the 1950s, the psychologist Solomon Asch demonstrated that the tendency to conform is so powerful that individuals will follow the crowd, even when the crowd is obviously wrong [Note 53]. A government that engages in mass surveillance cannot claim to value originality, innovation, or critical thinking.

Finally, mass surveillance actually undermines the role and influence of authority. Security chiefs might believe that mass surveillance gives them greater control over their population, but is this actually true? A recent study found that it is probably not the case. The study showed that if members of a team felt a common social identity with their leader, then surveillance in fact reduced the leader's influence by fostering resentment and distrust. On the other hand, if they saw their leader as belonging to a social outsider group [Note 3], then surveillance actually increased the leader's power [Note 4].

This pattern is interesting because it places politicians and the security services in conflict. For politicians to succeed in a democracy, they must be seen as part of the same "ingroup" as their electorate. We see this most strongly at election time, when politicians go to enormous lengths to emphasise their grassroots connections with their electorate. But by supporting mass surveillance, politicians undermine this relationship and put themselves in an outgroup. The security services, on the other hand, have the opposite motivation. For them, mutual distrust with the public is normal, so it is better to maintain a social distance from the public. In this way they are guaranteed to be perceived as an "outgroup" which, the studies suggests, increases the influence they can wield through surveillance.

This conflict between the motivations of elected representatives and security services can be resolved in two ways. One way is to simply embrace totalitarianism, thus breaking all bonds of a common social identity between politicians and the electorate. In this scenario, democracy is converted into a police state in which all parts of government are seen by the populace as an outgroup. The other alternative is to put an end to mass surveillance, thus obliging the security services to come in line with the parts of government that value liberty.

Political fallout: What seems clear is that no government can continue as both an ingroup and an outgroup - it can't claim to serve the liberty of its citizens while at the same time violating their liberties. If they achieved nothing else, Snowden's NSA revelations throw this contradiction into sharp relief. The sense of betrayal and disenchantment of many Western electorates with their traditional politicians is quite tangible at the present time. The consequence of this distrust is now beginning to manifest itself in quite dramatic political upheavals. We see signs of this, in recent years, as traditional 2 or 3-party democracies are being challenged by radical "upstart" parties that appear apparently from nowhere, but control vast numbers of dissident votes. Whilst the Snowden revelations didn't bring any immediate political revolution, the public mood became noticeably more radical within weeks of publication and threatens to undermine the political status quo.

A footnote to this ongoing story is the announcement that a coalition of nine organisations, including Wikipedia, Human Rights Watch and Amnesty International USA filed a lawsuit in March 2015 against the National Security Agency and the US Department of Justice. This alleged that the NSA's mass surveillance of internet traffic in the United States - often called "Upstream" surveillance - violates the US constitution's first amendment, which protects freedom of speech and association, and the fourth amendment, which protects against unreasonable search and seizure. The group collaborated with the American Civil Liberties Union and this is just one of several lawsuits stemming from the illegal surveillance revelations.

2.2.1.1.2 Manipulation of Public Opinion: Those in power tend to have a monopoly on knowledge to some extent. Not only do they have more guns than we do, they have more knowledge than we do - or so they hope. Controlling the narrative in a dishonest way is a classical abuse of power. As Joseph Goebbels, Reich Minister of Propaganda in Nazi Germany from 1933 to 1945 has been famously quoted as saying: "…If you tell a lie big enough and keep repeating it, people will eventually come to believe it. The lie can be maintained only for such time as the State can shield the people from the political, economic and/or military consequences of the lie. It thus becomes vitally important for the State to use all of its powers to repress dissent, for the truth is the mortal enemy of the lie, and thus by extension, the truth is the greatest enemy of the State".

This philosophy, as horrendously immoral as it sounds, is actually the mantra behind the way that most governments control public access to the truth. Yes, even in our "free", "liberal", "democratic" Western nations, our governments use their power to control the narrative, so that we are presented with a "truth" that fits their political agenda: they do this more or less constantly. This is a clear abuse of power in an attempt to manage public opinion by massaging the truth. During the last Iraq war, George W. Bush banned the screening of any video or photograph of the "coffin planes" returning dead soldiers from Iraq for burial in the USA. The imagery of hundreds of coffins with dead soldiers was considered by the Bush gang to be a threat to their right-wing war-mongering policies, and so these images had to be withheld from public view.

In a similar attempt to alter the story, in early 2015, the British Foreign Minister Philip Hammond blithely announced that it was time for the British public to "move on" from the uproar over mass surveillance by the NSA and GCHQ. Well, he would say something like that, wouldn't he, since his department is one of the parties guilty of this illegal spying. He is clearly attempting to alter the narrative. He obviously would like to "move on". The problem is that the rest of us want to keep protesting about this until we get some action. Sorry, Mr. Hammond, in a proper democracy Snowden would be honoured for bringing the illegal abuses of power to light. Instead, he's hounded by the Western political establishment, including British government ministers and vilified as a threat to national security. It's quite Kafkaesque.

2.2.1.1.3 Kidnapping and Torture: We put these two abuses of power together, since the United States and some of its allies (including the

United Kingdom) seem to have used this particular criminal cocktail in recent years as a means of furthering their own outrageous acts of war and state terror. There have been numerous documented and proven incidents where individuals have been seized by US and other collaborating intelligence services, without any legal warrant, and transported to various "black sites", often in allied countries, and then subjected to the most appalling torture, physical and psychological abuse in order to extract "confessions" or other "intelligence".

Counterproductive: Aside from the illegality under national and international law, the use of kidnap and torture is morally repugnant. But, regardless of our disgust that our governments could engage in such shocking brutality, they also don't seem to have realised how counterproductive such acts of abduction and torture are. It is quite amazing that our governments still do not seem to realise that torture does not provide good information, does not aid a war effort, and, indeed, may well send an intelligence service into a series of pointless wild-goose chases. Holding naked people in stress positions for 36 hours will certainly elicit a response and, indeed, that response may well be perfectly tailored to fit the expectations of the torturer, but is quite likely to be entirely synthetic. The relationship between the outpourings of a torture victim and the truth is quite often non-existent.

The use of torture alters the landscape of a conflict by dragging it into new realms of barbarism. The public exposure to prisoner humiliation and torture by US forces in Abu Ghraib in Iraq altered the nature of the insurgency movement in Iraq. It became much more angry, violent and vicious. It triggered a new level of generalised public outrage and high emotion amongst the Iraqi population. Of course, when one side descends to the use of physical torture against its prisoners, the other side sees this as a signal for all restraint to be removed. The war thus descended into a "no holds barred" conflict, as we are now witnessing with the more recent incarnation of Iraqi insurgent groups, such as ISIS, that are setting new standards of savagery.

Torture is a dark slippery slope that yields nothing but determined new recruits for the enemy, unreliable or useless "information" and the moral degeneration of the perpetrator. The USA can hardly be surprised that it has created so many enemies in the world, given that it has behaved with such inhumanity. The Geneva Conventions were constructed to proscribe the use of torture and to protect the basic rights of prisoners of war. America tore up the Geneva Conventions in the deserts of Iraq. It cannot then be surprised at the consequences for its own soldiers, now and in the foreseeable future.

2.2.1.1.4 Political Corruption: In general, this is an "indirect" form of abuse of power, in the sense that it doesn't directly hurt anyone. For instance, bribery and nepotism simply benefits someone else in a way which is illegal and unethical. Eventually, of course, political corruption does hurt the public, but short term there is no immediate direct pain. In this regard, bribery and nepotism tend to be tolerated until they start to eat into the economy or well-being of a population. This has happened in the case of various kleptocratic regimes around the world, where a politician or party is also accused of abuses that are more direct and threatening, when suddenly their corruption also rises up to the top of the agenda of an angry abused population. For instance, in a 2014 survey of voters in Spain, the issue of political corruption was found to be one of the public's greatest worries. The survey showed that many saw widespread political corruption as a major political issue and a threat to the future of the country.

Almost all politicians and officials trade on their authority for their own benefit. Friends gain favours from officials in positions of authority, politicians make promises to the electorate to gain votes and stay in power. Government jobs are often "designed" to perfectly fit a friend's curriculum vitae; juicy contracts are awarded to friends of officials or politicians, despite apparently transparent tendering processes. It's all old hat now, to the extent that the public is largely inured to political corruption and jobbery. It has become routine. We don't trust politicians anyway, so what's new? However, despite the cynical attitudes of the electorate, it is amazing how, when the public is angered, allegations of corruption suddenly begin to surface and are added to the litany of other accusations against those abusing their authority.

There are too many forms of political corruption to define them all here, but here are some contemporary examples which have infected Western democracies in recent years. They include the so-called "rotating door" system, the "cash for questions" system, the "cash for access" system, selling political contacts aka the "Tony Blair" system, the misuse of government funds for personal profit, the illicit allocation of government contracts to friends' companies, and the system of donations from corporations to political parties in return for political favours.

Rotating door system: The rotating door system is a form of institutionalised political corruption, where politicians move into well-paid roles in industry and commerce as a reward for "services rendered" whilst in public office. It is a form of barely legal bribery that no-one wants to challenge because for many politicians it is an important future source of income. The rotating door works in the opposite direction as well. Party donors from big business are often awarded knighthoods or other honours as payment for their huge cash donations to political parties [Note 43]. Sometimes they are awarded fat contracts as a form of direct appreciation for filling political party coffers. Clearly, having outside business interests is counterproductive to a politician's work on behalf of the public. Not surprisingly, a 2015 study found that British MPs with the highest outside earnings were much less active in Parliament that MPs dedicated to their political careers [Note 10].

Working for big business: Politicians these days are very frequently the mouthpieces of big business lobbyists. They accept money from big business to ask questions or take positions in their parliaments, or to grant access for businessmen to high-ranking politicians and civil servants. In Britain and Spain, such political corruption extends all the way to the royal households of those countries. At the level of members of parliament this form of corruption has become endemic, as recent journalistic "stings" have demonstrated. It appears that when members of parliament are not cheating on their expenses, they are pocketing money to sell their influence to the highest bidder. Politics in many Western democracies has descended into sordid and cynical money-grubbing. The British public has to bear the ignominious sight of ex-prime ministers, such as Tony Blair and others, selling their "services" to tin-pot dictators in Central Asia, whilst taking public money from international organisations for acting in various worthless symbolic roles or picking up huge director's fees from "grateful" client corporations.

A wide-ranging abuse: Such political corruption isn't confined to the Anglo-Saxon world. In Spain, the use of political patronage by members of the Francoist Popular Party to their friends in the property and construction industry has become so institutionalised, that it will take Spain's courts many years to investigate and prosecute those guilty of the acts of multi-billion Euro frauds and corruption which have been going on for decades. At the time of writing there are over 2000 cases of political corruption being investigated by the courts in Spain [Note 42]. Within Europe alone, a similar situation exists in Ireland, Greece, Portugal and Italy, but no country is free from political corruption, apparently even permeating the European Commission, up to the very highest levels. In conservative Luxembourg, the so-called "Lux leaks" scandal of 2014-2015 revealed how Jean-Claude Juncker, ex-prime minister of Luxembourg and now President of the European Commission, gave generous tax breaks to large multinational corporations. This was done apparently in contradiction to both Luxembourg and EU law. No legal action has ever been taken against Juncker and there seems little prospect that there ever will be.

2.2.1.1.5 Detention without Trial: This form of abuse is one which we have singled out for particular attention because it is a vicious, direct affront to the human rights of its victims. What's more, it is an abuse which almost always generates a violent public reaction, sooner or later. Detention without trial is in the same category as kidnap and torture, in the sense that it is obviously an excessively brutal act by a paranoid government that has lost the ability to act in a rational way under the rule of law.

Detention without trial is a statement of defeat in a sense because it demonstrates that a government has lost faith in the legitimacy of its own judicial system. It is an act of desperation, where an authority clutches at any way of attacking its political enemies, however inhumane, in the hope that it will gag its victims. It is an ineffective method of human control in a conflict because it creates powerful antagonisms against authority and acts as a recruiting sergeant for the authority's enemies. Indeed, every victim of detention without trial may recruit thousands of ordinary citizens into the radicalised ranks of "the enemy", simply by being the victim of this obvious barbarity. Not a word needs be spoken. The injustice speaks for itself.

In democracies: One might think that detention without trial is the sole domain of totalitarian regimes, like modern China or Nazi Germany, but, in fact, such detentions were and are in continuous use in many "democratic" countries. The USA has captured or kidnapped thousands, some just children, during its recent Middle Eastern wars. Many still languish in Guantanamo and other secret prisons years after the USA retreated from these countries. In often appalling conditions these prisoners are without the benefit or prospect of any proper legal process. Their status as prisoners of war was stripped by the George W. Bush regime in an act of unprovoked revenge, in direct contravention of the Geneva Conventions [Note 44] [Note 45].

There is evidence to suggest that the USA is still engaged in illegal detentions without trial and perhaps torture. As a consequence, there is also plenty of news to show that America's enemies are escalating their own brutality to match that of the USA. That, of course, is the natural consequence of violent abuses of power. They are infectious.

Colonial history: Britain has a long history of detention without trial and, indeed, collaborated with the USA in its widespread illegal detentions and torture after 9/11. This included sharing the techniques developed by British military intelligence over years of abuse in Britain's old colonies with CIA interrogators [Note 46] [Note 47].

During "the troubles" in Ireland, for instance, in 1971, several hundred suspects were detained without trial or any legal process [Note 5]. In the first wave of raids, called "Operation Demetrius" by the British army, 342 people were arrested. Many reported that they and their families were assaulted, verbally abused and threatened by the soldiers. Many claimed that soldiers smashed their way into houses without warning, firing rubber bullets through doors and windows. Many reported being ill-treated during their detention at holding centres. They complained of being beaten, denied sleep, threatened, starved, and harassed by dogs. Some reported being forced to run a gauntlet of baton-wielding soldiers, having their heads forcefully shaved, being kept naked, burned with cigarettes, having a sack placed over their heads for long periods, having a rope kept around their necks, having the barrel of a gun pressed against their heads, being dragged by the hair, being trailed behind armoured vehicles while barefoot, and being tied to armoured trucks. Some were hooded, beaten and then thrown from a helicopter after being told that they were hundreds of metres in the air, but were actually only a few metres from the ground.

These were not isolated incidents of poor military discipline; these were organised acts of deliberate state terror against unarmed citizens, who had not been charged with any offence. They were deprived of any form of legal representation, legal protection or legal process.

Behaviour like this makes it very hard for any citizen to accept that they must obey the law of the land to the letter, when their governments act in a fashion which is so inhuman and so blatantly criminal, not just once, but continuously over decades or indeed, in the case of Britain, centuries.

The similarities of methods of torture used routinely in Northern Ireland and those techniques used by the US military in Abu Ghraib prison in Iraq begs many questions about the "special relationship" between Britain and the US.

Blowback: Detention without trial tends to generate powerful reactions. This particular British outrage in Northern Ireland ("Operation Demetrius") triggered off an immediate upsurge of violence; the worst seen there since the 1969 riots. The British Army came under sustained attack from Irish nationalist rioters and gunmen, especially in Belfast. Factories were burnt and hundreds of vehicles were hijacked. Loyalist and IRA gunmen were everywhere. Kevin Myers, the journalist, commented about the public reaction to the detentions that "Insanity has seized the city".

People blocked the roads and streets with burning barricades to stop the British Army entering their neighbourhoods. In Derry, barricades were again erected around Free Derry and "for the next 11 months these areas effectively seceded from British control". Between the 9th and 11th August, 1971, 24 people were killed or fatally wounded: 20 civilians (14 Catholics, 6 Protestants), two members of the Provisional IRA (shot dead by the British Army), and two members of the British Army (shot dead by the Provisional IRA).

This particular incident of abuse by the British government also marked a deadly turning point in a conflict which could easily have been resolved peacefully. But that resolution wasn't to be. British government incompetence and hubris caused even more acts of lawless savagery against the Catholic population of Northern Ireland.

The consequence of these actions was a generation of insurrectionary war, with 3500 dead and 45000 injured in a conflict that was ultimately completely unnecessary and which ended in London's loss of control of much of Northern Ireland.

Detention without trial in Northern Ireland was a flashback to the way the British colonial army put down rebellious dominions in Africa and India, with the bullet, the bayonet, the concentration camp and the torturer. It ended in the same way, with Britain being a banished pariah, despised and ignored.

2.2.1.1.6 Collective Punishment: This is a form of retaliation by an authority where a suspected perpetrator's family, friends, acquaintances, neighbours or even an entire ethnic group is targeted for some form of punishment. The group being punished often has no direct association with the perpetrator or any control over their actions.

In times of war, collective punishment has resulted in appalling atrocities. Historically, occupying armies have used collective punishment to retaliate against local populations for acts of sabotage, or sometimes to deter attacks on their forces by resistance movements. This has often resulted in the destruction of entire towns and villages.

Collective punishment is a violation of the laws of war and the Geneva Conventions [Note 6]. Nonetheless, the technique of collective punishment is still in use by many signatories of the Geneva Conventions and some that are not. Israel is currently one of the worst offenders. The current blockade of Gaza has been criticized by the International Committee of the Red Cross, in a United Nations report, and by various other organisations as collective punishment aimed at the Palestinians [Note 7]. The Israeli army's practice of demolishing the houses of Palestinians who are detained has also been considered to be a form of collective punishment, as their families are also punished for the acts of the detainees by losing their homes. This is in direct violation of international law [Note 8].

The comparisons between the Nazi fenced Warsaw ghettos and the Israeli fenced Palestinian ghettos are shockingly unmistakable. But, given that the use of collective punishment was a favourite atrocity of the Nazis against anyone who helped the Jews in Poland during WWII, it beggars belief that Israel now also uses the very same techniques against the Palestinians.

Not to be outdone, of course, when it comes to barbarism and punishment, Britain has a long colonial history of exacting collective punishments. One notorious example was the British use of collective punishment as a widespread and official policy to suppress the Mau Mau uprising in Kenya, in 1952. During this period, between 320,000 and 450,000 civilian "suspects" were moved into British concentration camps. Most of the remainder - more than a million - were held in "enclosed villages". Although some were Mau Mau guerrillas, many were simply peasants, innocent victims of the collective punishment that British colonial authorities imposed on large areas of the country. Thousands suffered beatings and sexual assaults during "screenings", intended to extract information about the Mau Mau. Later, prisoners suffered even worse mistreatment in an attempt to force them to renounce their allegiance to the insurgency and to obey British colonial law. Significant numbers were murdered and even official accounts describe some prisoners being roasted alive [Note 9]. Prisoners were questioned by British forces with the help of "slicing off ears, boring holes in eardrums, flogging until death, and pouring paraffin over suspects, who were then set alight, and burning eardrums with lit cigarettes". Castration by British troops and denying access to medical aid to the detainees were also widespread and common [Note 48] [Note 49].

Of course, collective punishment is not only an outrage against human decency, but it is also usually totally counterproductive. It generally has the effect of galvanising a group into an even more close-knit association. Moderates become radicalised, and nonviolent elements take up arms. In the case of Britain's war crimes in Kenya, the Mau Mau carried out a number of atrocities against British sympathisers and, despite the uprising being suppressed, Kenya finally became independent in 1963 with the Mau Mau celebrated as national heroes. Meanwhile, the British government is still fighting litigation in UK courts by Kenyan victims of British atrocities, despite decades of British attempts to cover up these crimes. Needless to say the appalling behaviour of Britain as it lost its empire has permanently expunged any illusion that the country has any real respect whatsoever for the rule of law. Outside of its own shores, Britain is largely perceived as piratical and is almost universally despised.

In Israel, the constant brutalisation of Palestinians in collective punishments does nothing to bring about either the submission of the Palestinian people or the prospect of peace. The Israelis, of all people, should know that such outrages have just the opposite effect to the one intended. Clearly, Israel's collective memory is somewhat cloudy about its own recent history.

2.2.1.1.7 Rigging of Elections: There are several ways in which elections can be rigged. Electoral areas can be manipulated to favour one party over another (so-called gerrymandering). Votes can be split by an opposition party by the deliberate creation of a new similar party in an election. Votes can be bought by politicians promising favours or money to parts of the electorate. Votes can be deliberately lost by an electoral committee and votes can be forged (ballot stuffing). Selected members of the electorate can be deliberately disenfranchised from voting. Voters can be coerced or frightened into voting in a particular direction. Some of these methods are illegal, all are immoral.

We shouldn't get the idea that election rigging is the sole preserve of dodgy authoritarian states or third world countries. Indeed, rigging of elections happens in western democracies quite often and would happen even more often if politicians could get away with it.

Both the 2000 and 2004 US presidential elections (in which George W. Bush claimed victory) are still mired in controversy. In the 2000 election, Florida was a key state for Bush to win and his brother Jeb Bush, who was governor of Florida, knew that the only way George could win was if tens of thousands of Democratic voters were removed from the electoral rolls. So Jeb ordered his Secretary of State, Katherine Harris, to purge tens of thousands of largely Democrat-leaning African-American voters from the rolls, which she did. In fact, she removed nearly 60,000 voters from the rolls, claiming that these people, who comprised 3% of the entire African-American electorate in Florida, had been convicted of felonies and were thus ineligible to vote. It transpired that this justification was untrue. The list of felons was actually based on a Texas felon list. Nonetheless, when the day of the election arrived, these voters were denied a vote. The Florida vote was close and the Florida Supreme Court ordered a recount of all votes. However, George W. Bush sued in the Supreme Court, in the infamous "Bush versus Gore" case, claiming that if the entire state vote was recounted, it would create "irreparable harm to the complainant (George W. Bush)." And so the conservative Supreme Court gave the presidency to Bush. It wasn't until a year later, in November of 2001, that a group of newspapers completed their total recount of the Florida ballots. The New York Times reported on the vote recount, but the facts buried in the 17th paragraph of the story was the bombshell that, had the U.S. Supreme Court not intervened, and had all the ballots been recounted in Florida as the Florida Supreme Court had ordered, Al Gore would have won the presidential election, no matter how the ballots were recounted. Apparently, the press played down the recount because of the 9/11 incident. The events of that election have moved into history as one of the world's most notorious election frauds and these frauds were indeed committed as a result of a conspiracy led by the two Bush brothers.

Election rigging is another form of indirect abuse of power. Firstly, it's often hard for the public to see if elections really have been rigged and secondly, the effects of a rigged election are slow to be felt. There is no immediate "pain" involved and, indeed, the public may remain completely unaffected by the fraud. However, when it is revealed, it severely undermines trust in the perpetrators and in the political classes in general.

2.2.1.1.8 State terrorism: The word "terrorism" is one of the most misused in the English language. Especially over the last 20 years the word has been devalued by overuse. The word is often dragged out by governments as a means of justifying draconian laws restricting the rights of law-abiding citizens in Western democracies. Governments have created this monster that they call "terrorism" as a means of justifying everything, from forcing people to take off their shoes before boarding a flight to tapping and storing absolutely everyone's emails and telephone call data.

Nonetheless, the word "terror" in this context originated in 18th century France and referred to the use of terror by governments against their own citizens and their political enemies. And it is in this context that we refer to terrorism here, i.e. to state terrorism. Definitions are a little loose, but a starting definition might be "the use of violent actions with the intention of causing terror in civilian populations".

State terror can be directed at civilian populations in any country, including a country's own population. One of the distinguishing features of state terror is that it has no direct military objective. For example, the firebombing of Dresden or Coventry in WWII had no military objectives. These were acts of large-scale destruction of civilian areas, designed to terrorise. In neither case were there strategic objectives to achieve. The same could be said of the bombing of Guernica, or Hiroshima. These were acts targeted at non-combatants, with the sole aim of terrorising large numbers of civilians in so-called "Shock and Awe" tactics.

On a smaller scale, the British army in Northern Ireland in the 1970s employed a strategy of engendering conflict between Catholics and Protestants by means of the so-called "Military Reaction Force" (MRF). This unit operated in small cells, shooting and killing Catholic civilians indiscriminately in order to deflect nationalist Catholic anger away from the British army and towards the Protestant Unionists, who were blamed for the killings. This was clearly a series of acts of state terror. The targets in these killings were innocent civilians with zero military or strategic value or involvement. The British military objective was simply to create a climate of enmity and fear between Catholic and Protestant communities [Note 11].

Other examples of state terror include the French bombing of a Greenpeace ship in New Zeeland in 1985. The ship was part of a wider protest against French nuclear testing in the area and was blown up by a unit of France intelligence services. A Greenpeace photographer died in the attack. The agents responsible pleaded guilty and were sent to prison for 10 years, but were given a secret early release in a deal between France and New Zeeland [Note 12].

Chomsky on state terror: During the 1970's, the USA was intimately involved in covert activities in many Latin American countries. Led by the CIA, the US collaborated in numerous acts of state terror. All Latin American countries that historically employed death squads were also US client states and this was no coincidence.

Noam Chomsky and Edward S. Herman, in a series of works on the subject of US State terrorism, claimed that 74% of regimes that used torture on a routine basis were U.S. client states, receiving military and other economic support from the US in order to retain power. They concluded that the global rise in state terror was largely the result of US foreign policy. In Latin America, right-wing regimes, such as those in Chile, El Salvador and Guatemala, killed hundreds of thousands of their own civilians using death squads, supported by US funding, training and equipment.

Chomsky concluded that all the major powers backed state terrorism in client states. At the top was the USA but others, notably the United Kingdom and France were and are not far behind the US in their use of state terror. Both these latter have provided financial, military and diplomatic support to Third World regimes, often kept in power through violence against their own people. These Western governments acted together with multinational arms and security corporations [Note 13] to support some of the world's most brutal terrorist regimes.

Naturally, US law refuses to acknowledge the existence of "state terror". Terror is defined by US law as being an act carried out "by *sub national* groups or clandestine agents usually intended to influence an audience" [Note 14]. But then, of course, a concept of "state terrorism" could prove quite uncomfortable for the USA, given that they are close to the top of the list of global state terrorist nations.

State terrorism involves violent and direct attacks on civilians by an authority. Whether the authority is our own government or whether our own government is being financed by an outside government, it makes no difference to the victim. State terrorism is morally outrageous because it offends the social contract between those that should defend the civil population (our governments) and their actions in terrorising their own people.

Blowback: The blowback from state terrorism can be extremely violent and as a strategy for long-term political control of a population it is totally ineffective. At some point after an act of state terror there will be revenge. In the meantime, acts of state terror against a large number of people serve only to unite them in a common hatred and disgust for the terrorist regime. In those not directly affected by the terrorism, it engenders deep enmity. The idea of a government deliberately plotting to terrorise its own people is deeply offensive and as we can see it has little long-term effect.

In the case of the Latin American client countries of the USA, barely a generation later (almost) the whole of Latin America is now governed by democratically elected left-leaning or socialist governments. The USA has lost all semblance of respect or influence in Latin America, as well as losing access to much of its natural resources. The word "Yankee" has entered the vocabulary of much of Latin America as one its greatest insults.

In a similar way, under pressure from a horrified public, France no longer tests nuclear weapons in the Pacific. In Northern Ireland, the Catholics and Protestants govern the region together in a delicate peace, but regularly side together against a British government that cares little for either community - the communal divisions caused by British military intelligence have finally begun to heal. Solidarity is the not only the enemy of state terrorism and it is very often the direct result of such terror.

2.2.1.1.9 Impoverishment: This is an abuse of political power where an authority deliberately impoverishes a sector of society as a means of punishment or as a method of social or political exclusion. The methods include attempts to increase the supply of labour, reduce the cost of labour or simply to debilitate a political group with poverty, so that they cease to have political influence.

Feudal systems throughout history have employed a strategy of deliberate impoverishment as a method of social control. When a whole social class is preoccupied by their primary needs, such as shelter, nourishment and basic security, it is incapable of rising to levels of personal or political awareness, never mind large-scale political organisation. In feudal times impoverishment provided a powerful means of social control, where a local landlord could easily command the allegiance of the hungry masses to work for little and fight for him in exchange for protection and a basic subsistence living.

Modern conservative political parties in Western democracies still misguidedly employ much the same tactics as their feudal antecedents. They are convinced that poor civilian populations will behave in the same way as feudal serfs did 1000 years ago and will be grateful to have work of any kind, at any wage, just in order to sustain themselves and their families. Gladly, much of the world and its population have moved on somewhat since then and serfdom has become unacceptable to the vast majority, even in the poorest developing nations. There are few slaves left in the Western democracies, willing to tolerate any working or living conditions just to stay alive. Fortunately, such lack of dignity is rare and the modern workforce understands the power of collective bargaining and how to drive the labour market.

Examples: As examples of the abuse of power to cause deliberate impoverishment Britain, France and the USA provide fine models. Britain is a country that is currently trying to demolish its social welfare systems as a means of deliberate impoverishment of its working classes. By removing social safety nets and universal healthcare, successive Conservative governments believe that they can recreate a new, "cheaper" underclass, which will drive economic growth by manning business and industry with low-cost labour. The entire motivation for such a policy is the concept that low labour costs propel economic growth and that, somehow, Britain can regain its lost glory as an economic powerhouse. This strategy in turn is driven by international corporate interests that demand that British governments maintain low labour rates and low taxes in order to encourage inward investment from non-EU sources. Of course, the reality is that Britain is creaking under the strain of a completely dysfunctional post-industrial economy, dominated by uncompetitive tertiary industries with poor economic sustainability and little long-term future.

Meanwhile in the USA, more than 40 million people live below the poverty threshold including 20% of American children. Since the 1980s, poverty in the USA has greatly exceeded that of most industrial nations. The latest figures show 1.5 million households in the US living on less than $2 per day and this includes almost 3 million children.

However poor the citizens of Britain or the USA become, they will never (in the foreseeable future) be quite as poor as sub-Saharan Africans or Southern Asians. And so, labour-intensive manufacturing will always gravitate to these super low-cost regions, far away from the UK or the USA. In the case of British commerce, all that remains is a dodgy financial services industry and the even more ethically challenged arms industry. (Britain is the world's 4th largest global arms exporter [Note 15]).

The poor are excluded: The policy of impoverishment in Britain and other industrialised countries, such as the US, serves the purpose of re-establishing and maintaining the docility of the "starving masses", but it also hides more sinister purposes. Protest and dissent are a luxury of the middle-classes or at least the financially secure working class. Maintaining a large underclass close to poverty serves two purposes: Firstly, it provides a cautionary tale to anyone threatening to rebel against the status quo, with every poor person's war cry being "any job is better than no job!" Secondly, it guarantees that millions subjected to poverty are unable to get an opportunity to participate in any type of political process or civil resistance. This underclass becomes socially excluded from better off citizens who collaborate with the government and are allowed to share some of the profits. They become politically "non-people", too absorbed by trying to swim against a tide of crushing poverty.

Whilst impoverishment has been a tactic of authoritarian governments for centuries, it also has a habit of turning very sour. Popular rebellions arising from poverty also evolve over time, as the nature of poverty and entitlement evolve. Thus, the levels of poverty that triggered civil rebellion in 14th century England were a great deal more acute than those that triggered the French Revolution in the 18th century, or various anti-austerity riots in the 21st century. This is because the sense of entitlement to basic living standards acceptable by the poor also evolves over time.

In this respect, government authorities make fundamental miscalculations. Feudally-minded conservative governments assume that the potential for impoverishment is much greater than it really is. They assume that populations will only become violently rebellious when they are deprived of primary needs, such as food, for long periods of time. The reality is that the modern fuse is a great deal shorter than that of our mediaeval counterparts. The recent, very temporary, loss of water supplies in Sao Paolo in Brazil demonstrated how quickly a civil society moves from order to chaos when the population experiences deprivation. No-one expected that people would rampage through Madrid and Athens when ordinary citizens were evicted from their homes. No-one expected that London, Birmingham, Manchester and Bristol would experience unprecedented rioting and looting in 2011 as a result of a young black man being shot dead during a police traffic stop in a poor part of London.

2.2.1.1.10 Denial of Justice: Denying justice to a political enemy or the socially dispossessed is an ancient form of abuse of power. In modern times it has been extended to whole groups, such as the so-called "illegal immigrants", the poor, disabled and those relying on social security help from the state.

Hidden courts: Another means by which justice is denied is when it is hidden from public view. For instance, in Britain, there have been many high-profile trials which, the government has insisted, must be held in private for "reasons of national security". In 2014, a British judge declared he would try two suspected terrorists entirely behind closed doors, for the first time in centuries. The trial judge, Mr. Justice Nicol, ruled that the case would be held in secret and, in fact, the public would not even know the men's names for unknown 'national security' reasons. A draconian gagging order even prevented the media from reporting on the existence of the case. So much for open justice! This Kafkaesque perversion of British justice brings the quality and safety of that judicial system to a new low point. These developments have given rise to the suspicion of political interference in the judiciary and caused consternation in legal and liberal political circles.

Manipulated courts: Political manipulation of judicial systems is not a new strategy for Britain. In 1973, the British government suspended the right to trial by jury in Northern Ireland and established a special type of court with just a single judge - the so-called Diplock courts. These courts continue to operate to this day and are another example of a government that lacks confidence in its own judicial system. The British government abandoned the age-old principle of trial by one's peers in favour of trial by a government appointee - a single judge. A similar system exists in the Republic of Ireland and is an equally repugnant degradation of natural justice. Of course, governments know that it's easier to bribe or intimidate a single judge than it is to corrupt a 12 person jury of ordinary citizens.

Expensive justice: Interfering in the judicial process is not the only means by which justice is denied to the citizenry. This can also be done by making access to justice too expensive for ordinary citizens. In most civilised countries it is normal for poor people to receive economic or professional assistance to ensure they are properly represented in court. Legal services are expensive the world over and for this reason democratic countries provide help with the costs of criminal or family law actions.

When conservative governments hold power, even in democracies, they find that equal access to justice by rich and poor to be a dangerous precedent. For instance, the British Conservative party in government started in 2011 to dismantle large parts of the legal aid system, with the result that many defendants were unable to find lawyers to take their cases. The effect of these cuts hit the poorest hardest. Even legal aid to assist children in cases of divorce or separation and in cases of domestic abuse was dramatically cut. Some legal actions taken by the police have also been dismissed from the courts because judges ruled that defendants were unable to represent themselves properly, and at the same time were unable to pay for barristers in the absence of adequate funding, and they therefore could not receive a fair hearing. This effectively led to defendants accused of various crimes being released - an unintended consequence of the government's policy. The cuts also triggered strikes by solicitors and barristers and a boycott by human rights groups of the 2015 Magna Carta commemorations; not that important, but somewhat embarrassing, nonetheless.

Inaccessible justice: Other methods of denying access to justice are not so subtle. Australia's method of handling unwanted asylum seekers is to confine them in overcrowded concentration camps on several islands, including Manus and Naru, with little access to basic services. The practice of isolating immigrants in this way was roundly condemned by the United Nations Refugee Agency and the United Nations Committee on Torture, in March 2015. It has led to dozens of accusations of sexual and physical abuse of detainees, including children, by immigration officials [Note 17] and the deliberate use of physical and psychological attacks on the immigrants, amounting to torture [Note 18]. Other medical personnel or officials making complaints about the appalling conditions have been fired or told to shut up by the Australian immigration authorities.

The (right-wing) Australian government has been operating a system of immigrant racial discrimination for decades, favouring Caucasian or wealthier non-Caucasian applicants. Many of those detained in Manus and Naru are impoverished Vietnamese people, escaping crushing poverty by taking to the sea in an attempt to reach Australia. They are held on these islands in a state of legal limbo, unable to access proper legal services. Australian authorities appear to hope that the poor conditions will persuade refugees and asylum seekers to give up their attempts and return to their countries of origin. Both UN reports condemning Australia conclude that the offshore processing of emigrants constitutes "arbitrary and mandatory detention under international law"; that no offshore processing centres offer "safe and humane conditions of treatment in detention", and none provide a "fair, efficient and expeditious system for assessing refugee claims...," according to UNHCR's director of international protection. Both reports are particularly critical of the government's new 48-hour target turnaround time to send emigrants offshore, which, one report says, does not allow "an adequate individualised assessment of health concerns or vulnerabilities". The UN reports outraged Human Rights campaigners in Australia and around the world, but was met with a furious reaction from Australia's Prime Minister (Abbott) who roundly condemned the UN agencies involved. The UN has obviously exposed some very unjust and illegal practices and caught out the Australian government in a very embarrassing position - hence Abbott's fury at the UN revelations.

Delayed justice is no justice: Another favourite method of denying justice to a particular group uses judicial delay, to ensure that victims and perpetrators are dead or very old before justice is done. In legal circles, this method of denying justice is often referred to as "Justice delayed is justice denied".

Britain has a long history of doing this. For instance, the Bloody Sunday atrocities committed by the British army in Derry in 1972 were not investigated properly for 30 years. Only in 2010 was the inquiry report published and did the British prime minister apologise - 38 years after the event. Most of those involved were either dead or too old to be reasonably prosecuted for murder. The British government adopted a similar strategy to cover up and delay investigation of the atrocities it committed in Kenya in the 1950s during Kenya's war for independence. The strategy continues to this day, with the miraculous disappearance of government documents concerning the atrocities and the government fighting continuous legal rear guard actions against Kenyans demanding an apology and compensation.

A more contemporary example of attempts to delay justice concerns long-standing and widespread allegations of a paedophile ring in Westminster. Despite repeated reports and specific accusations against MPs and senior officials (including a senior MI6 officer) being handed to Margaret Thatcher and Leon Brittan (Home Secretary) in 1984, no action was taken to investigate. The dossiers were subject to a "file and forget" policy, especially as some of the accused were very senior government and political figures. There is increasing proof that the Metropolitan police also hid or destroyed evidence and refused to investigate the allegations. In 2013, the accusations arose again, but two years on, the present British Home Secretary has yet to prosecute a single perpetrator. A commission of enquiry has collapsed twice under the weight of accusations of establishment connections with members of the enquiry committee.

After Leon Brittan died in January 2015, he was accused of "multiple child rape". Labour MP Tom Watson said he had spoken to two people who claimed they were abused by Brittan, including a man who alleged he had been attacked more than a dozen times as a boy. The alleged victim also said he had seen Brittan assault others. This would seem to explain why this Home Secretary appears to have "lost" the dossier containing evidence of the paedophile ring and why Margaret Thatcher decided not to demand further investigation. There was clearly a conspiracy of fear and silence at the highest level, designed to cover up these offences. And so the victims of this horrendous plot (including at least two children murdered by members of this Westminster ring) have been denied justice, apparently in an effort to protect senior members of the political and civil service establishment from prosecution. At the time of writing, victims who have come forward to restate their claims have been receiving anonymous death threats as a result of their statements and accusations [Note 19]. The plot continues and, 30 years later, there is still neither justice nor any immediate prospect of it.

On a larger scale, the right-wing Spanish Francoist "Popular Party" has long engaged in a similar strategy of delay in investigating the atrocities committed by Franco and his fascist (Falange) party between 1936 and 1978. These atrocities included the arbitrary detention and murder of hundreds of thousands of political prisoners, the kidnapping of thousands of children of socialist families in collaboration with the Catholic Church and, after the civil war, the institutionalisation of slave labour camps for dissenters and the routine use of torture and imprisonment without trial.

After 30 years of delays in dealing with the perpetrators of Franco's atrocities, a Spanish judge finally opened a case into these crimes against humanity in 2008. Many of the Franco regime's victims, witnesses to atrocities and, indeed, perpetrators are now either quite old or dead. So time was of the essence. In this case, Baltasar Garzón, the judge, argued that there was a systematic campaign by the Franco regime to eliminate his opponents and hide their bodies, and that this was grounds for a crimes-against-humanity case, which, he claimed, had no statute of limitations.

Garzón named Franco and 34 other wartime generals or members of his government as the instigators of their campaign of state terror and sought to investigate and indict the many thousands of other living Franco collaborators. In 2010 however, the judge was suspended by the Supreme Court pending allegations of abusing his authority. The Supreme Court, dominated by right-wing PP supporters, preferred to let the Franco atrocities lie dormant, since this political party's own roots are firmly associated with the fascist Falange party and many of its present supporters are themselves old fascists. In 2012, in a move which shocked the international legal community, Judge Garzón was suspended from his post for 11 years, on the pretext of using a (legitimate) wiretap against suspects in a separate case involving a number of high- ranking PP official (many of whom are now in prison). Clearly Garzón was getting far too close to prosecuting the Franco-supporting fascist old-guard of the PP and had to be removed.

Thus, the case against Franco and his collaborators was effectively shut down in Spain, despite the insistence in 2013 by the UN that mass graves and the atrocities that led to them must be investigated by the Spanish authorities. However, the case has since moved to an Argentinean court. This court applies a system of "universal jurisdiction" to crimes against humanity and is qualified to carry out the investigation and judge defendants. Clearly, the PP's attempts at sabotaging Garzón and his investigation were aimed at causing further judicial delays, in order that even more victims and perpetrators would die before justice was done. They hadn't, however, banked on the case moving to another jurisdiction (Argentina) over which they have no control. Witness statements have already started to be compiled by Argentinean judge María Servini de Cubría, in Spain and in Buenos Aires. Subpoenas and international extradition warrants have now been issued against alleged fascist torturers and other Franco collaborators in Spain. The story is far from over. Justice may yet be done, at last.

Hiding of victims: Finally, authoritarian governments can deny access to justice by denying access to facilities where prisoners are detained. This happened when the United Nations' top investigator on the use of torture, Juan Méndez, accused Washington of refusing him proper access to prisons and inmates at Guantánamo Bay. Méndez had been waiting for more than two years for the United States to give him access to a range of state and federal prisons where he wanted to probe the excessive use of solitary confinement [Note 20]. Clearly, Washington did not want their criminal activities in Guantanamo exposed to legal scrutiny.

In a similar incident, in 2014, a UN special rapporteur investigating violence against women was denied access by the UK government to the controversial Yarl's Wood Detention Centre after the suspicious death of an inmate. The UN official reported: "A visit was facilitated and I was accompanied by a staff member of the inspectorate of prisons. When I reached Yarl's Wood I was notified by the director that she had received a phone call (probably from the Home Office) that I would not be allowed in."

The UN rapporteur was particularly interested in visiting Yarl's Wood after a Jamaican woman, Christine Case, died on March 30 after allegedly being denied medical treatment. Hers was just the latest case of alleged mistreatment at the facility. In 2012, a total of 6,071 women applied for political asylum in the UK. Of this number, nearly one-third, or 1,902 of them were detained, according to official Home Office statistics. The conditions in UK detention centres have been widely condemned as inhumane and there have been persistent allegations of physical and sexual abuse of detainees by staff. At the time of writing, the centres are run by a private company (Serco) under contract and supervision of the British Home office.

In March 2004, the Prisons Ombudsman published a report of evidence of racist incidents by staff. In October 2004, the same ombudsman published an inquiry into a disturbance and fire in 2001. In February 2006, the Chief Inspector of Prisons found substantial gaps in health care at the centre. Also in 2006 the group Legal Action for Women investigation into Yarl's Wood found that: 70% of women had reported rape, nearly half had been detained for over three months. 57% had no legal representation, and 20% had lawyers who demanded payment in advance. Women reported sexual and racial intimidation by guards. "Self-Help Guides" given to inmates were confiscated by guards, thus depriving detainees of information about their rights.

In April 2009, the Children's Commissioner for England published a report which stated that children held in the detention centre were denied urgent medical treatment, handled violently and left at risk of serious harm. The report detailed how children are transported in caged vans, and watched by opposite-sex staff as they dress. This follows earlier allegations in 2005 by the Chief Inspector of Prisons that children were being damaged by being held in the institution.

Clearly, there are lots of reasons why the British government doesn't want a visit by a representative of the United Nations investigating violence against women. Obviously, there is something very bad going on in

Britain's asylum seekers' detention centres. If the British authorities had nothing to hide, then they would have nothing to fear from high-level UN visits. The authority's brazen refusal to allow access to UN personnel is a shockingly blatant attempt to hide the crimes taking place in these detention facilities and to deny these detainees their basic legal rights.

2.2.1.1.11 Perversion of Justice, Show Trials: A show trial is a public trial in which the judicial authorities have already determined the guilt of the defendant(s). The objective of a show trial is to present the accusation and the verdict to the public as a political justification and a warning to others. Show trials tend to be a form of political retribution and/or propaganda rather than having any judicial or correctional function. Such trials are an abuse of judicial powers, in order to make a political point.

In times of conflict or when a regime feels threatened, governments frequently resort to actions designed to bolster their credibility in an attempt to hold on to political power. Such was the case in several show trials that took place in Britain at the height of "the troubles" in Northern Ireland between 1975 and 1976. The trials arose after the Provisional IRA escalated its attacks on mainland Britain in 1973. This escalation gave rise to an attack, on average, every three days during this period and placed a lot of pressure on the British authorities to catch the perpetrators. These attacks included a series of pub bombings in England in 1974, targeting pubs used by British soldiers. The bombings of two Birmingham pubs resulted in 21 deaths and 182 injuries. The Provisional IRA denied responsibility for the bombings and apparently claimed that the IRA leadership and IRA supporters were "horrified" by them. Nonetheless, the attacks caused public outrage in Britain. The same night, six Northern Irishmen travelling by train to catch the ferry to Belfast, were arrested and interrogated. It was later revealed that these men were also beaten, attacked by police dogs and subjected to mock execution during their detention. These beatings continued until their trial. The men came to trial in 1975, and based on forensic evidence that they had handled explosives, the six were convicted of murder and sent to prison for 21 years. They all protested their innocence. Their convictions were finally quashed in 1981. It transpired that the forensic "evidence" was deeply flawed (the six had been handling a new pack of playing cards coated with a chemical which caused similar forensic results to nitro-glycerine) and it was demonstrated that none of the men were IRA members or could have been involved in the attack.

In October and November 1974 more bombs were detonated in pubs in Guildford and Woolwich in England, again targeting places frequented by British soldiers. In December 1974, under severe pressure to act, the police arrested three men and a woman, later known as the Guildford Four. The Guildford Four were falsely convicted in October 1975 of the bombings and sentenced to life in prison. Another group of Irish immigrants, later known as "the Maguire Seven" were also arrested and falsely convicted in March 1976 of providing bomb-making material and other support and sentenced to terms varying between four and fourteen years. The Guildford Four were held in prison for fifteen years, but Giuseppe Conlon died near the end of his third year of imprisonment.

All of these convictions were overturned years later in the Appeal court after it was proved the Guildford Four's convictions had been based on confessions obtained by torture (as were some Maguire Seven confessions), whilst evidence specifically clearing the Four had been deliberately covered up by the police.

All three trials were amongst the most disgracefully manipulated and deliberate miscarriages of justice in the last generation in British justice. Clearly, the police were politically pressured to get convictions - any convictions - to save the necks of their political masters. It appears, with hindsight, that they simply "fitted up" some rather harmless Irish immigrants with fabricated cases by deliberately manipulating evidence.

The effect of these show trials and later acquittals caused further Nationalist outrage in Ireland and a further weakening of trust in the British political classes and judicial system. The real culprits were never caught, despite various high profile confessions from other Republican groups to British authorities, which emerged during the time that these innocent people were incarcerated. The truth appeared to be of no interest to the British authorities. They had their convictions and the real criminals were apparently irrelevant.

2.2.1.1.12 State and Corporate Censorship: Censorship is the suppression of speech, public communications or other information which might be considered harmful, politically incorrect, sensitive, objectionable, or inconvenient by authorities, governments, corporations or by parts of the media or other institutions.

Censorship is not the exclusive domain of governments. Corporations also impose systems of censorship on their employees. These are usually backed up with threats of dismissal or legal sanctions. Governments and corporations sometimes collaborate to impose various forms of censorship. For instance, internet censorship is driven by governments and implemented by corporations. Sometimes corporations refuse to collaborate with government attempts at censorship, as in the case where several US technology companies provided technical methods of bypassing state internet censorship.

Legality: Direct censorship by authorities may or may not be legal, depending on the jurisdiction, type of censorship and content. Some countries provide legal protections against censorship, but none of these protections are absolute. Frequently, a claim of "necessity" to balance conflicting rights is made, in order to determine what can and cannot be censored. There are no laws against self-censorship anywhere in the world.

Ubiquity: According to the OpenNet Initiative, all of the world's major powers carry out various forms of internet censorship with the USA, UK, China, Russia, Saudi Arabia, India, Australia and Central Asia as the forerunners of the most intrusive internet censorship systems in the world.

Counterproductive: Censorship is considered counterproductive to human development, as it prevents a censored topic from being discussed [Note 22]. It has been argued that censorship is used to impose moral values on a society, for example, the censorship of material considered obscene or politically radical. As a form of abuse of power, censorship operates by excluding selected parts of society from selected information or literature available to other parts of society, solely on the basis of some imaginary moral right. Concepts of obscenity or political opinion are subjective and, within certain social norms, should be considered a matter of choice, provided that the material does not and has not impacted upon the rights of any other individual. Censorship is often accompanied by flimsy moral or security justifications, whereas most forms of censorship are really political rather than practical or protective.

Corporate censorship: There are many cases of corporate censorship, where corporations have suppressed negative stories. In recent years we have seen Monsanto refusing to publish crop food safety test results for their GM products [Note 23]. Pharmaceutical companies routinely hide unfavourable product test information so as to make their products seem more effective or safer than they really are. For instance, in January 2007, Eli Lilly obtained a restraining order from a US court forbidding activists in the Psychiatric Survivors' Movement from posting links on their websites to leaked documents, which reportedly showed that Eli Lilly had intentionally withheld information regarding the lethal side-effects of the drug Zyprexa [Note 24].

Corporate and political collaboration in censorship: Corporate censorship isn't confined to protecting large industrial corporations. In 2004, Walt Disney prevented Miramax from releasing Michael Moore's politically controversial movie Fahrenheit 911 because the documentary was highly critical of the Bush administration. In a similar vein, in December 2010, Amazon cut off WikiLeaks services 24 hours after being contacted by the staff of Joe Lieberman, Chairman of the U.S. Senate Committee on Homeland Security. This was an act of censorship carried out by a pliant corporation under pressure from a right-wing government. As a footnote, the censorship was useless and in fact caused the WikiLeaks database to be copied and spawned on websites around the world.

Ineffective: With the advent of the internet, censorship has become less and less effective. This is because what is censored in one country may be freely available in another, and it's technically quite difficult to absolutely censor the internet (as we shall demonstrate later in the book).

Indeed, even an attempt at censorship tends to trigger a "Streisand Effect", where suddenly everyone wants to publish the censored material, discuss it, download it and distribute it as much as they can. It's the nature of the internet (and human beings) that when something is forbidden, it acquires a premium value and, of course, distribution of material on the internet is a very simple matter these days, whether it's a document, photo, video or audio content. Even banned books can be electronically published and sold or given away by a myriad of independent eBook publishers at virtually no economic cost to the publisher. At a local level there is also the use of peer-to-peer file sharing, using the BitTorrent protocol, which is virtually impossible for any government to control or block, since files are spread between 100 and 300 million users around the world. This all makes censorship a lot more difficult for governments or corporations. Even when court orders block publication in one country, a non-national website can publish freely and without legal implications. The internet, in this regard, seems likely to become the final nemesis of censorship.

2.2.1.1.13 Covering-up misdeeds: In the same way that authorities like to control information or media using censorship, they also like to cover up their own misdemeanours from the gaze of the public. This applies just as much to authorities in "liberal", democratic countries as in overly authoritarian regimes. A "cover-up" is an abuse because it allows an authority to use its power to deceive the public for its own benefit or self-preservation.

At least in theory, governments are supposed to operate in the interests of the public good and in a transparent way. Corporations are also supposed to act responsibly, legally and transparently. When they commit misdeeds, these should be exposed to public scrutiny and dealt with by the legal system. Of course, we know that this doesn't actually happen and that both governments and corporations constantly commit crimes that they then try to cover up.

Duplicity and bad faith: Sometimes authorities cover up relatively trivial incidents, and when caught out they attract more criticism for the cover-up than for the original offence. The act of covering up by an authority is very offensive to the public, for it demonstrates a high level of duplicity and bad faith, which undermines public trust in all their future dealings. To some extent this accounts for the high levels of public apathy and cynicism towards politicians and big business which we are currently experiencing in the Western world. We know we can't trust authorities to act honestly, so we ignore them - in protest. It's not the correct solution to the problem of dishonesty in government, but it is an understandable public reaction.

Truth almost always comes out: For many reasons covering up has become quite a bit harder than it used to be. Information has a habit of seeping out and sensitive information is more prone to leaking than most.

It's almost impossible to guarantee complete secrecy, even in a small group in any organisation. An overheard conversation, a thrown away memo, a loose email, a drunken comment, a gossiping spouse or a spurned partner are just a few possible sources of a leak, not to mention those personnel whose specific task it is to infiltrate and spy on an authority or company.

Technology liberates the truth: Technology has added to the problem of cover-ups by authorities. Mobile phones with cameras and voice recorders make everyone a potential documentary maker or spy, anytime, anywhere. In a recent case of attempted corruption by a UKIP candidate in Britain, an aid was caught red-handed on camera by a restaurant employee, trying to obtain an inflated restaurant invoice so as to make a fraudulent expense claim to the EU. It led to her suspension and a criminal investigation [Note 37] and was an excellent example of how we can all capture and expose corruption.

Judging by the amount of material posted on YouTube every day, it seems that the whole world is constantly filming or photographing something or somebody. It's hard to cover up an act of police brutality when 200 people are simultaneously making and posting a video of the police beating someone up. Once upon a time (about 10 years ago) we relied on investigative journalists to set up sting operations to entrap corrupt politicians, corporate officials and criminals, and to film or record them caught red-handed. Now we can all do it! This has to be a good thing for the political health of any country. It's another example of how communications technology, and especially the internet, have been politically liberating in many ways.

The rise of the whistleblower: The growth in whistleblowing creates another difficulty for those who are trying to cover something up. Whistleblowers were once considered to be disloyal traitors by society. Now they are public heroes and role models. The change in public attitudes to whistleblowers has come about because of a general public distrust in authority. Where once we used to think that "they" (our politicians) would look after us, we now know that "they" are just trying to line their own pockets at our expense and that "they" couldn't care less about the greater good. Thus we rely on whistleblowers to keep politicians, businessmen and officials reasonably straight, the logic being that if they feel that there is someone watching them, they are less likely to misbehave.

The rise in stature of the whistleblower has surely saved the public from some of the worst excesses of authority and blown many a cover-up. For this reason, authorities tend to react very severely against whistleblowers. Rather than understanding the reason for the revelations, most authorities make matters worse with gross over-reactions and attempts at revenge. This thirst for vengeance is highly counterproductive. When Edward Snowden, hiding in Hong Kong, participated in an online chat to explain his motives, he was asked whether the treatment of other whistleblowers influenced him. He responded; "[Previous whistleblowers] are all examples of how overly-harsh responses to public-interest whistleblowing only escalate the scale, scope, and skill involved in future disclosures. Citizens with a conscience are not going to ignore wrongdoing simply because they'll be destroyed for it: the conscience forbids it. Instead, these draconian responses simply build better whistleblowers."

So, again, we see that authorities are often their own worst enemies. Their natural authoritarian instinct to control and dominate blinds them to managing whistleblowers in a more subtle way. The tendency to a heavy-handed response simply sets the scene for more and bigger future revelations of political misdeeds.

2.2.1.1.14 Suppression of Dissent: When an authority tries to directly or indirectly censor, persecute or oppress another party or individual with which it doesn't agree politically or ideologically, it may employ various methods, as follows:

• Direct action against the dissenters, which may include legal actions, dismissal, ostracism and coercion to halt expressions of dissent.

• Indirect actions against dissenters include actions such as negative publicity, disinformation, and attempts to discredit dissenters and their arguments.

• The suppression may lead to self-censorship, with the dissenting person or group deciding to halt their expression of dissent out of fear of the consequences, such as violence, dismissal, legal action or other punitive actions by an authority.

Attempts at suppression of dissent may involve any of the following strategies:

• Denying a dissenter the right to speak freely. This may include imprisonment or even assassination of dissenters in extreme cases, but more usually it includes denying them access to the press.

• Cutting the dissenter off from their audience by denying them a platform. Techniques go all the way from shouting down dissenters, to exiling or imprisoning them.

• Undermining dissenter groups by infiltration, spying, etc. This is the favourite for modern authoritarian governments and corporations. Spying on dissenters gives an authority a strategic advantage by knowing and foiling dissenters' plans in advance.

• Controlling academia: deciding what can be written and published. Both corporations and governments finance much of what takes place in the academic world and they feel that they have a right to politically control the output of academia. Luckily, many academics are free-spirited and many refuse to accept constraints on their work.

Suppressing dissent is an abuse of power because an authority takes advantage of the relative weakness of the dissenter in comparison with the power of the authority to control expressions of political or moral opinions. It is a direct attack on what is considered to be a basic human right: to hold personal beliefs without being subject to threats or coercion of any kind. The suppression of dissent is one of the first steps in the establishment of an authoritarian state, as it seeks to neutralise public opposition.

The suppression of dissent is considered a foundation stone of authoritarian dictatorships, but it is also common practice even in modern liberal democracies. Fortunately, many consider dissent itself to be the basis of a healthy democracy and a fair society. As Karl Marx wrote in 1843: "if constructing the future and settling everything for all times are not our affair, it is all the more clear what we have to accomplish at present: I am referring to ruthless criticism of all that exists, ruthless both in the sense of not being afraid of the results it arrives at and in the sense of being just as little afraid of conflict with the powers that be".

Examples of suppression of dissent: The suppression of political dissent is as old as human history. In modern times though, with improved media and communications, the role of the dissenter is a much more profound threat to an authority than it was, say, in Roman times. The availability of mass communications means that dissenters can disseminate their message globally and easily. For an authority the use of the mass media makes the suppression of dissent much more important and urgent.

An early example of an attack on the media took place in the McCarthy period in the USA, which lasted from the end of WWII until the end of the 1950s, when Hollywood became a target of suppression. During those times of extreme political paranoia, the USA entered a period where any form of dissent was construed as "un-American" and therefore quite likely part of a Communist plot to overthrow the country. McCarthyism was largely driven by very right-wing Republican politicians and implemented by the FBI, supported by a range of draconian legislation. It was similar in many ways to the wave of paranoia that has swept the United States since the events of September 11th 2001 and its subsequent military losses in Iraq and Afghanistan.

During the McCarthy era, thousands of Americans were accused of being communists or communist sympathizers. They became subject to aggressive investigations, which often involved questioning before government or private-industry panels, committees and agencies. The main targets of such suspicions were government employees, entertainers, teachers and active union members. Suspicions of communist sympathies were taken seriously on the flimsiest of evidence. The accused were often painted as dangerous subversives, "leftists", determined to overthrow the 'American way of life'. Many people suffered loss of employment, with their careers left in ruins, some even suffered imprisonment. Later, many of these show trial verdicts were overturned, with the laws used to enforce the verdicts declared unconstitutional. The reasons for citing dismissals from employment were later declared illegal or un-actionable, with the extra-legal procedures deemed at the least unethical and open to question.

Famous examples of McCarthyism include the Hollywood blacklist, associated with hearings conducted by the House Un-American Activities Committee (HUAC) and the various anti-communist activities of the Federal Bureau of Investigation (FBI) under Director J. Edgar Hoover. Hollywood was specifically targeted because dissenters in Hollywood clearly had access to the mass media and were therefore an urgent threat to the right-wing.

McCarthyism was a widespread phenomenon, affecting all levels of society, and was successful in stifling dissent to some extent. During this period, some argue, the USA descended towards becoming a police state - an experience from which it has never fully recovered.

To this day, the FBI continues to suppress activists that the US government considers a threat to either its power or to corporate interests. Targeted groups include unions, peace movements, green groups, and anti-capitalist groups such as Occupy. In the last decade the FBI have used anti-terrorism laws to target and disrupt completely peaceful protest movements in a totally cynical way [Note 25].

Suppression of dissent happens everywhere and there are many contemporary examples. In Britain for example, it has become daily fare to read stories of appalling public services being exposed by concerned whistleblowers, who are then bullied, fired, sued or ostracised by those they have accused of incompetence or abuse. For instance, in March 2015, Dr Hayley Dare, a clinical psychologist with an unblemished 20-year record in the NHS, spoke out against poor patient care at the West London Mental Health Trust. She was then subjected to a campaign of bullying from senior managers. Her concerns were upheld in court, yet the employment tribunal found against her because it said she had not made her claim "in good faith", a legal tactic often used to dismiss whistleblowing cases. She now faces costs of £93,500, despite the fact that the issues she raised were totally valid, very serious and upheld by the court [Note 26].

Whilst the suppression of dissent may have the immediate affect on slowing or temporarily stopping open opposition, unless those opposed to the authorities are actually removed from the scene completely (i.e. exiled or murdered), repressive tactics almost always backfire. Suppression may actually draw more attention to the issue in hand. The enemy of the suppressor is the power of public information, through the conventional press or the internet. When the oppressor realises that the dissident cannot be silenced, he will give up.

2.2.1.1.15 Pork-Barrel Politics: Political immorality: a politician siphons the allocations of government spending for local projects into his particular political constituency or areas sympathetic to his party, to curry the electoral vote in favour of himself or the current government. It is an abuse of power because it uses public money to benefit a political party or an individual politician. It can be confined to a single area, a region or an entire country. It can be refined to target certain types of spending. For example, public transport spending, a sensitive issue in certain areas with many commuters can be used to "buy" votes from commuting residents. Whilst this practice is difficult to control and is technically not illegal, it certainly does need to be highlighted to the electorate - both to the beneficiary electorate and those who will lose as a result of funds being selfishly sidetracked by politicians with vested interests.

Diverting public spending just before an election to "buy" votes is a common abuse of the democratic process. Many traditional political parties in most democracies are guilty of this abuse.

2.2.1.1.16 Misuse of Police Powers: Society grants members of law enforcement agencies enormous powers to enable them to keep the peace and to preserve social order. They are granted a great deal of discretion in using their judgment regarding which laws to enforce, when and against whom. This wide range of options and authority can lead to the abuse of police power. Some police officers come to see themselves not simply as enforcers of the law, but as the law itself. Such abusive police officers frequently remind their victims that it is within their power to deprive them of freedom, privacy, safety and security at any moment they choose.

Some authorities take advantage of this abusive tendency in the police force in order to make the police appear to be more coercive than is actually permitted under the law. Police rely on the general rule that officers do not testify against each other or prosecute each other and this perpetuates the culture of the police being "above the law". This systemic behaviour is often enforced by prejudices within the judicial system that tend to take the word of a policeman over that of an ordinary citizen.

The abuse of police power may be part of a larger conspiracy within an authority or it may simply be acts of abuse by individual policemen or small groups of policemen. In 2012, the Guardian newspaper compiled an extraordinary snapshot of 58 cases from 2011-2012 taken against British police officers. The majority of the abuses they committed were sexual offences against women detainees. A disturbing number were sexual offences against children, some as young as eight. A few cases involved the misuse of police databases to obtain information for personal (often sexual) reasons. The list makes horrendous reading and demonstrates that, regardless of safeguards or political guarantees, the abuse of police power is alive and well (in Britain at least). Some commentators remarked that the report was just the tip of a huge iceberg of abusive behaviour, which is routinely covered up by police and the establishment [Note 27].

Examples of misuse of police powers: Examples of the more institutional abuses of police power in Britain include the misuse of stop and search powers, which are often used to racially harass ethnic minorities. A raft of studies has shown that the level of stop and search is much higher amongst black minorities than in the general population. Home Office figures show that black people are seven times more likely to be searched on the street than white people. One report points out that 27% of these searches were "unjustified based on any evidence". Another study showed that only 9% of the searches led to an arrest and even less to a conviction. Given that the British police conduct 1.2 million such searches a year and that they are so racially biased, it is little wonder that young black people have almost no faith in the British police. In July 2013, the official police watchdog in the UK described the street stop and search powers under the 1984 Police and Criminal Evidence Act (Pace) as "some of the most intrusive and contentious powers granted to the police". They warned that, although some might think it will help to "control the streets" in the short term, its heavy-handed use may lead to major disorder in the long-term. We may well look forward to more large-scale riots in Britain for this very reason [Note 28].

2.2.1.1.17 Discrimination against certain Groups: Authorities may decide to discriminate against certain groups in society for reasons such as ethnic origin, religious belief, age, gender or sexual orientation. Indeed, authorities, even in Western democracies, do this all the time. In less liberal jurisdictions the level of discrimination may degenerate into acts of physical violence against such groups. In Russia, for example, the level of institutional discrimination against homosexuals is extreme and often violent. The government actively encourages public discrimination.

In more "moderate" regimes, discrimination tends to be legally banned, but informally embedded in institutions of the state or within a corporate ethos. In the last section, for instance, we saw how the British police are 700% more likely to stop and search a black person than a white person, despite the British black population being only around 4% of the total British population: with total non-white population being only 13% of the population. This imbalance in the use of "stop and search" is no coincidence. This is pure racial discrimination at work. The law may say discrimination is illegal, but the reality is that it exists within the institutions of authority and clearly these institutions turn a blind eye to it for political or ideological reasons.

Discrimination of this kind contravenes the UN Charter of Human Rights and is despicable. Even when it is legally forbidden, the existence of such discrimination indicates that an authority tacitly tolerates it and may even applaud it. If an authority was serious about eliminating such discrimination, it would do so without further delay. This tolerance of discrimination, in itself, represents an abuse of power. As was the case in Nazi Germany, anti-Semitism was first tolerated and then encouraged because it achieved a political objective. An authority that allows such discrimination is an accessory to the act itself. It is guilty of allowing its power to be employed in discrimination. In the stop and search example, the police have powers vested in them by the state, therefore the crimes of the police are indeed crimes of the state. For instance, the British Home Secretary is guilty of the discrimination by the police because her office fails to sanction the unbridled misuse of "stop and search" tactics against young black people. In effect, the government is guilty of a crime of omission by refusing to correct the problem within the police force. The excuse "we didn't realise" doesn't work; not after decades of studies, internal reviews and expert reports highlighting the discrimination. The truth is that nothing changes because the British government actually finds this informal discrimination acceptable. The police force act as the "bully boys" of the white British establishment, keeping a foot on the throat of a downtrodden black community.

Targets of discrimination: Discrimination by an authority, even when it is unofficial, has many targets. Many countries discriminate against asylum seekers, migrant workers, the poor in general, ex-convicts, gypsies, travellers and the disabled and not solely because of ethnic origin (some of these groups may well have the same ethnic origin as the authority), but also because of social prejudices. In Britain's rampant xenophobic society, at the time of writing, all of these groups are targets for institutional discrimination, quite often with the tacit support of large sectors of the general public.

Migrant workers: For instance, certain EU migrants into Britain are demonised by the right-wing press and there are plans to "legally" discriminate against EU migrants in Britain's social welfare system. This is despite the fact that EU citizens are legally entitled to live and work anywhere in the European Union, as are British citizens who also travel and live freely in many EU countries. However, in Britain, the perception is that a British citizen has a right to live in another EU country, but EU citizens can only reside in Britain if it suits Britain. In other words, some British citizens perceive themselves to have a higher value than other EU citizens and certainly a higher value than those originating in certain Eastern European countries. This is an attitude of pure discrimination, based on ignorance and supported by political opportunists, conservative politicians and certain xenophobic institutions of the state.

Asylum seekers: Similar prejudices relate to asylum seekers. This group of often traumatised individuals and families, rather than being cared for and helped, is incarcerated in camps not dissimilar to concentration camps, where they are abused, mistreated, often deprived of legal assistance and prepared for often summary repatriation. Any reputation Britain may have had as a place of sanctuary for the oppressed has long since gone. The reality is that public and institutional attitudes and behaviour towards asylum seekers is one of proven and sometimes vicious discrimination.

The poor: A similar level of discrimination afflicts the poor in Britain. Those who are unable to find work or who work in the millions of low-paid jobs find themselves victims of institutional and social discrimination. They are often type-cast by the middle-class, right-wing press as being lazy, welfare fraudsters. The strategy is clear. Successive governments have helped their corporate friends to create a supply of low cost labour and in order to do this they needed to create a poor underclass that is desperate enough to work for slave wages. This underclass must then be whipped into work. This is achieved by means of draconian social welfare sanctions and the manipulation of middle-class attitudes by the government to cause the public to act as proxy agents of government discrimination. Any concepts of "dignity in labour" have been ground into dust by the cynical collaboration between big business and the corrupt political classes, whilst the middle-classes shrug their shoulders.

A means of control: For an authority, discrimination plays a powerful role in controlling populations. It is a divisive mechanism which denies solidarity and therefore keeps ordinary people divided and weak. It also tends to set one part of society against another, thus one group does the authority's work for it as a proxy. Very often the working classes are used as a proxy by being convinced that their poor living conditions are the fault of migrant workers or asylum seekers. Many forms of discrimination provide excuses for an authority's incompetence. It's much easier to blame a few thousand Romanians or sub-Saharan Africans for the state of the nation than it is to understand and correct the endemic incompetence and decades-long mismanagement of the country's economy by a bunch of inept public school boys.

2.2.1.1.18 Blackmail by Authority: Government agencies and other authorities sometimes take part in blackmail attempts against their own citizens or against other officials in government. For instance, it now seems clear that the US National Security Agency is engaged in spying on members of the US Congress [Note 29], along with all other US citizens. It was also revealed that the NSA routinely shares telephone metadata with other intelligence agencies, including Mossad in Israel, thus leaving open the possibility that law makers and other officials could, it has been suggested, be blackmailed into making decisions which are pro-Israel. In a completely separate development, in 2013, it was revealed that the NSA were collecting data on access to various pornographic websites by Muslims in order to be able to blackmail or morally discredit them [Note 30].

This kind of surveillance for blackmail purposes is nothing new. The FBI collected secret dossiers on the sexual and other behaviour of dangerous "enemies of the state", such as Martin Luther King Jr. and President John F. Kennedy, in case such information was needed for the purposes of blackmail. We don't know if it was ever used.

An authority's use of public resources to carry out surveillance to provide material to be used in blackmail is a gross abuse of power, especially if the final objective is to aid a political agenda.

At a lower level, members of the public are frequently the victims of blackmail by police investigators that use private information they have obtained about individuals in order to extract confessions or other incriminating information from informants or defendants.

2.2.1.1.19 Theft of Citizens' Property: There are several ways in which a government authority may steal the property of its citizens. The obvious example is the case of excessive or unjust taxation. A second case involves the compulsory seizing of land for a government or other project. Both may be completely legal within a jurisdiction, but may involve some degree of abuse of power. The case of the Boston Tea Party illustrates how over-taxation by a government, without delivering any benefits to the public, can be construed as an abuse of power. Seizing land for the purposes of an unnecessary and speculative development may also be construed as an abuse of authority or at least maladministration.

In some countries, governments can seize not only land for public ownership, but may be legally able to seize property such as contract rights, patents, trade secrets, and copyrights from citizens. In the EU, the possibility of expropriation of private property by the state is effectively controlled by the European Convention of Human Rights in Article 1 of the First Protocol to the Convention, which states that "Every natural person or legal person is entitled to the peaceful enjoyment of his possessions." However, this is subject to exceptions where state deprivation of private possessions is in the general or public interest, is in accordance with law, and, in particular, to secure payment of taxes.

2.2.1.1.20 Miscellaneous Abuses of Power

The list of abuses of power described above is not exhaustive. The following abuses of power also exist in various forms:

- Manipulation of markets (labour or products) by government or corporation to promote a political agenda or commercial interests.

- Human Manipulation: Abuse of knowledge, statistics and information.

- System Manipulation: "Gaming" the system and its institutions for political advantage.

- The abuse of rank by officials and politicians to obtain personal or political favours.

- Persecution: religious persecution, ethnic persecution and political persecution as a means of gaining political advantage.

- The abuse of trust. This happens when an authority dealing with a trusting public deliberately abuses this trust to gain some political or pecuniary advantage.

2.2.2 Negligence in Authority

Negligence as a form of social control: Being a victim of an abusive government authority is often traumatic and may be fatal for dissidents living in authoritarian states. However governments have developed alternative ways of controlling civil populations. Negligence is one of them.

Neglect is a passive form of abuse in which an authority, responsible for the well-being of its population, disregards some or all of its duties. It may deliberately overlook an entire population or a small part of it.

Whereas one may be able to forgive an official for occasional neglect, routine institutional negligence is a different matter. No government or other institution is ever innocent in such a case because such dereliction really is a deliberate act. Negligence happens when an authority consciously ignores the interests of certain citizens, employees, customers, etc. with a view to weakening their position. It doesn't happen by accident, it happens by design.

Negligence as a form of oppression: Politically motivated negligence is often seen as a "sin of omission", whereas a deliberate abuse of power might be perceived as "sin of commission", which makes it useful as a political tool of control.

One could argue that negligence is just another form of abuse of power because it involves a deliberate act, but we can distinguish it from other abuses of power because negligence carries such a high level of deniability. Nonetheless, negligence can cause enormous suffering to a population or minority. Abuses of power leave evidence of actions and of conspiracy. Negligence just leaves victims. Negligence is therefore a favourite means of oppression where an authority doesn't want to be blamed. It's hard for an authority to explain why it is rounding up dissenters and throwing them in prison for a few months without trial. But depriving a group of people of basic services, such as healthcare, education and social security is something an authority can quite easily explain away.

Negligence in government is a powerful, subtle and pernicious tool of oppression for several reasons: It can be applied temporarily, with varying degrees of effect. It can be reversed at a moment's notice. In this way, large sectors of the population can be oppressed, but their suppression can be carefully controlled so that they do not "come to the boil". Indeed, when an authority actually stops being negligent, affected populations often express gratitude to their authorities for allowing them the benefits that they should have had all the time. Negligent governments can also hide behind necessity, such as shortage of funds, personnel, or time. There are lots of ways in which failing to do something can be explained or excused.

How negligence is used by authority: Negligence can be a very effective way of controlling populations; for example, by damaging their economic potential. A government can easily economically disadvantage a specific area simply by refusing to build basic infrastructure, such as water supplies, roads, public transport, telecommunications systems, schools, hospitals or shops. By disregarding the maintenance of such infrastructure, an authority can act to disadvantage a target population because, as these infrastructural systems begin to break down, the area becomes less and less habitable or economically viable.

Examples of institutional neglect have occurred when a government wishes to displace populations from areas which have oil, gas or other mineral reserves. For instance, the Brazilian government has deliberately failed to provide medical services to various indigenous tribes, such as the Yanomami, in areas where there is also a significant (illegal) gold mining industry, or potential cattle land being eyed by ranchers. The result is the steady decline of Yanomami populations in their traditional homeland [Note 51].

A government can also target certain socio-economic groups for neglect. For instance, a government can refuse to pay for teachers to work in schools in certain inner city districts, home to a certain social (and political) strata of society. By reducing the quality of education, this form of neglect damages the educational and career prospects of this particular social group, effectively condemning them to ignorance and poverty.

A government reducing access to medical services for the poor by omitting to fund public healthcare directly impacts the well-being and life expectancy of an entire social class.

Neglecting public transport to a particular area can effectively isolate that area economically and socially from neighbouring areas. A local government wishing to isolate a poor, rundown area from more affluent suburbs may well cut public transport budgets for services linking the two districts and divert funds away from building roads connecting deprived areas.

Governments often use subtle forms of negligence to control populations. For instance, keeping the price of internet broadband services high or making rural broadband expensive or inaccessible deliberately targets the economic well-being of poor and rural dwellers and fosters social exclusion and poverty. Refusing to finance childcare facilities in rural areas may obstruct rural women from entering the workforce and oblige them to remain in the home.

Examples of neglect: Ireland is a good example of how negligence is used in the service of political ideology. The country has a very conservative political class, with both major parties trumpeting right-wing, nationalist agendas, strongly allied to the Roman Catholic ethos.

Rural parts of Ireland and depressed inner city districts are notoriously ignored [Note 31]. Ireland has many small farmers, often in remote areas. In line with traditional Catholic policy of keeping peasants in their place and women at home, poor, ignorant and pregnant, the Irish government provides negligible public transport and almost no childcare facilities or adult educational facilities in rural areas. Many farmers are economically marginalised, i.e. poor, and their families survive on a mixture of subsidies and "farmers dole".

In Ireland, internet connections in most rural communities are either non-existent or of a very poor quality. Medical services are concentrated in urban areas, far from rural communities, and are very basic, at best. Core infrastructure, such as roads, is neglected to the point of complete decay; apart from major toll routes used by business travellers and tourists.

Drinking water in large parts of rural Ireland is contaminated, mostly by untreated agricultural waste, and has been so for decades. In inner city areas, alongside shiny new office blocks in the capital's financial district, Dublin's poor sleep in shop doorways or live in dilapidated 1970s slums amongst the debris of a generation of neglect, crime, drugs and depravity, lacking schools, hospitals and other basic facilities.

When someone does manage to enter an Irish hospital, it is quite likely that, as an inpatient, they will spend a considerable time (possibly days) on a hospital trolley because the government has neither the beds, the premises nor the staff to manage the levels of patient demand. This is nothing new [Note 53]. This situation hasn't fundamentally changed for decades, despite the "Celtic Tiger" period of affluence. The reason for this is simple.

In Ireland, the elite political classes care little about the poor, rural or working class urban populations, except to keep them under control. They have adopted one of the methods of control from their ex-colonial masters, the British, namely a system of institutional neglect. The British drew a wall around the Dublin area and called it the Pale. Everything outside was "beyond the Pale" and that is pretty much how Ireland is governed today. Certainly, there are some very rich people living in rural Ireland, but they don't concern themselves with the lack of local services. Their children are in boarding schools, their internet connections arrive by satellite uplinks, their medical care is private and they arrive on their estates by helicopter or expensive 4-wheel drive vehicles, untroubled by the neglect around them.

Keeping the Irish poor, badly educated and socially excluded has maintained a high level of unemployment, emigration and low-paid work. Emigration acts as a safety valve, ensuring the country's population is low, poor and divided. Meanwhile, Ireland's political and economic elites reap the huge profits from Ireland's corporate tax fiddles and "brass-plate" corporate scams. During the "Celtic Tiger" years the country boasted about its huge budget surplus. But on the same front page of the Irish Times one could also read the tragic story of a pregnant woman that had to walk 19 miles from her village in the Dublin Mountains to get to a hospital to deliver her baby because there was no ambulance to collect her; just one more story of how Ireland's wealth is inequitably divided.

When it comes to government by neglect, Ireland sets new standards. However, in a similar vein we could cite the British government's neglect of those living in industrial zones in the North of England, the Australians' wilful neglect of their aboriginal people or the US government's institutional negligence of African-American and Hispanic populations and the vast numbers of underemployed poor in the USA.

Negligence and civil rebellion: Negligence may be a less aggressive strategy than the deliberate abuse of a population, but it is equally potent as a trigger for civil rebellion. When negligence is recognised by its victims, it may reach a point where unorthodox means, such as civil disobedience, are used to attract attention to their cause. Those suffering may even try to unseat and replace a government. At the time of writing, Ireland is undergoing huge changes in its political landscape, triggered by the government's severe austerity measures driven by three generations of government neglect and corruption.

2.2.3 Government by Hubris: Many state authorities suffer from a disconnected view of their own country and people. For instance, some post-colonial governments still see their countries as superpowers and waste vast sums of money and energy trying to maintain their grand international image and military prowess. They do so at a cost to domestic policies, such as education or healthcare. Such authorities don't exactly abuse power deliberately, but their decisions are based on delusion. Hubris is sometimes called the "pride that blinds" and in the examples below it is hard to believe that the policies described can be the decisions of entirely rational human beings, never mind modern national leaders.

Britain is a good example of government by hubris. Despite its once large empire, the UK is actually now a very small country on the periphery of Europe, both geographically and politically. Unfortunately, this reality hasn't been fully understood by large parts of the public and political classes. Despite the economic problems which bedevil the country, and the fact that the country cannot economically support its basic National Health Service or state school system properly, it still spends much more of its GDP on its military than any other country in Europe (2.3%) [Note 32]. Britain supports a nuclear armoury which needs constant expensive refurbishment and a submarine nuclear force which needs periodic replacement, as well as a large conventional ground army, air force and navy, none of which it can afford. Apart from privations caused to social spending by expenditure on a useless military, these hubristic policies lead to absurd situations.

Take for instance Britain's new and very expensive aircraft carrier, named amongst great pomp in 2014, the HMS Queen Elizabeth. The only little problem is that the aircraft carrier has no planes [Note 33] and one might say that an aircraft carrier without planes is not really much of an aircraft carrier! The planes will not be purchased until 2020, at the earliest. The

Harrier planes that Britain did have were sold to the USA to raise money several years earlier.

This is a painful reminder of Britain's diminished global status, exacerbated in the aftermath of its retreat from Iraq and the almost constant financial crisis. Deep defence cuts mean that for all that Britain struts about the world pretending to be important and dictating what should happen in other countries, the country simply doesn't have the money to fund armed forces to match its aspirations of global influence. The two aircraft carriers being built will only be able to carry helicopters. This lack of aeroplanes somewhat defeats their objective. The second carrier will be mothballed almost immediately after launch. Some have even suggested using them as mobile football pitches! However, at £3 billion each, there are some in the British public that begin to wonder why the country is being told to accept more and more austerity measures and cutbacks in services, whilst the defence industry is being awarded multi-billion pound contracts for military hardware that is effectively worthless. A similar tale surrounds the Trident nuclear fleet, now due for renewal at up to £100 billion [Note 34]. Given that this expense is for a military technology that cannot ever be used, the British citizen is understandably upset at the prospect of declining services and poorer living standards they must bear in order to pay for these shiny new missiles.

Apart from its military delusions, Britain delights in refusing to participate in the European project to bring the nation states of the continent together in a proper union. It can truly be said that Britain has dragged its feet on every progressive social or economic measure introduced by Europe. Whether it is open borders, common human rights laws, a common currency, common health and environmental regulations or common security, Britain is generally against cooperating to unite Europe. Britain periodically "threatens" to leave the EU and immediately starts to become dewy-eyed about how it will return to trade with the British Commonwealth countries (old colonies) - the nearest of which is in West Africa. Meanwhile, the Commonwealth countries are busy trying to disassociate themselves from Britain, its flag, its queen and its unfortunate history. It's a sorry sight to watch [Note 50].

Britain is not alone in its hubristic government, but it is certainly one of the most extreme cases, where much of government policy and expenditure is driven by delusion rather than hardnosed reality. It ignores the fact that its main trading partners are European nations and also the reality that militarily Britain is completely irrelevant - as witnessed by ignominious defeats in Iraq and Afghanistan.

Hubristic government might appeal to that part of the electorate prone to nostalgia. However, eventually popular opinion will turn against a government squandering money on a delusion, a lost empire, a dream of glory, long past.

When a populace is being pressed to accept two week waiting lists to see a GP, eight hour waiting time to get into Accident and Emergency or a six month waiting list for vital surgery, it's hard to accept tax payers' money being wasted on useless military hardware. There are limits and at a certain moment civil rebellion will demand an end to such madness.

Hubristic government is often its own worst enemy because it likes to publicise its expenditure with much pomp and circumstance. Rather than hiding military expenditures, it boasts about them, it rubs the noses of the poor in the grandeur of royal or presidential palaces, carriages, guards of honour, overflights and 21 gun salutes. This might fool some of the people some of the time, but it certainly does not impress all of the people all of the time, and hubristic regimes often experience tumultuous and unexpected social rebellions and upheavals. When the pomp is over, the poor return to their hovels and wonder why they are poor and dispossessed. It doesn't take long for them to put two and two together.

2.2.4 Lack of Ethics in Government: Poor standards of ethical behaviour by officials and politicians have a corrosive effect on public confidence in government authority. Even if poor ethical standards have no immediate economic impact on a population, they erode trust and confidence in the political system, the political classes and the civil service. Poor ethical standards create a climate of antagonism between an authority and its subjects. There are many forms of unethical behaviour in government:

Economic corruption: All government agencies suffer from some degree of economic corruption, carried out for reasons of personal gain. In some parts of the world, public administration is completely or partly hijacked in the interests of local "mafia". This type of corruption is far from the heady world of political corruption which may, at least, be driven by political or ideological motives. This is purely about money for favours. Favours may include turning a blind eye to dealing in drugs, to organised crime, organised prostitution, organised begging, or even unauthorised street trading. In less extreme cases, even in Western democracies we have countries where getting something done involves knowing a government minister or a high-ranking official. The process of awarding government tenders seems particularly prone to corrupt practices. Politicians reward large corporate donors with government contracts, which, in turn, provide funding for kickbacks as party donations and "presents" for political friends. This form of toxic economic corruption is a source of much public anger and disillusion in the political classes. This anger has been translated into electoral action and is currently altering the political landscape in several European countries, as traditional parties are replaced by new radical anti-corruption parties. Spain's Podemos and Ciudadanos parties are examples of this, and the dramatic rise in support for the Socialist Party and Sinn Fein in Ireland represent a similar rejection of the traditional two-party status quo.

Disregard for the public: Public officials exist to serve the public, who, in theory, pay their salaries. In reality though, public officials inhabit a world far apart from their public clients. For example, public officials working for the department of social welfare tend to be middle-class and have secure, life-long, pensionable jobs. On the other hand, their clients may live on the street, may be habitual drug users, may have psychiatric problems or may be educationally "sub-normal". They may live on the edge of society, quite disconnected from the norms of bourgeois etiquette. To expect the twain to meet requires exceptional qualities of empathy and experience of the officials involved, which means paying for expensive, highly-trained and experienced specialists. In reality, many government officials in such roles are the antithesis of "specialist". They tend to be hired according to the limits of a low budget, or to be staff left over after the talented ones have found "proper" jobs.

Civil services in most countries are staffed by those who simply don't have the talent to find "real" jobs, thus ending up in mediocre government posts where job security is more important than a challenging career. Talented people who accidentally "slip through" are quickly obliged to "conform or leave". Thus, civil service departments everywhere are centres of mediocrity, with most employees on a race to the bottom, where most staff members are intent on "keeping their heads down" and "covering arse". Civil service departments are rarely global centres of excellence in their chosen discipline.

The poor quality of human resources in the civil service, taken together with the inherently conservative, rule bound institutions and attitudes found in government departments, creates a perfect climate for shockingly poor public service. And, lo and behold, that is exactly what most public services deliver and what most members of the public report. Some examples of this are so excruciatingly frustrating for members of the public that they actually trigger off acts of civil rebellion.

Ultra Vires: There is one form of unethical behaviour which is particularly provocative to the general public and which occurs when an authority acts outside of its legal powers.

For example, an authority may make a judgement or decision that it has no legal right to make, exact an illegitimate tax or charge or seize private property without a proper legal basis. Such behaviour ranges from illicit seizure of illegally parked cars all the way to illegal imprisonment or execution of a citizen.

Sometimes a "legal" justification for an illegal act can work temporarily to placate the general public. For instance, when an authoritarian state justifies repressive acts against some citizens, that it has categorised as "terrorists", it becomes self-evident that the legal state has complete justification to act against such insurgents for the greater good. However, if it emerges that these "enemies of the state" are actually a political fantasy and that there is no legal right to act against them, then suddenly the legal basis of an authority is quite undermined.

Such a situation occurred in Spain, in February 2003, when the country was on the brink of becoming seriously involved in the Iraq war. Despite the lies of its government, the country's population rose in heated street demonstrations of millions and demanded the end to Spain's involvement in the military adventure. Massive urban demonstrations, well beyond the control of civil authorities, effectively contributed to displace the conservative government and caused Spain to withdraw from the Iraq war effort shortly afterwards.

2.2.5 Other Motivations for Civil Disobedience: Governments often behave in the most perverse way when trying to control their subjects, and they often provoke acts of civil rebellion simply because they are incompetent or perverse. Sometimes it seems that governments are deliberately trying to make life as unpleasant as possible for the citizen. At a certain moment it all may become too much and the citizen, independently or in groups, rebels against the authority. Here are three different motivations for this:

2.2.5.1 Arbitrary Government: This is a phenomenon in which a citizen is treated in a seemingly arbitrary or absurd way by the state or other authority. It is manifested in laws, regulations, prohibitions, rules and conventions deliberately designed by a powerful authority with the express intention of inflicting indignity and hardship on ordinary citizens as a means of control. By imposing absurd rules and insisting that the rules are "normal", this strategy replaces common sense with a set of arbitrary regulations which undermine and degrade the citizen and allow the authority to control ridiculous narratives.

The underlying tendency of governments that make and enforce such ridiculous laws is authoritarian. Part of their reasoning is that they need to constantly reaffirm that they have the power and that the citizen has to obey - however absurd the rules. There are many examples; some are just cases of the "nanny state" on steroids, but others are quite sinister attempts at corralling and manipulating civil populations.

The growth of annoyingly absurd regulation in the last generation has been prolific. Even taking out those, sometimes dubious, initiatives which are honestly designed to protect the citizen, such as smoking restrictions, food safety regulations, and health and safety rules, we are still left with a mountain of legislation that seems to have been designed by someone with a bizarre sense of humour.

The problem is that for the ordinary urban, time-poor citizen, already stressed by a busy life, huge economic pressures on top of the normal commitments to manage their life and family, it's a bit rich when a school authority starts actively monitoring the contents of their child's sandwich box and rejecting what they consider unhealthy. Arbitrary rules such as these, however well-intentioned, are a red rag to a bull for the average citizen. They are often the very trigger mechanisms for individual protest, which may lead to more organised forms of civil rebellion. Here are a couple of examples. There are many more.

The airline security circus example: For contemporary examples we have to look no further than the increasingly bizarre regulations regarding airline passenger security. Restrictions on carry-on liquids, shoes, belts, and nail files are supplemented by naked full body scans, invasive searches, arbitrary watch lists, and racial profiling of passengers. These are all examples of absurd, worthless and arbitrary regulations which serve only to annoy and humiliate passengers, but have zero effect on aircraft security.

For instance, it is still legal and quite normal to carry litres of highly inflammable alcoholic liquors onto aeroplanes around the world (we call it duty-free), why would a terrorist bother trying to secrete similarly inflammable substances in his underpants? He and his colleagues can just bring their handy duty-free shopping right into the cabin when they board a plane and no questions asked. A couple of litres of cognac, decent vodka or polish spirit ignited in an aircraft cabin or toilet would cause quite a conflagration. And if you forgot to buy your inflammable booze at the airport duty- free, don't worry; the hostesses will be around in a minute with little bottles of it, served right to your seat! It really doesn't get more absurd. A mother and baby may have their milk bottle confiscated, or an old lady may have her mineral water seized, or a teenager may have a jar of peanut butter ceremoniously taken out and subjected to a controlled explosion, but hey, bring as much inflammable alcohol as you like onto the plane and boxes of matches, no problem. To add insult to injury, airline security regulations allow everyone to carry on several lithium batteries in their phones, cameras, laptops, tablets etc. without any restriction, despite the fact that these are amongst the most dangerously explosive batteries that exist and are prone to cause violent uncontrollable fires under certain conditions. That's all fine, but, for God's sake, don't bring a jar of your favourite sandwich spread or a bottle of water - they're really dangerous!

The net effect of this and similar airline security fiascos are a huge amount of delays, discomfort and inconvenience when trying to board a plane. Go to any airport and watch the enormous queues of human lemmings taking off their belts and shoes, their jewellery, looking for loose change, opening and starting their laptops, phones and tablets, putting tubes of toothpaste in regulation size plastic bags, and getting full-body pornographic X-rays. And God help you if your phone battery is flat, they'll just confiscate your new iPhone without a moment's hesitation. It is a vision of circus-like absurdity, on a par with the images conjured up in the Magic Christian of perfectly normal businessmen jumping into a swimming pool full of sewage to retrieve a few dollar bills. And this global pantomime contributes zero to airline security, whilst making travel a complete nightmare for millions of regular air passengers.

As the destruction of Germanwings Flight 9525 in March 2015 demonstrated, there is a great deal more to flight security than making passengers take off their shoes and locking cockpit doors.

Leaky border control example: Another example of absurd security measures is to be implemented at Britain's ferry ports. The conservative government of David Cameron intends to implement a system whereby all passengers leaving Britain by ferry have to have their identity verified. It is a system of exit control not unlike those used in China, Saudi Arabia, the former Soviet Union or North Korea. The objective, the British government claims, is to control the movement of terrorists.

The fact that all of the terrorist acts committed in Britain since 9/11 were committed by British citizens doesn't seem to have deterred the Tory lawmakers' enthusiasm for inflicting pain on the general public. However, the only problem is that these exit checks double the passenger processing time and severely impact the already long queues to board the ferries. Every coach and car has to disgorge its passengers for individual passport checks. One university of Kent study has shown that the new exit checks, during peak times, will cause 9 km long traffic tailbacks from the ferries, effectively closing access to the whole port of Dover.

The government's response to this scenario is that during peak periods the home office may allow the exit checks to be waived. This obviously sends a very clear message to would-be terrorists planning a day trip to Calais, which is "always travel on peak period days and then you won't be checked!"

The absurdity of the new regulation doesn't end there, though. Neither Britain nor Ireland are members of the borderless European zone called the Schengen area. However, under separate arrangements, British citizens can travel to and from the Republic of Ireland without passport controls or other border checks. Indeed, there are no border posts at all between the two countries. This means that our would-be terrorist can simply drive to Dublin without any border controls whatsoever, and then take a ferry to France or wherever, without the British government knowing he has left Britain. He can also return in the same way. Similar routes also exist via the Channel Islands. In other words, the government regulations assume that all terrorists leave Britain via Dover or the other east coast ports and not via Ireland, for instance. That's one hell of an assumption!

Such a leaky system of exit control, which is so easy to bypass, is effectively worthless as a means of catching terrorists or managing border crossings. It will certainly cause havoc, annoy a lot of holidaymakers and cost haulage companies a fortune in wasted time on the road. It will damage the British tourist industry and increase the costs for exporters, but it will not improve national security one jot, nor deter a single would-be terrorist from travelling [Note 35].

2.2.5.2 Institutional Incompetence: Incompetence is an integral part of all bureaucracies. Governments, politicians and civil servants live far apart from "normal" society in many ways and have little practical experience of how the real world works. They build administrative systems that are focused on control and compliance monitoring, rather than on good, human design and ease of use.

Creating an impression of control: Many systems are designed to give the user the impression that citizens are being carefully monitored by government whereas in reality, the information the user provides is unusable for any form of control. For instance, governments ask for information which is not and cannot ever be used, but where the request alone is enough to create a climate of fear for the user. In Spain, for instance, it is common practice to ask a customer for an identity card when issuing an invoice. This is then photocopied and added to the mountain of other photocopies of identity cards and then, after a few months, these are discarded. The shop is obliged by the tax authorities to identify the customer in this way, but has no means of processing the millions of photocopies. The act of taking the copy is purely symbolic and designed to give the customer the impression that their economic activity is being controlled, when obviously, it is not.

Control freaks are incompetent: The desire to exercise control and demonstrate the power of authority blinds the average civil servant to the primary objective of their job, which is to be a servant of the public. They become ensnared in their own web of bureaucratic rules, losing any sense of "the bigger picture", any concept of common sense, and any feeling of humanity. Civil servants begin to see themselves as custodians of the rules and users as mere fallible mortals that understand nothing. The relationship between civil servants and the population thus descends into a game, where the civil servant tries to entrap an unsuspecting civilian, and where the public delights in "gaming the system" to get one over on the authority. This climate of antagonism makes dealing with institutions of state a highly laborious, labyrinthine and inefficient experience. For this reason, the vast majority of the general public in countries around the world will agree that the civil service is institutionally incompetent.

Limits of public tolerance: At some levels this incompetence is tolerable. Spending two days to have your new car registered in Germany is annoying, but not the end of the world. However, if you happen to be a single mother with 3 small children, without work or money to feed your family, and your application for social security has mysteriously disappeared, then institutional incompetence comes into very sharp relief. It becomes, literally, life-threatening and there are many such examples.

When incidents of institutional incompetence impact a larger group of the public, they can trigger anger and eventually organised civil rebellion. For instance, delays by a government to pay subsidies to small farmers may well trigger some organised farmer protests. Government incompetence at a higher level, such as the mishandling of a conflict or economic crisis, may well trigger large-scale protests. Many of the recent anti-austerity protests in Greece, Spain, Ireland, Germany and Portugal have arisen because the public blames the incompetence of their governments for the mishandling of their economies and the lack of banking regulation. This, the public believes, is what has plunged Europe into an economic recession. These protests are gradually turning into a slow-motion political revolution which promises to displace many of the traditional political classes from their jobs.

2.2.5.3 Hypocrisy in Government: There is no doubt that one of the most irritating acts by an authority is one which demonstrates obvious hypocrisy. It's almost guaranteed to trigger outrage from the public.

In 2015, there were large-scale demonstrations in Frankfurt, Germany, which degenerated into rioting at the opening of the new European Central Bank building. Demonstrators were complaining about the excessive austerity measures being taken against some poorer Euro members, but one particularly antagonistic fact was that the new shiny glass-and-steel ECB tower office block cost the European tax payer over €1 billion, at a time when many people in Europe literally had no income at all and were living out of rubbish skips. The hypocrisy was not lost on the demonstrators and, taken together with some police overreaction, the protests turned into car burning riots.

Similar resentments continually smoulder in most countries, but especially when governments make harsh demands on their population whilst, simultaneously, their political classes are themselves enjoying lives of privilege and affluence. This hypocrisy provides fertile feeding ground for the venting of strong popular emotions and demands for change amongst the economically and socially excluded. It is not difficult to see how an attitude of "let them eat cake" can quickly tip an angry crowd into a murderous insurgency.

2.2.5.4 Disrespect in Government: We know that many of those that govern or employ us have little respect for us. For them we are just the "little people" that must be tolerated and controlled. We are just "the 99%", the outsiders and no-hopers, excluded from the powerful elites that control capital and run governments.

Most governments try at least to keep their disrespect under cover in public. However, occasionally their real feelings slip out and we plebs get a glimpse of what people in authority really think about us. In a similar way to hypocrisy or political corruption, such disrespect may not in itself be enough to base a civil rebellion upon, but it may be enough to trigger and validate other protests against an authority. The disrespect of an authority gives a protest group a good reason to say "Look, I told you so!" to the public and gather support and validation. Here are a few examples from which it is easy to see how the disrespect of our political leaders can quickly trigger public anger and frustration.

In late 2014, a Conservative Welfare Minister (Lord Freud), no less, was actually recorded at a public meeting as saying that disabled people are "not worth" the full national minimum wage. His answer was in response to a question from a Conservative councillor at a fringe event at a Tory party conference. He even went on to suggest £2 per hour might be considered! (The minimum wage of £6.50 is generally considered to be below what is considered a living wage in Britain, and so £2 per hour would be equivalent to a starvation wage).

The comment triggered a shockwave of outrage. There is something particularly hurtful and distasteful about a government minister saying that one group of people are not worth the same as the rest of society. It's a comment that is more than faintly fascist, like something that might be being explored at a Nazi party meeting. It says much about the attitude of the conservative political elite towards the rest of us mere mortals, disabled or otherwise. The comment coincided with four years of the British Conservative government's attacks on disabled people and put it into words. "You are disabled and that means you are not worth as much as other people." It is really something to hear a government minister articulate the belief that the disabled are not as good as other citizens, that they are not of value, in fact, less a citizen and more fair game to be exploited with low wages. For many, the comments demonstrated again that the government was colluding with big capital to build an underclass based on the desperately poor and disabled. The same minister was on video record in the House of Lords during a debate in which he described the changing number of disabled people likely to receive the employment and support allowance as a "bulge of, effectively, stock". After a furious response by the disabled community, Hansard, the official record had to be altered to remove the offending word. Nonetheless, the word "stock" was used and, most likely, in the context of the employment of disabled labour in government employment programs, which in turn provide cheap, disabled labour to generate profit in a number of large companies.

In another sinister act of disrespect, in 2013, the police of the Irish Republic seized two children (aged 2 and 7) from a Roma family, simply because they were blond and blue-eyed. For this reason, the Irish police assumed that the children must have been kidnapped by the Roma family (all Roma have black hair, according to well-informed sources in Irish police intelligence). After several days and DNA tests on the parents and children the authorities returned the children to their distraught family. This act of "disrespect" would have been quite at home in the Nazi Germany holocaust, especially since the police were acting partly on public tip-offs. It says much about the ignorance and embedded fascist attitudes of that country's authorities that they had the arrogance to assume that a Roma child couldn't possibly have blond hair and blue eyes. Does that mean that all Irish children that do not have red hair and freckles must be the victims of kidnapping? Clearly, this was simply just an act of total disrespect by the authorities against a traditional scapegoat community, based on mindless government prejudices. Plainly, the Roma community in Ireland is not going to view the police (Garda Síochána) as "guardians of the peace" after an incident like this [Note 52].

2.3 Civil Disobedience and Trigger Events. What makes it suddenly happen?

The degree and variety of civil rebellion against maladministration depends on assorted factors. What do we know?

• **Fundamental threats cause strong reactions:** We can see that threats to fundamental human needs, such as shelter, security and food, generate profound and potentially violent acts of rebellion. Threats to higher needs, such as creativity or self-esteem, may be annoying, but they generate less profound reactions. We also know from observation that any threat to any human need has the potential to trigger off or compound civil rebellion of some kind. For instance, threats to our "sense of justice" may trigger off some form of civil rebellion, such as a protest demonstration, even though this is not a threat to a very basic human need.

• **Threats and injuries are added together:** We know that the severity of civil defiance is proportional to the sum of the injuries inflicted by an abusive authority. We don't react to a single injury; we react to an accumulation of injuries. The fewer and less serious the injuries, the less severe the reaction. Governments misguidedly often implement repressive measures piecemeal, in the hope to lessen public reaction to them. We see this in the way in which the USA, UK and Russia have gradually implemented more and more surveillance measures on their civilian populations in the last decade. They have done so in tiny steps, hoping that no-one will notice that civil and human rights and freedoms are being undermined. Fortunately, civilian populations are not so easily fooled and when protest does begin, all these offences are rolled up into a popular indictment of the authority.

• **Abuse is historically cumulative:** We know that, in almost all cases, acts of abuse are cumulative and are not readily forgotten or forgiven. Abuse is like a bank account. Every oppressive act is added to the victim's balance of grudges against an offending authority. We know that there will always be a reckoning of sorts - big or small, sooner or later. For instance, seventy years after WWII, countries or groups who suffered at the hands of the Nazis are still settling scores and harbouring a desire for revenge. In 2015, for instance, an impoverished Greek government, with much popular support, demanded €11 billion from Germany in reparation for the Nazi invasion of Greece in the Second World War. Old crimes cast long shadows and are not so easily erased. The same goes for a civil population's grudges borne against authorities. They tend to accumulate until they are properly confronted, either by the authority or by a rebellious population. For instance, the crimes of General Franco in Spain, still largely unresolved, continue to surface on a daily basis. This historical memory of abuse doesn't suit governments very well. They would really prefer if we just forgot about previous misdeeds. Unfortunately for them, the public never forgets an offence.

• **There is almost always a day of reckoning:** We know that often a "settling of accounts" tends to occur during civil rebellion, insurgency or revolution. Often this revenge seems disproportionate to the apparent authoritarian crime, but in reality this "payback" is the sum total of all abuses against all victims, for however long they have occurred. The acts of retribution are condensed into a shorter period of (often bloody) revenge. Every victim wants to punch the abuser, so we often end up with physically and politically violent results. The violence of the French Revolution largely reflected the duration and depth of suffering of the French peasants, which had lasted for centuries. The bloodletting was not the result of a few months of bad government; it was the pent-up anger of many generations, expressed in just a few years.

• **The victim may not always attack the right perpetrator:** We know that acts of civil disobedience are not always clearly aimed at the obvious perpetrator of the oppression or abuse. An uninformed victim may lash out at authority in general, in a frustrated attempt to damage their abuser.

Alongside these characteristics there also appears to be subtle trigger mechanisms at work in the relationship between acts of oppression and retaliatory reactions from an abused individual or civil population. For example, very often we see long periods of fairly steady oppression taking place without any retaliatory action at all by the abused. Then, suddenly, we see a rapid (and often dramatic) change in mood as the victims become mobilised and begin to take action in the form of some kind of civil rebellion. This sudden change often appears to have no apparent cause, or is the result of some quite minor escalation in abuse. Thus, there is obviously much more involved in learning to understand why some threats to our basic needs turn into serious civil rebellions, whilst others do not.

In the following section we will attempt to explain the relationship between a citizen's fear of authority and why it is that suddenly some citizens will decide to attack an authority.

2.3.1 Catastrophic Changes of State: What causes these sudden, often explosive reactions to upset apparently stable abusive regimes? For instance, history has many theories about what triggered the French and Russian revolutions or the Protestant Reformation. But the excesses of the Romanovs, Bourbons and Papacy were old news, and in all these and many similar cases, none of the explanations really account for the causes and timing of the sudden violent chain of events that overthrew two millennial empires and the world's largest Christian church.

This brings us to an important point about popular rebellion, including civil disobedience, and that is its spectacular unpredictability, both in timing and in consequence. This lack of predictability is what terrifies would-be authoritarians so much. The unpredictability of civil rebellion generates authoritarian paranoia, which itself often leads to even more abusive oppressive government and creates an escalating feedback to amplify a potential conflict between authority and civil population.

An understanding of the complex, apparently unpredictable relationship between oppression and rebellion lies in the concepts of catastrophe theory. This group of ideas and mathematical models studies and classifies phenomena characterised by sudden shifts in behaviour arising from small changes in circumstances. The theory analyses how qualitative changes in systems or behaviour may sometimes depend upon very small qualitative changes in conditions. These models show how tiny changes in one or more parameters may lead to sudden and dramatic changes, for example, the unpredictable timing and magnitude of a landslide [Note 40]. They apply to the oft-quoted example of the effect of the flap of a butterfly's wing, which may trigger a hurricane on the other side of the planet.

Within catastrophe theory there are several well-defined "geometries" which describe how apparently stable systems can very rapidly alter their state given very small changes in conditions. One of these, the "cusp" or "butterfly" geometry, is often used to model human and animal psychology and behaviour when threatened or stressed by an external influence (such as an oppressive authority).

In particular the cusp catastrophe is often used to model the "flight or fight" behaviour of a stressed dog, which may respond to outside threats by becoming cowed or becoming angry. [Note 41] The threatened dog passes through a series of complex mental states as it is progressively threatened. Initially it feels confident to attack, and then fear alters this state, until the dog alternates between snarls of aggression and whimpers of fear. This dynamic and the "catastrophe" models used to explain it, work pretty well for human beings as well as for dogs. The suggestion is that at moderate stress levels, the dog will exhibit a smooth transition of response from cowed to angry, depending on how it is provoked. But when a new threat occurs at higher stress levels, we start with a situation where, if the dog is initially cowed, it will remain cowed as it is irritated more and more; until it reaches the so-called "fold" point, when it will suddenly, discontinuously snap through to its "angry mode" without any smooth transition, not gradually, but instantly. Once in 'angry' mode, it will remain angry, even if the direct irritation or threat is considerably reduced. This behaviour is easy to demonstrate, provided you have the confidence to confront a potentially angry dog (or person)!

In human psychology, the gradual application of moderately oppressive behaviour against a victim will lead to a smooth transition from relative contentment (social contract) to relative anger (social conflict). Withdrawing the oppression will reduce the level of anger. These gradual changes in the level of oppression can be repeated ad infinitum. However, when a person or group is severely abused or oppressed, i.e. is living with a background of continuous oppression, then initially the victim(s) will conform out of fear (they are in "flight mode"). However, if the oppression continues, the victims will suddenly and unpredictably snap into a state of great anger ("fight mode") and remain in that state for an indefinite time. In this state, removing the oppressive threats will no longer alleviate the anger or aggression. The victim is now in full "attack mode" and the abuser had best take care not to be bitten (or guillotined)!

In real world examples, this trigger phenomenon is easy to identify. For example, the excesses of the French aristocracy were legendary and long standing at the time of the revolution. However, a succession of contemporary economic problems, poor harvests and sudden high food prices came on top of many generations of political repression of the French peasantry. These additional hardships suddenly triggered off a hellish, unstoppable reaction, the consequences of which we all know. The revolution was by no means preceded by greater oppression or abuse of the peasants, but other unconnected factors combined to create a catastrophic change of political state, from stable feudal repression to bloody revolution. We will now take a closer look at how cusp catastrophes explain civil conflict.

2.3.2 Fear, Conflict and Authority - Flight or Fight and Catastrophe Theory

It is reasonable to assume that authoritarian threats to human needs are the basic underlying causes of civil rebellion. What isn't quite so clear is why these civil conflicts only arise in some cases. What is it that suddenly tips a person or group from being obedient, law-fearing citizens into becoming rebellious protesters? There is an inclination to assume that more oppressive government always leads to more rebellion, in a simple linear sense. But, clearly, this is not so because in some cases more oppressive government sometimes results in more subservient populations. In reality, the relationship between authoritarian threat and popular reaction is a great deal more complex than a linear correlation between oppression and rebellion or oppression and obedience.

To understand this phenomenon we have to examine the relationship between the citizen and their authority, both in terms of catastrophe theory and the behavioural psychology of fight or flight reactions. In the "fight or flight" scenario, the relationship between moods of aggression and fear is contrasted with fight or flight behaviour under various levels of threat.

Mathematically, a catastrophe is a sudden, discontinuous change in a system and in its environment. It is an event that may be anticipated, but cannot be predicted with any accuracy as to when or where it will take place, or how severe it will be. This lack of predictability makes people generally overly optimistic about the likelihood of a threat actually taking place, its severity, the vulnerability of their own systems, and the consequences of a threat coming to fruition. For the most part we live in a world of mundane risk and opportunity; a little gain here and a little loss there, with most fluctuations in the environment taking place at the margins. Authorities are notoriously optimistic that they are in control and they are often blinded to risks of civil rebellion, until these risks actually and suddenly materialise.

Catastrophic events become highly likely when a population's grievances are not attended to for a long time and then some unforeseen outside force triggers a civil revolt. It works like this: in neutral conditions, a citizen feels neither fear nor anger towards their governing authority. However, as an authority alters its behaviour in a way which is perceived to threaten the needs of the citizens, the citizen's feelings begin to alter. In one case, citizens may feel increasingly fearful and apprehensive about the behaviour of an authority. This fear increases to a point where the inclination is for the citizens to run from the authority's threats or oppression. However, as fear increases, a new factor begins to enter the dynamic and that is anger. With time, or increased oppression, a frightened citizen becomes increasingly angry about their situation, to a point where they feel anger and fear in equal amounts. In an alternative, but similar, scenario, a civil population being oppressed by an authority may at first feel great anger towards the authority. Gradually this anger becomes tinged with fear and apprehension, until the population again reaches a point where sentiments of anger and fear exist to an equal degree. This is a very perilous place for both a civil population and its governing authority because it indicates proximity to a catastrophic event. The following graphic goes some way to illustrating this complex relationship.

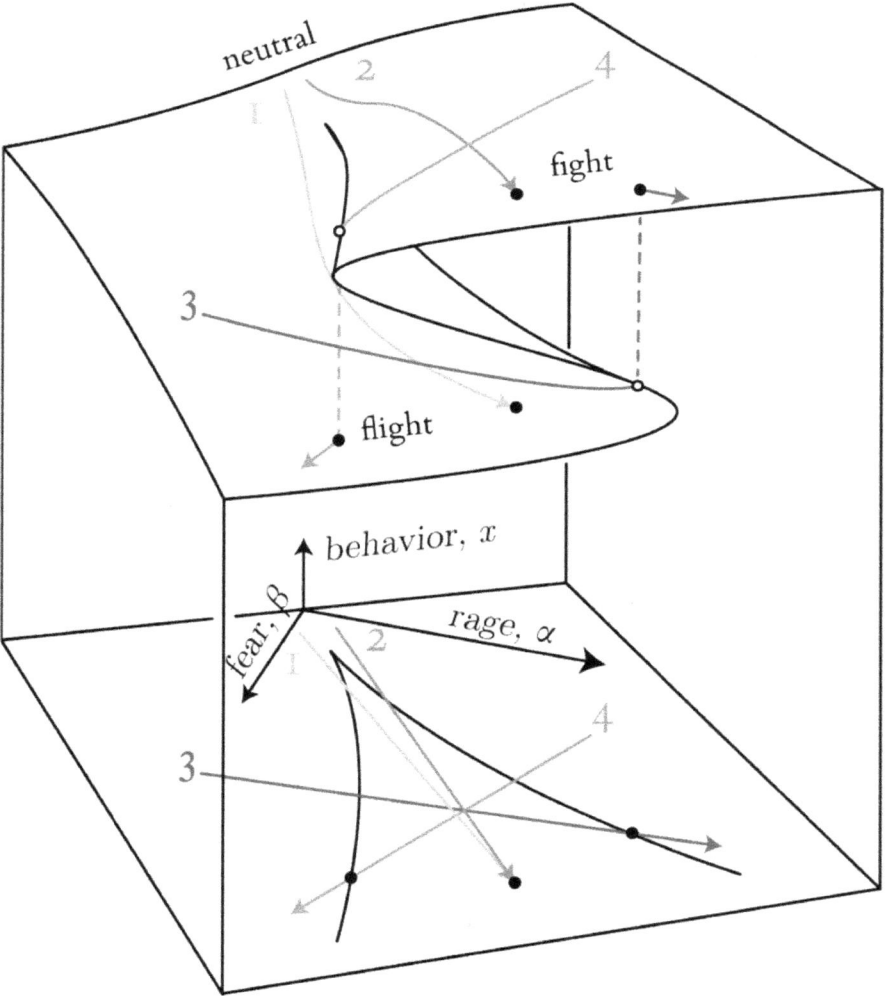

Note that the two cusps (or folds) are the points where additional fear leads to flight and where additional anger leads to fight.

In both cases, at this point a civil population is at the critical juncture where it may either flee from the authority, thus losing ground completely, or it may turn around and fight. The population is now close to the so-called "cusp" of a catastrophe, where even a very tiny change in the amount of fear or anger it experiences will trigger a dramatic alteration in the behaviour of the citizens. It is in these near catastrophic circumstances that very small, seemingly insignificant events can trigger a full-blown civil rebellion (or complete retreat).

For instance, an authority becoming increasingly oppressive at this point may trigger additional anger, which will then lead to the civil population attacking the authority. However, equally, additional oppression may lead the civil population to become more afraid, in which case the oppression may trigger a fear reaction, leading to the complete retreat of the civil population.

How these slightly altered circumstances (the additional oppression or some outside influence) affects the civil population is actually impossible to predict for either an authority or a protest leader. At this critical point in a conflict, a small change in the stimuli affecting a civil population produces a large and dramatic change in their behaviour, ranging from a full-scale civil rebellion to complete retreat and conciliation, but it is impossible to say which.

How authorities and protest groups behave to channel responses to these small changes can have an important affect on the outcome of a conflict. A protest group may attempt to convert small increases in threat into greater popular anger, in the hope of triggering an attack on the authority. An authority may try to convert their threats into greater popular fear, in the hope of triggering a full-scale climbdown and retreat by the civil population. In either case, what happens next will be quick, dramatic and largely unpredictable.

Before leaving the topic, it's worth mentioning that we have only considered the behaviour of a civilian population under threat and how its reaction may be strong and seemingly unpredictably in some circumstances. We should not forget that authorities also feel threatened by civilian populations, and an authority's behaviour is subject to similar rules. Their behaviour can be influenced by fear and anger in exactly the same ways. This needs to be remembered by the leaders and planners of civil rebellions. Sometimes it may suit a protest leader to keep a government relatively placid; in other cases it may be useful to trigger either a climbdown or an attack by an authority.

Notes on Chapter 2

Note 1: International Journal of Law, Crime and Justice, Volume 40, Issue 2, April 2012, Pages 65-81The social consequences of a mass surveillance measure: What happens when we become the 'others'?

Note 2: Stanton, Jeffrey M.; Barnes-Farrell, Janet L. Journal of Applied Psychology, Vol. 81(6), Dec 1996, 738-745, "Effects of electronic performance monitoring on personal control, task satisfaction, and task performance."

Note 3: In sociology and psychology, an ingroup is a social group to which a person psychologically identifies as being a member. An outgroup is a social group with which an individual does not identify.

Note 4: The Leadership Quarterly, Volume 22, Issue 1, February 2011, Pages 170-18 "Leadership, power and the use of surveillance: Implications of shared social identity for leaders' capacity to influence", Emina Subašića, Katherine J. Reynoldsa, John C. Turnera, Kristine E. Veenstraa, S. Alexander Haslamb

Note 5: Internment: A chronology of the main events. Conflict Archive on the Internet (CAIN)

Note 6: Article 33 of the Fourth Geneva Convention specifically forbids collective punishment.

Note 7: ICRC says Israel's Gaza blockade breaks law". BBC News. 14 June 2010.

Note 8: Shane Darcy, 2003, Al-Haq,West Bank affiliate of the International Commission of Jurists: "Israeli's Punitive House Demolition Policy: Collective Punishment In Violation Of International Law"

Note 9: Guardian, Wednesday 8 May 2013: "The sun is at last setting on Britain's imperial myth", Pankaj Mishra

Note 10: Guardian, Tuesday 10 March 2015:"MPs with highest outside earnings are less active in parliament, study finds", Frances Perraudin

Note 11: Murray, Raymond. The SAS in Ireland. Mercier Press, 1990. pp.44-45

Note 12: Reports of International Arbitral Awards XX: 215-284, especially p 275. 30 April 1990.Case concerning the difference between New Zealand and France concerning the interpretation or application of two agreements, concluded on 9 July 1986 between the two states and which related to the problems arising from the Rainbow Warrior Affair".

Note 13: Monthly Review, 2001, Volume 53, Issue 06 (November): "The United States is a Leading Terrorist State: An Interview with Noam Chomsky - An Interview with Noam Chomsky" by David Barsamian

Note 14: Country Reports on Terrorism - Office of the Coordinator for Counterterrorism". National Counterterrorism Center: Annex of Statistical Information. U.S. State Department. April 30, 2007.

Note 15: Stockholm International Peace Research Institute, Top List TIV Tables-SIPRI. Armstrade.sipri.org.

Note 16: 28 November 2014, TeleSur: Australia Gains Reputation as 'Law-Breaker' for Refugee Policy, Two U.N. agencies condemned Australia's hardline asylum seeker regime in the space of just a few hours.

Note 17: September 30, 2014: Sydney Morning Herald: "Detention centre child sex abuse claims number in dozens"

Note 18: Guardian, Monday 4 August 2014: Australia's detention regime sets out to make asylum seekers suffer, says chief immigration psychiatrist

Note 19: Mirror, 29 January 2015: "Westminster paedophile ring victims suffer death threats after Select Committee published their details online"

Note 20: AFP, Wednesday 11 March 2015 "UN torture expert refused access to Guantánamo Bay and US federal prisons".

Note 21: OpenNet Initiative "Summarized global Internet filtering data spreadsheet", 8 November 2011 and "Country Profiles", the OpenNet Initiative is a collaborative partnership of the Citizen Lab at the Munk School of Global Affairs, University of Toronto; the Berkman Center for Internet & Society at Harvard University; and the SecDev Group, Ottawa

Note 22: According to the social commentator Michael Landier.

Note 23: Global Research, December 19, 2012, "Cancer of Corruption, Seeds of Destruction: The Monsanto GMO Whitewash", F. William Engdahl

Note 24: Lawyers and Settlements, November 21, 2007: "Zyprexa Side Effects are Deadly", By Heidi Turner

Note 25: Guardian, Saturday 29 December 2012: "Revealed: how the FBI coordinated the crackdown on Occupy", Naomi Wolf

Note 26: The Telegraph, 11 Feb 2015: "Meet the NHS whistleblowers who exposed the truth", Laura Donnelly

Note 27: Guardian, Friday 29 June 2012: "Police officers and abuse of powers: the list, Police officers in court for harassing individuals listed", Sandra Laville

Note 28: Guardian, Tuesday 9 July 2013: "Misuse of stop and search powers risks undermining police, says watchdog", Alan Travis

Note 29: Washington Post, January 4, 2014: "The NSA refuses to deny spying on members of Congress"

Note 30: New York Times, November 27, 2013: "The N.S.A. Dips Into Pornography"

Note 31: Irish Times, Fri, Mar 20, 2015: "Income divide between Dublin and regions rises again"

Note 32: Defence Data Portal, Official 2012 defence statistics from the European Defence Agency

Note 33: Telegraph, July 4th, 2014: "An aircraft carrier without planes is the perfect metaphor for Britain's diminished global status"

Note 34: Guardian, Richard Norton-Taylor,Tuesday 20 January 2015: "Trident: Parliament debates £100bn project - at last"

Note 35: Guardian, Alan Travis, Tuesday 17 March 2015: "Ferry companies: immigration checks will cause travel chaos at Dover"

Note 36: RT, March 17, 2015: "Unintended consequences: Obama traces origin of ISIS to Bush-era Iraq invasion"

Note 37: Guardian, Friday 20 March, 2015 "UKIP faces crisis after suspensions and racism claims - MEP Janice Atkinson, UKIP 's candidate in Folkstone and Hythe, was suspended over claims that a member of staff attempted to overcharge EU expenses", Rajeev Syal

Note 38: Gene Sharp, ed., Waging Nonviolent Struggle: 20th Century Practice and 21st Century Potential (Boston: Porter Sargent, 2005), pp. 41, 547.

Note 39: Maria J. Stephan and Erica Chenoweth: "Why Civil Resistance Works, The Strategic Logic of Nonviolent Conflict". International Security, Vol. 33, No. 1 (Summer 2008), pp. 7-44 Harvard College and the Massachusetts Institute of Technology.

Note 40: Catastrophe Theory In Social Psychology: Some Applications To Attitudes And Social Behavior, Oregon State University by BR Flay - 1978

Note 41: E C Zeeman, Catastrophe Theory, Scientific American, April 1976; pp. 65-70, 75-83

Note 42: Guardian, Monday 3 November 2014: "Corrupt Spanish politics faces shock therapy from an angry electorate", Miguel-Anxo Murado

Note 43: Saturday 21 March 2015 "Revealed: the link between life peerages and party donations", Daniel Boffey: "Ground-breaking study reveals the link between seats in the House of Lords and donations"

Note 44: Guardian, Wednesday 2 April 2003: "Mesopotamia. Babylon. The Tigris and Euphrates", Arundhati Roy

Note 45: Guardian, Thursday 17 January 2002: "The Geneva convention" by Simon Jeffery

Note 46: Guardian, Friday 12 December 2014: "Britain convulsed by its dirty secret in wake of CIA torture report", Ian Cobain

Note 47: Guardian, Sunday 14 December 2014: "CIA torture report: at least the Americans came clean. In Britain, no one is held to account"

Note 48: Daily Mail, 5 June 2013: "Mau Mau fighters raped, castrated and beaten in Kenya's uprising against Britain get £14million compensation but no apology"

Note 49: Guardian, Wednesday 29 October 2014, Katie Engelhart "40,000 Kenyans accuse UK of abuse in second Mau Mau case", "Castration and inhuman treatment among claims of 41,000 Kenyans seeking damages"

Note 50: Independent, 24-3-2015: "Barbados plans to remove the Queen as head of state almost 400 years after British colonisation"

Note 51: Survival International, 3-7-2014: "Amazon Indians join forces to reject 'devastating' mining": http://www.survivalinternational.org/news/10333

Note 52: Guardian, Thursday 24 October 2013: "Irish police return blonde girl to Roma family".

Note 53: Irish Times, 21-4-2015: "The trolley emergency: when will they ever learn?"

---o0o---

3. The Morality and Legality of Civil Disobedience

A lot has been written on the subject of the morality of peaceful civil rebellion, especially the use of civil disobedience. It has been a hot topic in political philosophy since Plato and to this day it remains a source of some controversy. The connection with legal justification clouds and complicates moral considerations because it begs the question when it is legitimate to disobey the law. In the following sections we will examine these moral and legal issues and how these apply to those engaged in peaceful civil rebellion.

3.1 The Moral Issues involved in Peaceful Civil Rebellion

Because civil disobedience involves breaking the law, many philosophers have argued that it needs special justification. However, we can argue that this only applies when we have an obligation to obey the law. If, for example, the state is not legitimate or is behaving very unjustly, then perhaps we don't have any political obligation to obey its laws. If we aren't obliged to obey the law, we do not need a special justification for breaking it. This doesn't automatically mean that civil disobedience would always be justified, but it does mean that justifying it is no different from justifying any other actions we may take.

3.1.1 The Concept of Political Obligation

Political obligation refers to a citizen's moral duty to obey the laws of his country or state. This is an important concept in the morality and legality of participation in actions such as civil disobedience where it is very likely that laws are going to be broken, so it is worth spending a little time understanding the meaning of political obligation.

The discussion of what political obligation means to the citizen has gone on for thousands of years. Plato had Socrates refusing to obey the city elders in favour of divine rules, which he considered higher than his obligations to the civil authorities. The concept of political obligation took another step with the advent of Christianity, which accepted that the citizen owed certain duties to Caesar and others to God. Christian doctrine seemed to make it clear that what the rulers command may be at odds with what God wants done. However, parts of Christian gospel also implied that rulers were given the right to govern by God and therefore should be obeyed almost without exception.

By the 17th century, new theories defined the relationship between a citizen and the state in terms of a social contract in which (put briefly) the state agrees to protect the citizen in return for the citizen's obedience and subservience to the state. Breaches of social contract by either party would, according to this theory, lead to social conflict. The question of whether a law should be obeyed was further developed when the Utilitarians of the eighteenth century proposed that, morally, only good laws should be obeyed and bad laws could be ignored. Their reasoning for this was that bad laws are those that have little use (utility) to society and therefore should be ignored. Good laws are those that bring human happiness, pleasure, economic well-being and the reduction of human suffering. Bad laws are those that do not bring such benefits. By the end of the eighteenth century there were several conflicting views on political obligations; with Kant arguing that the citizen had an absolute obligation to obey the law of his government, good or bad, simply because law and order were better that the chaos of ungoverned society.

By the end of WWII, after the moral hand-wringing of the Nuremberg trials, the question of political obligation had come to include a discussion of when a political obligation exists and when it may be ignored for moral reasons. The so-called Nuremberg defence, which was often used by the Nazi war criminals on trial, was that they were not guilty of the charges against them as they were "only following orders." Thus, the Nuremberg principles set out guidelines for determining what constitutes a war crime. The principles were created by the International Law Commission of the United Nations to codify the legal principles underlying the Nuremberg Trials. Under Nuremberg Principle IV, the "defence of superior orders" is explicitly excluded as a defence for war crimes, as it states: "The fact that a person acted pursuant to order of his Government or of a superior does not relieve him from responsibility under international law provided a moral choice was in fact possible to him."

The negation of the Nuremberg defence clearly lays the moral responsibility for an act squarely on the shoulders of the individual and indeed enjoins the citizen to disobey an order if it is immoral.

Thus, the long evolution of the concept of political obligation has firstly altered the meaning of the moral principle from being one of simple obedience to the law into a moral question about whether a law should be obeyed on conscientious grounds. Then the concept has further evolved into a positive injunction and legal obligation to disobey a law if the law is patently immoral.

Despite this new conditional definition of political obligation, every authority in the world believes that its citizens have a political obligation to obey all the laws and orders that they make, without exception. The arguments for this are that there are other ways of bringing about changes using the law, such as political lobbying etc. Nonetheless, the Nuremberg principles still exist as international law and provide several justifications for a citizen to break the law when justified by moral objections.

3.1.2 Breaking the Law in an Illegal or Unjust State

If a state is not legitimately constituted or is legitimate but behaving unjustly, then there is a strong moral case to justify a citizen's refusal to obey the laws of that state. Therefore, in this case the issue of political obligation doesn't arise: there is no political obligation on the citizen of such a state, because the social contract has been broken.

We need look no further than Nazi Germany to find a case of a legitimate state that behaved very unjustly, both to many of its citizens and to its neighbours. In such a case, as an extension of Nuremberg Principle IV, the citizen has both a moral right and obligation not to obey the laws of the state and, in fact, if they do obey, then they may, under international law, be held morally and legally accountable for their actions.

In this case, no further discussion of the morality of civil rebellion is required because there is no moral or political obligation to obey the country's laws and, indeed, there is actually a moral imperative to engage in civil rebellion. In this example, we might even argue that there is an ethical justification that civil rebellion should be escalated to violent insurrection, as was the case in several Nazi-occupied countries.

3.1.3 Breaking the Law in a Democratic Society

The background assumption in most of this discussion on the morality of peaceful civil rebellion is that we are referring to democratic states. We assume that the state is reasonably just, and sufficiently fair-minded in general to imply a political obligation on us to obey its laws.

In this case, the fact that we are breaking the laws of a just state counts as a moral reason against engaging in civil rebellion, simply because we are breaching our legitimate political obligation. In addition, of course, many laws are supported by several other independent moral reasons, such as benefiting "the greater good". To morally justify civil disobedience then, we will need to provide a justification that can outweigh these moral reasons as well.

But one can argue it can sometimes be morally justified to break our political obligation for the sake of some greater moral value. In "A Theory of Justice", John Rawls, the moral philosopher, argues that if the aims of an act of civil disobedience are important enough, the act can be justified on certain conditions. One of these conditions is that all legal attempts to change the law have failed. Civil disobedience must be a 'last resort'. The second condition is that civil disobedience must be nonviolent. These conditions may seem reasonable, but they do have some important limitations. How, for example, do we know when all legal means are actually exhausted? How can this work in an emergency when there is no time for legal action or lobbying? Who decides and how do we decide that it is clear that legal action has failed and civil disobedience must begin? Regarding violence, we may argue that the issue should not be violence v. nonviolence, but whether the consequences of the action are justified by its aim. Sometimes the consequences of nonviolence can be just as bad as violence, e.g. ambulance drivers going on strike. And sometimes, it may be that limited, directed violence can make a point where nonviolence would not succeed, e.g. when the civil disobedience occurs in a brutal, violent, unjust state.

3.1.4 Do we have a Right to Civil Disobedience?

Some philosophers have argued that in a democracy we have a right to civil disobedience as part of our democratic rights. For example, some have argued that whenever the law wrongly violates one's rights, then one has a right to civil disobedience. This right is not explicit, but it is entailed by our other rights, including those that the law has violated.

But do we have a right to civil disobedience? Certainly, we have a right to political participation and if our political obligation rests on our consent of the state as legitimate, then we must also have a right to dissent. If we have no right to dissent, the idea of our "consent" would have no meaning because we have to be consenting partners in the social contract for the social contract to have meaning. If we have no right to dissent, we live in an authoritarian state which is unjust and for which we have no political obligation to obey its laws.

But having the moral right to express one's dissent does not logically guarantee a right to civil disobedience. It may only give us the right to legal protest actions and not illegal acts of civil disobedience or direct action. Some have argued that when we have a political obligation, i.e. when we reside in a liberal or just democratic state that protects the right to legal dissent and maybe the right of conscientious objection, then there is no right to civil disobedience as well. The argument is that we have as much rights to protest as we need, but stepping further into acts of civil disobedience is a breach of our political obligation to our decent liberal state.

But if this is the case, then under what circumstances may a citizen morally engage in civil disobedience in such a liberal democratic state? Indeed, is civil disobedience ever morally justified in a just, democratic state that tolerates dissent? To answer these questions we have to examine what we mean by the words "liberal", "just" and "democratic".

3.1.4.1 The Democratic Deficit: In reality, no state is all good, just, liberal and democratic and the corollary is also true of authoritarian states. The truth is that there are streaks of authoritarian instinct within the political establishment of even the most liberal Western democracy. History and human nature have bequeathed us a sizeable number of autocratic politicians who would rather rule with an iron fist than with a humanistic concern for the citizen's rights and well-being. For them democracy is an inconvenient obstacle which has to be tolerated. Sometimes these would-be tyrants find themselves in government and they waste no time in implementing laws that satisfy their authoritarian tendencies, degrading the rights of the citizen and helping enrich fellow elite members. If we look at any modern Western democracy we can see plenty of laws, government orders and regulations made in circumstances which clash directly with the rights of the citizen and concepts of government for the greater good.

In such circumstances citizens may find themselves in conflict with a just, democratic state. The conflict is not total, the citizen doesn't object to everything the state does, but does strongly objects to specific laws, orders or attitudes of the state. Some basic needs of a citizen may be at risk, some civil or human rights may be undermined or the safety of future generations may be threatened, but that doesn't mean that everything the state does is unjust. Such outbreaks of authoritarian behaviour are common in all democracies. Democracy is an inclusive form of government, open to all opinions and political colours, and the risk of electing a government with authoritarian ambitions is therefore rather high.

These cases of a democratic state acting unjustly or autocratically, also known as the "democratic deficit", provides the very moral basis for citizens to suspend their political obligation to obey the laws of the state and, as we have already said, there is no moral obligation for a citizen to obey the illegitimate laws of an unjust state. In the same vein, we can logically argue that there is no moral or political obligation for the citizen to obey the laws of a just state when the laws themselves are unjust or when the state is behaving unreasonably or has undermined its primary responsibility to protect its citizens.

For instance, it could be argued convincingly that a democratic government that uses tax-payers' money to buy unnecessary military hardware in times of peace whilst taking essential funds away from public health care has breached its primary responsibility to protect the interests of its citizens. There are numerous similar examples, where a normally just government becomes unjust. The government hasn't broken any laws, it is simply that the laws it has made are unjust. In such circumstances, the citizen has the moral right to use all forms of peaceful civil rebellion to register their dissatisfaction.

3.1.5 Violence versus Nonviolence: In a just, democratic state, if we compare the consequences of violent and nonviolent action, we can see how the consequences of nonviolence are "better" than those achieved with violence. Violence tends to breed violence whereas nonviolent protests do not encourage others to use violence. Nonviolence does not antagonise those opposed to an act of civil disobedience as much as violence does, so nonviolent actions are less socially divisive. Therefore, from a pragmatic point of view, in the case of a just state, peaceful civil rebellion is a superior strategy to the use of violence, which tends to be counterproductive.

A powerful argument also exists for nonviolent action at a moral level. In the same just, democratic or egalitarian society the most important interest that the law and state protects is the safety of the citizen. This is a primary component of the state's duties in the social contract. To threaten this with violence is to act unjustifiably, in general.

Nonetheless, the use of violence in civil rebellion is sometimes triggered by the same authoritarian streak found even in fair democratic states. Sometimes, as we have seen, normally democratic states exhibit authoritarian streaks leading to physical violence by the state against protest or civil disobedience. Often authorities over-react in the hope of "teaching those protesters a lesson". In an ideal world our well-disciplined, patient protesters will calmly accept the violence and turn the other cheek. Sadly, we don't live in a perfect world and often the violent escalation of conflict by an authority will trigger off a defensive and then an aggressive reaction from a group of disobedients or protesters.

How justified is this violent reaction by protesters? Well, again, a government which reacts to a peaceful protest with violence forfeits its right to be referred to as a "just state". The use of violence by state authorities against peaceful dissenters makes that state, at least temporarily, an unjust, authoritarian state. In these circumstances, again, the citizen's political obligation to obey the law is suspended until government regains its legitimacy. During this time citizens may feel justified in defending themselves from the violence of the state and this, in turn, may involve the use of limited acts of violence against the state by protesters. The use of such violence may be counterproductive if it is sustained, but it may be quite effective if the violence is short and sharp. The shock effect may help bring a government to its senses and return it to a more democratic and just state.

3.1.6 Moral Justifications of Civil Disobedience

Even when we consider acts of civil disobedience morally legitimate, we are still not free of moral considerations when carrying out such acts. Acts of civil disobedience have consequences with moral implications. The morality of our motivation in committing acts of civil disobedience also needs to be questioned; we may be doing the right thing for the wrong reasons and this may make a protest morally indefensible. Here we examine these two moral questions.

3.1.6.1 Consequences: An act of civil rebellion, such as civil disobedience, has consequences which are sometimes far-reaching. It may damage a society economically, socially and politically. It may be divisive and may unintentionally encourage general disrespect for the law. Civil disobedience can increase political instability, and it may even lead to reprisals on people who do not support the protest. All of these potential consequences have a moral implication.

Moral calculations: For instance, how much economic damage is tolerable to achieve a particular protest objective? Causing widespread job-losses and bankruptcies in order to achieve a small pay rise for a selected group of workers may well be construed as morally indefensible. Triggering off social divisions between groups supporting a development and those opposing it may be more damaging than the development itself. A responsible protest group needs to understand the moral issues connected with the consequences of their actions and make appropriate moral calculations when planning a peaceful civil rebellion.

Morality of failure: Having acknowledged that all forms of civil rebellion have consequences with moral implications, we must also consider what happens if an act of civil rebellion fails. This may well be a nightmare scenario for two reasons:

Firstly, no protester wants a campaign to fail. Failure triggers disappointment, frustration and perhaps hopelessness and a feeling that the campaign was a gross waste of time and energy. Organisers of the protest are morally responsible for managing these sentiments in the event of a failure.

Secondly, as we discussed above, a campaign of civil rebellion comes with economic, social and political costs to society. This is the case whether the campaign fails or succeeds. Perhaps these costs are considered morally justifiable by the higher moral objective of the protest; however, that moral calculation only works if the campaign succeeds. The justification falls apart if the campaign fails, in which event society has to bear all of the costs incurred by the protest and none of the benefits of the campaign succeeding.

This brings us to an important moral consideration: To undertake civil rebellion without a good chance of achieving the desired change in the law or policy is morally irresponsible. The objective can only justify the means if it has a realistic chance of success.

The costs of failure, both to society and to a protest group, are high and therefore protest organisers have a moral responsibility to ensure that their objectives are reasonably attainable. In terms of practical planning, this means adopting a strategy which divides big and difficult objectives into smaller, achievable ones.

Mitigating moral dangers: The moral risks of civil rebellion shouldn't for a moment dissuade the protester from proceeding with their plans, but they should provide food for thought. The moral dangers should be discussed and taken very seriously in the practical planning of a campaign, right down to individual actions. A campaign which isn't grounded on well thought-out and properly morally justifiable actions will arouse the contempt of the public and will have limited long-term support. The ends do not justify the means. Both means and ends must be separately and properly morally justified.

However, there are other features of a protest campaign which can mitigate the moral dangers of the action:

A willingness to remain peaceful, disciplined and to submit to punishment (in the case of an unlawful act of civil disobedience) makes clear the protesters' general respect for the authority of the law in a democracy. This minimises any encouragement of unjustified disobedience, general disrespect for the law or incitement to violence. It also indicates the protesters' strength of feeling and the fact that they are not acting for personal gain. These sentiments diminish the antagonism and resentment that others may feel if they disagree with the protest. This policy also cancels out an authority's possible claim that the protest is simply a cynical political wrecking action with no moral principles, a favourite authoritarian attack strategy. This can be neutralised if the protest group has a well-developed moral evaluation and justification to hand.

3.1.6.2 Motivation: The morality behind the motivation for a campaign or action is another important factor. For example, part of the definition of civil disobedience is that it is motivated by a genuine sense of a law being morally wrong. However, this may not be enough.

Justice offended: Some moral philosophers [Note 1] claim that protesters must specifically seek to address society's sense of justice, arguing that justice is the most important and fundamental value in political society. People may legitimately disagree about moral values, so these cannot be the basis for laws or for changing laws. Laws should be based on justice, and arguments about laws should therefore refer to justice.

In this scenario, civil rebellion can only be morally justified if the motivation is based not just on an objection to a single, simple bad law or regulation, but must be based on a defence of justice itself. This raises the bar a great deal because it means that civil disobedience, for instance, could only be used when justice itself is threatened by an authority. In this case there would need to be a clear and substantial injustice, as only such a serious wrong could justify the grave act of breaking the law.

Not just justice: Many moral and political philosophers disagree with this assertion. They argue that political society concerns other values apart from justice. Politics may concern itself with human well-being, human rights, sustainability, economics, etc., as well as justice. These values may also provide strong morally correct motivations for the use of civil rebellion. An example might include a situation where a population lives in a state that's just, but their very existence is threatened by poverty; they have a great justice system but they are starving. The state may find itself incapable of dealing with the cause of the poverty, even though it attempts to maintain justice. A similar scenario might exist where a perfectly just state threatens the environment because of ignorance of the consequences. In both cases there is no obvious injustice intended, but there is a prima facie case that the state has failed to act reasonably and to satisfy its part of the social contract to protect the citizen. In these scenarios civil disobedience clearly does not need to be motivated by or appeal to a sense of justice. It can be justified on the simple political grounds that the authority has failed to protect its citizens. The social contract has been broken.

A middle road: One way of reconciling the two opinions on this is to ensure that the means of civil rebellion is proportional to the end. If a group of parents illegally blockade a street as part of a campaign to have a safe crossing installed for their children, this is obviously justified, even though the issue is not socially 'substantial' and has little to say about injustice. A small protest for a small aim is obviously not wrong. Similarly, there would seem to be good moral justification for a general strike to protest nation-wide austerity measures forcing millions of people out of work and obliging many families to sleep on the streets in abject poverty. A general strike in protest would seem an eminently proportionate response; moderate, in fact.

Planners of civil rebellion need to give careful thought to the appropriateness of their action. Their conclusions depend on being sensitive to the social and political context. How unjust is the government generally? How unjust is the law? How much protest can society take? These questions cannot be answered in general but they must be considered by a campaign group upfront because obviously they have both planning and moral implications.

3.1.6.3 Political Health and Civil Rebellion: One of the most convincing moral justifications for civil disobedience and protest is that peaceful, but powerful, civil challenges to authority improve the political health of society. Thus, instead of looking at peaceful civil rebellion as an irritant and disruptive influence on the smooth running of society, we should actually see it as essential for the political health of the state and therefore a demonstration of good citizenship by its members. There are several reasons for this:

• Authorities that are challenged become less complacent. A complacent government that ignores public sentiment is in danger of failing in its primary role of defending the public good.

• Authorities that are challenged are obliged to confront their own policies. An authority that remains unchallenged begins to believe its own propaganda. Strong challenges to an authority eventually oblige the authority to review their own policies against a different (protest) narrative. This can, and often does, have the effect of dismantling long accepted propaganda.

• An authority that is frequently challenged is constantly reminded that power ultimately resides with the people. Authorities are quick to forget that, even in totalitarian regimes, they govern at the pleasure of the masses. Mass actions that are defiant of authority remind our leaders that what separates the corridors of power from the passage to the hangman's noose is the goodwill of the people. Frequent peaceful civil rebellions are good reminders of this.

• Acts of civil rebellion drive difficult issues into the public domain. They oblige the public to think and to consider sometimes complex subjects that affect them and the political life of the state. In a world where the public are increasingly disengaged from party politics, acts of civil rebellion often engage the public in issues of the wider political world. When the citizen realises that there is a direct connection between their current living conditions and the high price of oil caused by a certain war, then they become involved in politics again. Civil rebellions such as anti-war protest actions, for instance, can help achieve this re-engagement of citizens.

3.1.6.4 Can Civil Rebellion be Immoral? Acts of peaceful civil rebellion are not confined to those of a left-leaning temperament. Indeed, there are no political limits to who may engage in peaceful civil rebellion, ranging from the far left to the far right. Even those attempting to establish authoritarian states may use peaceful civil rebellion as a means to achieve this end.

Obviously the objective of peaceful civil rebellion may be in itself immoral. Also, as we have discussed, the motivation for and consequences of civil rebellion may also be construed as immoral. By definition therefore, civil rebellion is not necessarily a principled action taken by highly moral citizens in pursuit of the greater good. During the time of the Sandinista governments in Nicaragua (1979 to 1990) there were continuous campaigns of civil rebellion, sometimes very violent, ostensibly carried out by anti-government dissenters, but actually financed by the US government via the CIA in an attempt to destabilise the revolutionary government.

So, clearly, peaceful civil rebellion can be immoral. It all very much depends on the motivation.

3.1.7 When is Civil Disobedience a Moral Obligation?

Sometimes there are moments when civil disobedience is not an elective political action, but becomes a moral and even a legal obligation. Such cases occur where an individual or group of citizens are confronted by an authority which is engaged in acts of such obviously abusive and oppressive behaviour that it is morally impossible for the citizen to ignore this behaviour. This concept of a moral and (sometimes) legal responsibility on the individual to defy the orders of an authority in cases where natural justice and human morality are being abused by a government is now enshrined in international law and, indeed, occasionally in national laws in some countries.

Do no wrong: Whilst we cannot all significantly change the world or challenge all the oppressions of our fellow human beings, we can ensure that we do not, at least, contribute to their oppression. As Thoreau said in his famous lecture "Resistance to Civil Government", in 1849:

"It is not a man's duty, as a matter of course, to devote himself to the eradication of any, even the most enormous wrong; he may still properly have other concerns to engage him; but it is his duty, at least, to wash his hands of it, and, if he gives it no thought longer, not to give it practically his support. If I devote myself to other pursuits and contemplations, I must first see, at least, that I do not pursue them sitting upon another man's shoulders. I must get off him first, that he may pursue his contemplations too."

This is the concept of "do no wrong". In other words, if you can't do anything good, at least don't do anything bad. If you can't do anything to stop the evils and injustices of the world, at least do not contribute to them. This is an important moral principle which drives many morally responsible citizens to disassociate themselves from collaboration with oppressive and abusive regimes.

The Nuremberg defence: Under the heading of moral obligation to disobey we return again to the most startling modern example, which is that of Nazi Germany. The participants in the Nazi WWII atrocities on trial in Nuremberg realised that they could not shift blame or moral responsibility for these crimes to their superiors. The UN, at that moment, made it quite clear (in the Nuremberg principles) that the defendants should have refused immoral orders. This clear statement by the UN actually moved civil disobedience out of the realms of moral choice and into the realms of moral and legal obligation.

As mentioned, many Nuremberg defendants claimed they were not guilty of the charges laid against them as they were "only following orders." This is often referred to as the "Superior Orders" defence. The important legal point defined during the Nuremberg trials was that the defence of superior orders was no longer considered enough to escape punishment; it merely could lessen punishment. The concept of direct legal responsibility, regardless of superior orders, remains somewhat unclear in international law, but generally speaking, there lies a clear responsibility on any individual to refuse an order which breaks international law, including breaches of the UN Charter of Human Rights and a large group of other treaties such as the Geneva Conventions.

In such cases, an individual or group is legally (and morally) bound to take actions of direct civil rebellion by disobeying or ignoring orders issued by a legal authority, be it government, military, police etc. This imperative over-rides issues of whether a state is just and democratically constituted. As it happens, Nazi Germany was, by and large, a legal and properly constituted democracy. Nonetheless that counts for nothing, according to the UN, when that same state breaches natural law and international laws in its treatment of civilians, conquered regions and prisoners of war.

3.2 Other Moral Justifications for Civil Rebellion

3.2.1 Survival, Self-Defence: In extreme cases, such as wartime occupation, the use of civil disobedience may be a means of survival or basic self-defence. The right to life provides moral cover for civil rebellion when survival is at stake.

The citizen's right to self-determination when suffering an occupying force, or when one's government is a puppet for an alien power, also provides a moral justification for rebellion.

The situation gets a bit complicated when a citizen's government is being controlled by a foreign power. Such was the case in much of Latin America in the 1970s and 1980s when the USA dominated weak fascist governments. Their countries were run effectively by the CIA (El Salvador, Chile, Columbia etc.) In such cases there is no obvious occupying force, but the national government had effectively betrayed its own citizens by selling out to an alien power and thus breached the social contract. In this case the citizen certainly has no political obligation to the state such as it is.

3.2.2 Civil disobedience as a Form of Defiance: There are arguments that a citizen has a right to protest when an authority refuses to take their complaints seriously or when an authority attempts to suppress their dissent. This protest takes the form of an act of defiance against an authority which has, temporarily at least, decided to ignore the voices of its citizens and even attempts to silence them. In this case, the state has ceased to be a just state, and the political obligation on a citizen to obey the state is removed. The state becomes temporarily illegitimate. The social contract is partly and temporarily broken. In such a case the citizen has the right to demonstrate their defiance against the unjust state and may justifiably use civil disobedience to do this.

3.2.3 Religious Justifications: Religion and the underlying ethics of a religion may provide a moral justification for civil rebellion in the same way as any other sincere moral conviction, provided that it is not motivated by self (or group) interest.

The history of civil disobedience has many examples of principled groups driven by religious and philosophical ideologies. Martin Luther King, Gandhi and the fathers of the Christian Reformation were all motivated by ideology and religion in combination with a liberating vision of humanity which brought them into conflict with conservative establishment authorities.

3.2.4 War and Civil Disobedience: In a war the rules for the morality of civil rebellion are somewhat altered. For instance, we may find ourselves as citizens of a conquered country where the occupying force behaves in a just and respectful way to the population. In such circumstances it may be that there is little point or moral justification in carrying out acts of civil rebellion. They may, indeed, be counterproductive. In these circumstances civil rebellion could be construed as an aggressive act of war against a conquering nation, solely because they are conquerors and not because they have breached the social contract. Indeed, they may govern in a perfectly decent way.

On the other hand, if an occupying power treats a defeated population unjustly, then it forfeits the right for its government to demand political obligation from the civil population. Peaceful rebellion can be easily justified and may indeed be essential to improve conditions for the greater good.

The other important moral consideration of civil disobedience in times of war is when the citizen comes from the country waging war on another. There are those that would argue that it is immoral to engage in civil rebellion at a time when their country is fighting a war, because it is divisive, distracting and encourages disloyalty. This, of course, is too simplistic an analysis.

We have to return to the same acid tests to find a proper moral analysis. Is the state engaged in a "just war"? Is it a war of defence or aggression? Did the state do everything in its power to avoid war? These are the questions which allow a protester to decide if civil rebellion during time of war is morally justified or not.

Obviously, in the case of a defensive war against an aggressor, where the state has tried but failed to negotiate a peace with the aggressor and is now fighting for its very survival, there is a strong case to argue that now is not the time for civil disobedience. The state is trying to defend its citizens as best it can under the terms of the basic social contract and the political obligation of the citizen should be at its strongest. The stakes for survival are thus too high to permit the luxury of local civil rebellion.

On the other hand, a state may itself be engaged in an unjust war of aggression against another country, and be the active aggressor in this war. In this case, the state is behaving in a way which is unreasonable and may be illegitimate. To a greater or lesser degree the state is being unjust, both to the victim nation and to the future security of its own citizens. It thus relinquishes the right to the political obligation of its citizens and leaves itself open to civil rebellion on the issue of the unjust war and any other issues afflicting the civilian population.

Contrary to what our governments would like, i.e. blind obedience and jingoistic enthusiasm for all their military adventures, the one circumstance we mentioned earlier is the only instance when we can morally (and legally) justify support for war, i.e. a war that is clearly defensive. In these extreme conditions, it is hard to find moral justification for civil rebellion. However, conversely, when aggressive wars are conducted by our own state, it is indeed morally insupportable not to engage in civil rebellion against our state government.

3.3 The Legal Issues involved in Civil Disobedience

There are lots of definitions of civil disobedience, but in a legal sense the following definition is quite clear: "An act of civil disobedience is an illegal public protest, nonviolent in character" [Note 2]. From a legal point of view there are two aspects to civil disobedience: a/ the nature of the act which makes it recognisable as civil disobedience and b/ the evaluation of the acts in a legal sense

3.3.1 The Legal Nature of Civil Disobedience

For an act of protest to be classified as civil disobedience it must display the following characteristics:

• An act of civil disobedience must break the law. However noisy, lawful protests cannot be referred to as civil disobedience. To be classified as civil disobedience a participant must explicitly break a law or refuse to obey a law.

• Acts of civil disobedience must be public. By its very nature an act of civil disobedience needs to communicate with the authorities and public, since its main reason is to change a public policy or law. Civil disobedience must therefore become public.

- An act of civil disobedience has to be motivated by an act of protest. Public illegalities which do not represent a protest objective are not acts of civil disobedience, they are just criminal acts.

- An act of civil disobedience is, by definition, nonviolent.

3.3.2 A Legal Justification for Civil Disobedience?

If we accept that civil disobedience involves the wilful breaking of a law as a means of protest and that this unlawfulness is an integral part of the act of civil disobedience, then it is impossible to find a legal justification for civil disobedience. The law cannot justify the violation of the law. It is a contradiction in terms. If there is a legal justification for an action, that action is not an act of civil disobedience, it is merely an act of legally justifiable protest, which is something different from civil disobedience.

The law, self-sacrifice and civil disobedience: According to traditional views of legal obligation in a just, legitimate society applying the rule of law, anyone who deliberately breaks the law should be tried and punished for that offence. The civil disobedient deliberately breaks a law he knows is applicable to him and he is no exception to the rule. He is subject to the normal punishment for the offence he commits. Participants in civil disobedience understand this and accept it fully. They break the law with the express intention of pleading guilty to a minor crime, and with the expectation of being punished for it by a fine or jail sentence. In acts of civil disobedience, a legal punishment is more than just a possible consequence of the act; it is the natural and proper culmination of it. Because the act is one of protest, the disobedient's submission to public punishment is vital in demonstrating the protester's intense concern over the issue at hand.

Prosecution of a case against participants in acts of civil disobedience increases the publicity of the act and demonstrates commitment to the protest cause, thereby demonstrating the dissident's willingness to self-sacrifice on behalf of that cause.

Civil disobedients should, and normally do, realize that punishment for their infraction is not and cannot be bypassed because of the noble motivation of their disobedience. Indeed, it is just because it is a crime, and known by protester and public to be punishable, that the act is chosen and serves as a dramatic form of protest. If we take away the illegality of the action, we take away much of the value of the protest action.

Punishment: Whilst there may be no logical legal justification for civil disobedience, how does the principled action of a civil disobedient affect their punishment? Again, in a society applying the rule of law, the punishment of an individual engaged in civil disobedience should be determined solely by the severity of the infraction. There is no crime of civil disobedience and so there is no fixed punishment for it. In addition, it would be unjust for the law to treat an offence committed by a disobedient differently from the same infraction carried out by an ordinary citizen - neither more harshly nor more leniently.

Having said that, a trial court has some discretion over how a defendant is sentenced and may consider the circumstances of the disobedient act and the attitudes and character of the accused. It may find that he broke the law deliberately, perhaps defiantly, but it may also weigh the honourable motivation of the act. While that motivation cannot properly cancel the guilt, it can affect the response of the community to the offence. It would be reasonable to treat a case of civil disobedience as a simple infraction without looking at any special circumstances. But if a court does consider special circumstances in terms of punishment, then all circumstances, including those in the protester's favour may also be considered.

3.3.3 Breaking the Law to Test the Law

Sometimes an apparently unjust law may be tested by a deliberate infraction to determine its legal status in court. The participants may look forward to being vindicated if the tested law is proven to be invalid and the protesters can go home happy. However, if the court decides against them, they can expect no thanks for testing the law and will be subject to the full rigours of the judicial system, despite the morally motivated reasons for their actions. There is no judicial basis for any form of legal mitigation just because the defendant is trying to clarify the law by testing it.

3.3.4 When does Legal become Political? - Size matters

In principle, in a state that operates under the rule of law, it doesn't matter whether an offence is committed by 1 person, 100 people or 10,000 people; they should all face the rigours of justice equally. This applies to illegal acts of civil disobedience just as much as it does to any breach of the law.

In reality however, when the number of citizens committing an illegal act is large, then somehow, at some point, the offence moves from the legal domain to the political arena. There are several obvious reasons for this: a/ the state feels incapable of processing legal actions against thousands of defendants without triggering further citizen action, b/ the legal systems and physical facilities of the state are overwhelmed by the numbers of defendants, c/ the sheer volume of support by citizens indicates a political base for the protest cause, which the state feels insecure about challenging at a judicial level.

Even the most just democratic state will act as a judicial bully when its officials think they can get away with it. They will gladly prosecute small numbers of protesters that break the law. In fact, many states will deliberately target small numbers of protesters for prosecution to "make them an example" to others. However, as in all cases of bullying, the state will think twice about taking on several thousand organised protesters. In such circumstances, authorities may suddenly decide to use the rhetoric of conciliation rather than that of prosecution.

This is an important principle for the organisers of various forms of civil rebellion: what is a criminal offence for 10 demonstrators may well be construed as a "political statement" when 10,000 are involved.

3.3.5 The Right to Civil Disobedience

We have discussed the concept of moral justifications to carry out acts of civil disobedience in certain circumstances: when a state behaves unreasonably and oppressively and has thus breached the social contract with its citizens. We know that this can be morally reconciled with a citizen's political obligation in a just state to obey its laws. Unfortunately, the same calculation cannot be made in terms of the law.

The right to use civil disobedience is a moral right and not a legal right. Nonetheless, many have argued that civil disobedience is a vital means of maintaining the stability of a just constitution [Note 3], and some have gone even further, defining which types of laws could be "legitimately" disobeyed and which laws must be obeyed regardless.

Disobedience and types of law: Gandhi distinguished between "moral laws" which may not be broken, for instance, laws forbidding the murder of innocent people, and what we might call "pragmatic laws", such as revenue laws that are justified as being useful for the governance of a country but are considered neither moral nor immoral. Such laws might be useful or harmful and may be disobeyed for symbolic purposes under certain conditions. Gandhi also said that immoral or unjust laws, where obedience would involve directly compromising one's own self-respect or committing immoral acts, could also be disobeyed. The laws that we could break, in principle, are the purely state-made laws, as opposed to those laws which reflect morality and justice. Our duty to obey moral laws remains, regardless of how wicked the state is.

Disobedience and the health of the constitution: Gandhi went on to argue that civil disobedience was not just a right, but that it was also invaluable in the workings of a constitutional state. Sometimes when someone disobeyed a government ordinance or law, Ghandi argued that the executive or the legislature could be acting unconstitutionally. This could be so, even if the highest court came out in favour of the state, simply because the interpretation of the constitution was not infallible. Civil disobedience, when conducted properly, could play a valuable role in the just working of the constitution. In fact, Gandhi claimed that the true civil disobedient "is a philanthropist and a friend of the state..... Pure civil disobedience, therefore, must not be carried beyond the point of breaking the unmoral laws of the country". Gandhi thought that civil disobedience, when properly conducted, could work as a safety valve because in its absence there would be violent threats to the constitutional system. He, like John Rawls, believed that honest civil disobedience worked as a stabilizing device for the constitutional state.

A right, but only in unjust states? Other philosophers and legal specialists, such as Joseph Raz, have argued that civil disobedience should be legally confined to illiberal, non-democratic and non-participatory societies, where the citizen has no chance to help formulate the laws that govern him. He argues that in a liberal, democratic state the citizen has enough access to the law-making process to negate any right to civil disobedience as a method of persuasion. However, Raz does admit that even in liberal democracies there may be a case for civil disobedience when it is the morally right thing to do. Thus, Raz grants that even liberal societies may contain any number of bad and iniquitous laws, but he is anxious to deny that there is any right to civil disobedience because such a right permits people to indulge in civil disobedience, even when it is wrong to do so.

As a last resort in self-defence: One other argument in defence of a right to civil disobedience centres on self-defence of the citizen. Some have argued that administrative and legal failures often place a citizen in a position where they have no alternative but to constructively break the law in order that they can be heard and defend themselves. Certainly, there are plenty of examples these days where access to proper legal services for citizens is limited by their relative poverty, even in modern Western democracies, and thus citizens become excluded from the proper workings of legal process. The legal system becomes the preserve of the wealthy. In such cases there may well be a legal argument that the citizen's constitutional rights are violated and that acts of civil disobedience are actions of the last resort.

A better alternative to violence: Most liberal political philosophers have argued that, whilst civil disobedience may never become a "right" in a system based on the rule of law, nonetheless it should be treated leniently in the courts, as the dissenters are acting out of principle, perhaps self-defence and (generally) in the interests of the common good. Lawyers will honestly argue that civil disobedience is a peaceful (if disruptive) act of protest that allows a frustrated citizen to draw the attention of authority to protest issues and that it is an act of last resort. One potent argument is that civil disobedience acts as a fairly harmless democratic safety valve, without which violent rebellion could well ensue. Surely peaceful civil disobedience is preferable to that.

3.3.6 Legal Necessity - When is Civil Disobedience a Legal Obligation?

There are no national laws which explicitly permit the breaking of the law. However, there are some laws which allow a citizen to act disobediently.

Nuremberg revisited: The Nuremberg Principles clearly oblige us to be disobedient to authority when the orders are immoral and in breach of international law. These principles carry force of legal precedent.

- Principle I: "Any person who commits an act which constitutes a crime under international law is responsible therefore and liable to punishment."

- Principle II: "The fact that internal law does not impose a penalty for an act which constitutes a crime under international law does not relieve the person who committed the act from responsibility under international law."

- Principle III: "The fact that a person who committed an act which constitutes a crime under international law acted as Head of State or responsible government official does not relieve him from responsibility under international law."

- Principle IV: "The fact that a person acted pursuant to order of his Government or of a superior does not relieve him from responsibility under international law, provided a moral choice was in fact possible to him".

- Principle V: "Any person charged with a crime under international law has the right to a fair trial on the facts and law."

- Principle VI: "The crimes hereinafter set out are punishable as crimes under international law:

  (a) Crimes against peace: (i) Planning, preparation, initiation or waging of a war of aggression or a war in violation of international treaties, agreements or assurances; (ii) Participation in a common plan or conspiracy for the accomplishment of any of the acts mentioned under (i).

(b) War crimes: Violations of the laws or customs of war which include, but are not limited to, murder, ill-treatment or deportation to slave labour or for any other purpose of civilian population of or in occupied territory; murder or ill-treatment of prisoners of war or persons on the Seas, killing of hostages, plunder of public or private property, wanton destruction of cities, towns, or villages, or devastation not justified by military necessity.

(c) Crimes against humanity: Murder, extermination, enslavement, deportation and other inhumane acts done against any civilian population, or persecutions on political, racial, or religious grounds, when such acts are done or such persecutions are carried on in execution of or in connection with any crime against peace or any war crime."

- Principle VII: "Complicity in the commission of a crime against peace, a war crime, or a crime against humanity as set forth in Principle VI is a crime under international law."

Other international law: The Nuremberg principles of the United Nations are important, but they are not the only examples of supra-national laws, treaties or conventions which may be used as legal justification or even legal obligations to break local national laws. There are many similar precedents:

EU directives and regulations: For instance, in the European Union there is a wealth of legislation governing all aspects of modern life. This legislation is supposedly transposed into national legislation in every European member state. In reality, many EU directives are not properly transposed and many more that are transposed into national laws are either ignored or misinterpreted locally. This leaves open a vast swathe of possibilities where a protest campaign can actively disobey a national law, simply on the basis that the national law is itself illegal and non-conformant with EU legislation. Such cases are becoming increasingly common and after legal arbitration in a member state, these cases often end with the European Commission and the European Court of Justice (in Luxemburg), the final arbiter of European law and its implementation in the national law of a member state.

European Charter of Human Rights: Many existing laws in European countries remain in breach of articles of the European Charter of Human Rights, which is binding at least in all EU member states (and others). This again provides abundant opportunities to defy national laws which fail to conform to the articles of the charter. The final arbiter of such disputes is the European Court of Human Rights in Strasbourg.

Notes on Chapter 3:

Note 1: Notably John Rawls, "The Justification of Civil Disobedience." In Hugo Adam Bedau, ed., Civil Disobedience: Theory and Practice, pp. 240-255. New York: Pegasus Books, 1969.

Note 2: Carl Cohen, "Civil Disobedience and the Law", 1966, Rutgers Law Review

Note 3: John Rawls, "A Theory of Justice", Oxford University Press, 1971

---oOo---

4. An Analysis of Civil Rebellion

The phrase "civil rebellion" refers to a whole spectrum of human behaviour towards authority, ranging from simple acts of refusal to obey an order by an individual, right through to popular armed insurrection. The great differences in method and outcome between such diverse acts of rebellion belie the fact that both are driven by a similar sense of defiance and a refusal to conform to the will of an authority.

The common thread of "refusal to obey" implies that there are relationships between lesser acts of rebellion and the more dramatic acts of armed revolution. The following sections describe peaceful civil rebellion, the relationships between types of rebellion and how, under some circumstances, civil populations may transit from peaceful protest to violent rebellion.

4.1 The Spectrum of Civil Rebellion - from Peaceful Protest to Bloody Revolution

Here are some basic definitions for acts of rebellion and defiance against an authority, classified by whether they use violence or not.

Nonviolent methods:

• Civil disobedience, protest, intervention and direct action are completely peaceful forms of civil rebellion widely available to populations as a means of protest in both autocratic and democratic regimes.

Limited violence used:

• Subversion: Subversion is a hidden method used to sabotage a government, carried out by spies and relying, normally, on nonviolent methods to destabilise an authority.

• Mutiny: Mutiny may or may not involve acts of violence. It involves members of a close-knit group defying authority and may include their taking control of their own immediate environment.

• Civil Disorder - Riot: Civil disorder, such as rioting, may involve some limited acts of violence and property damage by participants. It is largely spontaneous in nature and often stems from popular outrage at authoritarian behaviour.

Violent methods of rebellion:

• Coup d'état: This may or may not be violent (bloodless coups are not). It involves a sudden attempt by a small group of insiders to seize control of a state. A coup is often organised by parts of a country's military.

• Armed resistance is most often a form of informal rebellion by armed civilians against an occupying force or the puppet government of a larger power.

• Revolt is a form of localised rebellion rather than a full-scale revolution. It is frequently spontaneous and violent.

• Terrorism involves violent acts carried out by radical groups, aimed at terrorising a civil population and its government.

• Armed insurrection: This is a limited armed rebellion against a state, carried out by armed civilians rather than military personnel and with the intention of overthrowing the government of that state.

• Revolution: This is the overthrow and replacement of an established government or political system by its citizens. Revolutions can be bloodless, but more often than not an incumbent government will mount an armed defence, thus leading to violent confrontation and bloody revolution.

4.2 Types of Peaceful Civil Rebellion

Many schools of thought have defined nonviolent civil rebellion as being divided into four main categories of activity:

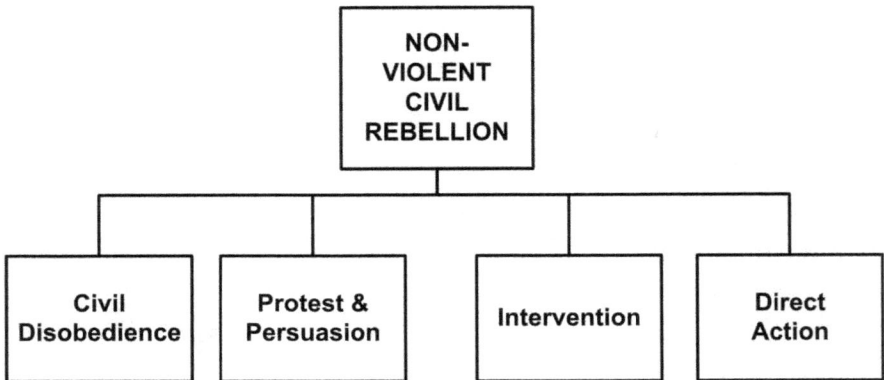

The definitions of these categories are somewhat ambiguous and overlapping, since "protests" are also sometimes acts of "civil disobedience" and vice versa ". Direct actions" are forms of "intervention" and the opposite is sometimes true. All of these are also categories of "protest" in some sense. But we have chosen to stick with these commonly used terms, simply to try and clarify the spectrum of civil rebellion, which actually encompasses deeds from the least profound protest actions to the most radical acts of defiance against authority. What all categories have in common is that they are physically nonviolent.

4.2.1 The Spectrum of Civil Rebellion

These categories indicate a wide spectrum of nonviolent civil rebellion, from "civil disobedience", the most latent form of civil resistance, to "direct action", the most active form of civil non-cooperation.

As we will see below, some forms of "intervention" and "direct action" get very close to open insurrection and metamorphose beyond the realms of "legal" protest into a full-scale challenge to the legitimacy of the state, albeit nonviolently at first.

All forms of non-cooperation (economic, political and social) can be found in "Civil Disobedience". Overt acts of protest and persuasion are classified as "Protest". Actions which seek to protest and bring about practical changes at the same time are referred to as "Intervention". Finally, "Direct Action" consists of a group of techniques which involve and encourage deliberate acts of political (though not physical) violence against an authority.

The genesis of civil rebellion: Before they reach the stage of active "civil disobedience", civil populations often complain of dissatisfaction and feel distressed by certain decisions of an authority. This might include being ignored by government or management in policy planning or it may refer to government policies that are socially divisive or which lack popular support.

Later, after this initial phase of discomfort, citizens begin to feel socially excluded, with a growing sense of disassociation from the political process. They begin to protest and complain. If authorities recognise this low level dissent and deal with it, the problems can generally be hastily and quietly resolved. However, when an authority decides to ignore the discontent, low-level protests begin to develop into acts of disobedience. This may manifest itself as a lack of cooperation, causing deliberate delays or low level sabotage of administrative systems.

Governments that fail to recognise that there is a problem at this point, further antagonise the population by failing to take them seriously. As this situation progresses, popular protest groups become more and more focused not simply on stating their grievances, but on bringing about real practical or political change. Protest becomes organised and acts of civil disobedience become planned, alongside acts of "intervention", where protesters start to provide their own alternative solutions in protest at the neglect of the authority.

Further along this spectrum of activism, if authorities still fail to deal with the underlying causes of discontent or if authorities attempt to repress the protests, protest groups will resort to using "direct action", much of it illegal, in a much more combative and provocative way.

If authorities continue to ignore the demands of their populations and mishandle the problems of exclusion, civil populations will be tempted or provoked to enter the realm of violent insurrection and revolution. In the same way that a peaceful demonstration, when violently attacked by the police or military, can morph quite rapidly into a violent, armed and very dangerous riot, so too can an entire population make the decision that the route of nonviolence is not delivering change and, in an act of collective anger, frustration and hopelessness, turn to violence.

Bad government and violent rebellion: There is a fine line between nonviolent civil protest and more violent methods of opposition to authority. The crossing of this line by an aggrieved population is more often triggered by the unsympathetic behaviour of an authoritarian government than by any deliberate plan of the discontented populace to escalate matters. Despair of any change in the foreseeable future is a primary catalyst for a civil population to take up arms. If this is then mixed with aggressive attempts at repressing a peaceful protest, the end result may be quite explosive.

Few, if any, civil rights groups of the last two centuries were founded with a "military wing" as part of their early organisation. A case in point would be the civil rights movement in Northern Ireland in the 1960s. It was founded as a peaceful movement to win more rights for the socially-excluded Catholic population. It was largely un-militarised until the British government took the decision to open fire on an unarmed civilian demonstration in Derry on what became known as "Bloody Sunday". At that point the military wing of Sinn Fein, the provisional-IRA, was born. A similar story surrounds the civil rights movement of the USA. The Black Panthers were not part of the original civil rights movement; they were formed as the direct result of police brutality supported by the government's refusal to protect America's black population. The MK, military wing of the ANC was not part of the original anti-apartheid movement. It evolved from a frustration that no-one was interested in the rights of the oppressed South African black population. Faced with the increasingly vicious behaviour of successive South Africa's white apartheid-supporting governments, the ANC took up arms as a form of self-defence.

Thus, peaceful protest morphed into armed insurrection; all thanks to stupid and intransigent governments. We will now examine how this happens.

4.2.3 Violent Escalation in Civil Rebellion

Rarely do bloody revolutions erupt spontaneously without any warning. The French revolution was preceded by decades of rumbling dissent from the peasantry manifested in marches, popular declarations, tax strikes and food riots. A unique series of poor harvests and increased taxes pushed the already hard-pressed working and tradesman classes into desperation, but their complaints were largely ignored by the monarchy and the feudal aristocracy. Within months the situation had deteriorated into open defiance and the country embarked on a period of upheaval that saw the creation of a national assembly of the people, the abolition of feudalism, the creation of the first French constitution, a "declaration of the rights of man", and an attack on the power of the church. It culminated shortly afterwards in bloody revolution and the infamous "reign of terror", which saw the execution of the king and much of the aristocracy.

History shows us many similar examples of how a country may slide into revolution as a result of unjust and oppressive behaviour triggering popular protests that are then ignored or, worse, violently repressed. The obvious examples are the Christian Reformation and the Russian revolution, but more contemporary instances include the Cuban revolution of 1959, the Portuguese revolution of 1975, and the Tunisian revolution of 2011. All were characterised by an overthrow of authoritarian regimes that cared little for their citizens or their opinions, blatantly ignored the warning signs of impending civil rebellion and then attempted to brutally repress dissent.

Tipping points: Clearly there are tipping points in civil rebellion where an aggrieved citizenry are primed to escalate their action to the point where it ceases to be protest and becomes some form of violent revolt.

Based on historical observation we might conclude that escalations usually occur more often than not as a result of the actions, reactions or inactions of the authorities and are rarely the result of some grand plan by the protesters. Authoritarian states are convinced that they can force a popular protest movement to disperse by force or coercion, whereas these strategies have the very opposite effect. They tend to trigger escalation rather than retreat.

Tipping points are often characterised by attempts at violent or legal repression by authorities against protesters. Such strategies may spark civil disturbances, such as riots which are not organised and which may become violent and be hijacked by other groups. Rioting is very often a symptom that nonviolent protest has passed into the early stages of violent insurgency. This simple schematic shows how a "just" state can quickly descend into violent rebellion. There are many such scenarios:

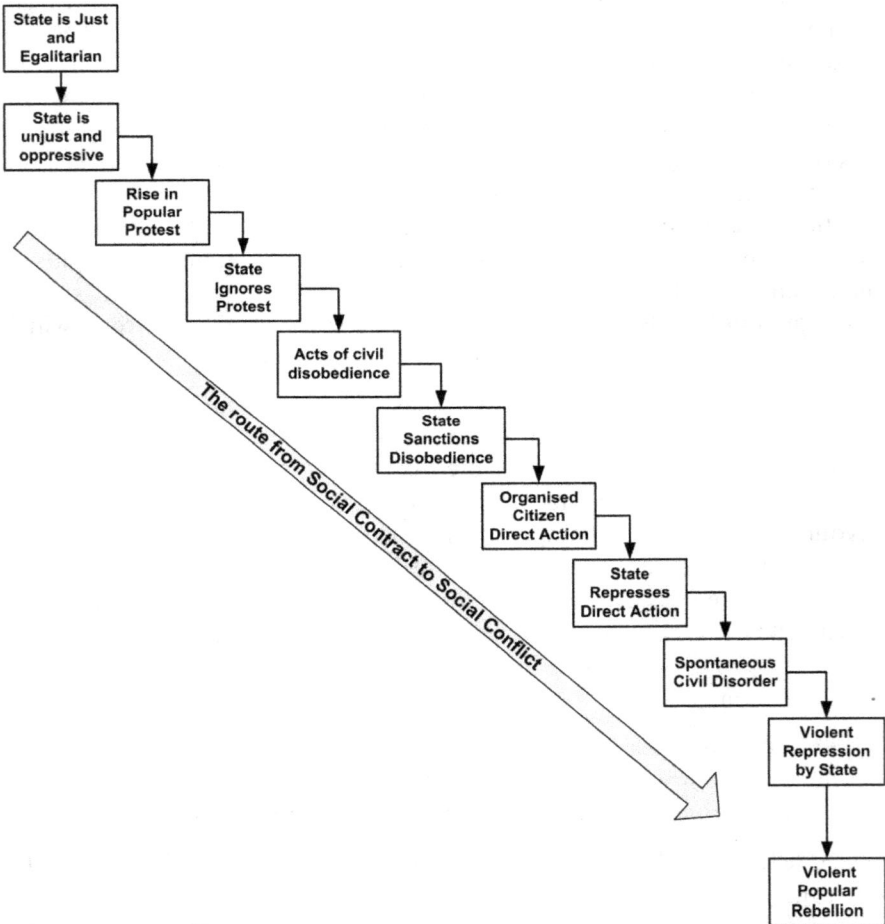

The route from Social Contract to Social Conflict

- State is Just and Egalitarian
- State is unjust and oppressive
- Rise in Popular Protest
- State Ignores Protest
- Acts of civil disobedience
- State Sanctions Disobedience
- Organised Citizen Direct Action
- State Represses Direct Action
- Spontaneous Civil Disorder
- Violent Repression by State
- Violent Popular Rebellion

The human factor: It would be a grave error to believe that there is some physical or psychological difference between those of us that may attend a peaceful rally to protest about some environmental issue and those of us who find themselves locked in a violent insurgency against a brutal totalitarian government. There is not. The only differences that exist are the conditions that place individuals in very different circumstances. No-one in our rich Western society could honestly deny that they would take up arms and fight in self-defence if they were faced with horrendous physical oppression and an existential threat to their own life and that of their families by some brutal authority.

State at war with its own people: In a peaceful civil society it is easy to expound the principles and effectiveness of peaceful civil rebellion. But when faced by a merciless genocidal regime of murder squads that come knocking on the door in the night with the objective of making you and your family "disappear", it's hard to see how peaceful civil disobedience answers to the need to protect oneself, one's family and civil society. In a world without any concept of constitutional rights or rule of law, the concept of nonviolent protest as a means to alter a bad law or to help change a government's mind is somewhat absurd. Civil disobedience and protest imply some possibility of dialogue with an authority, which does not exist in such circumstances. Clearly, from a moral perspective, such an authoritarian state deserves neither the allegiance of the citizen nor the benefit of a nonviolent dialogue. The state is effectively at war with all or part of its own population and the rules of nonviolent rebellion cease to apply.

Plainly, between the two examples above there is a world of difference. In the case of a civil protest against a normally just and democratic state, there is no existential threat, the risk that exists is not immediate and the consequences of failure in the protest are not fatal. In the second case of an insurgency against a violent authoritarian state, the risks are mortal and immediate. Failure to overcome the state may mean certain death. The use of limited violence in self-defence seems morally and legally justified. But at what point does peaceful rebellion become violent self-defence?

Continuity of rebellion: Despite the differences in circumstances outlined in these two extreme scenarios, there is something which links the two lead characters in these examples: neither accepts the power of what they both consider an unjust oppression being imposed upon them from the outside. The environmental protester refuses to accept what they consider an environmentally dangerous development and the insurgent guerrilla refuses to become just another body in a shallow grave, courtesy of a nocturnal death squad.

Both are motivated by a strong sense of justice, a desire for a decent life for themselves and their families, and a common willingness to fight against injustice. The differences in the forms of defiance and rebellion are simply those of degree, the method of defiance and the political environment that they find themselves in.

It is thus very likely that someone willing to protest to protect the environment or human rights may very well be capable of escalating their role in a rebellion to that of an armed insurgent in defence of their home, family and principles if placed in a position where they are confronted by injustice, repression and a threat to the lives of their loved ones.

Rebels are not born, they are made. And they are made by the injustices of authoritarian governments. The more violent the injustice, the more violent will be the rebel.

4.2.4 Is Peaceful Civil Rebellion Effective?

Returning to the subject of peaceful civil rebellion, and considering that some governments may be inclined to repress or ignore such peaceful protests, we have to ask ourselves if peaceful civil rebellion is really effective as a means of political change. Most of us would imagine that forceful violent rebellion would be much more effective in combating an authoritarian regime than peaceful protest and disobedience, but it would appear that the opposite is actually the case in most instances.

Based on much post-colonial modern history, it is easy to demonstrate that organised peaceful civil rebellion is effective; there seems no doubt of that. The liberation of India from British colonial rule, the fact that the USA voted in a black president after years of civil rights protests, and the transition of South Africa to a majority rule government all attest to the fact that peaceful civil rebellion is effective. In all three cases the main campaigns that brought about these radical changes were generally (though not entirely) peaceful and characterised by a desire for peace and reconciliation by the protest groups.

Various studies have demonstrated that peaceful protest actions strengthen political conviction and re-energise a citizen's interest in politics, which in itself is a form of success. Policymakers are also affected by protest, as politicians respond to large protests in their constituencies by voting more in line with the protesters' demands.

Peaceful rebellion is more effective: Political scientist Erica Chenoweth carried out a study comparing success rates for various types of peaceful resistance and protest actions versus violent campaigns aimed at the overthrow of a government. She compared hundreds of cases and the results of her study are startlingly clear [Note 2].

- She found that there was more than double the number of successful nonviolent campaigns than there were violent actions.

- There were three times as many failed violent campaigns than failed nonviolent campaigns.

- She found that even in the case of a partial success, nonviolent campaigns were more than twice as successful as violent actions.

- She also found that the trend towards the success of nonviolent campaigns was increasing over time and that the success rate of violent campaigns had more than halved in the period 1940 to 2006, whilst the success rate of nonviolent campaigns had almost doubled in the same period.

- Her research indicates that when 3.5% of the population joined a campaign, the chances of success were almost 100%. She also noted that campaigns with this number of participants were exclusively peaceful campaigns.

Other research indicates that an uprising becomes about 50% more likely to fail if it turns to violence. It seems to be the case that once protesters pick up guns, it legitimises the state's use of overwhelming violence in response. Using violence also tends to reduce public support for any form of uprising. Erica Chenoweth thinks this is because a violent uprising is more physically demanding and dangerous and thus scares off participants. But, in addition to this, a violent uprising can end up polarising people in support of the government, whereas a government crackdown against a nonviolent uprising will often reduce public support for the regime [Note 3].

Another important point which arose from the Chenoweth research was that violent resistance movements, even if they do succeed, can create a lot of long-term problems. Nonviolent rebellions tended to encourage democratic solutions, whereas the use of force, no matter what its driving ideals, is all about legitimising power through force. Thus it's not hard to see how its victorious participants would end up keeping power primarily through violence.

One important point to bear in mind in reading the results of this study is that very often violent rebellions are staged against violent regimes, and this may skew the results of the study because violent regimes have few scruples against deploying their (well-equipped) military against their (badly equipped) civilian populations. This often leads to the failure of a violent uprising, simply because of the military supremacy of the state rather than an inherent failure in violent uprisings.

Popular rebellions are complicated events and it is impossible to completely predict the outcome based solely on whether the rebellion is violent or not. Even if most violent uprisings fail, some do succeed, so it's not a hard-and-fast rule that nonviolent movements are always more effective [Note 4]. Clearly, there are cases where self-defence against violent repression requires the use of force to be effective.

4.2.5 Alternatives to Civil Rebellion

There are those that argue that in a just, democratic society the use of peaceful civil rebellion is redundant, that many alternatives exist allowing the citizen to communicate with their government and participate in law-making and challenges to decisions of government. Therefore, they argue that civil rebellion has no place in a democratic society. In an ideal world there may be something to be said for this contention, but, alas, we live in a world that is politically far from ideal; including even the best and most effective democracies around the world.

Nonetheless, in some cases an effective protest should also include these alternative methods as part of a group's strategy:

• **Lobbying:** This is an attempt to influence politicians or political appointees in an effort to have them alter their position on a political topic over which they have some control, such as a vote or a recommendation. Lobbying is carried out by individuals, associations, protest groups, other politicians, corporate interests and professional lobbying companies, often working on behalf of private business interests. Lobbying may involve letter-writing, presenting petitions, meeting law-makers and making statements to the press.

• **Legal action:** This is the use of legal structures, such as the courts, to challenge items of legislation or an authority's application of the law in practice. Aside from the courts, most democracies also have a structure of regulators and ombudspersons whose role it is to protect the interest of the citizens against certain authorities and against certain industries such as energy and telecoms companies.

• **Conscientious objection:** This is applicable mostly to the citizen's right to refuse military service for reasons of conscience.

• **Legal protest:** This is citizen protest which has been legally sanctioned by the government.

• **Political action:** Joining a political party or starting a new political movement.

4.2.5.1 Reasons why Democratic Structures Fail the Citizen: The world of politics is largely inhabited by career politicians and there is little space there for the campaigning citizen. The same goes for big business. Both arenas are elitist clubs which are, by and large, closed to the general public. Public administration has its own species of civil service elite, who are no less hostile to the public, and especially to those with a grievance.

Hostile and disinterested politicians: Political authorities represent a rather hostile and alien environment for the layman who has an issue or grievance that needs resolution. At a legislative level, politicians are loath to involve themselves in individual issues, preferring to see themselves as law-makers rather than law-keepers or guardians of the citizen. Indeed, citizens are seen as something of a nuisance and an obstacle to the politician's pursuit of his party dogma and the constant game of point-scoring against political opponents.

Duplicitous corporations: Big business will tolerate citizen representations so long as it brings them some PR kudos and not too much hassle. Since capitalist companies are under no obligation to keep their promises to individual citizens, they can basically say anything they like to a citizen, without any repercussions. Even in negotiations with their workforce a company can make all kinds of promises, without any absolute obligation to fulfil them. They can always walk away from a promise on the basis of "changed economic conditions".

The Civil Service: More than my job's worth: The civil service is in quite a unique league when it comes to antagonising the general public. They refuse to engage in topics which even remotely relate to legislation, since that is the domain of the politician, they claim. In terms of procedure, likewise that is not their fault but that of the senior officials who translate law into public processes. Civil servants are trained not to think "outside their pay-grade" and they refuse to do so. They operate in cocooned, disconnected isolation from the outside world and even from their own colleagues. Their authority and responsibility is severely limited. Their only interest is in implementing narrowly construed regulations in a way which causes them the absolute minimum of discomfort, mental fatigue or work. As a good place to start when complaining about a grievance, the civil service in most countries is pretty much at the very bottom of the list.

Into this unhelpful landscape our aggrieved citizen arrives to bring his problem to the attention of the authorities, with hopes of a resolution.

Obstacles to democratic change: Apart from the obvious constraints in dealing with different parts of government and public administration directly, there are many obstacles to using the standard means of attracting political attention to a protest cause. Here are just a few limitations in the legal structures that are available to the citizen:

• **Lobbying:** Lobbying can be summarised as a way of influencing political decisions where the largest amount of influence is attributed to those with the largest bank accounts.

Lobbying by individuals or small protest groups can never be as effective as the well-financed commercial lobbying that goes on and that is paid for by big business. In a dispute in which a large company is involved, the strength and quality of political lobbying used by a protest group can never match that of professional lobbyists paid for from some company's generous slush fund.

In this respect, lobbying as a means of political persuasion is almost a form of corruption. Lobbying is often used by those with inordinate social or economic power to effectively influence the law-making process in order to serve their own interests. Politicians have a duty to act equitably on behalf of their constituents' interests and the public good. When they stand to benefit by shaping the law to serve the interests of some private party, this creates a huge conflict of interest. The failure of government officials to serve the public interest as a consequence of lobbying by special interest groups that provide them with benefits comes very close to illegality.

• **Legal actions:** As a means of airing a grievance the conventional national legal systems in most Western democracies are outside the price range of most small protest groups. Legal actions, such as taking injunctions, launching legal challenges against authorities or corporations are shockingly expensive, apart from being slow and intimidating. They are also very time-consuming, and for the layman a labyrinthine experience with little guarantee of success. In a conflict with a company or authority, the small protest group finds itself in a David and Goliath-style struggle, where the main weapon is money. Justice in modern democracy has become a commodity for the rich rather than a right available to all.

Many protest issues need instant attention and protest groups often can't afford the luxury of months or years in court. Even when a protest has access to legal systems, such as the European courts, the processes are extremely slow.

• **Legal Protest:** Legal protests have little to do with effective activism. This is really "protest light" because it conforms to the conditions laid out by an authority against which the protest may be directed, which somewhat dents its impact. Legally sanctioned protests are toothless affairs where protest groups are corralled into areas at times of day decided by and most convenient for the authorities. Given that the protest may well be targeting the authority, it makes any ideas of surprise action impossible.

As seen above, it is clear that the dice is stacked against the aggrieved citizen, despite all the theoretical methods for political and legal participation and dialogue available to him. For this reason many protest groups are formed with the intention to short-circuit political and legal systems and try to fast-track their issue up the political agenda. For this they resort to some form of civil rebellion.

4.2.6 Advantages of Civil Rebellion

As a means of getting an important issue in front of the politicians it's hard to beat some form of protest or civil disobedience. One well-attended and politically embarrassing demonstration, splashed all over the television and newspapers, is worth an awful lot of irate letters to "The Times" and one's Member of Parliament. Given the obstacles of institutional intransigence that confront attempts to bring about change in the conventional way, it is quite understandable that many take the route of civil rebellion. Here are just some of the obvious advantages:

• Civil rebellion brings immediate attention to an injustice. Lobbying politicians is slow and usually ineffective. However, protest and civil disobedience brings immediate attention to a problem or an unjust law.

• Civil rebellion demonstrates the strength of popular feeling to an authority.

• Civil rebellion is a form of asynchronous conflict between a weak public protest group and a powerful authority. A protest group can use their flexibility and numbers to defeat a monolithic authority in an otherwise unequal contest.

• Civil rebellion is cheap. The cost of an organised protest may be high overall, but if the cost is borne by many, it is relatively low cost per capita. This is especially true when making a comparison between using the courts to challenge an injustice and taking to the streets.

• Civil rebellion reminds authorities of their role in society as the servants of the people. Authorities are by nature authoritarian and acts of rebellion remind them to curtail their autocratic tendencies.

• Civil rebellion gets media coverage and helps to spread the word about protest issues to the general public.

• Civil rebellion excites the public to take an interest in an issue, thus putting pressure on politicians and officials to address it.

• Civil rebellion provides a rallying point for the socially excluded. Often those with few resources are excluded from conventional politics. Popular civil rebellion is much more accessible to every one in a community than party politics.

• Civil rebellion generates international interest and pressurises a government into dealing with a problem.

4.3 Authoritarian Attitudes and Responses to Civil Disobedience

Authorities are universally antagonistic towards any form of disobedience, even when its aim is one of protest. Civil disobedience is high risk for governments because a relatively small, poorly-resourced, but determined group can create a high profile protest from virtually nothing and turn it into a politically dangerous issue. Therefore, governments (or other authorities) will use almost any weapon in their armoury to overwhelm a group of disobedients or protesters. They will even resort to illegal actions, such as illegal surveillance or blackmail, if they can get away with it (ask the London Metropolitan police). The typical responses to civil disobedience from an authority may include the following strategies:

• **Divide and conquer:** An authority attempts to weaken a protest movement by trying to induce disunity and conflict to the group.

• **Infiltrate and sabotage:** Many authorities now routinely infiltrate and spy on activist groups and NGOs. They do this to stay ahead of protest campaigns and to obtain information which may be damaging to the protest group and its members.

• **Spread disinformation:** Governments in conflict with a protest group will do anything to win the propaganda war for the sympathy of the general public. This includes spreading disinformation about the group and its members in an effort to discredit the protest campaign.

• **Control the narrative:** An authority that is attacked by a protest group will try to seize and control the narrative. They will use the press and various media to try and damage the integrity of the protest group and undermine their arguments. An authority will attempt to stop a protest group from having any form of stage to address their audience.

• **Silence the protest:** Governments that cannot control a protest narrative will attempt to stifle protests by other means. This may include the use of police forces or new legislation to forbid protest manifestations or make incitements to demonstrate illegal.

• **Coerce the protesters:** In desperation, an authority will use coercion or physical violence to intimidate or confine protesters. In the case of a government, they will use the police to harass, detain and violently physically assault protesters.

Anyone planning a protest campaign must be cognisant of these threats from a target authority and find ways to manage them.

Notes on Chapter 4

Note 1: Harvard University, July 2, 2013, "Do political protests matter? Evidence from the tea party movement", Andreas Madestam, Daniel Shoag, Stan Veuger, David Yanagizawa-Drott

Note 2: "The success of nonviolent civil resistance", Erica Chenoweth, TED lectures

Note 3: Washington Post, By Max Fisher November 5, 2013, "Peaceful protest is much more effective than violence for toppling dictators"

Note 4: "Why Civil Resistance Works", Chenoweth and Maria Stephan, E-ISBN 978-0-231-52748-4

---o0o---

5. A History of Civil Disobedience

We tend to consider civil disobedience to be a modern concept, but this is not a correct assumption. The term "civil disobedience" is a modern one, but the phenomenon is by no means new. In fact, the history of civil disobedience is as ancient as humanity. Extensive and complex, the concept and methodologies of civil disobedience have evolved over millennia using ideas drawn from different eras and cultures.

The conflict between authority and "subject" is an ancient dynamic. The techniques used by civilians to respond to authority have developed to meet the needs of the times, but the driving motivation is unchanged. The misuse of power in hierarchical societies has long elicited similar responses from the abused subject towards the abusive authority.

Even though we may have tolerated authority differently in the past, there has never existed a period of complete harmony between the forces of authority and those who exist as its subjects. Thus, the history of civil disobedience is actually the history of the changing relationship between authority and civilian population, between the ruler and the ruled. Here we are going to provide some milestones in the history of civil and human rights and in the development of civil disobedience.

The exercise of authority always generates some form of reaction from the subjects of that authority. These interactions may, in some cases, lead to conflict between the authorities and their subjects which can give rise to acts of civil disobedience. Civil disobedience is generally triggered by some particularly excessive authoritarian behaviour or an offence against some popular sensitivity.

As a means of dealing with the excesses of authority, civil disobedience is one amongst many traditional techniques available to redress the grievances of civilians that feel oppressed. These techniques range from the violent overthrow of governments in a revolution, the assassination of leaders or other armed insurgency, a coup d'état, right down to simple acts of individual non-compliance and or minor anti-government sabotage.

The origins of rebellion: But what is it that gives us the right to disobey the authorities that rule over us? The idea that there is a law that transcends the laws of the state is found in the works of Socrates (ca. 470-399 BC), in some of the classical Greek tragedies, and in the ancient Indian concept of dharma (duty). In these traditions the principle was established that if certain higher 'natural' laws conflicted with the laws of the state then the individual had the moral right and indeed perhaps a moral obligation to disobey the laws of the state.

In the Middle-Ages, Thomas Aquinas (1225-1274) defended the natural-law view [Note 8] when he argued that unjust laws did not bind the conscientious citizen to obey. In a similar vein, John Locke (1632-1704) taught that government derived its authority from the people, that one of the purposes of the government was the protection of the natural rights of the people, and that the people had the right to alter their government should it fail to discharge its fundamental duties to protect these natural rights [Note 9]. This is strong stuff compared with today's absolute faith in the concept of parliamentary democracy as the 'nirvana' of human freedoms cherished by the Western world. By the 20th century the "right to disobey" had become highly developed and was augmented with the additional radical concept of the "responsibility to disobey" in cases where the orders of an authority were morally repugnant [Note 10]. Simultaneously, by the end of the 20th century the use of protest and civil disobedience as a tool to control authority had become prevalent. Various technological advances such as the internet, personalised blogs, global electronic petitions, electronic whistleblowers, secret drop boxes have all modernised civil disobedience. We now coordinate street protests by social networking systems, we publish our demands on electronic newspapers and we hunt offending politicians in electronic packs on Twitter or Facebook. There is no doubt that recent technological developments have made the use of civil disobedience much more available to the ordinary citizen. There is also little doubt that our leaders are just as authoritarian as they ever were. Perhaps the real difference is that the citizen is now a little better equipped and more confident in his or her ability to control our leaders' totalitarian instincts.

Let us take a look at some historical trends and their role in the development of personal freedom and our human and civil rights.

5.1 Social influences on Human and Civil Rights, Technology and the Hierarchy of Needs

Hierarchy of Needs: Without doubt the citizens' attitudes to basic human and civil rights have evolved in tandem with radical improvements in socio-economic conditions over the centuries. When primary physiological and safety needs such as having enough food and reasonable physical security are met they become less critical to us and we tend to refocus on those personal needs that centre on the need for love, belonging, esteem and self-actualization, including personal freedom. Thus, as living conditions improved during and after the Middle Ages, there was a growing interest in the concept of the individual, personal freedoms, good governance, a fulfilled life, and not merely a pre-occupation with staying alive [Note 7].

Clearly, these changes have been much more profound in the last 5 centuries than they were in the preceding millennia. The two hundred years since the Industrial Revolution has seen a marked acceleration in our focus on the civil and human rights of the individual in society. It seems that as living conditions improve, our demands for more and more individual freedoms increase simultaneously. In parallel with this increased focus on the personal liberty and self-fulfilment of the citizen, there has also been a shift away from blind acceptance of authority by the public, whether by the authority of the state, the church or commercial interests. We have morphed from a society overawed by the power of authority to one that is largely distrusting and challenging of authority.

Technological influences: Intertwined with improvements in living conditions are the technological influences that have brought these improvements. One could argue that technological advances were and are the driver of the process of "enlightenment". When you don't suffer from constant famines or plagues of disease you surely have more opportunity to conceive of your world as being a place in which you can love and be loved, where you can be creative and respected and achieve a degree of equality with your fellow human beings.

The unleashing of such ambitions in the last centuries by means of various technological advances is undoubtedly one of the most profound changes in the human condition since we started to farm and founded the first civil societies. No longer is knowledge the exclusive preserve of the authorities of church or state. Those days are well and truly over.

Whether the advances in our ambition and achievements in social liberation will continue to march side by side with technological progression is impossible to know. Technology is amoral - it can be used for good or evil, and indeed it is.

What we can say about the present day is this: information technology is now in the hands of the people and it seems unlikely that any authority on earth can regain total control of it again. This cat is out of the bag and systems such as the internet attract a wealth of rapidly changing, highly diverse interests; some good and some less so. Nonetheless, short of disconnecting the internet and all other forms of electronic communication, there is actually no way in which authority anywhere can ever significantly control high-speed communications ever again, and certainly not if they have any desire to continue generating wealth for themselves or remaining in power. The very internet technology that creates wealth is the same technology that is also liberating citizens around the world. In this sense the internet is one of the most democratic of technologies.

Authority and control of technology: Clearly, many governments now realise that the release of information technology has been far too democratic. Because of this, we are now seeing large corporations and governments desperately collaborating to try to regain control of these resources in an attempt to re-establish their dominance and our subservience. This is generally motivated by economic interests and a desire to control civilian populations and markets. Why else would companies such as Cisco Systems, the world's largest internet router manufacturer, deliberately provide "back-door" access into all their routers to the US National Security Agency?

We now know that governments spy on their entire civilian populations in order to control and manipulate them. They do this with the active cooperation of large corporations that control the internet and the telecoms networks whilst simultaneously profiting from customers who pay them for the privilege of being spied upon. Gladly, we also know how to stop them.

These authoritarian tendencies to control human populations are not confined to communications and internet technologies but extend to all aspects of human life. In the past, as in the present, authorities can and do attempt to leverage any important resource in an attempt to control their citizens.

For instance, governments make the provision of food aid to civil populations contingent upon the "good behaviour" of the population. It used to be "Rice for God" when the church dished out charity in return for faith. Nowadays, it's "food for collaboration" in the hands of government and private enterprise. Government aid agencies in the Western world have long since been discredited as simply external wings to their ministries of foreign affairs, economics and/or defence. At a corporate level, pharmaceutical companies use their control over drug technology to impose draconian patent restrictions to limit access to important drugs which save human lives. They do this with the cooperation of elected governments for one simple reason: to maximise their own profits.

Limiting factors: The increasing supremacy of the individual over the interests of our community in recent years is a double edged sword; it is both liberating and destructive. It liberates by giving the individual more rights and more personal control over their own destiny, but it is also destructive because it creates a "society of individuals" with less social cohesion, fewer strong connections and less need for solidarity. This individualism may one day present a natural limit to how much more benefit humanity can derive from technological change and economic growth as we begin to see the quality of our lives decline in an increasingly lonely world. More importantly, our lack of solidarity may well make us less able to defend our new-found freedoms and protect our rights against authoritarian regimes, simply because ordinary citizens may become too self-interested and therefore unable or unwilling to form powerful, united groups in defence of these liberties.

Whilst we can certainly generalise that "technology is liberating" we cannot assume that technological advances always guarantee our social advances as individuals or as a society as a whole. Ultimately, whilst technology may open new paths to potential freedoms, only a "switched-on" civilian population can seize and keep these freedoms. Nothing is automatic and all the technology in the world does not made our governments more moral or more trustworthy. Technology does not change human nature. A socially connected and caring population with strong principles and a high degree of solidarity is more potent than any technological gadget.

The history of civil disobedience is immense and what follows is just a sample of some of the key moments in a very long and on-going struggle between authority and the citizen. These sections will attempt to deal with the timelines and influences which have shaped our attitudes to authority, our own personal freedom and how we see the need and uses of civil disobedience in society.

5.2 No Going Back: The Evolution of Human Freedom

One recurrent theme which you will see in the following history is that there has been a gradual evolution and spread of civil and human rights which have led to increasing numbers of the world's people enjoying greater freedoms. In tandem there has been a rise in the quality of those freedoms. What drives this evolution and will it continue?

There is one important phenomenon at play in the evolution of human freedoms: once a liberty is granted or won, it is very hard to remove it from those who are its beneficiaries. In the case of citizens' freedoms, attempting to take away a freedom will generate a reaction, often a very negative one, as soon as the people realise what is happening to them.

That isn't to say that governments therefore do not and cannot remove freedoms. Indeed, they have always tried to do this during certain dark periods of our history. Governments today use fear (of terrorism, for instance) to trick people into relinquishing freedom in return for safety. These authoritarian tricks do sometimes work temporarily, but they also have a habit of unravelling and at the earliest chance the lost freedom is seized back again by the people.

This constant granting and losing of liberties is a dynastic process that has taken centuries. It resembles a crab-like evolution of appearing to move sideways but in fact progressing forwards in almost imperceptible forward steps. To demonstrate the truth of this evolutionary progress, simply compare any particular freedom we have in Western nations to the circumstances pertaining 200, 500, 1000 years ago. Just consider access to education, decent housing, medical services, and freedom of movement, electoral franchise, and social mobility. Today, we may complain about all of these being inadequate, but just imagine what most of us would have had in any 16th century rural or urban setting anywhere in Europe: squalor, ignorance, hunger, brutal government and a very short life. We are moving forward, though sometimes it feels like we are actually in reverse when we consider the excesses of various totalitarian regimes even in the last 100 years. Authoritarianism and fascism are social (and often psychological) illnesses that have a habit of popping up in our leaders from time to time. Whether it is the authoritarian excesses of the House of Bourbon, the Tsarist regime, Adolf Hitler, Joseph Stalin, Tony Blair or George W. Bush, it is every citizen's responsibility to stand up to and destroy these regressive pathologies when they occur. Nonviolent civil rebellion, including civil disobedience and protest, are just one group of weapons in the citizen's armoury.

5.3 Classical Ideas of Civil Disobedience in Europe

Socrates was probably the most famous of the classical "disobedients" when he stood up to the city authorities of Athens by refusing to conform to their religious, political and social norms. His difficult relationship with Athens finally came to a head when, at the age of seventy, he was arraigned, tried, and sentenced to death by a city court.

The case was brought against him in the usual Athenian way by a group of his fellow citizens who took it upon themselves to prosecute him on behalf of the city. The charges against him were threefold: a/ failure to acknowledge the city's gods, b/ introducing new gods and c/ corrupting the young.

Each of these charges carried a political dimension in Athens at that time, given the centralised civic control of religious cults and the political importance of educating the young to take their place in the "normal" civic order, without question.

The trial came just a few years after a short-lived oligarchic coup in which several of Socrates' associates took part, and after the ignominious Athenian defeat in the Spartan wars. The trial stank of political revenge against Socrates for his criticisms of Athens' government.

The accounts of Socrates' trial and his speeches, produced by Plato [Note 5] and others, make interesting reading in the context of civil disobedience because Socrates' arguments directly address his morality and motivation. He was a highly moral person and felt obliged to confront the authority of Athens in a way which ultimately ended in his murder (forced suicide) by the state.

Socrates played his part as an ordinary Athenian citizen, allowing his name to go forward for selection to serve on the Council and serving in the army when required. But he had not engaged actively in "public affairs", he had not spoken in the Assembly, nor, so far as we know, brought prosecutions or volunteered for selection for jury service in the law courts. These omissions were perceived as a deliberate snub to Athens by Socrates.

Plato's version of Socrates' trial says that, after countering the religious accusations, Socrates acknowledged his lack of participation in public affairs, but goes on to claim to have had a more important mission than just fulfilling his civic obligations. Socrates claimed his mission was given to him by the god Apollo. His mission was to "stir up the city", to "discuss virtue and related matters", and to benefit the citizens by "trying to persuade them to care for personal morality and virtue rather than personal wealth or the wealth of the city". In his defence, Socrates went so far as to claim that as a civic benefactor, he deserved not death but the lifetime of free meals commonly awarded to an Olympic champion.

In these speeches of defiance Socrates depicts himself as a new kind of citizen, defining the concept of "public good" in a new way which he claimed was best served through unselfish acts by officials and politicians. This idea of public good was in complete contrast to the conventional Athenian definitions of virtue which centred on conflict, victory, political and economic success. These latter, of course, were and are some of the traditional values of authoritarianism and totally incompatible with Socrates' new vision of the "public good" as a new moral obligation of authority versus the traditional Athenian idea that authority was more important than personal morality.

But Socrates went further. During his defence he made several remarks which in modern times are often quoted as indications of the limits which he put on the requirement of a citizen to obey the law. The first remarks related to various political incidents in which Socrates was involved. In one incident Socrates had voted against an illegal proposal of the state council and in another, during the short-lived coup, he refused an order of the ruling body to arrest a democratic partisan for execution.

In a second remark in his defence, Socrates muses hypothetically that if the jurors were to say to him, "we acquit you, but only on condition that you spend no more time on this investigation and do not practice philosophy, and if you are caught doing so you will die". To this Socrates retorts that his reply would be: "I will obey God rather than you, and as long as I draw breath and am able, I shall not cease to practice philosophy (regardless of what you order)".

To a modern reader, such actions and words of defiance smack very much of a citizen engaged in active civil disobedience. This is one of the earliest documented cases where civil disobedience is actively endorsed when certain circumstances exist; in this case a breach of "natural" justice by authority. Sadly, this disobedient philosopher obeyed finally and drank the poison given to him by his executioners.

Plato often returns to the subject of the relationship between the citizenry and their rulers, particularly in "The Republic". There he discusses whether rulers can ever be really moral (given their reasons for being in power in the first place) and why citizens must always be more moral than their rulers. Plato comes to some fairly surprising and rather modern ethical conclusions. Many of Plato's conclusions have laid the modern foundations for the morality underpinning civil disobedience and the concepts of moral obligation being supreme to authority rather than the other way around.

5.4 Christian Influences on Concepts of Civil Disobedience

Much of the world's pre-Christian (and much post-Christian) history has been dominated by the belief that rulers were divinely ordained to rule. Roman emperors often became deified. This idea was so strongly endorsed that for most people the concept of disobeying their ruling political elites was entirely alien to them. Christianity was one of the influences that helped to change this blind obedience to power.

Christianity altered these attitudes by clearly dividing the power of the state and the power of the divine. This concept of human versus divine power is most evident in the gospel of Matthew where Jesus defines a clear distinction between the tributes owed to Caesar and those owed to God [Note 11]. Clearly the implication is that what our rulers command may be at odds with what God wants.

Unfortunately, however, this division of material and moral power was not ultimately all that clear and other pieces of Christian doctrine are somewhat ambiguous on the subject. For example, the apostle Paul seems to contradict the clear distinction about our obligations to state and divine authority when he states in the Epistle to the Romans: "For there is no authority except from God, and those that exist have been instituted by God. Therefore he who resists the authorities resists what God has appointed, and those who resist will incur judgment." [Note 12]

These contradictions caused moral difficulties for Christians, especially during the early centuries of the religion as it spread through the old empires of the world and Christians became the victims of various persecutions. But these moral problems were short-lived. The more radical questioning of authority which Christianity seemed to advocate was quickly subsumed when Christianity became one of the tolerated official religions of the Roman Empire under Emperor Constantine [Note 13]. It wasn't long before Christianity was receiving imperial patronage and extraordinary material favours from Constantine and the line between religious and imperial allegiances became increasingly complex. It is one thing to know we should give to Caesar that which is Caesar's and to God that which is God's but it is quite another matter to know what exactly is Caesar or God due!

For Christians being persecuted by hostile rulers, the main challenge was to reconcile Paul's text about obedience to authority with the uncomfortable reality of their own suffering. Similarly, it was difficult for early Christians happily receiving imperial patronage to avoid towing the imperial line. This conflict of interest continued into the time of the Holy Roman Empire. It was finally challenged in part by the Reformation when the Roman church's excesses and material corruption became intolerable even to its own priesthood and their distaste morphed into a full-scale rebellion and schism.

This conflict between moral and material obligations arose with the emergence of Protestantism in the sixteenth century, where two branches of the same religion were mutually hostile to what the other took to be true Christianity. Protestant adherents suffered at the hands of their Catholic rulers and Catholics found themselves persecuted in Protestant regimes. One response to the moral conflict of how to reconcile the religious obligation with the civil obligation to obey the law was simply to believe that vicious rulers must be endured because God had given them power as a sign of His displeasure with a wicked people. But others within Christianity took a different position.

One such position was to distinguish the divinely ordained office from the officer who occupies it. That is, God ordains that political authority must exist because the condition of human life (since our ejection from the Garden of Eden) requires such authority, but God does not ordain any particular person to hold a position of authority. More importantly, God certainly does not want to have rulers that abuse their authority by ruling tyrannically. This distinction, employed as early as the fourth century by John Chrysostom [Note 14], was invoked throughout the Middle Ages and somewhat undermines the idea of divine right to rule. It is an important concept because it asserts that a particularly abusive authority figure is not divinely appointed and can be disobeyed if necessary.

Another response to the problem of the division of moral and secular authority was to distinguish disobedience from resistance. According to Martin Luther and others who drew this distinction, Christians may not actively resist their rulers, but they must disobey them when the rulers' commands are contrary to God's.

However he moves further when in the "Magdeburg Confession" of 1550 [Note 15] he argues that the "subordinate powers" in a state, faced with the situation where the "supreme power" is working to destroy true religion, may go further than non-cooperation with the supreme power and assist the faithful to resist". This moral concept of resistance is even more potent and revolutionary than the first because it calls upon a Christian to actively resist immoral rulers, not to simply just disobey them. This moves us closer to a justification of active rebellion as a form of self-defence and away from a mere justification of passive disobedience. It has been called "the first Protestant religious justification of the right of defence against unjust higher authorities." [Note 16]

Another response to the moral problem of civil disobedience dealt with the management of possible conflicts between two or more of our rulers. Thus, if more than one person holds political authority over a subject and if they issue conflicting commands, then the subject may satisfy the Apostle Paul's injunction by obeying the authority whose commands are more congenial to the subject's understanding of true Christianity, even when such obedience entails resisting the commands of others in authority. This concept seems to give us the right to use our moral judgement to take up a partisan position to set one ruler against another. These last two responses played an important role in the many regional political disputes that accompanied the Protestant Reformation.

Most importantly, the Protestant Reformation also gave rise to a new form of response to the moral conflict as Protestants came to rely on the belief that political authority derives from the consent of the governed and actually has no divine component at all. In Europe this idea of the supremacy of human rights over civil or religious authority was the foundation of modern humanism and indeed the foundation of European ideas of democracy, civil and human rights.

5.5 Concepts of Civil Disobedience in Medieval Europe: Thomas Aquinas

One of the most important ideas developed during the medieval period in Europe concerned the relationship between law and morality and how this impacted on the individual. One of the most dominant theories was that developed by Thomas Aquinas in his "Natural Law Theory" [Note 8]. This is a complex set of principles, but it effectively defines a personal morality (natural laws which are God-given and undeniable and which cannot be disobeyed). These natural laws are effectively Christian principles and Aquinas goes to some lengths to discuss how these principles may come into conflict with civil authorities and the law.

This principle of a set of natural moral laws was not so revolutionary in itself, but what was new in Aquinas' political writings was his belief that if a human law diverged from the principles of "Natural law", it was quite legitimate to break that law. This principle also became known as the "Unjust Law is No Law" concept and is still an important legal principle in many jurisdictions.

He explains as follows: "One does not need to consider the worst sorts of regimes to see the difficulty inherent in achieving good citizenship. In any regime that is less than perfect there always remains the possibility that promoting the interests of the regime and promoting the common good may not be the same. To be sure, good men are often called to stand up heroically against tyrants [Note 17], but the full potential of the good citizen will never be realised unless he lives in the best of all possible regimes. In other words, only in the best regime do the good citizen and the good human being coincide" [Note 18].

Generally, Aquinas does not seem to advocate armed revolt and believes that an act of civil disobedience requires four characteristics:

- It must be public
- It must be nonviolent

- It must be either direct or indirect deliberate unlawfulness
- It must be conscientiously aimed towards the "good of society"

Therefore, a reasoned act of "conscientious refusal" is what Aquinas seems to advocate in his Natural Law Theory as a means of civil disobedience.

What is most extraordinary about Aquinas is that he was very much a pillar of the church and indeed is considered a saint in the Roman Catholic Church. Yet he propounded a very well-respected argument for judging civil states and in some cases resisting them if they proved to be acting immorally against a universal standard of "natural law" that was effectively a basis for modern humanism. This was fairly revolutionary thinking in the context of 13th century European Catholic society.

5.6 The Peasants' Revolt

What started as peaceful protests and acts of civil disobedience became an all-out armed revolt in England in 1381. It is a classic example of how a popular protest, can, if ignored, rapidly morph into a full-scale, bloody rebellion.

A combination of economic and legal factors caused the original protests. The government, alarmed by rising labour costs for workers after the 1348 Black Death plague, decided to implement a series of measures to control wages and curtail the movement of workers from one place to another [Note 19]. This interference by the Crown in rural affairs infuriated the workers and some trades people and the laws were openly flouted. However, struggling to finance its war in France, the English Crown began to raise increasingly higher poll taxes on the population. These taxes hit the poorest particularly hard and were enforced by teams of collectors that had extraordinary powers.

The discontent began to give way to open protest. In 1377, what was called the "Great Rumour" occurred in south-east and south-west England. Rural workers organised themselves and refused to work for their landlords, arguing that, according to the Domesday Book, they were exempted from such requests [Note 20]. The workers made unsuccessful appeals to the law courts and the King for support. The troubles increased again in 1380, with protests and disturbances across the north of England and in the western towns of Shrewsbury and Bridgwater. An uprising occurred in York, during which the city's mayor was removed from office, and fresh tax riots followed in early 1381. Despite the increasing protests, parliament refused to act to diffuse the problem.

The protest and civil disobedience turned to armed revolt on May 30th 1381, when a tax collector arrived in Brentwood to demand unpaid taxes from several nearby villages [Note 21]. The villagers in question arrived to be examined, but with the well-organised support of a group of men armed with sticks and bows. When their leader again refused to pay the taxes, the collector attempted to have him arrested, at which moment violence broke out and the tax collector and his men were forced to escape. Warrants were issued for the villagers but by then they had joined forces with several thousand other protesters, now armed, and divided into two columns; one marched on London and a second marched North to raise more rebels and spread the news of the rebellion.

The elected leader of the rebels, Watt Tyler, was a charismatic and able leader. The rebels quickly overran several strategically important places such as Rochester Castle and Canterbury where they caused much destruction, executed several agents of the Royal Council and deposed the Archbishop, taking control of the cathedral and monasteries.

The rebels then turned towards London, forcing the King and entourage to move to the Tower of London in fear of their lives. After some failed negotiations and unable to raise any military support, the King found himself besieged. The rebels refused all negotiated offers and marched into the city where they were met by crowds of sympathisers and more incoming bands of rebels from Kent and Essex. They tore through the city, opening and destroying prisons, attacking, looting and burning various courts, monastic houses loyal to the Crown, and several palaces, carrying off large amounts of gold and silver plate. Little was actually looted by individuals and most ended up in the river or was added to finance the rebel exchequer.

The next day the assault on the King's supporters and government buildings continued as the rebels advanced to the Tower. At some moment King Richard decided to leave the Tower with a small group and talk directly to the rebels. After some negotiations almost all of the demands of the rebels were met, including a general amnesty and, most importantly, the abolition of serfdom for which the king issued a decree immediately [Note 22].

Meanwhile, the rebellion had taken hold in all other parts of the English countryside and violence flared in several county towns. However, in London, the rebels had begun to disperse. The King, taking advantage of this, raised a militia and after a brief exchange Watt Tyler was executed. The king then rapidly raised an army and began the suppression of the rebellion. He rescinded his abolition of serfdom and set out to hunt down the rebel leaders. By July the rebellion was effectively at an end.

Whilst the King betrayed most of his promises to the rebels, the government and local lords were relatively circumspect in restoring order after the revolt, and continued to be worried about fresh revolts for several decades. When negotiating rents with their landlords, peasants frequently alluded to the incident of the revolt and the threat of repeated violence [Note 24]. There were no further attempts by Parliament to impose a poll tax or to reform England's fiscal system. Unable to raise fresh taxes, the government had to curtail its military expeditions and began to examine the options for peace. The wages of labourers continued to increase and serfdom began to die out. Over the course of the 15th century, the institution vanished in England completely.

Clearly the poll tax protests and acts of civil disobedience sent a message to Parliament and King that negotiation was necessary but it had fallen on deaf ears. The monarchy and aristocracy of the time set high standards for their brutality towards the labouring classes. In reply to one further appeal by the rebels for the king to abolish serfdom, King Richard rejected them all, allegedly telling them that "rustics you were and rustics you are still. You will remain in bondage, not as before, but incomparably harsher" [Note 23].

In the end, such attitudes cost the regime a large fortune in gold and future taxes, victory in the war with France, the respect of its subjects and rapidly hastened the end of the feudal system in England. Sometimes things have to get worse before they get better.

5.7 Religious Civil Disobedience in 16th Century Europe

Obviously not all acts of disobedience are aimed at governments. Often they can be directed at other high authorities such as religious (or educational or corporate) institutions. Such was the case during the great Christian reformation of the 16th century. The conflict that ensued was cataclysmic for European Christians and the cause of violent conflicts that smoulder on to the present day.

The Reformation was not the act of a single individual but was actually a cumulative action of theological disobedience towards the Roman Church and the monarchies that supported it.

The original argument surrounded a number of claims by the Augustinian friar Martin Luther about abuses in the Roman Catholic Church and was supported by John Calvin, a French theologian, and several others in the early years of the sixteenth century. The Reformation spread rapidly throughout Europe and the accusation of corruption in the Catholic Church was taken up by populations from the Baltic States, to Britain, Switzerland, France and Scandinavia.

What is interesting about the Reformation is that it coincided with (and partly gave rise to) several other technological events, such as the invention of the printing press and the publication of the Bible in vernacular languages. In a sense these technological advances both derived from and fed into this social revolution.

The Reformation had started its life modestly as an internal attempt to reform some of the more excessive systemic corruption within the Catholic Church, such as the selling of indulgences etc. Very quickly it became clear that the corruption within the church reached all the way to the Pope himself. The Reformation then moved outside of the internal reform of the church when Luther finally nailed his 95 arguments to the door of the castle church in Wittenberg in 1517 in an act of supreme civil disobedience to the Church [Note 25].

In general, Luther charged the Pope as an anti-Christ and many of the practices of the Church he condemned as corrupt and un-Christian. This single brave (or foolhardy) act of rebellion triggered off a revolt against the Church which spread like wildfire, causing alarm in the highest levels of the Catholic hierarchy and their supporting princes. However, it simultaneously galvanized many civilian populations en masse against the ecclesiastical abuses and brought many disgruntled princes to the side of the reformers against the Church and Rome's chief supporters at the time: the Habsburg Empire.

As momentum against the Catholic Church (and the Habsburgs) grew, the reformers made clever use of inexpensive pamphlets as well as vernacular bibles, using the relatively new printing press, so there was swift movement of both ideas and documents to the public. This use of the printed media was the 16th century equivalent of modern internet-based social media, in effect, getting the word out to the general public quickly and understandably.

The Reformation gave rise to a series of tragic conflicts and a great deal of persecution on both sides, finally culminating in a series of religious wars, including the Thirty Years war. This conflict devastated central Europe and ended in 1648 with the Treaty of Westphalia. The Treaty essentially guaranteed religious freedoms [Note 26], finally eliminated the papacy's European political power forever and ended the large-scale military conflicts between religious adversaries.

The Reformation is officially considered to have ended around 1750, almost 250 years after it had begun as an act of defiance against a huge corrupt institution by a tiny group of morally principled individuals.

Not only did it represent a huge blow against immoral leaders and church corruption, it also heralded new ideas on authority and human rights. It brought to the table the obligations of princes to rule morally and protect the rights of their subjects. It firmly established humanist morality on the agenda of European politics and finally dismantled the idea of a divine right to rule. If nothing else, the end of the idea of divine right was one of the most profound changes in the relationship between authority and the governed, bringing Europe to the end of one of its darkest periods.

In addition to the end of concepts of divine right, the persecutions of Protestants in various atrocities such as the massacre of French Huguenots in the St. Bartholomew's Day Massacre in 1572, led to a new concept of civil resistance developed by various Calvinist thinkers. One of the most prominent of these was François Hotman who constructed the basis of what has become known as "Calvinistic Resistance" [Note 6]. He wrote that the king is to be "a tutor and guardian of the people who also defends their liberties and that if that ruler becomes a tyrant and no longer a tutor and guardian of the people, then they (the people) have the right and responsibility to remove him. If the king does not protect the people's welfare and rights, which is the highest law, then popular assemblies could legitimately resist him".

Other Calvinist resistance philosophers, such as Beza and Daneau went further and asserted that all power ultimately comes from the people and those rulers who failed to acknowledge this truth can be legitimately disobeyed and forcibly removed [Note 27]. This endorsement of conditional revolutionary behaviour was a radical philosophical step at the time and opened up the concepts of individual civil and human rights and the moral legitimacy of self-defence of these rights through militant actions. This was quite a quantum leap in 16th century Europe.

5.8 The Diggers of 1649 - the First English Hippies

The Diggers were an interesting group of civil dissidents because they founded their philosophy on a love of nature, a belief in the complete equality of man and adopted a modern form of socialist principles based on fundamentalist Christian readings [Notes 28, 33].

The year 1649 was a time of huge social disruption in England. In the struggle between Crown and Commons, the Parliamentarians had won the First English Civil War. However, they had failed to negotiate a constitutional settlement with the defeated King Charles I. So, when members of Parliament and the upper echelons of the New Model Army were faced with King Charles' perceived duplicity, he was tried and executed and Parliament declared a "Commonwealth", basically a republic. It was a momentous occasion, unprecedented in English history, and it sent shock waves through the established aristocracy and the church.

Government by means of the King's Privy Council was replaced with a new body called the Council of State which was controlled by the Army. In this new environment, many people were active in politics, suggesting alternative forms of government to replace the old order. Royalists wished to place King Charles II on the throne; men like Oliver Cromwell wished to govern with a plutocratic parliament voted in by an electorate based on property, similar to that which was enfranchised before the civil war.

But there were several groups of agitators with a variety of demands. One such group, the "Levellers", was influenced by the writings of John Lilburne who wanted parliamentary democracy of sorts based on an electorate of every male head of all households. Yet another group, called the "Fifth Monarchy Men", advocated a theocracy and another group, called the "Diggers", led by Gerrard Winstanley, advocated an even more radical plan for the future government of England. They were one of a number of non-conformist dissenting groups that emerged around this time.

The Diggers were a group of Protestant English agrarian socialists, founded by Gerrard Winstanley in 1649. They were originally known as the "True Levellers". This original name came from their belief in economic equality based upon specific passages in the Acts of the Apostles [Note 29, 30]. They became known as Diggers because of their attempts to farm on common land. Their radical philosophy is believed to be the basic inspiration which gave rise to later movements such as alternative society movements of the 1960s, including the hippie movement [Notes 31, 32]. The Diggers tried (by "digging" common land) to reform the existing social order by founding an agrarian lifestyle with the creation of small egalitarian rural communities.

The Diggers' beliefs were imbued by the writings of Winstanley in which he envisioned an ecological interrelationship between humans and nature. Acknowledging the inherent connections between people and their surroundings, Winstanley declared that "true freedom lies where a man receives his nourishment and preservation, and that is in the use of the earth". In 1649 Gerrard Winstanley and 14 others published a pamphlet in which they called themselves the "True Levellers", to distinguish their ideas from those of the Levellers [Note 28].

A frequent undercurrent of the Diggers philosophy was that the "common people of England" had been subjugated and exploited by a foreign, Norman feudalism and that the actions of the Diggers were a re-assertion of their ancient land rights.

The acts of civil disobedience of the Diggers began in 1649 when food prices were at a record high. In Surrey a general invitation was issued by the Diggers to "all to come in and help them, and promise them meat, drink, and clothes." They intended to pull down all enclosures and encourage the local populace to come and work with them. They claimed that their number would be several thousand within ten days. Within a month, the Diggers issued their most famous pamphlet and manifesto, called "The True Levellers Standard Advanced", which claimed a divine right to freedom for all mankind and in particular the Diggers right to "Digge up, Manure, and Sow Corn upon George-Hill in Surrey".

Despite the Diggers' calls for universal brotherhood, the local landowners with the support of the commander of the New Model Army, Sir Thomas Fairfax, duly arrived with his troops and interviewed Winstanley and another member of the Diggers. Fairfax, having concluded that Diggers were doing no harm, advised the local landowners to use the courts.

Winstanley remained and continued to write about the treatment they received. The harassment from the lord of the local manor was deliberate and systematic, including organised attacks on the Digger community and a trumped up court case which the Diggers lost. Unable to resist a military assault to enforce the court's decision the Diggers abandoned the land they had squatted upon. But that was not the end of the Digger movement.

Some of the evicted Diggers moved a short distance to Little Heath in Surrey and took over some acres of land for cultivation. Six houses were built, winter crops were harvested, and several new pamphlets published. After initially expressing some sympathy for them, the local landlord became their main enemy. He used his power to stop local people helping them and he organised attacks on the Diggers and their property. By April 1650, the landlord and other local landowners succeeded in driving the Diggers from Little Heath.

Again, this wasn't the end of the Diggers. Another community of Diggers close to Wellingborough in Northamptonshire sprung up as a result of informal contacts with the Surrey Diggers. Delegations of Diggers spent time raising support through the counties of Surrey, Middlesex,

Hertfordshire, Bedfordshire, Buckinghamshire, Berkshire, Huntingdonshire and Northamptonshire before being apprehended.

Simultaneously, the Council of State was losing its patience with the Diggers and ordered that the courts should proceed against them. Nine of their leaders were arrested and, though not charged, were held without trial. Unrepentant, more Digger colonies were founded in Iver, Buckinghamshire, in Barnet in Hertfordshire, Enfield in Middlesex, Dunstable in Bedfordshire, Bosworth in Gloucestershire and a further colony in Nottinghamshire. All faced a similar reaction from the local landlords and often from other local farmers and labourers, frightened of this radical affront to authority.

During these constant conflicts with authorities, the Diggers adopted the strategy of nonviolent disobedience. When violently confronted, they would simply pack up and move on a mile or so to other common land and set up again. Finally however, the constant barrage of state legal action, local harassment and financial depravation drove the Digger movement out of existence. Except that it didn't.

The Digger movement left a wealth of writing and folk lore behind, including pamphlets, ballads and a doctrine which still represents an attractive idyll for many seeking a simpler and freer life. Indeed, during the middle and late 1960s, the San Francisco Diggers (who took their name from the original English Diggers) opened stores which simply gave away their stock; they provided free food, medical care, transport and temporary housing, and they also organised free music concerts and exhibitions of political art. They were self-confessed "community anarchists" who blended a desire for freedom with a consciousness of the community in which they lived. Many believe that the historical origins of the 1960s Hippie movement and the later "New Age Traveller" movement are to be found in the Digger philosophy. The Hippie movement flourished in many parts of the world and still exists on the periphery of many Western societies, to some extent. For example, since the revival of anarchism in the British anti-roads movement, the Diggers have been celebrated as precursors of land squatting and communalism.

To this day there is still a vibrant community of "new age travellers" driven by environmental concerns that act as nonviolent "flying squads" to attend demonstrations and blockades against all kinds of environmentally damaging acts of government and big business. These range from the annihilation of badgers, protests against blood sports, the destruction of ancient forestry to fracking for gas and a sad litany of other environmental and social abuses.

5.9 Pre-Revolutionary Ideas of Civil Responsibility and the Social Contract

The subject of conflict between civilians and their rulers was again addressed in the 17th century by philosophers Locke and Hobbes and later by the French philosopher Rousseau. They developed the concept of a civil responsibility to obey the authorities in what was called an obligation of our "social contract" with our rulers. This was a political theory riddled with logical faults and incorrect assumptions, but it does have some value because it represented another step in the development of our collective understanding of the relationships between civil populations and authority.

The basic theory of "the social contract" ran like this: authority is essential to maintain order and some semblance of peace in an otherwise anarchic world full of murderous and greedy human beings. Therefore rulers are required, nay, essential. The "social contract" is what we enter into with our rulers in return for the maintenance of peace and public order. In return for the benefits of their good governance we (the public) relinquish some of our natural freedoms to our rulers. One of these acts of submission is our basic right of self-governance. Therefore, in the social-contract model, we voluntarily submit our individual rights of self-determination and have an obligation to obey these sovereign rulers, regardless of how their sovereignty has been instituted or acquired [Note 34].

The idea of the social contract is attractive in some respects because it places responsibility on both the ruler and the ruled to fulfil their parts of the contract. Rulers must be just, maintain order and security and the ruled must be obedient and obliging to their government.

Despite the propositions of the social contract providing a neat way of defining and maintaining an ordered world, the theory is obviously full of logical problems. Firstly, it assumes that we all have entered into a social contract explicitly and that we consent to all parts of it. This is obviously not the case since most of us just find ourselves born into a particular society without any discussion of our consent at all. So there is no sense of explicit consent.

Secondly, the theory provides no recourse for those of us who do not agree with all or parts of the particular social contract into which we have been born. What should we do if we disagree with the behaviour of a particular regime, leave the country or start a revolution? How should we behave when our government acts immorally or obliges its citizens to act immorally? Do we ignore their immorality? Do we collaborate with the immoral actions or do we defy our government and breach the social contract?

Clearly, the simple idea of a mutually beneficial social contract fails to deal with real world conflicts between the ruler and the ruled. But the idea of a "social contract" isn't without redeeming factors. It can be a very useful concept in several respects when discussing civil disobedience.

For Locke, there are some things to which we cannot consent. In particular, we cannot allow ourselves to live under an absolute ruler, for doing so would defeat the very purposes for which we enter the social contract: to protect our lives, liberty, and property. He also argues for the right of revolution on the grounds that overthrowing an unjust government will not immediately return the people to that frightening, anarchic "state of nature" that we all fear so much (apparently). Instead, Locke suggests that it may lead to a new, better government which can be substituted for the previous tyranny. In this way, Locke begins to define a more nuanced idea of the social contract, where the recourse for the dissenting citizen is defined all the way up to violent revolution and the overthrow of a tyranny.

And so, the idea of a balanced relationship between the citizenry and its government and their mutual rights and responsibilities begins to emerge from the original simplified theory. Within this more sophisticated concept the citizen has the right to a maximum amount of freedom within his or her duty to help maintain order and peace, coupled with the responsibility of obeying any reasonable laws in order to maintain this order and peace. By the same token the government has the right to be obeyed if their laws and behaviour are reasonable and designed for the public good. Thus, when a ruler ceases to govern in a reasonable way a citizen was not obliged to obey the law, and something between dissent, civil disobedience and revolution became morally legitimate reactions, according to Locke and Rousseau [Note 35].

5.10 The Whiteboys

The Whiteboys were a secret agrarian organisation in 18th-century Ireland who used various tactics to defend land rights for subsistence tenant farmers. Their name derived from the white smocks the members wore in their nightly raids. They sought to address the complaints of excessive rents, tithe collection, excessive church dues, evictions and other oppressive acts. As a result they targeted landlords and tithe collectors [Note 37].

Their initial activities were limited to specific grievances and their tactics were nonviolent, such as the levelling of ditches that enclosed common grazing land, the digging up of ley lands and orchards and the theft of cattle from enclosed common land. As their numbers increased, the scope and violence of the Whiteboy activities began to widen, and proclamations were clandestinely posted stipulating their demands. Threatening letters were also sent to debt collectors, landlords, and the occupants of land gained from eviction, demanding that they give up their farms.

The Whiteboys operated in small local groups, often at night, and they were very hard to detect. The level of popular local support for the movement ensured that few would betray them. Later a sophisticated network of supporters made them somewhat bolder and they led attacks on prisons and other British government buildings. Today they would probably be termed a terrorist organisation because they operated subversively and often resorted to property damage. They employed an asymmetric strategy in their attacks. The Whiteboys knew that they were less well equipped than the British militias, but they also had the advantage of popular support, good intelligence and communications and an ability to move very quickly in familiar territory. Hence they used a strategy of hit and run under cover of darkness and were long dispersed before the slow moving military machinery could react.

Instead of dealing with their fairly legitimate claims, the British government of the time over-reacted with a huge, though ineffective, campaign of general intimidation, arrests and show-trials against the Whiteboys. The result of this was that the countryside was very quickly emptied of working-age males who fled and refused to work the land, which, in turn, triggered off huge losses in agricultural production.

Many of the Whiteboys in the west of Ireland joined up with French revolutionary forces and United Irishmen when they landed an expeditionary force in County Mayo in 1798 and engaged in an unsuccessful guerrilla war against the British, having declared a Republic of Mayo [Note 36].

5.11 The Enlightenment (I): The Utilitarians and Atheists

One philosophical concept which emerged during the 18th century and deals with the relationship between citizen and government is called "Utilitarianism". The most famous protagonists of Utilitarianism were Jeremy Bentham and John Stuart Mill, and the early philosophy was much influenced by the Scottish philosopher David Hume [Note 38].

The basic principle of the philosophy is that we should always act to maximize expected utility, minimise negative consequences and promote the greatest happiness of the greatest number of people. Implied in this ideal is the conclusion that all other obligations have little or no binding force - including automatic obedience to the law or act of government.

In "A Fragment on Government" Bentham summarises the theory of utilitarianism by stating, "it is the greatest happiness of the greatest number that is the measure of right and wrong"[Note 38]. Nonetheless, in general, the Utilitarians were not anarchists and they mostly believed that we should strive to have a society which has good, just laws that are easy to obey and generate the maximum human benefit.

This philosophy represents a dramatic shift away from the concept that moral codes are somehow disconnected from their effect on society. For example, moral codes such as Christianity make no connection between a moral law and whether or not it brings happiness or benefit to its adherents. For instance, a priest's celibacy clearly brings unhappiness to many priests but has been part of the moral code of the Catholic Church for centuries. For the Utilitarians, celibacy would be considered a bad law because it has no utility and in general brings only unhappiness to many people.

The Utilitarian philosophy spawned many varieties and discussion continues to the present day with philosophers including Karl Marx, Karl Popper and Richard Brandt all adding their contributions.

Hume extended his distaste for bad laws and tyranny to his views of religion and he included the behaviour of both the Protestant and Catholic Church. Despite the fact that he never admitted being an atheist, he had a strong sense that both the archaic superstitions of Catholicism and the fervent tub-thumping enthusiasm of Protestantism were extreme and brought no value to society or to the members of those churches. He spoke of curtailing the powers of the clergy in his ideal society [Note 39].

In terms of civil disobedience the basic Utilitarians' theory is important because, in more extreme forms, the theory undermines a citizen's political obligation to obey the law if the law has little or no utility. In other words, whether we should obey or disobey the law becomes a matter to be settled by considering what will do more good for society, obedience or disobedience, not by determining whether we have a simple, general obligation to obey the laws of our government or not.

5.12 The Enlightenment (II): Kant and the Right to Revolution and Disobedience

In contrast to Utilitarianism, the practical philosophy of the eighteenth-century German philosopher Immanuel Kant plays a major part in contemporary debates about "political obligation", i.e. the citizen's basic obligation to obey the law. Kant's views often seem contradictory and hard to reconcile at first sight, but that is because he is intensely pragmatic in some respects.

Kant argued that the "organised" civil state is the only way that coercive power can be centralised and controlled in a civilised world. He believed that it was the "social contract" which determined the stability of the civil state. He also argued that the citizens of the state were, in general, bound to obey the laws of the state because any organised state was always better than the dangerous and uncivilised "state of nature" from which human beings had emerged into the civilised world.

Kant seems to be one of the early believers in the "political responsibility" of the citizen to obey the laws of the state. However, this idea also appears to contradict his views on human freedom when he states that "there is only one innate right, that is freedom (independence from being constrained by another's choice), insofar as it can coexist with the freedom of every other in accordance with a universal law".

These apparently conflicting sentiments are not such a contradiction from Kant's perspective when we realise that Kant actually rejects any other basis for the existence of a state other than "for the protection of human freedom". He assumes that a state exists primarily for the protection of its citizens. With such a pre-condition it is easy to see why Kant believes that it is the citizen's obligation to obey the laws of such a state because it is that very authority which is the defender of the individual's freedoms.

Thus the idea of a right to rebel against such a moral government is incoherent, Kant argued, because the embodiment of all that is right is actually the existing state. By this, Kant did not assume that any actually existing state is always completely just, or that merely by virtue of having power, the state could determine what justice is. He meant that the opposite of the most abhorrent "uncivilised state of nature" is possible only when there is some means for individuals to be governed by the "general legislative will". He asserted that any kind of state embodies the general will better than no state at all. Kant was definitely not an anarchist but he did believe in the concept of "the greater good".

While he argues that the people cannot rebel against the state, Kant does not insist that citizens always obey the state. He allows, at least, for civil disobedience and, though he doesn't approve of revolutions, he makes some pragmatic exceptions, especially when the revolutions are successful and bring about human progress. He argues that if a revolution is successful, citizens have as much obligation to obey the new regime as they had to obey the old one. Since the new regime is in fact a new state authority, it now possesses the "right to rule".

Further in his theory of history, Kant argues that progress in the long run will come about in part through violent and unjust actions such as wars and even revolutions. Kant even takes it as a sign of progress that spectators of the French Revolution had greeted it with "a wishful participation that borders closely on enthusiasm". Kant is not pointing to the revolution itself as a sign of progress but to the reaction of people such as himself to news of the revolution. The spectators endorse the revolution not because it is legitimate but because it is aimed at the recreation of a civil constitution. Revolution then, for Kant, is wrong but may still contribute to progress.

When it comes to the idea of civil disobedience Kant argues that a form of acceptable resistance applies to individuals and he even asserts that citizens are obliged to obey the sovereign "in whatever does not conflict with inner morality". He does not elaborate on the term "inner morality" but clearly he is advocating disobedience in cases where laws conflict with his concepts of humanistic morality.

5.13 Modern Times: Utilitarianism and Libertarianism

Utilitarianism is still an important political philosophy in modern times. It has spawned some important political movements, such as modern traditional classical liberalism, which is a political philosophy and ideology where the primary emphasis is placed on securing the freedom of the individual by limiting the power of the government. However, Utilitarian principles are also a foundation for modern libertarianism which ranges in political colour from left-wing anarchist groups to some extreme right wing neo-fascist groups.

The common belief for these diverse groups is that government should have only a minimal role in the running of the state and that the liberty of the individual should be paramount. For the Left-libertarians, Marxists or Anarchists this means the right of the individual to be allowed to live as they wish without state interference, provided they harm no-one else. This includes the abolition of wage labour, private property, capitalist economics, organised religion, and state interference in education or private morality.

The Right-libertarians place a high value on "self-ownership" which leads to strong support for private property and free-market capitalism, while rejecting most or all state functions and controls on their ability to gain and dispose of personal wealth. They use the same arguments of "utility" to demand freedom of capitalism from all government regulation, the ability of the citizenry to police themselves and punish wrong-doers in society, to exploit natural resources without state interference and to defend their private property with arms if they see fit to do so. They also demand freedom of religion, education and personal morality. Much of their world view is based on the assumption that society is self-regulating and the advocacy of the idea of the survival of the fittest.

Very often in modern times libertarianism and utilitarianism have been used by various cynical groups as a cover for implementing more selfish agendas, generally to achieve power or make money.

Both right-wing and left-wing libertarians have frequently resorted to acts of civil disobedience when they feel that an authority has overstepped its limits and is impacting on their freedoms. Whether or not such acts of civil disobedience are justifiable is another matter. Sometimes they are genuine acts of revolt against an unjust authority, sometimes they are simply motivated by the self-interest of a group of individuals with little interest in the common good. Some examples of such populist political groups are Greece's Golden Dawn party, Britain's UKIP or the Tea Party in the United States. All of these parties are demonstrably driven by the self-interest of their ruling elites rather than the political well-being of ordinary citizens of their countries.

5.14 Anarchist Challenges to "Political Obligation"

Anarchist philosophies have been around in various forms for a long time, but modern anarchism actually sprang from the secular and religious thoughts of the Enlightenment in the 18th century, particularly Jean-Jacques Rousseau's arguments for the moral centrality of human freedom.

Rousseau challenged the medieval concept that there is an automatic obligation, often referred to as a "political obligation", to blindly obey the laws of one's government. Over the centuries, there have been many dissenters who believe that there is no general obligation to obey the law, not even on the part of the citizens of a reasonably just society. These dissenters argue that there is a moral and logical obligation to act autonomously as an individual or in collaborating groups, but absolutely no moral or logical reason to blindly obey any form of authority.

The most obvious of these dissenters have been anarchists proper; that group of political philosophers that insist that all states and governments are inherently wicked, coercive institutions that ought to be abolished.

Yet another group of sceptics have concluded that the fundamental anarchist is wrong about the need for the state but right about the obligation to obey the law. Like the anarchist proper, these "philosophical anarchists" hold that the state is illegitimate, but they deny that its illegitimacy entails "a strong moral imperative to oppose or eliminate states; rather they typically take state illegitimacy simply to remove any strong moral presumption in favour of obedience to, compliance with, or support for our own or other existing states" [Note 1].

These philosophical anarchists represent a group that have emerged forcefully over the last century and a half. The basis of their philosophy is that there is no logical or moral case to be made for the idea of a general obligation to obey the law - or any authority for that matter. Their reasoning is that such an obligation would violate the "primary obligation" of human autonomy which is a refusal to be ruled [Note 2] and the capacity for individual human freedom of choice.

If we accept this idea of human autonomy as a "primary obligation" for every individual, then the idea of "political obligation" is obviously doomed, except in the highly unlikely case of a direct democracy in which every law has the unanimous approval of the citizenry. Under any other form of government apart from anarchy the idea of personal autonomy and deference to authority are simply incompatible.

Anarchist philosophy also insists that it is logically and morally impossible to make a case for the idea of any "political obligation" for citizens to obey any particular authority. Short of fear of physical violence, why should citizens relinquish their autonomy and freedom to conform to an obligation that has no a priori or a posteriori basis except the threat or use of violence against those who refuse to obey? The anarchist argues that civil authority based fundamentally only on violence or threats of violence is a form of barbarism and tyranny [Note 40].

The principle of philosophical anarchism goes further at a moral level by stating that authority is "the right to command, and correlatively, the right to be obeyed" [Note 2] which entails that anyone subject to authority has an obligation to obey those who have the right to be obeyed. But, the anarchist argues, if we acknowledge such an authority, we allow someone else to rule us, thereby violating our fundamental moral obligation to act autonomously.

According to this philosophy, we must therefore reject the claim that we have an obligation to obey the orders of those who purport to hold authority over us and conclude that there can be no general "political obligation" to obey the laws of any authority that falls short of a unanimous direct democracy. That conclusion pretty much consigns modern methods of statehood to the bin of immoral government.

Whilst there are few ardent, full-time adherents to the entire anarchist philosophy in modern society, it is remarkable how the development of anarchist ideas has shaped public opinion and attitudes in the last century.

Authorities and establishment groups and individuals that were unchallenged and untouchable 100 years ago are now open season for attacks by the general public, the press, activists and NGOs. Power-wielding elites such as the land-owning gentry, large corporations, governments, their ministers, parliament, the church and our royal houses are now the butt of continuous attacks from those that resent their power or their abuses of power. We sneer at and accuse our government, politicians, religious leaders and aristocracy in a way that was unthinkable a century ago and whilst we may not call ourselves anarchists, most of the general public in Western society is quite capable of being quite anarchic when and if it deems necessary.

The vitriolic and anarchistic reactions to authority seem to be increasing in frequency and vehemence in Western societies. Or is it that the constant exposure of our systems of government to continuous libertarian and even anarchist criticism has finally managed to deconstruct and expose the lies upon which our post-feudal and now capitalist societies have been built? Could it be that these truths are now filtering down to civil society in general and that this is generating a more aggressive questioning of authority by the public?

There are plenty of objections to the various political theories of anarchism. Some are credible and some are just political double-speak aimed at suppressing individual freedoms. Amongst the more honest objections is that human beings are essentially social creatures and tend to cooperate rather than to operate as highly individual autonomous units. Thus, the idea of autonomy as an absolute moral imperative for the individual is seen as undesirable and therefore somewhat undermined.

We know that, in reality, human beings are more effective when they operate in groups of collaborating individuals. Indeed, without human cooperation, it is unlikely that we would have survived and prospered as a species at all. Moreover, the idea of many individuals operating with complete autonomy is fairly bizarre when we consider it in the context of basic needs, such as human reproduction, food and physical security and so on. Inevitably these imperatives involve the creation of nuclear families with interlocking relationships with other conjugally-related families operating a system of collaboration and self-defence.

Very quickly a group of entirely autonomous individuals would find themselves in a tribal environment where conflicts of interest would inevitably be resolved by some form of collective or authoritarian action.

However, despite objections to the practicality of anarchists' political ambitions, the fact is that anarchist sentiment can be a potent force in opposition to authoritarian societies. When a government is collective, transparent and inclusive, anarchism holds far less appeal as a political system.

5.15 Civil Disobedience in the Aftermath of the French Revolution

Once the concept and mechanism of popular revolution had been established in 1789 in revolutionary France, political philosophers found that they had a lot of catching up to do in order to define the new relationship between civil authority and its subjects.

The idea of an undeniable "political responsibility" to obey the state had been torn to shreds, in France at least, with the storming of the Bastille and the destruction of the monarchy and aristocracy. Concepts of Liberty, Equality and Brotherhood had moved centre stage, pushing aside ideas of citizens' "political responsibility", not to mention any remaining ideas of divine right to rule!

The repercussions of the French Revolution spread quickly throughout the old imperial worlds, triggering further revolutions in the old Spanish colonies, North America, Russia and other European nations. The concept of the revolution as a successful means of changing either a regime or an entire system of government had been definitively proven.

The important principle of "people power" being ultimately sovereign to any external tyranny was born during this revolutionary epoch and many a monarch or dictator went to the block or firing squad lamenting the end of the era of absolute power.

Today, of course, revolution or coup d'état remain the ultimate means of dealing with tyrannical or unjust governments and these mechanisms are still in use where no other means are available. The family of Romania's

President Ceausescu learned this fact most violently in recent European history. The threat of armed popular movements is still the nightmare of all governments, even of the more liberal regimes in the Western world. Thankfully, the threat of revolution or popular uprisings acts as a break on the worst excesses of our more totalitarian leaders. In other words, even the threat of revolution is sometimes enough to focus the mind of a potential totalitarian government.

But there is also an interesting side effect of the revolutionary era of the last 200 years and that is an alteration in the public perception of power. The general public is no longer quite as afraid of authority as it once was. In feudal times, power was wielded at the end of a sword or pistol by those that controlled the entire means of coercion. That generally came down to elite groups, such as monarchs supported by their aristocracies and churches. Suddenly, after the French and American revolutions, we collectively realised that these authorities had, in reality, no God-given rights to govern at all and were just as fallible and beatable as any of us mere mortals. Indeed, in countless revolutions the ordinary citizen has demonstrated that these elites could be beaten and completely overthrown by popular, organised uprisings with quite limited resources. The ordinary folk of this new, post-revolutionary world found that they had finally lost their fear of authority.

Together with the realisation that our leaders could be beaten and removed, came the other important revelation that real power actually and ultimately resides with the will of the people. The myth of our sovereigns being ordained by God was bloodily shattered. Suddenly we realised that a centuries-old plot existed to protect the interests of a corrupt elite by constructing some pseudo-religious mumbo-jumbo around royal succession and coronation.

This new-found knowledge of the fallibility of authority and an enhanced sense of our betrayal by those we trusted has engendered a resentment and distrust towards all authority. So today we arrive at a period in our history where politicians and rulers are openly despised, mistrusted and ignored. Corporate greed and government corruption are taken as read and the remnants of monarchy, aristocracy and the church are redundant and in total disgrace, lurching continuously from one corruption scandal or abuse revelation to another [Notes 41, 42].

Even in stable periods these constant revelations of the corruption of those in power plays into the development of a sense of popular indignation and an acceptance of civil disobedience as a means of controlling or altering government. We no longer blindly obey our governments or authorities;

rather we defend our own personal or local interests and we have become more prepared than ever to use whatever means of civil disobedience we have to hand. Since the French, American and Russian Revolutions, the threat of violent revolt and civil disturbance has become an ever present option in civil rebellion, albeit as a last resort.

5.16 Shelley: The Masque of Anarchy, the Massacre at Peterloo and Nonviolence

Shelley was a radical British poet of the early 19th century. Though he only lived until he was 30, he was immensely influential and admired by contemporaries and figures such as Oscar Wilde, Thomas Hardy, George Bernard Shaw, Bertrand Russell, W. B. Yeats and Karl Marx. He was an atheist, anti-monarchist, pacifist and in many ways a subversive. He was a vegetarian and obeyed few of the conventional limits when it came to sexual relationships.

Thoreau's civil disobedience and Gandhi's passive resistance were influenced and inspired by Shelley's nonviolence in protest and political action. It is known that Gandhi would often quote Shelley's poem "The Masque of Anarchy" to vast audiences during the campaign for a free India. The Masque of Anarchy is a political poem written in 1819 by Shelley following the Peterloo Massacre of that year. It is probably the first modern statement of the principle of nonviolent resistance and had a great influence on the philosopher Thoreau in his work "Civil Disobedience".

Other thinkers and campaigners such as Paul Foot describe the poem as "the greatest political poem ever written in English". Aldous Huxley, in his book "An Encyclopaedia of Pacifism", noted the poem's call that the English protesters should resist assault without fighting back, stating "The Method of resistance inculcated by Shelley in "The Mask of Anarchy" is the method of nonviolence".

The poem was inspired by the British Government massacre in 1819 at St. Peter's Field in Manchester (Peterloo) of a number of unarmed civilians holding a meeting of protest to demand improvements in their appalling living conditions and a number of political reforms. The assault by cavalry and hussars left 15 dead and 600 injured.

The poem begins with powerful images of the unjust forms of authority of his time by "God, and King, and Law". Shelley then goes on to imagine the beginnings of a radical form of social action: "Let a great assembly be, of the fearless, of the free". In the poem's narrative, the crowd at this gathering is met by armed soldiers, but the protesters do not raise an arm against their assailants. He then goes on to describe the psychological consequences of violence met with pacifism. The guilty soldiers, he says, will return shamefully to society, where "blood thus shed will speak... in hot blushes on their cheek". Women will point out the murderers on the streets, their former friends will shun them, and honourable soldiers will turn away from those responsible for the massacre, "ashamed of such base company".

The poem mentions several members of Lord Liverpool's government by name: the Foreign Secretary, Castlereagh who appears as a mask worn by "Murder", the Home Secretary, Lord Sidmouth whose guise is taken by "Hypocrisy", and the Lord Chancellor, Lord Eldon whose ermine gown is worn by "Fraud".

Led by "Anarchy", a skeleton with a crown, they try to take over England, but are slain by a mysterious armoured figure that arises from a mist. The maiden "Hope", revived, and then calls to the people of England, with the last 2 stanzas summing up the sentiment of the poem and the public response to the atrocity, which is that ultimately the masses outnumber the ruling classes and that tyranny is ultimately defeated by "people power":

> *The old laws of England - they*
>
> *Whose reverend heads with age are grey,*
>
> *Children of a wiser day;*
>
> *And whose solemn voice must be*
>
> *Thine own echo - Liberty!*
>
> *Rise, like lions after slumber*
>
> *In unvanquishable number!*
>
> *Shake your chains to earth like dew*
>
> *Which in sleep had fallen on you:*
>
> *Ye are many - they are few!*

5.17 Slavery in the United States, Thoreau and Civil Disobedience

Henry David Thoreau was an American philosopher born in 1817 and celebrated as one of the most innovative and radical thinkers of his time. He is considered by many to be the father of the environmental movement and by others to be a political anarchist (which he denied). His interests ranged from politics and history to the natural world, and human rights. He is most famous for his work "Resistance to Civil Government" (also known as "Civil Disobedience"), an argument for public disobedience to an unjust state. He was certainly one of the first political philosophers to develop the idea that the power of popular disobedience could be a means of large-scale political change [Note 43].

The accusation of being an anarchist was somewhat extreme and Thoreau himself always argued that what he wanted was "not *no* government but *better* government". In this philosophy Thoreau saw civil disobedience as a powerful weapon in the citizens' armoury against bad government; not as an end in itself, but rather as a means to the end by involving the civilian population in improving government. In this respect Thoreau was a left-leaning libertarian. However, it is true that his philosophies do embody a streak of anarchism.....as he says himself "That government is best which governs not at all" [Note 3].

One of the driving personal philosophies of Thoreau was his interest in "Transcendentalism". This was a loose religious and philosophical movement that developed during the late 1820s and the 1830s in the eastern region of the United States. It began as a protest against the general state of spirituality and intellectualism at Harvard University and the doctrines of the Unitarian church. The Transcendentalist movement was influenced by certain important Hindu writings and some of the precepts of German idealism. It reacted against the mentality of the Calvinists of the time, which sought to rationalise all human morality and spirituality by introducing a new level of mysticism into spirituality. Among the Transcendentalists' core beliefs was the inherent goodness of both people and nature. Transcendentalists believed that society and its institutions, particularly organised religion and political parties, eventually corrupt the purity of the individual. They believed that people were at their best when truly "self-reliant" and independent. They believed that it is only from such individuals that true community could be formed.

For Thoreau these semi-religious beliefs confirmed his belief that neither government nor church was an indisputable authority which had to be obeyed; rather, he saw both as unnecessary evils that required constant control and continuous reform to rein in their tendencies to be excessive and oppressive. At the same time, Thoreau saw the role of the individual as being responsible for controlling these institutions and bringing about their constant reform.

In this sense, Thoreau had a very mature, post-revolutionary view of political power, human rights, civil liberty and disobedience. For him, civil disobedience was not a one-off act of rebellion but rather a routine obligation for every citizen with a conscience. The concept of permanent revolution developed by Marx and Engels found quite a resonance in

Thoreau's political attitude towards civil disobedience. Civil disobedience is something you do every day of the week when you experience an injustice by authority.

The basic precepts of Thoreau's book "Resistance to Civil Government" include the following arguments:

• Governments are inherently corrupt and unjust: Governments, according to Thoreau, are not just slightly corrupt or unjust in the course of doing their otherwise important work, but in fact governments are primarily agents of injustice and corruption. It is in their nature. Because of this, it is "not too soon for honest men to rebel and revolutionise", he argued

• Democracy is not the solution: Thoreau asserts that because governments typically do more harm than good, they therefore cannot be justified. Democracy is no cure for this because majorities, simply by virtue of being majorities, do not also gain the virtues of wisdom and justice. Democracies are just as capable of being corrupt and unjust.

• Right is Might: The judgment of an individual's conscience is not necessarily inferior to the decisions of a political body or even a majority of the population, and so "it is not desirable to cultivate a respect for the law, so much as for [what is] right."

• Personal moral obligation: Thoreau exhorts us to be moral in our dealings and that includes in our dealings with states and their laws:

"The only obligation which I have a right to assume is to do at any time what I think right.... Law never made men a whit more just; and, by means of their respect for it, even the well-disposed are daily made the agents of injustice."

For instance, on the topic of slavery (which he abhorred) he adds: "I cannot for an instant recognize as my government (that) which is the slave's government also." This is a powerful statement of how far personal moral responsibility extended in Thoreau's philosophy. More than 100 years before the Nuremberg trials, Thoreau expounded a clear understanding of the concept of how we can easily become the servants of an evil tyranny if, first and foremost, we fail to observe a clear understanding of our personal moral obligations to our own conscience above any other consideration, and that includes obeying the law.

• No expense justifies injustice: Many political philosophers of his time counselled caution against revolution because revolution typically causes a lot of suffering, expense and inconvenience. Thoreau contends that such a cost/benefit analysis is inappropriate when governments are actively facilitating an injustice (in his case it was the existence of slavery). Such fundamental immoralities absolutely justify any difficulty or expense to bring such injustices to an end. As Thoreau put it, "This people (the USA) must cease to hold slaves, and to make war on Mexico, though it cost them their existence as a people."

• The crime of omission and hypocrisy: Thoreau spreads the blame to those who do nothing against injustice. He explains to his audience that they cannot blame problems of injustice solely on those that commit injustices, but also on those that fail to do anything about them simply because of their own apathy or self-interest. He says that the audience cannot just blame the pro-slavery Southern politicians, but must put the blame on those, for instance, in Massachusetts as well, who do nothing to fight these injustices. As he puts it, we can also blame those "who are more interested in commerce and agriculture than they are in humanity, and are not prepared to do justice to the slave and to Mexico, cost what it may.. There are thousands who are in opinion opposed to slavery and to the war, who yet in effect do nothing to put an end to them."

• Everyone can act: Thoreau exhorts people not to just wait passively for an opportunity to vote for justice, because voting for justice is as ineffective as wishing for justice; what the people must do is to actually be just. This is not to say that you have an obligation to devote your entire waking life to fighting for justice, but you do have a moral obligation not to commit an injustice and not to give injustice your practical or economic support.

• Practical examples of how we cooperate with or fight injustice: Paying taxes is one way in which otherwise well-meaning people collaborate in injustice, Thoreau contends. People who proclaim that a war is wrong and that it is wrong to enforce slavery contradict themselves if they fund both policies by paying their taxes. Thoreau points out that the same people who applaud soldiers for refusing to fight an unjust war are not themselves willing to refuse to fund the government that started the war. Thoreau is clear that there is a complete moral obligation not to assist a government or economic system which commits acts of injustice or tyranny.

• Practical stances to civil disobedience: Thoreau went into some detail about what government actions he considered legitimate and those he did not. For example, Thoreau said he was willing to pay the highway tax, which went to pay for something of benefit to his neighbours, but that he was opposed to taxes that went to support the government itself - even if he could not tell if his particular contribution would eventually be spent on an unjust project or a beneficial one. "I simply wish to refuse allegiance to the State, to withdraw and stand aloof from it effectually."

• When and how the individual should disobey the government: In a constitutional republic (like the United States in Thoreau's time), people believe(d) that the proper response to an unjust law is to try to use the political process to change the law, but to obey and respect the law until it is changed. However, Thoreau points out that if the law itself is clearly unjust, and the lawmaking process is not designed to quickly obliterate such unjust laws, then the law deserves no respect and it can and should be broken by conscientious citizens.

In Thoreau's days, and in the case of the United States, the constitution itself enshrined the institution of slavery, and therefore falls under this condemnation. Therefore slavery abolitionists, in Thoreau's view, are morally obliged to completely withdraw their support of the government and stop paying taxes, even if this means imprisonment. Thoreau asserts that under a government which imprisons anyone unjustly, "the true place for a just man is also a prison.... where the State places those who are not with her, but against her, the only house in a slave-state in which a free man can abide with honour....cast your whole vote, not a strip of paper merely, but your whole influence", demands Thoreau.

• Popular action: Thoreau argued for the strength of popular action and hints at asymmetrical strategies to use against an unjust system: "A minority is powerless while it conforms to the majority; it is not even a minority then; but it is irresistible when it clogs by its whole weight. If the alternative is to keep all just men in prison, or give up war and slavery, the State will not hesitate which to choose. If a thousand men were not to pay their tax bills this year that would not be a violent and bloody measure, as it would be to pay them, and enable the State to commit violence and shed innocent blood. This is, in fact, the definition of a peaceable revolution, if any such is possible."

• Moral well-being and avoiding retaliation: Thoreau was under no illusions about the vindictive nature of authorities in the face of civil disobedience. He counselled activists to make sure that they could not be morally or physically damaged by authority. Because a government will retaliate, Thoreau says he prefers living simply, because he therefore has less to lose. "I can afford to refuse allegiance to Massachusetts.... It costs me less in every sense to incur the penalty of disobedience to the State than it would to obey. I should feel as if I were worth less in that case."

• On a more positive note: Thoreau did see some signs that there was progress in the evolution of human government. Because government is man-made, not an element of nature or an act of God, Thoreau hoped that its makers could be reasoned with. As governments go, he believed the U.S. government, with all its faults, was not the worst and even had some good qualities. But he felt that the American citizen could and should insist on better, and he clearly believed that American democracy was not the end of the evolutionary process for human government, however proud the American people may be of it. As he stated: "The progress from an absolute to a limited monarchy, from a limited monarchy to a democracy, is a progress toward a true respect for the individual. Is a democracy, such as we know it, the last improvement possible in government? Is it not possible to take a step further towards recognizing and organizing the rights of man? There will never be a really free and enlightened State until the State comes to recognize the individual as a higher and independent power, from which all its own power and authority are derived, and treats him accordingly."

Thoreau's writings were and are a great source of influence to those struggling to achieve freedom and independence from some form of tyrannical system. Mahatma Gandhi [Note 44], Martin Luther King, Tolstoy, Proust, Yeats and Hemingway were all much impressed with his well-developed philosophies and he remains essential reading to anyone interested in human and civil rights and the relationship between the state and the citizen.

5.18 The Luddite Rebels and Worker Disobedience

The story of the Luddite movement is an interesting one because the Luddites found themselves in dispute with an entire class of factory owners in the early 19th century. It is also noteworthy that what started as a legitimate concern by skilled workers rapidly deteriorated to deliberate sabotage of machinery, property damage and then into open violent and deadly clashes between groups of civilian workers and the military. It is a classic case of what happens when governments fail to deal fairly with legitimate grievances from their civil population. In this case the complaint resulted from the mechanisation of the ancient craft of weaving and the loss of work and dignity for hand-loom weavers during the Industrial Revolution.

The modern use of the word Luddite is very corrupted and implies that Luddites were backward and opposed to the use of technology. The original and more accurate use of the word referred to a group of textile workers (hand-loom weavers) who protested against newly developed labour-replacing machinery in the period 1811 to 1817 and consequent wage reductions.

The Luddite movement was in fact part of the much larger picture of increasing labour activism that had begun a hundred years earlier with actions by miners and other industrial workers from Cornwall to Durham who plundered granaries after intolerable rises in food prices. At around the same time, other workers in other trades began to organise themselves into cooperative "friendly societies". This was done in order to pool economic resources in an attempt to save themselves from unemployment, illness, old age and destitution in the new and heartless environment of industrial England.

The most radical Luddite actions occurred during the extreme economic conditions of the Napoleonic wars and very quickly spread throughout England. Frustrated by having their demands ignored, members of the Luddite groups took to burning down mills and destroying the new machinery that put them out of work or cut their wages.

Rather than attempting to address the grave hardship and the grievances of the workers, the response of the British government was to confront the workers with military violence and a number of show trials, ending in the execution or penal transport of protesters. Of course, this further exacerbated the situation and the sabotage of machinery soon descended into pitched battles with mill owners and militia in which lives were lost on both sides [Note 45].

Although the Luddite movement itself was pretty much extinguished by the brutal and draconian actions of the government, the movement itself inspired several similar groups and emboldened workers to form the earliest organised unions to defend their jobs and to fight to improve working conditions. Thus, even after the Luddite rebellions were crushed, similar protests occurred in the agricultural sector in the 1830s, where new agricultural machinery was sabotaged or destroyed because it caused the loss of agricultural employment.

The Luddites had clearly touched a nerve of the new capitalists by demonstrating that their "productive capital" (machinery) seemed to be more important than their "human capital" and sabotage became a by-word in later industrial disputes - a "spanner in the works" one might say.

5.19 Daniel O'Connell, the start of the Land League and the Monster Meetings.

Daniel O'Connell, born in 1775, was a famous orator, lawyer and agitator for Catholic emancipation and the end to British rule in Ireland. O'Connell was convinced that pacifism combined with civil disobedience was the best route to achieve his goals.

He is famous for (amongst other things) his development of a new nonviolent technique to agitate, which became known as the "monster rally" or "monster meeting".

Catholic emancipation became law in 1829 as a result of a complex series of events, including O'Connell's winning a seat in Parliament but unable to take the oath as he was a Catholic. He then turned his attention to the issue of British rule in Ireland, which was a thorn in the side of most of the Irish population, and for this he employed his monster rallies as a means of showing the huge level of popular support for the British to leave Ireland.

The first monster meeting was held on 9 March 1843 at Trim, Co. Meath and attracted 30,000 people. By the next meeting, in Mullingar on 14 May, the numbers had increased to 100,000. A week later in Cork the crowd had swelled to half a million. The meeting at Tara held on 15 August was said to have attracted a full million people.

The effect of these huge rallies was twofold: Firstly, it demonstrated to the ruling British that a vast "army" could be raised to support independence and full-scale Catholic emancipation. Secondly, these meetings raised considerable amounts of money to support O'Connell's campaigns.

The culmination of the campaign was to be a meeting on Sunday 8th October at Clontarf, near Dublin. On the Saturday evening, Sir Robert Peel proscribed the meeting as illegal. Warships entered Dublin Bay beside the venue and Clontarf itself was surrounded by cavalry.

O'Connell cancelled the meeting to avoid violence. Despite this he was arrested for sedition and spent three and a half months in prison [Note 46]. On appeal, he was released to a rapturous populace. Despite the largely symbolic significance of these rallies, they sent a powerful signal to the ruling British government.

These monster rallies were an early example of modern-day protest demonstrations. They combine the "demonstration" of strong popular support with a thinly veiled threat of popular insurrection and send these messages to government.

5.20 Land Wars and the Boycott

Late in the eighteenth century when the Irish Land League was formed in the west of Ireland to help poor tenant farmers, large-scale rallies were also a feature. The Land League's primary aim was to abolish landlordism in Ireland and enable tenant farmers to own the land they worked on. The period of the Land League's agitation is also known as the Land Wars. As well as large demonstrations of disciplined protesters, the Land League's more famous forms of protest were rent strikes and boycotts. Indeed, the first use of the word "boycott" was the result of an action against a land agent named Captain Boycott.

Captain Boycott was employed on the estates of Lord Erne in County Mayo and he attempted to evict tenants refusing or unable to pay their rents. Charles Stewart Parnell, a Land League leader, proposed that anyone who took over a farm from which another tenant had been evicted should be totally shunned. While Parnell's speech did not refer specifically to land agents or landlords, the tactic was first applied to Captain Boycott when the evictions began.

Despite the short-term economic hardship to those undertaking this action, Boycott soon found himself completely isolated. His workers stopped work in the fields and stables, as well as in his house. Local businessmen stopped trading with him, and even the local postman refused to deliver his mail [Note 47].

This concerted action meant that Boycott was unable to hire anyone to harvest the crops in his charge. Eventually 50 Orangemen from Cavan and Monaghan volunteered to do the work. They were escorted to and from the land by one thousand policemen and soldiers. The costs of protection for this workforce ended up being far more than the harvest was worth. After the harvest, the "boycott" was successfully continued.

The idea of a "boycott" caught on very quickly. Within a few weeks Boycott's name had travelled the world. The New York Tribune first wrote of the "boycott" in the international press. It was used by The Times in November 1880 as a term for organised isolation. The Daily News wrote on December 13, 1880: "Already the stoutest-hearted are yielding on every side to the dread of being 'Boycotted'." The boycott - a new technique of civil disobedience was born.

5.21 Marx, Engels and the birth of Modern Socialism

Whilst Marx and Engels were certainly not the only great philosophers concerned with the relationship between capital and human freedom, they certainly developed the most complete definition of modern socialist theory currently in existence. Both are considered to be amongst the most influential philosophers and sociologists of modern history and no discussion of the history of civil disobedience would be complete without them.

There are several parts of Marxist philosophy which have influenced the ways in which citizens perceive authority. Clearly Marx saw the domination of capitalist elites as part of a historical class struggle, which would ultimately end in revolution and sweep away the "exploitative classes of capitalism" [Note 48].

Marx saw the capitalist system as transitory and inherently unstable and he believed that this economic and social instability would become greater over time. He considered religion to be "the opium of the people. The abolition of religion as the illusory happiness of the people is the demand for their real happiness."

For Marx the downfall of capitalism as a system was a historic inevitability, just as the end of feudalism was the natural result of the ascendancy of capitalism and the Industrial Revolution. Marx believed that the structural contradictions within capitalism necessitated its end, giving way to socialism, or a post-capitalistic, communist society.

In this new society the self-alienation between worker and capital would end, and humans would be set free to act without being bound by the labour market. It would be a democratic society, enfranchising the entire population.

In such a Utopian world there would also be little, if any, need for a state because the only role of the state (as we know it) is actually to enforce the alienation between worker (proletariat) and capital.

Marx believed that if the proletariat were to seize the means of production, they would encourage social relations that would benefit everyone equally by abolishing the exploiting classes, and by introducing a system of production which is less vulnerable to cyclical crises ("boom and bust" economies).

In terms of civil disobedience, Marx used the phrase "permanent revolution" to describe a strategy of a revolutionary class to pursue their class interests independently, without compromise, even if faced with the political dominance of opposing sections of society. Trotsky later extended this idea to suggest that in late developing capitalist countries the working and middle classes can and must seize social, economic and political power, and form alliances with the peasantry.

Since the days of Marx, socialism and communism have been through a series of radical evolutions and splits. Some parts of the socialist movement have followed a strictly revolutionary course towards a society free of capitalism and class distinction. Other parts of the movement have sought to work within the capitalist system to reform society in an evolutionary rather than revolutionary way. The latter has given rise to all kinds of compromises such as "compassionate capitalism", and movements such as the "social democratic movement", a sort of watered-down socialism.

Despite all the hybrid forms of socialism which have evolved throughout the world the fundamental Marxist principles remain central to all serious socialists, even to this day. These principles centre on the fact that capitalism is an exploitative economic system, which seeks to control the working classes with the help of a collaborative state authority and various other institutions, such as religion.

From the point of view of any form of rebellion, this provides the socialist with a perfect explanation and justification for all honest acts of civil disobedience, since the conflict between proletariat and capitalist state is inevitable according to Marx - until we achieve full revolution.

5.22 Trade Unions and Worker Direct Action

The Luddite rebellions were just one manifestation of a wider radicalisation of workers that took place during the Industrial Revolution. The concentration of workers from rural areas into often squalid urban areas, the intensive use of child labour, the downward drive on wages and often dreadful working conditions triggered a widespread but uncoordinated movement to organise the labour force across Europe in the 18th century.

In Britain, the concept of worker unions and collective bargaining had been outlawed since the 14th century, in part giving rise to a violent rebellion: the Peasant's Revolt in the latter years of that century. However, the huge increases in population density necessitated by the industrialisation and urbanisation of 18th century manufacturing made the formation of organised labour inevitable.

The first (illegal) trade union in Britain was formed in 1810, followed in 1820, in Scotland, by the first general strike. By 1871 in Britain, trade unions were finally legalised. In other European nations, the earliest trade union movements date from the mid 18th century [Note 49].

To this day, few governments or corporate administrations in Europe have a positive relationship with labour unions and the history of the labour movement is fraught with conflict, mostly as a result of assaults on unions by governments or managements. Over the years, governments have legislated to "box in" unions so that their actions are somewhat limited. Improved living conditions also made unions less vital and less popular. However, even with less popular support than they had 50 or 100 years ago, and even within newly implemented legal limits, a well-organised and motivated union or organised workforce can be a formidable adversary in the face of an unreasonable employer.

The two primary acts of disobedience that a union can manifest are a/ a strike and b/ a "work to rule". A strike is a total withdrawal of labour by members of a union for a definite or indefinite period. A "work to rule" is when workers apply the terms of their contract strictly and without flexibility, thus maintaining their income but creating operational problems for the management of a company.

Additional strategies adopted by unions over the years have included picketing. This involves a blockade by union members in an attempt to persuade workers and customers not to deal with a target company, thus cutting off their supplies and sales.

Still further strategies for industrial action include the occupation of factories, "slowdown", and bans on overtime.

Unions manage industrial actions to make them as effective as possible. This includes paying basic "strike pay" to participating workers so that they are not forced back to work because of poverty. For this, workers regularly pay into a fund that is used for this eventuality.

Unionised strikes are a primary example of large-scale collaborative civil disobedience [Note 50].

5.23 Feminism and the Suffragette Struggle for Women's Equality

Far from the bustling European capitals with their salons and parliaments hotly debating the latest political events, rural New Zealand was in fact the first sovereign country to grant women the right to vote in 1893, when all women over the age of 21 were permitted to vote in parliamentary elections.

In contrast, the USA had to wait until 1920 before there was universal suffrage for adult women, whilst England, 'the mother of parliaments', dithered until 1928 before all women over 21 years of age could vote. It sounds incredible but it is indeed one of the great shames of our modern history that this basic emancipation of half our population took so long in coming.

The term "suffragette" is particularly associated with activists in the British Women's Social and Political Union (WSPU), led by Emmeline Pankhurst. Their protest tactics included chaining themselves to railings to provoke an arrest, pouring harsh chemicals into mailboxes, breaking windows at prestige buildings and night-time arson of unoccupied buildings.

Many suffragettes were imprisoned in Holloway Prison in London, and were force-fed after going on hunger strike. The suffragettes' means of protest triggered strong reactions of disgust by certain conservative establishment figures, but also outpourings of sympathy and support from those that agreed with their cause [Notes 51, 52].

The group's early militancy used nonviolent forms of protest. The WSPU organised rallies, made speeches, gathered signatures for petitions and published a newsletter called "Votes for Women". The group convened a series of "Women's Parliaments" to coincide with official government sessions. When a bill for women's suffrage was filibustered on 12 May 1905, Pankhurst and other WSPU members began a loud protest outside the Parliament building. Police immediately forcibly dispersed them. However, they regrouped and demanded passage of the bill. Although the bill was never resurrected, Pankhurst considered it a successful demonstration of militancy's power to capture public attention.

The exclusive focus of the WSPU on votes for women was a hallmark of its militancy. It was a single issue group. Whilst other organisations agreed to work with individual political parties, the WSPU insisted on separating itself from, and often opposing, political parties which did not make women's suffrage a priority. The group protested against all candidates belonging to the government's ruling party (Liberals) because it refused to pass women's suffrage legislation.

Members of the WSPU were sometimes heckled and derided by the public for spoiling elections for Liberal candidates. On 18 January 1908, Pankhurst and her associates were attacked by an all-male crowd of Liberal supporters who blamed the WSPU for costing them a recent by-election. The men threw clay, rotten eggs, and stones packed in snow and the women were beaten. Similar conflicts later developed with the Labour party. Until party leaders made the vote for women a priority, the WSPU vowed to continue its militant activism. Pankhurst and others in the union saw party politics as a distraction from the goal of women's suffrage and criticised other organisations for putting party loyalty ahead of women's votes.

On 21 June 1908, half a million suffragette activists rallied in Hyde Park to demand votes for women. Faced by amused indifference from the government, a small group proceeded to Downing Street and threw rocks at the windows of the Prime Minister's residence. The next year the movement began a campaign of hunger strikes. The prison authorities' response was a policy of brutal force-feeding which caused almost universal condemnation.

By 1912 the WSPU, utterly frustrated and radicalised by the inaction of government, police and prison brutality, coupled with frequent negative public opinion, decided to escalate their acts of sabotage by adopting arson as another tactic. The issue of property damage caused a minor rift in the movement. But the events of 1914 and WWI soon overtook the movement and in 1918, partly as a result of the decimation of the male population in Britain resulting from the war, about 8.4 million women gained the vote. 10 years later, the franchise was extended to all women over the age of 21.

The Suffragette movement is an extraordinary story of civil disobedience and bravery, where activists refused to hold their tongue, went to prison and in some cases died for their principles.

Historians generally argue that the first stage of the militant suffragette movement under the Pankhursts in 1906 had a dramatic mobilizing effect on the suffrage movement. Women were thrilled and supportive of an actual revolt in the streets. The extraordinary violence which was meted out by the (male) authorities to the original peaceful protests was brutal and resulted in a powerful popular awakening. Thus the movement for complete female emancipation and equality was born and continues the struggle for complete gender equality to this day.

5.24 Pacifism and the Anti-War Movement

The philosophical origins of pacifism include Buddhist and Hindu traditions, Christian teachings and contributions from some groups within Judaism and Islam that refuse to participate in violence.

Pacifist actions against militarism were first recorded in the 3rd century AD, when a Christian refused to be conscripted into the army and was martyred as a result. Since then the idea of conscientious objection to violence has become a major source of civil disobedience in many societies throughout the world.

Philosophically the concept of absolute nonviolence is difficult and many conscientious objectors exclude the need for self-defence from their pacifist philosophy. The so-called "Just War" [Note 53] theory postulates that whilst war may be horrendous, the spectre of unbearable loss of freedom and life may justify the use of war.

One group which believed that all violence was abhorrent was the Cathars in the 13th century. Although this sect was Christian, it was also a rival to the Roman Catholic Church, which proceeded to wage a crusade against the Cathar population in southern France, leading to its complete annihilation [Note 54]. Sadly, this is not the only example where complete pacifism which excludes self-defence has led eventually to genocide.

The post-Reformation world gave rise to a new wave of pacifist ideas and new churches, such as the Quaker and Amish congregations, who adopted a strictly pacifist Christian interpretation. The following centuries saw pacifism develop still further and by the end of the Napoleonic Wars pacifism was no longer an isolated opinion.

By the mid 19th century the rise of socialism began to merge with increasingly vocal pacifist values. Tolstoy, for example, a self-dubbed "Christian Anarchist", was staunchly pacifist and hugely influential in his refusal to accept the use of violence in either warfare or in resistance.

However, at the time of the First World War, many socialist groups and movements in Europe were anti-militarist, arguing that war by its nature was a type of governmental coercion of the working class for the benefit of capitalist elites. Nonetheless, those who refused to fight were often treated harshly, imprisoned or executed [Note 55].

After WWI, the destruction and carnage dramatically altered the thinking of many who had entered the war full of nationalist pride. Pacifist sentiment became much more acceptable as a result of the horrors of the war with the post-WWI years heralding a period of strong anti-war idealism; however this soon ended with the rise of fascist militarism in Germany, Italy, Spain and Japan.

The bellicose actions of Nazi Germany in the 1930s and the outbreak of war in Europe in 1939 effectively put pacifist beliefs into full reverse, with many pacifists feeling obliged to admit that there was no alternative but to fight the Nazis and their fascist allies or face extermination.

Even pacifist moralists argued that WWII was a "war of self-defence" and a "just war", the inevitable result of aggressive German territorial expansionism; others argued however that the war could have been avoided with astute political and diplomatic actions.

Since WWII though, the world has seen a series of wars which were not as existential in their threats as the Second World War. The USA and its allies have engaged in a number of armed conflicts which were pure acts of aggression deliberately aimed at nations far from their shores merely to satisfy their economic or other geopolitical objectives. Thus the wars in Korea, Vietnam, Iraq and Afghanistan were not conflicts of self-defence however one stretches the definition of self-defence. These were wars of aggression designed to protect the strategic interests of the USA and its allies, rather than wars of self-defence. These were wars of greed rather than acts of military defence. Such "immoral" conflicts have now given rise to a new generation of pacifists.

Despite the slight liberalisation in attitudes towards pacifism, it is hard to see a great difference between the attitudes of modern day jingoistic US or British governmental policy and those of the militaristic Nazis towards war and pacifism. For instance, Hermann Göring described, during an interview at the Nuremberg Trials, how denouncing and outlawing pacifism was an important part of the Nazis' seizure of power: "The people can always be brought to the bidding of their leaders. That is easy. All you have to do is tell them they are being attacked and denounce the pacifists for lack of patriotism and exposing the country to danger. It works the same way in any country" [Note 56]. Ring any bells? George W. Bush, emulating Göring's advice, asserted: "You are either with us or with the terrorists" in an address to a joint session of Congress on September 20, 2001.

Nonetheless, post WWII pacifist protests have been increasingly more powerful. They have included the mass burning of draft cards by Vietnam "refuseniks", huge mass anti-war demonstrations in Europe (some of several million demonstrators) and in the USA as a result of the second invasion of Iraq by the USA and its allies.

Lesser known anti-militaristic protests include the Larzac plateau protest in France in 1972 where 103 peasant landowners took an oath to resist the proposed extension of the existing military training base on the Larzac plateau. Using a mixture of civil disobedience, including hunger strikes, they were ultimately successful when the base extension was cancelled by President François Mitterrand immediately after his election in 1981.

Another prominent anti-war protest began in 1981 when the "women's peace camps" were established in protest at the deployment of cruise missiles centred on the Greenham Common airbase in the UK. "The Greenham Women" or "peace women" and their 19-year protest drew worldwide media and public attention. Finally the base was closed and in 1997 Greenham Common was designated as public parkland [Note 57].

Many anti-war activists hold strong ideological beliefs and many who practice civil disobedience also do so out of religious faith. Notable examples of such religious anti-war activists include Dorothy Day, a co-founder of the Catholic Worker Movement and member from the 1930s to the1970s, Philip and Daniel Berrigan, Catholic priests, who were arrested dozens of times in acts of civil disobedience in anti-Vietnam war protests in the 1960s and 1970s.

5.25 Fascism, War, Religion and Resistance: Dietrich Bonhoeffer

One of the most famous modern stories of wartime disobedience relates to Dietrich Bonhoeffer, a Lutheran pastor and anti-Nazi dissident. Educated in Germany and the USA, Bonhoeffer was vehemently anti-Nazi and was disgusted by the acceptance of the Nazi regime by other parts of the German Evangelical Church [Note 58].

Bonhoeffer is unique in the sense that he committed his acts of disobedience against the Nazi government of Germany by means of the most secret subversion possible, i.e. by infiltrating a part of the Nazi intelligence service.

He was an amateur in these matters, not a professionally trained spy, and it must have demanded the most extraordinary bravery, intelligence and dedication for a civilian to operate without detection within the very heart of the detested Nazi intelligence apparatus.

Earlier, Bonhoeffer had helped found an underground church in Germany called the "Confessing Church" and he assisted in the training of pastors in secret seminaries. This church was strongly anti-Nazi and under constant threat of suppression by the Nazi party. Bonhoeffer wrote and spoke widely on the Christian obligation to human rights, but he was finally forced by the Nazi regime to curtail his public writings and speeches.

By 1941 it was clear to Bonhoeffer that nothing he could say or write could in any way alter the course of the Nazis' fascist agenda in Europe. He decided therefore, via his brother-in-law, to join the Abwehr, a German military intelligence organisation, which was also secretly the centre of the anti-Hitler opposition and resistance.

The same brother-in-law became actively involved in several plots to assassinate Hitler with other co-conspirators in the Abwehr. Bonhoeffer's experience in the Abwehr gave him access to a fairly complete picture of the full horrors of Nazi atrocities and using the Abwehr as a cover, he acted as a courier for the German resistance movement hoping to garner their support. Through his ecumenical contacts abroad, he hoped to secure possible peace terms with the Allies for a post-Hitler government.

His visits to Norway, Sweden and Switzerland were camouflaged as legitimate intelligence activities for the Abwehr. He made contacts with high-ranking members of the British government and the Church of England but, like all previous contacts with German resistance, the British government unfortunately chose to ignore these contacts.

Meanwhile, Bonhoeffer and his brother-in-law were involved in Abwehr operations to help German Jews escape to Switzerland, and he maintained a network of anti-fascist former students with whom he communicated.

On 5 April 1943, Bonhoeffer and his brother-in-law, Dohnányi, were arrested. This was not due to their conspiracy however; rather it was the result of long-standing rivalry between SS and Abwehr for control of the Nazi intelligence administration. Bonhoeffer was imprisoned at the Tegel military prison to await trial. However, after the failure of the 20 July plot on Hitler's life in 1944 and the discovery in September 1944 of secret Abwehr documents relating to the conspiracy, Bonhoeffer's real connection with the conspirators was discovered.

He was transferred from the military prison in Berlin to the detention cellar of the Gestapo's high-security prison. In February 1945, he was secretly moved to Buchenwald concentration camp, and finally to Flossenbürg concentration camp.

On 4 April 1945, the diaries of Admiral Wilhelm Canaris, head of the Abwehr, were discovered, and after reading them, in a rage, Hitler ordered that the Abwehr conspirators be executed. Bonhoeffer was led away just as he concluded his final Sunday service. He was condemned to death on 8 April 1945 by SS judge Otto Thorbeck at a court-martial without witnesses, records of proceedings or defence.

He was executed in Flossenbürg by hanging at dawn on April 9, 1945, just two weeks before soldiers from the United States army liberated the camp, three weeks before the Soviet capture of Berlin and a month before the capitulation of Nazi Germany [Note 59].

Despite the tragic death of this very brave and principled man, his last years underline an important reality for all, which is that there is always something that we can do to oppose tyranny, whether openly or subversively, even in the most appallingly risky conditions. It also illustrates the very real personal risks of opposing a despotic and inhuman regime.

5.26 Mahatma Gandhi and Nonviolent Civil Disobedience

Civil disobedience clearly is not the same as revolution, even though a political crisis may rapidly descend from civil disobedience into full-scale revolution if a government does not deal with the grievances of its citizens quickly and effectively.

The ultimate end-game for civil disobedience, as every activist knows, is escalation, which means moving from passive disobedience to violent acts of rebellion. A wise political leader knows this and will attempt to avoid such an escalation at all costs. A wise activist also understands this and knows how to optimise civil disobedience to be effective, whilst hinting at the consequences of being ignored or oppressed by government.

Such an activist was Mahatma Gandhi in his struggle against British rule in India between 1921 and 1947. Gandhi was a barrister and civil rights activist in both South Africa and India. He espoused a pluralist view of India where Hindus and Muslims could live together and collectively fight for independence from Britain. He developed a radical nonviolent form of civil disobedience which included periods of fasting and a simple lifestyle, and he used mass action to make British-controlled India as ungovernable as possible [Note 60]. He managed to appeal, at least for a while, to both Muslim and Hindu populations. He became leader of the Indian National Congress and was considered a great unifying influence. He was a great believer in equality for all human beings regardless of gender, race, religion or class.

Part of Gandhi's strategy of nonviolent civil disobedience included mass boycotts against British products, British educational institutions, British courts and British government jobs. Other actions included the Salt march of 1930, a protest against the British salt taxes, where thousands of Indian supporters accompanied Gandhi on a 400 km march to the sea to make their own salt in defiance of the government tax. The British government responded by imprisoning 60,000 Indians.

Gandhi's most potent campaign was the "Quit India" campaign during WWII. This brought Gandhi into direct conflict with Britain on the subject of India's role in the war, as the independence movement explicitly refused to support India's participation in the war. Gandhi asserted that India could not be party to a war, ostensibly being fought for democratic freedoms, while that freedom was denied to India itself. The "Quit India" campaign became the most forceful movement in the history of the tragic Indian quest for independence from Britain, with mass arrests and violence on an unprecedented scale.

Over the years, Gandhi was arrested and imprisoned by the British authorities on numerous occasions, sometimes for years at a time. Despite the violent atrocities committed by the British against Indian civilians, such as the Amritsar massacre, where hundreds of unarmed, peaceful Indian civilians were gunned down by British troops in an act of collective warning and punishment, Gandhi maintained his stance of peaceful non-cooperation to the very end [Note 61]. India was granted independence in 1947.

Though his nonviolent attitudes were admired by many, Gandhi also infuriated those who wanted to move to a more active and more violent struggle against the British and those who were becoming impatient with the slow pace of the movement.

Others were frustrated by Gandhi's compromising and inclusive stance to the Muslim population, the untouchables and to women. In 1948 Gandhi was tragically assassinated by a Hindu extremist who accused him of favouring Pakistan and who refused to accept his doctrine of nonviolence.

Gandhi is revered today as one of the most influential advocates of nonviolent protest.

5.27 Fascism, Religion and Resistance (II): Martin Luther King Jr.

One of the modern world's most respected thinkers and orators on the subject of human rights, Martin Luther King Jr. was born in 1929 in Atlanta, Georgia. He became a pastor and is renowned as an activist, a humanitarian, and as the leader of the African-American Civil Rights Movement. He is best known for his role in the advancement of civil rights, using nonviolent civil disobedience based on his Christian beliefs.

Martin Luther King was assassinated on April 4, 1968 in Memphis, Tennessee whilst on a speaking appointment. The identity of the assassin is still a subject of controversy.

King became a civil rights activist early in his career in the 1950s. During his short life, he led numerous nonviolent protests against segregation between black and white citizens in the United States. He was a superb orator and won the Nobel Peace Prize for combating racial inequality through nonviolence. In his final years, King expanded his focus to include poverty and the Vietnam War. He alienated many of his (white) "liberal" allies with a 1967 speech titled "Beyond Vietnam". He was assassinated the following year.

His philosophy was straightforward and clear. It was a simple affirmation of the US constitution and the basic human rights guaranteed by the United Nations Charter. He was a great advocate of peaceful civil disobedience and had no problem in advocating that laws should be (peacefully) broken in the process of defending human rights. As he points out in one of his speeches, "the Boston Tea Party", a celebrated act of rebellion in the American colonies, "was illegal civil disobedience", and, conversely, "everything Adolf Hitler did in Germany was 'legal'". He became increasingly frustrated by the attitude of the American liberal white population to radical liberation politics.

King also expressed his frustration with white moderates and clergymen too timid to oppose an obviously unjust system. As he says, "I have almost reached the regrettable conclusion that the Negro's great stumbling block in his stride toward freedom is not the White Citizen's Councillor or the Ku Klux Klanner, but the white moderate, who is more devoted to "order" than to justice; who prefers a negative peace which is the absence of tension to a positive peace which is the presence of justice; who constantly says: 'I agree with you in the goal you seek, but I cannot agree with your methods of direct action'; who paternalistically believes he can set the timetable for another man's freedom; who lives by a mythical concept of time and who constantly advises the Negro to wait for a 'more convenient season'".

Martin Luther King's leadership of the Civil Rights Movement was extraordinary both for its bravery and its restraint. Appalling crimes were (and still are) committed against black populations throughout the United States by supremacist whites. In the face of these atrocities, Martin Luther King maintained his Christian-driven policy of peaceful protest actions only. Even more remarkable was that most of his innumerable dedicated followers obeyed his orders to avoid violence. His influence on his supporters was almost absolute and he is certainly the most loved and revered leader of ordinary black Americans that has ever lived in that country [Note 62].

Whilst the problems of racism in the USA are far from over, the situation has improved since the 1960s and there is no doubt that Martin Luther King's restraint and deeply felt humanist views are the most important reasons for this.

5.28 Nelson Mandela, the ANC and the Overthrow of Apartheid

The ANC was a famous movement, led by Nelson Mandela together with Archbishop Desmond Tutu and Steve Biko, which initially advocated the use of civil disobedience as a means of overthrowing the dominant apartheid system during whites-only rule of South Africa.

The ANC rose to prominence after 1948 when a system of extreme apartheid was implemented by the white supremacist South African government. The white government made no apologies for being overtly racist. Their system disenfranchised black South Africans, placing strict, racist travel and residence restrictions on non-white citizens whilst also curtailing almost all their political activity.

Because of the use of violent repression on any form of demonstration against apartheid in South Africa, the ANC was initially obliged to use methods of passive resistance against the apartheid regime [Note 62].

In June 1952, the ANC joined with other anti-Apartheid organisations in a "Defiance Campaign" against the restriction of political, labour and residential rights, during which protesters deliberately violated these oppressive laws. They followed the example of Mahatma Gandhi's passive resistance in Kwa Zulu-Natal and in India.

However, the disobedience campaign was called off in April 1953 after new laws were passed which prohibited protest meetings. In 1958, the ANC first called for an international academic boycott of South Africa in protest against its apartheid policies. The call was repeated the following year in London.

In 1960, the ANC undertook a campaign against the so-called "Pass Laws". These laws required black people to carry an identity card at all times to justify their presence in white districts. This campaign was to begin on 31 March 1960. The Pan Africanist Congress, a parallel protest organisation, pre-empted the ANC action by holding unarmed protests 10 days earlier, during which 69 protesters were killed and 180 injured by police fire in what became infamously known as the Sharpeville massacre.

Following the Sharpeville massacre, the ANC leadership concluded that methods of nonviolence such as those utilised by Gandhi against the British Empire in India were ineffective against the apartheid regime in South Africa. Therefore, in 1961 a military wing of the ANC was formed (known as MK), with Nelson Mandela as its first leader. This marked the transition from civil disobedience to armed revolt.

MK operations during the 1960s primarily involved targeting and sabotaging government facilities. Mandela was arrested in 1962, convicted of sabotage in 1964 and sentenced to life imprisonment. These acts of sabotage escalated until they included a number of fatal bombings. The ANC was finally classified as a terrorist organisation by the South African regime and some Western governments, including the United States of America and the United Kingdom. This was despite the fact that the apartheid regime of South Africa was clearly deeply unjust and the ANC and most ordinary black citizens had been provoked into violence by the repressive and inhumane measures of the government.

In the succeeding years, the South African government found itself under increasing internal and external pressure, and this, together with a more conciliatory tone from the ANC, resulted in a change in the political landscape.

Finally, on 2 February 1990, the State President F.W. de Klerk removed the ban on the ANC and other organisations, and began peace talks for a negotiated settlement to end apartheid. In 1994, the ANC and its allies won resounding victories in the democratically organised elections and apartheid in South Africa came to a definitive end.

Whilst the ANC is not an example of an organisation that exclusively used civil disobedience as its main method to challenge unjust authority, it is a very good example of an organisation that tried to use peaceful means to bring about social change in the face of a tyrannical authority, but was ignored by the latter.

The result of this contempt for peaceful protest was inevitably the bomb and the bullet and ultimately the overthrow of the authoritarian regime.

5.29 Hippie Culture and the Movement of '68

Various forms of informal alternative counter-culture philosophies have long existed and some have been more clearly defined than others. One of the less clearly defined is the Hippie movement of the 1960's and early 1970's. Hippie (or Hippy) culture was originally an unstructured youth movement that arose in the United States during the mid-1960s and quickly spread to other countries around the world and was connected with the popularity for contemporary protest music and culture, alternative art and the theme of youth rebellion, free-thinking and free love. The Hippie movement was largely confined to the emergent middle classes of the Western world's baby-boomer generation, though not exclusively.

Several characteristics are common to all Hippie groups or movements, but it is very difficult to define an exact philosophical origin for the phenomenon. Some would argue that the origins lay with a sudden antagonism towards capitalism and growth-based economic systems during the post war booms in the West. Others maintain it was a "back to fundamentals" reaction to rapid urbanisation. Some consider it was a desire to re-establish a more transcendental understanding of our lives that drove the movement, and hence the common interest in mind-altering drugs. Yet others blame a form of bourgeois hedonism on the growth of the movement. Probably all of these influences played a part in the growth of the Hippie movement [Note 64].

What can be said for certain is that the growth of the Hippie movement was powered by a common set of philosophical and behavioural norms which expressed a certain distaste for the dominant and conventional morality of the times and contempt for the systems of government and economic elites that enforced them.

The movement originally emerged during the post WWII period when the United States and its allies were entering a protracted war in Vietnam, not that long after a previous ignominious war in Korea. This gave a legitimate target of protest to the Hippie movement (which was unreservedly pacifist).

In addition, the West was locked in a continuous Cold War with the Communist nations, with the threat of nuclear holocaust just a button's press away (allegedly). It is quite certain that this constant fear of nuclear war and the rapacious capitalism that the United States was developing during this period were immense sources of antagonism to the libertarian youth of the time, alienating and driving ever increasing numbers of young people into the arms of those seeking an alternative society. Faced with the possibility of continuous war, and/or a sudden and final nuclear winter or a bright, free, open and peaceful world what would you choose?

The Hippie movement didn't provide a particular alternative political solution, but it did offer a different narrative which included many of those things which most young people find important, such as personal freedom, beauty, nature, love, equality, peace, community, and art. In a world steeped in a state of continuous war with a hard-faced capitalist economic system rapidly destroying the global environment, it was obvious that any alternative would seem to be more attractive by the youth of the time.

Hippie culture was wide-ranging. It included an interest in eastern religions, foods and philosophy. It embodied radical political ideas taken from the early Libertarians, Marx and Thoreau and from the earliest "back to nature" activists of Europe and the United States. It could simultaneously be revolutionary, radical, passive or subversive and from the authorities' point of view, the Hippie movement was a dangerously asynchronous threat to their authority. It was highly communicative but completely disorganised.

In terms of real acts of civil disobedience the Hippie movement set new standards in the post WWII era. Hippies squatted in empty buildings, refused to pay taxes, travelled at will and were generally uncooperative with the authorities they encountered. They worked the system to extract money from the welfare and social benefits authorities, openly used illegal drugs, lived in communes, campaigned against wars and sometimes (in the USA) even burned their draft cards in public acts of defiance against the authority of the state. They organised their own alternative musical events on a huge scale and communicated through a network of impenetrable channels of friends and associates which were invisible to the "modern" security services of most Western countries [Note 65].

One of the most important aspects of the Hippie movement was the prominence of middle-class people who could move seamlessly between an establishment background and radical activism as needed. This fluidity confounded the authorities and the police and makes the movement important in any study of successful civil disobedience. Indeed, it teaches us that some of the most potent forms of civil disobedience are those initiated by the middle classes. We will discuss why this is at a later point.

Generally speaking, the Hippie movement was a peaceful one though this did not stop various government authorities becoming paranoid about their various activities. Clearly the Hippie alternative way of life (real or imaginary) was seen as a real threat to the more conventional lifestyle offered by the capitalist system and clearly the Hippie movement needed to be removed. This was partly achieved when the musical counter-culture of the Hippie movement was monetised by the media industry and began to descend into a cynical money-making industry. But this attack on the idealism of the Hippie movement was not entirely successful and a whole generation went on to develop and propagate their ideas to others.

After a generation and a half of social change it is hard to say what the outcome of the Hippie movement has been. One can say that it was an artistic renaissance of sorts and that its moral principles (loose as they were) still resonate almost 50 years later in the political forces such as the green movement, "New Age Travellers", and the "Occupy" movement. Indeed, Hippie principles and ideals are deeply embedded in the psyche of many of former participants, people who are now bank managers and corporate managers. Therefore, if nothing else, we have to thank the Hippie movement for opening up our social attitudes to gender and sexual equality, to a more open discussion of human relations and human morality. The Hippie movement succeeded in undermining the last vestiges of supremacy of state power and they effectively triggered off the most radical critique of modern capitalism in the last 100 years. Some of what we perceive as modern Western morality is grounded in the warm, cosy, communal decency defined during the Hippie era.

5.30 Greenpeace and New Forms of Environmental Protest

Greenpeace today is a highly influential global environmental NGO with activists campaigning on all major environmental issues throughout the world. The organisation developed both as a response to nuclear weapons' testing in the 1960s and to the rapidly deteriorating global environment.

Greenpeace's early protests involved its use of ocean-going vessels to bring protests directly to the site of an environmental problem and this method has evolved over the years to engage in some of the most high-profile protests the world has ever seen. Greenpeace has become synonymous with peaceful civil disobedience and is well-known for its fearlessness in confronting environmental misdeeds, regardless of the risks to the activists involved. The violent arrests of vessels and activists over the years by governments around the world are a testimony to this courage. Sadly, this harassment of Greenpeace by governments ended in the bombing of one of Greenpeace's vessels - the Rainbow Warrior - in 1985 by the French Intelligence Service, with fatal results, on the direct orders of French President Mitterrand.

Greenpeace has always avowed a policy of nonviolent protest. Despite this, the organisation has often been referred to as being a group of "eco-terrorists" [Note 4], an accusation which somewhat undermines the serious use of the word "terrorism".

One of Greenpeace's greatest "crimes" and one of the main reasons that it is so detested by both corporate and government authorities is its sheer effectiveness. Greenpeace has a highly professional media management team and is very competent at publicising its campaigns. In many senses Greenpeace has learned a lot from the capitalist world about campaign management and effective public relations.

The organisation was an early adopter of internet technology and operates a continuous system of internet-based protest, communication and petitions. This is done alongside a more conventional approach to protests which includes such activities as legal actions, "normal" street protests, boarding oil-rigs, scaling government buildings in high-profile media demonstrations, acts of non-lethal sabotage of corporate installations and many other actions. Publicity is high on the Greenpeace agenda and getting activists mobilised effectively and quickly is one of the organisation's talents.

Whilst Greenpeace may be one of the high-profile environmental NGOs, there are, of course, many others and their techniques for highlighting, delaying or stopping environmental crimes vary. There are many different examples.

In the UK, road protesters stopped forest destruction by digging tunnels under ancient woodlands and camping in the trees, thus stopping or delaying construction work. Elsewhere, protesters against blood sports harassed hunters by blocking access roads or warning foxes of the arrival of a hunt, or deliberately disturbing the scent of a fox to throw off the hunting dogs. In other protests in the UK, government hunters were frustrated in their efforts to kill badgers by protesters deliberately and noisily alerting badgers to the arrival of the gunmen and thus leaving almost nothing for them to shoot.

Most of these actions were carried out by small cells of demonstrators acting independently without any form of centralised coordination. This strategy of asynchronous disruptive action is an important development in the concept and efficiency of civil disobedience.

The infiltrations of green protest groups by police and other agents of the state started almost immediately after the environmental movement became a mainstream threat to modern industrial corporations and governments. It was also recognised by protest groups quite rapidly and their response was to de-centralise their groups and operate within a common strategy but otherwise without too much central coordination. This meant that small groups of trusted friends or colleagues working at a very local level began to operate autonomously. Police and other authorities find this type of small autonomous group very difficult to identify or track because they simply don't appear on their "radar". They exhibit no patterns of communication and very often their protests or acts of sabotage actions are informal, covert and sometimes quite spontaneous. For highly structured police forces or agents trying to infiltrate protest groups, such behaviour is a nightmare scenario. Protesters and saboteurs can strike quickly, without any pattern of behaviour or any standard method, without any warning and at any moment. There is often no "communications chatter" before or after an action and they can simply disappear into the night without detection. In a sense, many of these environmental groups now most closely resemble the Whiteboy saboteurs of 18th century Ireland; a close-knit local group, loosely organised and largely autonomous.

5.31 Stéphane Hessel and Time for Outrage

Stéphane Hessel (1917 - 2013) was a diplomat, ambassador, writer, and philosopher. He was born a German citizen but emigrated to France as a child. During the Vichy fascist regime of France he fled to London and joined the French Resistance. He then returned to France to help organise communications networks together with the allies. He was captured by the Gestapo and sent to Buchenwald concentration camp where he was tortured. He survived by escaping whilst in transit to another camp.

After WWII, Hessel became an observer of the editing of the "Universal Declaration of Human Rights" in 1948. In later years his activism focused on the Israeli / Palestinian conflict, human rights and economic inequality, for which he has received many honours and awards. In 2011 he was named by Foreign Policy magazine in its list of top global thinkers.

In 2010, Hessel published a short book called "Indignez-vous!" which was translated into English as "Time for Outrage!" The book was an instant hit and is believed to have sold 4.5 million copies worldwide in some 30 different languages. Hessel and his book were linked and cited as an inspiration for the Spanish Indignados, the American Occupy Wall Street movement and many other radical political protest movements that are currently taking political actions around the world [Note 66].

In the book, Hessel asserts that indifference is the worst of all human attitudes. He speaks of his experience in the WWII French Resistance, his role in drafting the Universal Declaration of Human Rights and he exhorts young people to be active in politics and indeed to look for topics of indignation. He then presents his own current principal source of indignation: the suffering of the Palestinians at the hands of Israel (Hessel's grandparents were Jewish).

Hessel rails against the assaults on global human rights and the huge global disparity between rich and poor which he believes is the direct result of uncontrolled capitalist greed and a betrayal of the anti-fascist principles which were the basis of the post war world order. He ends the tract by calling for nonviolent action ("a peaceful insurrection") and for an uprising against the powers of capitalism and political corruption. The writing is powerful and straightforward and goes very much to the heart of the subject.

The book was published in the midst of the economic crisis which began in 2008 with the near collapse of the global banking system, general loss of confidence in the political system and revelations of endemic corruption in the financial and political centres of power. Thus the book tapped into popular anger around the world. It was most notably popular in Spain, where unemployment was at catastrophic levels and the right-wing government and banking sector were implementing draconian economic measures.

In Spain on May 15, 2011 a new mass protest movement began simultaneously in 58 cities with the instigation of huge urban demonstrations against the failure of capitalist economics, partisan politics and widespread corruption in government. One of the names given to the 2011 Spanish protest movement was "Los Indignados" (The Outraged), taken from the title of the book's Spanish translation (¡Indignaos!).

The Spanish protests later inspired other protests all around the world, including Greece, Israel and indeed the Occupy Wall Street movement in the United States. Hessel's work also inspired the book "Manifiesto de los Indignados de la Cruz del Sur", written by philosopher Eduardo Sanguinetti, released in Montevideo in December 2011. The book remains an immensely popular work and a source of inspiration to many currently engaged in various ongoing protest movements.

5.32 Movement 15M, the Indignados and the Anti Eviction Movements in Spain

Since the ongoing economic crisis began, Spain has had one of the highest unemployment rates in Europe, reaching a record of 27% with youth unemployment at a catastrophic 56%. Many of Spain's problems are perceived to have arisen because of the actions of an uncontrolled banking sector that irresponsibly advanced credit and created a huge property bubble.

Simultaneous with the economic crisis came a series of high-profile revelations of political corruption, mostly aimed at right-wing Popular Party members and officials (though not exclusively). These events coincided with a general lack of confidence by the Spanish population in the political classes. This followed several scandals at various levels of government and opposition with events such as the suspension of Balthazar Garzon, a generally trusted and well-liked examining judge who was investigating crimes against humanity committed by the previous fascist Franco regime [Note 67]. Garzon was also investigating high level corruption in the Popular Party. Given that the Popular Party (PP) arose from Franco's fascist party, it was clear that the PP had to remove Garzon before he was able to get these damning cases into the courts. So, in 2010, Garzon was suspended as a judge by the PP-dominated Spanish Supreme Court. This obvious political interference sent shock waves through an already traumatised national psyche.

In 2010 the PSOE (centre-left) central government began a series of unpopular economic reforms, including a rise in the retirement age. A general strike took place in September 2010 and by early 2011 there were violent clashes in Madrid. But the government continued to announce more and more social program cutbacks.

In January 2011, a loose collection of individuals and groups began to organise, using social networks (Twitter and Facebook). They called for a national demonstration to take place on May 15th (hence 15M) in every major town and city in Spain.

Protests took place in all the planned cities, with protesters demanding more democracy, a new electoral law and an end to political corruption, as well as other reforms, such as the nationalisation of banks. According to the website of the movement, 50,000 people gathered in Madrid alone on the first day of the demonstrations. The first protest was called under the motto "we are not goods in the hands of politicians and bankers" and was focused on opposition to what the protesters called "antisocial means in the hands of bankers." The motto referred partly to the changes made in 2010 to contain the ongoing European sovereign debt crisis through a bailout of the banks which Spanish society saw as responsible for the crisis.

At the end of Madrid's demonstration, protesters blocked the Gran Vía avenue and staged a peaceful sit-in in Callao street, to which police responded by beating protesters with truncheons. As a result of the clashes a group of 100 people headed to Puerta del Sol and started camping in the middle of the square, which would result in the following days' protests.

The police brutality and the attempts to ban the demonstrations spurred a rapid escalation of protest with large-scale demonstrations around all regional and provincial capitals in Spain in a sign of solidarity with the demonstrators occupying the Puerta del Sol Square in Madrid. By the night of the 19th May to the following day, the number of demonstrators in Madrid had grown exponentially, with the Guardian newspaper reporting that "tens of thousands" had camped out in Madrid and throughout the country. On the 20th May the Supreme Court banned the demonstrations but the demonstrators voted to stay, in defiance of police, city authorities and the courts. In the coming days occupations of government buildings escalated and violent clashes broke out in Barcelona when police attacked a peaceful protest camp in the city.

On July 25, 2011, Nobel Prize-winning economist Joseph Stiglitz participated at the "I Foro Social del 15M" organised in Madrid, expressing his support for the protests. The generally peaceable behaviour of the protesters contrasted with the frequent display of violence by some of the police - firing rubber bullets and tear gas. The protesters retaliated by throwing rocks, attempting to surround parliament and attacking banks, heckling and blocking politicians of all parties and blockading city and town centres.

Under severe pressure to respond to the street protests, the left-wing government called a snap election for November 2011 and was defeated. Many of its supporters abstained in protest at the government's austerity measures and mishandling of the demonstrations. The result was that, by default the right-wing PP was elected. Their election inflamed the situation, with the PP introducing new laws banning demonstrations.

The original demonstrations spawned many new groups with assorted styles of protest including sit-ins, surrounding parliament, and long marches across the country converging on the capital. Generally they have been peaceful demonstrations, except where national police have intervened violently. One series of demonstrations by the left-wing miners of Asturias was violently attacked by Madrid police. The retaliation was a barrage of explosive charges from the well-armed miners and many demonstrators and miners were injured.

Since the beginning of the 15M movement there have been, and continue to be, waves of protests from various sectors, i.e. the medical profession against cuts in healthcare, (the so-called "White tide"), protests by firemen (with fully equipped fire-engines) facing off against the police, and strikes by every branch of the public service including strikes by students and school children and their parents together with their lecturers and teachers, known as the "Green Tide".

In August 2012 the mayor of Marinaleda led protests to get the Spanish government to end the austerity measures. The protesters entered and openly stole food from several large supermarkets to feed jobless people. The objective of these actions was to stress that the government was ignoring the hunger and despair of the middle and working classes.

An interesting offshoot of the 15M movement was a national group of activists made up of retired people and calling themselves "Yayoflautas" basically meaning "Grandpa Flautists" or, as they are sometimes referred to, "Seniors at War". This group comprises many who distinctly remember the days of Franco's terror and now feel the need to stand alongside their children and grandchildren to ensure that they have a better life. The group is well-organised and has the avowed aim to support "any just movement against injustice with nonviolent action". They assist the 15M movement and PAH group by helping collect signatures, participating in demonstrations, lobbying politicians and writing letters and petitions in support of these movements. Despite their generally peaceful activities, they have been known to force certain banks to close their doors during angry protests against the banks' fraudulent mishandling of their customers' deposits. The Yayoflautas groups exist in many parts of the country and are living proof that, regardless of age, it's never too late to become an activist!

One particular lasting initiative which did emerge from the 15M was a group called PAH (Plataforma de Afectados por la Hipoteca), dedicated to helping the victims of mortgage defaults who were being evicted from their homes by the banks. Ada Colau, the founder of the movement in Barcelona in 2009, won notoriety when she publicly called a representative of the Spanish Banking Association "a criminal" during a parliamentary hearing in 2013. Her book "Mortgaged Lives" is scathing about the system of debt and property ownership in Western capitalism. Branded a terrorist by at least one member of Spain's right wing governing PP party, she has won numerous international prizes for her defence of human and civil rights. The PAH movement she founded campaigns for housing rights and takes direct action to stop evictions. It operates in local cells which work with residents struggling or unable to pay their mortgages. In the case of residents about to be evicted, the group organises demonstrations and blockades of homes to physically stop bank agents and police enforcing an eviction. In the 4 years up to October 2014 the group has stopped over 1100 evictions from being executed.

Whilst the actions of PAH are in defiance of legally enforceable evictions, few banks have had the temerity to oppose the group in the climate of intense public hatred of the banking sector in Spain. All the same, hundreds of thousands have been evicted since 2008, with an average of nearly 100 houses lost per day in 2014.

At the time of writing the 15M movement and direct action groups like PAH continue to be very active. The general viewpoint of the groups involved is that all the main political parties in Spain have failed the people - some more than others. They accuse all the political classes of being guilty of some degree of corruption and refusing to deal properly with the country's fascist past. The movements claim the political parties are disconnected from the ordinary citizen and are unable to manage the Spanish economy and protect it from the rapacious interests of big capital.

For these reasons the 15M movement insists that it is apolitical and completely inclusive and is more of an abstentionist movement than a left-wing or anarchist group. Nonetheless, it is pretty clear that there are very few members of the ruling right-wing Popular Party manning the 15M barricades or attending their "people's assemblies".

Despite their apolitical position, some political movements have arisen from 15M's actions. Some new left-leaning parties (such as Podemos) have emerged and been relatively successful in the polls though it is difficult to know if they will ultimately succeed. The main left-wing party (PSOE) has vowed to reform itself and move back to the left again under its new leader.

Probably the most important victory for the 15M movement is that it has sent shock waves through the political and economic establishment in Spain. It has demonstrated that a relatively loose grouping of fairly diverse citizens can organise mass nationwide protests, causing serious economic and political disruption and blocking the efforts of banks to seize property. If nothing else, it has set limits on the excesses of central and regional governments in Spain and curtailed the power of the banks and the bad behaviour of the police forces. The misconception of a compliant Spanish citizenry is gone for ever.

The 15M movement has been an inspiration to many other movements, notably the global Occupy movement and various other generally anti-capitalist activist groups which have sprung up around the world in recent years.

5.33 A New Generation of Disobedience: The Whistleblowers - Assange, Snowden, and Manning

The concept of a "whistleblower" is a fairly modern idea. The whistleblower is a person or group that exposes misconduct, dishonest or illegal activity in an organisation. The organisation can be corporate or government.

The misconduct may be classified in many ways. For example, it can be a violation of a law, rule, regulation, or it may be some form of corruption, a direct threat to the public interest, such as health and safety violations or fraud.

Whistleblowers operate in three possible ways:

- They may make allegations internally to other people within an organisation.

- They make public accusations or report externally to regulators, law enforcement agencies, the media or other interested parties.

- They can make their accusations via a dedicated third party organisation which exists only to investigate and manage accusations made by whistleblowers. WikiLeaks and similar organisations fall into this category.

Whistleblowers may have a specific accusation or sometimes they simply provide large amounts of information (as a leak perhaps), which taken together represents an indictment of the organisation's behaviour.

Whistleblowers often face fierce reprisals, either at the hands of the organisation or group which they have accused or from related organisations, and sometimes under the laws of the countries they have offended.

One of the reasons that whistleblowing has become quite a powerful tool in the hands of our most modern civil disobedient protesters is because it requires very little effort to execute. The use of highly available technology to get an accusation into the right hands or into the public domain is available on every PC or mobile phone. Modern, high speed communications and information technologies mean that vast amounts of supporting documents and data can be copied and transmitted in just a few moments by a myriad of different methods. All that is required for a whistleblower action is a motivated individual to be in the right place at the right moment.

Another reason that whistleblowers serve an important role in modern society is that they effectively, single-handedly remove the veil of impunity which many governments and certain corporate managements have used to hide their activities. No longer can a military unit commit an atrocity in a far-away country and be sure that they will get away with it. No longer can a drugs company "lose" damning drug test results with the absolute certainty that someone didn't keep a copy.

Such immoral acts have been stock-in-trade in governments and corporate organisations for centuries, but the arrival of the whistleblower armed with modern technology makes this kind of behaviour very risky and very hard to hide. It is no wonder that whistleblowers face harsh measures when they make their revelations; Julian Assange was forced to flee into political asylum in the Embassy of Ecuador in London in 2012, Edward Snowden was obliged to seek asylum in Russia in 2013, and Bradley-Chelsea Manning was sentenced to 35 years imprisonment in 2013 in the USA.

All three of these high-profile whistleblowers had committed the ultimate crime in the eyes of the United States government - they had leaked vast amounts of information which was embarrassing to the USA. None of the information leaked actually threatened US security or risked any lives, but it certainly hurt the ego of the government and undermined confidence in the military and security systems of the USA. This, above all, is what caused such a furious reaction by the US government. No-one likes being caught out in a lie and the US government, US intelligence apparatus and US military are no exceptions, except in these cases it wasn't just one lie, it was tens of thousands of historical and current deceptions, misdeeds, atrocities, plots, betrayals and breaches of national and international law. In just 4 years, these three people have undermined the world's most powerful military, intelligence and diplomatic agencies by revealing their darkest secrets. It's easy to see that they have been effective in their whistleblowing because the US government is incandescent with anger and plotting violent revenge against these people.

Interestingly, none of the three, Assange, Snowden, or Manning is a professional spy. Manning and Snowden had access to secret material but they held only quite junior positions and Assange ran a third party agency to receive and investigate leaks. All three are young people and apart from Assange, not known activists. But they share a common idealism and all were deeply disturbed by the antics of the US government and its agencies. Manning and Snowden were both security-cleared to quite a high level, but clearly they were all "under the radar" of US intelligence and were able to steal secrets on a huge scale for quite a long time. Obviously, being white Anglo-Saxons they didn't match the CIA's profile of what a subversive should look like.

All three were able to publish their revelations to the public using various internet-based systems. This perhaps explains why successive US governments are so determined to gain more complete control of internet traffic. Professional terrorists clearly don't send emails to each other or chat about their plans on their mobile phones, so why is the US government so interested in monitoring email and mobile traffic? Is this a manifestation of the paranoia of the security services rather than anything to do with national security?

The problem for those who are the subject of a whistleblower's accusations is that no security screening in the world is completely fool-proof, or should we say whistleblower-proof. No system of confidentiality is completely leak-proof. Wrong security decisions are common even in the strictest security regime. For example, Guy Burgess, Anthony Blunt (and several other colleagues) were British spies who leaked secrets to the USSR for ideological reasons for years. They were establishment figures and security-cleared by British intelligence at the very highest level - indeed they were high-ranking members of that very intelligence apparatus themselves!

The methods of security screening used by governments and corporations are tremendously unsophisticated and simple to circumvent. Often security clearance is finally dependent on a small group of "trusted" executives interviewing someone and getting a feeling for the candidate's attitudes, and then, if reasonably satisfied, signing off their clearance. Background checks are part of this process, but irrelevant since they say nothing about an individual's current thinking. Apart from the inadequacy of the security clearance process, the security of an organisation is almost always leaky.

There is always someone to overhear a conversation, glimpse a document on a desk, or some IT administrator who "borrows" some data, or someone who takes a photograph or makes a video on their mobile.

So, throughout the world, there are probably tens of thousands of potential whistleblowers in all kinds of privileged positions with access to colossal amounts of sensitive data. They may not even be active yet. They may never act at all but they are there, and should an appropriate set of circumstances arise they may become active whistleblowers.

The very idea of a government or corporate organisation being riddled with potential whistleblowers sends profound shivers down the spines of our political and corporate masters. Nonetheless, on the basis of recent events, we can assume that this is precisely the situation that exists.

It is interesting to note that the level of whistleblower activity increases as authorities become more draconian and unreasonable. An open, transparent authority is no place for a whistleblower; they simply have no material to work on and little motivation to betray their employers. But in a closed-up, aggressive and paranoid environment where misdeeds are common and employees are treated badly, there is a huge threat that the authority will be attacked by a whistleblower. Indeed, in these circumstances the authority is actually breeding whistleblowers.

Edward Snowden was known as a fairly conservative young man. He became a whistleblower because of his exposure to what he found was the completely unacceptable behaviour of the US government's intelligence agencies. The chain of events which led to Manning's whistleblower activities is an amazing litany of institutional personnel management and security failures by the US military, but finally Manning acted (according to the message accompanying the leaked material) to reveal "one of the most significant documents of our time removing the fog of war and revealing the true nature of 21st century asymmetric warfare." In other words, the leaking of the secret files was an ideological act by a young person against an unreasonable authority.

Despite the risks entailed in becoming a whistleblower, it is certainly a growth activity at the moment. Corporations and governments have moved quickly to make the practice as dangerous as possible for the whistleblower. Despite the insincere rhetoric about protecting whistleblowers, the truth is that many a whistleblower is and has been threatened, fired, demoted, bullied and imprisoned, tortured or assassinated for their activities. In recent times however, the practice has been made safer for the whistleblower by the use of file cleansing, encryption, and the use of secure drop boxes by journalists. These techniques often allow the whistleblower to remain anonymous, thus removing most of the risk of repercussions.

5.34 The Present Day: Technology, Communications and Civil Disobedience

Many aspects of civil disobedience rely on an ability to communicate effectively. Several Protestant religious movements in the 16th century took advantage of access to the printed word and by the 1970s nearly everyone in the Western world had access to a phone and a photocopier.

Of course, since those days we have experienced an even more revolutionary development with the advent of the internet. It is hard to exaggerate just how dramatic a change the internet has made to modern activism. It has truly revolutionised speed of communications, the movement and storage of data and how we disseminate information. Social networks, blogs, email, messaging services and access to modern, super-safe encryption systems have all been at the heart of a number of popular movements for civil and human rights in many parts of the world. Despite attempts to control such technology by authoritarian forces, the prospect is that the internet will actually become freer and less controllable as alternative technologies find new ways of circumventing authority's attempts at control.

In the same way that it was impossible for the Roman Catholic Church to "un-invent" the printing press, it is also impossible now to "un-invent" the internet. Anywhere where there is a telephone line and a PC there is a potential internet connection, one way or another. Apart from dismantling the planet's entire telecoms system, there is no absolute way that this technology is ever going to be removed or effectively controlled by government ever again. What is astonishing is that something which was designed to make money for the large capitalist nations has been transformed into something that has such potential for human and personal liberation.

Notes on Chapter 5

Note 1: Simmons 2001, p. 104

Note 2: Robert Paul Wolff (1998 (1970), p. 18)

Note 3: Thoreau, H. D. Resistance to Civil Government

Note 4: 2001, when the Institute of Cetacean Research of Japan called Greenpeace "eco-terrorists".

Note 5: Plato in the Apology (Apologia Socratis) presents his version of the speech given by Socrates as he defended himself

Note 6: See Franco-Gallia, François Hotman (1574)

Note 7: Maslow, A.H. (1943). A theory of human motivation. Psychological Review 50 (4) 370-96.

Note 8: Aquinas: Summa Theologica, First Part of the Second Part, Question 94 Reply Obj. 2

Note 9: John Locke (1689): Two Treatises of Government

Note 10: Nuremberg Principle IV, "defence of superior orders" is not a defence for war crimes, although it might influence a sentencing authority to lessen the penalty. Nuremberg Principle IV states: "The fact that a person acted pursuant to order of his Government or of a superior does not relieve him from responsibility under international law, provided a moral choice was in fact possible to him."

Note 11: Matthew 22:21: "Therefore render to Caesar the things that are Caesar's, and to God the things that are God's."

Note 12: Romans 13:1-7

Note 13: In 313AD, Constantine and Licinius issued the Edict of Milan decriminalizing Christian worship.

Note 14: St. John Chrysostom (347-407AD): Homiles from Antioch (386-397AD)

Note 15: Officially, "The Confession, Instruction, and Admonition of the pastors and preachers of the Christian congregations of Magdeburg" (1550)

Note 16: Witte, John (2007). The Reformation of Rights: Law, Religion and Human Rights in Early Modern Calvinism. Cambridge University Press, p.106.

Note 17: Thomas Aquinas: Summa Theologiae, II-II, 42.2, ad 3

Note 18: Thomas Aquinas: Commentary on the Politics, Book 3, Lecture 3 [366]

Note 19: Dunn, Alastair (2002). The Great Rising of 1381: the Peasants' Revolt and England's Failed Revolution. Stroud, UK: Tempus. ISBN 978-0-7524-2323-4.

Note 20: Faith, Rosamond (1987). "The 'Great Rumour' of 1377 and Peasant Ideology". In Hilton, Rodney; Alton, T. H. The English Rising of

1381. Cambridge, UK: Cambridge University Press. pp.43-73. ISBN 978-1-84383-738-1.

Note 21: Dunn, Alastair (2002). The Great Rising of 1381: the Peasants' Revolt and England's Failed Revolution. Stroud, UK: Tempus. ISBN 978-0-7524-2323-4, p.73

Note 22: Oman, Charles (1906). The Great Revolt of 1381. Oxford, UK: Clarendon Press. OCLC 752927432

Note 23: Saul, Nigel (1999). Richard II. New Haven, US: Yale University Press. ISBN 978-0-300-07875-6.p74

Note 24: Dyer, Christopher (2000). Everyday Life in Medieval England. London, UK and New York, US: Hambledon and London. ISBN 978-1-85285-201-6, p 291.

Note 25: Martin Luther: 95 Arguments - "Disputatio pro declaratione virtutis indulgentiarum" were written by Martin Luther in 1517 and are widely regarded as the initial catalyst for the Protestant Reformation

Note 26: All parties would recognize the Peace of Augsburg of 1555, in which each prince would have the right to determine the religion of his own state, the options being Catholicism, Lutheranism, and Calvinism

Note 27: Theodore Beza (1574) De jure magistratuum (Right of Magistrates).

Note 28: (1649) The True Levellers Standard ADVANCED: or, The State of Community opened, and Presented to the Sons of Men

Note 29: Acts 4:32, Today's English Version: "The group of believers was one in mind and heart. No-one said that any of his belongings was his own, but they all shared with one another everything they had."

Note 30: Acts 2:44, 2:45: "All who believed were together and had all things in common; they would sell their possessions and goods and distribute the proceeds to all, as any had need." Winstanley argued that "in the beginning of time God made the earth. Not one word was spoken at the beginning that one branch of mankind should rule over another, but selfish imaginations did set up one man to teach and rule over another."

Note 31: Hippies: A Guide to an American Subculture by Micah L. Issitt

Note 32: Droppers: America's First Hippie Commune, Drop City by Mark Matthews

Note 33: Lewis Henry Berens: "The Digger Movement in the Days of the Commonwealth"

Note 34: Patrick Riley, The Social Contract and Its Critics, chapter 12 in The Cambridge History of Eighteenth-Century Political Thought, Eds. Mark Goldie and Robert Wokler, Vol 4 of The Cambridge History of Political Thought (Cambridge University Press, 2006), pp. 347-75.

Note 35: Jean-Jacques Rousseau: Du contrat social (1762)

Note 36: Flanagan, Thomas. The Year of the French, ISBN: 978-1590171080

Note 37: Richardson, W. Augustus (1979). "Levellers in their White Uniforms;" Whiteboyism in southern Ireland, 1760-1790. University of Essex, MA Thesis Social History.

Note 38: Bentham, Jeremy (1776). "A Fragment on Government".

Note 39: David Hume: Treatise of Human Nature (1739-40), Enquiry Concerning Human Understanding (1748), History of Religion (1757) and Dialogues Concerning Natural Religion (1779).

Note 40: Stanford Encyclopedia of Philosophy Political Obligation First published Tue Apr 17, 2007; substantive revision Thu Aug 7, 2014

Note 41: Jenkins, Philip, Pedophiles and Priests: Anatomy of a Contemporary Crisis (Oxford University Press, 2001). ISBN 0-19-514597-6

Note 42: Berry, Jason and Gerald Renner. Vows of Silence: The Abuse of Power in the Papacy of John Paul II (Free Press: 2004) ISBN 0-7432-4441-9

Note 43: Henry Thoreau (1849) "Resistance to Civil Government"

Note 44: Gandhi, M. K. "Duty of Disobeying Laws", *Indian Opinion*, 7 September and 14 September 1907.

Note 45: Binfield, Kevin (2004). Luddites and Luddism. Baltimore and London: The Johns Hopkins University Press.

Note 46: Boylan, Henry (1998). A Dictionary of Irish Biography (3rd ed.). Dublin: Gill and MacMillan. p. 306. ISBN 0-7171-2945-4.

Note 47: Marlow, Joyce (1973). Captain Boycott and the Irish. André Deutsch. pp. 133-142. ISBN 0-233-96430-4.

Note 48: Karl Marx (1867) Das Kapital, Kritik der politischen Ökonomie

Note 49: G. D. H. Cole (2010). Attempts at General Union. Taylor & Francis. p. 3.

Note 50: Aleksander Smolar, "Towards 'Self-limiting Revolution': Poland 1970-89', in Adam Roberts and Timothy Garton Ash (eds.), Civil Resistance and Power Politics: The Experience of Nonviolent Action from Gandhi to the Present, Oxford University Press, 2009, pp. 127-43

Note 51: Crawford, Elizabeth. The Women's Suffrage Movement: A Reference Guide, 1866-1928. Routledge.

Note 52: Sophia A. Van Wingerden. The women's suffrage movement in Britain, 1866-1928 (Palgrave Macmillan, 1999)

Note 53: Guthrie, Charles; Quinlan, Michael (26 Sep 2007). "III: The Structure of the Tradition". Just War: The Just War Tradition: Ethics in Modern Warfare. United Kingdom: Bloomsbury Publishing PLC. ISBN 978-0747595571.

Note 54: Barber, Malcolm (2000), The Cathars: Dualist heretics in Languedoc in the High Middle Ages, Harlow: Longman, ISBN 978-0582256620

Note 55: Hochschild, Adam (2011). To End All Wars - a story of loyalty and rebellion, 1914-1918. Boston, New York: Mariner Books, Houghton Mifflin Harcourt. pp. xvii. ISBN 978-0-547-75031-6.

Note 56: "Nuremberg Trial Proceedings, Volume 9: Eighty-fourth day, Monday, 18 March 1946, morning session". The Avalon Project. New Haven, Connecticut: Yale Law School, Lillian Goldman Law Library.

Note 57: "Records of Greenham Common Women's Peace Camp (Yellow Gate)". National Archives.

Note 58: Michael J. Martin, Dietrich Bonhoeffer. Champion of Freedom series. (Morgan Reynolds Publishing, 2012). ISBN 978-1-59935-169-8.

Note 59: Eberhard Bethge, Dietrich Bonhoeffer: Theologian, Christian, Man for His Times: A Biography Rev. ed. (Minneapolis, Fortress Press, 2000).

Note 60: Bondurant, Joan Valérie (1971). Conquest of Violence: the Gandhian philosophy of conflict. University of California Press.

Note 61: Sofri, Gianni (1999). Gandhi and India: a century in focus. Windrush Press. ISBN 978-1-900624-12-1.

Note 62: Fleming, Alice (2008). Martin Luther King, Jr.: A Dream of Hope. Sterling. ISBN 978-1402744396.

Note 63: Pillay, Gerald J. (1993). Voices of Liberation: Albert Lutuli. HSRC Press. pp. 82-91. ISBN 0-7969-1356-0.

Note 64: Grunenberg, Christoph; Harris, Jonathan (2005), Summer of Love: Psychedelic Art, Social Crisis and Counterculture in the 1960s, Liverpool University Press, ISBN 0-85323-929-0.

Note 65: Carmines, Edward G., and Geoffrey C. Layman. 1997. "Issue Evolution in Postwar American Politics." In Byron Shafer, ed., Present Discontents. NJ:Chatham House Publishers.

Note 66: Indignez-vous! essay. Indigène, Montpellier (21/10/2010) 32 pages, ISBN 978-2-911939-76-1 (French)

Note 67: El Pais, 14/05/2010
http://elpais.com/elpais/2010/05/14/actualidad/1273825020_850215.html

---o0o---

6. Strategic Considerations in Civil Disobedience and Protest

Jumping into a protest campaign without working out the protest objectives and appropriate strategies is almost certainly a formula for failure. All too often very good protest movements fizzle out because of a lack of any kind of strategic vision, organisation or pre-planning.

Large authorities and corporations are well-financed and well-informed and they are staffed by well-trained specialists. A disorganised, chaotic, amateurish protest group is no match for such powerful organisations, whereas a well-organised, flexible group of activists can be very effective at running rings around large monolithic authorities.

In this respect, most protest groups need to realise that they are actually engaged in a series of highly asymmetric struggles. Innovative tactics in conducting their assault on the target authorities are essential. One common error many NGOs and other activist groups make is focusing on the action or tactic rather than on the objective and strategy. As the famous military strategist Sun Tze said: "Strategy without tactics is the slowest route to victory. Tactics without strategy is the noise before defeat." Protest organisers need to remember the mantra: Objectives, then Strategies, then Tactics - in that order!

How to define the objectives of a strategy? Not all strategies achieve the objectives of a protest group. Strategies need to be monitored. They also need to be realistic and well-defined. It is important to decide in advance what a protest group expects to achieve from each strategy it defines for a particular protest. It's important firstly because a protest group needs to determine if a strategy is achieving its goal. If a strategy has succeeded, the group can move on to the next objective. If it is failing, then the group can decide whether to abandon it or to change the methods being used. If a strategy seems to be working, but has not yet succeeded, then the group can continue with the same strategy for some time longer. For instance, a "boycott call" may not be working because the call is not being heard by the right people, or it may be too weak or too unspecific. How do you know if the strategy is working or not?

Obviously, each strategy should be part of a defined objective. For instance, a boycott call against a particular company should cause a clear, quantifiable reduction in its customers and generate press activity which reinforces the boycott. This can be measured and should be noticed by customers and the target company. These strategic objectives need to be clearly defined by a protest group. An example might read as follows: "The boycott call against Dirty Oil Ltd seeks to reduce its retail sales by 10% to 20% within 6 months".

This kind of organised strategic thinking and planning may seem alien to the average protest group, but it is essential to a successful action.

Management techniques in protest: Another hang-up for many protest groups or small NGOs is their reluctance to use any modern management techniques to run their protests. There is a pervasive idea that anything that smacks of organisation, planning, management, public relations or branding is the work of the Devil. This is unfortunate because it ignores the usefulness of these techniques and conflates the tool with the user. Some bad capitalist organisations may use public relations to lie to people or employ efficient organisations to carry out their dirty work, but that does not mean that public relations and an efficient organisation are intrinsically evil and to be avoided. These tools are simply in the wrong hands or being used for the wrong purpose. Numerous protest groups run shy of these techniques in a completely irrational way and it damages their ability to fight for their cause.

In a similar way, much technology is seen as either unnecessary or "far too organised" by traditional protesters. This "down-home" attitude to protest is a leftover from the 1960s and 1970s protest tradition when the world was, in some senses, a more innocent place. In those days, a flower in a soldier's gun was a profound act of protest. These days such actions are the easy part. The real battle with an authority is taking place on the internet, or in controlling knowledge and public opinion. A lot of protest struggle comes down to having and using information. Authorities have vast stores of data about protesters and NGOs and they have the resources and expertise to infiltrate and destabilise protest groups. What information do the NGOs have about the authorities and their personnel? Often NGOs have none at all. And this is simply because of an absurd aversion to the use of technology to aid the cause.

The future ambition for the successful protester should be to overcome these hang-ups and learn to be as or more effective at using the available tools and technology as "the bad guys". In the following chapter we are going to elaborate some of the ways that protest organisations can do this, by looking at some important strategic aspects of campaign organisation.

6.1 The Design and Management of an Effective Protest

Without doubt, many protest groups and campaigns start their life in a pretty chaotic way. Often, protests arise from a group of emotional activists being confronted in some way by an authority's behaviour. They may be angry, disappointed, sad, bereaved, outraged, hurt or frightened, but most of those forming the genesis of a protest group will not be particularly concerned about the management of their group, or how they are going to proceed with a protest, never mind how they are going to design a strategically effective protest which delivers change. At this stage they are 95% emotional and 5% rational.

When these early reactions have passed (and this may take some time), a motivated protest group has to eventually get down to organising themselves and considering how best they can respond to the offending authority.

Generally, those that participate in protest groups are not specialists. They are usually not career activists. Probably few participants will know anything at all about organisation, management, leadership, communications and logistics, or have even the first idea where to begin to run an effective protest campaign. What they will have is a lot of motivation and solidarity.

There is no standard template to explain how a protest should be organised in terms of leadership and member participation. This very much depends on the circumstances of the protest. It may be very local, it might be global. It could be aimed at a single organisation, such as a local factory, or it may be addressed to a huge institution, such as the Roman Catholic Church. Also the seriousness and type of issues affect how a group will be arranged and who needs to be involved. A problem with water contamination would seem to demand the presence of certain specialists, whereas an anti-war protest needs only a strong moral public position, since the issue is a moral rather than a technical one.

Thus, it is hard to generalise and be prescriptive about the organisation of a protest group. However, over the years protest movements have learned a great deal about being effective in their campaigns and there are quite a few principles that apply to all protest groups. Here we have identified some of these guiding principles that can be applied in virtually any environment:

6.1.1 Management of the Group

As with all human endeavours, a protest group requires some form of management in order to function. Often with voluntary organisations the management and membership of a protest group is non-professional and driven by ethical motivations. For this reason the level of member participation in the group management needs to be much wider than it would be, for instance, in a commercial enterprise. Members are highly motivated and expect to be heard and to participate in steering the protest.

The other aspect of voluntary (and some small non-voluntary) NGOs is that they may be staffed by people of immense goodwill but with little experience in management of the usual processes of communications, meetings, decision-making, office management, public relations, technology, fund-raising, membership management, etc. This creates some unique challenges in making sure that the group has the correct skills to be effective and is sufficiently structured. Many protest groups suffer from an endemic lack of formalised management and organisation, and this can be fatal.

• **The tyranny of lack of structure:** Finding a balance between informality and structure in a voluntary protest group is difficult and the inclination is to maintain an informal structure. However, lack of structure can be a critical weakness in a protest group. Jo Freeman's seminal 1970 essay "The Tyranny of Structurelessness" put a name to the persistent problem that plagues decision-makers in non-hierarchical organisations. She explains how sometimes the least structured group can be the most tyrannical. In structureless environments such as meetings or day-to-day management, Freeman explains how powerful individuals tend to dominate with their own agenda, exclude others and effectively kill participation. This "hegemony" is often not even a conscious act, but just the tendency of stronger individuals to "fill the vacuum". The problem can be countered by promoting accountability within the group and establishing rules for participation, a proper management structure and well defined roles which guarantee that everyone gets an equal hearing. A lack of hierarchy does not mean a lack of structure; indeed, the less hierarchical a group is, the more structure it requires; just look at any democratic parliament.

• **Delegate tasks:** One of the most common failings in unstructured groups occurs when participants are unclear about what actions they are personally responsible for. It's fine having a group meeting to decide on a series of actions or initiatives, but in the final analysis, groups don't get things done, people do. For this reason, a group needs to have structures where decisions are made and members are allocated a task with clear objectives and deadlines. Thus, an effective protest group delegates work to its own members. Again, in a voluntary environment there is a tendency to be somewhat reticent about anyone formalising members' roles and allocating tasks. In reality though, this is exactly what needs to happen. To ensure that the right people are getting the right tasks it is, of course, vital to discuss the delegated tasks to ensure those allocated the work are comfortable about completing it. It is also worth building up a database of in-group skills, so that tasks can be matched properly to talents and experience.

• **Equality of leaders:** Protest groups don't have to be run on the lines of a corporate or civil service hierarchy. This would certainly be counterproductive. So how is it possible to reconcile the need for structure and efficiency without a hierarchy? Who is the boss? Clearly, a distrust of hierarchy can lead to negative attitudes toward all forms of leadership. This can be just as counterproductive in a situation where a protest campaign absolutely needs leadership and clear direction. The answer of course is to design an efficient democratic system which allows decisions to be made by an elected managing group in consultation with ordinary members. Such a managing group can have a rotating or elected chairman to conduct the day-to-day business, but with no seniority over any other members. All decisions are still only made collectively by consensus where possible and the chairperson acts purely as a facilitator or coordinator.

• **Don't command: Enable:** Power struggles are the antithesis of collaborative action. A protest group which is taking its direction from grassroots members should have one objective, and that is to deliver on the intentions of a majority of those members and to encourage other members to participate as they see fit. Group leaders should be supportive and enabling in order to awaken the creative potential of protest participants. They are not there to act as managers delivering orders to subordinates. Such attitudes are guaranteed to lead to damaging splits and antagonism within a group. Members who have a tendency to command rather than consult may prove disruptive and need to be controlled.

• **Consensus is just a means and not an end in itself:** The idea of consensus within the management of a protest campaign is a modern and attractive one. The implication is that the group always moves forward in unity. The idea is that, after discussion, all issues are resolved by sensible, intelligent people and a unifying consensus is found and decisions are made.

In reality, there are plenty of problems with attempts to manage a protest with complete consensus. Firstly, consensus also requires a vote and rarely, if ever, is true and complete consensus ever achieved. Human beings being what they are, there are always contrarian views, special interests, subliminal signals, sub-conscious prejudices that cloud our judgement or make our decisions different from our peers. Inevitably, a vote after discussions ends with one group voting for the proposal and another group voting against it and this degrades the idea of only working with a consensus of opinion. Often "consensus" boils down to a division of opinion which is just as divisive as in a simple, traditional committee voting system.

But all is not lost. There are actions which can be taken when consensus is not achieved. For instance, a modified form of consensus allows those members most affected by a decision to get a higher priority in explaining their position - in effect having a double or casting vote on the basis that they are the most affected. Other ways of trying to achieve consensus is to form smaller representative (break-out) groups to discuss the issues informally and then bring their conclusions back to the larger group.

Ultimately, however, if consensus cannot be achieved, this must be accepted. After all, the consensus method of management is just the means of decision-making in a group and not the end objective of a protest group.

6.1.2 Clear Strategy, Good Tactics, Simple Rules and Careful Planning

When a protest group has established its own management and is in a position to start designing its protest campaign, the real work begins. This includes establishing objectives for the protest and strategies to achieve these ends. This should be done in a formal way, in writing. One method of doing this would be to ask for submissions from the entire protest group and then collate these proposals into a set of proposed objectives, which can then be debated and voted upon. After this process, the agreed objectives become the formally accepted aims of the group. A protest objective might read "To delay and then permanently stop the destruction of ancient forest at location X".

The next step is to develop strategies to achieve the protest's goals. Again, all members can be asked to contribute suggestions for strategies to achieve each objective and, again, these can be collated, discussed, short-listed and voted upon. One typical strategy might read: "To physically impair workers' access to the forest in order to stop felling of trees", another might read: "To make legal submissions to the European Commission regarding the protection of this important habitat".

Whatever process is used, it is obviously vital that the objectives are clear, realistic and achievable and that the strategies to be adopted have been fully discussed and risk assessed, so that the entire group is clear on the direction being adopted by the group and what lies ahead. Now is the time for any reservations to be discussed - practical, moral, political or personal.

At this stage of a protest organisation there are many imponderables. The campaign has yet to start and the reaction of the authorities, the behaviour of targets, the attitudes of the general public and the ability of the protest organisation have all yet to be tested in action. However, at this point in the start-up there are a number of important principles which will help in planning a protest:

• **Choose tactics (protest methods) that support your strategy:** Very often there is a tendency for one or more tactics (methods) to dominate a campaign. For instance, mass sit-ins may attract huge media coverage, but that doesn't mean that that method should dominate the entire campaign. It is just one protest method. It is much more vital to keep an eye on the main strategy and not let an individual tactic distract from the larger strategy. Strategies represent the overall protest plan; protest methods (tactics) are just those actions used to implement the strategy. This is a distinction which is critical for structuring effective campaigns.

Deciding which protest methods are best employed requires that protest groups consider risk, cost, public opinion, the press, the moral and legal implications and the consequences of error as part of their strategic planning.

In the above example, the strategy "To physically impair workers' access to the forest in order to stop them felling trees" might cause one to consider using protest methods such as "Nonviolent obstruction (Blockade)" of the site, "Motorcades" to stop machine entry to the site, and, perhaps, "Refusal to let or sell property" to frustrate workers or developers on the site, and so on. The choice of tactics also depends very much on what is achievable and practical for the group. There is no point trying to stage a large-scale sit-in in a tiny village, where the number of participants is small and there is no real audience.

• **Choose the target carefully:** The chances of victory in a protest action are greatest when the actions target the person or entity with the institutional power to meet the protest demands. When designing a protest action, it is often tempting to choose the most obvious target. For instance, in a planning dispute the obvious target might be the local planning authority that allowed a development on a protected site without due diligence. However, in reality, the real perpetrator might be the government ministry that issued the planning guidelines to all local planning agencies. In that respect, the real target with the power to make a change is the government ministry, and attacking the local authority is a much lower priority. In some cases it may be a complete waste of energy.

• **Don't mistake your protest group for "society"**: There is always an inclination for a protest group to start to believe its own propaganda. After months or years of beating the drum on a particular issue with other like-minded protesters, it often becomes difficult to have realistic perceptions of public opinion which are not conflated with the "truths" that have become totally "self-evident" to the protester.

This is a dangerous inclination. A protest group is a hothouse of very specific opinions and it is far from being "society". To avoid this problem it is good for a protest group to meet and have discussions with members of the public, unconnected with the protest, in open days or, better still, just on the street. The further away from public opinion a protest group moves, the less likely it is that its views will resonate. Indeed, very often it is necessary to stealthily build up a case with the public, whilst earnestly listening to their concerns at the same time. Even if a protest group is diametrically opposed to popular public opinion, it is very unwise to ignore it. A disconnection between a protest group and wider society creates the risk that protest strategies and methods actually antagonise public opinion and lose support for the protest. Something that might seem quite reasonable for a seasoned protester might outrage the public. Care must be taken to stay grounded and open to public commentary.

• **The real action is your target's reaction:** It is not always true, but it is worth remembering that the success of a protest can often be measured by looking at the reaction of the target. "No reaction" may mean that the protest methods chosen were the wrong ones or that the strategy adopted is incorrect and may need to be reconsidered

The second part of this principle relates to managing a target's reactions. This is important because anticipating a target authority's reaction gives the protest group an opportunity to manage it, plan around it, make use of or circumvent it. Therefore, in advance of a protest action, the protest planners need to sit down and work out the likely reactions of the target authority and what they will do in various scenarios.

For instance, if a protest group plans to blockade a road to a site with cars and protesters, how will the authority react to this? What will they do? Who will they use as their agents (police, private contractors)? What can be done to make use of or circumvent the target's reaction? What are the risks? Is there a "Plan B"? How should the press be involved? Are there safety issues? These and many more questions should be asked and the responses anticipated. Then the protest group can decide (in advance) how to react when the authority responds. Perhaps the protest group will move in heavy machinery to retain the blockade or perhaps they will just call off the blockade after the photo call with the media. Whatever the plan, this needs to be decided in advance and agreed by all. There is not much point being confronted by a powerful reaction from an authority, such as the arrival of riot police, and then starting to wonder what is the best thing to do about it.

Protest actions need to be scripted to some extent and the script should belong to, and be under the complete control of, the protesters - NOT the target authority.

• **Escalate strategically:** Protests which start off "hot and heavy" tend to alienate public opinion by making protesters look extreme. They also tend to harden positions in the target authority and make early compromise more difficult. Therefore, as a general rule, protests should be escalated strategically. It is definitely easier to escalate than to de-escalate; ask any conflict negotiator.

One potential problem with this principle is that an authority may perceive restrained early protest actions as indicating a lack of support or weakness in the protest group. But this is a minor risk, and the benefit of bringing moderate popular opinion into the protest movement in the early days is more important. Also, with time, a gradual escalation will be understood, even by the most conservative or moderate members of the protest group, to be justifiable, so that what would have been considered an "extreme" action in the early days of a protest may later be viewed as quite justified and moderate (see "Moving the Overton window").

A long process of escalation also has a corrosive effect on a target authority. Intensive and extreme protest actions are hard to sustain by most campaign groups and cause campaign fatigue. An authority will often wait for a group to exhaust itself rather than engaging in real negotiations. However, a gradually escalating campaign can erode an authority's credibility over time and is much more likely to lead them to negotiate with the protesters. In the meantime the protesters don't suffer from "burn-out".

• **Pace the protest:** In the same vein as the principle of "Escalate Strategically", the principle of "pacing the protest" is important for the survival and success of a protest group.

Most people involved in a protest campaign are unpaid volunteers who give their time and energy freely to the cause. But each participant also has another life, outside of the protest movement, which requires time and commitment. This is one simple reason why a protest needs to be paced. A very intensive protest may only be possible for semi-professional campaigners who have the time to devote to such a movement. Demanding too much of voluntary protesters is likely to cost their involvement. Therefore, planning a campaign to allow for normal personal life to continue is important to keep the protest reasonably enjoyable, communal and sustainable. This is one good reason to pace it carefully. A slow campaign that is effective is better than an intense protest that bombs out after a few weeks because of lack of supporters.

• **Moving the Overton window:** What is considered outrageous and unthinkable in one political landscape may well be considered absolutely reasonable by the same group of people in other circumstances.

For instance, if in 2015 an activist attempted the assassination of a democratically elected prime minister in a Western European country, we would unanimously agree that the activist was a dangerous psychopathic terrorist that must be caught and incarcerated at once. However, how do we judge people like Johann Georg Elser who, in 1939, staged an elaborate assassination attempt on Adolf Hitler, or, for that matter, all the activists and members of the German aristocracy who attempted to kill Hitler in numerous assassination attempts between 1939 and 1945. Hitler was a democratically elected leader of his country, and yet today we perceive those who tried to murder him almost as saints. Clearly, there are no hard and fast rules about what is universally morally acceptable in all circumstances. Running a left-wing guerrilla operation in the jungles of Columbia is considered by the USA to be morally repugnant. However, the USA financed and supported guerrilla operations in much of Central America during the 1970s and 1980s, albeit that these were right-wing guerrilla armies, supporting a US agenda. Even large parts of the conservative Catholic Church found US support for these right-wing murder squads impossible to accept.

Obviously, what is thought to be reasonable or acceptable at one time and in one set of circumstances can be considered outrageous and beyond the pale in other eras and places through different eyes. This concept of what is acceptable is a moveable feast. It is referred to as the "Overton Window", named after its originator James Overton [Note 1].

As applied to peaceful protest movements, changing the Overton window can cause the public to alter their perception of what is a reasonable protest action and what is not. The Overton "window" defines the limits of what is considered reasonable or acceptable within a range of public options.

A protest group can move the window of acceptable debate or protest action by focusing the attention on a position or action that is more radical than their own. For instance, police brutality against peaceful protesters can alter public opinion to make physical sabotage against police vehicles "acceptable" rather than outrageous. Protest groups need to understand this principle and use it when planning a protest action and choosing protest methods.

• **Know your cultural terrain:** In traditional guerrilla warfare, the fighter needs to understand their own terrain and use it to their advantage against their less knowledgeable adversary. In the world of protest the terrain is not simply the physical terrain of protest action (although this is important as well), but also the cultural environment in which the protest is being launched.

For instance, running a successful protest campaign to overcome racial prejudice in an environment where the population is largely racist, and where racial minorities are marginalised and abused, requires both courage and an exceptional understanding of the "cultural terrain" of the area and its society.

Generally speaking, a well-managed protest campaign will attempt to identify and redirect the strong emotions underlying a particular behaviour or prejudice into more positive attitudes.

For example, England is famous for the prejudices and ignorance of its so-called "working-class Tories" and "right-wing Labourite" groups. These large sections of English society are politically similar in their attitudes and often in their background. They may vote for different parties and read different newspapers, but their prejudices and preconceptions are largely identical. Both groups exhibit similar racist and xenophobic attitudes, are preoccupied by immigration, morally affronted by unemployed people claiming state benefits and convinced of the probity of their own aspirations to be part of the middle class. Generally, they are poorly educated, but even when educated they remain deeply parochial and entrenched in a narrow set of inherited attitudes. Mostly, they lack experience of other cultures and ways of life and they are morally hidebound by their own perceptions of "decency". They are often referred to as "Little Englanders" and they are certainly the most reactionary social groupings in England. One thing they share in common is their working-class background and the value they place on communal society, now swept away by post-industrial life. A good protest organiser can use this common pride in coming from labouring families to redirect negative attitudes to people of different backgrounds or ethnicity to positive attitudes and sympathy towards immigrants who, for instance, work hard to send money home to their families.

In a similar way, understanding the cultural landscape of both younger and older sections of society helps a protest organiser to connect with those sectors. Especially understanding mass culture can help a protest organiser in gathering support. Appealing to common moral elements may also allow an ethical bond to be established between the objectives of a protest group and even the most conservative religious adherents. There is much more in common, for example, between Christianity and Socialism than actually separates the two moral philosophies, despite the often expressed enmity between the two schools.

• **Keep it simple:** There is a natural tendency to try to completely choreograph a protest campaign and not to act at all unless this is done. This kind of "total planning" is practically impossible in most cases, even when a management group can work out many possible scenarios that might arise in planning a particular action.

Rather than trying to stage-manage a protest action, it is often more effective to just set some simple rules for the participants. These rules might include: where to meet, what to bring, what is encouraged, what is forbidden, what to do if confronted and what is the message and objective. After that it is often better just to leave it to the people to organise themselves.

6.1.3 Participation and Motivation of a Protest Group

Getting supporters is only part of making a protest campaign successful. Getting the supporters to actively participate and to feel involved and motivated in a protest is another matter and requires particular skills and personality. However, there are some useful principles that are helpful in encouraging participation and in motivating a group of volunteers:

• **Anyone can act:** In a voluntary movement participants very often have to be flexible and adventurous. It is more than likely that volunteers have to do work for which they have had no training or experience. In such an environment participants need to be highly motivated and they need to have plenty of self-confidence and be given plenty of encouragement.

Certainly there are some skills which are so highly specialised (such as IT, security, and legal matters) that these really need to be left to the experts, but there are many other less specialised skills where volunteers can be trained or train themselves to be quite accomplished. And, of course, No-one expects a citizen action group or small NGO to be as polished as a professional organisation. It is allowed to be a bit amateurish in lots of areas; indeed, it is expected from a citizen protest movement.

In a world where everyone is some kind of specialist, one of the most oft-spoken statements is "oh, I couldn't do that" or "that's not for people like me". Many people are convinced, for example, that to write a press release you need a MA in journalism and fifteen years as a war correspondent for the New York Times. The reality is that most of the skills required for practical tasks, like managing the press, can be self-taught, simply by looking around at similar organisations and reading about the subject. The internet is replete with all kinds of educational material on every subject under the sun. Most of this is open-source and free. With a lot of reading and a little practice and friendly critique from colleagues in a protest group, a layman through and through can become the group's public relations representative. If you have a professional journalist you can talk to, even better. Practice makes perfect. The same thing goes, for example, with protest theatre actions. Whilst it might be easier to hire professional actors to do some guerrilla theatre, ordinary volunteers should also be encouraged to get involved in such activities. They may find they have hidden talents!

Good team management should encourage participants to be confident and to learn as much as they can about the protest itself and the management of the group. The management should also encourage the more expert protest participants to impart as much of their knowledge as possible to their less informed colleagues. Knowledge is power.

• **Take leadership from the most impacted:** It's all too easy for a protest movement to lose sight of why it exists and to forget to listen to those most affected by the protest issues.

A protest group can become preoccupied by day-to-day campaigning work, managing its public relations, lobbying and all those other time-consuming activities. In the heat of all this often stressful activity it is easy to forget to maintain a contact with those most affected by the issue at hand.

For instance, protests which seek to protect a natural environment should find time to listen to the biologists and ecologists who know what will be lost if the development goes ahead, or to the farmers or villagers whose lives and heritages will be destroyed or damaged. Indeed, it is vitally important to be guided by contacts with these highly affected groups because their strength of feeling will help to galvanise a protest campaign, and their passion will strengthen the emotional language of the protest messages. New words and sentiments enter the protest narrative, driven by those with most at stake. Also, of course, these people may also have many new ideas for strategies to make the protest campaign more effective.

• **Use praxis as a method of decision-making and active participation:** The word praxis refers to the act of applying a theory in practice. Protest groups are inclined to spend a lot of time hand-wringing about the issues they are concerned with and how best to carry out their protest. Ideas for new strategies come and go. Some get adopted and turned into protest actions; some are successful, some fail. This is normal enough in all protest movements. However, one negative aspect of this informal approach is that rarely is there any real analysis of why one strategy was successful whilst another failed, and rarely is there any means of quantitatively analysing the degree of success.

Praxis is a process, much discussed by many of the great philosophers such as Aristotle, Kant, Marx etc., which seeks to resolve these problems by applying a cycle of theory, action and reflection that helps analyse our efforts in order to improve our ideas.

Thus, using praxis, a group might discuss a range of ideas for new protest strategies or methods. It selects a strategy for trial. Then, before taking any action, the group analyses the critical success factors associated with the strategy. How is success to be measured? Perhaps this is a numeric measure, such as the number of new members joining, or perhaps this is a public relations achievement, such as coverage in the "national press". The group has to decide how to measure the success in a clear and objective way.

The next step is the implementation of the strategy into practice and for it to be monitored at appropriate regular intervals. When the strategy has been implemented for a pre-defined period, the group meet again to assess the success of the strategy. Has the strategy achieved the objective according to the pre-defined measure of success? If not, why not? Has the strategy achieved part of the objective and, if so, to what extent? What has affected its success rate? What lessons can be learned?

Using praxis in this way is both educational and motivating for participants in a group. It teaches participants about what works and why it works and it gives them a sense that they can control, to some extent, the narrative of a protest action. They can apply objective techniques to achieve political goals and understand why some techniques work in some circumstances and others do not.

Theory without action produces armchair revolutionaries. Action without reflection produces ineffective or counterproductive activism. That is why praxis is such a useful management technique.

• **Brainstorming is good:** Despite all the talk about maintaining some level of structure, that doesn't mean that a protest group shouldn't have informal sessions of brainstorming.

Brainstorming is an excellent, creative way of finding new ideas and getting them out into the open. A period of free-form brainstorming should be part of all protest group meetings. There are lots of ways that ideas and suggestions can be tabled. This can even be done anonymously. Brainstorming needs no chairperson and the only thing to watch is that it is confined to a pre-agreed period of time.

• **Challenge patriarchy and prejudice in the protest organisation:** There is no place in a protest group for any form of exclusion or elitism. Both are divisive, often unjust and counterproductive. As a protest group becomes more organised, it is important that prejudices be actively challenged. Such sentiments are destructive and should be openly exposed, if necessary by exclusion of the offending participants.

6.1.4 Message Delivery

One of the greatest challenges to a protest campaign is to get the message out to the public, the target authority and the press. Misunderstandings bedevil protest movements and can be fatal to gaining support and to negotiating with a target authority. Therefore, making sure that there is a clear message being delivered is vital. There are several principles which should be considered when deciding how to deliver a protest message.

• **Think about the narrative:** Sometimes the best response to a powerful problem is a powerful story. When describing protest issues, tell the whole story, but keep it brief. Obviously, if there is a lot of history, this needs to be condensed with just the key points being emphasised. Ignore the side issues, details and squabbles that happened along the way and make the story develop and flow, so that the reader reaches the same conclusion as the protest group has - preferably before hearing the end of the story. Once the narrative has been defined, stick to it. Don't confuse the public or press by altering the history; just update it with the latest events.

• **Show, don't tell:** Highly visual communications are far more effective than stand-up speech making. The sound of someone talking for 30 minutes is guaranteed to cause many listeners to lose interest or simply be overwhelmed by the volume of words. Many listeners may feel that they are being preached to or are being patronised by speakers, regardless of how impassioned the speaker is. Good protest communication needs to combine plenty of imagery and metaphor to be effective. Therefore, the use of visual material, such as charts and photos and visual action, such as theatre, film, recordings and art add to both the experience of the participants as well as delivering a much clearer and more tangible message. No speech should last longer than 5 or 10 minutes without the introduction of some additional visual media.

• **Make the invisible visible:** In a similar vein to the previous principle, it is clear that many injustices and protest issues are invisible to the general public. When a protest group brings these wrongs into full public view, it changes the game by making the need for the audience to take action much more compelling.

Take an issue such as fracking. Many people are very much opposed to fracking because they have become convinced that it carries many risks of contaminating ground water supplies. On the other hand, the narrative of the oil industry is that fracking provides a way of becoming energy-independent. So many people are tempted to believe that "they" (the oil companies) have the technology to safely exploit the gas, without any risks, and that "they" will take good care of all any possible problems because "they" are careful and "they" are overseen by our good, clever government that always looks after us. And, anyway, it's very deep underground and therefore quite invisible to anyone. After all, how could drilling for gas affect water supplies?!

Then one watches a 90 second video of a rusting and debris-strewn fracking site in the middle of the Irish countryside, abandoned 10 years ago, but which is still steadily leaching creamy, oily toxic, radioactive slurry directly into the pristine wooded headwaters of the River Shannon. The cameraman pans through the ancient deciduous forest to focus on this appalling aberration, bubbling up between the rocks and trickling into the crystal-clear waters of the little river. The full horror dawns on the viewer. This is what really happens when you pump millions of tonnes of toxic chemicals into the ground at high pressure. The 90 second clip is a real game-changer for anyone that sees it. It's so obviously real and the contamination so obviously deeply hidden that this little film's revelation is spine-chilling.

Such illustrations are shocking and speak thousands of words to the viewer. To make the invisible visible is one of the primary roles of a protest campaign. It doesn't have to cost much money. There is much high quality material available on the internet, as well as the (often free) tools to create and edit videos, photo collages and presentations. These days anyone can be a documentary or program maker, and a powerful two minute video put on YouTube can be extremely potent in revealing invisible horrors to huge numbers of people.

• **Put movies in the hands of the protest:** Continuing the theme of revealing the invisible, the use of documentary film is also a powerful means of communication. Filmmakers and activists, working together, can collaborate to make a documentary film a potent method of telling a story and bringing about change.

Professional documentaries can combine personal stories, demonstrative imagery and interviews to address complex and sensitive issues and present them in a thought-provoking way.

Making a documentary doesn't require a huge budget. Many art and media studies schools have degree and post-graduate students looking for projects who are often more than happy to participate in producing a documentary together with a protest group. It does require a lot of planning and preparation, such as defining story boards to plan the sequence of the documentary, scripting of the dialog, location selection, finding participants and working out interview questions etc., but a well made documentary is a powerful reusable asset to a protest campaign.

• **Bring the issue home:** Whenever possible, protest issues should be personalised. Very often, a campaign issue can seem remote and somewhat abstract. The public may find it difficult to understand the issues or empathise with victims. A good communicator will seek to bring these subjects into everyone's living room. This is easy if the protest concerns a tangible subject that directly affects an audience, such as air pollution, a new road development or a new airport in the next town.

However, an issue such as the effect of GM crops on peasant farmers in India, is a subject that is both complex and far away for many of us. Nonetheless, a good communicator can gain the sympathy of an audience by showing how ordinary peasant farmers are driven to suicide by poverty and how they are tricked by large multi-nationals into using expensive GM seeds. Such a narrative will then explain what the viewer can do to help these victims; for example, by boycotting certain household products or foods, certain companies and by lobbying various companies and government agencies. In this way, a protest becomes localised as a link is created between the exploited peasant farmer and our local boycott of GM cotton or Monsanto.

• **Avoid perfectionism:** There is a natural inclination to try to make all our communications as perfect and professional as possible. Activists will argue for hours over the last 5% of the wording of a press release to get it just right. This often causes delays and takes a lot of energy and time. Whilst communications of any kind should be of decent quality, there is a limit to the amount of time that should be devoted to them. If a communication is clear, honest, verifiable and to the point, then it is basically ready. It is, after all, only a communication of some kind, whether it is a bit of street theatre, a presentation, a flyer or a press release. It's important to know when to "let go".

• **Play to the audience that isn't there:** Very often protest actions don't take place in front of the audiences that are really the target and it is important to remember this when carrying out an action. An extreme example would be the Greenpeace protest boarding of Russian oil rigs in the Arctic. The oil workers were NOT the target audience for this action. The footage of this confrontation was very clearly destined for Western public and governments' consumption. Greenpeace, being masters of such demonstrative actions, turned the issue of high risk Arctic oil exploration into a piece of nail-biting live action theatre for millions; professionally documented for delivery by the main news outlets.

In a highly media-oriented world, the protest audience is often not in the "same room" as the protest action, but it is an audience that will be reached through mass and social media. Therefore it is important to design protest actions with this distant audience in mind.

• **Make actions both concrete and communicative:** Some forms of protest action are purely symbolic, without any physical connotations. They are often designed to be thought-provoking, such as a silent protest. Such communicative actions need have no specific target authority, though they have a specific audience. They usually do not expect any concrete response. Most authorities simply ignore them. However, it is important to make sure that such communicative actions are highly visible to the desired audience. Erecting a banner in the forest will have no effect whatsoever, either as a communicative act of protest or as a concrete act of protest. Communicative acts need the protester to consider the audience and delivery to that audience very carefully. Who is the audience and how is the audience to be addressed? Also in this calculation, the designer of a communicative action needs to balance the "art" of delivery with the strength of the message. Too much "art" may distract from the message and too much message neutralises the art of delivery.

Other, non-communicative, protest actions are designed to have a clear direct physical effect, such as a blockade or strike. They have a concrete objective, like stopping machinery arriving at a site. These tangible actions have a clear authoritarian target and are seeking a definite response, for example, a confrontation with police.

It is important for a protest group to understand which type of action it is planning because expectations need to be unambiguous. Protesters are often discouraged when they take part in a communicative action expecting a concrete result, which never comes. Therefore, it is much better to be clear from the beginning about what the expected results of an action are.

An action can be both concrete and communicative, as in the case of a blockade of a symbolic building, for instance, a particular tax-evading bank. The physical blockade will trigger off a physical reaction from the authorities, but it will also send an important message. The physical reaction and the message are both results that can be expected from such a hybrid action.

• **Lead with sympathetic characters:** Authorities are past masters at using sympathetic characters as a means of selling their policies. For example, a Conservative government policy to give grants to create new elitist private schools is sold to the public as making more places available in elite schools to "hard-pressed working class families trying to get the best for their kids". In a similar way, reducing welfare payments to the long-term unemployed is sold as a way of "getting people back into the world of work". These somewhat Orwellian tricks take advantage of the fact that the "kids of hard working families" and "the world of work" conjure up characters that are seen as positive and provide a means of delivering a story with sympathetic characters to whom everyone can comfortably relate. The authorities know very well that this makes for a more acceptable and credible story. The facts are the same; all that is manipulated are the characters used to communicate the story.

Protest movements need to take advantage of this phenomenon when delivering their story to the public. Gaining the sympathy of the public is often important and it is the job of a protest movement to ensure that an authority is not allowed to take control and manipulate the characterisation in a story.

To this end, in communication with the public, it is important to choose sympathetic characters. For instance, in the protest documentary "Gasland" about the evils of fracking, the filmmakers chose their characters carefully. These were ordinary hard-working farmers' families, having their farms and water contaminated in their sometimes heartbreakingly naïve struggle with large oil companies. These were not highly educated activists making political statements, but just decent, plain-speaking working people struggling to make a living whilst being abused and deceived by heartless profit-seeking capitalists. Few viewers could fail to empathise with these tragic storytellers.

• **Brand or be branded:** Despite the corporate connotations associated with the word "branding", it is actually simply a way by which the public associate a concept (in this case a protest campaign or group) together with a set of expectations, stories, memories, and relationships.

If a protest group doesn't explicitly manage its own branding, then it is quite certain that the group will be branded by the public anyway, based on what stories and images filter through the press. This uncontrolled branding is not a good thing because the messages that the public receive can be managed and manipulated by an authority that may want to paint the protest in a bad light. Therefore, in general, the branding of a group or campaign needs to be handled pro-actively and group management needs to sit down and decide what the group stands for and how this should be communicated or "sold" to the public.

Clearly, it is important to be honest in this. Also, protest branding should not be overdone otherwise the public will feel pressured and react negatively. The kind of considerations in managing protest branding are similar to commercial branding and include having an effective and recognisable logo (like a trademark), snappy and pointed slogans, a common style and colour-scheme and a policy for promoting the group by various means.

• **Manage Anger:** Most protest groups grow up out of a sense of outrage at some authoritarian act or some negligence which antagonises or angers the protesters. This anger is normally translated into resolve and action, but it can sometimes spill over into public view. This visible anger needs to be managed because it can either come across as normal moral indignation or as annoying self-righteousness.

On the one hand, suppressing anger can have the effect of emasculating common and honest indignation, which should be expressed. On the other hand, constant angry outbursts give the impression that a protest group is not in control and has yet to learn to channel its anger into action in a mature way.

The British Labour party is a good example of emasculated anger. During the 1980s and 1990s, the party leadership became so afraid of being labelled as the "Looney Left" by the powerful British right-wing press, that they severely limited any form of public expressions of outrage by party officials. This had the effect of alienating much of the left-wing party membership. It displaced what had always distinguished the Labour Party, which was a sense and expression of moral outrage against oppression and inequality. Without this "core anger" the party gradually morphed into a middle-class, non-controversial, fairly meaningless shadow of the Tory party, totally lacking any expressions of moral emotion.

This unfortunate development came about because of the sometimes extreme behaviour of some sectors of various left-wing groups in the 1980s, which were reacting to the constant assaults being carried out by Thatcher's Tory party on the working-classes, the unions and the poor. These left-wing groups were rightly angry, but were unable to manage and channel this anger, so these emotions tended to overflow into public view, with some fairly unfortunate incidents that were played upon by the Tory press and establishment.

A protest group needs to allow natural expressions of anger, but must also seek to channel it into dignified and controlled actions that demonstrate the strength of emotion, the reasons for the anger, as well as demonstrating the discipline of the group.

In other words: "Calm down. Don't get angry, get even!"

6.1.5 Designing Mass Appeals for the Protest and Attracting Supporters

Second only to planning and carrying out protest actions, a protest group needs to be much concerned with appealing for public support and gaining new membership and donors. This is no easy task, but there are a few principles that should be kept in mind which can help:

• **Become a welcoming organisation:** Recruitment and retention of volunteers and other supporters go hand in hand. Gaining new participants into a protest group is hard work, time-consuming and expensive, so it's important to hang on to new recruits once they have joined. This means taking the trouble to personally introduce them to other group members before they participate in a meeting. Alongside these introductions it's useful for both parties to find out what motivates a new member, what they are good at and what they think they can contribute to a protest campaign. Also, once a new member has joined the group, it's important to monitor how they are fitting in and whether they are happy to be helping. This involves having frequent informal interviews to discuss these things and get and give feedback to new members.

In most protest groups members are generally entirely voluntary. They give their time freely because they believe in a moral cause. Just ignoring new members and expecting them to just fit in to a protest group is a sure way of losing most of them fairly quickly. So, whilst all the additional work in helping new members to integrate is time-consuming, it is also essential if a group wants to hold on to them.

• **Building mass movements:** Building a mass movement is a means of uniting large groups around a common interest and/or a common enemy, and is an important way of building and maintaining powerful transnational grassroots protest movements.

Mass movements tend to be united by a social evil, such as debt or poverty, but can also be mobilised by many other common evils, for example the rejection of government surveillance, environmental crime, modern slavery, political corruption and many other forms of institutional discrimination or inequality.

Hence the cry of "*Debtors of the world, unite!*" would entice supporters from all kinds of backgrounds, including students that suffer from huge educational loans, hard-pressed mortgage debtors, and poorly-paid workers taking short-term debt to supplement their low wages. All would rally to such a call. Spinning off such a mass movement we can see many forms of potential protest actions: eviction blockades, tax and debt strikes and boycotts of banks, for instance, all supported by potentially millions of sympathisers around the globe.

Mass movements now exist in many arenas of protest and they grow by means of support from protest groups. It is in this way that a new protest group can not only support a growing mass movement, but can also expand itself by association with a mass movement. A protest group that is associated with a larger movement is likely to attract followers much more effectively than one that is working in isolation from the rest of the world.

• **Reframing: Recapture the flag and retake the streets:** There is always an inclination to believe that protest groups are organised by hard-line anarchists or extreme subversives intent on the overthrow of the establishment.

In reality, many protest groups consist of eminently respectable members of the middle-classes. For example, groups like the Campaign for the Protection of Rural England (Patron is Queen Elizabeth II), the Ramblers Association, SEO Birdlife, the RSPB and 38 Degrees in Britain have done important campaigning work to protect the environment, freedom of movement and defend public services. And yet they are dominated by a largely comfortable middle-class membership. The same can be said for groups such as the "Yayoflautas", the loose group of elderly protesters in Spain that routinely blockade banks and stage eviction disruptions, or the

"Marea Blanca" group of doctors and nurses that stage large-scale and noisy protests against Spanish government health service austerity and privatisation measures.

Members of these groups could hardly be described as system-wrecking anarchists. They are just decent people who have become outraged and motivated by the bad behaviour of various authorities. Every country has such middle-class protest groups and, indeed, the really radical protesters are in the minority.

But despite the preponderance of middle-class (and often middle-aged) protesters, most government authorities try to characterise protesters as being dangerous trouble-makers that border on being terrorists. Not only is this extremely unjust to those ethically motivated protesters, but such attitudes also have a negative effect on public opinion and reduce public support for a protest group. Therefore, this negative characterisation needs active management by a protest group.

To neutralise negative sentiments directed at a protest movement it is useful to sometimes "reframe" a protest around various moral values that are held by the majority of the general public. For instance, an environmental or human rights protest movement in a conventionally Christian country might well frame its protest in the context of Christian morality by quoting supporting words from a church leader or a high-ranking member of the establishment. A labour protest may remain legitimate by appealing to a common belief in the right to earn a "fair day's pay for a fair day's work" and an abhorrence of deliberate exploitation by an employer. Protests can even be framed in the context of national pride in defence of "our traditional fairness and equality", "traditional freedom of speech", constitutional rights, or international prestige etc. There are many ways in which protest messages can be reframed so as to appeal to a particular sector of the public, and some of these may be highly unexpected. For example, the conservation of wild animals is sometimes framed as an essential role for the "responsible hunter" who wants to maintain a sustainable environment and a plentiful supply of game. This may seem like a completely unlikely alliance and yet it can be an eminently sensible and workable one.

The constant reframing of a protest message in various ways is not only a powerful way of countering the manipulation of a group's image by an authority, but it is also a way of appealing to different segments of the public, simply by repackaging the same honest message in contexts which appeal to other parts of society.

There is nothing dishonest in this. After all, virtually all modern ethical systems have similar views on most basic moral questions, such as civil and human rights, environment, dignity in labour etc. All that a protest group needs to do to widen its appeal is to point out this common ground.

• **Encouraging participation: Using cultural assets:** Following on from the principle of reframing a protest to find common ground with different sectors of the public, a protest also needs to deepen participation by taking full advantage of the shared cultural links which unite a society. These include art forms, music, stories, symbolism, local knowledge, mythology, language, local humour and other common practices that bind a community together and define its identity.

Perhaps a protest group plans a protest meeting centred on a concert by a popular rock band or on the performance of some well-liked traditional music. The music may attract the attention of non-members and then generate an interest in the protest itself. The very familiarity of the culture in the event makes it less intimidating to an observer. Similar cultural manifestations may be as modest as public meetings held in a bar with a public raffle for non-members, seasonal celebratory dances or a party run by a protest group, but open to the public, or walks in the local countryside, organised as protests, but doubling as recreation and also open to the public. There are lots of possibilities for a protest group to use its common cultural assets as a means of attracting new supporters whilst building solidarity within a protest group.

6.1.6 Managing Public Relations and the Press

The press can be a reactionary bunch when it comes to a new protest movement. They often have fairly cosy relationships with government ministers, senior members of the civil service and local authorities, who quietly brief them on what they want the press to know and print. These authorities make life easy for journalists by writing the press releases for them. The press are all too often happy to quietly acquiesce and just publish what they are given verbatim.

Then come along some angry, principled protesters that want to "kick ass", "stir up the pond" and generally cause trouble for the authorities and who don't care who likes it or not. Such events unsettle journalists because they threaten their sedentary lives and oblige them to actually get up and go out and do some real journalism with all that tedious in-depth investigation, asking questions, being inventive and writing serious original copy. It is not surprising, therefore, that getting a journalist to even acknowledge a protest campaign is not easy. They really would prefer if protesters just went away and left them in peace. And when the press does start to take notice, there is a strong inclination to characterise protest groups using a standard set of clichés that tend to attract public suspicion. After all, it's easier to trot out some tired old clichés than to actually try to understand and explain a load of difficult protest issues.

To manage all of these public relations problems there are some principles that a protest group can use to good effect to get the press to work in their favour and to boost public relations:

• **Do the media's work for them:** As we have said, the press can be quite a sedentary bunch and many journalists would really prefer to simply recycle already written press releases. It saves a lot of work and time. Governments are happy to oblige the media by trotting out pro-government press briefings that can be easily translated for immediate publication with only a few editorial adjustments.

But two can play at that game, and a good protest organisation should nominate at least one person to be responsible for press and public relations, liaising with the press, writing and delivering "press-ready" public statements as press releases.

Press releases should be clear and not too obviously partisan; otherwise the journalist has too much work to do to remove the partisan bits from the text. One way of delivering the partisan parts of the message in a neutral way is for the press release to *quote* from a protest official. For instance, a press release can say something like "a spokesman for the group emphasised that they are concerned by the risks of fracking to drinking water reserves, based on US studies showing widespread groundwater contamination". This lets the journalist off the hook because he is just quoting a verifiable source and yet the press release also delivers an important protest message about fracking and ground water.

Nowadays, journalists are expected to combine news with entertainment and some human interest content in their copy because the perception is that the public has only a very short attention span and needs to be entertained. Whether this is true or not, it is important to humanise press releases and make the narrative relevant to "ordinary folk", even adding a touch of humour or scandal to the story, if possible.

Another way of encouraging the press to publish is to provide photographs or any explanatory graphics. This saves journalists from having to do the research and dig out existing images, request permission to use them, etc. If the images are owned by the protest group, then a simple letter granting permission to publish should accompany the press release and image files. This saves a journalist a lot of hassle.

Something to remember is that all news outlets like to be either sole publisher or the earliest publisher of a story. For this reason it is worth considering whether a protest group should give a story to all the media or whether it is better to be selective and give a story only to those media that are going to be sympathetic. For instance, a group protesting climate change is wasting its time trying to get the right-wing press interested in their actions.

Finally, when delivering a press package to a news outlet, give them a contact person and telephone number for comments. Most journalists will at least make a telephone call to verify the source of a story. Make it easy for them.

• **Stay on message:** It is notoriously easy to be deflected from a group's message when giving an interview or when making public statements under duress. This risk must be actively managed. To this end, the first task of a PR manager is to define the precise messages that the protest group wishes to communicate to the public and press. These don't have to be complex, but they do have to be clear.

For instance, the anti-GM movement has an immensely complex environment in which to operate and the public is quite confused about many of the scientific, agricultural and economic issues concerned with the topic. However, a protest group can build a limited set of verifiable statements which define their position and which appeal to public "common sense". As an example, in terms of health risk, a protest group can honestly state: "Studies have shown that there are health risks associated with eating GM foods.", "More health studies are needed", "The precautionary principle should apply if there is any doubt about GM food safety". All of these statements are true, verifiable and simple to understand. Having built up such a series of statements on the protest issues, the next important step is to ensure that these, and only these, messages are delivered.

Staying on message in the written word is relatively easy. The written monologue is controlled by just one party; in this case the protest group. This is not quite so simple in a debate or interview environment or when taking questions in public. In this more hostile environment it is very easy for a spokesperson to be dragged off course and to make some serious errors, or to be undermined or manipulated by antagonists. To avoid this happening, a spokesperson should use what is called the "ABCD technique of question response". The ABCD technique refers to a technique of press management which works as follows:

First, a spokesperson keeps a list of the protest group's messages close to hand. Then when a question is asked, they use the "A" from the "ABCD", i.e. to "**A**cknowledge" the question and thank the questioner for asking it. For instance: "Thank you for your thoughtful question".

Next the spokesperson uses the "B" from the "ABCD", which refers to building a "**B**ridge" to a standard response. He decides which part of the group's standard messages most nearly fits the question or can be used to respond to the question in a more oblique way, with a response such as "That is a question that is often asked, but the underlying point is [make a bridge to the message you want to deliver]......"

Now using "C" from the ABCD technique, i.e. **C**ommunicate the appropriate standard message which best fits the question. Keep it clear and give examples, if necessary.

Finally, steer the questioner away from negative questioning by using "D" of the "ABCD" technique, i.e. **D**angle information designed to steer questions into positive territory.

In an example from the GM debate, an antagonistic interviewer might ask an anti-GM protest spokesperson: "How can you oppose a technology that could increase global food production and reduce poverty?" Here is one possible response thread:

- **Acknowledge the question**: The spokesperson should first acknowledge the question, "An interesting question, especially if GM really did increase crop yields".

- **Bridge to health risks**: "The jury is still out on the question of increased yields from GM, but the real point is not so much quantity but quality." The subject is moved from indemonstrable yield claims to demonstrable health risks.

- **Communicate the message**: Now the real message is delivered. "There are numerous peer-reviewed studies indicating that there are many health risks associated with GM foods. Until we can be absolutely sure that these new foods are completely safe, it really is too early to talk about GM production alleviating poverty. To avoid yet another food scandal we must apply the precautionary principle to GM technology."

- **Dangle new information**: "On the other hand, though, recent long-term US studies have proven that organic agricultural systems can deliver yields that are as high as or higher than GM techniques and organic farms can do this sustainably, without chemicals, at a lower cost and without health risks to workers or consumers. Some even argue that organic foods taste better as well!"

In this example, the contentious issue of crop yields is dumped. It is a trick question anyway because there are so many contradictory studies, so the spokesperson decides to ignore it, converting the question instead into an opportunity to discuss health risks and the precautionary principle. Concluding the answer by apparently coming back to the original question, the spokesperson throws in the fact that organic yields can also be increased to match or beat GM, with no health risks. The subject is now refocused to the benefits and sustainability of organic farming and away from the contention of GM solving the world's food security problems.

• **Don't dress like a protester:** From a public relations point of view the main objective of a protest group is to communicate with, and convince, as many people in as many social groups as possible of the validity of the protest message. The objective is certainly not to engage in personal grandstanding, or to make fashion statements about protester clothes design!

If protesters look like stereotypical protesters, it's easy for people to write them off. Dressing in a "strange" way to attend a protest action just separates ordinary people from participation in a protest. Thus, it is important (within limits) to dress and behave in a reasonably "normal" way. Obviously, in some circumstances (such as when facing tear gas assaults) a protester may need to bring some specialised clothing, but deliberately adopting a stereotyped image is childish and counterproductive.

6.1.7 Managing Authority, Direct action and the Law

Governments and other authorities put a lot of time and energy into managing protests, using a mixture of carrot, stick and various manipulative methods to channel and control the activities of a campaign. But this strategy is not exclusive to an authority and a protest group can manage target authorities as well. Here are some principles that can help in this:

• **Put the target authority into a decision dilemma:** Protest actions that are seeking a concrete outcome (rather than just delivering a message) need to force a target authority into making a decision. A well-designed protest action will limit the decisions that an authority can make, so that all their available options play to the protest group's advantage. This is called a decision dilemma.

For instance, an anti-fracking movement in Spain staged some well-supported protest actions in 2 villages which were run by conservative (pro-fracking) councils. The anti-fracking demonstrations began 3 months before local elections and there was strong, demonstrable, local support for the protest. As a response, the conservative councils felt it would be political suicide to support the fracking plans and instead refused to give permission for the fracking tests to take place in their villages or for the fracking companies to use council land.

In this example, the councils had many possible choices. They could, for instance, ban the demonstrations, give permission for the fracking and then confront the villagers when they took direct action. Any of these actions would guarantee that the councillors would be removed from office by the electorate within weeks and replaced with anti-fracking councillors. The other possible decision option was for the council to ban the fracking and have a chance to stay in power. Either way, the anti-fracking faction had won.

Similar decision dilemmas occur when an authority has to deal with peaceful mass demonstrations. If they allow the demonstrators to stay, they risk future public order problems with further demonstrations. If they confront peaceful demonstrators with tear gas and water cannon (or worse), the authority risks being accused of over-reaction and authoritarian behaviour. Either way they lose.

• **Use the law:** Protest groups are often characterised as being fairly anarchic. The judicial system is often perceived as being pro-establishment. Both generalisations are incorrect. In reality, protesters can make very good use of the legal system to promote their cause. Indeed, frequently it is the establishment that has stepped outside the law, whilst those who protest remain very much within the law and their right to challenge an authority's behaviour.

This principle needs to be taken into account when designing a protest. Marches, demos, blockades, boycotts are excellent means of communicating protest messages and forcing an authority to react. But there is nothing better to focus the attention of an authority on a protest group's demands like a High Court injunction against that authority or a decision from an international court condemning or fining a government.

Clearly, it is not a case of one or the other, protest versus law. In fact, using the law should be seen as just another form of protest. In some cases, an authority may be persuaded by mass demonstrations that public opinion is against them and they may concede ground. In other cases, a stubborn authority may refuse to give in and may need to be obliged to do so by legal force. A well-designed protest campaign should combine all legal options in protest actions, just as it would use a boycott or demonstration.

• **Use authoritarian prejudices to your advantage:** The prejudices of an authority or its personnel are a weakness that can be exploited to the advantage of a protest group.

Essentially, a prejudice is a mental shortcut that leads a person or group to make assumptions about others. These assumptions are usually false and predictable, and so they can be useful in a protest action to trick an authoritarian target. They include sexism, racism, homophobia, ageism, class distinction and all the other associated stereotypes.

-   **Racism:** In a well-known example from Chicago in the 1950s, in a campaign to improve slum conditions in an organised black ghetto, the organisers decided to take their demonstrations outside their own neighbourhoods into the white suburbs where the slum landlord lived. The presence of lots of black men and women picketing the landlord's house led to a flood of phone calls from his white neighbours who didn't care at all about the slums. They would not have become involved otherwise, but wanted to keep their own neighbourhood segregated, and thus they pressured the landlord into capitulating.

-   **Class distinction:** Along with classism goes all the paraphernalia of belonging to a particular class. Businessmen wear suits and carry briefcases or laptops, high-class waiters wear bow ties and diner jackets, labourers wear overalls, male protesters have long hair and holey jeans, people who play golf are middle class, etc., etc. Any one of these stereotype assumptions can be used to fool an authority or its personnel. Go to any conference centre and dress like the other invitees and you have a fighting chance of being admitted with just the mildest of deceits to the receptionist.

-   **Ageism:** Old people are generally considered to be harmless and "dotty". Kids are thought to be selfish and incapable of discipline. For many authorities these groups become almost invisible because they just don't count. Such prejudices have been used to trick an authority on many occasions. Elderly Palestinian goatherds moving their herds between villages and Palestinian children travelling freely between cities have both helped in communicating memorised information between units of the Palestinian resistance movement to assist in the coordination of boycotts, demonstrations, labour and other strikes.

-   **Sexism:** One of the oldest uses of prejudice in the world is when a girl or woman deliberately distracts a guard or official whilst something else is going on behind their backs. Try the experiment: Get a male friend to ask a (male) policeman the way. Then have a pretty girl ask the same question. You will notice that the directions given to the girl will be much more lengthy, comprehensive and detailed than those given to the man. This provides a ready means of distraction.

• **Apply makeshift solutions:** This principle relates to the strategy where a protest group takes practical direct action itself to remedy a problem as best it can, in order to pressure authorities to fix it properly.

Imagine that there is no kindergarten in your area and the local authority has no money or plans to open one. Apart from the usual protest actions to pressure the authority to take action, one possibility would be for a group of protesters to get together and open one. Certainly it will be illegal, it will not be very well equipped, it will not be in an appropriate building and will not have professional staff. Nonetheless, it will exist and will function to some extent. The existence of this makeshift solution puts pressure on an authority in several ways:

Firstly, it demonstrates commitment by the protest group to their own demands. They obviously mean business. Secondly, it embarrasses an authority by making the authority seem inadequate or incompetent. If a bunch of amateurs can do this, why can't the people to whom we pay our taxes? It also attracts public sympathy for those who committed their time and money to a public act. Finally, of course, it results in opprobrium towards the authority from the general public.

• **Kill them with kindness:** Authorities often overreact to a protest, especially when they are "in the wrong" themselves. They will frequently use too much force in an attempt to suppress a peaceful protest, or they may attack a protest argument too violently in the media.

In these circumstances it is important for a protest group to remain calm and hold on to the moral high ground. For one thing, it is unlikely that the protest campaign will be decided by any single action or by the authority's unwise reaction to it, so whatever happens needs to be kept in perspective. More importantly, if a protest group immediately retaliates in response to the authority's overreaction, then it provides an excuse for the authority to use excessive force against them. In the "fog of war" no-one will remember who started it, and inevitably the protest group will be blamed.

A much better strategy for the protesters to adopt when an authority initially overreacts is to issue a simple public statement to that effect. The statement should be conciliatory rather than threatening. The protest group should behave calmly, with dignity and good will, and offer to negotiate.

In this way, every authoritarian action that is more violent, unfriendly or unyielding is automatically painted as being unreasonable in the eyes of the general public. In this way, by simply being calm and magnanimous, a protest group can accrue a lot of public support.

• **If a protest is made illegal, make daily life a protest:** Authorities, for some irrational reason, believe that protests can be curtailed simply by making the manifestations of protest illegal. For instance, by banning strikes, demonstrations, pickets, boycotts, etc. Needless to say, a protest movement continues, with or without protest actions, as long as the reasons for the protest continue to exist. And clearly, human beings that are motivated to protest will be sufficiently motivated to find other ways of demonstrating, aside from the conventional methods that authorities sometime choose to ban. Thus, when standard dissent is made impossible by overwhelming state repression, protesters find other ways to make ordinary acts subversive.

One frequent response to the banning of protest is to move the protest into daily life, in all kinds of unconventional ways. For instance, the collective banging together of kitchen pots (indoors or hidden from view) at a pre-determined time every day is an example of a coordinated protest action, not in the public view, but very much a collective public act of defiance, as happened in Pinochet's Chile in 1983. In themselves, such protests have no effect, except to demonstrate to an authority that the protest lives on and that it may take on a different, more threatening form at any time. Other examples of this kind of protest include coordinated large-scale turning on and off of house electrical supplies, deliberately driving slowly or the slow payment of bills and taxes; there are indeed many more opportunities for protest within seemingly mundane daily life.

• **Using the power of ritual:** Rituals can be powerful because of their familiarity. They may have special meaning and carry certain connotations for many. New rituals can be imbued with significance.

Rituals can be used by protest movements in various forms. For instance, the space outside a church, mosque or synagogue takes on a special status after a religious ritual has taken place and the area is filled with participants. It (and its proceeding ritual) can be used to deliver important protest messages to potentially sympathetic groups. The same can be said of funerals, where the dead and their funeral may be deliberately associated with a protest message.

A protest group can also invent its own rituals, such as silent protests, vigils or other ritualised demonstrations to communicate a protest message, to encourage and demonstrate solidarity and to show collective discipline, outrage or sympathy.

• **Turn the tables:** One of the most potent methods of managing the narrative of a protest in the face of an unreasonable and unyielding authority is to subject the authority to the very injustice being protested about. An example, which recently took place in Ireland, saw an Irish TD (Member of Parliament) demanding in the Parliament that the Prime Minister drink a glass of water that he poured from a bottle. The water came from the TD's own constituency and, although contaminated by various bacteria, was a sample of the water still being delivered to thousands of residents for months on end. The Prime Minister declined, of course, but the message was loud and clear: "You won't drink it, but you expect us to!"

Greenpeace has consistently used this tactic to shed light on toxic dumping. In 2003, they collaborated with families and victims of the chemical plant disaster in Bhopal, India, and attempted, unsuccessfully, to deliver seven barrels of that toxic waste to the Dow Chemical Company HQ in Amsterdam. The action addressed basic questions of fairness and power: "If you can dump this toxic sludge on the people of India, then we can dump it back on you." Why is one act illegal while its analogue goes unpunished?

• **Confidence in protest:** It's vitally important that a protest group remains confident of its own righteousness and doesn't behave too cautiously. Confidence inspires confidence in others and, indeed, fear tends to be contagious. Therefore, within the legal limits of a regime, a protest group needs to remain focused and confident. Amazingly, this confidence will not only inspire support, but it will also frighten and undermine an authority.

6.1.8 Managing Protest Discipline and Safety

This is an important area of protest organisation, because it directly affects the legal position and physical safety of protesters and supporters. Many protests can become highly emotive and may degenerate into violence by protesters and/or authorities. For this reason, organisers have to have strategies and plans for dealing with protester discipline, physical and legal safety. Here are two basic principles to keep in mind when designing protest campaigns:

• **Maintain nonviolent discipline:** Nonviolent action works best when it stays nonviolent. Authorities, even in "liberal" Western countries, often use heavy-handed tactics on peaceful protesters. They trap them for hours in "kettles", beat them up, tear gas and pepper spray them. Sometimes they hit them with water cannon, baton rounds and they generally use escalating coercion as a standard means of stopping physical acts of protest. Very often these acts of brutality are designed to trigger off retaliation and violent escalation by protesters, with the sole purpose of giving the authorities the pretext they need to escalate a violent repression of protest.

For this very reason it is important that protest organisers maintain good discipline in the ranks of the demonstrators. It is vital to ensure that demonstrators are not provoked into doing what the authorities want them to do, which is to become violent. Such provocations are quite obviously dirty tricks designed to discredit a protest campaign and violent retaliation plays right into the authority's hands, generally on camera. It is worth reminding protesters, in advance of an action, that they can get their revenge on another day and that often it is better to simply walk away from a deliberate provocation rather than hand a moral and PR victory to the authorities by engaging in violent actions. The motto "our day will come" is an important one.

• **Take risks, but take care:** It is important to be bold and daring in protest actions, but that does not mean being foolhardy. Most protesters in citizen groups are volunteers who give freely of their time and enthusiasm. It is good that they have the confidence to confront unreasonable authorities, but they should not put themselves at risk of injury or death. For this reason protester safety and security has to be carefully considered when designing protest actions.

Lets face it, most protest campaigns come down to a long-drawn-out slugging match with authority, where endurance is often more important than anything else. Therefore, it is most important for a protest group to stay "in the ring" as long as possible, rather than demonstrating fast and furiously and then having to drop out because of injuries and losses of support. A safe protester will continue the struggle another day, a bloodied one may not.

6.1.9 Managing Alliances

It is often useful for protest groups to build alliances that can support a protest. For example, a protest group may affiliate itself with a political party or another NGO. These alliances may bring additional supporters, new expertise or maybe just bring some new ideas into play. Alliances need to be managed however, because an alliance may require compromises with views which are not completely consistent with those of a protest group. There are some basic principles which can help with managing these alliances.

• **Seek common ground:** When looking for allies, it is important to realise that a protest group will probably not find allies that have identical policies or even identical worldviews. If such allies existed, one or other of the groups would be redundant. Therefore it's clear that some degree of compromise is going to be necessary. For instance, an alliance between a green protest organisation and an organised church may generate an area of common ground, but an even larger area of dissent. If an issue is sufficiently important for both groups, it should be possible to forge an alliance on the main issues, whilst ignoring differences of opinion on other points.

This brings us to the main principle, which is: in seeking allies, a group's management, together with its membership, needs to seek common ground with potential allies. This common ground has to be sufficiently profoundly important to both parties that any differences become irrelevant. If this test of importance fails, then the alliance will not work and will simply waste time and energy. A failed alliance is more destructive to a protest group than no alliance at all, so these considerations are important.

• **Team up with experts:** A protest group needs to be properly supported by independent experts that can help to substantiate their claims. A protest group cannot hope to take on the role of independent experts because their "expert" advice will always be suspected of being biased. Therefore it is important to cultivate relationships between protest activists and experts, in order to organise effective protests and interventions when complex issues are involved.

• **Shift the support of allies:** Protest movements rarely win by overpowering the opposition; rather they win by shifting support away from the target authority. In this respect it is vitally important to understand the basis of an authority's support, in order that their allies can be shifted to favour the protest objectives.

For instance, during the anti-hunting campaigns in England over the last two decades, the pro-hunting faction was largely supported by the main pillars of the rural establishment, i.e. the landed gentry, their workers, the local established Church, the Tory party, and local pubs and businesses benefiting from hunting activity. The anti-hunting lobby was largely urban, supported by left-wing factions, mostly middle-class animal rights supporters.

Gradually, anti-hunt lobbyists began to shift the support of the main fox-hunting allies. In 2000, the Church of England "Board for Social Responsibility" released a report, coming out clearly against fox hunting when it stated that "Christians have a clear responsibility towards animals". The view that they were incapable of suffering was "no longer seriously supported". Christians would have to take seriously their responsibility towards animals in not inflicting gratuitous pain. "That must be the starting-point for all Christian discussion". Similar realignments of allegiance continued to take place with the formation of a group called "Conservatives against Fox Hunting", an anti fox-hunting lobby within the very Tory party itself, and then there is the "Pubs against Bloodsports" faction, a group of publicans that help hunt saboteurs and refuse access to fox hunts. The erosion of establishment support continues to this day.

• **Reframe:** As we discussed in another part of this chapter, the concept of reframing is an important way of winning supporters from unlikely quarters. The same concept of reframing a protest in the context of another group's moral philosophy is also a powerful way of building alliances with other groups. As in the case of the fox hunting protests, it is quite easy for an environmental lobby and an established Christian church to find common ground on an ethical question, such as hunting wild animals.

6.2 Protest Group Organisation

There is no prescriptive formula for determining how protesters should be organised. It all very much depends on the issues and protest objectives, the expected duration of the struggle and the target authority. Therefore, understanding different group organisations is important to allow a group to decide on the most appropriate structure to use in their particular case. Even leaderless protest groups have some form of informal organisation.

6.2.1 Getting Started

The very first step is to meet with your collaborators and form a steering committee to try to define the objectives of any organised protest campaign. Try to get some idea about the expected duration of the protest. Then decide together on a type of organisation that best suits your protest objectives (see below). For this there needs to be consensus.

Next, if a protest group is to be formed or joined, the steering committee should take an honest look at your group's potential members - its assets. Not everyone has the same level of commitment to a protest cause. They may have other personal commitments or they may have other political agendas. They certainly will have different levels of experience in any kind of protest activity. Protesters can generally be divided into the following categories:

- Novices (Joining a protest for the first time)
- Returners (Protesters of moderate intensity and commitment)
- Repeaters (Protesters with moderate intensity, but greater persistence)
- Stalwarts (Persistent, frequent, intense and experienced protesters)

It's important that everyone knows which category they and their colleagues belong to. This will alleviate potential complaints of unfair sharing of workload later on.

Finally, the steering committee evaluates the skills that exist in the group and which roles might fit each individual. Define job descriptions for all the managing roles that are envisaged in the protest group. Discuss the range of available roles and ask for volunteers for each role.

If the group is going to be around for a long time, formulate a management structure and a constitution. For this there needs to be complete consensus in the founding committee. After that, the protest organisation is formed and the steering committee is dissolved. You are in business!

6.2.2 Structures of Protest Groups

Despite the title of this section, a protest doesn't have to be carried out by a group and it doesn't have to have much of a structure. One-man protests are a case in point. There are many forms of protest, which range from the one-man activist who operates entirely alone, through informal and often anarchistic groupings of like-minded individuals acting loosely together, to one-off protest groups, single issue campaigns, through to highly traditional, well-funded NGOs. Groups can be community-based, national or global. They may last for a day, for six months or they may be around for decades. When beginning a protest movement, it's important to understand what kind of protest you are engaged in and what structure, if any, is best suited to your objectives. Here we examine some common organisational structures.

6.2.2.1 Hierarchical Structure: This is the most traditional structure for an organisation. It is based on a board of directors that have overall responsibility for the organisation. These directors are elected or appointed by an assembly of ordinary members of the organisation. The strategic decisions made by the board of directors are passed to the executive director of the organisation who, together with a group of co-directors, implements the board's strategic decisions via a group of managers (who may also be directors). Each director has responsibility for one area of the group's activities, such as PR & Press, Membership, Logistics, Legal

Affairs, Finance, Technology, Protest Operations, etc. Here is a typical structure for a hierarchical management for a campaigning NGO:

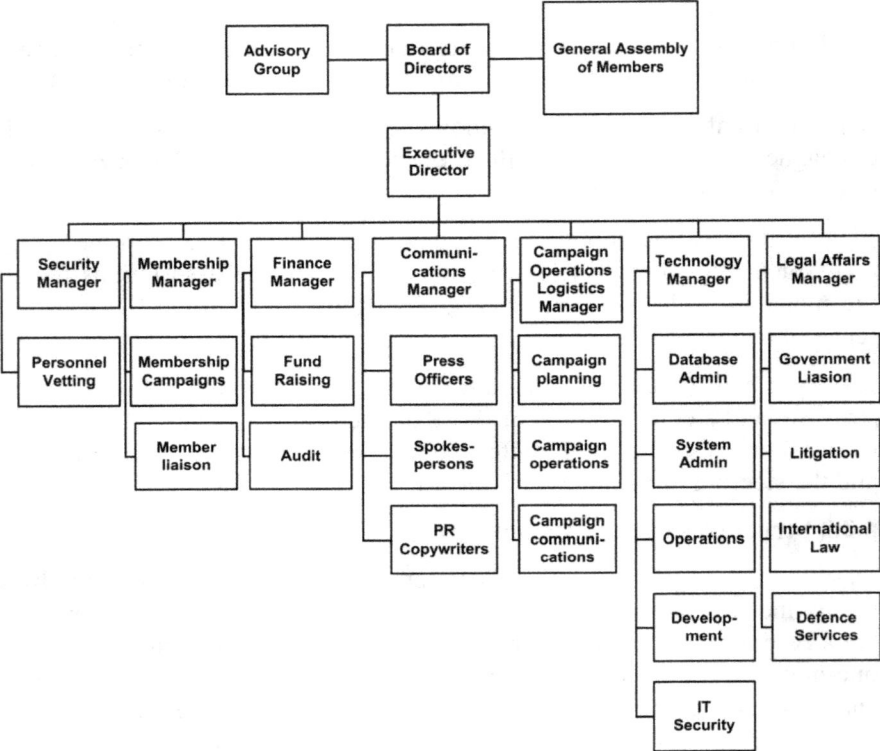

Hierarchical organisational structures are best suited to permanent NGOs with a formal legal status, employing large numbers of full-time staff and volunteers. For many small, single-issue protest groups such a structure is much too "top heavy" and inflexible.

6.2.2.1 Leaderless Groups: At the other extreme, some protest groups operate without any form of leadership. Such a group shares a common set of objectives and values and some basic rules of engagement, but for the rest each member operates autonomously, only coming together with other members as required to carry out protest actions that require collective effort. Anonymous, the so-called "hacktivist" network, is such a protest group. Members are theoretically anonymous, but share some common ideals, without any leader or command structure. Actions are suggested by members in various internet forums. They are discussed and then members go off to carry out the actions. Often the actions take the form of attacking an offending website with Denial of Service (DoS) attacks, or hacking servers belonging to a corporation or government to release information or show embarrassing failures in security.

Leaderless groups such as Anonymous are the highpoint of asynchronous struggle. The individuals themselves are relatively powerless, but together with pooled technological knowledge they can be quite a formidable opponent against even the largest and most powerful organisations in the world. Because they have no command structure, they are almost impossible to infiltrate or disrupt. Even when a member is exposed, that member is just one of many that can be rapidly replaced by other anonymous volunteers. The nearest natural comparison is that of a swarm of bees. They can and do operate independently, but with the interests of the greater good. Attacking the hive causes a significant backlash, whereas killing one member has no effect on the overall strength of the community.

Leaderless structures only work in certain protest environments and with certain protest tools. Hacktivism and internet actions are a perfect environment for such a protest group structure. However, such a structure simply would not work so well when dealing with long-term tangible protest targets, such as winning human rights or drawn-out environmental protests, where physical actions, such as blockades, or legal actions are required. The exception to this is when a more structured protest group calls in support from other - leaderless - groups, such as informal flash mobs or flying pickets to help with a protest action. Here the two types of group can work very well together.

6.2.2.2 Team Structured Protest Groups: This is an organisational model based on management by consensus (or near consensus) of an entire group. A management team acts as facilitators to the group to make suggestions and to execute the decisions of the group. Regular structured meetings (assemblies) of the entire membership consider policy, objectives, strategy, plans and problems, and then vote on propositions to govern the actions of the group. The decisions of the assembly are passed to the management board to be implemented. The management board then coordinates the implementation of these instructions by passing the tasks out to those responsible for different areas of activity.

For instance, a team assembly may decide that a new protest action should carry out a blockade of a factory. The management team takes up the decision and converts it into a concrete set of plans and actions to carry out the protest. This includes issuing press releases, organising personnel to man the blockade, looking after supplies and logistics (transport, etc.), briefing the demonstrators and making any legal arrangements. The tasks are then handed out to those responsible and the facilitators of the management team oversee the whole proceedings, to make sure that it is properly coordinated. Small teams may be built "on the fly" to deal with a particular plan.

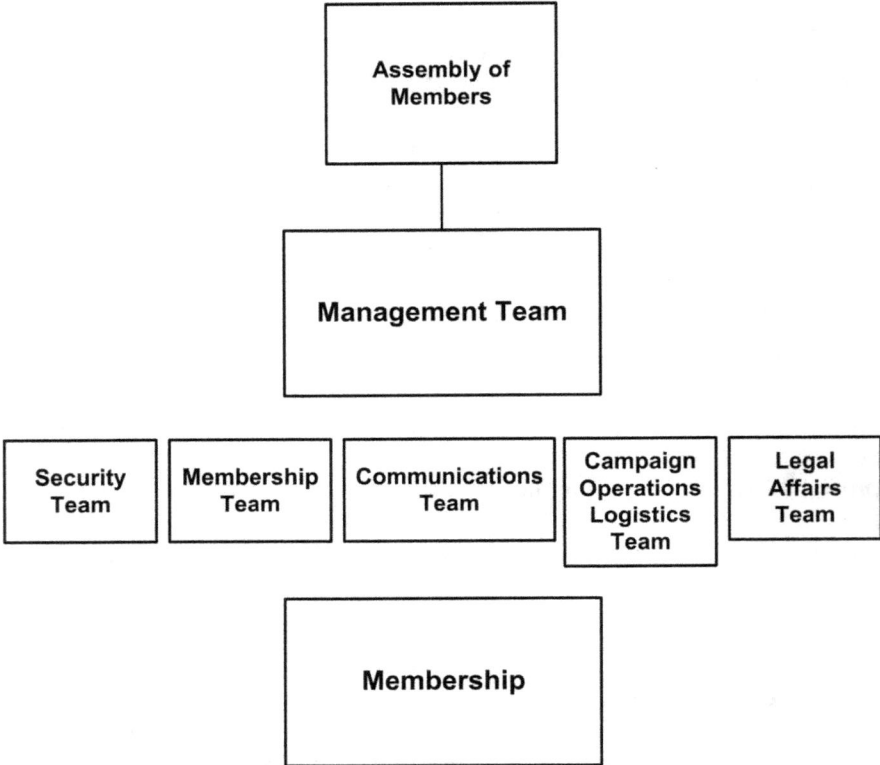

```
                        ┌─────────────────┐
                        │  Assembly of    │
                        │    Members      │
                        └────────┬────────┘
                                 │
                   ┌─────────────────────────┐
                   │                         │
                   │    Management Team      │
                   │                         │
                   └─────────────────────────┘

┌──────────┐ ┌────────────┐ ┌───────────────┐ ┌────────────┐ ┌──────────┐
│ Security │ │ Membership │ │ Communications│ │  Campaign  │ │  Legal   │
│   Team   │ │    Team    │ │     Team      │ │ Operations │ │  Affairs │
│          │ │            │ │               │ │  Logistics │ │   Team   │
└──────────┘ └────────────┘ └───────────────┘ │    Team    │ └──────────┘
                                               └────────────┘
                   ┌─────────────────────────┐
                   │                         │
                   │      Membership         │
                   │                         │
                   └─────────────────────────┘
```

Members of the management team are referred to as "directors", but in fact they have no more decision-making role than other members in the assembly. Their role is simply to implement the decisions of the assembly and manage day-to-day operational details and administration.

A team structure works well in volunteer-based protest groups (not permanent NGOs), where individuals may have to manage several different tasks or areas of responsibility. The structure helps to unite a group, since it seeks to work with near consensus of the membership, where decisions are open to everyone's input and vote. Note that in such an organisational structure there are no formal hierarchical relationship between teams and management.

6.2.2.3 Pop-up Protest Group Structures: Some protests are deliberately short-lived affairs, where the objective is to make a short, sharp point to the target authority and the public and then close up shop and disappear. Such groups have no legal status and no formal structure. They are generally led by a small cadre of experienced protesters who have already worked out their strategies and protest methods and simply carry out the protest actions with the help of some supporters and members of other sympathetic groups in an informal alliance.

These are not leaderless groups, indeed, the inner cadre is completely autocratic - you join them if you like what they are doing, but the agenda is already fixed and not open to discussion. Such "pop-up" protests are useful when a rapid response to quickly unfolding events, such as revelations of scandals, court decisions, government announcements, etc. is required. They are particularly annoying for authorities because they disappear as quickly as they arrived and infiltration is basically impossible.

6.2.2.4 Network Structures: In some instances, independent or semi-independent organisations form loose affiliations in which they share resources, information, data, and responsibility for joint projects. An example of this kind of cost-effective organisation is a neighbourhood alliance, in which organisations working on different aspects of community development coalesce as an umbrella organisation, hiring a senior program manager and sharing office space and material resources. There are many variations on network structures, ranging from small, totally independent groups coming together for a common cause to affiliates of international organisations that share the same principles and can work together on large projects.

Protest networking can be useful because it aids efficiency in the following areas:

- A small core infrastructure provides services needed by all.
- Groups with a common cause can be highly responsive and flexible.
- Decision-making occurs with all groups in the alliance involved.

6.2.2.5 De-Centralised Protest Structures: Many large protest and campaigning organisations are global. Greenpeace and Amnesty International are two examples. However, they are also highly devolved organisations, having national offices with a high degree of autonomy in terms of fund-raising, local campaigning, local membership, etc.

Of course, local branches of these organisations operate within the legal and philosophical framework of the parent organisation. But these de-centralised structures help to make a protest organisation much more relevant and effective, locally. Members feel they are both part of a global organisation, which gives them confidence, but they also act locally, which makes their work highly relevant and instantly rewarding.

In some cases, rather than forming a new protest group, it may be worth considering joining an existing group if they are willing to take on your campaign. Offering the services of your little group of supporters may be an incentive for an existing campaign group to allow you to operate under its auspices. This can save a lot of hard work, money and organisation.

6.3 Knowledge is Power - The Strategic Importance of Information

Authorities: Authorities have long been well aware that the more they know about their citizens, the better they can control them. Thus, their appetite for even the most trivial details is insatiable. Governments use this information to tax, intimidate, blackmail, litigate against and sometimes convict their citizens. Now, in the post-NSA-revelations world, this government spying is well and truly out in the open and there is now open public discussion about anti-surveillance tactics for ordinary citizens. We have entered an era where the public know that they are being spied on by their governments (and others). But not only are they fully aware of the snooping, they are now actively taking counter-measures to avoid this surveillance, and some are even deliberately spreading disinformation to confuse government spies and corrupt their data. To some extent we are all now involved in widespread and quite deliberate civil disobedience. The moment that we encrypt a file or email, use SSL security to browse the web, or use a secure messaging service, we are actively refusing to be spied upon by our government. We are protesting.

In strategic terms, the intelligence which is held about members and organisations of protest groups by government authorities is particularly crucial. Protest groups are the vanguard of democracy and freedom. They are at the very front of the clash between authoritarian ambition and civic freedom. Any attempt to spy upon a protest group is a direct affront to democratic principles. Nonetheless, infiltration of and spying upon peaceful protest groups happens constantly everywhere in the world, regardless of the political system that's in place.

Protest groups and authorities: Unfortunately, in general, protest groups are not so adept at or interested in spying on their own authorities as said authorities are in spying on them. Protest groups tend to be too preoccupied by their own campaigns and protest agendas to be interested in keeping tabs on government or corporate adversaries. But this is actually a big oversight on the part of the activist. Knowledge of an adversary's organisation is so strategically important that intelligence gathering about and basic espionage on target authorities should be considered amongst the very high priorities of a protest group.

Imagine how valuable it would be to have a good understanding of the business relationships between government officials and private companies, or to be privy to the confidential plans, discussions or memos of a government agency. Some items of information could be so powerful that they could literally be complete game-changers in a protest campaign. A protest group which fails to gather, store and collate information about its adversary is guilty of a great oversight.

Protest groups and useful knowledge: Another area in which information needs to be managed by a protest group is in keeping track of contacts, communications and data on other campaign assets such as journalists, specialists, relevant research material and documents. Unless there is some means of storing such data, it very often happens that, after the passage of time, people forget contacts and they mislay or forget documents, letters, and emails etc. Potentially useful knowledge is simply gradually lost, and very often this results in wasted time and missed opportunities, simply because a protest movement has no central database where this kind of information can be stored and shared. In such cases, a group has to rely on very fallible human memories. This would be unimaginable for any government authority or corporation, so why should a protest group be any different? The answer, of course, is that a protest group should be just as assiduous as a government in properly storing useful information and making it available to others as a permanent campaigning resource.

The practical aspect of intelligence gathering is addressed in the next chapter in much more detail.

6.3.1 Acquiring, Storing and Retrieving Data

Know thy enemy: Gathering and storing information about an authority is an important task. Much of this involves publicly accessible information available from conventional media and the internet. Some information may also need to be obtained covertly from within an organisation, using inside sympathisers, or by getting a member of the protest group to infiltrate the authority and siphon information back to the group. Social media such as Facebook, Twitter and professional services such as LinkedIn may also provide an interesting source of information about government or corporate officials. Gathering gossip, and direct spying methods (which we discuss under "Espionage and Intelligence Gathering") will all yield information of varying quality.

These days, with modern database technology, storing and indexing this kind of information is eminently straightforward. Relational databases offer an excellent method of storing and retrieving any kind of data or even copies of original documents. Such database systems are freely available to anyone and, with some help, a protest group can build their very own data-mining system, which allows all kinds of data to be indexed, collated and stored and then retrieved, using standard queries and ad-hoc "data-mining" requests.

When data is received it can be instantly added to a central database and "tagged" with what is referred to as metadata. This is data which defines the contents of what is being stored. For instance, a copy of an internal memo might be tagged with various freeform keywords that characterise the document's content, its date, a short description of the documents, the source, a list of names of persons that are connected with it, etc. If an item of gossip is being reported, it can be entered as a descriptive text and tagged with its associated metadata. Similarly, with information picked up from social media, or from databases of corporate information, it is simply stored together with some identifying metadata. Data can also be qualified as "reliable" or "hearsay". The metadata that is stored with a piece of intelligence helps to rapidly identify related data. It creates an intelligent index to actual data, rather like the index in a book. When, for example, a protest group researcher wishes to find all the connections between or references to "Person A" and "Company X", the researcher simply creates a database query which searches the metadata for records where these two values occur or occur together. The search then yields all the documents, gossip, Facebook references, Tweets and memos where these names occur. Of course, all this data needs to be stored in the first place and this takes effort and time, but eventually a very powerful and useful intelligence database can be established.

Know your assets: In the same way as it's important to know as much as possible about an adversary, it's also vital for a protest group to keep on top of and share its own group's knowledge. Protest groups quickly build up a wealth of information, contacts and documents which is relevant to their campaigns, but is usually widely dispersed across many PCs, in many formats, and may be only very narrowly shared. This is a gross waste of resources and knowledge that can be easily overcome using relational database technology.

Here are some examples of what should be stored and made available to protest group members (security issues being taken into consideration, of course) from a common database:

- General contacts database with metadata for each contact
- Media publications and contacts database
- Journalists and their specialities and contact details database
- Correspondence database with relevant metadata (emails, letters, faxes, etc).
- Document database with relevant metadata
- Skills database for members and external expertise
- Lobbyist database of sympathisers
- Membership database

It may seem completely obvious to store this information in a database, but amazingly many protest groups do not use database technology of any kind at all. This means that every time they have a new campaign, they have to find the contact information for their press contacts and the group's members and then manually select appropriate addresses. They'd then email those press releases manually instead of using a database to automatically send mails to a reusable and pre-defined list of addresses. Again, when the group needs to find all the relevant documentation about a particular subject, they have to manually search for these documents, ask their colleagues if they have anything relevant and then hope that they have found the right paperwork, instead of executing a 10 second search of the metadata on a document retrieval database.

6.3.2 Using Information to Undermine or Attack Authority

Clearly, having information about an authority is not enough. It has to be used to the advantage of a protest group. Here are some examples of how knowledge can be used to a protest campaign's advantage:

• **Revealing corrupt or suspicious connections:** Governments in every country in the world are riddled with corruption. From the usual cases of civil servants taking bribes to awarding contracts to business friends, it goes all the way to the top, where parliamentarians take money to vote in a certain way or political parties take donations from corporate donors to buy their political support. Indeed, it extends into the very bosom of several royal families, whose members have been known to take money and favours from big business in return for using their name or covering up corrupt business or sexual activities.

Even at a very modest level, a revelation or even a suspicion of corrupt practice by a civil servant can seriously damage an authority and undermine its decisions. Planning departments and government tendering are two areas where corruption tends to be rife. If a social or economic relationship can be demonstrated between officials and the beneficiaries of building permits, government contracts or other benefits, then this can potentially cause permits to be revoked or contracts to be cancelled. Indeed, it may even lead to criminal prosecutions.

• **Revealing maladministration:** Governments are not only corrupt they also tend to be endemically incompetent. The civil service doesn't generally attract the most talented members of the population and the general standard of work in the civil service is poor. This accounts for the almost complete inability of the British civil service, for instance, to effectively manage to bring in a project on time and on budget, whether it's a battleship or an IT system. Anything the civil service touches becomes a running disaster. Billions have been wasted in gargantuan project failures, with the only beneficiaries being the large private contracting companies, such as arms manufacturers.

Revelations of tax-wasting acts of maladministration are an important method of undermining authorities. Authorities try very hard to cover up these kinds of scandals, but ultimately they tend to be revealed - usually by an internal whistleblower.

Such revelations of incompetence can be very useful when formulating an argument about security. Claims by British government officials that they could be trusted to safely store personal ID card data were finally shattered when it was revealed in 2014 that 2,000 NHS patients' records are lost every day, and that there have been more than two million serious data breaches logged in the health system since the beginning of 2011. Such revelations play straight into the hands of those who are protesting against the privatisation of parts of the health service (NHS), who demand to know: "Where will this lost data end up if the NHS is privatised?"

• **Revealing prejudice by authority:** Most government agencies exercise various forms of prejudice or discrimination against members of the public, and even against their own employees. These practices often go uncorrected for years. A protest group with enough evidence can leverage revelations of institutional prejudice to undermine an authority and cause organisational changes.

• **Doxxing officials:** Apart from using public revelations of an authority's misdeeds as a way of undermining it or forcing a change of decision, there are other ways of using information to pressure an authority or an official. Collecting, compiling and publishing information about individual officials in a single document can be rather disturbing for the official and the authority concerned. Governments routinely collect and store such information about citizens, but are somewhat averse to citizens doing the same to their own officials.

The technique, when applied by an ordinary citizen, is called "Doxxing" and it can be quite distressing to a victim because it collates lots of widely distributed data about one person in a single document, which is then published somewhere on the internet and indexed with the major search engines. As a means of undermining a government official or politician it can be quite chilling and it shouldn't be used without very good moral justification.

The kind of information contained in a doxxing attack against an individual would be basic personal data, social security information, career history, business connections, photos, banking and housing information. The published document may contain information about friends, family, holidays, hobbies, and opinions. For many people, all this kind of material is available on the internet in fairly accessible places, such as Twitter, Facebook, LinkedIn, etc. Other websites, such as registrars of companies, electoral registries and registrars of births, marriages and deaths provide additional verifiable public sources of information.

Doxxing doesn't prove anything. It doesn't accuse anyone of anything. But, what it does do is to "turn the tables" on officials in an authority that are engaged in intelligence gathering against a protest group or individual protesters. It demonstrates, in a sense, that information is democratic: anyone can collect and anyone can publish it.

6.3.3 Frustrating Intelligence Gathering by Authority

Disinformation is the dissemination of false information with the express intention of confusing, discrediting or undermining the intelligence gathering efforts of an adversary.

We have already mentioned that intelligence has variable quality. Poor quality intelligence refers to a questionable source, and information which cannot be verified independently of that original source - it might be fabricated, in other words. Good quality intelligence comes from a reputable source and has multiple possible methods of independent verification. Reducing the quality of information using junk "disinformation" has a debilitating effect on the quality of an authority's database of intelligence because it drags down the quality and reliability of its overall intelligence activities. This fact can be used by a protest group to its advantage.

The strategy works by pumping out poor quality information (disinformation), so that it is collected by those spying on a protest group. This intelligence is poor quality, but if there is enough of it, the authority's spies find that they have a very high "noise to signal" ratio and are unable to distinguish junk from quality.

It's not complicated to engage in this surveillance counter-measure. Large numbers of mock emails, social media postings, blog postings can be used to send whatever junk signals the group decides upon. This can even include random obfuscated messages that send an authority's cryptographic specialists on fruitless wild goose chases to decode meaningless messages. See the later section in "Methods of Civil Disobedience, Protest, Intervention and Direct Action" entitled "Disinformation" for more details.

6.4 The Strategic Power of Time and Place in Protest: The Art of War

The timing and location of a conflict in a protest campaign often determines the outcome. The rules for deciding when and where to stage a confrontation with an authority in a protest are remarkably similar to the guidelines that have been used in military strategy for thousands of years. It's useful to remember them.

Especially in asymmetric conflicts, timing is everything. That doesn't mean that all protests revolve around short-lived, sudden conflict. Indeed, sometimes attrition is a better strategy to beat an authority. Sometimes, an all-out assault is better, in order to occupy the attention of an authority temporarily. Other times a combination of attrition and the occasional surprise attack is the better approach. Ideally, no conflict at all is the best solution. As Sun Tzu reminds us in "The Art of War", "To fight and conquer is not supreme excellence; supreme excellence consists in breaking the enemy's resistance without fighting at all". This is especially true in protests against authorities, where conflict often makes future compromise and resolution more difficult.

Nonetheless, conflict is sometimes inevitable when dealing with an intractable authority. In such cases, a protest group needs to take over the narrative and choreography of the conflict. It is vital to be flexible and be capable of rapid redeployment. Again, Sun Tzu comments in "The Art of War" how "swift chariots are superior in attack to the heavy chariots designed for defence". In other words, government authorities are monolithic and slow and can be overwhelmed by speed and flexibility. In the same vein, it is vital that a protest group decides when and where a confrontation is to take place. The protest group needs to control and frame the confrontation to its advantage and not allow the confrontation to be controlled on the grounds by the authority. Sun Tzu comments: "The rule is, not to besiege walled cities if it can possibly be avoided." Here's another sound piece of military theory that should be applied to a protest campaign by its organisers.

Obviously, every protest is quite different. Some campaigns benefit from a noisy start, followed by a long period of quiet subversive activity. Other campaigns may be more effective if the campaign works towards a crescendo of protest activity.

One key element in planning is making sure that the target authority is unable to seize the initiative. In general, this means making sure that the protest group is prepared for all eventualities. In some cases there may be arrests; how will the group manage these at a practical level and in terms of publicity? Authorities frequently attempt to demonise protesters. How will this be managed and neutralised? What is the optimal order in which to execute each part of an action? What is the best time to start the action? Sometimes maximum effect may be had during holidays, sometimes the opposite. How are the press to be handled, when and by whom?

For a successful action, all of these details, and more, need to be investigated and coherent, clearly-timed plans need to be formulated.

Notes on Chapter 6

Note 1: Joseph Lehman. "A Brief Explanation of the Overton Window". Mackinac Center for Public Policy.

---o0o---

7. Planning Civil Rebellion

As we have seen in the preceding chapter, the planning and organisation of a campaign is vital to its success. This is especially true in campaigns against well-organised, well-resourced and unscrupulous authorities. We are now going to examine in more detail the kind of pre-action planning and preparation that is required for a protest to be successful.

7.1 Analysis and Planning a Peaceful Protest

The Process of Analysis and Planning of a Campaign looks like this:

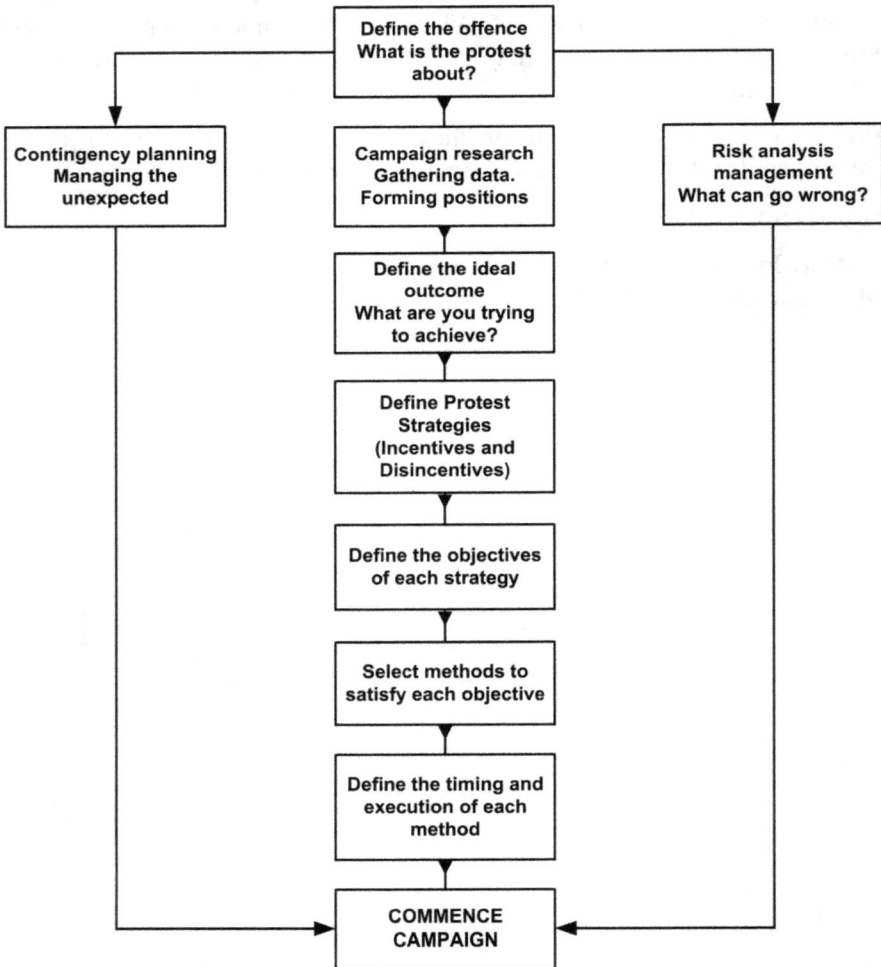

```
                    ┌──────────────────┐
                    │ Define the offence│
                    │ What is the protest│
                    │      about?       │
                    └──────────────────┘
┌──────────────────┐ ┌──────────────────┐ ┌──────────────────┐
│Contingency planning│ │ Campaign research │ │  Risk analysis   │
│  Managing the     │ │ Gathering data.   │ │   management     │
│   unexpected      │ │ Forming positions │ │ What can go wrong?│
└──────────────────┘ └──────────────────┘ └──────────────────┘
                    ┌──────────────────┐
                    │ Define the ideal  │
                    │     outcome       │
                    │ What are you trying│
                    │   to achieve?     │
                    └──────────────────┘
                    ┌──────────────────┐
                    │ Define Protest    │
                    │   Strategies      │
                    │ (Incentives and   │
                    │  Disincentives)   │
                    └──────────────────┘
                    ┌──────────────────┐
                    │Define the objectives│
                    │ of each strategy  │
                    └──────────────────┘
                    ┌──────────────────┐
                    │ Select methods to │
                    │satisfy each objective│
                    └──────────────────┘
                    ┌──────────────────┐
                    │Define the timing and│
                    │ execution of each │
                    │     method        │
                    └──────────────────┘
                    ┌──────────────────┐
                    │    COMMENCE       │
                    │    CAMPAIGN       │
                    └──────────────────┘
```

264

In this phase of a protest action, we first need to establish and examine the protest objectives. These can range from relatively small actions aimed at a corporate management, designed to bring a negotiated solution to a labour dispute, right through to huge national or international protests directed at governments and designed to bring about maximum political change.

Obviously, the underlying cause of any protest act and the motivation of protesters determine the general objectives. To find the correct methods to use in a particular context requires a careful analysis of the situation. Much valuable energy can be wasted by a failure to understand the objectives of a protest correctly, resulting in an attack on the wrong targets or even the right targets using the wrong methods.

7.2 Defining an Offence. What is the Protest About?

Many a protest action has failed because it wasn't well thought out. Often the emotion surrounding a particular protest tends to overshadow and cloud the planning of a campaign. Many collaborators may also have personal agendas or be too ambitious in their objectives. This can divide the limited energy of a protest group across too many initiatives. It is also very common in the febrile atmosphere of a protest for an action about one issue to spread to a raft of associated disputes. This "protest drift" is very damaging because it can terminally dilute the focus of a protest group. So it is important to be very clear as to what a protest is actually about and to define the very definite limits to a protest.

Mission statements: The reasons for a protest action need to be clearly defined in writing, together with the protest objectives and the main principles of the protest group. A typical example of such a mission statement might read:

"Our protest is against the increase in the number of working hours and reduction in hourly rate by company X. We consider the actions by company X to be an affront to our legal rights under regulations Y, a breach of previous agreements and a direct assault on the living standards of our members by the company. A majority of the members of this union have voted to withdraw their labour completely until the management of company X restore the status quo and enter into negotiations with this union over any future changes in working conditions".

7.3 Campaign Research - Gathering Data and Defining Positions

A badly informed campaign is very likely to fail to bring about change or may just fizzle out. If the organising group isn't fully informed of all the aspects of the core issues of their protest, they will have great difficulty persuading anyone else that their demands are justified, never mind negotiating a solution with an authority.

The target authority against which a campaign is aimed is probably better resourced than the campaigning group and will be better informed and organised than the protesters. They will have specialist researchers dedicated to defending their position and strategists working on ways of undermining the protesters. Faced with the formidable strength of most corporate or government authorities, any protest group beginning a campaign without a fully researched and fully nuanced position is effectively wasting their time and a lot of people's energy.

7.3.1 Understanding your Subject is Vital

The curse of many protest groups is that they are frequently well-intentioned and motivated, but often lack good organising skills and an understanding of how large organisations, such as corporations or government authorities, work. This naivety is the reason for the failure of many a worthwhile protest campaign.

Another weakness in many civil protests is a faith that governments and corporations are basically law-abiding and fundamentally decent. This is a grave error, since they are neither. Again, to be successful, campaigners should not underestimate their corporate or government opponents. Campaigners really must assume that their opponents in government or business will play all manner of dirty tricks on them and on the public. One such trick revolves around the strategic reality that "knowledge is power". Corporate and government opponents often rely on public ignorance or a "lack of provability" as a method of defence. The only way that this "trick" can be bypassed is for protest campaigners to ensure that they are better informed than the authorities.

Being well-informed involves a lot of disciplined and well-organised research work. It may involve using sophisticated and automated techniques, such as databases to store and collate data. It may require professional help by specialists such as statisticians, lawyers, scientists, IT personnel and public relations specialists, etc. It will certainly require a lot of hard work and late nights.

7.3.1.1 Information as a Weapon of Protest:
As an example of this concept we can quote from a protest action in the last 10 years, which centred on poor drinking water quality in the Republic of Ireland. As a result of various historical water contamination incidents one protest group became engaged in gathering vast amounts of nationwide water quality data.

Despite decades-long public announcements to the contrary, there appeared to be many water quality anomalies showing up in laboratory test results. Indeed, to the naked eye, these "quality exceptions" seemed to be more often the rule than the exception being claimed by the authorities. The official line was that the incidences of contamination were within the normal margins of quality variation. Given the volume of data, it was hard for anyone to disprove this assertion.

The main problem for the campaign group was that the amount of data involved was colossal. The lab reports involved millions of daily and weekly test results from hundreds of water supplies for dozens of different contaminants, going back at least a decade. It seemed that the government was hiding behind an impenetrable mountain of raw data. The assumption seemed to be that no campaign group would be able to get to the bottom of the real national contamination incidence, simply because of the sheer volume of data.

However, the campaign group mounted a technological assault on the "data mountain" by building a sophisticated database, uploading the data to it and then carrying out its own statistical analysis of the water contamination.

The results were startling. Within a few weeks the group had published the shocking fact that more than 65% of the nation's water had suffered contamination within the previous 12 months, often with potentially fatal bacterial and parasitic agents. Moreover, the campaign group was able to prove that the nation's water had been illegally contaminated for at least a decade without public knowledge or government action, and that drinking water quality was in dramatic and long-term decline.

This news was a body blow to the authorities and it triggered off a number of other spontaneous reactions which culminated in nationwide street protests organised by affected citizens, a legal action in the European Court of Justice, questions in the European parliament, water utility payment boycotts and a lot of government embarrassment. The protests continue to this day.

It's worth noting that this campaign centred on research and understanding the data behind the core issues. The campaign group didn't set one foot outside its offices or organise a single protest march. The power of a simple analysis of the raw data was enough to prove that a huge problem existed and to trigger widespread public anger and protest.

7.3.1.2 What Kind of Research is Needed? There are basically two areas of research which need to be carried out before and during a campaign:

• The issues: The first type of research deals with the protest issues and what can be realistically achieved by the protest action.

• The opponents: The second set of research deals with understanding the protest's opponents, i.e. the organisations against which the protest is aimed, aka the "target authority".

The following sections deal with these research activities in detail.

7.3.2 Campaign Research

7.3.2.1 Issue-Based Research: The following schematic shows some of the most essential areas of issue-based research:

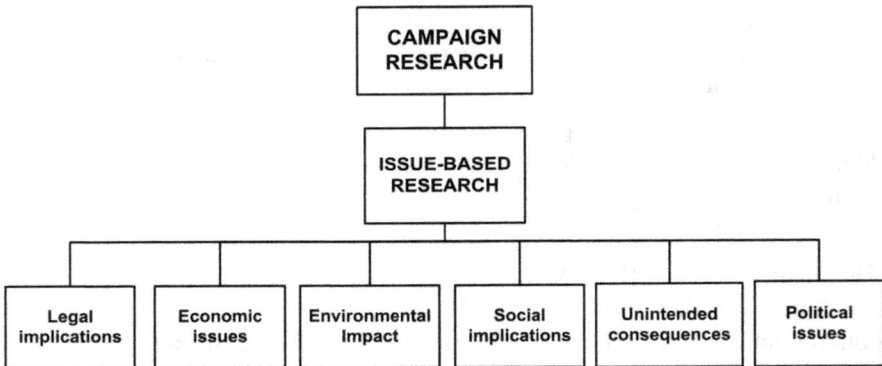

```
          ┌─────────────────┐
          │    CAMPAIGN     │
          │    RESEARCH     │
          └────────┬────────┘
                   │
          ┌────────┴────────┐
          │   ISSUE-BASED   │
          │    RESEARCH     │
          └────────┬────────┘
```

Legal implications	Economic issues	Environmental Impact	Social implications	Unintended consequences	Political issues

There is always a lot more to a protest issue than appears on the face of it. Whether the campaign is part of an environmental, economic, social, political or legal conflict, there are without exception aspects, apart from the main issue, which may affect the direction of a protest. The objective of good protest research is to uncover all of these aspects and present them in a ready to digest way with properly supporting cross-referenced evidence.

As an example, let us take the recent protests against fracking in various parts of Europe and the demands for a complete ban by many environmental activist groups. Apart from the emotive demand to stop all fracking, what else could we know about this subject?

For instance, what are the unique risks of fracking? What are the legal, social, environmental, economic consequences of an accident? Would an accident have cross-border or political implications to neighbouring countries or regions? Realistically, how great are the risks? What is the accident record of fracking in other countries? How economically viable is fracking? Where does it fit in with climate change? How much energy is used to extract the gas, relative to other energy sources? What are the legal implications of long distance horizontal drilling under other properties far from the licensed site? Who bears liability for clean-ups and reparation? Who decides on licensing for operators? What are the implications on agriculture and the agricultural economy of the use of large amounts of clean water to carry out fracking? How does fracking affect rural areas, house prices, local businesses, roads and other infrastructure? What chemicals are used in this process? How will waste be disposed of? How long do these gas reserves last? How will landscapes be repaired, what will it cost and who will pay? What are the government contingency plans in the event of groundwater contamination? What is the design lifespan of the pipeline? What happens afterwards? What are the relevant European directives and regulations and how do they affect this technology? Are their local laws or by-laws which might block this activity? Are their noise abatement implications? Are their human rights issues at stake? How does the activity affect conservation and planning strategies? What is public opinion on fracking? Who benefits from fracking and how?

Such a list of questions is potentially huge! And, without a doubt, the oil companies and governments will already have considered some of these questions without our knowledge, so that they can head off any protest attacks.

It is impossible to be totally prescriptive about the precise research necessary for a particular campaign, but as a general rule the following areas should be addressed in carrying out research:

- Legal implications
- Economic issues
- Environmental impact
- Social implications
- Unintended consequences
- Political issues

7.3.2.2 Legal Implications: This area of research deals with both the legal implications of the core protest issues and any possible legal impacts arising from the protest itself. This means considering local laws, national laws, and international laws.

Local laws: In terms of local laws, the researcher needs to investigate if there are any local or regional "by-laws" which are related to the core issue. This might be a planning by-law, some ancient right (like access rights), or other local legal custom which might impact. For example, the ancient right of shepherds to pass through the land on which Madrid is now built gives rise to the surreal annual sight of thousands of sheep passing through the centre of the city for the payment of a few cents in taxes. Such oddities exist in many countries. Similar ancient rights of passage were the basis of the protest movements in Britain defending the public's "right to roam" and were the founding principles of the Ramblers Association, which sprang from a combination of environmental awareness and the British Communist party. Their knowledge of the ancient network of public paths is a good example of how local laws assisted the group in their struggle to defend the rights of everyone to access to the countryside.

On the other side of the coin, at a local level, a protest group needs to understand if there are any legal inhibitions to the type of protest they are planning. For instance, there may be some bizarre local laws dealing with loitering, trespass and assembly which could curtail mass demonstrations in some circumstances in some places. It's best to fully understand such laws in advance so as to better circumvent them or ameliorate any possible consequences.

National laws: In terms of national laws, a protest group should be familiar with the appropriate legislation related to their core protest issues, and their research should seek to examine opportunities for the use of national laws as part of their protest campaign. Examples of such laws may be environmental regulations dealing with waste disposal, land use, labour law, health and safety regulations, civil rights, access rights, trespass laws, property ownership laws, etc.

In terms of a protest campaign, the protest group needs to fully understand what national laws may be used to curtail the group's activities and how these should be dealt with if there is a direct confrontation with the authorities. This is particularly important when employing tactics of direct action where the perpetrator is clearly visible to the authorities and probably breaking the law. It's best to be clear about which laws the protesters are likely to be breaking.

International law: In the investigation of international law all supra-national laws, such as the many EU directives, Human Rights law, International law and the many International Treaties which deal with subjects as diverse as working conditions (ILO), military responsibility (Geneva Conventions), the treatment of prisoners, and the Law of the Sea should be considered.

There is an assumption that international law is mainly aimed at resolving cross-border conflicts. This is not so. International laws, such as EU directives, apply equally to the behaviour of a single member state as they do to cross-border disputes. But, indeed an authority's actions in one country may also have cross-border implications. For example, plans by one EU government to build a dam may well have downstream effects on the environment in another country. Perhaps the dam reduces water flow to an SPA (Special Protection Area) 100 km away. SPAs are managed nationally, but under the auspices of an EU Directive (Habitats Directive). Failure to protect an SPA suddenly becomes an international issue and a dispute may up in the European Court of Justice.

In a similar way, we should understand the context of our protest campaign in terms of international law, in particular in terms of human rights law. Perhaps we are inhibited from taking action in one EU country, but can possibly claim our rights by recourse to the European Court of Human Rights.

Legal process: There is a plethora of legal methods which can be used to frustrate or delay an opponent or to increase their costs. These include the use of legal challenges to legislation (in the UK called a judicial review), temporary injunctions to delay an authority from taking action, the launching of formal processes with a national or international regulator, or simply filing a formal objection with the appropriate authority to trigger a delay (such as a planning objection or appeal). To run an effective campaign where the activists are setting the agenda and defining the timescales, it is vital to know what legal processes can be used against an authority, if only to cause a delay or as a diversionary tactic.

Legal access to information: Though legislation varies from one country to another, most Western nations now provide some legal guarantees of citizens' rights of access to information. These rights can be used to demand access to much information which is relevant to the protest campaign. Not only may the information be directly relevant to the campaign, but it may also be instrumental in getting a desired result when combined with a broader strategy, as the following example explains: A protest group was running a campaign centred on getting local authorities to repair dangerously un-maintained roads. The campaigners noticed that they were having little effect in persuading local authorities to respond to their complaints, so they adopted a different strategy. Firstly, for each case they demanded a complete history of maintenance of a particular road from the local authority under their right of access to information (EU Freedom of access to information Directive 200/4/EC). Then they gathered information / photos about the current state of a particular road. Finally, they presented a formal report to the local police with the full package of written evidence and a formal warning that any accident occurring on that particular piece of road could well be fully or partly attributable to the documented state of the road. The effect of this strategy was instant and universal. The police contacted the local authority and, using the local authority's own reports, explained the complaint and the risks of local authorities being held legally liable in the event of an accident. Without fail, the campaigners claim, the local authorities responded by sending out maintenance crews within 24 hours. This was a good example of how information can be a very effective leverage in a protest campaign. It is also incidentally a good example of how a proxy can be used to achieve campaigners' demands. In this case, it was, ironically, the authority of the police which was used as a proxy, to force another authority, the local council, to take action - which, as it happens, exactly satisfied the campaign's objectives.

7.3.2.3 Economic Issues: Given that money is almost always at the heart of authoritarian excesses, most protest campaigns will have to deal with issues which have some economic implications. The core issue may affect local or national taxes, economic development or growth. It may alter the level of economic activity, the value of public or private assets such as house prices, or it may have an impact on revenues and employment in other sectors, for instance damage to the tourist industry by a large building development. Other economic considerations may revolve around how a core issue affects personal incomes, living standards, healthcare costs, economic well-being, demographics, etc.

For example, a government policy of allowing banks to foreclose and evict mortgage holders in arrears has a negative impact on the families affected, but also causes sudden surpluses of vacant property in an already saturated market - thus further exacerbating the effects of a burst property "bubble" and the "negative equity" phenomenon. In addition, mass evictions force a large number of people to become homeless and dependent on the state for housing and social security support. Those campaigning against such economic evictions rightly argue that the evictions simply socialise the costs of the banks' greed and lay these costs on the public purse. The evictions, they argue, achieve nothing but higher social security costs for the government, more unsold assets for the banks, whilst exacerbating the housing surplus and creating a great deal of human misery. Apart from the immorality of the actions, anti-eviction campaigners correctly claim that it is an economically stupid policy to evict defaulting mortgage holders. In fact, we all know that such evictions are a form of spiteful punishment against those who fail to obey the rules of capitalism. Evictions rarely have anything to do with recovering losses.

A protest group may also need to discuss the economic "sustainability" of a disputed activity in terms of cost and benefit, and define the complex economic costs of damage, for instance, to an environmental resource, such as a river or forest, as part of a disputed development. Conversely, a protest group also needs to fully understand the economic benefits of some developments and comprehend the nuanced relationship between poverty and development, which argues that poverty retards economic development, and rather than providing cheap labour, it merely produces impoverished non-consumers.

In any case, a protest group needs to have a thorough understanding of all the economic arguments, including those being used by the opposing authority. The group's researchers need to be sure that the numbers used by the authorities are correct and based on reasonable assumptions. Any disparities detected in the economic arguments need proper examination and need to be fully documented and cross-referenced. If necessary, a protest researcher can use their legal right to access information to obtain source documentation for the calculations and assumptions being used by an authority in their economic assertions.

7.3.2.4 Environmental Impacts: There is a wealth of environmental law in most Western nations these days, especially in Europe, where there is now a host of EU environmental regulations and directives. National laws in most Western nations (including in the EU, where EU directives are transcribed into national law) provide some reasonable basis for justifying most environmental protest campaigns. However, there are still plenty of cases where national laws are interpreted in a partial way and still more cases where an environmental issue is not well covered legally at any level.

There are also those cases where nobody actually knows what the environmental impact of a development might be. In this latter instance, the campaign group is put in the difficult position of having to carry out independent research into the probable outcomes and the levels of risk of an environmentally sensitive development.

In any of the above scenarios, the opposing authority and/or developer will almost certainly have made a "best case" evaluation of the development. In this case, it is the role of the campaign group to research the historical and contemporary facts of the case and also to adopt a "worse case" evaluation of a development. Most jurisdictions demand a so-called independent "Environmental Impact Assessment". The resulting document provides a good starting point for a protest group to build a case against a damaging development.

The GM experiment, a cautionary tale: The protest movement against GM crops and foods demonstrates the above principles. The large GM interests, with the support of various parts of the US government, made the case that their products were safe from both a health and an environmental point of view. The pro-GM lobbyists argued that they would reduce pesticide use, increase yields per hectare and would not interfere with other forms of agriculture or impact other species. They provided scant documentation to demonstrate any of these assertions and in the spirit of self-regulation (which means no regulation), a lot of business-friendly Western governments allowed this behaviour to proceed with few questions asked.

After two decades, the global GM experiment is nearly over. We now know that some or all GM food products cause various health problems, including increased cancer incidents. We know that GM production levels are not higher than conventional or organic methods. We also know that herbicide application rates rose dramatically, rather than declined as claimed by the GM companies. This has had dramatic impacts on other plant and animal species and water ecologies, and has given rise to well-documented and serious human health problems, from grown adults to the unborn.

The effect of GM products on the general ecology and agriculture has been quite disturbing with the evolution of monster weeds which are resistant to conventional herbicide control, thus requiring a dramatic escalation in the toxicity of the herbicides being used to contain them, including the recent adoption of "Agent Orange" known as a cause of gross birth defects in humans.

Other non-GM farmers (conventional and organic) have been forced out of business by GM activity contaminating their land and seed. Now, the GM industry is fighting a rearguard action to try to stop GM food labelling in the USA by pouring millions into pro-GM advertising to persuade voters to vote down state resolutions to oblige GM food to be labelled as such. The entire situation is a complete disaster for the environment, for public health and for trust in the food industry. Despite the marketing hype, GM food products are now effectively banned in Europe.

In this example, we have a large corporate group supported by corrupt or ignorant political classes, manipulating a spineless regulatory authority in the US (the FDA) into abandoning the central pillar of the "precautionary principle". And this was done for the sake of corporate profits for the few at the cost of the health of the general public, the defence of the wider environment and the integrity of the food safety and good farming practice.

Alas, when the GM industry started to introduce commercialised GM seed into the public domain, protest groups were entirely unprepared to challenge the assertions of the GM lobby. To this day many protest groups are still unable to grasp the full implications of a development which seeks to patent the means of production of food.

Many environmental protest groups find the issues around GM hard to understand because they have failed to inform themselves, "It's all so terribly complicated and, after all, a GM corn looks pretty similar to a conventional one." seems the common misconception. Many campaigners who normally get animated about the loss of a forest and its biodiversity were unable to comprehend a technology that could potentially reduce global biodiversity on an industrial scale. They fell into the gentle PR traps set by the GM lobbyists because they failed to challenge the scientific assertions being made and to keep up with the developments and contrarian research that was taking place.

This is a salutary tale when it comes to thoroughly researching a potential issue because, at the time, there were plenty of well-qualified dissenting scientists warning of the risks of GM. These experts were shouted down, isolated, fired, dismissed and vilified by the GM lobby and largely ignored and misunderstood by many badly informed, nay ignorant, green campaigners of the time.

The result of this lack of proper preparation by the green movement is that the GM industry "stole a march" on the campaigners. 30 years on and the green movement is still (yes still) trying to get to grips with GM development and all the lies that surround it.

Specialist research: Environmental science is a highly complex and nuanced subject and it is quite likely that a campaign group will need the help of specialist researchers.

Large corporate entities and government authorities, when dealing with complex scientific material in the public domain, love to "simplify" the issues and make trite, easy-to-believe statements to keep the public quiet. For instance, with the contaminated water case mentioned earlier, government scientists were quick to point out that "Water contaminated by bacteria can be treated with chlorine and will be 100% free of bacteria". Sounds great, a silver bullet to cure all ills. Sadly, it belies the scientific reality that the reaction between chlorine and organically contaminated water produces chemicals called THMs as a by-product of the chlorination. These are just one of a group of dangerous carcinogenic organohalides. So no, indeed the water won't have (most) bacteria anymore, but it may well be carcinogenic after treatment. So if the bugs don't get you, the toxins will!

Thus, it should be clear from these examples that, when researching environmental issues, it is vital to understand the nuances, have the full facts, be completely thorough and deliver the information in an unambiguous way. Knowledge is the enemy of deceit.

7.3.2.5 Social implications: Authorities tend to play down negative social implications and exaggerate positive social implications. So, typically, we find governments telling us that they are "getting record numbers of people into employment" without telling us that half of them work for nothing and the rest work for a pittance. The use of this so-called "weasel" language is popular amongst the political classes when trying to promote some draconian hidden agenda such as "we are short of cheap labour to staff our expensive residences or work as serfs on our country estates." This gets dressed up as "the necessary liberalisation of the labour market".

Research into social impacts is probably one of the more difficult areas to be absolutely definitive about, and carrying out social research can be challenging, especially in the context of a protest against something which hasn't yet happened - a government proposal, for instance. On the other hand, we can always adopt a heuristic approach. History provides us with plenty of well-documented examples of the social impacts of various government or corporate "initiatives". In a protest against a coming war, we know, for example, that there is very rarely (never) a war where civilians are *not* the main victims. We can even extrapolate the levels of civilian deaths and casualties resulting from a certain type of military campaign. Urban warfare costs much civilian human misery. Tactical military actions against another military tend to incur fewer civilian losses. Military strategists make these calculations all the time. An anti-war campaigner can also make such projections based on historical precedents and the current situation.

In other circumstances we can easily defend a more causal-mechanistic evaluation of social impacts. For instance, it is self-evident that reducing or freezing the minimum wage is going to increase child poverty. Why? This happens simply because such a policy takes money away from poorer communities where child poverty is a dominant feature and is constantly looming over every family that exists on a fragile domestic economy. We can demonstrate this causally and we can prove it heuristically based on many historical examples of similar actions. We can even determine the number of families and children affected by a particular level of poverty and the social security costs to the state in providing emergency social services to them. We can also accurately estimate the damage to economic activity caused by such a policy and make accurate predictions as to how it will affect commodity prices, the housing market and even demographic changes. Thus, a campaign against such a policy should research and investigate such projections as part of the process of developing a detailed and coherent position for their campaign.

Social impacts are obviously an important part of most protest campaigns. Environmental campaigns frequently have a strong social element, such as loss of amenity, degradation in living conditions, deterioration in health standards, well-being, economic security, etc. Campaigns against the use of military force or other forms of forced occupation clearly have an abundant social content. Plainly, changes in working conditions, pay or social security conditions have direct social impacts, as do alterations in consumers', workers' and other civil and human rights.

In any campaign it is vital to emphasise the social impacts of the activity being protested against. Some elements of the public would be shocked by a reduction in minimum wages from a moral point of view and sympathise with the victims. Others will be outraged that it simply moves the cost of dependency from abusive employers onto the long-suffering taxpaying public (them). These two views are equally true and it is a protest group's responsibility to appeal to all possible views of the general public, regardless of what affects their sensibilities most. And this is the most important reason for good, detailed and reliable research.

7.3.2.6 Unintended consequences: The idea of "unintended consequences" is an interesting and important concept. It is important in protest campaign planning because it often provides very powerful arguments against a particular unpopular initiative or act by an authority. Unintended consequences are grouped into three types:

- A positive, unexpected benefit (usually referred to as luck, serendipity or a windfall). We are not so interested in these.

- A negative, unexpected detrimental effect which occurs simultaneously with the desired effect of a plan. For instance, while irrigation schemes provide people with water for agriculture, they can increase fatal waterborne diseases. Such events are moderately interesting to a campaign planner, but don't deliver a coup de grace and may be somewhat too nuanced to deliver a clear message.

- A perverse effect contrary to what was originally intended when a planned solution actually makes a problem worse. This has been dubbed the 'cobra effect', as a result of a British policy in colonial

India offering a bounty for killing cobras. The policy caused people to breed cobras especially to pick up the reward. These types of results are very useful in protest campaigns because they illustrate the wrongness of the initiative and the intense stupidity of the authority in their lack of foresight.

Clearly, it's important when evaluating a protest issue that the subject is evaluated in terms of possible unintended consequences which the authority have not considered or has not publicized

Taking a contemporary example: in the UK the idea of sub-contracting social services administrative work to private contractors looks like a really clever economy - on paper. The cost to process an applicant is fixed and reduced, the processing is efficient and streamlined, the automated systems and other infrastructure are owned and run by the contractor, and the government can simply sit back and devise incentives to offer to the private contractors. They can (and did) create incentives to the contractors to be very stringent in their evaluation of social security applicants by paying a premium to the contractor for detecting "those abusing the system".

The unintended consequences of such a policy should be fairly obvious from the inception to anyone with any understanding of human nature, but, plainly, they weren't to the best and brightest in the British government. Firstly, to achieve the maximum throughput of applicants for the minimum cost per applicant the contractors skimped on time per applicant. This in turn, lead to dramatic increases in very expensive legal appeals by wrongly assessed applicants and a huge cost to the exchequer.

In a similar vein, the financial incentives to detect disability allowance "abusers" drove the contractors to dramatically increase the rejection rates of disabled people. It wasn't long before completely absurd situations developed and began to make their way into the press; an elderly applicant lying in his hospital bed was called on his mobile by the social services contractor to attend a "work placement course" immediately. This was despite his being registered as critically ill and needing a quadruple bypass. Even worse and more bizarre cases saw huge numbers of patients with degenerative disorders, such as multiple sclerosis and Alzheimer's disease being classified as "available for productive employment" within 6 months after being reassessed by social security contractors "evaluating" their fitness.

Clearly, these systemic privatisations were the cause of these very costly and hurtful aberrations. Actually, anyone with an ounce of imagination could have predicted these "unexpected" outcomes in advance. But "government" and "imagination" don't seem to mix, somehow.

For the protest campaign planner, information of this kind is vital and insightful. It can make or break a campaign. Even those members of the public who are not immediately that sympathetic to the old, the unemployed, the homeless or the disabled may well become animated when they realise that idiotic, self-serving or malicious government policies have cost the taxpayer hundreds of millions instead of reducing costs, and the cash benefits have probably largely filled the coffers of political allies of the government in the private sector.

Thus, a campaign planner can use this kind of information to widen the appeal of a campaign. This really optimises the damage done to the politicians and bureaucrats that were responsible and it highlights the private contractors' disgraceful behaviour. Such errors can be emphasised to the point where a well-orchestrated campaign can force an enquiry, resignations and even a reversal of policy.

One of the simplest ways of discovering if such unintended consequences have actually happened or could happen is to apply some simple "game theory" to the question.

In the example above, simply asking some basic "what if" questions would have elicited a fairly clear understanding of the very likely unintended consequences. For example:

-   Q. What happens when you incentivise a profit-oriented company with processing applications with a fixed price per application?

    A. Volumes will tend to rise to maximise profit and quality will tend to fall.

-   Q. What happens if applicant processing quality falls and more applicants are rejected in error?

    A. Applicants will feel cheated and demand an appeal or take legal action against the authority.

-   Q. What happens when you incentivise the rejection of applicants by the same company by paying a premium for rejected applicants?

    A. Applicant rejections will tend to rise as a percentage of the total number in order to increase profit yield.

-   Q. What happens when you incentivise the same company to reduce the number of disabled people receiving social security benefit?

A. The company will find large groups of disabled benefit recipients that it can declare "able to work" in order to receive the cash incentive, which in turn will tend to reduce the quality of the contractor's assessments and increase the number of apparently miraculous recoveries amongst the disabled population and cause costly legal appeals.

These types of examinations of a protest case should always be conducted as an initial way of discovering unintended consequences. They may prove to be very powerful.

7.3.2.7 Political Issues: All protest campaigns have political motives and cause political outcomes, one way or another. Political consequences may be within a corporate structure or in a government authority. There are various aspects regarding the political context of a protest action which need to be researched and understood as part of the campaign preparation.

Political motivation of an authority: Firstly, we have to examine the political attitudes and motivation of the target authority. The answers to some basic questions can have an important influence on further research and on planning which parts of an authority to target in a protest. For instance, these are some salient questions one might ask about the political stance of the target authority:

• Who in the target authority is responsible for managing those issues which the protest group is targeting? For example, if the protest is about an environmental problem, who in the government is responsible for causing or allowing this problem. It is important to have the names, positions and connections of the officials and politicians involved.

• What are the political consequences for the responsible persons if they are defeated by the protest? Resignation? Demotion? Ignominy? Hurt pride? Embarrassment? In other words, what is at stake? The answer to this question will determine the extent to which those responsible will struggle to defeat the protest. How much are those responsible willing to defend the core issue from the negative effects of a protest campaign? Not that important? Vital interests at stake? To the death?

• What are the main motivations for the political support for the contentious issue? Do the officials or politicians gain materially by defending their position? Does it serve their political ambitions? Are the officials or politicians afraid of the consequences if they do not defend their position and if so, why? Are politicians and officials just talking tough to the public to show who's in control or do they really believe in their position, or are they just closing ranks? Is their position being taken because they are trading favours with a 3rd party? Would losing the conflict cause economic loss to the organisation?

Political context of a protest: Secondly, we need to turn our attention to the political context of the protest issues in terms of the general public. Some relevant questions include:

• How high on the public political agenda is the core protest issue?

• What is the political mood of the public? Apathetic? Antagonistic to the responsible authority? Sympathetic to the authority? Spoiling for a fight with the authority?

• What political issues are high on the public agenda? Does the campaign issue fit within the public agenda?

• Is the public antagonistic to protest campaigns in general or to certain protest campaigns?

• What political approach would be most effective in motivating the public to support the protest campaign?

• What characterises the public that is targeted by the protest campaign? Are they of a particular socio-economic group? What are their traditional political affiliations? Do these political attitudes coincide with any of the objectives of the protest campaign? Can the campaign be reframed to appeal to this target group?

• Are there sections of the general public that are likely to vehemently oppose the protest campaign? If so, how? How can they be managed or converted?

• Are there political parties likely to support the protest campaign? Are these political parties that a protest group would be happy to be associated with? Would their support alienate other sectors of the general public?

Political research is important to a campaign planner and may alter the approach taken to a protest campaign. Depending on the results of this research, a protest campaign planner may soften the approach to a political establishment whilst taking a tougher position with a sympathetic general public, or vice versa. The emphasis of the campaign may be altered to reflect weaknesses in the target authority's political position or to optimise public support for the campaign by focusing the campaign on a particular context, such as political corruption, incompetence etc. All of these options can be evaluated only when the protest group has a good picture of the political landscape.

7.3.3 Researching the Opposition

The following schematic shows the most essential areas of opponent-based campaign research:

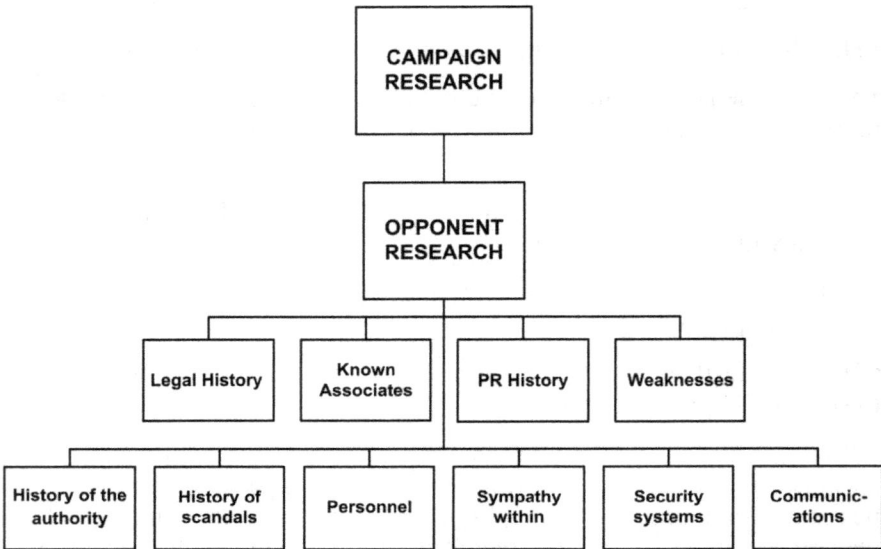

```
                    ┌─────────────┐
                    │  CAMPAIGN   │
                    │  RESEARCH   │
                    └──────┬──────┘
                           │
                    ┌──────┴──────┐
                    │  OPPONENT   │
                    │  RESEARCH   │
                    └──────┬──────┘
```

Legal History	Known Associates	PR History	Weaknesses

History of the authority	History of scandals	Personnel	Sympathy within	Security systems	Communic-ations

It's vital in a protest campaign to know as much about the target authority as possible. We can be sure that the authority will use its power and resources to gather as much information as possible about the organisers of a protest campaign. They will certainly use this information to mount a defence, to discredit, infiltrate and divide a protest group and to spread disinformation about it.

The only strategy to deal with this is to be as efficient (or more efficient, if possible) as the authorities at mining and gathering intelligence on the target organisation. This can then be used in the course of the protest campaign to attack the authority and deflect attacks on the protest campaign.

Here are some areas which should be researched and which may yield useful information:

- History of the authority or company
- Legal History of the authority or company
- History of scandals
- Known Associates

- Personnel
- PR History - Previous public statements
- Sympathisers within
- Weaknesses
- Security Systems
- Communications

We will now examine each of these areas of research in more detail:

7.3.3.1 The History of an Authority or Company: A useful insight may be gained into the attitudes of an authority by understanding its history, its management structure and financial status or budget. If it's a company, its origins, current ownership and relationships with other companies may be very revealing.

The following questions will be relevant:

• When was the organisation founded? In the case of a company, when was it registered and what kind of company is it? What is the ownership history of the company?

• What is the management structure and who are the key players in the organisation? What are their backgrounds? What are their relationships with other parts of government or other businesses?

• What is the budget of the organisation? In the case of a company, what is its capital and how is it financed (private, public, etc.), what is its annual turnover?

• What are the activities of the organisation? If it is a government department, semi-state or quango, what are its terms of reference? If it is a company, what are its registered business activities?

• What relationships exist between the target organisation and other organisations? In the case of a government department, are there close links with semi-state bodies or other government departments? Are there strong commercial links with private business? In the case of a company, are there subsidiaries, is it a subsidiary, are there cross-investments or are holding companies involved? The researcher needs to define these relationships in detail.

• In the case of a company, does the company make political donations? What are the political affiliations of the company's directors?

Having completed this research, a protest group should have a clearer picture of how the target organisation came into being, who is running it and how it relates to other organisations. With luck, the researcher may even have revealed some interesting nuggets of information which may be useful in a protest campaign, such as directors with interests in tax havens or government department heads with dodgy corporate friends and lavish lifestyles.

7.3.3.2 The Legal History of an Authority or Company: It's important to build up a picture of an authority or company in terms of its legal history. It may be that they have quite an extensive history of litigation and this needs to be documented at least in a headline form. Government departments will almost certainly have a colourful background and this information, properly collated and presented, can be very powerful in developing a position for the protest campaign and for communications with the press. The following are relevant questions:

• Has the organisation taken legal actions against similar protest groups in the past? What were the outcomes and costs of these prosecutions?

• Has the target organisation been involved in any previous litigation which reflects badly upon it? For example, has the company or government agency lost any litigation; was it found guilty of any form of abusive behaviour? A list of the cases and outcomes will be valuable.

• Has the organisation been guilty of using bullying legal behaviour? For example, has the government department or the company used its power to attack those who are perceived to be weaker than they? For example, banks constantly chase and persecute defaulting private customers, many of whom are old, poor and weak. Government departments, the courts and the police often take draconian measures against those unable to defend themselves, such as the sick, unemployed or disabled. If so, protest groups should find and document examples of these legal actions.

Legal advisors: It may be useful for a protest group to know something about the authority's legal personnel, just in case a legal conflict develops during the campaign. What kind of legal opponents will the protesters be dealing with and how are they likely to behave? Having a wealth of accurate information about these lawyers may be helpful in undermining their probity. Here are some typical questions to lead the research:

• Does the authority employ their own legal staff and/or use external advisors?

• What are the identities of these advisors and what are their legal backgrounds? For example, all legal firms (and individual specialists) have a history. They may have represented some notorious villains or defended companies against claims for abuse or negligence, be involved in providing advice on dodgy tax evasion structures or have any number of undesirable clients.

• Have any of the target organisation's legal staff or their legal firm's staff been involved in or publicly accused of any wrong-doing? What does the internet and their social media profiles reveal about them: LinkedIn, Facebook, Twitter, etc.?

• Does any of the target organisation or their legal firm's staff have any political connections or other business dealings, share holdings, directorships? Are there any possible conflicts of interest?

7.3.3.3 History of Scandals: Every authority and company has some skeletons in its cupboard somewhere. It might be a case of discrimination, complaints from customers or the public, an abusive management, a discredited executive, a disgruntled employee blowing the whistle, a breakdown in industrial relations, tax avoidance, an environmental accident or a myriad of other possibilities. Knowing this history of scandals is essential to a protest campaign. One can be certain that the target authority will be busy building up a dossier of every childish student prank recorded against the campaign organisers since they were infants. In the name of self-defence the campaign group needs to be prepared to do exactly the same thing with regards to the target authority.

Large organisations have no collective memory about their past crimes or scandals. Every new generation starts with a clean sheet. This attitude to the past can be useful to a campaign organiser because over the years all organisations build up a litany of often horrendous scandals of all kinds that they tend not to remember. Take Monsanto, for example, that bright, shiny agrochemical corporation that was not long ago responsible for the misery of millions of Vietnamese, whose babies are still being born with birth defects to this day, caused by Monsanto's "Agent Orange" herbicide. Or take BASF, that respectable manufacturer of all things plastic, which only a few decades ago joined forces with IG Farben to develop and manufacture the chemical Zyklon B, used to murder millions of innocent civilians in Nazi Germany's gas chambers.

Governments are frequently scandal-ridden, and though they often try to cover up their misbehaviour, they rarely get away with it. Take, for instance, the case of the atrocities, torture and collective punishments committed by the British army against civilians in Kenya during the Mau Mau insurgency against British colonial rule in the 1950s, or the British and American use of torture in Iraq and Afghanistan in recent years. The litany of dishonour for most government is enormous and damning.

If a protest group knows about the past crimes of an authority, it can use this information both to defend the campaign from an authority's dirty tricks (personal attacks on campaign organisers being a favourite tactic) and also to launch swinging counter-attacks against the authority and its management. The campaign organiser may have stolen a policeman's helmet or got fined a few quid for smoking hash at university, but at least he didn't turn a blind eye to the long-term and widespread sexual bullying and abuse in his government department or to the deliberate use of illegal detention or torture. He also didn't look the other way when 20,000 tonnes of contaminated water wiped out 30 km of pristine trout stream. And, indeed, our campaign organisers were probably never found guilty of using privileged information to buy land that was about to be rezoned for building in order to enrich themselves.

In the current GM debate it is pretty difficult for anyone to believe that Monsanto is a "responsible member of the corporate community", when the very same company knew in advance that Agent Orange caused birth defects in mammals, but still sold thousands of tonnes of it to the American Air Force to spray on occupied Vietnamese villages. Was that "responsible", one might ask? The scandals of the pasts of these companies can have a dramatic impact on the way the public views them today, and the same goes for government authorities. When the British military talks of its honourable past, compare and contrast that to that same "honourable" British army that opened fire on, and killed, unarmed civilians in the streets of Derry or Amritsar, or the force that tortured prisoners by hanging them upside down in a bath of water in Baghdad or Belfast. Is that "honourable"?

Such counter-attacks from the protest group need to be fairly vicious. Anything less will just generate revenge attacks and be seen as a sign of weakness. Hopefully, such tactics aren't necessary very often. Nonetheless, governments and corporations are increasingly reduced to using various underhand methods against protesters, such as spreading disinformation. This needs an effective response and therefore campaign organisers need good quality information about the target authority's own scandals.

Timing is important when planning mud-slinging attacks on a target authority. There is no point trying to dig out information about scandals when the campaign group itself is actually being attacked by an authority. The delay in response will be too great. The management of a protest needs to have its ammunition ready at the beginning of the campaign as a form of insurance against what might happen later in the protest action. The information needs to be factual, fully documented and verifiable. Scandals can be categorised and packaged, ready to use. For instance, the following categories may be used: financial scandals, environmental scandals, conflicts of interest, tax scandals, employee abuse, sexual scandals, human rights scandals, criminal acts and cover-ups. There are more such categories. Each scandal should be written in a summary form, ready to send to the press with an appropriate "wrapper" to put the scandal in context, as and when the need arises.

Here are some ideas as to the kind of research to carry out:

• Have any of the authority's management team or their immediate family been convicted of a criminal offence at any time in the past? What are the details?

• Do any of the authority's management team or their immediate family have political connections? Are they donors to any political party or have relationships with any past or present politicians? Are there any possible conflicts of interest?

• Have any of the authority's management team or their immediate family been implicated in or investigated for any form of fraud, tax evasion or corruption, whether proven or not?

• Has the authority been the subject of any scandal which did not involve litigation? This could include employee abuse, breaches of health and safety rules, breaches of workers rights, environmental incidents, expenses or tax frauds, discrimination (sexual, racial, religious, ageism, or political). Define the details.

7.3.3.4 Known Associates: All authorities have formal and informal alliances with other organisations. Chief executives may rub shoulders with other executives, chief constables, government department heads, cabinet ministers and other associates with whom they communicate either officially or informally. Some may be members of the same club, the same religious group or the same political party. They may live in the same village or even the same street. Whatever the association, it's important to understand the connections between these members of the target authority and the outside world.

This kind of research is difficult, but it can prove very useful in a protest campaign. In the real world things often happen because someone who knows someone else gets a favour. It might be a local businessman getting a favour from a local councillor, or a government minister rubber-stamping a grant application for an old school pal or, indeed, it might be having a protest leader arrested, their credit rating slashed or their kids refused a place in the local school. Unfortunately, these shenanigans of nepotism, corruption and dirty tricks happen all the time, normally "under the radar" of any scrutiny by the general public.

Unofficial actions by an authority are very often the result of informal relationships with known associates and therefore, building up a picture of the social, professional and business connections of key members of the target authority is important. A simple and useful way of demonstrating these relationships is to use a sociogram.

Here is a very simple example. Guess what's going on here! Real sociograms are usually much larger, more complex and often more sinister.

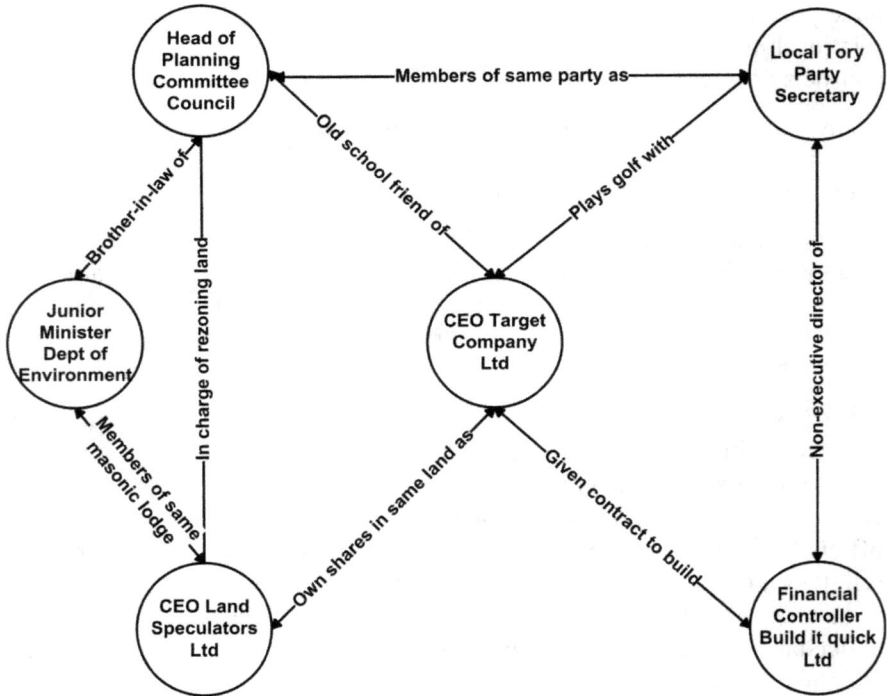

7.3.3.5 Personnel: As with external relations of a target authority, it is useful for a protest group to have a good understanding of the human resources employed within the authority.

Organisational structure: Firstly, a group needs to understand and document the relevant parts of the organisational structure of an authority. Very often authorities hide behind a bewildering organisational structure, which seems entirely opaque to the general public. How many times have we complained of being passed from one person to another when we are trying to make a complaint or have some problem resolved? Authorities can be particularly obtuse when it comes to fulfilling their duties or promises or handling public complaints, but extremely efficient when it comes to controlling or extracting money from us! Their organisational structure reflects this propensity.

The managements of large organisations very often use defensive "layers" of personnel to insulate themselves from the public. Try, for example, complaining to a utility company about your service or bill. You will almost certainly spend some unhappy hours on the phone, talking to a completely disinterested, poorly-paid call-centre operative in some far away land, whilst being deliberately antagonised by endless renderings of a very ancient and crackly recording of Greensleeves. You know that if you could just speak to the accounts manager, you could get the thing sorted out in 2 minutes, but no, you have to be tortured on the rack of customer services for hours over several days or weeks, just to get them to correct the results of their own incompetence. Sometimes, dealing with large organisations can become a complete Catch 22 situation, as you are told that you cannot make a complaint because you haven't got an incident number and you can't get a number until you lodge a complaint!

Why is this relevant to a protest campaign? And what can we do to remove or circumvent organisational barriers? Well, very often protests originate as a result of the failings of a government agency or company to fulfil their duties or behave in a reasonable way. Escalation often takes place because the offended party is unable to penetrate the protective layers of human handlers and speak with real decision-makers. We simply don't know who or where these decision-makers are. So, in any protest it is very useful to know how an authority's organisation hangs together. If a dispute escalates into a protest it is also very helpful to know exactly who needs to be attacked by the protest. There is really no point blaming the boy or girl on the end of the phone in a call centre.

It is also important to know who works for whom. If, for example, we are receiving poor treatment at the hands of some bureaucrat it is handy to know who his or her boss is and who are the boss' superiors. With this information we can then plot ways to neutralise the offending agent by, for instance, setting them up in compromising situations and then reporting this to their bosses.

Getting information about an organisation's management structure should be relatively easy. Many authorities and companies actively provide this information, but usually without names or contact information. Documenting such a structure is a relatively simple matter, using an organisational diagram such as the one shown below.

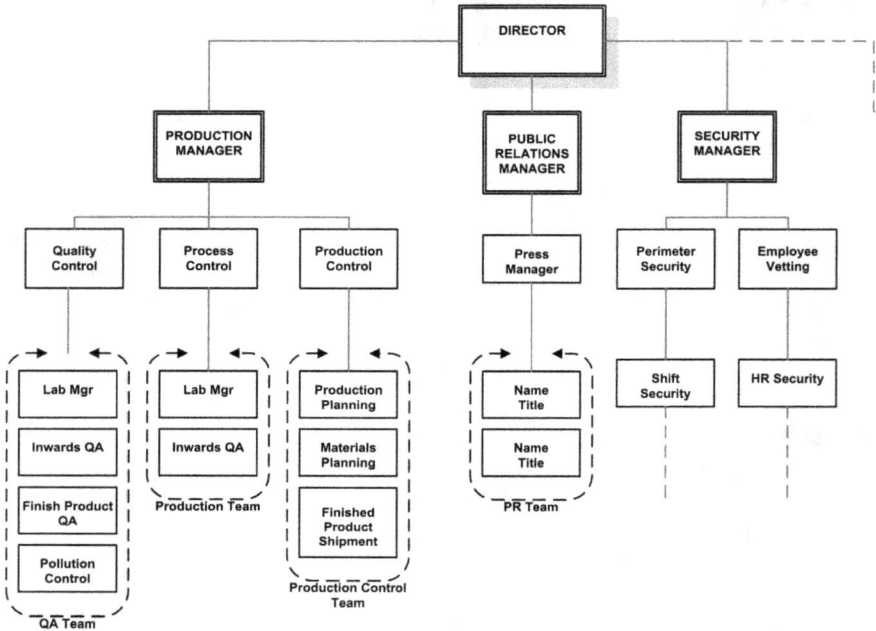

Human resource information: The next part in the research of an organisation's personnel is much more difficult and calls for a degree of guile and patience, or, better still, an insider to spy for the protest group. This involves gathering information on key personnel within the authority or company. But why would a protest group researcher be interested in an authority's personnel? How could this be useful to a protest movement?

As we discussed in the section on "Known Associates", the personalities of the staff and their relationships in the authority may be important to the protest campaign. For example, it may be that there are sympathisers within the authority and the protest group needs to identify them. It may also be that the protest organisers have friends or family within the authority who could be persuaded to use their position to aid the protest campaign, one way or another. In any case, the protest group needs to "open a file" on anyone that is in anyway connected with the issues or the campaign, and gather as much information as possible on these individuals.

The following information should be collected as a bare minimum:

- Name
- Gender
- Age
- Qualification
- Position
- Time in position
- Anything interesting (criminal convictions, past scandals)
- Known connections of interest (inside and outside the authority or company, political connections, etc.)

Conflict mapping: The subject of internal conflict is another area where it is useful to gather information about a target authority. This involves finding out which parts of the organisation or which individuals are sympathetic or antagonistic to other individuals or groups within the authority. For this kind of detailed knowledge a protest group needs to infiltrate the organisation and to have someone on the inside long enough to gather this sort of information.

Mapping relationships is done using a "conflict diagram". These diagrams show contacts, conflicts, alliances, broken connections and influences. Here is a simple example:

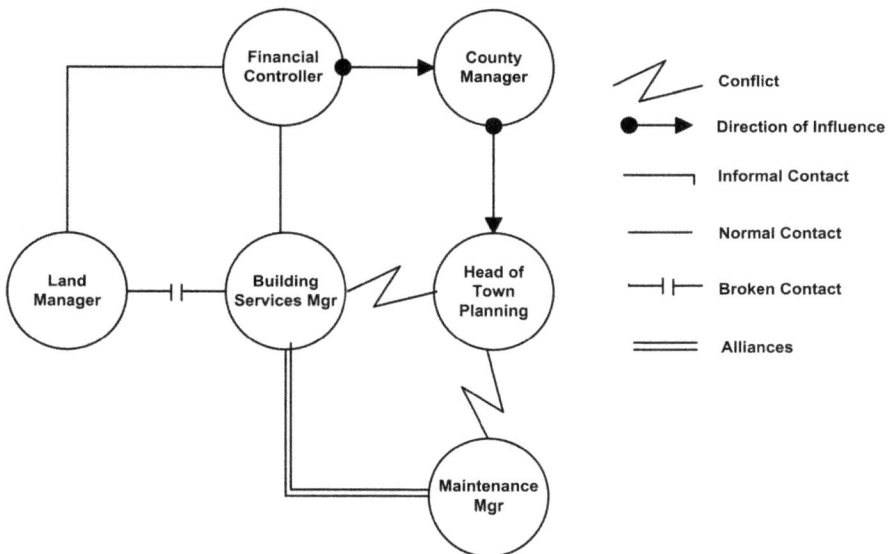

Understanding the relationships within a target organisation helps a protest group to engineer and inflate conflicts in strategic parts of the target at appropriate moments. As the biblical adage says: "a house divided against itself cannot stand." And thus, uncovering existing conflicts and other fragile relationships offers opportunities to create or exploit damaging rifts within a target organisation.

7.3.3.6 PR History - Previous Public Statements: Large organisations make many public statements over the years and they tend to have a very short memory regarding their past statements. These previous public statements can often come back to haunt them. It is very definitely worth carrying out a thorough search of the newspaper archives and the internet to gather references to all the authority or company press releases, going back as many years as possible, and sort them by content (economic, environment, human rights, labour relations, etc.).

A protest campaign can gain some good PR leverage at appropriate moments by dredging up some inappropriate or embarrassing press releases that directly contradict the organisation's present stance or which put the organisation in a bad light, makes it look heartless, hypocritical, untrustworthy or corrupt.

7.3.3.7 Sympathisers Within: Having sympathisers within a target authority is immensely useful. They can spy on the organisation on behalf of a protest group, take copies of incriminating documents, record conversations and help in any sabotage efforts. They may also be able to act as provocateurs, triggering off unwise actions by the authority. Equally, they may even be able to influence a target authority to be sympathetic to the protest objectives.

The only way to know if the protest group has any sympathisers is to identify their personnel and sift through their names, looking for friends or family etc. Another alternative is to plant a member of the protest group within the organisation. This is more difficult and time-consuming, of course, but not impossible. We will deal with the practicalities of infiltration in a later chapter (under "Subversion of Authority").

7.3.3.8 Weaknesses: All government or corporate organisations have their own particular set of weaknesses, and it's important for campaigners to fully understand and exploit these as necessary.

For example, an authority may suffer from poor labour relations, weak internal communications, a shortage of funding, conflicts of internal management, bad customer relationships, shoddy planning, old or inflexible work practices, lack of investment, substandard corporate PR management or inadequate corporate security, etc. etc.

A protest group needs to evaluate and define the weaknesses of a target organisation as part of the strategic planning of its protest campaign; to see how these weaknesses may be exploited. For instance, if an organisation has poor labour relations, this flaw can be exploited by recruiting disgruntled employees to spy on the organisation from within and provide useful material for the protest group. Similarly, mediocre internal communications can be exploited to trigger contradictory behaviour from different parts of the organisation, thus discrediting the organisation in the public eye. Poor security may provide opportunities for the copying and leaking of embarrassing documents, such as incriminating emails or memos. An unprofessional PR management provides opportunities to attack an organisation publicly, quickly and by surprise, in "hit and run" exercises designed to smear or discredit them.

7.3.3.9 Security Systems: Modern organisations have multi-faceted security systems that manage the following areas:

- Physical security of property and equipment
- Security of data and systems (IT security)
- Security of personnel
- Security of communications
- Document security
- Counterintelligence

It is important for a protest group to a have a fair understanding of the security systems within a target organisation. Some of this can be established by observation from outside, but in general this is work for an insider. One fast way to get an insider into a position of trust quickly is via the security department itself or via a trusted department, such as an IT department. Fortunately, both security and IT are activities that many executives foolishly believe they can safely contract out to perfect strangers, who then are given super-user passwords and the keys to the front door! Amazingly, contract cleaners also share many such privileges. So, getting someone on the inside isn't as hard as it may seem.

Understanding (or, better still, infiltrating) the security of a target organisation is immensely useful to a protest organisation. Access to physical paperwork, network or mail servers provides a wealth of confidential documents which may relate to a protest or which may be incriminating or embarrassing to a target authority.

Understanding the physical security systems of an authority provides an insight into areas where sabotage may be possible and effective or where physical blockades may be placed.

Access to communications systems provides ample possibilities for the placing of surveillance devices on voice and email systems, and even the installation of spyware, should it be necessary. The next section elaborates on this.

7.3.3.10 Communications: Tapping or otherwise monitoring the communications of a target organisation is not an easy feat, although in recent years the availability of phone and email tapping technology has increased dramatically. Thankfully, many government authorities are fairly amateurish and undisciplined when it comes to communications security. Recent incidents have shown how easy it is to get hold of mobile numbers for the British prime minister and the director of MI6 (military intelligence in the UK), and to tap mobile phone voicemails.

Gathering information on a target authority's communications may provide a huge source of high quality intelligence for a protest group. Even if the contents of calls cannot be found, telephone records and email contact lists can be useful. This so-called metadata allows a protest researcher to show connections between individuals in an authority and their "known associates".

In a similar vein, social networks, and especially professional networks like LinkedIn, make finding distant connections between a target and their contacts very simple. Setting up false identities in such social / professional networking systems is quite easy and requesting connections with members of a target authority or their associates is really straightforward and can be made very plausible, with a little imagination.

7.4 Defining Ideal Outcomes. What can be realistically achieved?

It is important that acts of protest or civil disobedience have realistic, well-defined objectives. A protest against a planning proposal for a nuclear power station can only hope to overturn the plan to construct that particular power station although success in such a venture may impact other similar plans. However, it is important to confine the protest objectives to what can be reasonably achieved by a particular protest action, rather than having more ambitious plans than there are resources to manage. The adage "he who fights and runs away, lives to fight another day" is the keynote. One small victory is worth ten big failures!

To define "Ideal Outcomes", we need again to be analytical about what can be achieved. In the planning example, a particular protest group may only have the resources to force a legal review. Thus, it may well be necessary to divide up a problem into separate components to achieve anything at all. In this example, the ultimate "ideal outcome" may be to have the entire plan abandoned, but first it may be necessary to have it delayed in order to buy time, for instance. In that case, a protest organiser has to focus the group's energy on the short-term objective of gaining a delay to the project, whilst simultaneously planning the main objective of total abandonment of the entire plan, or getting another group to work on that.

So, in our example of the nuclear reactor protest, the definition of the "ideal outcome" might read: "To force the delay of the planning application for this nuclear reactor for at least 6 months, as a means to allow time to prepare a secondary campaign to force the plan's complete abandonment". This objective is clear and realistic.

7.5 Planning Protests: Incentives and Disincentives

Protests work when they motivate authorities to alter their behaviour. Like most other human institutions, all authorities, even the most liberal, are conservative about changing course. In general, attempts at persuasion by protesters are rarely enough to bring about any change. We almost always need to create a strong incentive to actually force change.

An incentive grants a reward to those that act in a desired way. A disincentive punishes those that behave in an undesirable way. All protest actions should use systems of incentives and disincentives to persuade an authority to alter its behaviour. Picking the right incentives and disincentives is critical to an effective protest. The entire issue revolves around cost and benefit. To be effective, a protest needs to increase the cost to an authority adhering to its plans, up to a point where the costs of proceeding with the plans exceed the benefits of the plans to the authority. Costs may be economic, social or political, or all three.

For example, a protest against an environmental crime, such as fracking, being carried out by a corporation and permitted by a government, has several opportunities to identify and use various forms of motivation to stop the crime. An analysis of the situation would suggest that there are many disincentives available to the protesters. Corporate entities are very shy of publicity which may damage them economically. They are very afraid of boycotts by customers, secondary boycotting of their suppliers and corporate customers, lengthy legal actions in local and international courts, widespread bad press, legal injunctions, shareholder rebellions, complaints to regulatory authorities and similar disincentives. These types of action focus the corporate mind and personalise it, so that members of corporate managements start to take a more urgent interest in the protest.

Several incentives also exist. Corporate authorities like to be seen as responsible and responsive to public opinion, so they start to calculate the economic and public relations costs of ignoring a protest versus the economic benefits of proceeding with their plans.

Simultaneously, governments are sensitive to bad international press and this can be turned into an important disincentive. An environmental crime could also be construed as damaging to tourism, future investments or long-term human health. This may raise the prospect of future compensation claims, damage to other sources of GDP, such as agriculture, and possible breaches of international legal obligations. Governments are sensitive to being taken to international courts and the huge economic consequences if they lose.

As an incentive, on the other hand, governments do like to be seen to be listening to the public, to be seen as responsible and forward looking. Ultimately, government members like to hold on to their jobs, so when these jobs are put at stake because of a powerful protest, then members of the government begin to feel uneasy and start to take action to mollify the protesters.

So, one of the tasks of a protest planner is to identify in detail the factors that either incentivise or disincentivise target authorities to conform with the protest objectives. Then the protesters must find ways of designing and implementing the appropriate incentives and disincentives. These need to be clearly defined and turned into practical protest methods.

For example, one reason why a government might reconsider its support for fracking could (in theory) run as follows: "The UK government could be dissuaded from its support for the fracking exploration were it to find that such exploration places the UK in contradiction of the Water Framework Directive in the European Union, regarding the protection of Ground Water Sources."

A reason why an oil exploration company may think twice could be their investors threatening to take their money out. For instance, an oil exploration company thinking about moving into fracking may have a large part of its shareholding held by high street banks or by other public institutions. Supporting a dirty technology could persuade customers or stakeholders in such institutions to take their business elsewhere, into more ethical investments, in an effort to refuse finance for a dirty industry.

7.6 Risk Analysis and Management

One technique of great value to a protest group is that of formalised "risk management". This technique seeks to identify risks and then take assertive action to manage such risks. Easier said than done, one may think, but there are a series of techniques which are actually quite effective in helping a protest management team to have more or less control over the risks they are confronting in the protest campaign.

In its simplest form, risk management works by having a small "risk management committee", led by a "risk manager". This committee represents all of the key parts of the protest group, such as fund-raising, public relations, operations, legal services, membership services, logistics, protest operations, etc. Each member is responsible for identifying risks in their own area of activity and for managing these risks. The risk management committee meets regularly (once per month, perhaps). The main task of this committee is to establish, maintain and review the "risk register".

The risk register defines all the known risks to the organisation, brought together by each separate member of the committee. A risk may be virtually anything that threatens the effectiveness of the protest group. For instance, a risk might read "Falling membership levels is threatening the availability of funds for operational purposes" or "Legal manoeuvres by the local authority seek to place injunctions on further land occupations by the protest group".

Each risk is registered, together with the level of risk (Low, Medium or High), by the person responsible for managing the risk and the latest actions taken to mitigate the risk, and the current status. For instance, the risk to funding might be classified as a "Medium risk". The manager for this risk may have decided on the following action to mitigate the risk: "A new internet and social network appeal for members and donations will run for the next 60 days".

Risk management systems like this don't make risks go away, but they do provide a rational framework to define and manage them in a coherent way.

7.7 Contingency Planning - Handling the Unexpected

Someone said that wars are like eating peas with a knife: you never know which way they will go! The same could be said of conflicts between a protest group and a target authority. It is a good idea to try to plan as much as possible, but in reality it isn't possible to choreograph absolutely everything. For this reason a properly run protest campaign needs to plan for contingencies. Ideally, this planning should happen before things go wrong rather than when the group is actually in the middle of a catastrophe.

What can go wrong? In a similar way to risk management (which operates at a higher level), a group can protect itself from various practical contingencies by considering them in advance. This is sometimes called "downside planning" because it provides for plans when things go wrong and it considers what to do in "worst case scenarios".

"Games theory" provides some complex methods of predicting outcomes from unexpected events, but even at a more basic level it is possible to define possible contingencies when implementing a strategy or carrying out a protest action. For instance, a peaceful street demonstration may be blockaded by riot police, with supporters trapped in one area being threatened with police violence. What is the group's response to this? A protest group receives an injunction to desist from an occupied site. What is the group's response?

There are many possible contingencies possible in the dynamics of a protest conflict. Most of them are fairly obvious and many of them are unpleasant, which is one reason why protest planners prefer not to face up to them in advance. However, it is a major failing of a protest organisation if it does not have plans for the main contingencies that are likely to occur. Such a failure is a dangerous oversight because it may literally put lives at risk. It certainly puts the credibility of the protest group at risk.

For instance, everyone may agree that when a street demonstration is blockaded by police, perhaps the strategy should be to disperse peacefully and regroup elsewhere. Or perhaps the plan is to abandon the action completely. It doesn't matter what is decided, but clarity and advance planning do matter. They are essential. All protest actions require planning and this must include downside planning to handle a realistic range of contingencies in a safe and coherent way.

7.8 Select the Methods to Satisfy each Objective

There are many methods of protest, which are described in some detail in the following chapter. Obviously, not all methods of protest action are appropriate in all cases and choosing the correct method alters the effectiveness of a protest.

For example, many protests begin with street demonstrations; they seem the obvious way of galvanising a protest group. Whilst they may be useful to publicise a cause and garner support in the early days of an action, such demonstrations are largely just symbolic and rarely bring about change by themselves. Authorities become inured to such demonstrations and they often end in an anti-climax.

The problem with symbolic actions is that they don't exact a high enough "cost" from the target authority, whilst they do cost the protest group a great deal of energy and money. Thus, when choosing what methods of protest or civil disobedience to use, it is vital to balance the cost of the action to the target with some benefit to the protesters and to choose methods that, whilst resulting in a high cost to the target, give a big benefit to the protesters, though costing them little.

For example, a simple internet denial of service action has a relatively low cost to the protest group, but can exact a very severe cost to the target authority by temporarily closing down an internet service. Such a method is high profile, achieves a lot of publicity, is nonviolent, has a low cost to execute and is a lot easier than organising a demonstration on the street that the authorities will probably just ignore or brutalise. In a similar way, a product boycott can have a very profound effect on a target company and costs the activist group almost nothing, apart from some publicity.

---o0o---

8. Methods of Civil Disobedience, Protest, Intervention and Direct Action

There are many methods of civil disobedience, associated protests and interventions available to the activist and the following chapter is a description of these methods. We are grateful to Gene Sharp, the political philosopher, for his work in identifying a list of 198 basic methods of nonviolent action. We have modernised and extended this list of methods to include many new techniques now available to the contemporary protester. We present them here with detailed descriptions of how they work in a contemporary context with some historical examples of their use and the risks and considerations associated with using them.

The following schematic summarises the categories of civil disobedience, acts of protest, interventions and direct action. Each of these categories of techniques will then be examined in turn:

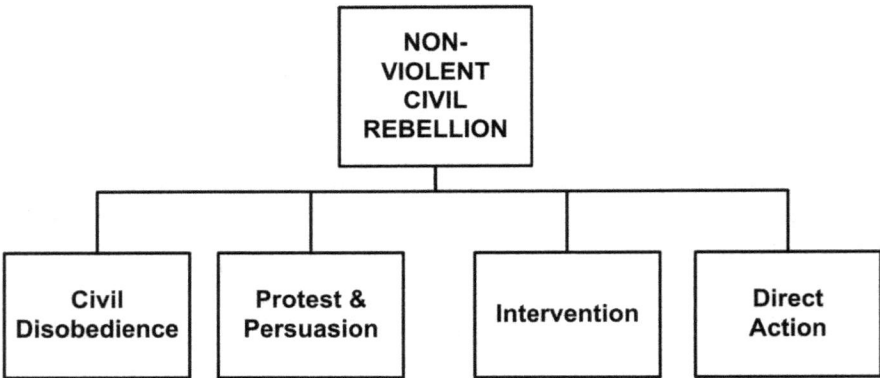

```
                    ┌─────────────┐
                    │    NON-     │
                    │  VIOLENT    │
                    │   CIVIL     │
                    │ REBELLION   │
                    └─────────────┘
       ┌──────────────┬──────┴──────┬──────────────┐
┌──────────────┐┌──────────────┐┌──────────────┐┌──────────────┐
│    Civil     ││  Protest &   ││              ││   Direct     │
│ Disobedience ││ Persuasion   ││ Intervention ││   Action     │
└──────────────┘└──────────────┘└──────────────┘└──────────────┘
```

8.0 Civil Disobedience

Methods of civil disobedience can be divided as follows at the highest level:

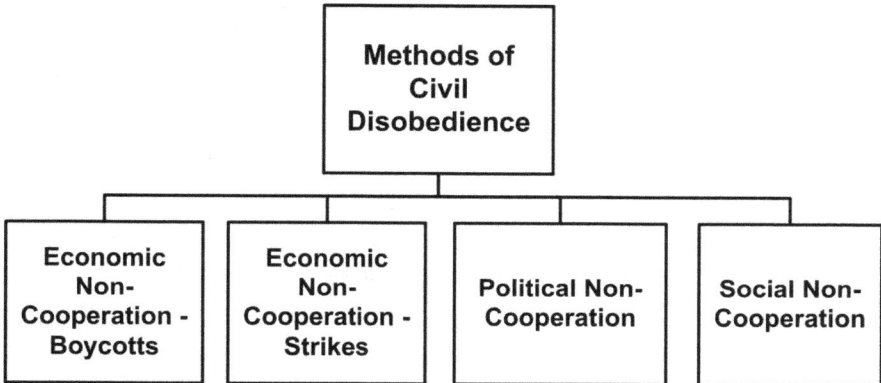

```
                    ┌─────────────────┐
                    │   Methods of    │
                    │      Civil      │
                    │  Disobedience   │
                    └─────────────────┘
        ┌──────────────┬─────────┴──────┬──────────────┐
┌───────────────┐┌───────────────┐┌──────────────┐┌──────────────┐
│   Economic    ││   Economic    ││              ││              │
│     Non-      ││     Non-      ││Political Non- ││ Social Non-  │
│ Cooperation - ││ Cooperation - ││ Cooperation  ││ Cooperation  │
│   Boycotts    ││   Strikes     ││              ││              │
└───────────────┘└───────────────┘└──────────────┘└──────────────┘
```

8.1 Civil Disobedience: Economic Non-Cooperation - Boycotts

This group of methods involves all those actions which impact a target authority economically, and includes boycott actions by consumers, workers, producers and intermediaries.

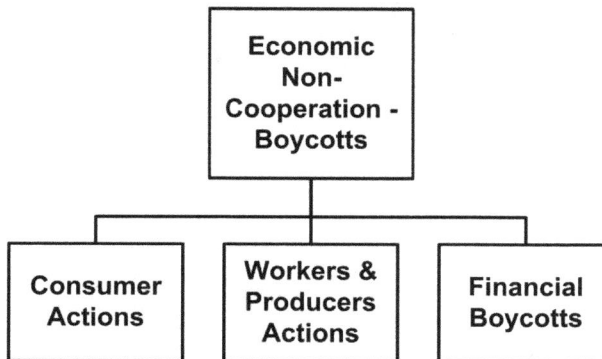

```
              ┌─────────────────┐
              │    Economic     │
              │      Non-       │
              │  Cooperation -  │
              │    Boycotts     │
              └─────────────────┘
       ┌─────────────┼─────────────┐
┌──────────────┐┌──────────────┐┌──────────────┐
│   Consumer   ││  Workers &   ││              │
│   Actions    ││  Producers   ││  Financial   │
│              ││  Actions     ││  Boycotts    │
└──────────────┘└──────────────┘└──────────────┘
```

8.1.1 Consumer Actions

Consumers are a powerful group when motivated and organised to take action. Consumer actions hurt the target in the most sensitive place: the pocket - without the consumer running any particular risks or being unduly affected by their own actions.

```
                    ┌─────────────┐
                    │  Consumer   │
                    │  Actions    │
                    └──────┬──────┘
        ┌──────────┬───────┼───────┬──────────┐
┌───────┴──┐ ┌─────┴────┐ ┌┴─────┐ ┌┴───────┐ ┌┴────────┐
│Consumers'│ │Secondary │ │Rent  │ │Refusal │ │  Bill   │
│ Boycott  │ │Consumer's│ │Strike│ │to Rent │ │ Payment │
│          │ │ Boycott  │ │      │ │        │ │ Refusal │
└──────────┘ └──────────┘ └──────┘ └────────┘ └─────────┘
```

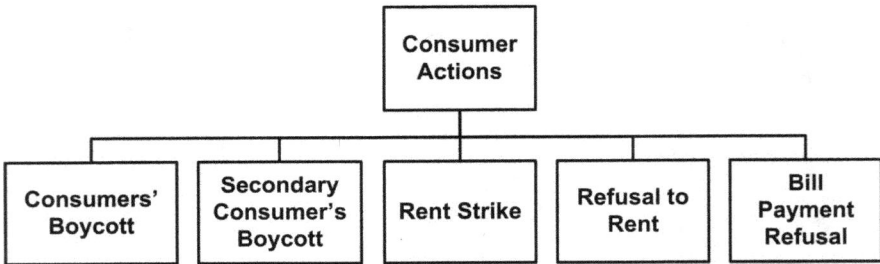

8.1.1.1 Consumers' Boycott: A consumers' boycott is an organised campaign against a product, a producer, a group of producers or even a whole country. The method calls for participants in the campaign to refuse to buy or consume one or more boycotted goods.

Consumer boycotts are organised for a variety of reasons. A product may be manufactured in an unethical way, by an unscrupulous company or originate in a country with poor labour or human rights standards. The reasons for the protest action may be that there are failings, for example, to protect human rights, civil rights, labour rights or the environment.

Considerations and risks: It's obviously vital to be sure of the identity of the product or manufacturer being boycotted. Accidentally hurting an innocent party is unforgivable and will discredit a protest campaign. Also, consider that there may be legal implications in accusing a company of certain behaviour. Make sure you have a complete case file which demonstrates the truth of what you are saying beyond legal doubt.

When giving product boycott advice, it is a good idea to offer the consumer some practical alternatives. If one boycotts Nestlé because it uses palm oil from areas where virgin tropical forests have been destroyed, then suggest a sustainable alternative to the consumer, such as some certified fair-trade or organic chocolate producers.

Historical and contemporary examples: Famous "country-based boycotts" include the long campaign against apartheid in South Africa, which started in 1959 and ran very successfully until the 1990s. All South African goods were targeted.

Current "corporate boycotts" include a complete boycott of Royal Dutch Shell and its products. This boycott originally arose because of the appalling suppression and execution of environmental protesters by the Nigerian government, in collaboration with Shell, starting in 1995. Despite UN accusations of breaches of human rights in 1998, Shell continues its operations in much the same way to this day. The company has such a bad environmental and human rights record that in the last 20 years Shell has been the subject of almost continuous consumer boycotts. At the time of publication, there are literally dozens of "Boycott Shell" campaigns taking place [Note 1].

A well-known "product boycott" is against bluefin tuna. According to Greenpeace, bluefin tuna is an endangered species which could soon be extinct. Despite this, it is still being served in sushi restaurants in the UK, which are now the target of a full-scale boycott [Note 2].

The most widespread consumer boycott in operation at the time of writing is a large group of boycotts against products or services originating in Israel because of that country's well-documented illegal mistreatment of Palestinians and the theft of their land. This has already become an economically very costly boycott for Israel. Throughout 2013 Israeli settlements in the Jordan Valley lost 14% of their income, solely because supermarkets in the UK and Scandinavia shunned their products [Note 3]. Here are just a few examples of the consumer boycotts against Israel since 2009:

• In 2009, Britain's Trade Union Congress voted to endorse an initiative to boycott products originating from the Israeli-occupied territories [Note 4].

• At around the same time, the UK Fire Brigade Union and Britain's largest trade union, Unite, and the UK's largest public sector union, Unison, called for a complete boycott of all Israeli products.

• In October 2009, the University of Sussex Students' Union became the first in Britain to vote for a boycott of Israeli goods [Note 5].

• In June 2010, the British Methodist Church decided to boycott products originating in Israeli settlements, thus becoming the first major Christian denomination in Britain to officially adopt a boycott against Israel [Note 6].

• In July 2010, in the State of Washington (United States) the Olympia food co-op decided to stop selling products from Israel in its two large grocery stores [Note 7].

• In 2010, the World Council of Churches called for a boycott of products originating in Israeli settlements [Note 8].

• In April 2012, the United Kingdom's Co-Operative Group said in a statement that it had decided to stop buying products from companies known to source from the settlements. The retailer had already stopped selling goods originating from the settlements themselves in 2009 [Note 9].

• In July 2013, two of the largest supermarket chains in the Netherlands stopped selling all products manufactured in Israeli settlements. A third chain, which had already stopped selling settlement goods, sought confirmation that goods it sold as "Made in Israel" didn't originate in the settlements [Note 10].

8.1.1.2 Secondary Consumer Boycotts: Secondary boycotts are actions taken against those who assist the target. Such secondary boycotts may be aimed at suppliers of a boycotted company or customers that purchase from a boycotted company, or from a boycotted origin.

Considerations and risks: A secondary boycott only requires that you can definitely prove that a supplier or other business relationship exists with the primary boycott target. But make sure that you have hard evidence of this before making any accusation. If you are sure of the facts but cannot prove them, publish them anonymously to avoid the unlikely risk of legal action for corporate defamation.

Historical and contemporary examples: Currently there is a boycott of Israeli goods originating in the occupied Palestinian territories and any of the companies which supply these manufacturers or handle their products.

Another boycott aimed at the Israeli Defence Forces targets Motorola [Note 11]. The New York Campaign for the Boycott of Israel has called for a boycott of Motorola over the company's business dealings with the Israeli Defence Forces.

Secondary boycotts can extend to all kinds of supplies. The campaign 'Shut Down H&K' is boycotting financial services company Mutual LV, aka London Victoria Friendly Society [Note 12]. Activists discovered that LV owns a small business park on an industrial estate in Nottingham which is home to arms manufacturer Heckler & Kochs' UK head office.

A high profile case of a secondary boycott occurred in 2014 when the Hollywood actress Scarlett Johansson faced severe criticism for leaving her job as ambassador for Oxfam in order to continue to work for SodaStream. This Israeli company has a factory in an illegally occupied Palestinian territory; an occupation expressly criticised by Oxfam [Note 3]. It seemed apparent that the Hollywood actress was under pressure from what cameraman Steve Rankin referred to as US-Israel "zealots" stating that they are "so powerful...... especially in the entertainment industry... what they could do to her career....". Nonetheless, it was clear that Oxfam refused to allow Johansson to continue to work for them because of her alliance with SodaStream and its Israeli owners [Note 13].

8.1.1.3 Withholding Rent - Rent Strikes: This method of action can be high risk in some jurisdictions where withholding rent may give a landlord the right to evict. In other jurisdictions withholding rent is a legally justifiable action in certain cases.

Considerations and risks: In general, rent strikes should be a part of a large-scale protest where many participants act in unison rather than a one-person action. Landlords may still try to intimidate activists into paying up by threatening mass evictions, but the costs of doing so may become too high for the landlord if enough tenants are involved.

It is usually advisable to place the withheld rents in a separate bank account so that, if and when payments resume, the funds are available to the tenant without delay.

Rent strikes are frequently used to force bad landlords into behaving more responsibly but they are also used to support other actions. For instance, in Northern Ireland, civil rights activists organised rent strikes to protest against internment without trial carried out by the British government in the 1970s.

Historical and contemporary examples: Britain has had its fair share of rent strikes over the years, probably because the country has a long and miserable history of landlordism.

In the late 19th century the appalling behaviour of absentee landlords in Scotland and Ireland gave rise to a wave of rent strikes organised by their respective Land Leagues. The causes of these strikes were similar: the landlords wanted to clear their land for intensive grazing and to obtain higher rents, so they set about to get rid of tenants by increasing rents, carrying out illegal evictions and terrorising small farmers. The farmers organised quite quickly and withheld rents. In the case of Ireland, this movement led directly to the events of 1916, which saw the beginning of the complete expulsion of the British and their aristocracy from Ireland within a few years.

Meanwhile, during the First World War, the landlords of Glasgow used the huge influx of shipbuilders to raise rents and exploit their tenants in a cynical ploy to make money from the poor on the back of their war effort. The victims were often the women who were left behind by their men going to war. As a result of these rent increases, there was a popular backlash against the landlords and a rent strike ensued, led by Mary Barbour, who with her "army" would forcibly prevent the bailiffs from entering the tenements, pelting them with flour bombs. The strikes soon spread within Glasgow. In fact, they became such an overwhelming success that they spread to other cities throughout the UK. Under increasing pressure, the government, on 27 November 1915, introduced legislation to restrict rents to their pre-war levels.

The pro-democracy demonstrations in Hong Kong in late 2014 also gave rise to a series of coordinated rent and tax strikes to allow non-demonstrating protesters a way of contributing to the campaign for universal suffrage. Under the demonstrator's non-cooperation plan, Hong Kongers were urged to express their displeasure with the government by splitting their tax payments into small sums to lengthen administrative processing. Tenants of public housing flats were urged to delay paying their monthly rent until the last possible moment [Note 14].

8.1.1.4 Refusal to Rent: Refusal to rent is the act of refusing to rent property from a particular landlord.

Considerations and risks: Normally these actions need to be carried out on a large scale to have any effect. They are usually the result of dissatisfaction with a landlord, the price or quality of property being leased, but they can also be in support of other actions.

In a tight accommodation market, this is going to be a difficult protest action because certainly some tenants will be tempted into taking up a lease, either through ignorance or desperation to find housing.

Historical and contemporary examples: Shelter is a long-established UK housing charity which routinely names and shames bad landlords in Britain in order to save tenants from landlord abuse. In 2010, the charity conducted large-scale research into landlord abuses, naming and accusing one large landlord with over 200 properties of a wide range of shocking tenant abuses. Needless to say, the landlord was almost instantly boycotted by the public [Note 15].

8.1.1.5 Bill Payment Refusal: This is a similar action to a rent strike, where one or more consumers refuse to pay a particular bill. An example of this would be a group of customers refusing to pay a utility bill. Generally, this happens when a supplier makes unreasonable demands on the consumer in terms of price or delivery. The objective is to upset the cash flow of the supplier and oblige them to rethink their policy.

Considerations and risks: This is another of those cases where it is best to act collectively. Different countries have differing legislation, but in some cases there is a legal liability to settle a bill even when the account is in dispute. Acting in a large group may not alter the legal facts, but it does provide some level of persuasive leverage and a level of public support.

Bill payment refusal shouldn't be undertaken in isolation. It should be part of a suite of actions. If a group is refusing, for example, to pay a utility bill, it should also be taking judicial (or political) action to refute the legal rights of the utility company, otherwise the protest smacks of some people trying to get out of paying a legitimate bill.

Historical and contemporary examples: An example of this protest method took place in Ireland in 2014, when a large number of water consumers collectively refused to pay their water bills in protest against excessive charges and the low quality of water supply. This was a classic case of unintended consequences because the Irish government had stubbornly refused to deal with the problems of contaminated water and problems of poor supply. However, later it decided that it needed to charge for water to raise funds during the economic crisis. The public, reeling from years of austerity measures and aware of the poor quality of their water supply, were unable to stomach the charges. They took to the streets. Similar payment strikes in Ireland have occurred when local authority taxes have been introduced without the provision of any tangible services. At the time of writing the Irish government's popularity is catastrophically low and it is not sure how much longer it can remain in power. The mass refusal to pay the water charges extends to more than 50% of the population of Ireland [Note 16].

8.1.2 Action by Workers and Producers

Worker and producer boycotts are similar to consumer boycotts with the proviso that workers and producers refuse to work or produce in certain conditions or with certain materials, rather than refusing to consume a product.

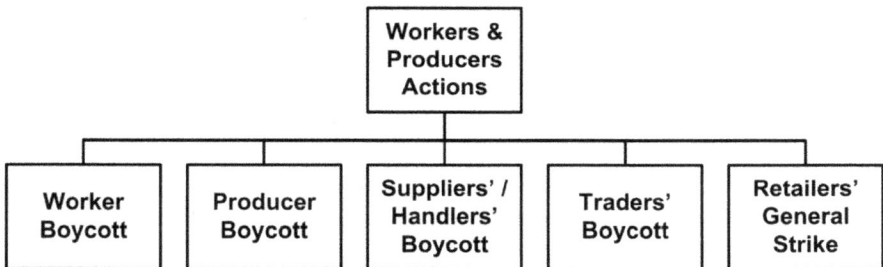

8.1.2.1 Worker Boycott (of materials, tools, customers): A worker boycott involves a group of workers who refuse to work with a particular set of materials, tools or to carry out work for a certain customer. This is different to a strike because it is motivated by ethical considerations rather than economic issues or problems with the workforce's own conditions. In a worker boycott, a group may decide certain materials or tools should not be used. They might be hazardous, or of unethical origin, for instance.

Considerations and risks: Obviously, taking a principled approach may give rise to reprisals. Thus, worker boycotts have to be carried out en masse. All negotiations must include amnesties for participants. Often employers will try to pick off the "weaklings and ring-leaders" during a boycott to weaken the overall resolve of the non-cooperation. The standard response to such a strategy should include painful escalations by the protest group. So, instead of simply boycotting a part of the employer's work, it may be necessary to boycott larger parts of the business activities of the employer until the company agrees to negotiate. This escalation may, of course, end in an outright strike.

Historical and contemporary examples: One hybrid of this type of action is when a group of workers refuse to work for a particular customer because they have some ethical or economic objections to that customer. Such was the case with the original boycott in County Mayo in Ireland in 1880, where all the local workers, including the postman, and even his house servants refused to work for Captain Boycott, the local land agent for the large Mayo estates of Lord Erne. This withdrawal of labour took place because of Boycott's attempts to evict small local farmers due to rent arrears after a catastrophic harvest. After the boycott, this large estate was left in a completely unmanageable condition [Note 17].

A more violent protest took place when the hand-loom weavers of England started to break up mechanised looms during the Luddite rebellions of the Industrial Revolution, in a protest at reduced wages and deteriorating working conditions. The damage to the machines meant that factory owners had to spend large amounts of capital to re-equip their factories. The Luddite rebellions were largely propagandised as "ignorant weavers destroying machines because of a fear for progress". However, the reality was that the weavers destroyed the machines in an effort to damage the economic strength of the mill owners in a protest at the appalling working conditions imposed upon them [Note 18].

8.1.2.2 Producer Boycott - Selling Strikes: A producer strike or production boycott occurs when a producer, such as a farmer or fisherman, refuses to produce for the market. Very often such strikes are triggered off by poor market prices or new legislation affecting small producers, such as new fishing quotas or reduced agricultural subsidies. The objective in a producer strike is to withdraw products, causing shortages which may in turn create a price rise or pressure an authority to make changes to the law.

One variant of the selling strike is when producers dump large amounts of produce on the market at a very low price or free of charge. This has been done in recent years by small producers attacking large, monopolistic supermarket chains because of their shabby treatment of small producers; they hope to cause a collapse in prices.

Considerations and risks: Small producers can become quite dependent on single large corporate customers. This dependency creates an existential risk to a small producer if they attempt to get a better price by withdrawing production from the market. This is something that needs to be done in a large, collective protest action.

Alternative supplies from other producers or countries may break a supply boycott. Therefore a secondary action to stop transportation of substitutes may also be necessary. A coordinated boycott may need the cooperation of colleagues in other parts of the country or in other countries or in other sectors (such as road haulage) to block the customer's alternative supplies.

Historical and contemporary examples: In 2012 during one of the so-called "milk-wars", dairy producers asked customers not to buy milk from the supermarket chains Morrisons, Aldi, Lidl or Londis and to think twice about buying from Asda and the Co-operative.

The row centred on the "farm gate" price paid to Britain's 14500 dairy farmers, most of whom received just 25p a litre for the milk they produced compared with around 30p before. The producers' organisations claim that the price cut would force many farmers into bankruptcy and they demanded a minimum 30p a litre as the least the producers would need to survive. This running battle between producers and large supermarket chains continues at the time of writing. Similar producer strikes in the UK have been held by small fishermen and other agricultural producers [Note 19].

8.1.2.3 Suppliers' and Handlers' Boycott: These are boycotts by intermediaries such as suppliers or handlers of certain activities. For example, dock workers may refuse to unload a ship carrying certain toxic or boycotted materials.

A similar boycott by suppliers occurs when they refuse to deal with certain customers or nations. This may happen to avoid secondary boycotting by being associated with an unethical customer. It can also be that suppliers don't want to do business with a particular customer for other ethical reasons.

Considerations and risks: As with many such boycott actions, this is an initiative to be entered into as part of a unified group. Clearly, the main risk to a supplier or handler is that the target customer just finds an alternative supplier. Be ready, therefore, to use a secondary boycott of those suppliers and handlers that are trying to break the boycott. They may need to suffer a boycott as well. Identify them in advance and be ready to put pressure on them to respect your boycott.

Historical and contemporary examples: An example of a handlers' strike occurred in February 2009 when dock workers in South Africa refused to unload an Israeli ship "as part of a refusal to support oppression and exploitation". The Congress of South African Trade Unions, COSATU, compared Israel to "dictatorial and oppressive" states such as Zimbabwe and Swaziland. COSATU also drew parallels to events in 1963, when dock workers across the globe boycotted vessels from South Africa to protest its apartheid regime [Note 20]. The Western Australian members of the Maritime Union of Australia also supported the move and called for a boycott of all Israeli vessels.

In a separate protest, and as a response to an Israeli military raid of a relief ship approaching the Gaza Strip, Swedish port workers decided to refuse to process Israeli ships for a period in June 2010 [Note 21]. Similar boycotts in response to the Israeli raid were launched by port workers in Norway and California.

8.1.2.4 Traders' Boycott: A traders' boycott occurs when retailers refuse to stock or sell certain goods. This may occur when the suppliers or countries of origin are boycotted, or when the goods are considered unethical in themselves (such as some forms of pornography or types of food, duck pâté, for instance).

Trader boycotts can be actions by single retailers or by groups of retailers collaborating in a large-scale boycott.

Considerations and risks: A trader needs to ensure that he has alternative product lines before starting a boycott against a particular supplier, product or country of origin. It is, after all, important to offer customers an alternative, both for their sake and for the sake of the trader's own survival. Being an ethical trader is only useful if the trader manages to stay in business. Thus, a trader boycott needs some preparation of alternative supplies before it can begin. For example, a recent boycott of duck liver pâté offered customers pâté which was ethically produced without force-feeding and cruelty to the animals involved.

Historical and contemporary examples: In a recent incident (2012) involving the online business community, a protest was launched against so-called internet copyright legislation in the U.S. congress (SOPA & PIPA). Critics of the legislation insisted that the legislation was too far-reaching and threatened freedom of speech as well as the internet industry as a whole. As part of the protest, websites such as Wikipedia, Reddit and Boing Boing disappeared for 24 hours in a "go black" protest. This temporary disappearance was both a symbolic gesture of protest as well as a practical one. Critics say that if the current legislation passed, it could result in the permanent disappearance of many websites. The protest black-out was designed to show what life would be like without such websites. Those protesting the legislation hoped that the fall-out from the 24-hour disappearance of even a few large websites would give pause for thought to decision-makers regarding the fate of the proposed legislation [Note 22].

8.1.2.5 Retailers' General Strike: A great deal of inconvenience and economic disruption can be caused when retailers collectively decide to close all their outlets for a time. This is often motivated by political or economic conditions.

Considerations and risks: Closing the shop doors for a hard-working retailer is a difficult decision. It is vital to inform customers of the reasons for the action and to gain their solidarity, otherwise the retailer risks losing its customer base. Again, this is an action that needs to be carried out en masse. No individual retailer should be obliged to risk their livelihood alone. When a retailers' strike is widespread it receives more popular approval and understanding than when it is an isolated act.

Historical and contemporary examples: In 2013 in Greece, small shop keepers staged a strike in protest against 7-day/week shop opening which, they claimed, would favour larger shops over family businesses [Note 23]. Another example of a retailer general strike took place in July 2014 in East Jerusalem where all shops were closed on a business day as a protest against Israel's actions in Gaza.

8.1.3 Boycott Actions by Holders of Financial Resources

This is an area of great potential for influencing where and how money is invested. Clearly, the theory goes that if capital flows away from immoral corporations towards more ethical companies, the world should be a better place. This concept has spawned a whole new industry in ethical financial services such as ethical funds, ethical corporate and national bonds and ethical banks with all the services of a high street bank but none of the "dirty money".

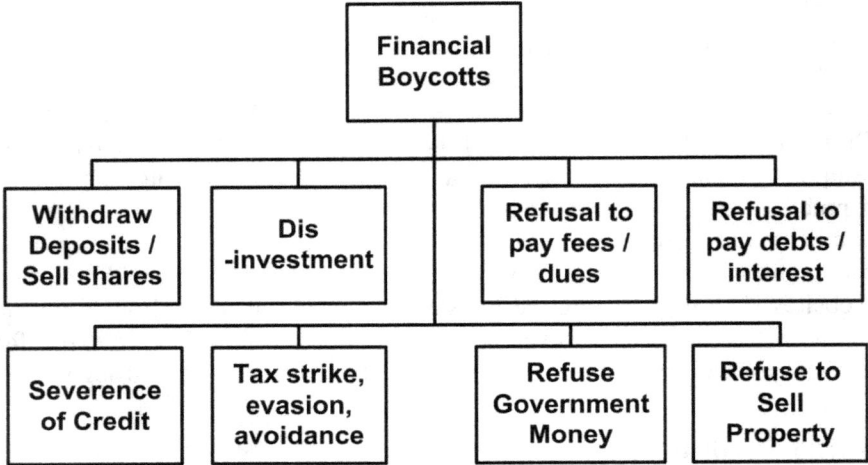

```
                    ┌─────────────┐
                    │  Financial  │
                    │  Boycotts   │
                    └─────────────┘
```

| Withdraw Deposits / Sell shares | Dis-investment | Refusal to pay fees / dues | Refusal to pay debts / interest |

| Severence of Credit | Tax strike, evasion, avoidance | Refuse Government Money | Refuse to Sell Property |

Considerations and risks: There are not that many risks in moving capital into ethical investments (on the contrary, they tend to perform rather well). This is one of the more straightforward protest actions against conventional capitalism that anyone can take without much effort or risk.

Historical and contemporary examples: The origins of (modern) socially responsible investment are to be found in the actions of the Society of Friends (Quakers). In 1758, the Quaker Philadelphia Yearly Meeting prohibited members from participating in the slave trade. An early proponent of the idea of boycotting certain investments was John Wesley (1703-1791), one of the founders of Methodism. His famous sermon "The Use of Money" outlined his basic rules of social investment - i.e. not to harm your neighbours through your business practices and to avoid industries which can harm the health of workers (in those days that meant industries such as tanning and chemical production).

Some of the best-known historical cases of socially responsible investment were religiously motivated. Investors would avoid "sinful" companies, such as those associated with products such as guns, liquor and tobacco.

These days, there is a proliferation of ethical investment companies and funds. It's relatively easy to move investment capital into funds opposed to the arms industry and dubious regimes whilst simultaneously injecting capital into renewable energy and /or sustainable industry or businesses which espouse women's rights, minorities' rights, organic agriculture etc.

8.1.3.1 Withdrawal of Bank Deposits / Shares: This action is designed to shun one particular financial institution or instrument such as a share, bond or fund in order to favour another. Usually the ethical motivation for withdrawal of bank deposits or sale of shares is that the financial institution is operating in a disreputable way or has an investment in a 3rd party company which is behaving improperly.

Considerations and risks: There are not too many risks here. Moving cash away from one financial institution or investment to another is a relatively simple matter. There are plenty of alternative, ethical institutions and financial instruments with excellent moral references and a history of service and performance.

Historical and contemporary examples: In 2011, an online campaign in Holland overturned the Dutch bank ING's executive pay policy and proposals to give huge bonuses to bankers. ING had been rescued using Dutch taxpayers' money and angry customers mobilised on Twitter and other social networks to protest at the huge bonuses being paid to bosses at the bank, one of the biggest in the country. The threat of direct action of mass withdrawals from the bank raised the spectre of a partial run on ING, terrifying the Dutch establishment. A union organiser at the bank, referring to the proposed executive bonuses said: "People are outraged. We heard about the bloated sums being paid again in the City (London) and in New York; but suddenly the issue exploded on our own front door." So severe was the public reaction to these proposed bonuses that within days the executives of the bank had agreed to waive their awards and told other ING directors to do the same [Note 24].

In February 2014, in Thailand, a mass withdrawal of funds by customers of the Government Savings Bank (GSB) protesting at the bank's loans to a controversial rice pledging scheme, forced the resignation of the bank's president. The protesters suspected that he had been placed in his position by the government and was making the controversial loans on government orders. The bank was forced to rescind the controversial loans after protesters withdrew more than 40 billion baht (€960,000,000) in just one day [Note 25].

8.1.3.2 Disinvestment: This is a form of boycott which involves an investor or group of investors refusing to purchase investments in a particular company or group of companies. It also involves selling such interests if the investor currently owns them. The disinvestment may be targeted at a specific company (Shell for instance) or it may target a type of company such as all arms manufacturers or tobacco producers.

A further variant of disinvestment is to target other financial institutions, such as banks that may have unethical investments. Recently, for instance, Barclays Bank was subject to a boycott call by the Ethical Consumer organisation for its involvement in destructive Canadian Oil Sands projects.

In recent years, this has become a popular mode of action. Indeed it is so popular that many financial institutions have designed "Ethical Funds" that provide a guarantee to exclude certain types of immoral investments. These funds have proved popular and successful, specialising as they do in investments in areas such as renewable energy. This lead has been followed by several retail banks.

Disinvestment damages the target organisation by removing funding capital, thus pushing down its share price.

Considerations and risks: Forcing down share prices by organised disinvestment creates buying opportunities for other investors and may not be powerful enough to permanently drag down the market value of a security to the extent that the target company reconsider their behaviour. This is therefore an action that needs a lot of support to be effective. It may even mean that the protest group has to buy shares in advance of an action in order to make the disinvestment larger and create more market selling pressure. Also, selling a share isn't enough; it's important to have a coordinated buying policy as well. So selling shares in an unethical company to reduce its market value and capitalisation should be mirrored by the purchase of shares in an ethical equivalent to raise its market valuation and cause momentum for others to invest in it.

Historical and contemporary examples: During the apartheid years of South Africa, protesters forced many financial institutions to disinvest from the country.

In modern times, Israel has taken over from South Africa as the bête noire of the international community because of its appalling treatment of the Palestinians and breaches of both international humanitarian law and the Geneva Conventions. As a response there has been large-scale disinvestment, much of which has been voluntary, but some offloading has been undertaken to avoid the attention of various movements condemning Israel's behaviour. Here are just a few examples. At the time of writing the widespread disinvestment in Israel continues and is growing:

• In July 2004, the General Assembly of the Presbyterian Church (USA) voted to initiate a process of divestment in businesses that it believed bear responsibility for the suffering of Palestinians. In 2014 the Presbyterians decided, by a vote of 310 to 303, to divest from Caterpillar, Hewlett-Packard and Motorola Solutions which, the church said, supply Israel with equipment used in the occupation of Palestinian territory [Note 26].

• In 2009, a Norwegian government pension fund sold its shares in Elbit Systems because of its role in building the West Bank barrier. In 2010, the Norwegian government announced that based on advice from the Norwegian Council on Ethics, it had excluded two Israeli companies from a government pension fund. According to the government, the firms Africa-Israel Investments and Danya Cebus were involved in developing settlements in occupied Palestinian territory, action which is prohibited under the Fourth Geneva Convention. However, in 2013, after a review of Africa-Israel's activities, the Norwegian government announced that they could now re-invest in Africa-Israel and Danya Cebus as they were no longer involved in the construction of settlements. The ban was reinstated in 2014 after Norway's Council of Ethics received information Danya Cebus was in fact involved with the settlements.

• In September 2009, 14 Belgian municipalities closed their accounts with the Franco-Belgian bank Dexia, which was financing Israeli settlements through its Israeli subsidiary [Note 27].

• The New Zealand superannuation fund, which invests money on behalf of the New Zealand Government, excluded two companies because of their involvement in Israeli settlements, and one company for its involvement in the West Bank barrier in December 2012. A spokesperson cited UN findings of illegality concerning both the barrier and settlements as central to the decision to exclude the companies.

• In 2011, the German rail company Deutsche Bahn decided to withdraw from a project to build a rail link between Tel Aviv and Jerusalem. This decision was made following pressure from German lawmakers because the rail link cuts through the Palestinian West Bank [Note 28].

• In 2012, Caterpillar Inc. was removed from three "socially responsible" stock indices by the American investment firm MSCI. MSCI cited Israel's use of Caterpillar bulldozers in the Palestinian territories as a key reason for its decision. MSCI also cited employee safety concerns, environmental issues and a plant closing in Canada [Note 29].

• In 2014, Danish Danske Bank said Israeli Bank Hapoalim was acting against the rules of international humanitarian law by engaging in settlement construction and that consequently Danske could not invest in that bank. Danske had already decided to sell its investments in Africa-Israel Investments and Danya Cebus for the same reason [Note 30].

• The Dutch pension fund PGGM sold its holdings in five Israeli banks in January 2014. The banks were allegedly involved in financing illegal settlements on Palestinian land [Note 31].

8.1.3.3 Refusal to Pay Fees or Dues: This type of protest is directed against professional organisations or other member-based associations when a group of members decide en masse to boycott the organisation by refusing to pay their annual fees or membership dues.

An example of this could be when a cooperative or union is failing to represent its members' interests and a group of members decides to pressurise the co-op or union by refusing to pay membership charges. This puts pressure on the organisation's finances and is an embarrassment.

Considerations and risks: Provided this action is taken by a group of members, there is little risk. In a union, association, club or cooperative, it should be a last resort.

8.1.3.4 Refusal to Pay Debts or Interest: Debt repayment strikes occur when a debtor or group of debtors refuse to repay their loans or associated interest payments to a financial institution or other creditor. The primary motivation for a debt strike is to fight back against financial exploitation when many people feel crushed by debt.

With wages in many countries stagnant since the 1970s, citizens have increasingly turned to debt financing to pay for education, housing and health care. Banks and other credit organisations have aggressively pursued and profited from this explosion in debt, fuelling economic inequality, inflating a huge credit bubble and trapping millions in a form of indentured servitude.

Most people feel obliged to pay back loans no matter what the cost, and they fear the lasting consequences of default, such as a damaged credit rating and/or becoming a social pariah. However, the latest financial crisis has begun to change this attitude towards debt repayment, especially after the spectacle of Western governments pouring trillions of Euros in bailouts and cheap loans to the big banks.

Large parts of the population now view our debt burdens as a structural problem and part of a corporate/government scam rather than a personal failure or a legitimate obligation. Clearly, asking politicians or banks for debt forgiveness is unlikely to achieve anything and many have now realised that what the indebted masses really need is some form of leverage. And this brings us to the concept of the debt strike, which is really an experiment in collective bargaining for debtors.

The idea is quite simple: En masse, a large part of the population stops making repayments to the banks until the banks renegotiate their loans. Because banks can't operate without these debt repayments - for student loans, mortgages, or consumer credit - they are placed under severe pressure to negotiate in a debt strike.

Considerations and risks: As with tax strikes, refusal to pay a debt or interest payment carries many legal risks. This is not an action to be attempted alone because the target will simply prosecute its claims against an individual and certainly win. However, if a group takes this action, then the issue stops being a simple legal matter and becomes a political one. Such a strike can be connected to demands to reform the financial system, abolish predatory and usurious loan conditions, or provide direct debt forgiveness. Generally, with such a coordinated action the participants should all sign a pledge - either public or confidential - to stop making certain bank repayments.

In debt or interest strikes it is considered wise to put the withheld funds into a properly administered bank account overseen by an independent accountant. It may well be that at some future point, the protester may be required to pay all or part of their debts and it is better not to run the risk of a real default. In some cases debt strikers can pool these funds and use them to create their own credit union or credit club which they can eventually use to take over their debts on more humane terms.

Historical and contemporary examples: There have been many examples of this type of strike in various Western countries during various economic crises. Most recently, such strikes have become quite common, especially since the beginning of the 2008 financial crisis, where many mortgage holders experienced severe "negative equity".

"Negative equity" occurs when the value of a mortgage debt substantially exceeds the actual value of the asset (dwelling) for which the mortgage was granted. This is often the result of a rapid drop in property prices after unsustainable property price rises. In such circumstances a mortgage holder may find that they cannot sell their property at a reasonable price and that their mortgage payments are for a property worth only a fraction of the mortgage value. Faced by this situation, a home-owner may decide to abandon his debt, interest payments and property, returning the property to the lending institution as a way of relieving himself of the debt. In some cases this strategy involves individuals declaring themselves to be legally bankrupt. In some countries, bankruptcy provides a way of securing the protection of the bankruptcy courts for the borrower against further legal actions from his creditors.

Banks are often quite keen to lend large amounts of money secured against property at rather speculative valuations. On paper the inflated assets which secure the loan are sufficient to guarantee repayment and for the banks to increase the value of their own asset registers to borrow money on the debt markets. In reality, as some banks have now realised, this may end in an inflated asset base and a pile of unrealistic debts which should never have been granted by the bank. In some circumstances, a consumer can escape the risk of losses by simply writing off the entire debt and loss of their house and starting again from scratch. In this case, the banks bear the loss - which is reasonable since it was they that failed to exercise due diligence in their lending procedures in the first place. Banks are professional lenders, whereas most retail borrowers often don't have the slightest idea of risk or what they can afford to borrow.

A contemporary example of refusal to pay a debt is occurring in England at the time of writing. Students in England have recently become confronted with huge fees (and therefore loans) to attend university, much to their consternation. They are provided with government loans to cover these fees but are expected to repay these loans when they have paid employment of a certain level. However, the actual level of debt repayment to the government is proving to be very low because students either refuse or are unable to repay.

The government now sees the likely level of repayment at only 50% of the amount loaned, making the system of charging fees actually more expensive than simply giving free 3rd level education - as used to be the case. This would appear to be a slow-motion victory for the protesting students.

By early 2014, the cost to the English government of these fee write-offs was close to the gains created by the government's tripling of the level of university fees. The British Conservative government has thus put itself into an impossible quandary: reducing fees would be an expensive political "climb down" for the government, but increasing university fees would simply increase the level of debt write-offs faced by the government.

Some would argue that the concept of "can't pay, won't pay" was somehow lost on the Tory party economists that designed the scheme for high student fees and loans. With short-term debt losses of 45%, the only obvious solution appears to be the re-nationalisation of 3rd level education in England, as predicted some years ago [Note 32].

8.1.3.5 Severance of Credit: This is an act by a supplier business against an unethical customer. The business refuses to provide credit to the customer and this creates inconvenience and possible cash-flow problems for the customer. This kind of protest only works in cases where the customer is dependent on the supplier for cheap or free credit.

In a more open market a customer can simply find another supplier. However, there are plenty of instances where this is not possible. For example, where a supplier has an exclusive right to distribute a product and the customer is obliged to buy from this supplier. In such a case the withdrawal of credit to the customer can be a cause for great annoyance and even cause real financial hardship for the customer. This strategy can be applied to large corporations and governments, even by very small businesses if they hold exclusive rights over their products or services and these products are in strong demand.

Considerations and risks: Clearly, cutting off a customer's credit may cause some negative repercussions to both parties. This is another of those actions, therefore, that need to be carried out together with others in order to make sure that the target is unable to retaliate or intimidate. However, the risk is that after this action, the target may find an alternative supplier. This could be avoided if the group makes it a condition of a settlement that there will be no retaliation against any supplier - on pain of a further boycott. Then again, if one were to lose an unethical customer, one may ask if that type of customer is that important after all.

8.1.3.6 Revenue Refusal - Tax Strike, Tax Evasion and Avoidance: These actions all involve a refusal to pay taxes to the appropriate government authority. These may be temporary acts, such as a tax strike, or they may be an ongoing policy of tax evasion (illegal) or tax avoidance (legal) used to reduce tax income to an authority.

Tax strikes tend to be high profile and carried out openly by a group of protesters to draw public and government attention to a particular issue. Tax evasion, because it is illegal, is more likely to be a covert act and tax avoidance may be either public or covert since it is not illegal - though it may be construed as immoral by some.

Tax strikes are effective at forcing a government into focusing on a dispute because they hurt the finances of the government and can be quite contagious. No government wants to run the risk of a generalised tax strike; such a strike could be economically ruinous to a country and to the political future of the government. For this reason, governments tend to try to nip tax strikes in the bud, which often means making some significant concessions to the protesters.

Considerations and risks: Failure to pay your taxes is considered a serious offence in most countries, so a tax strike is an action which must be carried out in a group. Tax evasion and avoidance can be carried out as an individual, since the idea is that such actions will never be detected by the tax authorities. The protester simply refuses to contribute tax to an authority of which he does not approve. Evasion is considered to be illegal because it involves deliberately misleading a tax authority. Avoidance is considered to be simply manipulating the tax system to make it work to someone's own financial benefit.

There is always a legal risk involved and tax strikes in particular must ensure that funds are placed on deposit in the event that the participants will one day have to pay part or all of their tax debts.

Historical and contemporary examples: Tax resistance has probably one of the most vivid histories of all forms of civil disobedience. One of the earliest and most famous cases took place at the time of Jesus Christ when the Jewish population of Judea were resisting a Roman poll tax. Jesus himself was accused by the Roman authorities of playing a role in the tax strike.

There have always been tax strikes. The people of Worcester in 1041 refused to pay what they considered to be unfair taxes to the Danes, and following the killing of two tax collectors their town was destroyed in retaliation. The Peasants Revolt of the 14th century started as a simple tax strike and ended in full-scale insurrection. In the 16th century in Germany, a similar revolt was built on a defiance of all "man-made" taxes and tithes.

During the 17th century, France experienced many tax revolts which often ended in violence against tax officials and wide-spread withholding of taxes by organised groups of peasants, sometimes with the help of local officials or clergymen. In the nascent United States in 1773, the Boston Tea Party, a famous manifestation of the American Revolution, was triggered by a backlash to what was seen as unfair taxation by the British Empire against the American colonists.

By the mid-nineteenth century, tax strikes were quite in vogue and even Karl Marx was prosecuted for publishing an article saying that it was every citizen's "primary duty" to refuse to pay his taxes [Note 33].

In modern times, tax strikes have been waged against governments engaged in what campaigners considered illegal wars. Many such tax strikes were staged in the USA by prominent anti-war campaigners during the Vietnam War. To this day in several countries, including the UK, there are movements which seek to withhold some part of their tax contributions as a means of refusing to pay for military expenditure (see the Conscience Campaign, for instance). Many such movements actively conspire to avoid tax payments with this moral justification as a motive, without the tax authorities being aware of their actions.

A most recent example of a tax strike took place in Greece in 2015 when a €1bn shortfall in tax revenues for January was caused by some Greeks delaying tax payments in the run-up to the elections, thus adding to the strain on the unpopular government's finances.

8.1.3.7 Refusal of Government Money: Refusing government money may seem like a fairly unlikely and ineffective protest action but it is a lot more widespread than one would imagine. It often happens that individuals or groups refuse to participate with a government compensation scheme, for example for mandatory relocation, compulsory purchase of property or as a means of compensation for some losses caused by a government. In such cases the protesting citizen or group may refuse to accept the money a/ because they find it an inadequate amount or b/ as a protest against the government's behaviour in the case.

Considerations and risks: If the protest fails, the participants may accrue financial losses and may exclude themselves from future payments from a government. For instance, compensation payments are often time-limited. Failing to accept a payment may have the legal implication that a government is not obliged to negotiate after a certain date.

Refusing to accept a payment by a single individual is unlikely to have a great effect politically. Refusal of a payment by many individuals in a large group, on the other hand, may well prove much more embarrassing and potent as a protest action.

Historical and contemporary examples: During the American Civil War, when black soldiers began signing up with the Union Army in early 1863, they were paid $10 a month. White soldiers were paid at least $13, with officers earning more. Black people were further insulted when only they were charged a $3 monthly fee for clothing, lowering their pay to $7. As a result, the highest-paid black soldier earned about half of the lowest-paid white soldier's salary. To protest these conditions, black regiments refused to accept their inferior wages. Finally, pressure from abolitionist congressmen coupled with the courage black soldiers had shown in combat persuaded the US Congress to rectify the pay structure. In September 1864, black soldiers finally received equal pay, retroactive to their enlistment date. For many, this meant they finally had enough money to send some home to their families.

In a 2014 protest in Burma, villagers refused to accept compensation for land expropriated for a mining development in Letpadaung. The villagers claimed that they wanted their land back and not more compensation. The protest led to the establishment of a commission of enquiry which has already uncovered some irregularities in land seizure and compensation. The protest continues at the time of writing [Note 34].

8.1.3.8 Refusal to Let or Sell Property: This happens when a property owner is being pressured to sell or lease property but refuses to do so.

This may happen for a number of reasons. A property owner may value the property sentimentally because it has family connections or he may believe it is worth more than is being offered for it by an authority, or the owner may have moral or ethical objections to the use to which the buyer will put the land (industrial development, for instance).

Refusal to sell often occurs in so-called "compulsory purchase" disputes, where a private owner refuses to sell some land to a government authority or developer.

Considerations and risks: If this is private property and there are no compulsory notices of expropriation then there are no real risks associated with refusing to let or sell a property, provided that the refusal is not based on the grounds of racial, sexual or religious discrimination. On this the law varies according to country.

If, however, a property is subject to some form of compulsory purchase order, the refusal to sell will need to be organised in cooperation with other property owners in the same position. A lone protester will probably lose in such an action and be obliged to sell the property anyway. A group of protesters acting together has a better chance of turning the protest into a political issue and not just a simple, individual's legal defiance.

Historical and contemporary examples: There are many examples where individuals and groups have refused, for various reasons, to sell or lease their property. One simple, touchingly brave example occurred in 2001 in Limavady in County Derry, when a large supermarket chain attempted to build an expansive store and car park. Part of the land they needed belonged to 78-year-old Helena Hunt, a local resident. When she was told that her garden was needed for this major town centre redevelopment project, a scheme involving the building of a supermarket and the creation of 200 jobs, she stood firm and said no. She loved her garden too much to sell out. The property developer then upped his offer by degrees from £40,000 to £250,000. And still Ms Hunt refused to sell - with the result that finally, the entire development fell through [Note 35].

8.2 Civil Disobedience: Economic Non-Cooperation - The Strike

This form of protest action involves the partial or complete withdrawal of labour in order to impact a target authority or company economically. By refusing to provide labour, the protesters are able to disrupt the production, operations or sales of the target and negatively impact their economic performance. It is useful (essential) for an organiser to have a good understanding of local employment law [for example Note 36]. The following diagram shows the many forms that a strike action can take:

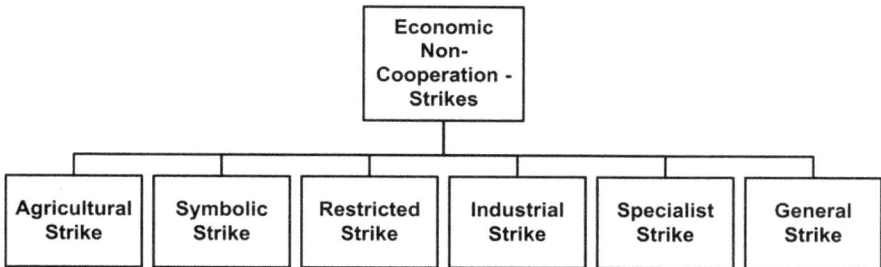

```
                    ┌──────────────┐
                    │   Economic   │
                    │     Non-     │
                    │ Cooperation -│
                    │   Strikes    │
                    └──────────────┘
```

Agricultural Strike	Symbolic Strike	Restricted Strike	Industrial Strike	Specialist Strike	General Strike

8.2.1 Agricultural - Fishery Strikes

Once upon a time, an agricultural strike meant that the peasantry were striking for better pay or working conditions. With the increasing domination of the global food industry by a small number of huge multinational companies, agricultural strikes in the 21st century are more likely to be farmers striking to be paid a living price for their produce. Price fixing and downward price pressure in the food industry is responsible for many of the protest actions in the agricultural sector. In the fishery sector, the problems are similar but protests usually centre on the forced reductions and division of fishery quotas and the domination of the sector by huge industrial fishing companies at the expense of small traditional fishermen.

```
                    ┌─────────────┐
                    │ Agricultural│
                    │  - Fishery  │
                    │   Strike    │
                    └─────────────┘
           ┌───────────────┼───────────────┐
    ┌─────────────┐ ┌─────────────┐ ┌─────────────┐
    │    Small    │ │    Farm     │ │    Farm     │
    │   Farmers   │ │  Workers    │ │   Product   │
    │   Strike    │ │   Strike    │ │ Price Strike│
    └─────────────┘ └─────────────┘ └─────────────┘
```

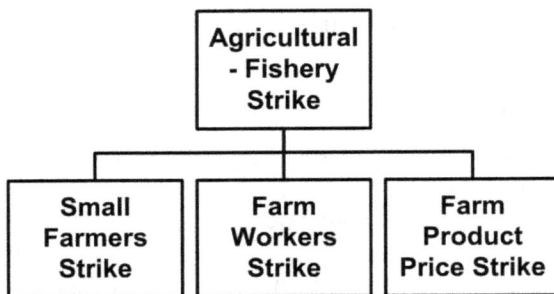

8.2.1.1 Small Farmers' / Fishermen's Strike: This is an action taken simultaneously by several small farmers or fishermen. Often, the protest is centred on poor prices being paid to farmers by large food corporations or, in the case of fishermen, the domination of their fishing grounds by industrial factory ships and government restrictions on catch sizes.

Farmers protesting against poor prices very often will target a supermarket chain and position themselves in front of their shops and give food away for nothing or sell it at wholesale prices. Of course, the public (and press) are very much attracted to this type of action (and by the very low prices). Farmers thus get an opportunity to explain their case to the public and bypass the supermarket "middlemen" to sell their produce.

Fishermen's protests tend to involve the dumping of rotten fish on the doorsteps of government buildings in a protest against what they see as unfair quotas and over-fishing. Sometimes fishermen also sell their catch directly to the public at very low prices. In both cases, the media is attracted to the protest action and this helps to get the story into the public domain.

Considerations and risks: For many farmers and small fishing operations, even a short interruption in agricultural production or fishing activities can have profound effects on their income and profitability. Thus, the primary risk of these types of strikes is that any loss of income may contribute to their bankruptcy. Hence, the most popular action is to continue production but to sell at cost price directly to the public. This keeps the funds flowing but punishes the "middlemen" or unfair competition that is really the target of the protest.

Historical and contemporary examples: The struggle to survive for the small-in-shore fishing fleet in Europe when faced by huge industrial fishing and extremely tight catch quotas has meant that many an artisan fishing family has lost its traditional income and been forced into bankruptcy.

In response to the imposition of catch limits on very small vessels, many fishermen have taken to giving away the surplus catches to the public for nothing. In 2012, Irish inshore fishermen began giving away thousands of Euros worth of prime fish to the public to protest the EU quotas. When confronted by Fisheries protection officers, fishermen who had exceeded their quotas for monkfish refused to dump the fish into the sea at the dock and instead openly unloaded it and gave it to passers-by and supporters on the quayside as a protest against the wasteful and unfair system of quotas (in the case quoted Irish fisherman have only 7% of the quota for fish in Irish waters, the rest being held by large international fishing operations) [Note 37]

French farmers have something of a reputation for giving away or selling produce at very low prices. However, occasionally they lose their patience and take rather more offensive (smelly) action. In November 2014, angry French farmers dumped hundreds of tonnes of manure and rotten vegetables on the streets as well as spraying a council water treatment office with slurry in a major day of protest. Members of the French Farmers Union (FNSEA) and the Young Farmers Union (YA) held demonstrations over worsening food prices as well as increases in the cost of fertiliser. Farmers complain that EU sanctions against Russia caused by the Ukrainian crisis led to the collapse in the prices of cereal and milk [Note 38]. During one protest in Chartres, farmers dumped 100 tonnes of manure along with rotting vegetables outside the offices of the agriculture department and the town hall. Around 300 farmers using 30 tractors took part in the protest. Union leader Jean Michel Gouache said his members were "fed up over increasingly crazy constraints and charges". In central Paris, farmers unloaded 50 tonnes of fruit and vegetables at the Place de la République and gave them away for free.

8.2.1.2 Farm Workers Strike: Farm workers in many countries are frequently amongst the most poorly treated in the workforce. Their working conditions are often very tough, and the continuous downward pressure on food prices means that they are generally poorly paid. Nonetheless, farm workers have a long history of taking strike action and the level of solidarity amongst farm workers is usually very high, which means that they can quickly and effectively close down a farmer's business without much risk of strike breakers interfering.

Farms are labour-intensive and a strike by dairy parlour workers, for instance, would have an urgent and dramatic impact on farm operations within 12 hours. The same goes for workers in other livestock farms. Animals need to be fed and cleaned out regularly or else they may well die quite quickly. Other types of farm workers, such as tractor and machine drivers may not be quite so critical. However during times of peak machine activity such as harvest and sowing times when every minute counts, the cooperation of drivers and machine operators is much more critical

Considerations and risks: Farm workers are often non-unionised workers because they tend to work in small numbers in remote places. For this reason these workers are often targets for bullying by their employers. Therefore it is best to ensure that a farm workers' strike is supported by a union and has the support of workers in other sectors that provide services, materials and fuel to the farm or farms involved. This includes delivery men, suppliers' employees, maintenance workers, customers' employees etc. Thus, when a strike is declared, the farmer must be made to realise that he cannot just bully the aggrieved farm workers. It needs to be made clear that he will be confronted with a unified front of workers that will not cooperate with him. In rural areas where there is a strong sense of community this kind of solidarity is often quite feasible. Many self-employed workers may also take a stand with the farm workers if they consider their demands reasonable. A union will support the workers, and other union workers will refuse to pass a picket line.

Historical and contemporary examples: Working conditions and pay for farm labourers are appalling in some countries and have been for centuries. There is a wealth of history of peasants' strikes and revolts in all cultures, some of which we have already mentioned.

To give a contemporary example, in 2012 in South Africa's Western Cape widespread strikes and acts of sabotage were carried out by farm workers protesting low wages, and poor working conditions. Much of the protest, involving thousands of farm workers, was aimed at Agri SA members, the farm owner organisation, which was accused of refusing to negotiate a living wage with the striking workers.

In the protests, damage by arson to farm machinery and buildings was caused by the strikers and protesters, running to millions of Rand. Despite farm owners' attempts to unite against the strikers, and because of their refusal to negotiate, the final result by 2013 was a government imposed minimum wage, which was actually in excess of what would have been a likely compromise wage. The arrogance of the farm owners left them far worse off than if they had simply negotiated properly with their workers at a local level [Note 39].

8.2.1.3 Farm Producer Price Strike: This is by far the most likely type of strike to take place in the agricultural sector in modern times. Resulting from the market dominance by a handful of large food companies, the downward pressure on food prices is constant.

In recent years there have been many price strikes, where groups of large farmers have come together to refuse to sell their produce to a particular cooperative, processor or supermarket. This is a different strategy to that of the small farmers described earlier, in that these large farming concerns simply stop the supply completely in order to force the supermarkets or processing factories to raise their prices.

Considerations and risks: The risks of ceasing production for an extended period are that the loss of income may permanently cripple a farmer. Farmers therefore should find alternative direct markets for their produce in order to maintain an income stream, whilst simultaneously punishing the customer cartels that are under-paying for their produce by cutting off their supply.

Historical and contemporary examples: There have been several such strikes in the European milk industry in recent years and the protesting farmers simply divert their milk away from their target company and use it to feed calves or sell it instead to be converted to milk powder. Whilst this does negatively affect their cash flow, it has the effect of successfully forcing up the price of the commodity. Similar actions have been taken with grain, wine, sugar beet, sunflower seed, rape seed and other produce.

8.2.2 Symbolic Strikes

As the name implies these are strike actions aimed at shocking or frightening a target authority. They are not specifically aimed at causing economic damage to the target. They are generally short and often without notice. The protesters in this case are basically sending a signal to the authority that they can and will strike in earnest unless their demands are taken seriously.

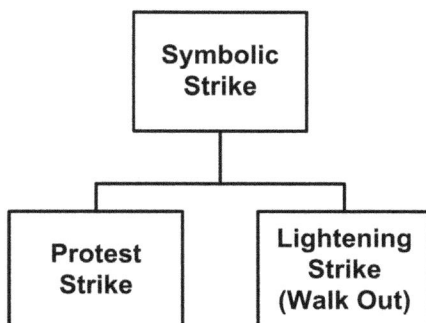

8.2.2.1 Protest Strike: A protest strike is (usually) a short strike planned to draw attention to a specific protest issue. The protest issue may or may not be connected with the workers' own pay and conditions. Indeed, such strikes are often called to protest an outside political or ethical issue.

Considerations and risks: One important factor with a protest strike is to make sure that the issues are made very clear to the public or to those suffering from inconvenience or disruption otherwise the public will just dismiss the strike as a selfish demand for more money.

Very often strike action is assumed to be something to do with money or working conditions. A protest strike often happens as a matter of principle and is unrelated to the strikers' pay and conditions.

Historical and contemporary examples: Protest strikes are often about wide-ranging issues affecting a whole society. In recent years, in many parts of Europe, such issues have revolved around austerity and the social evils of poverty.

In Greece in July 2013, tens of thousands of workers walked off the job and rallied in front of parliament in a huge protest against government austerity plans to sack public-sector staff. The Athens government had a list of between 12,500 and 25,000 workers slated for a "mobility pool" in which they are given eight months to find work in another department or get sacked. Over 30,000 demonstrators, including police and teachers facing dismissal, demonstrated in one of the biggest anti-austerity protests of that year. Civil aviation unions staged a four-hour work stoppage and Athens' transport system was badly affected, with bus and trolleybus drivers walking out. Trains stopped running and tax offices and municipal services remained shut. Rubbish collectors, commercial drivers, bank employees and journalists were some other groups that joined the walkout in solidarity [Note 40].

In 2014, thousands of nurses across the United States staged protest rallies and strikes over what they claimed was insufficient protection for health workers dealing with patients possibly stricken with the deadly Ebola virus. California-based National Nurses United estimated that about 100,000 nurses nationwide participated in the protest strike. The nurses are pressing hospitals to buy hazardous materials suits which leave no skin exposed, as well as powered air-purifying respirators, to properly protect nurses from exposure, and they are calling for more training to handle patients suspected of having Ebola [Note 41].

8.2.2.2 Lightening Strike - Walk Out: A lightening strike or "walk out" or "quickie walk out" is an unofficial strike that is not planned long in advance. It may be an almost spontaneous action where strikers leave their workplace without any advance warning to their employer.

Very often lightening strikes occur because management has caused serious offence to some or all of a workforce. This triggers an immediate withdrawal of the workers from the workplace, often to a nearby assembly area where workers gather to await an offer of resolution. Lightening strikes are usually short-lived but can develop into full-scale industrial strikes.

Considerations and risks: Sometimes lightening strikes are planned to coincide with periods when the target organisation is very busy or very dependent on its workforce. This instant withdrawal of labour can have a very dramatic effect on the organisation and its management. For example, such a strike occurring when a factory is fully occupied with an important and urgent order can be very effective at persuading the management to negotiate and cooperate with the workers' demands.

Of course, with all strikes there is a risk that the strike may lead to retaliation against "ring-leaders" later on and organisers should always demand amnesty for participants as part of any settlement.

Taking advantage of spontaneous labour rebellions: In an ideal world, there would always be structures in place for a workforce to be able to respond to unexpected disputes in the workplace. Unfortunately, this is hardly ever the case and such structures using unions tend to be weak and disorganised, slow and bureaucratic.

The situations that upset a workforce the most are likely to be unanticipated. Sudden rebellion is most likely to develop as a response to unexpected decisions or circumstances, such as unfair sackings, shift changes and other unilateral actions by the management. The workforce's reactions often need to be rapid and are therefore often fairly ad-hoc. The following describes some ways in which a local organiser can make the most of these spontaneous "work rebellions":

• **Act quickly.** In spontaneous disputes, the response needs to be very quick. Asking people to go to a meeting a few days later is worthless. In such an event, an incident is no longer at the forefront of people's minds. After a delay, a management's decision may have gained reluctant acceptance just by having been applied for some time and the initial fury will have passed, and so probably will the time to act. Action needs to be almost immediate.

• **Think carefully.** Although the activists need to act quickly, their actions also need to be considered and responsible, which is difficult in an emotive atmosphere. For instance, one has to consider if a further confrontation will lead to improvements or perhaps become a pyrrhic victory leading to even more job losses, for instance. In these circumstances it is much more important to think as workers rather than as political activists. In addition, at this critical moment it is vital to inform the people as honestly as possible about the likely consequences of further action and avoid giving other workers false hope.

• **Get everyone away from work.** The next most important action is to get the workers in dispute away from the workplace, to make them stop doing the things they are supposed to be doing. The routine tasks of daily work become ingrained responses and to get everyone to stop doing what they are supposed to be doing is a difficult but important step that opens the door to various possibilities.

As soon as the workers get away from their actual workplace they are effectively on strike. Then the management has to get the workers to go back. The longer the workers can stay away the harder that is likely to be. This works just as well for small as for large employers. Small companies sometimes respond more rapidly to this form of pressure than large ones. If two workers make up 66% of the workforce, the management is going to be a bit more pressured if the workers refuse to work. However, this depends on how easy it is for them to find new workers at short notice.

• **Don't talk to management.** In the early stages of such a spontaneous conflict it is better not to enter into dialogue with the management. It may seem a sensible thing to do, but in doing so a workforce inevitably gets drawn into a discourse about the future of the company and their jobs. This moves the debate into an area where the management is strong, whereas the strength of the workforce is in its collective ability to stop working. Thus, entering into negotiations stalls the momentum of a spontaneous action and is considered a bad move. The best action from the workers' perspective is to collectively refuse whatever decision has sparked off the rebellion and to forego all other discussions for the time being - until the management has had time to consider its precarious position.

• **Spread the struggle.** In a spontaneous situation like this it's important to spread the strike throughout the company and perhaps across geographical areas and industries, if appropriate. This entails communicating with different parts of the workforce telling them what's going on and persuading them to participate.

Even when they aren't totally successful, these sorts of spontaneous revolts can make management become somewhat circumspect about discussing their decisions with the workforce in advance. This opens up a certain amount of space for workers to negotiate properly with their managements.

Historical and contemporary examples: Lightening strikes have a long and infamous history. They are one of the strike actions most feared by employers. They cannot be easily planned around and they cause instant economic or organisational disruption.

In November 2014, for the third year in a row, a group of Walmart employees walked off their jobs at the retail giant on Black Friday, the US' busiest retail sales day of the year. The employees, with the support of their union, are calling for $15 minimum hourly wages, and fair work schedules. They also demand a reduction in their increasing workload as the company looks to hire fewer employees, while passing more work off to their current workers. Protests and unannounced walk outs took place at over 1600 Walmart stores [Note 42].

8.2.3 Restricted Strikes

Restricted Strikes are a form of strike which does not involve a complete withdrawal of labour as in a full-scale strike. The idea of a restricted strike is that it causes inconvenience and a reduced operating capacity to the employer, without causing a complete closure of the operations and without damaging the employees too much.

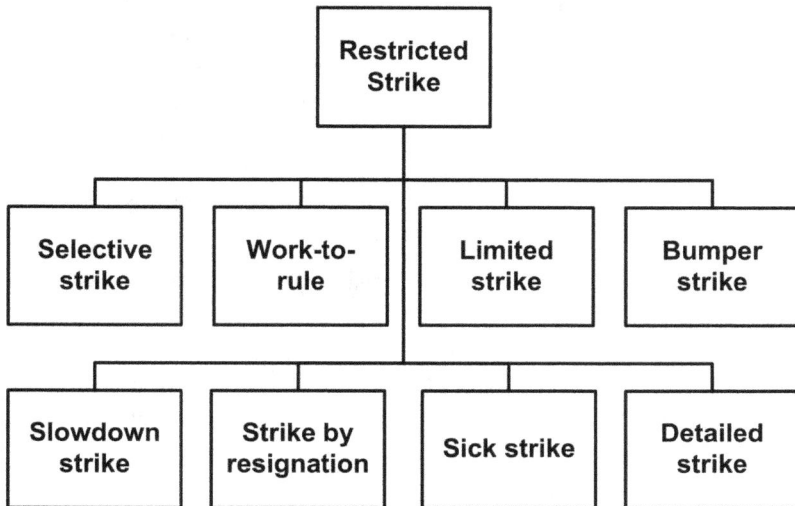

8.2.3.1 Selective Strike: This is a partial strike against a particular area of a business or against one employer or a small number of employers in a

331

collective bargaining situation. This type of strike is often designed to force several employers to bargain together. In fact, unions developed the selective strike specifically for this purpose.

The strategy of the strikers is to target sites that will cause a company the greatest economic harm and to discourage employers from either breaking away from a collective bargaining group or obliging them to join a collective bargaining group.

Considerations and risks: In a selective strike, the union strikes against one employer (or just a few employers) within a multi-employer bargaining group. The strike is usually of a short duration (a few days or a week at most). The union generally strikes against one employer at a time. Strikes may occur one after another (rolling strikes) and may overlap, or there may be a long period of inaction between strikes. The same employer may be struck repeatedly, with sometimes as little as 24 hours between strikes. Strikes are typically called off when an employer agrees to return to collective negotiation.

8.2.3.2 Slowdown Strike: A slowdown or "go-slow" is an action where employees carry on working but deliberately reduce productivity or efficiency in their performance. It is sometimes used as an alternative to a strike as it is seen as less disruptive, as well as less risky and costly for workers and their union.

Slowdowns are sometimes accompanied by intentional sabotage on the part of workers to cause further disruption. Sometimes slowdown actions are justified by the protesting employees by referring to legally binding but loosely interpreted health and safety rules. Employers frequently punish employees for "going slow", but it can be very difficult for an employer to dismiss an employee in such a case without running the risk of being accused of unfair dismissal and taken to an employment tribunal (in countries which have such legal protections).

Considerations and risks: The same risks apply to a slowdown strike as to other types of worker action against employers, i.e. retaliation and victimisation of participants. Such strikes need to be well organised and scalable. In other words, employers must realise that retaliation against strikers will trigger off an instant and escalated response strike action.

Historical and contemporary examples: During the 1970s, at Ford's car plant in Dagenham, in Britain, workers introduced a slowdown after Ford management unilaterally increased the production line speed from 18 to 21 feet per minute. This was the second speed increase of the production line and workers felt that this was unfair. After a slowdown by production line staff which caused major production disruption, Ford management reduced the line speed back to 18 feet per minute and work practices returned to normal.

8.2.3.3 Work-to-rule: A work-to-rule is an industrial action similar to a "go-slow" action. In a work-to-rule action, employees do no more than the minimum required by the terms of their employment contract. They may also precisely follow health and safety, quality and other regulations in order to cause a reduction in productivity. Such an action is considered less disruptive to the employee than a full-scale strike, but it is still very effective and can be very frustrating to the target organisation.

Simply "obeying the rules" makes an employee much less susceptible to disciplinary action. Examples of work-to-rule have included refusals to work overtime, travel for work or to agree to perform other tasks outside the employment contract which require employee assent.

Almost every job is covered by a maze of rules, regulations, standing orders, and so on; many of them are completely unworkable and generally ignored. Workers often violate orders, resort to their own techniques of doing things, and disregard lines of authority simply to meet the goals of the company. There is often a tacit understanding, even by the managers whose job it is to enforce the rules that these shortcuts must be taken in order to meet targets in a pragmatic way.

But what happens if all of these rules and regulations are followed to the letter? Confusion results, productivity and morale plummets. But best of all for the protesters, the workers can't get themselves into trouble with their employers using this tactic because they are, after all, "just following the employer's own rules."

Considerations and risks: Many of the rules contained in a contract of employment may be bent by either employer or employee. By adopting a work-to-rule there is a risk that employers may also demand adherence to rules which are less than advantageous to employees, such as punctuality, dress, conduct, productivity, and rest allowances. There is a risk that a work-to-rule may end in strikers shooting themselves in the foot, though generally this is not the case.

Historical and contemporary examples: Working to rule is a technique mainly of the 20th century and it has given rise to some bizarre manifestations.

Under the period of railway nationalisation, French railway strikes were forbidden. Nonetheless, rail workers found other ways of expressing their grievances. One French law required a railway engineer to ensure the safety of any bridge over which a train must pass. If after a personal examination they were still doubtful, then they were obliged to consult other members of the train crew. Of course, every bridge was so inspected, every crew was thus consulted, and none of the trains ran on time.

Then there was the case of the Austrian postal service. In order to gain certain demands without losing their jobs, the Austrian postal workers strictly observed the rule that all mail must be weighed to see if the proper postage was affixed. Formerly they had passed without weighing all those letters and parcels which were clearly underweight, thus living up to the spirit of the regulation but not to its exact wording. By taking each separate piece of mail to the scales, carefully weighing it, and then returning it to its proper place, the postal workers congested the office with un-weighed mail by the second day of their action.

8.2.3.4 Strike by Resignation: This strike action generally involves the mass resignation of a number of employees with the objective of forcing a company's management to negotiate new conditions. It is typically used by specialist employees that cannot be easily replaced by the company. There are many examples of specialists such as surgeons, scientists, technicians collectively resigning, knowing that their replacement would be almost impossible and thus forcing the employer to negotiate with them.

Very often highly specialist employees have little to lose from resigning because they know that they can easily find alternative employment. This causes additional pressure on the employer to act quickly to resolve the dispute before his top people find new (and better) jobs.

Considerations and risks: The obvious risk is that strikers may lose their jobs. If something goes wrong and the employer calls the strikers' bluff it may transpire that the strikers are jobless when the protest is concluded. On the other hand, a properly organised protest will demand that there are no job losses or recriminations after a settlement and the strike organisers need to build this contingency into their planning.

Historical and contemporary examples: In 2004, in France, some 2000 research workers resigned en masse in protest against the (under) funding policies of the government of Prime Minister Jean-Pierre Raffarin. These resignations largely halted the organisational work of research teams, including the ordering of new equipment, the search for new funding, the attainment of travel grants, etc. The daily La Croix found that over 80 percent of the public polled supported the researchers strike action [Note 43].

8.2.3.5 Limited Strike: A limited strike is a planned industrial action which has a time limit. Thus a teachers' union may declare 5 limited strikes of 2 days each on planned dates. The strikes are carried out for precisely the time for which they are planned and limited to this.

Considerations and risks: In Western countries these types of strike carry few threats. The strikes are legal, scheduled and normally organised by a recognised trade union. As always, in some less liberal countries, strike activists risk retaliation from their employers.

8.2.3.6 Sick Strike - Taking Sick Leave: Taking sick leave as a means of striking is often used by employees who are legally prohibited to strike. This strategy is frequently used by the police, fire-fighters, air traffic controllers, all of whom are legally forbidden to strike in some countries. It is often done en masse; leaving the employers in no doubt that this is an industrial action, however, it's impossible to prove that it is and the employers are unable to take disciplinary or legal actions against the strikers.

Considerations and risks: Sick leave becomes part of an employee's record and despite a settlement this sick leave data may remain on and damage an employee's record. It is important that organisers ensure that sick leave taken as part of a dispute is removed from an employee's record. This should be a part of the settlement reached in a dispute using this method.

Historical and contemporary examples: Obviously going sick is an easy and ancient way of refusing to work and it is just as popular as an industrial protest as it ever was.

In 2012, a surge in sick calls from Air Canada pilots led to disruption of travel schedules on one of the busiest weekends of the year [Note 44]. The inconvenience caused to thousands of travellers highlighted Air Canada's difficulties establishing a peace with its employees. Captain Jean-Marc Bélanger, chairman of the 3,000-member union, said that he had conducted a self-assessment and deemed himself unfit to fly, based on his personal workload and sleep deprivation. Air Canada said it had seen a surge in the number of pilots calling in sick since March 2012, after management tabled its final offer during protracted contract talks. The airline reported 23 flight cancellations across its network on the following Saturday. Air Canada alleged that some of its pilots had been absent from work in what it asserted was an illegal strike activity sanctioned by the union. More than a dozen pilots cited stress or fatigue for their absence on that Saturday in Montreal, for instance.

8.2.3.7 Bumper Strike: This is a strategy whereby a union organises strikes against a group of companies, but rather than striking in all of the companies simultaneously, the union focuses action on one company at a time to maximise the disruption and economic damage to the company before moving onto the next company. The idea of a bumper strike is to take out one company at a time and then move onto the next target to create sustained damage to the group as a whole, without putting the entire strike burden on the workers in one company alone.

Considerations and risks: In Western countries these types of strike carry few threats. The strikes are legal, scheduled and normally organised by a recognised trade union. As always, in some less liberal countries, strike activists risk retaliation from their employers. From a planning point of view, it's important to schedule the strike action to optimise its effect. Start with the weakest companies first in order to gain experience, maximise the effect and then escalate to the larger companies within the group.

8.2.3.8 Detailed Strike: This is a work stoppage or strike where employees stop work and/or leave the workplace one by one. The idea of this kind of action is to gradually increase the pressure on the employer until they agree to negotiate. Normally, the remaining employees' first demand is the reinstatement and a full amnesty for the employees who have already stopped work.

Considerations and risks: This method relies on the gradually increasing threat to disrupt production as more and more employees go on strike. It can be spread over any period but generally has been used over a few days or weeks. For this reason, this isn't a strategy used very often in industrial disputes because recent legislation in most countries demands that strike notices be issued by a participating union for an action in advance of its happening. However, in non-union companies (many farms, for example) it may still be a very good way of increasing pressure on the employer without actually completely stopping production. Retaliation against the "early leavers" is the main risk and any resolution must include an amnesty for all participants.

8.2.4 Industrial Strikes

Industrial strikes are full-scale work stoppages in an industrial context caused by the mass refusal of employees to work. There are various types of strike action. A strike usually takes place in response to employee grievances about payment and/or other working conditions.

Strikes are also sometimes used to pressure governments to change policies. Strikes are sometimes used to destabilise a government or a particular political party or ruler. In such cases, strikes are part of a broader social or political protest movement taking the form of a campaign of civil resistance and civil disobedience.

To win in a strike the strikers need to have a clear understanding of the target organisation and its vulnerabilities, and they need to develop a plan to exploit those vulnerabilities. Usually, no one single strike action or tactic provides enough pressure to beat a confident employer. There needs to be constant and creative escalation, using complimentary actions such as picketing, boycotts, secondary picketing etc. Strikes are more similar to conflicts of attrition than a knock-out blow.

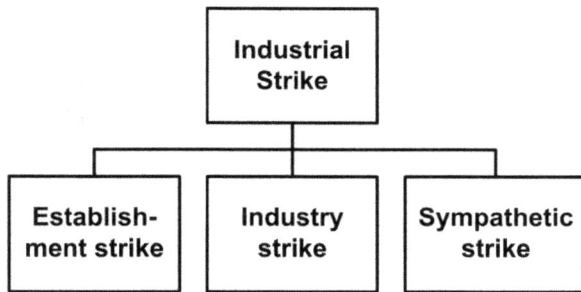

```
                    ┌─────────────┐
                    │ Industrial  │
                    │   Strike    │
                    └─────────────┘
          ┌──────────────┼──────────────┐
  ┌──────────────┐ ┌──────────────┐ ┌──────────────┐
  │ Establish-   │ │  Industry    │ │ Sympathetic  │
  │ ment strike  │ │   strike     │ │   strike     │
  └──────────────┘ └──────────────┘ └──────────────┘
```

8.2.4.1 Establishment Strike: An establishment strike is aimed at just one employer under a single management. These are the most focused strike actions and are usually restricted to grievances with that particular management.

Considerations and risks: In most jurisdictions there are legal limitations placed on strike action, which include prohibitions against strikes by certain groups of workers (police, for example), a minimum notice period for a strike, and various mandatory attempts at arbitration. Penalties for a union breaching such regulations are sometimes quite severe. On the other hand, strikes often occur almost spontaneously and without union organisers. In these cases, such regulations become somewhat irrelevant. Even in restricted professions, the excuse of sickness or personal commitment has often been used to absent large numbers of workers from their work. The legal regulation of labour attendance is pretty much a waste of time, except where the workforce is physically enslaved.

The risks of any form of strike addressing a single establishment are clear. After a strike there may be recriminations and attempts at revenge. During a strike the protesters will be without income or work. Strike organisers must be prepared to economically and socially support strikers and their families. This will take considerable resources and requires access to a "strike fund". These are normal in a unionised environment, but in a non-union dispute, a fund must be built in advance of industrial action. An average industrial family will start to feel uncomfortable after as little as six weeks without any income.

The perpetual risk to the strike organiser is the use of strike breakers by the company's management. Various methods are available to discourage strike-breakers, which include policies often referred to as "pickets to persuade" and "ostracism to exclude". Publishing the images and details of strike breakers in the press or on the internet may be illegal in some cases, but it is nonetheless a powerful disincentive to break a strike or betray your workmates.

Historical and contemporary examples: Since the Industrial Revolution, there have been thousands of company-targeted strike actions. They are certainly the most common forms of industrial action in Western industrial society.

The International Covenant on Economic, Social and Cultural Rights (ICESCR) is a multilateral treaty adopted by the United Nations General Assembly on 16 December 1966. Article 8 of this covenant ensures the worker's right to take strike action [Note 45].

8.2.4.2 Industry Strike: This type of strike action is aimed at an entire industry and all of the companies involved in that industry are affected by it. An example would be a coal mining strike or a fuel delivery driver's strike.

Considerations and risks: The normal legal considerations apply here as in all strike actions. The organisers' main strategy in this type of industry-level strike is to maximise disruption as quickly as possible with minimum pain for the striking workers.

So, for example, if the strike affects power-station workers, it is important to cause maximum supply disruption as soon as possible. This may take some pre-preparation to ensure that the moment the strike begins the management finds itself unable to cope. For instance, for several weeks / months in advance of a strike, it would be wise for the strike organisers to deliberately cancel or delay planned maintenance work so that when the strike begins there is a backlog of work to be done. This backlog will then cause either system failures or urgent maintenance work, both of which are disruptive.

Industry-wide strikes tend to trigger strong reactions from politicians that see essential services or industries being severely disrupted as politically calamitous. In such circumstances, politicians may use military or other government personnel to maintain basic systems. This is a risk to the success of the campaign, and again, some early planning before a strike can make external intervention less effective. Maintenance failures, for instance, may be insurmountable regardless of government intervention.

Historical and contemporary examples: One of the abiding images of post-industrial Britain are those of striking miners in 1984-1985 and their struggle with the Conservative government of Margaret Thatcher.

Although the miners lost their strike, the conflict revealed much about the methods of government and the morality of the British Tory party. To this day, the damaging effects to the credibility of the British Conservative Party are still impossible to gauge. Apart from anything else, the conflict polarised political opinion. The Thatcher government used every possible authoritarian dirty trick to defeat the miners. MI5 was involved in "counter subversion" against organisers and the police were clearly partisan to the Thatcher government in their treatment of demonstrators. Thatcher dominated the media coverage of the strike and her manipulation of public opinion was so ruthless and dishonest that it is has continued to provide reams of material for students to pore over and analyse. Morally, the miners are still perceived as the injured party, whereas the British Conservative Party is still referred to (even by its own adherents) as the "Nasty Party" [Note 46].

8.2.4.3 Sympathetic Strike (aka Solidarity Action): This is a strike action in support of a strike initiated by workers in another, separate enterprise. This type of solidarity action is illegal in many countries. Despite this, solidarity actions are still possible using some of the other tactics available to the workers, such as work-to-rule, sick strikes etc.

The term "secondary action" is sometimes used with the intention of distinguishing different types of dispute with a worker's direct employer. Thus, the term may be used to refer to a dispute with an employer's suppliers, a parent company, its financiers, or any other employer in another industry connected to the employer in the main strike action.

Considerations and risks: In most countries there are limits on the purposes for which people may go on strike. In continental Europe, solidarity action is generally lawful and the right to strike is seen as a part of broader political freedom.

However, in many English-speaking nations restrictions have been placed on organisations against which trade unions may strike. In the US, Australia and UK workers can typically strike only against their direct employer and the use of "sympathy strikes" is severely restricted. In the UK any form of sympathy action is basically outlawed. In reality though, it is impossible to stop a consumer or supplier boycott against a secondary target and legal attempts to control this are futile.

Historical and contemporary examples: Farm labourers in the United States are not covered by the same restrictions on sympathetic action as industrial workers. Thus, in the 1970s, the United Farm Workers union was able to legally use solidarity boycotting of grocery store chains as an aid to their strikes against various Californian food industries by means of boycotts of Californian grapes, lettuce and wine. The union's secondary boycotts involved asking consumers to stop shopping at a grocery store chain until such time as the chain stopped carrying the boycotted products.

In 2012, a rare sympathetic strike took place in Seattle in the USA when 250 drivers of Republic Services refused to work. Their action was in solidarity with 24 striking co-workers in Alabama. Because of certain clauses in their contracts regarding respecting a picket line and because the strike was seen as being instigated by the company's illegal demands, the sympathetic strike was seen as legal. It spread throughout this large garbage clearing utility and finally ended in executive resignations and an agreement with the strikers [Note 47].

8.2.5 Specialist Strikes

Over the years since strikes were first used to bring pressure to bear on employers, the technique has evolved into many hybrids designed to be used by various specialist groups in diverse circumstances. Here are some of them:

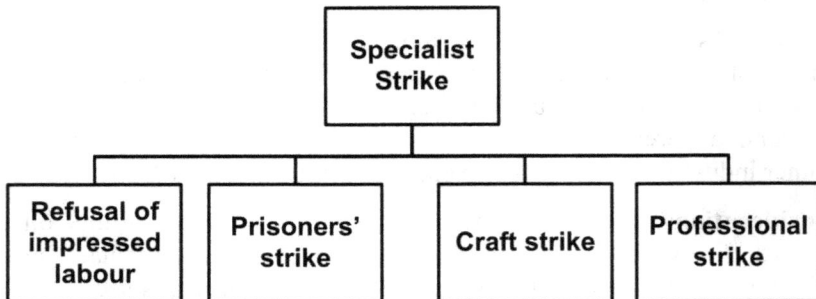

8.2.5.1 Refusal of Impressed Labour: Impressed labour is a labour-force which is obliged to work by an authority, usually a government. Very often social welfare systems oblige those receiving a benefit to do some work on community projects, such as maintaining public buildings and gardens, for example. Systems of obliging labour are generally very unpopular and akin, many argue, to a system of forced labour or slavery. These systems of employment often trigger off strike action where workers refuse to take part in such "projects".

Considerations and risks: If you are somehow forced into labour, then there is little to lose when protesting the conditions, apart from your life in some cases. You probably won't lose your "job", anyway. However, clearly, those working in impressed labour are already living under the worst possible conditions. Whether this is some form of gangster-organised slavery, a traditional caste system of slavery or Western government-sponsored "legal slavery", the victim is in a grave predicament. In general, any refusal to work should be part of a larger action with colleagues. If this is not possible, then the strike action will not work and may well cost someone their life or basic livelihood. In the case of Western, government-backed "work-experience" schemes, it is best to act in unison because the act of a single individual will simply attract victimisation and revenge.

Historical and contemporary examples: In 2012, the group "Right to Work" demonstrated at the small Tesco store opposite the House of Commons, protesting against a "workfare" scheme that pressed people to stack shelves for free for companies like Tesco. The group considered that there was no use demonstrating outside the Department for Work and Pensions; rather it would be better to attack the participating companies directly. Tesco (and other retailers) are highly sensitive about their image. "Workfare" is transparently unfair to most people, substituting slave labour for proper employees for big companies, (often corporate friends of the Tory party in Britain). Within a few days of the strike hitting the national press, several of Britain's largest companies had withdrawn from the scheme. The scheme was then fairly swiftly abandoned by the British government, much to the embarrassment of the coalition government parties. It has not been resurrected since [Note 48].

8.2.5.2 Prisoners' Strike: Not all strikes involve workers seeking better conditions for themselves. Prison inmates often strike to gain better living conditions within a prison. Frequently, these strikes combine a refusal to work with hunger strikes. Despite prison strikes being considered a serious offence in many countries, it is often the case that prisoners have very little left to lose and are therefore not discouraged even by further punishments or removal of privileges.

Considerations and risks: Prisoners' conditions are often so bad that they frequently feel that they can only gain by going on strike for better conditions or special treatment. In fact, they do run the risk of greater disciplinary actions, physical punishment, loss of privileges, or solitary confinement, so there is indeed much to lose.

As always, an action taken by a large group reduces the risk of revenge by prison authorities as they try to calm the situation. Whereas prison authorities can threaten and punish one or two prisoners, it becomes a lot more dangerous to punish several hundred prisoners.

The organisers of a prison strike need good communications with the outside world. A strike inside a prison is easy to hide by the authorities if no-one outside the prison knows about it. Therefore, at least one group of prisoners needs to remain outside of the strike action in order to report to the world on what is happening inside the prison.

Historical and contemporary examples: Prisoner strikes have a long history. Amongst the most high profile political prisoners' strikes in the Western world over the last 100 years are those by the English Suffragettes and the Irish Republican prisoners of the Maze prison, both of which included hunger strikes and led to loss of life.

8.2.5.3 Craft Strike: A craft strike is an industrial action by one particular specialist skill across all industries. Electricians or refinery operators, for instance, may decide to go on strike in all companies nationwide to obtain better working conditions and pay for their trade.

Considerations and risks: Craftsmen tend to be in demand and, generally, suffer a low risk of recrimination after a strike. Nonetheless, the use of contractors may alleviate the effects of a strike. As always, the organisers of a craft strike should embody an amnesty for participants in any settlement.

Historical and contemporary examples: The fear of being left without the really skilled workers upon whom an industry is dependent has long been a fear of capitalist organisations. Over the years there have been many strikes by skilled workers, protecting their own and their colleagues' interests.

Example: In 2013, electricians in St James' hospital in Dublin went on strike and caused serious disruption because the management was trying to loosen the regulation of electrical systems in the hospital and allow in freelance electricians with no experience of medical electrical installations.

8.2.5.4 Professionals' Strike: A professionals' strike is the withdrawal of labour of a group of salaried workers or self-employed professionals such as doctors, lawyers etc. The withdrawal of professionals isn't quite as rare as it may sound. Though the professional classes are often well-paid they do have other concerns which oblige them to strike.

Doctors may strike because of deteriorating conditions for patients and lawyers may take action (as they did recently in the United Kingdom) to oppose cuts in the legal aid systems for defendants. Strike action by professionals can have dramatic effects. In the case of the barristers' strikes in the UK, the action effectively suspended a number of high profile criminal prosecutions in several superior courts.

Considerations and risks: Strikes by doctors, lawyers, teachers and other professionals don't always carry as much public sympathy as strikes by ordinary workers. The professional classes are perceived as being affluent and comfortable and strikes are seen as out of place for "their class". Nonetheless, strikes by professionals are frequently motivated by social or ethical demands more than personal grievances. The strikes by barristers in England were about the cuts to the Legal Aid system and the undermining of the criminal justice system. Teachers often strike because they are concerned about cuts in education budgets and lowering standards, and similarly in the medical profession: doctors tend to strike (when they do) in an effort to protect the quality of what they do, rather than to demand more money for themselves.

Organisers of professional strikes need to be good communicators and ensure that the public understands the reasons for a professional strike. In some countries it is theoretically illegal for some professionals to strike (air-traffic controllers, for instance, may not strike in Spain or the USA). Professional strikers are usually treated more leniently by police in street demonstrations, probably because the police perceive that any acts of violence against a professional may well have more serious consequences than when beating up some poor workers.

Historical and contemporary examples: One professional group that are very effective when they decide to strike are air-traffic controllers. In September 2014, a four-hour strike by Italian air-traffic controllers caused the cancellation of hundreds of flights. Controllers belonging to the LICSA union were responsible for the short stoppage [Note 49]. They were angry about plans for a "Single European Sky," which they believed would jeopardise safety as well as costing jobs in air-traffic control (ATC). This controversial EU project has triggered many strikes over the years.

In a strike driven by moral principles in Spain, in 2012, hundreds of Spanish doctors and nurses registered their protest at a new law that requires them to deny treatment to illegal immigrants. The new law proposed that non-EU immigrants who did not have residency permits would be denied treatment at public hospitals and health care centres, unless they were under 18, pregnant, or in case of emergency. The ruling was part of a series of austerity measures brought in by a conservative (PP) government to cut public spending. Doctors, nurses and other healthcare professionals condemned the measures as "unethical" and "inhumane" and registered as "conscientious objectors" against the new law. The Spanish Medical College said the new law "violates the ethical principles of medicine and the code of professional ethics". The Spanish Association of Neuropsychiatry said it marked "a regression in human rights". Protests were staged outside hospitals and health ministries across Spain for several months. Some 300 organisations across Spain, including patient associations, immigrant advocacy groups and health workers unions came out against the move that overturned the then current law which guaranteed free healthcare for all. Some autonomous regions of Spain, such as Catalonia and Andalucía, amongst others, said they would defy Madrid and continue to provide free basic healthcare and medicines to all those that need it, whatever their residency status. At the time of writing, the new law has been effectively side-tracked and remains unimplemented [Note 50].

8.2.6 General Strikes and Economic Actions

General strikes are frequently launched as a political act and a direct assault on the authority of an incumbent government. They are often combined with economic actions to suspend the national economy for a short period.

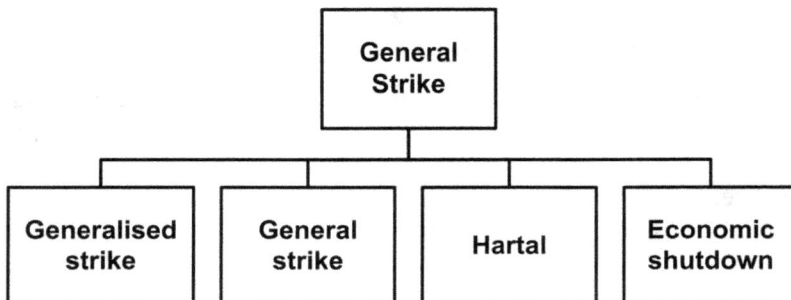

8.2.6.1 Generalised Strike Multi-Industry: This is a non-universal general strike. It affects many industries and many companies, but it is not completely universal like a general strike and it affects less than a majority of a nation's workers.

Considerations and risks: General and generalised strikes tend to be political protest actions rather than demands for changes in specific economic or working conditions. Because they are large-scale events there is some safety in numbers. Communications are, as ever, important in a generalised strike and it's important that everyone knows the reasons for the strike and what other protest activities will be held during the strike. To organise large-scale strike actions and demonstrations, to move huge numbers of people to a demo site, to make sure they are fed and watered, and kept safe requires professional organisational and logistical skills.

Historical and contemporary examples: Not all strikes are about personal working conditions; some have higher moral agendas, such as those that overthrew several Bolivian governments between 2003 and 2006.

Starting in 2003, workers and farmers in Bolivia began protests against the government, demanding redistribution of land and nationalisation of Bolivia's large natural gas reserves. The protests soon developed into blockades, and rolling generalised strikes in the gas, agricultural and mining sectors, followed by large-scale mass demonstrations in the capital. Police violence inflamed an already explosive situation and unions called for continuous strikes and the setting up of road blocks which virtually cut off supplies of food and fuel to the capital and closed the main airport. The strikers then demanded the resignation of the Bolivian president.

By October of 2003, the president called off the building of a contentious gas export pipeline to Chile, but he initially refused to resign. As columns of strikers from different parts of Bolivia then descended on the capital city, it took just four days for the president to step down. The vice-president took control of the government and promised reforms but by March of 2004, he had failed to deliver on any of his promises.

On March 18, 2004, activists again marched into La Paz to begin their action yet again with the erection of road blocks and blockades throughout Bolivia. The new president then made the mistake of signing a gas export deal with Argentina. This triggered further generalised strikes, affecting essential services and export industries. These strikes and blockades brought La Paz to a complete standstill. They continued for months until, in June 2005, President Carlos Mesa offered his resignation to the Bolivian

Parliament, citing popular protests paralyzing the functioning of his government as the reason for his leaving office.

Elections in December 2005 led to the decisive election of Movimiento al Socialismo's leader Evo Morales. On May 1, 2006, he signed a law fully nationalising the nation's hydrocarbon industry. It is now considered that the strong popular response to unions' calls for generalised strikes across multiple industries was one of the most effective actions taken by anti-government protesters, fatally undermining the authority of the president and his government.

8.2.6.2 General Strike: A general strike calls upon all workers to withdraw their labour and is considered to have achieved the full definition of a "general strike" when a majority of workers participate in it.

Generally speaking, general strikes are reserved as an important national political protest, but a general strike can also be applied to a city or other administrative or geographical zone. The main aim of a general strike is to damage the sitting government. Usually, a general strike is not aimed at damaging business. Therefore, general strikes tend to be initially short-lived. However, to harness this tactic's true potential, general strikes need to escalate from symbolic one-day protests to ongoing actions that last days and potentially weeks, with a clear goal of inflicting both economic and political damage until the strikers' demands are met.

Considerations and risks: General strikes are usually political protests rather than demands for specific economic improvements. Few governments have the temerity to send the police onto the street to harass strikers when they arrive to demonstrate in large numbers. Nonetheless, there have been cases where a government feels that it is being challenged politically and feels the need to deliver a violent response to strikers and protesters. Then there is a risk of confrontation with riot police, and the usual precautions and evasive actions need to be employed in street demonstrations.

It's important that organisers ensure that everyone knows the reasons for the strike and what other protest activities will be held during the strike. The press needs to be pro-actively managed and demonstration material such as banners need to be clear and unified in their message.

Organising large-scale strike actions and demonstrations requires professional organisational and logistic skills and quite a lot of funding. Therefore the organisers will need to start collecting money to finance mass demonstrations well in advance of the planned dates.

Historical and contemporary examples: General strikes have a long history, with the first examples being recorded in Roman times when there was a general strike by the plebeians (free Roman citizens) protesting against various injustices and lack of access to justice. Their general strike (known as a "secessio") took the form of the plebeians simply abandoning Rome en masse and leaving the patricians (upper classes) to themselves.

In modern times, the idea of a general strike was further developed by the Marxist philosopher Rosa Luxembourg in her 1906 book "The Mass Strike, the Political Party and the Trade Unions" and again by Ralph Chaplin, editor of the newspaper "Industrial Workers of the World". There is some difference in approach to general strikes between the trade unionist, who sees it as a means of persuasion and the revolutionary or anarchist who sees a general strike as part of a much more profound process of social and political change.

In the last hundred years, there have been scores of general strikes around the world. Britain has had two significant general strikes, France and Spain have had six and every other European country has experienced more than one general strike, as have Australia, most Latin American nations, Canada and various US states. The motives for these general strikes have included anti-austerity strikes against cuts in social spending, anti-war strikes (notably against the Vietnam and Iraq wars), strikes to protest changes in working conditions, pension rights, equality and strikes to dislodge unpopular governments.

8.2.6.3 Hartal - Suspension of Economic Life to make a Political Point:
The word hartal derives from the Gujarati word meaning "to strike", but has since passed into common use in Asia and globally to represent a combination of a general strike with a closure of unaffiliated businesses and government administration. A hartal is a total shutdown of economic and administrative activity.

Considerations and risks: This type of total shutdown originated during the long struggle to end British colonial rule in India and is still practiced in Pakistan, India and Bangladesh. In these parts of the world such complete shutdowns may be feasible, but in Western countries it would take a very extreme protest to be able to close down central and local government administration such as courts, councils, schools and all industry and private commerce at the same time.

Historical and contemporary examples: Apart from the famous strikes and economic civil disobedience of Gandhi and his followers in India, there was one other famous hartal in Ceylon in 1953. This was a country-wide demonstration of civil disobedience and strike action on 12 August

1953. It was organised to protest against the policies and actions of the incumbent (UNP) government. It was the first mass political action in modern Ceylon, the first major social crisis after independence and the first people's struggle against an elected government in the country. Led by a left wing grouping, it called on the labouring classes and public to resist the government and demonstrate civil disobedience and strikes. The hartal was open to all and there were no exclusions based upon caste, ethnicity or religion. The protests saw much sabotage and destruction of public infrastructure as a means of frightening and halting the government. The demonstrations lasted for only a day but with at least 10 people killed, it resulted in the resignation of the Prime Minister.

8.2.6.4 Economic Shutdown: This is an action sometimes combined with a general strike and it involves all economic sectors, even if they are not included in the general strike. This may involve private retailers, merchants and the self-employed. The combination of a general strike with an economic shutdown is a potent instrument of protest but very difficult to implement absolutely.

Considerations and risks: Organising a general strike and a coordinated shutdown of other economic activities is a tall order. Generally speaking, private independent businesses are apolitical and tend to be motivated by profit rather than principle. To persuade such businesses to close down even for a day is not going to be easy. However, there are issues which even the profit-hungry have to take note of. War is one such issue and many small businesses may well find themselves sympathetic to an anti-war protest, especially when it is explained that it will damage their business interests. In a similar way, government cuts or new regulations often have a knock-on effect on small businesses, and in this way it may be possible to gain the support of these types of business.

Economic shutdowns cause hardship. A campaign organiser must ensure that they do not cause hardship to those who are vulnerable, such as the elderly, the sick, the disabled, small children and the poor or homeless and that these groups have access to essential goods and services. Organisers also have to be very careful to explain the exact purpose of the protest to the general public and for this they need a strong proactive PR operation. The press must not be allowed to hijack such a protest for its own sensationalist agenda.

Historical and contemporary examples: In January 2014, as part of a long-festering political struggle in Thailand, a huge protest against the incumbent prime minister began causing the effective shutdown of the entire city of Bangkok. Seven key intersections around the city were besieged, blocking traffic and halting a population of over 6 million from going to work and disrupting major logistical movements of goods. The action also obstructed the thousands of tourists in peak holiday season hoping to enjoy the shops, temples and restaurants of the city.

The protests were designed to affect the service sectors, such as hotels, shopping malls and associated services. Hotel occupancy on the day was down to just 50% compared with the seasonal norm of 90%. Many shops and businesses didn't bother to open. Losses from the shutdown were estimated at 1 billion baht per day. Attempts to continue with the caretaker government and hold new elections were flouted by the ongoing demonstrations and economic shutdowns, resulting in increasing nervousness on the international capital markets and amongst Thailand's many export customers. However, the situation could not continue. On 22 May 2014, the Royal Thai Armed Forces, launched a coup d'état against the incumbent caretaker government, following six months of political crisis. The military established a junta called National Council for Peace and Order (NCPO) to govern the nation. This outcome, it may be argued, was probably one which the anti-government protesters were reasonably happy with, since the main antagonists of the protesters were removed from power by the military coup [Note 51].

8.3 Civil Disobedience: Methods of Political Non-Cooperation

Political non-cooperation occurs when citizens, agents of the government or other parts of political or administrative society (such as the judiciary) refuse to cooperate with a government executive. It can also occur as a result of diplomatic actions taken by external governments. Political non-cooperation is potentially the most explosive form of disobedience because some types of non-cooperation strike at the very heart of the governance of a country.

The following schema illustrates the classifications and methods of political non-cooperation.

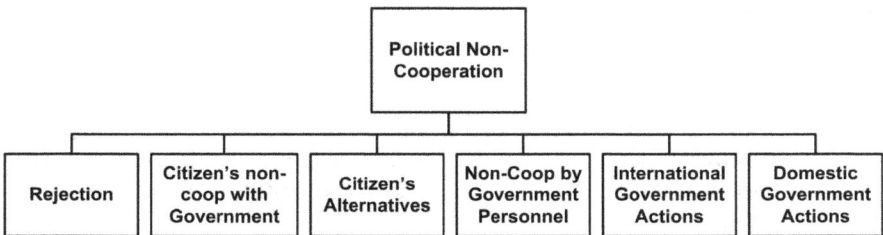

8.3.1 Rejection of Authority

The rejection of authority is a collection of acts of civil disobedience and protest wherein citizens refuse to acknowledge the authority of the state or other authority and advocate resistance and disobedience to authority.

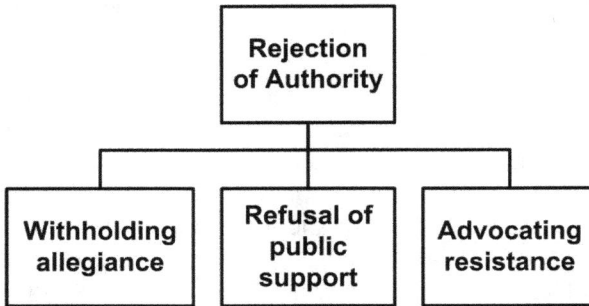

```
                    ┌──────────────┐
                    │  Rejection   │
                    │ of Authority │
                    └──────┬───────┘
          ┌────────────────┼────────────────┐
 ┌────────┴───────┐ ┌──────┴──────┐ ┌────────┴───────┐
 │  Withholding   │ │ Refusal of  │ │  Advocating    │
 │  allegiance    │ │   public    │ │  resistance    │
 │                │ │  support    │ │                │
 └────────────────┘ └─────────────┘ └────────────────┘
```

8.3.1.1 Withholding or Withdrawal of Allegiance: This is an act of rejection of authority where a citizen refuses to swear allegiance to a state or sovereign. It is the ultimate act of rejection of a state's power.

Considerations and risks: In many countries a refusal to give allegiance carries criminal liability and various punishments. In previous times (and still in some regimes, theoretically), it is tantamount to treason and may carry the death penalty.

Historical and contemporary examples: On many occasions in history, during the trials of those seeking political freedoms from what they considered an occupying power, the defendants have refused to acknowledge the authority of a state. During various trials of IRA operatives in British courts in the early 20th century and again between the 1970s and 1990s, the accused often refused to recognise the jurisdiction of the courts or the authority of the British government in Ireland. They thus refused to cooperate in their own defence. Despite the fact that many of the accused were legally British citizens they publicly renounced the jurisdiction of the British state or Crown in a public statement in which they denied all allegiance to the United Kingdom and Northern Ireland.

The refusal to take or accept the US pledge of allegiance has a long legal and constitutional history. There are those that argue that the references to God contained in the pledge breaches their constitutional right to religious freedom. Other objectors believe that the authors of the pledge of allegiance were socialists (which they were, in fact) and that this fact discredits the pledge of allegiance; a view very prominent during the Cold war era. Another group of objectors to the US pledge of allegiance claim that it is idolatrous and yet others insist it encourages blind patriotism without proper civic responsibility.

8.3.1.2 Refusal of Public Support: When individuals or groups become disaffected with their government they will quickly cease to express public support for that government or its policies. This creates a noticeable silence which in itself is a form of protest.

Considerations and risks: In authoritarian systems such a silence may well trigger off recriminations against those refusing to be enthusiastic for the government's policies. On the other hand, from the perspective of those wishing to make a protest, their silence and refusal to support the government is a clear sign of their position without having to engage in any form of dangerous overt confrontation.

Historical and contemporary examples: There are many examples where ordinary citizens refuse to cooperate with an authority with whom they do not agree. This non-cooperation often comes in the form of a failure to support an initiative. For example, doctors and nurses refuse to support an initiative to deprive unregistered immigrants of healthcare, as happened in Spain in 2012 [Note 50]. Then there are those professionals in the education sector that refuse to accept the "tinkering" interference of government in the education of a nation's children. Such refusals of support by teachers were directed at initiatives of Michael Gove during his period as Education Secretary in the UK government between 2010 and 2014.

A similar revolt took place (and at the time of writing is still ongoing) in certain US states where kindergarten teachers are refusing to administer certain tests (the FAIR test) to the children in their care. This defiance can result in a teacher being dismissed for a breach of contract. The primary reason for the lack of support for this testing comes from the fact that there are just too many performance tests of these small children being demanded (up to 9 batteries of formal tests a year) and this testing interferes with the teachers' core responsibility to educate the children. Also, teachers contend that the test results are largely irrelevant from an educational point of view. Many parents agree with this argument. Educationalists have long since refused to support these waves of new testing initiatives and teachers have now decided to refuse to administer the tests. Such was (is) the strength of feeling amongst teachers and parents that currently some of the pupil testing has been effectively suspended by at least one state (Florida) [Note 52].

Sometimes a failure of public support may come from another authority. In 2014, Liverpool City Council became the first council in the UK to boycott the government's new 'Help to Work' scheme which had been just launched. Under new rules jobseekers that had been unemployed for more than two years would either have to sign-on every day, undergo intensive training or take unpaid work. The work placements included six months of 30-hour weeks and could include activities such as gardening, running community cafes or restoring historical sites and war memorials. The Department for Work and Pensions announced that more than 70 organisations signed up to participate in the scheme. But a number of charities, including Oxfam, the YMCA and the Salvation Army made it clear that they would not be taking part. In Liverpool, the City Council joined up with Volunteer Centre Liverpool and other voluntary organisations in the city that have refused to support the scheme. Nick Small, cabinet member for Employment, Enterprise & Skills, described the government scheme as "immoral and unworkable" [Note 53].

8.3.1.3 Literature and Speeches Advocating Resistance: The publication of statements which openly defy a government and its policies is a clear form of citizen rejection which accompanies many other forms of protest, including civil disobedience. Whether in words or in writing: putting one or more names to a set of demands is a clear statement of attitude by an individual or group.

Considerations and risks: When an individual or group publish their views they place themselves on record. After that, any form of subversion is pretty much impossible. Thus, one of the greatest risks of publication is that a protester only has one chance to "play this card", after which everyone will know where they stand. In some countries this will mean that organisers will be investigated by the police or another part of the intelligence services, or perhaps by private investigators in the case of a dispute with a commercial authority. In some countries such an action may create an immediate risk to the safety and freedom of the protest group.

The risks inherent in publication mean that a protester should have everything ready for publication in advance before releasing any part of a campaign's portfolio. They should also ensure that they have security copies and alternative routes for publication (website, foreign press, blogs, social media, cloud servers etc.). It is wise to affiliate to a sympathetic press organ, such as a foreign newspaper, in advance of any publication. The timing of press releases is also very important.

Historical and contemporary examples: At some point all types of civil disobedience or other form of protest produce some kind of publication explaining a protest action, advocating a similar resistance to authority and issuing a call to others to join the campaign.

8.3.2 Citizens' Non-Cooperation with Government

There is a wide range of acts where a protesting citizen can demonstrate their refusal to cooperate with their government or other authority.

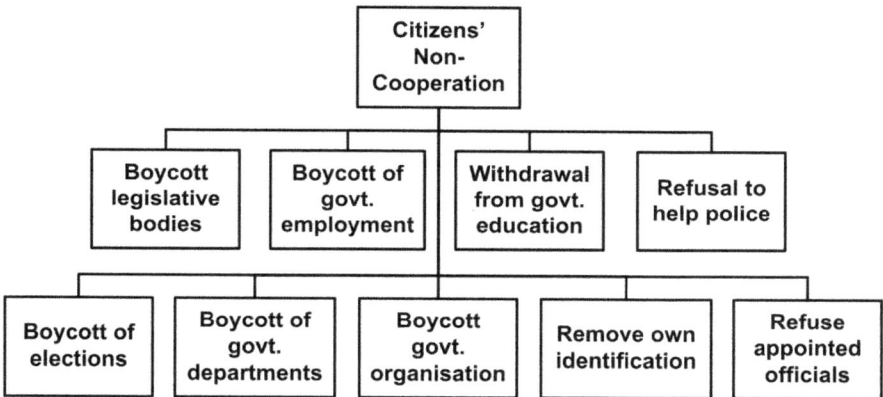

```
                    Citizens'
                      Non-
                   Cooperation

   Boycott       Boycott of     Withdrawal     Refusal to
  legislative      govt.        from govt.     help police
   bodies       employment      education

Boycott of     Boycott of      Boycott       Remove own      Refuse
elections        govt.          govt.       identification  appointed
               departments    organisation                   officials
```

8.3.2.1 Boycott of Legislative Bodies: This is the refusal by a citizen or group of citizens to acknowledge the supremacy of legislative bodies, such as parliament, local councils or the executive. Generally speaking, this has little effect on the legislature, except when those who boycott it are actually members.

Considerations and risks: There is a risk that the general public will simply accuse those who boycott the legislature of being undemocratic. It's important to explain to the public why the boycott exists and that the boycott is specific to the present legislative body as it is composed rather than the legislative body in general.

Historical and contemporary examples: There have been several instances of the boycott of Parliament in Britain, with the most recent occurring when members of Ireland's Sinn Fein were elected but refused to take their seats as a protest against British intervention in Ireland. This was during the "Troubles" of the 1970s and 1980s and was a repeat of a similar protest boycott by Irish Republicans shortly before the final independence of Ireland in the 1920s.

More recently, after flawed elections in Macedonia in 2014, the Social-Democrat opposition refused to recognise the legitimacy of the government, citing many electoral irregularities. The party confirmed that they would boycott the parliament unless new elections were held to international standards [Note 54].

8.3.2.2 Boycott of Elections: This involves the boycott of an election by a group of voters, all of whom abstain from voting. The boycott may be used as a form of political protest where voters feel that electoral fraud is likely, or that the electoral system is biased against its candidates. Voters may also believe that the election itself lacks legitimacy.

In jurisdictions with compulsory voting, a boycott may be illegal, so supporters of the boycott might cast blank votes or vote for "none of the above". Alternative strategies may call for particular political parties or candidates to refuse to run and their supporters urged to boycott the vote. In the case of a referendum, a boycott may be used as a voting tactic by opponents of the proposition if the rules of the referendum require a minimum turnout. In this case, a boycott may prevent a quorum being reached.

In general elections, individuals and parties will often boycott a poll to protest the ruling party's policies in the hope that poor voter turnout will deem the election illegitimate. This tactic, however, can prove disastrous for the boycotting parties. Lack of participation rarely nullifies election results and the distorted voting could actually make matters worse for the protesting group.

Considerations and risks: There is a risk that the general public will simply perceive those who boycott an election as being potentially poor losers. In this case, it is essential to inform the public as to why the election boycott is necessary. Boycotting an election may also give victory to a party antagonistic to the protest group and thus prove to be counterproductive.

Historical and contemporary examples: In recent times (2014), Bahrain's Shiite-led opposition boycotted the Gulf Kingdom's parliamentary elections. The opposition accused the reigning Sunni monarchy of manipulating elections to bolster its own power base. A coalition of Bahrain's four main opposition parties staged peaceful protests instead of participating in the November 2014 parliamentary elections, accusing the Sunni monarchy of failing to heed calls for genuine democratic reform. This Gulf kingdom's largest opposition party by membership, the Shiite movement, known as al-Wefaq, accused the royal family of ignoring the legitimate demands of the people. "The royal family retains all powers - executive, legislative and judicial, in addition to security, information and wealth," a representative of the opposition parties said. Although the Gulf kingdom is ruled by an absolutist Sunni king, the overwhelming majority of the population is Shiite [Note 55].

8.3.2.3 Boycott of Government Employment and Positions: In circumstances where a government no longer commands any real respect or moral power, such as authoritarian regimes, one form of protest is to refuse to work for these authorities by refusing to take government work. This protest becomes a boycott of government posts.

Considerations and risks: For many potential supporters, government work and contracts are often irresistibly treasured positions. Regular, well-paid, secure and often with a pension, it's never going to be that easy to find a lot of people willing to support a boycott of such positions.

Historical and contemporary examples: Boycotting government jobs because of poor conditions or pay is nothing unusual, but instances of moral boycotts of government jobs are somewhat less common.

One of the more high profile boycotts of government jobs in recent years concerns the refusal of citizens to serve in the Israeli army. Refusal to serve in the Israel Defence Forces (IDF) is a social phenomenon in which citizens decline to serve in the military or disobey orders when conscripted. These boycotts or acts of disobedience are made on the grounds of pacifism, antimilitarism, religious philosophy or political disagreement with Israeli policy. In particular, the occupation of the Palestinian territories has been a strong incentive for ordinary Israeli citizens to refuse to participate in that country's military forces. Conscientious objectors in Israel are known as "refuseniks". The history of this refusal goes back to the foundation of the state of Israel and continues to this day [Note 56]. Many brave young Israeli refuseniks have been instrumental in exposing a lot of the Israeli military's excesses in the occupation of Palestinian territories over the last decades.

8.3.2.4 Boycott of Government Departments, Agencies and Other Bodies: A citizen can refuse to deal with a government via its departments and agencies. We can, for example, attempt to drop out of the tax or social security system or refuse grant agencies, and ignore government-financed organisations such as libraries, schools, hospitals and other agencies.

Considerations and risks: A complete or even partial boycott of government institutions is quite a tall order these days when government is such an all-pervasive part of our lives.

In order to become totally independent of government in the Western world, we need to live anonymously in a very remote area. Sadly, these are in short supply. However, we can, in groups, selectively boycott a government department at least for short periods. The risks of such boycotts are that we may make ourselves liable to various penalties resulting from our failure to cooperate. At the same time, boycotting a government agency may have a negative financial implication. A farmer failing to cooperate with the Ministry of Agriculture may find that his agricultural grants are cancelled or delayed or that his land is forfeited for some breach of agricultural regulation.

On the other hand, there are various government agencies that we can safely boycott or ignore. For instance, the national census can be avoided or sabotaged easily enough; parents can refuse to collaborate with the plans of their children's schools; cooperative groups can run their own (uncontrolled) food business between members, thus bypassing Ministry of Health inspections; protesters can boycott government public inquiries or publicly funded activities. There are many such possibilities.

Boycotts of a government department may be selective; some activities of the department may be boycotted and some may not.

Historical and contemporary examples: In 1953, the government of South Africa passed the Bantu Education Act which provided some very rudimentary education for indigenous children. It was immediately condemned as being designed to keep the population ignorant and only allow the recipients enough education to be suitable for employment as factory or farm workers. In 1954 the ANC rejected the education plan and started to organise a boycott of government schools. Large numbers of children were withdrawn from their schools by angry parents. The children were then bussed by their families into the countryside and educated by volunteer teachers under the guise of "cultural clubs" (non-government schools and teachers were forbidden). Despite intimidation by the police, these cultural clubs survived until 1960, though many parents were gradually coerced into sending their children back to the "Bantu Education" schools.

One interesting way of boycotting a government was developed in 2014 by a group of Canadian veterans who were protesting their poor treatment by their government regarding the health and welfare benefits they were denied. They formed a coalition of veteran groups and boycotted all government photo-ops and participation in news releases to pressure the Canadian government to improve its treatment of veterans. Veterans are often used by politicians to reinforce their own patriotic image and the refusal of the veterans to cooperate sent powerful signals to the general public [Note 57].

In a radical attack on a government agency in 2014, nine leading human rights NGOs told the UK Parliament's Intelligence and Security Committee (ISC) that it was "not adequate" to the task of investigating the UK's involvement in rendition and torture, and said that the NGOs would boycott its inquiry into the issue as a result.

In a letter to the committee, the NGOs stated that "the [Intelligence] Committee has neither the powers nor the independence necessary to get to the truth of Britain's involvement in the rendition and torture of detainees abroad." As a result, they warned that "any investigation conducted by the ISC will be inherently flawed." Due to the "inherent" limitations of the ISC, which, the letter pointed out, is subject to a Prime Ministerial veto in terms of its membership, the evidence it is allowed to examine, and the information it is allowed to publish, the NGOs say they would be boycotting its inquiry.

The NGOs concluded that "we as a collective of domestic and international non-governmental organisations do not propose to play a substantive role in the conduct of this inquiry."

The human rights organisations that refused to collaborate in this obvious "whitewash" included Reprieve, Amnesty International and Liberty, three of the world's most respected NGOs. This boycott by Britain's leading human rights groups grievously undermined the controversial inquiry and any conclusions coming from the inquiry carried almost no credibility at all [Note 58].

8.3.2.5 Withdrawal from Government Educational Institutions: Since the 1960s, many protest movements have originated and been supported from schools and universities. The symbolism of classroom walk-outs and university mass sit-ins is still very potent.

Very often students have been the intrepid vanguard of larger citizen actions. Student withdrawals have been augmented by teaching staff in certain walk-out protests. Educational strikes and sit-ins often last for weeks on end. They are particularly difficult for governments to deal with. The sight of armed riot police attacking children or young people is imagery that is guaranteed to trigger off a violent reaction by the general public and for most governments it is best avoided.

Considerations and risks: Governments have long since feared large-scale student strikes. Students embody many of the characteristics that governments fear most: they are emotional, young, strong, well-educated, and energetic and generally display strong solidarity. They have a sense of justice and little tolerance for authority.

Students generally love a good fight for a moral cause. In recent years, governments have tried to dissuade students from their rebellious traditions by making education an elitist and expensive pursuit. For any student participant in a withdrawal or other strike or protest action there is some risk that they may lose their place in a particular educational establishment, which may cause an educational and economic loss to the individual - though this is much less likely (as with other strikes) with a large-scale withdrawal of students en mass.

Historical and contemporary examples: Whilst we may think that student strikes are a phenomenon of the modern era, the truth is that students have been rebellious for a very long time and very probably will be rebellious for centuries to come. Indeed, students are a form of social insurance for humanity against those regressive and reactionary forces that seek to control us. Students over the ages have somehow managed to stay above such conservative influences, frequently motivated by idealism and a healthy disrespect for convention.

In fact, one of the first recorded student strikes occurred in 1229 at the University of Paris when a bunch of rowdy students triggered off a dispute with a local bar which escalated into violence and some deaths. The civil authorities over-reacted and more students were attacked and killed. As a result, the entire university went immediately on strike, with students moving away from Paris to other cities; the normal life of the university came to a complete halt. It took two years to fully resolve the dispute and bring the university back to some degree of normality. Local bars are reputed to have been more tolerant of the students when they returned.

A more contemporary example of a complete boycott of state education took place in 1970 in the USA. In May of that year, just after the American invasion of Cambodia, National Guardsmen killed four students at Kent State University in Ohio [Note 59], and Jackson city police and Mississippi state troopers killed one student at Jackson State College and a high school passer-by in Mississippi. As a result, a national strike took place and more than 450 university, college and high school campuses across the USA were shut down by student strikes, with both violent and nonviolent protests involving more than 4 million students. Some students turned their anger on what was often the nearest military facility: college and university Reserve Officers' Training Corps (ROTC) offices. All told, 30 ROTC buildings went up in flames or were bombed [Note 60]. There were violent clashes between students and police at 26 schools and National Guard units were mobilized on 21 campuses in 16 states. The riots did not affect the US military position but they sent a shock wave through the establishment as they demonstrated the power of student rebellion.

These protests and strikes also had a dramatic impact on public opinion, convincing many Americans, particularly within the administration of President Richard Nixon that the nation was, at that moment, on the verge of insurrection. At one point, Nixon was taken to Camp David for his own safety.

8.3.2.6 Boycott of Government-Supported Organisations: When a government is being boycotted by a protest group, the effect of the boycott only becomes tangible when the protesters have an obvious target to boycott. "Government" is an abstract concept for most citizens, so very often protesters turn their attention to organisations directly supported by government. Protesters may resign from such organisations and encourage others to do likewise. The target organisations may include favourite NGOs, government-favoured charities, the established church, and various subsidised patriotic groups that support the established regime.

Considerations and risks: Not all government-supported organisations are bad. Despite the fact that an NGO receives money from a government, perhaps implying a degree of compliance with the wishes of that government, it does not mean that they are, by definition, corrupt. On the other hand, organisations funded by government must, at some point, show some sympathy with the government and are thus basically suspect.

For example, environmental NGOs that are part-funded by government cannot really be totally trusted to be as radical and objective as an organisation that is funded solely by its members. It is for this reason that it may be necessary to boycott such government-financed organisations.

The risk is, of course, that by boycotting well-financed organisations a protest group may itself be excluded from various potentially important discussions, decision-making and finance. These are purely ethical questions. On the other hand, the public is increasingly demanding more clarity and economic transparency, and a boycott of government-supported organisations is a logical extension to the increasing disillusionment with our systems of government.

Historical and contemporary examples: There are many anti-war campaigns that boycott Western commemorations of WWI and WWII. They do so because they believe that the commemorations have been hijacked and are no longer an honest remembrance of lost family members infused with anti-war sentiment; instead, they have been turned into a jingoistic way of justifying more wars.

Organisations such as the "Stop the War Coalition" actively campaign against events like "Remembrance Day" which is organised by various UK patriotic organisations that have been financially supported by a litany of British governments over many decades.

It's unpopular to stand up to and boycott these types of super-patriotic events, but nonetheless it is essential to stop them being converted from acts of grieving into a cynical justification for more bloodshed by opportunistic and bloodthirsty politicians.

8.3.2.7 Refusal to Help Police: Non-cooperation with the police has become more the rule than the exception in many Western countries. Decades of corruption scandals, miscarriages of justice, institutional racism, and proven acts of police brutality has left the public image of many police forces in complete tatters. They now face an antagonistic and largely uncooperative general public which tends to call the police only as a very last resort.

Not only does the public see the police as self-serving and corrupt, the police are also often seen as simply an instrument of state coercion with little connection to the people. Gone are the days of community policing, where citizens and police worked together to deal with local problems in a local way. Today, we live in the brave new world of CCTV cameras, infiltration of peaceful protest groups, armed police hit squads, tasers, pepper spray, rubber bullets and water canons. We are just fodder for the police; at best a nuisance that must be tolerated, but is never respected. Given the appalling record of many police forces, it is not surprising that few protest groups would ever consider cooperating with the police, unless in exceptional circumstances.

Considerations and risks: There isn't much involved in refusing to assist the police, unless one deliberately misleads them and this can be legally proven. In that case there may be a legal jeopardy. However, not knowing something is a difficult phenomenon to disprove and the eternal cry of "I saw / know / heard nothing" is generally impossible to disprove. On the other hand, it may be useful to assist the police in some respects whilst refusing to assist them in other matters, depending on the case.

Generally speaking, the police in most countries have put themselves so far "outside" normal society that they are rarely to be trusted. From a protester's point of view, there are risks from a police force that tries to "pick off" protesters one by one by using evidence, such as photographic imagery, to build a case against "uncooperative" individuals. The answer to this, of course, is to film any excessive behaviour of the police and make sure it is universally published. This kind of "tit for tat" countermeasure has now become the standard for dealing with police forces, even in the most liberal democracies.

Historical and contemporary examples: There are literally thousands of cases where groups of citizens refuse to help the police. In virtually every protest action, popular demonstration where the police have been involved, they have almost always provoked or attacked the participating citizens and thus caused ordinary citizens to refuse to cooperate with or trust them in future. Amazingly, quite middle-class protesters can become very antagonistic when being bullied by heavy-handed police tactics. In some respects, police forces have lost their way. They have forgotten that they are the protectors of the civil population and have instead often morphed into defenders of the interests of political elites.

8.3.2.8 Removal of Own Identification Signs and Name: This is a form of action where protesters take down street signs and other sign postings as an act of civil disobedience or as part of a linguistic protest.

Considerations and risks: Being caught defacing or removing street signs carries a penalty. Actions such as these antagonise local authorities (since they have to restore the signs) and may anger local populations. It is important therefore to carry out such actions as part of a limited campaign and provide the public with plenty of advance warning and information about the reasons for the campaign.

Historical and contemporary examples: In both Wales and Ireland during the last century, this has been a popular protest tactic. In both cases the motivations were nationalistic and linguistic. Signs in English were an affront to nationalist groups and were therefore removed, often under cover of darkness. In more recent years, dual language signs were often altered by painting over the English language place name, leaving just the native language name for a place.

8.3.2.9 Refusal to Accept Appointed Officials: One means by which a protest group can undermine a government or corporate entity is to refuse to accept and acknowledge the authority of officials appointed by the government or company.

Considerations and risks: In a company it is fairly easy to refuse the authority of an appointed official. If a group of subordinates choose to challenge the official's authority they can do so simply by questioning every order and decision to the official's superior. This will quickly lead to a review of the official's ability to manage and exercise their authority.

In government circles this is a more complicated situation, but a similar strategy of complaint and questioning to higher authorities can also help to undermine a particular government official.

For example, a particular bureaucrat can be "ganged up on" by a number of citizens and complaints can be lodged against him or her. With clever planning a case can be built against an official for incompetence, ineptitude or corruption and presented to that official's superiors. In some cases, it may only be necessary to prove a lack of independence, competence or some small suspicion of nepotism to eject an appointed official from their post.

Historical and contemporary examples: Governments frequently appoint a senior judge or "independent" official to chair a public inquiry into some scandal (such as the so-called "Historical Child Abuse" in Britain, Bloody Sunday, and the Iraq War etc).

Sometimes those appointed are far from independent and are in fact just "lackeys" of the governing political elites put in charge of an enquiry to make sure it reaches the "correct" conclusions and sides with the establishment.

Very often these political appointments are so extremely biased that participants in the enquiry and the general public refuse, en masse, to accept the appointment. Such was the case in 2014 when several chair persons of the enquiry into the "Westminster Child Abuse" cases in the UK were forced to resign because the candidates were considered to be too closely biased towards other politicians whose names had been linked to an establishment paedophile ring in and around the British parliament.

8.3.3 Citizens' Alternatives to Civil Obedience

In disputes and protest actions against governments or corporate authorities, citizens (or employees) may develop a set of alternative ways of dealing with authority which are designed to undermine the authority's effectiveness. These may be obvious acts of disobedience such as draft dodging or they may involve covert actions such as a worker reducing their efficiency.

```
                          ┌──────────────┐
                          │  Citizens'   │
                          │ Alternatives │
                          └──────────────┘
┌──────────┐ ┌──────────┐ ┌──────────┐ ┌──────────┐ ┌──────────┐ ┌──────────┐
│ Reluctant│ │  Popular │ │ Refusal to│ │   Non-  │ │  Hiding, │ │  Disobey │
│ and slow │ │disobedience│ │ disperse │ │cooperation:│ │escape, false│ │illegitimate│
│compliance│ │          │ │          │ │conscription│ │ identity │ │   laws   │
└──────────┘ └──────────┘ └──────────┘ └──────────┘ └──────────┘ └──────────┘
         ┌──────────┐ ┌──────────┐ ┌──────────┐ ┌──────────┐
         │Unsupervised│ │ Disguised│ │ Citizens │ │   Non-  │
         │disobedience│ │disobedience│ │  Sit-in  │ │cooperation:│
         │          │ │          │ │          │ │deportation│
         └──────────┘ └──────────┘ └──────────┘ └──────────┘
```

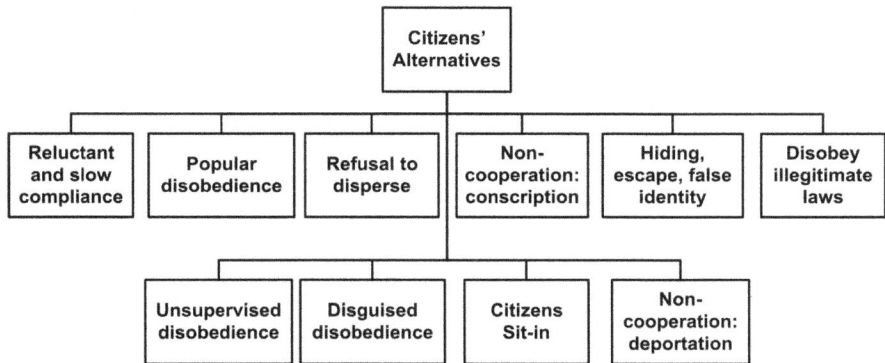

8.3.3.1 Reluctant and Slow Compliance: This is somewhat akin to the industrial strike action referred to as a "Go-slow" or "Slowdown", but rather than working slowly, the protesters refuse to comply with orders from an authority. If they do comply they do so very slowly and in a way which lessens the effectiveness of the order.

Considerations and risks: Sometimes orders from an authority fail to specify explicitly when an order must be completed or provide lots of opportunities to delay execution of the order. In both cases, there is a possibility to comply with an order but in a slow and inefficient way. This might involve continuous appeals, the use of deliberate administrative errors, or any number of excuses based on the failings of other parts of an authority or some legal or regulatory restriction. In other words, there is always a way to put a delaying spanner in the works of an order made by almost any authority.

Historical and contemporary examples: For the first time in 40 years, in 2012, doctors in the UK's National Health Service staged an administrative go-slow to protest against changes to their pension conditions by the government. The actions they took included refusing to fill in government forms, treating emergency cases only, and the extremely cautious referrals of thousands of patients to hospital. Whilst patient safety was not at risk, doctors carried out their administrative tasks in a pedantic and inefficient way which overloaded the administrative system [Note 61].

In 2014, in a protest against the activities of the unlicensed taxi system Uber, the drivers of the traditional black taxis of London staged a go-slow protest. Similar demonstrations were staged in Paris, Madrid, Berlin and Rome. Taxis continued to circulate, but the drivers reduced their speed to such an extent that they caused major traffic disruption. When asked to move on by police, taxis obeyed the orders but very slowly [Note 62].

8.3.3.2 Non-Obedience in Absence of Direct Supervision: This type of protest occurs when a group or individual refuses to obey an authority, but does so only when they are not being directly supervised or observed. The idea here is that the non-obedient person avoids the risks of being punished whilst simultaneously refusing to comply with the authority. So when given an order whilst being supervised, the protester complies with it, but as soon as the supervision stops he just begins to ignore the order.

Considerations and risks: Since those involved are being disobedient when there is no-one looking, this is a pretty low risk protest! The most important question is: does the disobedience have any tangible effect on the target of the protest? A protest must be felt, and in this case it has to be felt without the authority knowing exactly what or who is involved in the disobedience.

Historical and contemporary examples: There have been many examples of this technique down the years, but one well-known case was the Luxembourg general strike against Nazi occupation, in 1942. This came to a head on August 30, when the Nazis announced that all Luxembourg males of military age were to be conscripted into the Wehrmacht to fight against the Allies. It was this decision that motivated the people of Luxembourg from anger into action. As part of their campaign to resist the occupation they devised all kinds of ways of refusing to obey Nazi orders. They would pretend to work when Nazi officials were close by, but would then stop immediately they were unsupervised. School teachers stopped attending their schools and the production from the main national industries dropped dramatically. Despite the repressive backlash from the Nazis, many eligible males disappeared from their homes rather than fight, and industrial production didn't recover until the country was finally liberated.

8.3.3.3 Popular Disobedience: This technique of civil disobedience relates to acts of open disobedience by large numbers of protesters. The participants may refuse to comply with a particular law or regulation with which they disagree or they may simply refuse to comply with any instruction or order from a particular authority to which they object in total.

Considerations and risks: In a large protest group there is some safety in numbers. But remember this is not always true. Authorities have a history of committing atrocities against large groups in some cases. There are many examples of this, but take for instance the Sharpeville massacre in South Africa in 1960, when police opened fire on some 5000 unarmed protesters, killing 69 and injuring hundreds more. Many who died were shot in the back as they tried to escape the bullets.

Because acts of mass disobedience often face violent reactions from police or military, organisers need to have sophisticated and secret contingency plans. These may involve staging separate distracting demonstrations or attacks on other sites to draw police manpower away from the main event and to give demonstrators an opportunity to seize control of their main site and overwhelm police.

Historical and contemporary examples: Popular disobedience was a hallmark of the Indian resistance to British rule in the 1940s (See chapter "A History of Civil Disobedience") and it is still a most popular and often very effective means of protest.

For example, the mass occupation of the proposed Wyhl nuclear power plant site in Germany in the 1970s saw 20,000-30,000 people occupying the construction site, refusing to leave or to obey legal orders against the occupation. The ten months long occupation attracted international attention. Environmentalists, anti-nuclear activists, local farmers and residents, as well as some more radical political elements came. Mass meetings were held at the site with thousands of people in attendance. There are even reports of local police refusing to take part in the occasionally rough treatment of the protesters. In March 1975, the government responded by suspending the construction license and at the beginning of 1976, the government guaranteed that construction would not restart until all complaints had been heard and a final court decision had been reached. The occupation of the site ended, and in March 1977 the administrative court decided to ban construction altogether [Note 63]. The Whyl protests were a good example where safety in numbers was assured. Despite their rough treatment at the hands of the police, the number of demonstrators clearly outnumbered the police and the authorities were basically overwhelmed by the sheer numbers of protesters on site.

8.3.3.4 Disguised Disobedience: This is a form of political disobedience which is disguised to make it look as if the protester or dissident is actually being obedient. Many acts of sabotage rely on an infiltrator within an authority behaving in an obedient way, whilst simultaneously disobeying the authority and deliberately damaging its interests. In other cases, employees or citizens may simply pretend to comply with a law or a command and then quietly just ignore it. Bans on smoking in public places or bans on using a mobile phone whilst driving are typical informal examples of this. The laws on non-smoking in certain places or using a mobile phone whilst driving are clear and yet many people choose to ignore them as long as they think they can get away with it.

Considerations and risks: As a form of disobedience, you need to be fairly convincing to get away with this for very long and once a protester or group of protesters has been caught out it's unlikely they will get a second chance to pretend to be obedient. They will be eternally distrusted by the authorities and the only way around this is to morph identity, as did the many small Republican and Loyalist groups in the Northern Irish troubles as soon as they became legally proscribed.

Historical and contemporary examples: Examples of this tactic include avoiding being drafted into the army by getting medical exemptions from cooperative doctors. This was a popular ruse during the latter years of the Vietnam War, where potential recruits feigned various ailments to obtain a medical exemption. Pretending to be schizophrenic is relatively easy to do and quite difficult to disprove.

Similarly, banned organisations may disappear simply to pop up again with a different name but with the same objectives and membership. Such was the case in the 1970s and 1980s in Northern Ireland when various organisations were banned (proscribed). New organisations would simply be formed with the same membership and a new name.

8.3.3.5 Refusal of an Assemblage or Meeting to Disperse: This is a form of disobedience where protesters gather to demonstrate their views or discuss with other participants and then refuse to disperse when ordered to do so by the authorities.

Considerations and risks: In some jurisdictions the refusal to disperse may be considered an act of riot, leading to violent methods of dispersal, arrests and criminal charges against demonstrators. However, if the group is large enough, it should be possible to escalate the legal question of refusing to disperse into a political issue centred on freedom of association and freedom of expression.

Historical and contemporary examples: There are many examples of this form of disobedience, but one famous case known as the Rosenstrasse protest, showed the courage of the participants. It occurred in 1943 in Nazi Berlin when German, non-Jewish wives married to Jewish men gathered to demand the release of their husbands, 1800 of whom had been arrested to be deported to concentration camps. Despite being attacked by the Gestapo and the SS, the women's demonstration refused to disperse and their ranks were swelled to over 1000 women protesters. The protest became louder and more publicly obvious. The Nazis then deported scores of the men to concentration camps in the following days, but the demonstration continued and the women refused to leave.

Finally, the German leadership gave in, even as some of the Jewish men were being deported to Auschwitz. The Nazi Propaganda Minister, Goebbels, released the remaining intermarried Jews in an attempt to maintain appearances. The protests of these non-Jewish women against the internment of their Jewish husbands had shown open dissent to the Nazi pogrom, and for Goebbels it was more important to eliminate this dissent by releasing those Jews than to allow such dissent to be visible to other Germans or to the scrutiny of international bodies. Thirty-five intermarried Jews that had already been sent to Auschwitz were also returned [Note 64].

8.3.3.6 Sit-in: Also known as a "sit-down", it is an act of disobedience where a worker or protester sits down and refuses to leave their workplace or place of protest. In the case of a protest sit-in, the protesters normally choose a strategic place in which to sit, in order to create the maximum disruption and attract the maximum attention. The protesters remain until they are evicted, usually by force, or arrested, or until their requests have been met. Sit-ins have historically been a highly successful form of protest because they are easy to organise and peaceful, they cause disruption without damage and they draw public attention to the protest.

Considerations and risks: The obvious risk in a sit-in is that the authorities will simply pick you up and evict you. This strategy can be frustrated by the protester by also being chained to something solid. This will at least delay the authority in removing the protesters. Sit-ins are generally meant to be a peaceful affair, but in recent years in Western countries police have taken to using pepper spray on sit-in protesters to force them away.

A note on "crowd-control chemicals": Sit-in protesters should read the latest advice about managing the effects of pepper spray and CS gas and make sure that several participants are filming any police harassment activity and violent evictions.

The current suggested precautions against and treatments for pepper spray is as follows: Cover up well, use a hat and face mask and goggles to avoid contact. Use cheap rainwear to cover as much of your body as possible. If hit, resist the temptation to rub the affected area, this makes the situation much worse. Reduce the stinging by immediately saturating the effected area with full-fat milk using a spray or milk-wetted towel. An eye-wash may be needed for which a victim will need help. Eyewashes can be made with a pinch of salt dissolved in a litre of clean water. To remove the oils in the pepper spray, use a strong solution of cold water with washing up liquid and immerse the affected parts fully between 5 and 10 times for a few seconds to allow the detergent to dissolve the irritant oils. Gently rubbing skin to remove the pepper spray will trigger off temporary stinging. Change the detergent mix frequently. During contamination, avoid touching anything. Discard contaminated clothes and shower with lots of soap as soon as possible [Note 65].

With CS gas, wear a gas mask, cheap rainwear and try to stay upwind of the target area. If exposed to CS or tear gas, a bandana soaked in Apple Cider or Vinegar is reputed to help breathing for a few minutes. Gas canisters are hot and dangerous, so only pick them up with thick asbestos gloves and when wearing protective clothing. If they are still active drop them in a bucket of water. Throwing them back is a dangerous waste of time since the police will have gas masks. Never touch unexploded gas grenades.

Historical and contemporary examples: Between 1985 and 2014, the nuclear waste repository in Gorleben, Germany, was the subject of continuous and very strong protests by anti-nuclear activists. One of the weak links for the authorities running the nuclear waste dump was the transport of waste to the site by rail. The protesters therefore concentrated their efforts on stopping this transport. Thus, at all hours of the day and night and despite a huge police presence, the railway line to Gorleben was the target for protest closures. The anti-nuclear activists first staged sit-ins on different parts of the railway line, then, when they were forcibly removed, they upped the ante by chaining themselves in large numbers to the railway line. When forcibly removed again, they resorted to placing huge concrete blocks on the lines and later used hundreds of tractors chained to the lines to blockade the railway, often supported by thousands of demonstrators effectively overwhelming the police, despite the police presence rising to up to more than 20000 officers at times. The protesters would target different sections of the railway line and worked together with French anti-nuclear protesters to block the incoming transports from La Hague and on the French part of the journey to Germany. This protest is ongoing and has widespread popular support in the area and in Germany in general [Note 66].

8.3.3.7 Non-Cooperation with Conscription: This form of non-cooperation is concerned specifically with refusing to cooperate with the process of conscription into the army. Protest against conscription has occurred down the centuries and continues to this day. Some of the most famous contemporary protests against conscription took place in the USA during its unsuccessful military adventures in Vietnam.

Considerations and risks: In most countries the deliberate avoidance of a military draft is a criminal offence if it can be proven that the candidate is aware that he is being drafted and is deliberately attempting to illicitly avoid the draft. The ideal way to avoid a military draft is to leave the country and be incommunicado with no forwarding address or contacts. All other methods (exemptions) carry the risk that they may fail and the protester may be drafted anyway or arrested for attempting to avoid it.

Historical and contemporary examples: In the modern era non-cooperation with conscription was widespread in the USA during the Vietnam War, when many young men refused to be conscripted (drafted) into what they considered an unjust war. Many people opposed to conscription chose to either apply for assignment to civilian alternative services or non-combatant services within the military as conscientious objectors, or evaded the draft by fleeing to a neutral country.

In the United States around 1970, the draft resistance movement focused on mandatory draft registration. Some used their political connections to ensure that they were placed well away from any potential harm. Many others avoided military service altogether through college deferments, by becoming fathers, or serving in various exempt jobs such as teaching. Others used educational exemptions, became conscientious objectors or pretended to be conscientious objectors, although they might then be drafted for non-combat work. A simple route to avoid the draft was to get a medical rejection. A person could claim to have symptoms of homosexuality or mental illness and if enough physicians agreed that the draftee had such a "problem", he might well be rejected. For others, the most common method of avoiding the draft was to move into another country. Of the 210,000 US citizens that dodged the draft, 30,000 of them left the country. Canada and Sweden were favourite destinations for many of these young Americans [Note 67].

8.3.3.8 Non-Cooperation with Deportation: This form of non-cooperation relates to the refusal of an immigrant or group of immigrants to cooperate with orders for their deportation. This is a common form of non-cooperation, especially in richer countries where poor but illegal immigrants are desperate to try to avoid deportation back to their often impoverished homelands.

Methods of avoiding deportation vary widely. It may be that an immigrant fears political, religious or other forms of persecution in their own country. In most Western countries this may permit them the legal right to asylum. In this case an immigrant can present their case to the authorities if they have sufficient evidence to support their claim.

Where this is not the case, an "undocumented" immigrant may face deportation. The system of processing asylum seekers in most Western countries is a draconian one and many "illegal immigrants" realise that they have little chance to stay if they submit themselves to the authorities. Often, those who suffer horrendous persecution in their own country have little in the way of useable evidence to prove this. Then there are those who suffer from appalling poverty in their own country. However, acute poverty, however life-threatening, is not perceived as a reason for the granting of asylum in most Western countries. In this case, "illegal immigrants" may be obliged to simply disappear from "the system" in their new host country in order to avoid being detected and deported. This they do by working in the black economy, not using public services and living in unregistered accommodation. In some cases, organisations exist to help such "illegal immigrants" escape the authorities or help them manage legal interactions with authorities whilst their cases are being processed. In other cases these poor people fall into the hands of criminal human traffickers.

One desperate alternative to disappearing from the system is to organise a group action of immigrants to enter a country and defy deportation. This carries its own risks as we describe below.

Considerations and risks: The risks of being caught and deported are high if the victim has no local support, so it's important to seek out those that are willing to help. This generally means finding other persons of the same nationality that will provide material aid to those fearing deportation. Other organisations also provide food, safe shelter and legal assistance.

Historical and contemporary examples: One strategy to resist deportation is collective action by those facing deportation. This occurred with tragic consequences in the Warsaw ghetto in 1943, when it became clear to the surviving Jews that "deportation" for them meant certain death. They staged an uprising with some improvised weapons and decided to fight the SS rather than to be put aboard the "death trains". Sadly, their struggle against the Nazis failed, but they managed to hold out for 4 weeks and succeeded in killing 300 Nazi troops and injuring another 1000. The Jewish ghetto was completely destroyed by the Nazis in the process.

In 2014, there were a number of concerted efforts by a large group of immigrants to enter Spanish territory at the enclave of Melilla. In one case, more than 1,000 African migrants rushed toward the high fences topped with razor wire. They were met by the Moroccan and Spanish military police and many failed to enter. It was the second mass crossing to fail in a week and one of the largest since May 2014, when hundreds of migrants launched themselves at the fences on three separate occasions. Some of these attempts have caused tragic injuries with the exhausted immigrants torn and bloodied by the razor wire. However, 2500 made it over the fences between January and May 2014 and were received by the Red Cross in Spanish reception centres, able to at least win a chance to stay [Note 68].

The disappearance of migrants is by far the most common way to avoid deportation. For instance, in 2014, in Houston, Texas, it was reported that more than 6,000 immigrants who had come to the U.S. on student visas, were nowhere to be found on their school campuses. They had vanished. In a nod to the official policy of US paranoia, the Department of Homeland Security (DHS) said that the missing 6,000 students were of "heightened concern" because officials had not been able to successfully track down these individuals and one official stated that the immigrants "could be here to do us harm....my greatest concern is that they could be doing anything." Oklahoma Senator Tom Coburn added, "They just disappear. They get the visas and they disappear" [Note 69].

In a similar story in the UK, in 2014, the Home Office admitted that it had lost track of nearly 175,000 "illegal immigrants" and was struggling to find them. The Home Office was faced with fresh humiliation after MPs were told how many of those who had been refused permission to be in Britain had simply gone missing and disappeared. Officials were accused of "unacceptable complacency" after admitting they had no idea where the missing immigrants and failed asylum seekers were [Note 70].

8.3.3.9 Hiding, Escape, and False Identities: When an authority attacks one or more dissenters, it is sometimes necessary to evade the authority for reasons of self-defence by using some extreme measures. These may include hiding from the authority, escaping from the authority's control and the use of false identities to avoid recognition or apprehension by an authority.

Considerations and risks: The use of false identification documents carries the risk of criminal charges in most countries, regardless of the moral reasons for resorting to them. The informal use of a false name may not be a criminal offence.

There are many ways to obtain false identities. In the UK (and other countries) one of the most famous loopholes was the fact that birth certificates and death certificates were not linked. Thus the birth certificate of a dead person could be used to obtain various documents, such as an international driving licence or passport. This is called "ghosting". Then, in some cases, a utility bill or bank statement was sufficient to open other accounts or obtain a rental lease. Thus, a gradual escalation of documentary evidence provided a complete identity, from birth certificate through passport, driving licence, apartment lease, utilities bills and club memberships.

Some desperados have even been known to adopt the name and birth details of people who are still alive and have presumably left the country, since there are no records of the outward travel movements of citizens from most Western countries. Some have used the identities of living people who have no passport to obtain a passport in their name. Very often passport authorities need a signature of a "responsible person", such as a priest, policeman or justice of the peace to confirm an identity, not an insurmountable problem for someone determined to take on a new identity.

In general, obtaining a new identity is a relatively easy matter using this technique of gradual escalation of documentary evidence. Every piece of paper one gathers that has one's name on it provides additional evidence of identity to the next level of authority. Anything official with a name, date of birth (from birth certificate) and a photo is guaranteed to impress. The use of fingerprint databases (for criminals) and the cross referencing of databases makes identity theft more difficult but certainly not impossible.

Regardless of the mechanisms used and their legality, the greatest risk to an individual trying to hide from an authority is detection. Therefore, finding a place to disappear and "hide" is the single most important priority. This "hiding place" may not necessarily be a quiet place; a big city is often the best place to disappear. This is especially true of those cities with a large transient population, where locals are used to seeing a lot of outsiders coming and going.

The subject of disappearing is a big one and the right to be forgotten is only now being raised as a personal right of privacy. But there are a number of important considerations when a person wishes to disappear effectively:

• Before going into hiding, the subject needs to minimise social connections, the use of social networks, and contacts with friends and family. All traceable internet activity must cease and gradually all telecommunications as well. That means no PC, no fixed email, no mobile and no phone. Later, anonymous email accounts, public internet services and phone boxes can be used for essential communications.

• The subject will need to get rid of all credit and debit cards, and start to use only cash. This means disposing of any card with name or identity on it, paying cash for everything and not using anything that could link the "new life" to the "old life".

• Sowing disinformation. If someone wishes to disappear, it is important to prepare for this by creating disinformation for all of those with whom the subject had dealings, i.e. Government agencies, supplier companies, banks, clubs etc. This disinformation covers such information as social security, date of birth, marital status, place of birth, passport numbers, even the spelling of one's name. The disinformation can be spread by means of "mistakes" in completing forms or deliberately "seeding" the internet and social networks. It doesn't need to be too consistent or deliberate. Human error is generally not considered a criminal offence.

• Use a corporate shield: One way of managing money and legal arrangements for day to day life after disappearing is by means of a corporate entity. This entity, which can be established well in advance and using anonymous trusts and other mechanisms is an ideal way of administering financial affairs without being personally involved.

If all of this sounds terribly criminal to the modern Western middle-class reader, then a very cursory examination of recent European history will demonstrate that sometimes such extreme actions are not only necessary, but may be the difference between life and death. Hundreds of thousands of ordinary people survived the excesses of the Nazis, the Stalinist purges, Spain's General Franco, and the Vichy French regime using precisely these techniques over just the last 80 years.

Historical and contemporary examples: During the Nazi regime life as a Jew anywhere under Nazi control was extremely perilous. Parents, children, and their rescuers faced daunting challenges once the decision was made to go into hiding. Some children could pass as non-Jews and live openly. Those who could not, had to live clandestinely, often in awful conditions. Children posing as Christians had to carefully conceal their Jewish identity from inquisitive neighbours, classmates, informers, blackmailers, and the police. Even a momentary lapse in language or behaviour could expose the child, and the rescuer, to danger.

Living as a non-Jew required false identity papers, which were difficult to obtain in German-occupied Europe and were subject to frequent review by the authorities. Over the course of the war, children often had to move from one refuge to another in the most traumatic circumstances. For Jews to pass as "Aryans", it was essential to have quality false identity papers, which were often gained through contacts with the anti-Nazi resistance. Using forged or acquired papers, such as a birth or baptismal certificate, Jews sometimes could obtain other legitimate documents from the authorities under an assumed name. These ruses posed great risks to the bearer since the Germans and collaborating police forces closely examined identity documents in their frequent searches for Jews, resistance members and individuals evading conscript labour.

Not all Jewish children could pass as "Aryans" and enjoy the relative freedom of movement on the outside. Those who "looked Jewish," did not speak the local language, or whose presence in a rescuer's family raised too many questions, had to be physically hidden. Children were kept in cellars and attics, where they had to keep quiet, even motionless, for hours on end. In rural areas, hidden children lived in barns, chicken coops, and forest huts. Any noise, conversation, or footsteps could arouse neighbours' suspicion and perhaps even prompt a police raid. During bombings, Jewish children often remained hidden, unable to flee to the safety of the shelters.

Thousands of Jewish children survived the Holocaust because they were protected by people and institutions of other faiths. Dozens of Catholic convents in German-occupied Poland independently took in Jewish youngsters. Belgian Catholics hid hundreds of children in their homes, schools, and orphanages, and French Protestant townspeople sheltered several thousand Jews. In Albania and Yugoslavia, many Muslim families concealed Jewish youngsters. Children quickly learned to master the prayers and rituals of their "adopted" religion in order to keep their Jewish identity hidden from even their closest friends. Many Jewish youngsters were baptized into Christianity, with or without the consent of their parents, simply to save their lives.

8.3.3.10 Civil disobedience of "Illegitimate" Laws: There are many cases where an individual or group of protesters feel that they must disobey one or more laws because either the laws or the authorities that made them are illegitimate. This happens when there is a clear moral question and where the protester feels that they cannot ethically comply with the authority and its law(s). These circumstances provide a legal and moral argument and justification for illegal acts of disobedience.

In some countries, governments have created laws which oblige civil servants to refuse illegitimate orders under some conditions. Here is an example from part of the Croatian Civil Service code: "Civil servants shall be obliged to refuse execution of orders that are illegal or whose execution would run contrary to the rules of the profession or code of ethics, or whose execution could cause severe damages or whose execution may constitute a crime."

In other countries there are less explicit, but similar rules within constitutions and human rights laws which allow for, or even demand, refusal to obey an illegitimate law.

Considerations and risks: Whilst many Western countries preach human rights, ethical behaviour and transparency in government, they rarely allow it to be practiced in reality. Governments are inherently corrupt and will do a lot to hold on to the status quo and whatever power they have. Anyone refusing to collaborate with an unethical government will face swift retribution from the authority, even when refusing to carry out an immoral order or being forced to participate in some act of corruption. One should be under no illusion that such defiance of an authority by an individual will bring only harassment, dismissal or worse to their door.

However, there are ways of disobeying "illegitimate laws" or "immoral orders" which can be more successful. Primarily this involves four stages:

• Stage 1: Gather Information. This involves gathering evidence about the illegitimate law or order. How is it used, how often, by whom, for what reasons?

• Stage 2: Why is it illegitimate? Here one needs to understand why the law is illegitimate. Does it breach international law(s), natural law, local laws, or the constitution? Is it unpopular and if so, why?

• Stage 3: Gain support. If it seems that a law or order is illegitimate then obtain the proof that the law or order is illegitimate from higher authorities. If (in stage 2) you have demonstrated that a law is illegitimate in the eyes of a higher authority, it is important to enlist the support of this authority. For example, in the EU, if a law breaches the European Directive on Human Rights, then this needs to be demonstrable. In this case, access to the European Commission for an opinion or the advice of legal specialists with experience in this branch of European law may be required.

• Stage 4: Challenge the authority. With the collected evidence, a properly formulated case and support from a higher authority, it is time to challenge the illegitimate law or order by disobeying it. First enlist some sympathetic supporters, then inform the authority of your imminent action and then disobey the "illegitimate" law. Be prepared for a reaction and ensure that the higher authority has been briefed and is prepared to provide support.

Historical and contemporary examples: In 2013, the small town of Sugar Hill in New Hampshire joined a number of other towns, villages and the city of Pittsburgh in enacting local legislation (ordinances) to protect its own environment. In many cases this legislation directly and blatantly contradicted Federal and State laws and in some cases even defied the US constitution.

In the case of Sugar Hill, the local council reacted to the plans of a large electrical utility company to build a high tension line through their pristine (and protected) landscape. The council found it had no say in the planning of this development. So the council (with popular support) passed a local ordinance that banned corporations from acquiring land or building structures to support any "unsustainable energy system".

The local ordinance stripped those corporations of their free-speech and due-process rights under the Constitution, as well as protections afforded by the US Constitution's commerce and contract clauses. Judicial rulings that recognized corporations as legal "persons" would not be recognized in Sugar Hill. Any state or federal law that tried to interfere with the town's authority would be invalidated. "Natural communities and ecosystems" - wetlands, streams, rivers, aquifers - would acquire "inalienable and fundamental rights to exist and flourish," and any resident could enforce the law on their behalf. "All power is inherent in the people," the measure stated.

Certainly, this is not the end of this particular story, but it is an interesting and important development because it is indicative of a rising dissatisfaction with what are essentially illegitimate laws benefiting large corporations over citizens' interests. In this case, dissatisfaction with these illegitimate laws has risen to the level of local government and continues to spread [Note 71].

8.3.4 Action by Government Personnel

Civil disobedience and protest is not, of course, limited to ordinary citizens or professional protesters. Indeed, many acts of disobedience are initiated or carried out by government officials. Very often, government officials know much more of a government's intentions and secrets than the general public and this puts them in a position where they may feel morally obliged to act in a way which is politically disobedient.

```
                    ┌─────────────┐
                    │  Non Coop   │
                    │   by Govt   │
                    │   workers   │
                    └─────────────┘
```

Selective refusal of assistance	Stalling and obstruction	Judicial non-cooperation	Mutiny

Blocking of lines of command	Admin. non-cooperation	Deliberate inefficiency	Whistle blowing

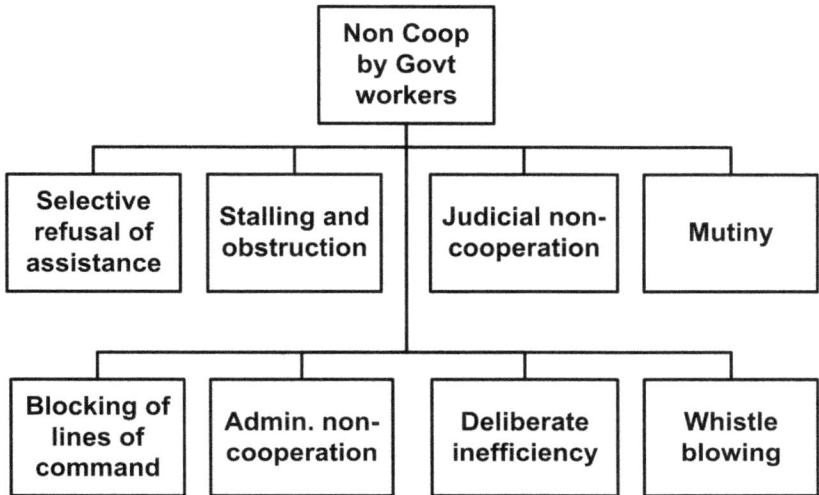

Considerations and risks: Governments have a naïve view of their civil services in general. In the era of George W. Bush, everyone assumed that the roller-coaster war on terror and the rising tide of fear would raise all boats. It did not. There is a common fallacy amongst politicians that all levels of government can be trusted, simply because self-interest dictates that each civil servant's duty to authority is bought and paid for, and that it is not in their individual interests to betray their authority and bite the hand that feeds them.

This simplistic view of human nature by our less intelligent politicians such as George W. Bush and Tony Blair, for example, comes at a price. They could do worse than heed the old Arabic proverb which advises to "Forget your enemies; it is your friends you should fear, for they know the tunnels to your very heart." In any large group of civil servants there will be at least one or two per thousand who couldn't care less about the narrow political interests at play or the interests of state. Indeed, they may well see the world in a broader sense, in which human interests have a higher value than this month's pay check. Without doubt the civil services of all nations contain those who despise the regime for which they work and, like "sleeper agents", they are simply awaiting an opportunity to damage it. In the meantime, they do little to promote the regime and spend their time engaged in low-grade sabotage, sniping and spying. Clearly, the main risk to a government official taking any kind of action against an authority, regardless of its moral probity, will be dismissal. However, in some regimes, betrayal of a government authority may be construed as an act of terrorism or a breach of national security.

Historical and contemporary examples: In modern times, the two shining examples of government officials that protested (loud and clear) against illegitimate actions by the authority of state must surely be Bradley Manning and Edward Snowden. These brave officials were not raving anarchists by any means, but they felt acutely that something was very wrong with the way the USA was behaving in the world, towards its adversaries, as well as towards its allies and its own citizens. They took action, which cost one exile and the other prison. Their contribution to modern human morality is immeasurable and they are shining examples of putting ethics before pay checks or personal security. I doubt that these two gentlemen were the only two such examples of liberated humanity in the US military and intelligence machine and so it is highly likely that at some point in the future we will be hearing from more government personnel who refuse to be bought off with a few dollars pay.

8.3.4.1 Selective Refusal of Assistance by Government Officials: This occurs when one or more government officials feel that they cannot obey some or all of the orders given to them by their government employers because the orders are ethically repugnant to them. Participants of such a protest action are sometimes referred to as "Refuseniks".

Considerations and risks: Depending on what a government official is refusing to do, they may receive more or less public support. In the example of the Israeli intelligence officers we mention below, they have received scant public support within their own country, but have been applauded by human rights campaigners internationally. Refusal to obey an order carries the risk of dismissal, ostracism and poverty or worse. If such actions are carried out by a large group, they cease to be single acts of defiance but become political acts and may carry more weight, and in some cases more savage revenge.

Historical and contemporary examples: An example of this method of action occurred in September 2014, when a group of forty-three Israeli military intelligence reservists signed a letter refusing to serve in the occupied Palestinian territories. In the letter they stated:

"We, veterans of Unit 8200, reserve soldiers both past and present, declare that we refuse to take part in actions against Palestinians and refuse to continue serving as tools in deepening the military control over the Occupied Territories. Millions of Palestinians have been living under Israeli military rule for over 47 years. This regime denies the basic rights and expropriates extensive tracts of land for Jewish settlements subject to separate and different legal systems, jurisdiction and law enforcement. This reality is not an inevitable result of the state's efforts to protect itself but rather the result of choice. Settlement expansion has nothing to do with national security. The same goes for restrictions on construction and development, economic exploitation of the West Bank, collective punishment of inhabitants of the Gaza Strip, and the actual route of the separation barrier. In light of all this, we have concluded that as individuals who served in Unit 8200, we must take responsibility for our part in this situation and it is our moral duty to act. We cannot continue to serve this system in good conscience, denying the rights of millions of people. Therefore, those among us who are reservists, refuse to take part in the state's actions against Palestinians. We call for all soldiers serving in the Intelligence Corps, present and future, along with all the citizens of Israel, to speak out against these injustices and to take action to bring them to an end. We believe that Israel's future depends on it."

The reservists were immediately denounced as criminal by the Defence Minister as the country's political and military leadership turned its fire on the refuseniks. The ferocity of the response was not unexpected by those involved. One signatory stated that he feared being portrayed as an enemy of the state after the letter was made public [Note 72].

8.3.4.2 Blocking of Lines of Command and Information (Jamming): Disobedience often escalates to acts of sabotage. In the particular case of sabotage by government or corporate employees this may take the form of sabotage of the lines of command and information. This might involve calculated failures to relay orders to subordinates, deliberately ignoring orders, or intentionally refusing to pass information to other employees or superiors.

This method may also employ deliberate technological sabotage of radio, telephone or internet communications, also known as "communications jamming". This type of technological sabotage requires specialist skills. Technological jamming may be useful to a protest for the following reasons: a/ to gain time in a fast-moving situation (like a physical confrontation) and b/ to deny the target authority the opportunity to communicate time-critical information within their organisation, such as police or military deployments.

Considerations and risks: This tactic of blocking command lines is best manifested as a form of institutional incompetence rather than running the risk of being accused of an obvious act of sabotage. In a busy department it's easy to show that communications are as efficient as they possibly can be in the circumstances, whilst making absolutely sure that they are as inefficient as can be without anyone detecting deliberate sabotage.

Technological jamming of government communications is considered illegal in most regimes and depending on the type of jamming; the jamming operator may be located and confronted using various detection techniques. However, specialists are also quite capable of evading detection whilst maintaining a more or less constant jamming attack, whether in an analogue or digital environment. Needless to say, the target of a jamming attack will resort to alternative communications methods and so a jamming attack needs to be designed to operate against all the possible alternative communications systems simultaneously and independently.

The risks of being caught deliberately slowing or blocking communications and command vary depending on the methods used. For instance, many government officials spend their entire careers explaining to their colleagues, the public and their superiors just how busy they are and why certain things didn't happen. Such excuses for incompetence are institutional in most government and corporate hierarchies. Few executives challenge such excuses for administrative incompetence, simply because they themselves rely on the very same excuses from time to time. More hi-tech forms of jamming may be harder to explain and carry greater risks and penalties.

Historical and contemporary examples: There are not that many highly publicised cases of deliberate sabotage of email servers or other computer systems in commercial or government circles. Such tales are far too embarrassing to be allowed to enter the public domain. However, a couple of publicised examples of such attacks include the case of Lockheed Martin's email system crashing for six hours after an employee sent 60,000 co-workers a personal e-mail message complete with a request for an electronic receipt in 1998. The defence contractor, which posts 40 million emails a month, was forced to fly in a Microsoft rescue squad to repair the damage caused by that one disgruntled employee.

On a smaller scale, a Forbes Inc. computer technician deliberately caused five of the publisher's eight network servers to crash as revenge for his termination from a temporary position. All of the information on the affected servers was erased, and no data could be restored. As a result of this one act of sabotage, Forbes was forced to shut down its New York operations for two days and sustained losses in excess of $100,000. Typical forms of simple IT communications sabotage involve using large file copies to fill up file systems, or using scripts to execute so-called "iterative copying", which can fill up even the largest disk systems in seconds rendering a system incapable of operation. The favourite method of attacking websites uses so-called "denial of service" attacks (DoS) to flood and overwhelm web servers with dummy requests for a page. These types of attacks are often carried out by many attack computers in different locations. This is referred to as a "Distributed Denial of Service" attack. It is difficult to pinpoint and stop because the source of the attack is not one but many single computers with unique and different IP addresses. This is a typical asynchronous attack strategy using many small attackers against one or two powerful servers. In database environments, so-called Cartesian joins can bring the most powerful servers to a virtual standstill in minutes.

In non-IT environments, there are many examples of how communications can be blocked or frustrated. For instance, one strategy has recently become popular in the USA when telemarketers call: Instead of hanging up, simply say, "Hold on please", then place the telephone handset in a drawer! This strategy costs the caller phone charges, their employees' wasted time and reduced efficiency. Similar strategies work with postal junk where a victim simply reposts the junk back to the sender with "return to sender" written on the envelope.

Other methods of jamming post rooms can be used where a group sends hundreds or thousands of letters to one or more addresses with unstamped or insufficiently stamped envelopes. This triggers demands from local post offices for surcharges on delivery, creating a huge load on human resources.

Jamming a switchboard uses a similar technique, where hundreds of calls can be automatically placed using many PCs' modem phone diallers, the incoming calls are then placed in a long queue, thus blocking or delaying any real business calls from getting attention. PC diallers can also be used to confuse those automatic robotic responders with their infuriating "Dial '1' for Customer accounts......" etc. Disconnected calls in these cases are continuously replenished automatically by the PC dialler. FAX machines and fax lines can be temporarily disabled or blocked in the same way.

Apart from the physical sabotage of communications systems, the only other means of interrupting command lines is when a person or group is part of the command organisation itself and is therefore in a position to delay or interrupt the communication of an order or an important piece of data. For example, an email can be ignored (don't sign the read receipt!) for quite some time, or "lost". A voice message can be missed, ignored or misheard or someone can often be unavailable, out to lunch, in a meeting, on a call, off sick or any one of a raft of reasons for being unavailable to pass on a call or order. One of the things that humans do best is incompetence. It comes naturally to most of us.

8.3.4.3 Stalling and Obstruction: Very often causing a bureaucratic delay has the same effect as stopping something completely. Civil servants are particularly well versed in causing delays and adept at creating obstructions. They are trained specifically to obstruct with a myriad of objections rather than to facilitate a request.

Considerations and risks: Stalling and obstruction is often difficult to detect or circumvent, especially when the activist is adept at "working the system" to create delays or obstacles. Very often this involves using legal regulation or legal methods to stall or obstruct. Sometimes a deliberate delay may be enough to derail an initiative completely, for instance, when there is a budgetary or voting deadline to be met. There are few risks involved here, except that after this kind of action the victim authority may seek some kind of retribution against the activists involved.

One generic form of obstruction is the use of an appeal to a higher legal authority against a decision (or lack of decision) by an authority. For example, a national decision by an EU member state authority may be appealed to the European Commission and thence to the European Court of Justice, thus triggering a legal delay.

In many countries it is also possible to take a legal action against a lower court or other authority to challenge the legality of one or more of their decisions. In British law this is referred to as a judicial review and allows for the courts to review the lawfulness of a decision made (or sometimes lack of a decision made) or action taken (or sometimes failure to act) by a public body. It is a mechanism by which a judge considers whether a public body has acted in accordance with its legal obligations and if not, declares a decision invalid. The grounds for reversing an administrative decision by way of judicial review in the UK (and elsewhere) include: a/ illegality, b/ irrationality (unreasonableness) and c/ procedural impropriety. Virtually every government authority may be the target of a judicial review. Normally during the conduct of a judicial review or a legal action in the European courts, the disputed decision of an authority is suspended.

Many governments around the world are in favour of weakening the concept of judicial review because it provides citizens with a legal method of challenging a government decision. At the time of writing the right-wing Tory-Liberal coalition government in the UK is in the throes of its latest attempt to make judicial review less available to the public [Note 73].

Historical and contemporary examples: In an anti-austerity action in 2014, Greek civil servants refused to carry out or complete employee assessments, fearing the loss of jobs for those not assessed highly enough. The union organising the action planned to hold out until the assessment deadline had passed 2 months later, thus effectively derailing employee assessments completely.

Judicial review processes have often been instrumental in obstructing a decision. In 2010, campaigners in the UK won a High Court battle over plans for a third runway at Heathrow Airport. Councils, residents and green groups had said the government's plan was at odds with climate change targets. Lord Justice Carnwath said the public consultation process used was invalid as it was based on out-of-date figures. The decision did not rule out a third runway, but called for government policy to be reviewed. The judge, sitting in London, said the government's public consultation did not take account of the latest information on economic benefits and climate change and was based on figures which were eight years old [Note 74]. The coalition that sought the judicial review into the government's decision, which was made in 2003 and confirmed in January 2009, includes six local authorities, Greenpeace and the Campaign to Protect Rural England (CPRE). By 2014, a further attempt to expand the airport was set to be delayed as the Airports Commission believed that a judicial review of its plans to build a third runway is "inevitable".

8.3.4.4 General Administrative Non-Cooperation: Governments may give the orders, but it is the civil service that makes things actually happen - if they choose to do so, that is. A group of disgruntled government officials can very easily thwart the directives of their government, at least for some time.

Considerations and risks: There is always the risk that a refusal to cooperate with a government authority will bring repercussions, such as dismissal or other disciplinary action. An insurance against such revenge actions is to ensure that key parts of the administration are collaborating in the action. It's unlikely an authority will risk firing its entire civil service.

Historical and contemporary examples: An example of administrative non-cooperation occurred in October 2014, when the Greek government attempted to sell off building stock to private investors. These attempts to sell public assets were thwarted by civil servants refusing to hand over the keys of the buildings and refusing to allow potential buyers to visit the properties. The officials claimed that the keys had been "lost" or that the visits were "inconvenient". These actions effectively thwarted the attempts to sell the real-estate.

In a potent act of administrative non-cooperation beginning in 2013, a new organisation of British civil servants working in employment offices throughout the UK voted to refuse to cooperate with the government's new policies of sanctioning the unemployed and benefit recipients for committing minor administrative indiscretions. Since they were introduced, these government sanctions caused widespread misery, poverty and homelessness amongst the unemployed and the new movement, "Civil Service Rank & File Network", called for solidarity with those claimants who had been affected. The movement already stated that it would act with or without the consent of its union and the initiative partly sabotaged the government's attempts to cut social welfare to Britain's poorest people. Their actions have included refusal to administer various forced labour schemes (aka "Workfare"), and various claimant sanctions [Note 75].

8.3.4.5 Judicial Non-Cooperation: When dissent reaches the judiciary, we can be fairly sure that a protest is coming to a head and that the outcome is not looking very good for the government or other authorities.

Considerations and risks: If a judiciary refuses to cooperate with the state, the risks to the judiciary are mostly limited to political revenge. Generally, this means that one or more judges may be replaced. The effects on the judges may be that their careers are terminated. When there is widespread support for an issue within a judiciary, it is much more likely that the authority will have to back down.

Historical and contemporary examples: In 2014, the British Government's plans for cutting criminal legal aid substantially were thrown into confusion when the High Court ruled that the Ministry of Justice consultation process was "so unfair as to amount to illegality". The decision was a significant setback for the Minister of Justice, who was in charge of the cuts in fees and reductions in the number of contracts for solicitors to attend courts and police stations. The protesting lawyers sponsoring the High Court case summed up the outcome:

"The way the government has handled this process means we no longer have any faith in their ability to conduct any further consultation with fairness and integrity. It has clearly not acted in the public interest as we would expect it to act; it has manipulated and schemed to the point where the high court labels its conduct as unfair and illegal."

"At a time when constitutional change is in the air, the right of citizens to defend themselves against state-funded prosecutions is not something that should be manipulated in a political way, but investigated impartially to appropriate savings and reforms that are sustainable and in the public interest."[Note 76]

Clearly having the judiciary on your side in a protest is a major boon to a protest campaign!

In early 2015, the Spanish judiciary refused to endorse the Conservative Spanish government's attempts to introduce a change to the law to allow governments to listen in on telephone conversations without a judge's approval. The PP government was obliged within 48 hours to remove this draconian attempt to spy on the entire population from its law reform simply because the Spanish judiciary made it clear that it was illegal and could not be implemented.

8.3.4.6 Deliberate Inefficiency and Selective Non-Cooperation by Police: The use of deliberate inefficiency and outright non-cooperation by the police is a protest tactic used by police who are either sympathetic to a protest action or who wish to reduce the risk of unnecessary violence or disruption.

Considerations and risks: In some (most) countries the police are obliged to obey the commands of their superiors on pain of criminal charges. However, police are not always very efficient or cooperative when they don't agree with the orders being given. They may decide to be slow in obeying orders and interpret such orders in not quite the way their political masters wish. When most of the police force takes the same attitude of selective non-cooperation it is fairly hard for a government authority to force them to obey and it is quite difficult to take legal action to punish them afterwards.

Historical and contemporary examples: In October 2011, in Albany, New York, the governor and mayor ordered state troopers and local police to enforce a curfew, and remove hundreds of the Occupy Albany protesters from state land. The police defied the orders to arrest the protesters. With the protesters acting peacefully, local and state police agreed that low level arrests could trigger rioting, so they decided instead to defy the orders. When the curfew hour arrived, the protesters quietly moved across an invisible line from state to city land. "We don't have the resources, and these people were not causing trouble," a state trooper official said. "The bottom line is the police know policing, not the governor and not the mayor." He added that State police supported the defiant posture of Albany police leaders to hold off making arrests for the low-level offence of trespassing, in part because of concern it could incite a riot or draw thousands of protesters in a backlash that could endanger both police and the public [Note 77].

In 2014-2015, a mutiny of New York police officers occurred when the Mayor of New York, Bill de Blasio, incensed rank-and-file policemen at the end of 2014 by seeming to side with those protesting the deaths of unarmed black men by white police officers. Regardless of the validity of either side's claims, the police in New York joined together in a quiet act of mass insubordination by turning a blind eye to every kind of low-level infraction. The go-slow took place during Christmas and the New Year and resulted in the almost complete cessation of issuing tickets for traffic or minor drug, public order or pilfering offences with recorded offences being the lowest in years [Note 78].

8.3.4.7 Mutiny: Mutiny is the refusal of members of the police or military to carry out orders. Mutinies may happen in response to specific government orders to repress protesters using violent methods. In other cases, mutiny may be used as a form of political non-cooperation against a government or in protest at a mutinous group's own unpopular officers, poor conditions, incompetent management, or unreasonable demands.

Considerations and risks: Mutiny often triggers off civilian actions, and in authoritarian regimes the suspension of the military or police may well spark a popular uprising which quickly makes it impossible for a government to rule. In most jurisdictions, mutiny is considered to be a criminal offence and often carries penalties of capital punishment. Mutinies are sometimes followed by violence against politicians or leaders by the mutineers although this is not inevitable. Mutiny in military circles is almost always a pre-cursor to a military coup d'état. The mutiny often originates with middle-ranking officers.

Historical and contemporary examples: There is a huge history of mutiny around the world, but a recent and somewhat amusing minor example took place in 2013, when fifteen soldiers from the 1st Battalion of the Yorkshire Regiment sat on the floor when ordered to stand to attention. They were subsequently jailed for 60 days for failing to obey a legal order. In their court martial for staging the mutinous "sit-in", their defence was that they were acting in protest at being "led by muppets". Their captain and sergeant had been found drunk and asleep during a training exercise and this had infuriated the soldiers to the point where they could no longer take their superiors seriously [Note 79].

8.3.4.8 Whistleblowing: The whistleblower is a person or group that exposes misconduct, dishonest or illegal activity occurring in an organisation which can be either a corporate or government entity. The act may be made as a powerful protest against the unethical behaviour of an authority or it may just be a private person revealing something which they personally find unethical.

Sometimes simply telling people the truth about what goes on at work can put a lot of pressure on a management or authority. In business, consumer industries like restaurants and food producers are very vulnerable to this, but all government and commercial interests are at risk from a whistleblower.

Whistleblowing can be as unsophisticated and low-key as a face-to-face conversation with a customer, or it can be as dramatic as the case of that engineer who revealed that the blueprints for a nuclear reactor had been accidentally reversed! Upton Sinclair, in his novel "The Jungle", revealed the scandalous health standards and working conditions of the meatpacking industry. Waiters can tell restaurant clients about the various shortcuts that go into creating the "haute cuisine" being served to them. When their complaints about poor hygiene were ignored, Starbucks union members in New York took photographs of rats and cockroaches in the coffee shop outlets and showed them to customers on picket lines. On a related topic, almost all businesses are very nervous about tax audits or health inspections and this provides opportunities for the whistleblower to leverage his particular story.

Considerations and risks: Despite the high-blown moralising statements of most modern politicians vowing to protect the whistleblower from any kind of retribution, the reality is that politicians are afraid of and hate whistleblowers. This is because a whistleblower exposes incompetence, corruption and stupidity in government or management and this reflects badly on the business and political classes. For this reason, despite the rhetoric to the contrary, whistleblowers are a primary target for political revenge. The old adage about shooting the messenger comes into clear focus when considering the treatment of whistleblowers in modern politics. Whistleblowers should be warned that there is a high risk of getting the sack - particularly in a small organisation - so it's wise to keep one's identity a secret if considering taking this route.

Historical and contemporary examples: Mordechai Vanunu (aka John Crossman), is a former Israeli nuclear technician who revealed details of Israel's nuclear weapons program to the British press in 1986. He was subsequently lured to Italy by a Mossad agent where he was drugged and abducted by Israeli intelligence agents. He was transported to Israel and ultimately convicted in a trial that was held behind closed doors. Vanunu spent 18 years in prison, including more than 11 in solitary confinement. Released from prison in 2004, he was then subject to a range of restrictions on speech and movement. Since then he has been arrested several times for violating those restrictions, including giving interviews to foreign journalists and attempting to leave Israel. He says he has suffered "cruel and barbaric treatment" at the hands of Israeli authorities while imprisoned. Vanunu has been characterised internationally as a whistleblower and by Israel as a traitor [Note 80].

8.3.5 International Governmental Action

Sometimes protesters can use their influence to persuade other governments or international organisations to act against their own or another government. In these days of globalisation such actions can have a dramatic effect and may undermine diplomatic, legal and economic relationships. Once upon a time, legal pressures could only be exerted by protest groups from within a country. Diplomatic approaches from outside regarding an internal matter would be seen as interference. But that has now changed, in Europe, at least.

In Europe, the institutions of the European Union are a powerful example of how international action may profoundly affect any member state's government. For instance, a citizen of Germany may complain to the European Union about poor environmental protection in, say, Ireland, even when not a resident of that country. In such a case the European Commission and eventually the European Court would be obliged to examine the case and may impose very substantial fines for breaching European laws. Similarly, a petition to the European parliament about a breach of European law in one member state could be supported by any number of MEPs from any other member states.

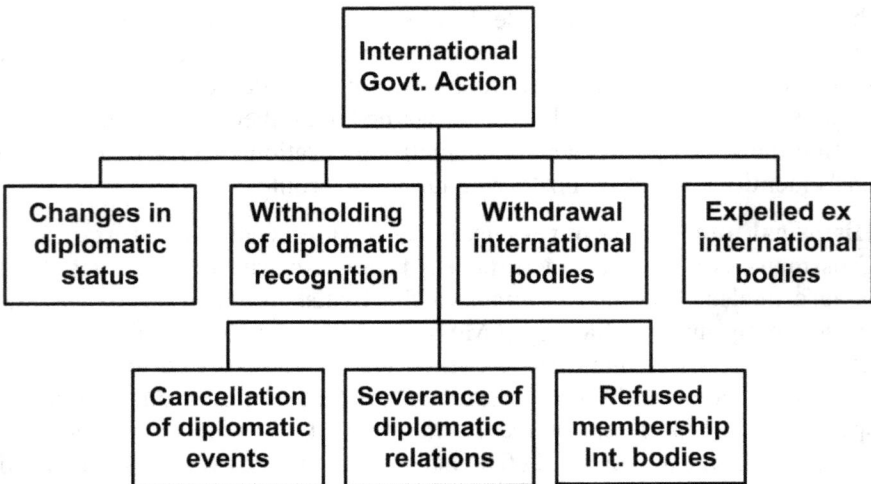

8.3.5.1 Changes in Diplomatic and Other Representations: Protests can sometimes oblige one government to review and alter diplomatic relationships with another government.

Considerations and risks: Persuading one government to diplomatically pressure another government is not something that is easy to do, although applying political pressure in the appropriate places can have this effect. There are few risks for those that attempt to alter diplomatic relations between countries, since in the final analysis it is a country's government that is responsible for its diplomatic relationships. Ordinary citizens can, however, influence diplomatic relations by releasing sensitive information about other countries, and by publishing information about another nation's human and civil rights behaviour.

Historical and contemporary examples: The leaking of the diplomatic exchanges between US embassies and the US government by WikiLeaks caused some serious and long-lasting diplomatic upsets and changes in diplomatic relations between many countries and the USA.

Spokesmen for the Pentagon and State Department cited recent exchanges with foreign officials that suggested some had suddenly grown reluctant to trust the U.S. with their secrets. "We have already seen some indications of meetings that used to involve several diplomats and now involve fewer diplomats," said State Department spokesman P.J. Crowley. "We're conscious of at least one meeting where it was requested that notebooks be left outside the room," Crowley told reporters.

Similar comments were made by the Defence Department, where spokesman Col. Dave Lapan said the military had seen foreign contacts "pulling back" and that "generally, there has been a retrenchment." "Believing that the U.S. is not good at keeping secrets and having secrets out there certainly changed things," Lapan said.

In some of the examples of the content of these diplomatic cables American officials were told to spy on the United Nations' leadership and get biometric information on its secretary general Ban Ki-moon. The cables detail claims of inappropriate behaviour by a member of the British royal family and criticism of Britain's military operations in Afghanistan and of David Cameron, a British prime minister. The cables also included requests for "specific intelligence" about British MPs.

Some leaks involved private diplomatic cables that included frank U.S. assessments of foreign nations and their leaders. Afghan president Hamid Karzai, for example, was described as turning a blind eye to corruption and releasing suspected drug dealers because of their powerful connections. In one particularly damaging cable, Yemeni president Ali Abdullah Saleh tells top NATO commander, general David Petraeus that his country would continue to pretend that American missile strikes against a local al-Qaida group had come from his military forces. The Yemeni government, seen as having only shaky control of a population in which anti-U.S. sentiment runs high, has since issued a denial. Nonetheless we have the cable as proof.

Bradley Manning, a young army intelligence analyst who had been stationed in Iraq, is suspected of downloading files using a Lady Gaga CD and a portable computer memory stick, then providing them to WikiLeaks. WikiLeaks' director Julian Assange has said the information provides valuable insight into the dubious work of the U.S. government by showing that it spies on its allies and ignores human rights abuses.

The Snowden NSA leaks have similarly caused diplomatic consternation amongst some of the US' closest allies with revelations that the US was tapping phones throughout Europe, up to and including that of German chancellor Angela Merkel.

8.3.5.2 Delay and Cancellation of Diplomatic Events: Protests can be used to trigger delays and even cancellations of diplomatic events. A diplomatic event might be something as minor as a state visit or something more profound, such as the signing of trade deals, international treaties or agreements.

Considerations and risks: The effort required to alter the schedule of a diplomatic event such as a treaty signing is huge. These events are often scheduled years in advance and are not easily cancelled or altered.

Historical and contemporary examples: In September 2014, the EU, under pressure from several international conservation groups, led an international démarche against whaling by Iceland. The EU, its 28 member states and the governments of the United States, Australia, Brazil, Israel, New Zealand, Mexico and Monaco, declared their opposition to the fact that the Icelandic government still permitted commercial whaling; in particular the hunting of fin whales and the subsequent trading of fin whale products.

Iceland has ignored all diplomatic criticism of its whale hunts by the IWC, as well as several strongly worded official diplomatic protests from a wide range of countries between 2003 and 2011. A recent decision by the US government regarding potential diplomatic action was prompted by the provocative resumption of Icelandic fin whale hunting in 2013 when a total of 134 fin whales were killed.

The EU's ambassador to Iceland, along with the diplomatic representatives of the United States, France, Germany and the UK delivered a démarche (protest) to this effect to the Icelandic government. The ambassador pointed out that public opinion in the countries that are Iceland's main trading partners is very much against the practise of whaling. This is evidenced by the public pressure put on companies around the world to boycott Icelandic goods, not to mention the pressure that voters and various organisations put on their politicians, encouraging them to send Iceland an increasingly stronger message.

Despite close economic relations with Europe, any future trade talks and cooperation between the EU / US and Iceland now hinge upon Iceland agreeing to change its whaling policy and respect the international ban on commercial whaling.

8.3.5.3 Withholding or Granting of Diplomatic Recognition: Diplomatic recognition is the admission of new states into the international community by states that are already members. The withholding of diplomatic recognition may be used in an attempt to force changes of policy on a new government, as illustrated by the non-recognition of the communist government of China in 1949 by the United States. Very often, new states have to wait a considerable time to gain diplomatic recognition, despite international support, as is the case with Palestine at the time of writing.

Considerations and risks: Persuading a government to withhold diplomatic recognition to another state is very difficult for a protest group. Generally speaking, a government will grant or withhold diplomatic recognition for a variety of reasons and will not be dissuaded by a particular lobby. Nonetheless, there may be good reasons to maintain pressure on a government to grant or revoke such diplomatic recognition to a particular nation. Eventually, other countries do "see the light", as has been recently demonstrated in the case of recognition of Palestine as a de-facto state.

Historical and contemporary examples: Protests in other countries can be used to bring pressure to bear to oblige a government to give or withhold diplomatic recognition to another state. The obvious example is that of Palestine, which has been pressing for diplomatic recognition for many years. At the time of writing Palestine has been recognised by over 130 countries in the world and in the last year has gained recognition by Britain, Spain, France, Ireland and others.

A further (unresolved) example is that of Tibet. The Tibetan government-in-exile maintains that Tibet is an independent state under unlawful occupation by China since its first incursion in 1949. Many protests have been staged around the world by Tibetans demanding recognition of their country's independence and sovereignty over the years. Similar protests in Tibet itself have been violently quashed by the Chinese government.

8.3.5.4 Severance of Diplomatic Relations: This is the cessation of normal diplomatic relations between two states, entailing the recall of diplomatic representatives and the shutting down of diplomatic missions. A severance of diplomatic relations usually occurs as a result of the onset of war (a declaration of war or an armed attack) or during serious complications in relations between states. The severance of diplomatic relations is quite a dramatic act and not undertaken lightly by most countries.

Considerations and risks: When a government or other organisation cuts off diplomatic relations, theoretically all communications between the disputed parties end. This might be the objective of the severance of relations, but it may also mean that important options for resolving a dispute may be lost. Cutting off diplomatic relations is thus a last resort. Generally, countries protesting the behaviour of another country will make a lesser diplomatic gesture to signal their displeasure. These include the summoning of an ambassador to explain their country's behaviour, it may include withdrawing an ambassador or it may escalate to expelling an ambassador, but it falls short of severing diplomatic relations.

Historical and contemporary examples: Imperialist powers frequently use the severance of diplomatic relations, or the threat of severance, as a means of interfering in the internal affairs of other states and as a means of exercising political pressure and provoking international conflicts. Such was the case when the USA and a number of Latin American countries severed diplomatic relations with Cuba in 1961-62.

Protest groups often demand the severance of diplomatic relations with countries against which they have an ethical objection. For example, in 2013, demonstrators in Bangladesh called for the severance of diplomatic relations with Pakistan because of the war crimes committed in Bangladesh's war of independence from Pakistan in 1971.

Currently, there are large numbers of protest groups around the world calling for the severance of diplomatic relations with Israel until such time as Israel recognises the rights of the Palestinian people to a homeland.

8.3.5.5 Withdrawal from International Organisations: This entails a state withdrawing its support and/or participation in an international organisation. States are often part of international organisations such as the

United Nations, the World Trade Organisation, NATO and various regional economic and political blocs such as the European Union. These associations often bring benefits for member nations, such as security guarantees, open trade deals, and international recognition. However, they also carry a number of responsibilities and obligations. Sometimes these obligations are objectionable to particular groups within a country. Europe, for instance, has many pressure groups and political parties (on the left and right) that would like their nations to leave the European Union or NATO and these groups lobby actively to achieve precisely these objectives, albeit for different reasons.

Considerations and risks: Becoming a member of an organisation, such as the United Nations or the European Union, is a long and complex process spread over many years of negotiation and adjustment. Thus, withdrawal from such an organisation may well entail an equally or more complex process for both parties.

To illustrate how difficult it is to leave an international organisation, consider the current anti-EU sentiment in some European countries. When populist anti-European groups in various countries blithely speculate about "leaving the European Union" they neglect to mention that their economies are almost entirely reliant on their membership. They also forget that they would face demands for aid repayments on a biblical scale, that the future of their expatriates living elsewhere in the EU would suddenly be undermined by withdrawal of residence rights. The volume of domestic legislative changes a departing country would need to enact and implement could keep their parliaments, courts and civil servants busy for decades. Sometimes leaving is harder than joining [Note 81].

Historical and contemporary examples: Certain World Trade Organisation rules demand that countries open their borders to the free-trading of goods. This may well affect the livelihood of local farmers and producers within their country. This in turn has triggered demands for the withdrawal from the World Trade Organisation by protest groups in many countries. These anti-WTO protests have now developed into a huge global protest movement demanding withdrawal from the WTO (and actually the abolition of the WTO). For instance, in 2014, the Via Campesina, the international peasants movement, launched another global protest against various free-trade initiatives between the US and EU and called again for their countries to withdraw from the WTO. This protest action involved occupations, marches and rallies across 30 countries, with hundreds of thousands of protesters. Forcing a withdrawal from the WTO is proving a very difficult objective, but the protest movement has a substantial and growing global momentum.

8.3.5.6 Refusal of Membership in International Bodies: International organisations have the right to refuse entry of a state into their membership. This fact is sometimes leveraged by national protest groups to force fundamental changes in the governance of their own countries or other countries perceived as acting in an immoral way.

Considerations and risks: Continuous and (sometimes) noisy pressure on a government by a protest group may oblige a government to refuse or veto the application of another government to join an important international body. This kind of pressure carries few risks to the activist group. On the other hand, trying to force one's government to act to veto another country's membership isn't usually that effective, unless the government has already decided to veto it anyway. However, a protest group can embarrass a government by exposing them to criticism or ridicule if they support the application of a pariah state.

Historical and contemporary examples: A contemporary example of this is the desire of post-Balkan-war Serbia to join the EU. Membership of the European Union is a slow, careful process, designed to allow countries to meet the minimum standards of open, democratic government as required by the Treaty of the European Union. After the Balkan wars, it was clear that certain emergent states were undemocratic and had supported various war crimes during that conflict. Serbia was one of the main perpetrators.

Under pressure from those wishing to avenge the war crimes committed by Serbia against them, the EU made further negotiation with Serbia dependent on the arrest and extradition of Ratko Mladic and Radovan Karadzic, two prime suspects of war crimes committed against the people of Kosovo. Serbia was obliged to comply. Pressure and protests from the new Kosovo government (and many street demonstrations) continued to make the entry of Serbia into the EU a very slow process. Croatia, in contrast, was able to demonstrate that it had reformed and, in 2013, entered the European Union with little difficulty [Note 82].

8.3.5.7 Expulsion from International Organisations: As well as refusing entry to an international organisation, a state can also be expelled from such organisations. This is a fact which is also used by protesters to bring pressure to bear on a government.

Considerations and risks: A protest group shouldn't make this strategy their main bulwark in a conflict against any government authority. International organisations are notoriously slow. They are slow to admit and slow to expel nations from their membership. Generally, minor indiscretions by member states are discussed when they occur and expulsion is really the very last resort.

Historical and contemporary examples: In the case of Palestine, in early 2014, demonstrators and the Palestinian Football Association chairman called upon FIFA to expel Israel for failing to abide by its conventions. In addition, the Palestinian Authority demanded Israel's expulsion from the International Olympics Committee. The protesters claimed that Israel does not want the Palestinians to have their own national sports entity and that Israel was seeking to break the Palestinians' athletic will. Israel's expulsion would represent a blow to the country's international standing [Note 83].

8.3.6 Domestic Governmental Action

Protesters are well aware that they can also achieve their objectives by making use of existing government and judicial structures, such as national law, local regulations, and regulatory guidelines. Here we take a look at some examples:

```
┌─────────────────┐
│    Domestic     │
│   Government    │
│     Action      │
└────────┬────────┘
         │
┌────────┴────────┐
│  Quasi-legal    │
│  Evasions and   │
│     Delays      │
└─────────────────┘
```

8.3.6.1 Quasi-Legal Evasions and Delays: Sometimes, protesters labour under the idea that nothing about their own government can be trusted and that no part of the state apparatus or judicial system can be used in pursuance of the protest objectives. This is an error because even the most corrupt system provides useful opportunities to further a protest using existing legal systems. There are almost always ways to use a legal system to evade or stall an authority.

Considerations and risks: Using legal mechanisms to evade or delay an action by an authority doesn't create that many risks to the protester. What is more important is to ensure that the evasion or hold-up is effective and cannot be circumvented by an authority.

Historical and contemporary examples: In most Western nations systems exist for challenging the legality of a law or the legality of an act by a government department or other body. In the UK and Ireland this process is called a judicial review. Judicial reviews are carried out by the judiciary in a court. They are often lengthy and deliver a binding ruling. Protesters can take advantage of this legal procedure to either overturn a government decision or to delay action by government.

Similarly, planning protests can use procedural processes to appeal planning decisions and cause delays in the approval of a planning application and even force a decision to be reversed.

8.4 Civil Disobedience: Social Non-Cooperation

Social non-cooperation is concerned with the behaviour of individuals or groups of protesters who refuse to abide by the norms of social participation and refuse to cooperate with one or other part of their society.

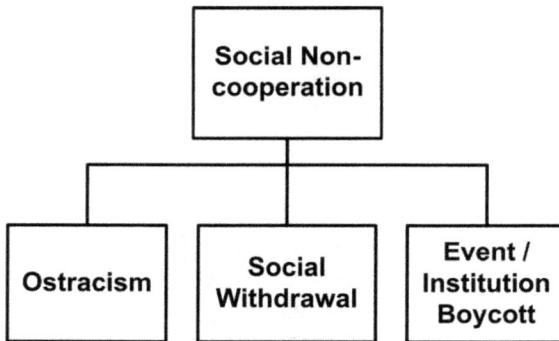

```
                    ┌──────────────┐
                    │ Social Non-  │
                    │ cooperation  │
                    └──────────────┘
        ┌───────────────┼───────────────┐
  ┌───────────┐   ┌───────────┐   ┌───────────┐
  │           │   │  Social   │   │  Event /  │
  │ Ostracism │   │Withdrawal │   │Institution│
  │           │   │           │   │  Boycott  │
  └───────────┘   └───────────┘   └───────────┘
```

8.4.1 Ostracism of Persons

The origin of the word and the practice of ostracism originated in ancient Athens, when one or more citizens could be exiled and excluded from society by the other citizens of the city. It did not necessarily involve a formal charge or allow any form of defence. In modern times, groups may ostracise other groups or individuals. In a protest, a group or individual may ostracise those that oppose them, be they individuals or another group.

```
                    ┌─────────────┐
                    │  Ostracism  │
                    └─────────────┘
```

| Social boycott | Selective social boycott | Lysistratic nonaction | Excommun-ication | Interdict |

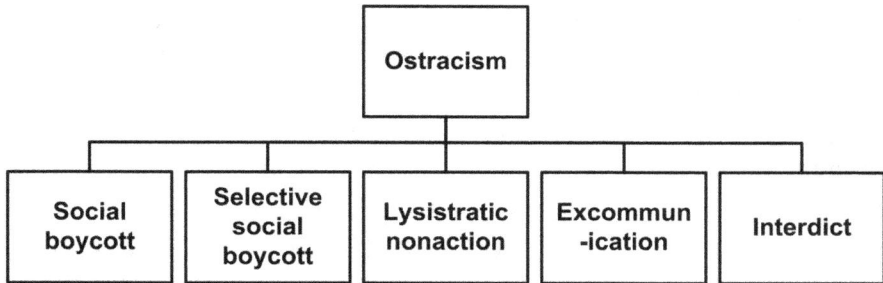

8.4.1.1 Social Boycott: A social boycott is the collective refusal by a group to engage in any form of social relations with particular persons. In the case of an occupying military force, for instance, a social boycott would seek to socially isolate the occupiers from the native population or part thereof.

In a protest, a social boycott is aimed at the protest target's personnel. For example, in a protest against hunting the social boycott would be aimed at the hunters, their employees, families and their supporters. It may take the form of refusing to socialise or communicate, or not allowing them to share a place of meeting, such as a bar or public building, and it includes a refusal to assist them in any way.

Considerations and risks: Social boycotts can backfire and expose the protesters themselves to a form of exclusion, simply because they take a principled position against an authority. Other (less principled) personalities may use the protesters' behaviour as an opportunity to capitalise on the target's isolation or even as a means by which they can attempt to ostracise the protesters.

Historical and contemporary examples: In close-knit rural circles in England, an issue as contentious as the ban on fox-hunting can have divisive results. Given that rural society often revolves around the local pub, it was inevitable that the powerful anti-hunt activists would target the village pub at some point in their dispute with the largely land-owning fox-hunting fraternity. In 2008, The North West Hunt Saboteurs Association posted a blacklist of country pubs on its website to put pressure on licensees to break all links with members of local fox-hunts. Customers were urged by the anti-hunting lobby to boycott pubs which allow hunts to meet on their premises. The website message reads: "Dying for a pint? - Hunt pubs perpetuate the myth of hunting as a harmless rural tradition. By providing a venue for hunts to hold social or fundraising events or by hosting a meet prior to a day's killing, these public houses are at the very heart of this callous, cruel and bloody 'sport'." The social boycott created a strong incentive for local pubs to refuse the use of their premises to local hunters rather than lose important local business from neutral or anti-hunt residents [Note 84].

8.4.1.2 Selective Social Boycott: This is a subset of a social boycott, whereby the protesting group refuses certain social interactions with the ostracised group.

Considerations and risks: There is always the risk of being called a hypocrite if a social boycott isn't complete. Refusing some social interactions whilst still cooperating with the target in other social activities may appear to be contradictory. On the other hand, in some circumstances it may be a very appropriate distinction which highlights the behaviour which is objectionable, but leaves a door open for negotiation.

Historical and contemporary examples: In the anti fox-hunting campaign referred to earlier, some protesters refused to assist the hunters or socialise with them during hunts, but did not refuse to speak to them at other times; nor did they refuse them access to facilities that they ran such as shops or bars. Naturally, this drove the point home to the ostracised group that what the protesters objected to was only one particular part of their behaviour: killing small defenceless wild animals for sport.

8.4.1.3 Lysistratic Non-Action: This is an ancient form of ostracism originating in ancient Greece. It involves the boycott, generally by women, of sexual relations with their partners as a protest against their spouse's actions.

Considerations and risks: Clearly, such actions may jeopardise the relationship between partners, which obviously is not the protester's intention. Such a protest may be perceived to devalue a relationship or be seen as an act of disloyalty and this perception may trigger unexpected results. For this reason, a protest like this is best undertaken en masse, so that one partner cannot claim they are being victimised by their particular spouse when clearly *all* partners are being targeted by their spouses.

Historical and contemporary examples: In one famous incident, during the 1600s, the Iroquois Indian Nations, a group of several indigenous tribes in North America, engaged in warfare with several other tribes. The men controlled when and against whom they declared a war. The Iroquois women decided that they wanted to stop this continuous warfare and to convince the Iroquois men to give them more power in deciding issues of war and peace.

Firstly, the Iroquois women boycotted sexual relations and childbearing. Iroquois men believed that Iroquois women knew the secret of birth, which made this a powerful tactic.

Secondly, the women began to restrict the warriors' access to supplies because the women also had complete control over the planting and cultivation of crops. The women prevented warriors from acquiring supplies by withholding commodities such as dried corn and moccasins. Although the Iroquois men controlled the politics and external relations of the tribe, they could not go to war without these essential supplies, which were controlled by the women of the tribe.

The men eventually gave in to the women's demands and granted them veto power concerning all wars. This nonviolent action has been considered the first feminist rebellion in the United States.

8.4.1.4 Excommunication: This is the institutional act of excluding one or more individuals from a church or a religious community. It is a form of exile used to punish and exclude someone who has seriously offended the moral principle of a religious community. Generally, excommunication is the act of an authority against a dissenting minority, but not always - it may also be an act of exclusion aimed at a large group of dissenters by a minority of protesting leaders in a religious authority.

Considerations and risks: Churches, like other clubs or associations, need members. No members - no club. Thus excommunication has to be used carefully and must not be seen as unreasonable by other members. If other members of a congregation feel that an excommunication was unreasonable, they may seek to take control from the current hierarchy of the church. Worse still, aggrieved communicants may just decide to leave the church rather than face the risk of excommunication. In both cases this is a direct threat to the church leadership.

On the other hand, in organisations like churches, excommunication is often seen as the only way to impose discipline. "Making an example" out of the offending members is often used to bring the congregation into line. Sometimes, however, excommunication or a similar exclusion may be used as a principled act of protest against another authority or immoral attitude.

Historical and contemporary examples: One of the most notable examples of excommunication was that of Henry VIII in 1538. After years of violent excesses against the Roman Church in England, including the destruction of monasteries and the murder and persecution of numerous members of religious orders, and the theft of Church land, Henry finally went too far when he started to destroy the relics of highly venerated saints, including that of Thomas Becket in Canterbury. He was finally excommunicated; not so much for his marital irregularities, as for his hunger for power and his attempts to usurp the spiritual authority of the Church when he declared himself to be head of the Church in England.

8.4.1.5 Interdict: This is a prohibition directed towards one or more individuals or groups forbidding them from taking certain actions. It may forbid movement, certain behaviours or associations and it usually causes restrictions in social interaction of some kind. An interdict may, for instance, ban political party members from travelling to certain countries.

Considerations and risks: Interdicts may be issued by an authority against its subjects, forbidding them from taking part in certain activities.

An interdict can also be used by others as part of a protest action. For instance, parents may forbid their children from participating in some morally unacceptable activity, such as receiving religious education at school, or participating in aggressive sports or military training. These are also interdicts, but in this case the interdicts are issued by those engaged in a protest. This use of an interdict in a protest action may bring the interdictor into social and legal conflict. For example, forbidding your child from participation in religious education may be legally challenged by a school and may lead to social ostracism of the child.

Historical and contemporary examples: There has been a long history of controversy in many Western countries where parents with conscientious objections to certain aspects of their children's education have made principled stands and forbidden their child from participating in certain school activities. Parents have often been opposed by schools for wanting their children to have a non-militaristic education, a humanistic education or an education with limited focus on physical sports. These disputes have sometimes come to the point where children have been removed from a particular school because of the interdicts of protesting parents.

A completely different use of an interdict in a protest occurred in 1955 after white parishioners refused to allow a black priest enter a chapel situated about 20 miles from New Orleans. Archbishop Joseph Rummel, a well-known fighter for equal rights, placed the chapel under an interdict. As he stated in his pastoral letters of 1955 and 1956: "Racial segregation as such is morally wrong and sinful because it is a denial of the unity and solidarity of the human race as conceived by God in the creation of Adam and Eve". Rummel's interdict was a clear case of a social liberationist using an interdict to frustrate a regressive public attitude to black people [Note 85].

8.4.2 Withdrawal from the Social System

This strategy involves a withdrawal from society by an individual or group of protesters. The withdrawal may be temporary (such as a stay-home protest) or long-term (such as a mass emigration to another country). The objective of protesters' withdrawal from a social system is to degrade the vitality of the society by refusing to participate in normal social life.

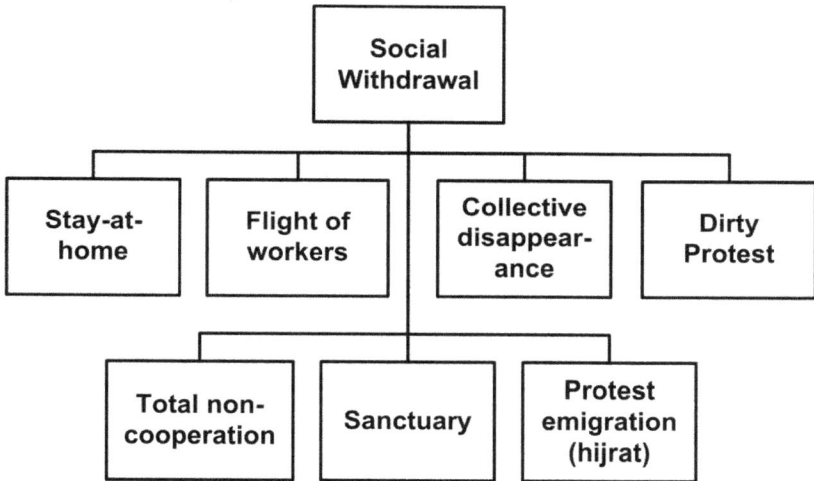

```
                        ┌─────────────┐
                        │   Social    │
                        │ Withdrawal  │
                        └─────────────┘
   ┌──────────┬─────────────┬──────────────┬──────────┐
┌────────┐ ┌────────┐ ┌────────────┐ ┌────────┐
│Stay-at-│ │Flight of│ │ Collective │ │ Dirty  │
│ home   │ │ workers │ │disappear-  │ │Protest │
└────────┘ └────────┘ │   ance     │ └────────┘
                      └────────────┘
         ┌──────────────┬────────────┐
    ┌──────────┐ ┌──────────┐ ┌────────────┐
    │Total non-│ │Sanctuary │ │  Protest   │
    │cooperation│ │          │ │emigration  │
    └──────────┘ └──────────┘ │  (hijrat)  │
                              └────────────┘
```

8.4.2.1 Stay-At-Home: This involves a refusal to go out of the home for the purpose of social interaction. This may entail refusing to go to a bar or restaurant, to concerts, sporting events, other types of entertainment or participating in social and religious gatherings. The protesters simply refuse to take part in outside social events and confine themselves to home life. For this kind of protest to work you need to have large numbers of dedicated participants and be well-organised.

Considerations and risks: Unless this is done on a relatively large scale, there is a risk that no-one will notice the protest. In a small community a relatively modest number of protesters may attract attention and cause disruption, but in large urban societies this needs to take the form of a truly massive action to have any effect.

Historical and contemporary examples: In November 2014, a group of consumers took part in a "Black Friday" protest over the death of an unarmed black teenager in Ferguson, Missouri. The "Black Friday" protesters urged consumers to stay at home on a day when Americans traditionally head to shops in large numbers for post-Thanksgiving bargain shopping. The protest movement aimed to highlight the perceived injustice of a grand jury decision not to indict the police officer for the shooting of 18-year-old Michael Brown on 9 August 2014. The shooting had led to violent protests in several American cities. The idea of the protest was conceived by Ryan Coogler. His 2013 Cannes award-winning drama "Fruitvale Station" tells the true story of a young black man shot dead by a white transport policeman in the early hours of New Year's Day 2009 [Note 86].

8.4.2.2 Total Personal Non-Cooperation: This is a form of non-cooperation which involves all interactions with society or the state. In particular, this includes a refusal to acknowledge or comply with the legal system of the state and it usually ends with a legal confrontation with the state. In order to complete this form of protest an individual or group must withdraw all cooperation with the authorities of a state, including when they inevitably confront and then pass through the legal system, from arrest through to imprisonment and release.

Total non-cooperation requires a complete withdrawal from the legal system, with some protesters as prisoners refusing to eat, drink or dress themselves; in essence, the prisoner completing the protest refuses to do everything - apart from breathe for themselves. Non-cooperation requires a protester to ignore all warrants issued for his arrest and not to attend willingly any courts for the hearing of their "offences".

Considerations and risks: This is very much a last resort for a protester who is being unjustly treated by an authority and has little recourse to real internal justice or external intervention on their behalf. Total non-cooperation often results in appalling acts of repression, including imprisonment, often in terrible conditions, as authorities use various escalating ways of punishment against the protester, such as solitary confinement and various other forms of torture and oppression.

Historical and contemporary examples: In the U.K., protesters taking part in the anti-nuclear weapons protests at Greenham Common withdrew their cooperation with the British legal system by refusing to speak during their own court appearances. By refusing to cooperate, many arrested protesters lost their rights to be released on a bond or bail and were usually sentenced to prison time equivalent to the fines that they refused to pay.

One well-known case of total personal non-cooperation is the case of the US conscientious objector Corbett Bishop, who withdrew all his cooperation with the authorities during World War II. After registering as a conscientious objector Bishop was required by the U.S. authorities to take part in a Civilian Public Service program. Bishop's beliefs were so strong he could not reconcile working in the program and thus withdrew from it. During his arrest for failing to take part in the CPS program Bishop let his body go limp and refused to assist those arresting him. Upon arriving in prison Bishop spent the time refusing to complete even the simplest tasks and was kept alive by force-feeding with a tube. Twice released on parole, Bishop refused to sign any documents or make any promises about his behaviour or participation in any programs. Corbett Bishop was finally released from prison in March 1946 after completing a protest of total personal non-cooperation that lasted 193 days.

8.4.2.3 Flight of Workers: Over the years, groups of workers have used cessation of work and flight from their jobs, homes, and sometimes their countries, to demonstrate to an authority their degree of unity and self-discipline. This is done in order to have an impact on the behaviour and economy of the target authority.

Considerations and risks: There is a considerable risk that authorities will simply replace the workers that have left with a workforce from a different area, thus rendering the protest ineffective. The return of workers after a protest is also fraught with risks, since there is a strong possibility of revenge attacks by the authorities, unless an amnesty is negotiated in advance.

Historical and contemporary examples: In ancient Egypt, using a combination of flight and sanctuary, workers would seek the "protection of their Gods" and go to the temples. Temples, churches and other holy sites have frequently been used as places of refuge for fleeing protesters. During 1968 the idea of flight to sanctuaries which included churches and universities, was revived in the United States in the context of resistance to the Vietnam War military draft.

In the 1860s and 1870s, Russian workers sometimes rebelled against severe working conditions by collectively leaving their jobs and returning to peasant life. The protest method continued to be used for some years as a means of collective resistance. There were forty-nine cases in which desertion of work was carried out in an organised way between 1870 and 1879 in the Russian Empire.

In the United States, temporary or permanent flight was used by African slaves. The flight of slaves played a role in bargaining with owners. Slaves would flee to swamps or forests and send back word that they would willingly return only if their demands (perhaps for better food, fewer beatings and shorter hours) were met or at least discussed. African slaves in the United States also undertook flight as a means of full escape from slavery by leaving a slave territory. In 1730 many slaves escaped into the Spanish territory of Florida where they received freedom under Spanish law, and were permitted to live there as freemen. During the American Civil War some slaves added a new demand as a condition for returning to the country as a soldier, i.e. the payment of real wages.

In modern times, workers suffering poor wages, poor conditions, few opportunities or intermittent work rapidly seek employment away from their own homes in other regions or countries. This movement of labour creates local shortages and an upward correction in the price for labour as employers become desperate to fill important roles. Often called the "brain drain", such flights of labour are usually not formally organised.

8.4.2.4 Sanctuary: Sanctuary is a way of protesting by means of social non-cooperation. An individual or a group of protesters withdraw from society and seeks refuge in a place where the authority cannot go without risking a contravention of religious, moral, social, or legal constraints.

In order to be successful, the action of seeking sanctuary must cause so much embarrassment to the authority that the protest demands are accepted. Historically, places of sanctuary were often sacred places or buildings that were believed to be untouchable, such as temples, mosques, synagogues or churches. These days, places of sanctuary might be more symbolic, such as union offices, embassies, schools, hospitals or political party offices. Sanctuary does not necessarily bring any legal protection, although acts of conscience may produce their own intrinsic protection by other parts of society, such as religious orders.

Considerations and risks: A place of sanctuary may not be as respected by an authority as a protester believes. St Thomas Becket was murdered in the confines of Canterbury cathedral by knights of King Henry II, despite the fact that the precincts of a church were considered completely sacrosanct at that time. The anger of the King was greater than his respect for the sanctuary of the church.

Another problem with taking sanctuary is the need to maintain contact with the outside world to keep up the protest pressure and to find a place which is suitable and can sustain a long period of exile in terms of basic living conditions and obtaining supplies. A successful sanctuary protest needs to consider the following issues: How long the sanctuary has to last before demands are accepted? How powerful is the symbolism of the act? Can the sanctuary be supplied if the protest drags on? How secure is the sanctuary? Can the protests resist eviction? How will communications and the press be managed from the sanctuary?

Historical and contemporary examples: In 1968, at a church in Boston, 300 men handed over their military draft cards to clergymen to protest U.S. military conscription. The support by the clergy fuelled the expansion of those opposing the draft, so that the Harvard Divinity School became a sanctuary. Next, the sanctuary movement spread to non-religious educational institutions, such as the Massachusetts Institute of Technology.

At the time of writing, two of the world's most wanted whistleblowers, Julian Assange and Edward Snowden, are both in sanctuaries. The former in an embassy in London and the latter benefiting from political asylum somewhere in Russia; both on the run from the revenge of the USA for revealing some of that country's government's international criminal activities.

8.4.2.5 Collective Disappearance: One type of social withdrawal that has been used to avoid participating in something the protester finds repugnant is to simply disappear. Collective disappearance can be used not only by individuals, but by entire populations of villages, for instance. The technique can be very disruptive for an authority and sends them a powerful signal that their authority is unwelcome.

Considerations and risks: There aren't that many risks involved, unless the authority has legally restricted freedom of movement, in which case there may be legal implications if and when one returns home. Moving away en mass may have severe economic implications and disrupt the infrastructure of an area for the immediate future. Agriculture and other forms of wealth creation may be severely disrupted and any future return home may be complicated by this.

Historical and contemporary examples: This strategy has been frequently used in wartime, such as when entire villages in China disappeared in 1939, as invading Japanese troops approached. This forced the advancing Japanese to bring many more supplies, labour and food with them, a costly and time-consuming exercise. Meanwhile, the local Chinese population simply disappeared into the hills with every ounce of their food and possessions.

8.4.2.6 Protest Emigration (Hijrat): Protest emigration, sometimes called hijrat, is the intentional emigration away from an area (usually a region, country or a particular government) as a protest against the behaviour of the government during periods of war or civil strife. The protest group migrates from the area controlled by the target authority. All social cooperation ceases as a form of protest. In some situations the emigration is permanent; in other cases the protest emigration is temporary and is intended to bring about some form of change from the authority. The mass emigration (temporary or permanent) can have a destabilising effect on the target government by undermining local economies or starving an economy of labour. The technique has a long history and was documented in the early years of Islam. It still occurs, but is generally one of the protests of last resort.

Considerations and risks: In areas of war or extreme civil strife, civil populations frequently abandon their homes to flee to another area or country as refugees. This tragic reaction is all too common in modern times, but has been a feature of human settlement for thousands of years. Abandoning an area may make it less economically attractive to an authority as infrastructural systems begin to fail and fall into disrepair. Agricultural land may become unusable, roads may become impassable, and services, such as supplies of water, food and fuel, will cease without a market. Reversing this damage may be a considerable challenge to a returning population.

Historical and contemporary examples: In modern times, many countries experiencing war or civil upheaval, or with unstable economies and corrupt governments, witness large-scale emigration. Very often, the emigration is not only an economic necessity, but also includes an element of protest. Ireland, a country which has a long history of poverty and political corruption, has suffered continuous emigration, even after it gained its national independence. Spain and Italy have experienced a similar phenomenon of the people "voting with their feet". There is a strong correlation between mass emigration and corrupt or unstable governments, mostly of right-wing persuasion.

8.4.2.7 Dirty Protest: A dirty protest is an act of disobedience carried out by prisoners when they refuse to comply with prison authorities regarding rules of hygiene and clothing.

Considerations and risks: Dirty protests carry the obvious risks to the health of the participating prisoners as reducing levels of hygiene increase risks of infection and disease. As always, publishing prison protests to the outside world is difficult. Generally, a small group of non-participant prisoners remains outside of the protest to act as a news gateway to the media outside.

Historical and contemporary examples: In 1976, as part of the policy of "criminalisation" of the IRA and INLA, the British Government brought an end to "Special Category Status" for paramilitary prisoners in Northern Ireland, which meant that they would be obliged to work and wear prison clothing. This triggered off a 5-year protest. The prisoners refused to wear the uniforms or to work. Eventually, they destroyed all their cell furniture and refused to leave their cells for any reason, hygienic or otherwise. Many ended up either naked or dressed in parts of their blankets. Simultaneously, the IRA ordered that prison officers should be executed on sight, and during the 5-year protest 19 prison officers were indeed assassinated by the IRA, often on their way to or from work.

The conditions in the prisons rapidly deteriorated into utter squalor, but the British government refused to concede the special status of the IRA and INLA internees. A hunger strike ensued and by October 1981, when it ended, ten men had starved themselves to death. Two days after the end of the hunger strike, the British government conceded to the demands of the protesters.

8.4.3 Non-Cooperation with Social Events, Customs, and Institutions

Another form of social non-cooperation relates to protests where the targets are social institutions, forms of behaviour and events:

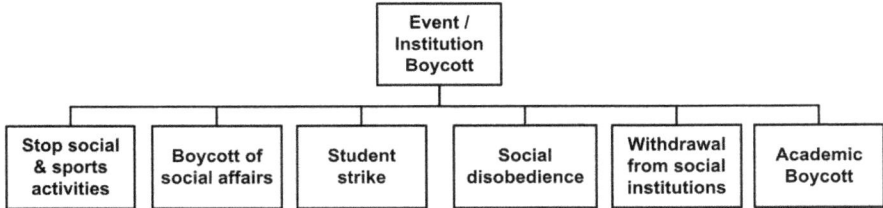

8.4.3.1 Suspension of Social and Sports Activities: An effective method of high profile protest is to force the suspension of a sporting or a social event.

Considerations and risks: There are few risks incurred by forcing the abandonment of a social or sporting event, except that it may generate the enmity of some socialites or sporting enthusiasts. For this reason, the causes of the protest need to be carefully explained to the public.

Historical and contemporary examples: One of the most famous historical examples of this is the boycott of the 1936 Olympics held in Nazi Germany. This hurt Nazi Germany because of loss of tourism, a compromised Olympic Games and a lack of support of their political ideals.

A similar protest was conducted in New Zealand in 1981 to prevent rugby games involving the white South African Springboks from taking place, and to gain publicity for the anti-apartheid cause.

In terms of art and cultural events, there have been many examples of artists refusing to perform in certain countries. For instance, in August 2010, 150 Irish artists launched a cultural boycott of Israel, declaring that they would not perform or exhibit in Israel "until such time as Israel complies with international law and universal principles of human rights". Organizers explained the boycott was motivated by what they saw as abuse of Palestinian human rights by Israel.

In August 2013, Roger Waters, the former front man of Pink Floyd, called in an open letter on fellow rock stars to boycott Israel. He said: "I write to you now, my brothers and sisters in the family of Rock and Roll, to ask you to join with me, and thousands of other artists around the world, to declare a cultural boycott on Israel. Please join me and all our brothers and sisters in global civil society in proclaiming our rejection of apartheid in Israel and occupied Palestine, by pledging not to perform or exhibit in Israel or accept any award or funding from any institution linked to the government of Israel, until such time as Israel complies with international law and universal principles of human rights" [Note 87].

In June 2013, the important British trade union GMB decided to ban its members from visiting Israel and the Palestinian territories on delegations organised by the Trade Union Friends of Israel (TUFI). A spokesman for GMB said the union didn't want to be associated with an organisation fighting a boycott of trade with illegal settlements in occupied territories.

8.4.3.2 Boycott of Social Affairs: The boycott of a social event means not showing up en masse. The absence of large numbers of participants may help a protest movement to demonstrate a point. Other social boycotts may involve refusing to meet certain people socially because of their opinions or affiliations, refusing to attend ceremonies, social gatherings, receptions or dinners.

In modern times, a boycott of social affairs may also include a boycott of an authority's presence at a social event and a campaign via the internet to encourage others not to engage with the authority at the social event.

Considerations and risks: There are few risks involved in a boycott of social affairs, except that you may not be invited again.

Historical and contemporary examples: In 2001, in the UK, dozens of Birmingham councillors tore up their invitations to the Lord Mayor's banquet in protest at the cost to taxpayers. The city's most glittering social occasion became an embarrassment with attendance at a record low. One of the main reasons for the boycott was the so-called "bed-blocking" scandal. Hundreds of old-age pensioners have been stranded in hospital beds because the city council claimed there was no cash to place them in care homes. A decision to spend up to £20,000 on a political banquet whilst these elderly people were suffering outraged many people, including many city councillors who boycotted the event [Note 88].

8.4.3.3 Student Strike: A student strike involves the refusal of a group of students to go to their classes. It is often used as a negotiating tactic to pressurise the governing body of a university or a local or national government. Where education is free, student strikes put pressure on governments to resolve disagreements in order to get the students back in their classes, so as not to disrupt the next term and following academic year.

Student strikes may concern the conditions and treatment of the students themselves or may be a political protest connected with government policy unconnected to the life of the students themselves.

Considerations and risks: As always, there is a risk of retaliation after a protest and students may be academically or financially penalised. For this reason, student strikes require a large turnout and plenty of solidarity.

Historical and contemporary examples: One of the most famous student strikes in modern history was the so-called May 68 movement in France. It is still considered as a cultural, social and moral turning point in the modern history of France. The unrest began with a series of student occupation protests against capitalism, consumerism, traditional institutions and their values, and against the forces of law and order. It then spread to factories with strikes involving 11 million workers (more than 22% of the total population of France was involved). The movement was spontaneous, de-centralized and resulted in the largest general strike in the history of France, the first ever nation-wide wildcat general strike.

Despite the fact that the French strikes did not dislodge the right-wing government (de Gaulle was re-elected), the size, rapidity and power of the student strikes and the ensuing solidarity from the labour force of France forever undermined the confidence of subsequent French regimes to bully or overbear their populations.

8.4.3.4 Social Disobedience: This is the act of disobeying the rules, expectations and custom and practice of a government or non-government authority. This may also be a club, a religious organisation or a company. Social disobedience has many possibilities and takes lots of different forms. It may involve dressing or behaving in an "unorthodox" way, disobeying rules or norms of behaviour, or even breaking company rules or ecclesiastic "laws". In small groups such behaviour is likely to lead to ostracism, in larger groups it may be effective in bringing about change in a social authority.

Considerations and risks: There are few risks in taking part in social disobedience, although in repressive authoritarian periods, unorthodox behaviour may trigger unreasonably vicious responses.

Historical and contemporary examples: Sometimes, social disobedience triggers disproportionate responses from an authority, as was the case when Pussy Riot (an unconventional all-female feminist band) made open and provocative attacks on Vladimir Putin and the Russian establishment (including the Church) during so-called guerrilla concerts in that country. These acts of social disobedience and musical protest raised public awareness regarding the problems of modern Russia, but landed three of the band members in prison [Note 89].

8.4.3.5 Withdrawal from Social Institutions: This is a form of nonviolent protest where one or more members of a social institution withdraw their membership. The social institution may be a club, a religious organisation, a movement, a part of an employer's organisation, a neighbourhood organisation, a professional organisation, or an academic organisation.

The withdrawal of membership by a substantial number of supporters can cripple organisations, both economically and in terms of their morale. This is particularly true if those who withdraw are considered valuable members of the organisation. Hybrid versions of this form of protest focus on just the withdrawal of "high value" members from an institution.

Considerations and risks: Having withdrawn from an institution, it may be difficult to re-enter it after a protest if one wishes to do so. The co-option of "high value" members in such a protest makes a later re-entry more likely, since they are much more highly valued than "ordinary" members.

Historical and contemporary examples: In 1992, the Church of England voted for the rights of women to become Anglican priests. As a result of this contentious decision thousands of lay members of the Church and Anglican priests who disagreed with the decision left the Church of England, mostly to become Roman Catholics. This large-scale withdrawal of senior and other members from the Church caused considerable disturbance and acrimony which continues at the time of writing.

8.4.3.6 Academic Boycott: The concept of an academic boycott involves a refusal by protesting teachers to engage with the academics or educational institutions of a target authority. The boycott may include refusing cooperation with the academic institutions in competitions, joint research projects, conferences, exchange programs, sharing research and technology, and sharing archives. Academic boycotts work by isolating a country from mainstream scientific and cultural movements, denying academics access to their colleagues and reducing the credibility of a country in academic and technological circles. It causes direct economic damage by reducing the effectiveness of economically important research.

Considerations and risks: Academic boycotts are most effective when the academics in the targeted institution agree with the boycott themselves. This is not as rare as one might think. Academics often share similar political attitudes and a desire to speak out, regardless of where they work. So organisers of an academic boycott should contact key personnel in the target organisations and see if they can garner their support.

The exact purpose of an academic boycott needs to be made very clear to the public. Solidarity with a boycott of this sort is important, so the organisers should canvass support amongst all the academic community in advance of the action. This is normally done using an open letter signed by many of the participating academics, making their protest and their demands clear before actually beginning the boycott.

Historical and contemporary examples: Israel is the most recent target of an academic boycott due to its behaviour towards the Palestinian people; actions which have caused revulsion especially in academic circles inside and outside Israel. Since 2009 the number of academic boycotts has grown rapidly in line with the intensity of Israel's attacks on Palestinian civilians. Here are just a few examples of academic boycott actions taken against Israel:

• In 2009, Spanish organizers of an international solar power design competition excluded a team from the Israeli Ariel University Centre. The reason given was that the Ariel University is located in the West Bank.

• In 2010, the US Campaign for the Academic and Cultural Boycott of Israel (USACBI) announced that it had collected 500 endorsements from US academics for an academic and cultural boycott of Israel.

• At its annual 2010 conference, UCU (University and College Union in the UK) members voted to support the boycott, divestment and sanctions (BDS) campaign against Israel and sever ties with the Histadrut (Israel's organisation of trade unions). At the UCU's annual conference in

Yorkshire, held in May 2011, the union again voted to adopt an academic and cultural boycott of Israel.

In April 2013, the following academic boycotts were launched:

• The Association for Asian American Studies in the US unanimously approved an academic boycott resolution against Israel.

• Sussex University students voted to continue a boycott of Israeli goods.

• The Faculty at Columbia University and Barnard College launched a divestment from Israel campaign.

• Belgian students called for an academic boycott of Israel.

• In May 2013, Stephen Hawking, the world renowned physicist, joined the academic boycott of Israel by reversing his decision to participate in the Jerusalem-based Israeli Presidential Conference hosted by Israeli president Shimon Peres.

• On May 9, 2013, The Student Representative Council (SRC) voted to support an end to all university ties with Technion University in Haifa, Israel.

• In July 2013, the European Union enacted a decision forbidding EU member states from cooperating with transferring funds to, or giving scholarships and research grants to bodies in the West Bank, the Golan Heights or East Jerusalem.

• On 4 December 2013, the American Studies Association (ASA) endorsed a boycott of Israeli academic institutions.

• In 2013, the Teachers Union of Ireland passed a motion calling for an academic boycott of Israel.

• In March 2014, The Council of the Royal Institute of British Architects voted to call on the International Union of Architects to exclude the Israeli Association of United Architects over its refusal to oppose Israel's construction of illegal settlements on occupied Palestinian territory.

• In October 2014, 500 anthropologists endorsed an academic boycott of Israeli institutions seen as complicit in violations of Palestinians' rights.

But Israel isn't the only academic boycott target. In 2013, there was also an extraordinary backlash by US scientists working for NASA after the US government decided to ban Chinese scientists who were working in the US from a conference because of a previous security law banning Chinese citizens from entering a NASA building. The planned international conference concerned the multi-national Kepler Telescope project. The ban angered many US scientists, who said that Chinese students and researchers in their labs were being discriminated against. A growing number of US scientists decided to boycott the meeting in protest, with senior academics withdrawing individually, or pulling out their entire research groups. Chris Lintott, an astronomer at Oxford University, called for a total boycott of the conference until the situation had been resolved. "I'm shocked and upset by the way this policy has been applied. Science is supposed to be open to all and restricting those who can attend by nationality goes against years of practice, going right back to Cold War conferences of Russian and Western physicists", he said. "The Kepler team should move their conference somewhere else - and I hope everyone boycotts until they do."

8.5 Protest and Persuasion

This group of methods deals entirely with expressions of objection to a particular action or policy of a government or corporate authority. "Persuasion and protest" are quite different concepts to those of "intervention", whereby an activist takes real practical action to change the situation. Persuasion and protest is about changing minds. Protests can be made up of single individuals, loose groups of people or formal protest organisations.

Methods of Protest and Persuasion

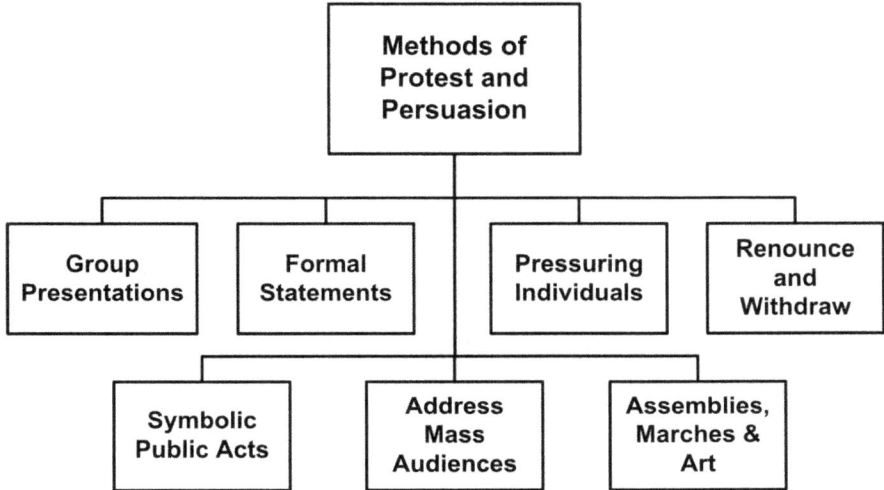

8.5.1 Group Presentations

This is a category of persuasion and protest where a group of like-minded activists take part in an action together.

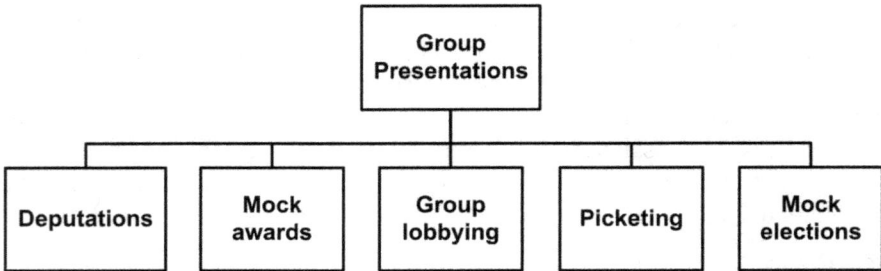

```
                    ┌──────────────────┐
                    │      Group       │
                    │  Presentations   │
                    └──────────────────┘
                             │
   ┌───────────┬─────────────┼─────────────┬───────────┐
┌──────────┐ ┌────────┐ ┌──────────┐ ┌──────────┐ ┌──────────┐
│Deputations│ │  Mock  │ │  Group   │ │Picketing │ │  Mock    │
│          │ │ awards │ │ lobbying │ │          │ │elections │
└──────────┘ └────────┘ └──────────┘ └──────────┘ └──────────┘
```

8.5.1.1 Deputation: A deputation is a group of people that is sent to a place to represent another, larger, group of protesters. In the case of a protest campaign, this normally means a small group that has been briefed to express the views of a larger body of protest. A deputation is useful to deliver a clear statement of the protesters' objectives and for the protesters to gauge the attitude of the target authority. The deputation acts as a form of diplomatic link between the protesters and the authority.

Considerations and risks: A deputation demonstrates that a protest group is willing to talk to the authority, thus showing some signs of being open to negotiation to both the authority and the public. However, this may not always be the message the protester wishes to send. Therefore, only send a deputation if there is some desire and prospect for dialogue. In extreme cases there is a risk that a deputation will be victimised (as the "bringers of bad news") and this may lead to arrest or other forms of persecution by an authority.

8.5.1.2 Mock Awards: A mock award usually refers to an award given as recognition that someone has achieved the worst (rather than the best) results in some field. This is a form of satire, in this case, aimed at an authority and designed to deride an authority's incompetence or incorrect policies in a clear, but humorous way.

Examples of mock awards could be "Dirtiest Streets of the Year Award" or "Most Contaminated Water Award". Normally, a small physical prize is prepared and the press is invited to the award ceremony, which is situated at or close to the authority's premises. A member of the authority will be invited to receive the award, but will probably not attend. The givers of the awards will prepare a press pack of information to justify the giving of the award to the particular authority. It is an effective way of undermining public confidence in an authority.

Considerations and risks: There are few risks associated with mock awards, apart from publicly offending an authority. Provided there is enough public support and interest in the subject this offence is unlikely to trigger any form of retaliation.

8.5.1.3 Group Lobbying: This is the process of representing the interests of a group to elected representatives or officials. Lobbying the elected is best carried out quite close to election time, when candidates are anxious to find and keep votes. It is important to have a well-prepared, properly reasoned and fully evidenced presentation to deliver as the centrepiece to your lobbying activity. Ideally, you should prepare a short visual slideshow which delivers your message clearly, quickly and powerfully to the representative or official you are lobbying.

Considerations and risks: It's important to know the people you are lobbying. It's useful to know their interests, priorities and political histories. Don't waste time lobbying candidates that are likely to be uninterested or antagonistic to your objectives. It is unlikely any amount of polemic is going to persuade them in a reasonable time. Focus on those that are somewhat sympathetic.

Make sure that the lobbying group is professional and disciplined. Everyone involved in lobbying should understand the strategy and know what their role is. It can be catastrophic if one member of your lobby suddenly picks a row on some minor issue and spoils an otherwise positive meeting. The group's objectives should be clearly presented, but be prepared to compromise. After a meeting, follow up with a letter of thanks and hopes to hold a short follow-up meeting to track progress.

8.5.1.4 Picketing: Picketing is a method of protest in which protesters (often strikers) assemble outside a targeted workplace or other target premises. Very often, picketing is designed to dissuade other workers from going to work, but sometimes pickets are designed simply to attract public attention.

The main objective of picketing is to put pressure on the target authority to meet particular demands and/or cease certain activities. This pressure is brought to bear by damaging the target organisation through loss of business, negative publicity, and discouraging workers or customers from entering the site, thus preventing normal business activity.

Picketing is commonly used by trade unions during strikes, when attempting to stop dissident workers and non-unionised workers from going to work. Those who cross the picket line and work despite the strike are frequently ostracised afterwards as a punishment for their lack of solidarity. In our internet age photos of those who cross the picket line are often published on various social networks as a further demonstration of their betrayal of their co-workers.

There are several forms of picketing:

• A mass picket is a demonstration of a large number of supporters. A demonstration of the extent of support is the primary reason for this kind of picket.

• Secondary picketing is where protesters picket sites which are not directly involved in a dispute. This may involve customer sites or supplier sites. The objective is to pressure other companies to cease business relations with the original target organisation, with the implied threat that their own employees may refuse to work.

• Information pickets. This is a form of picketing where the main objective is to pass on information to the public and other workers by means of speeches, brochures, banners etc.

• Flying pickets are a hybrid form of pickets that can be organised to picket a facility without any prior notice. This makes it difficult for a target authority to plan ways of circumventing the picket because they never know when or where they will arrive.

Considerations and risks: Some forms of picketing are illegal in some jurisdictions. Secondary picketing is still illegal in the UK. Picketing can cause strong emotions, especially when co-workers refuse to respect a strike. Discipline is important to avoid violence and picketers should be closely supervised and be aware that they will be expelled if they engage in acts of violence or intimidation.

8.5.1.5 Mock Elections: Mock elections are held to demonstrate the popular opinion of the state of the current political authority. They are organised informally and the participants have to vote for the real candidates in a mock poll. The results are then announced very publicly. Mock elections send strong signals to politicians regarding the general public's perception of them. In the case of student mock elections (they are very popular with students), the results demonstrate how that particular demographic group feels about the real political candidates.

Considerations and risks: Mock elections, though a bit of fun, also serve a serious purpose and therefore should be organised in a strict way. Electoral fraud should be forbidden and those who vote should have their fingers dipped in indelible ink so that they cannot vote again. Counting should be strictly supervised to avoid any cheating.

8.5.2 Symbolic Public Acts

A symbolic public act is a demonstrative action by an individual or a group of individuals, designed to indicate dissent against the behaviour or policies of a target authority. These public acts aim to register a protest; they have no impact on an authority's behaviour and may or may not influence public opinion. There are various tactics for symbolic public acts:

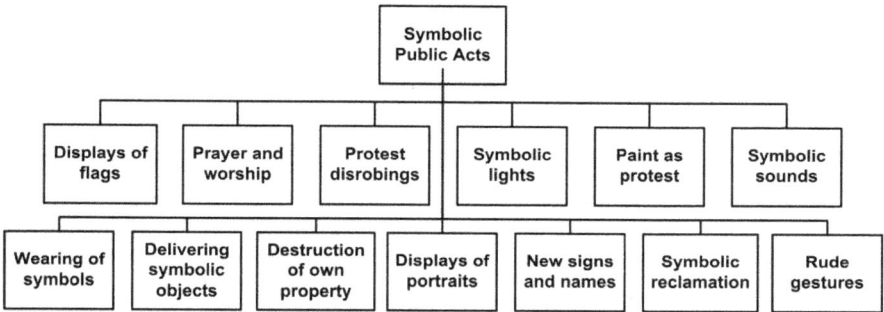

```
                         ┌──────────────────┐
                         │     Symbolic     │
                         │   Public Acts    │
                         └──────────────────┘
```

Displays of flags	Prayer and worship	Protest disrobings	Symbolic lights	Paint as protest	Symbolic sounds

Wearing of symbols	Delivering symbolic objects	Destruction of own property	Displays of portraits	New signs and names	Symbolic reclamation	Rude gestures

8.5.2.1 Displays of Flags and Symbolic Colours: In the aftermath of the British military's massacre of civilians on the streets of the Bogside in Derry on Bloody Sunday, 1972, the population of the area swung decidedly towards the Irish Republican movement, seen as protectors of the civilian population against the barbarity of the British government and its army.

This swing led to a much more extreme Republican sentiment and a natural affinity with the identity of the Irish Republic, just a few kilometres away across the border from the site of the atrocity. Simultaneously, the Bogside and other Republican areas in Derry began to be rapidly covered with murals of Irish Republican imagery and the green, white and orange tricolour of the Republic's flag, indicating that one was entering a Republican area. Even the kerbstones on the streets were painted in these characteristic colours.

This rapid affiliation with a particular flag and the symbolic colours of Irish Republicanism were a clear statement of extreme popular anger and protest designed to communicate defiance to the British government and a total denial of allegiance to the British Crown and flag.

Considerations and risks: Affiliating a protest movement with a particular flag may run the risk of accusations of jingoism. On the other hand, such symbols often create a unifying motif which is recognised by all.

8.5.2.2 Wearing of Symbols: The wearing of symbols is an ancient custom, which has long been used by all kinds of religious and political groups to identify other members. Some Christians wear crucifixes, some Jews wear a Star of David, some anti-war activists wear a "ban the bomb" symbol, and some anarchists wear the "circle A" symbol, etc. All such symbols are statements of personal belief that the wearer uses as a form of positive protest. Symbolism in protest movements is commonplace, and most people will recognise the symbols of Greenpeace, the Anti-Nuclear movement etc. without even thinking about them. The symbol triggers a subliminal reaction and symbols are often used as unifying motifs in large mass movements.

Considerations and risks: Wearing a badge doesn't make an effective protester. Indeed, it may be the worst possible action in a protest where it is important to separate one's identity from one's affiliation. In modern times, wearing certain symbols will certainly be recorded by police and other agents of state intelligence and it may ear-mark individuals for special attention. Generally speaking, the wearing of symbols should be confined to non-executive members of an activist organisation if they are going to be used in public demonstrations. In other words, the symbols are best associated with an organisation rather than a person.

Very professional looking symbols may (rightly) have the effect of making the public suspicious of a popular protest movement. If there is too much "branding" associated with a movement, it may give the impression that it is actually a well financed front for another political agenda. A popular protest movement needs to be allowed to be inventive when it comes to symbolism and it is better if it isn't too smart.

8.5.2.3 Prayer and Worship: This is not a subject of interest in most protest movements, but nonetheless it is a potent symbolic act in some scenarios.

In mixed secular or religious societies the support of religious organisations for a protest cause can provide a powerful positive symbol to supporters. To adherents of a religious faith, the use of prayer and worship in a protest adds a strong emotional appeal to a movement's principles and a divine aspect to their position.

The appearance of Orthodox priests in Ukrainian pro- and anti-government demonstrations, in 2014, added some degree of respectability to both sides of that conflict. The openly Republican role of Irish Catholic priests and the openly Unionist role of Protestant ministers in Northern Ireland lent credibility to both protest movements in the eyes of their respective conservative populations.

Considerations and risks: Whilst the use of prayer and worship in a protest movement may energise one part of the population, it may immediately alienate secular members of the public. In the Western world the latter may well be the larger group. Generally speaking, this means that you cannot please both secular and religious groups at the same time. The use of prayer and worship as part of a protest needs some careful consideration, depending on the character of the protest campaign.

8.5.2.4 Delivering Symbolic Objects: This is a favourite method of protest and can be a powerful reminder to a target authority of an ongoing dispute. French farmers are very fond of delivering huge quantities of vegetables (fresh or rotting) or manure to the offices of their government to remind them that, after all, French farmers feed French people and therefore need to be looked after.

More radical symbolic deliveries have been made, such as when a local housing improvement protest in Chicago piled up dead rats against the door of the city's mayor's office

Considerations and risks: It's important to decide which symbolic objects should be delivered and to whom. The objects have to be obviously connected with the protest. They have to be plainly symbolic and they must cause some degree of inconvenience to the target authority. The recipient also needs to be considered. Delivering something obnoxious to a prime minister probably won't work because they are isolated from such obvious protests. However, the same symbolic delivery to a junior minister at his private address (with the press present, of course) will probably work quite well and generate public interest.

8.5.2.5 Protest Disrobing (aka "Nude-Ins"): This is a method of protest that comes and goes over the years. Suddenly it's popular and then it's out of fashion and then, as years pass, it re-emerges. At the time of writing, it is fairly in vogue again, mostly amongst feminist protesters. It is clear that the protest act itself isn't really that shocking to the onlooker and it's not clear if taking off one's clothes actually influences anyone's opinions. It is a pure act of protest without any guarantee of persuasion. Nonetheless, it's a fairly harmless act of anarchistic behaviour which, if nothing else, attracts publicity, unsettles the routine of daily life of some onlookers and entertains others.

Considerations and risks: There is no doubt that participants in protest disrobing could be accused of bourgeois exhibitionism. In a world where hunger is endemic, it is hard to take such a protest action very seriously. It smacks of being childish and unimaginative, though it may well bring a smile to the face of the average member of the public. The question is whether it alters the way the average member of the public actually thinks about the main protest issue.

8.5.2.6 Destruction of Own Property: An unusual method of nonviolent protest is the destruction of one's own property in order to demonstrate the intensity of one's feelings of opposition.

One of the most publicised incidents of this method is the Boston Tea Party in the 18th century, when American protesters against British taxes dumped tea in Boston harbour and burned tea in Rhode Island as a protest.

Similar acts of destructive defiance were carried out during the Indian struggle for independence from British colonial rule, when imported cloth was burned.

One hybrid of this protest method is the destruction of documents issued by the target authority, such as passes, party membership cards, passports, identity cards and draft cards for conscription to the military.

These acts are powerful symbolic acts of defiance against an authority and indicative of very strong emotions amongst the protest group (as Britain found to its cost in America and India).

Considerations and risks: Destruction of personal property shows a high degree of commitment to defiance of an authority, but it clearly carries a cost and, in modern times, it may have a short lifespan in the public psyche. Whilst the Boston Tea Party may have been shocking in the 18th century, it is uncertain how impressed anyone would be by such a gesture in 2015.

8.5.2.7 Symbolic Lights: This action involves the use of lights such as torches, lanterns and candles etc. as part of protest marches, parades, demonstrations, and candlelit processions. They are used to send certain messages to the public and to authorities.

For instance, huge anti-racist candlelight demonstrations were held in Berlin in 1993 to mark the 60th anniversary of Adolf Hitler becoming German chancellor. The lights of the candles were said to demonstrate the light of civilisation in the darkness of fascism and racism.

A corollary of symbolic lights is symbolic darkness; an area is deliberately darkened as a sign of protest. This happened in January 2015, when the lights of the emblematic cathedral in Cologne were turned off by church authorities to protest against a demonstration by the Islamophobic PEGIDA organisation that was taking place in front of the cathedral.

Guerrilla Projection: A variant on this theme is the use of large-scale projectors on a building, turning it into a huge advertisement for a protest cause. Projecting the protest messages onto a spot that would otherwise be out of reach as a platform for the protest campaign can be strikingly effective. The technique is legally less risky than many other large-scale actions. It is relatively cheap and risk-free compared to, say, trespassing onto a building's roof to hang a banner. Modern, large projectors are capable of producing moving images of very good quality. Most importantly, this technique is visually powerful and often attracts large crowds.

Light Messages (aka Light Brigades): Another variation on the use of light involves the use of large illuminated letters formed by participants holding a letter each in strategic positions, such as government buildings, sides of main roads, bridges etc. Together the letters form a word or sentence such as "Stop the War NOW" and form an impressive night time display. The letters are available in various sizes and illuminated by LEDs.

Considerations and risks: For a candlelight demonstration to be effective it has to be big. Practical considerations such as safety are also important and ensuring that there are sufficient stocks of candles to complete the demonstration is clearly vital.

In the case of guerrilla projection, the legalities may make it reasonably safe, but it still relies on one or two projectors that can be seized or damaged by an authority and this immediately ends the protest by extinguishing the lights. That is not so easy when there are thousands of protesters carrying candles.

8.5.2.8 Displays of Portraits: The display of portraits or photographs of lost loved ones or political martyrs is a powerful way of humanising a protest. The Mothers of the Plaza de Mayo in Argentina have been gathering weekly for more than 35 years in the Plaza de Mayo in Buenos Aires to demand to know what happened to their relatives who were abducted by the fascist death squads of the military dictatorship between 1976 and 1983. Most were dissidents of socialist leaning and it is believed that 30,000 "disappeared" during this time. Until recently, the Mothers used to gather every Thursday with photographs of their loved ones to demand answers.

Considerations and risks: Giving a name and a face to someone who has been abused or wrongly detained or executed is a powerful way to personalise and communicate the heart-rending horrors of such abuses of authority.

8.5.2.9 Paint as Protest: This protest medium has been in use for a long time. Works from the Bruegel family, Bosch and Dürer are plainly brimming with moral caricatures and powerful moral messages.

In modern times, visual art continues to be used as a potent medium of moral protest. One of the most famous and talented protest street artists is the activist known as Banksy. His real identity is not entirely known, but despite this anonymity his works are considered very distinctive and powerful. His art work involves social commentary on many contemporary issues such as poverty, capitalism, the British royal family, political corruption, the police state and surveillance, amongst many other issues. His works rarely fail to shock and sometimes amuse.

One interesting variant of protest art is the method developed by Bill Drummond, who created his own grey paint to cover billboards that offended him. He paints these billboards with what he calls "international grey paint", often leaving spaces so that the original offending ad peeps out provocatively. His current targets, at the time of writing, are offensive ads from British extreme right wing party UKIP.

Considerations and risks: Much modern street art is not very good and most of it isn't very political, resembling vandalistic doodles from bored teenagers. It is more annoying than thought-provoking.

However, works from talents such as Banksy are quite different and many of his works are now carefully protected as cultural icons. Thus, quality is all-important. If you can't produce good quality protest art, it's probably better not to produce any at all.

8.5.2.10 New Signs and Names (see also Culture Jamming): This is an interesting method of protest, whereby the meaning of existing symbols is altered in the public perception. It might be a stars and stripes where the stars are tiny and sinister human skulls or images of the British currency where the Queen's face has been transformed into that of a monkey. Such transformations of household symbols have several effects on the viewer: they undermine the perceived "sanctity" of these images of state authority, they ridicule the state's authority and they negate the ability of the state to use these symbols as part of its means of control (well, not without raising a smile or two anyway).

Considerations and risks: In some jurisdictions, authorities are aware that this form of symbolic deformation can have a serious impact on their credibility. They are rather sensitive to such protest actions against the national currency or the national flag or the head of state. There may be laws forbidding these types of protest, which may be a very good incentive to use these methods to antagonise such an authority, but this may carry some legal risks.

8.5.2.11 Symbolic Sounds: Protest movements often adopt a tell-tale symbol early in their history that stays with them and becomes emblematic of the protest movement. Sounds are often used in this way.

In Republican areas of Northern Ireland, the banging of dustbin lids was a favourite way of warning IRA members of the presence of police and army in their area. It later became a form of protest symbol in itself, as the army rapidly realised its significance. The women of an area would deliberately bang dustbin lids to antagonise the soldiers or police and make any idea of a covert military operation impossible.

The "cacerolazo" is another form of noise protest practiced in Spain and many Latin American countries and involves the banging of metal cooking pots. It is particularly popular because people can participate from within their own homes without being observed and it thus draws a high level of participation. The practice has now spread to other countries, including Turkey and Iceland. In one mammoth cacerolazo during the 15M protests in Madrid the noise protest lasted for 12 hours. Given its auditory force, a cacerolazo of sufficient size can be incredibly effective in drawing people onto the streets, and massing them in public spaces. It also costs nothing and requires no previous activist training or skills. A cacerolazo is driven by shared discontent; the tactic is fundamentally participatory and democratic. People can also participate without being on the streets, simply by leaning out of their window and banging a cooking pot in solidarity.

Other symbolic sounds used in protests include whistling and the use of fog horns to antagonise an authority.

The corollary of a symbolic sound is a symbolic silence. The "grito mudo" (muted scream) was used by so-called "15M" protesters over the last few years in Spain, where thousands appear to scream, but there is absolutely no sound.

Considerations and risks: There are few risks involved in using symbolic sounds as part of a protest. Indeed, with the Spanish traditional method you can even participate from the comfort of your own kitchen if it has an open window!

8.5.2.12 Symbolic Reclamations: This is a form of protest concerned with disputed land use, whereby a group of protesters occupy or use the disputed land in a way which is very different from its actual or indented use. One popular example would be the planting of trees on land destined for an unpopular development or the deliberate spreading of wild plant seeds on a golf course. The objective of this type of protest is to demonstrate that the intended use of the land is in dispute.

Sometimes, land reclamations take the form of turning a disputed piece of land into a park or playground (including swings and other children's playthings) to make the point that the land would be better used as a park than for the disputed purpose.

Considerations and risks: Many jurisdictions take a dim view of protesters interfering in land they have ear-marked for other purposes and there may be legal risks involved. On the other hand, a large enough action provides some degree of protection against arrest or harassment.

8.5.2.13 Rude Gestures: Every culture has its own set of rude gestures and sometimes popular culture (TV, cinema) creates new gestures which are meant to be offensive or rude. Sometimes protests make use of such gestures to show their defiance of an authority.

In 2012, in protest against the austerity measures in Greece, promoted by Germany, Chancellor Merkel was greeted by thousands of angry protesters in a banned demonstration, many giving a Nazi salute and two dressed as Nazi officers with a large swastika flag (which was later burned).

In early 2015, the Chinese authorities in southern China seized a large amount of toilet paper bearing the unflattering image of Hong Kong's pro-Beijing chief- executive Leung Chun-ying. The toilet paper had been ordered by one of the protest parties.

Considerations and risks: Rude gestures achieve little, apart from satisfying protesters' desire to show defiance. Sometimes they are seen as offensive and a little childish. This should be avoided. Some thought needs to go into delivering a rude or offensive gesture to give a degree of political subtlety. On the other hand (as in the examples above), they can be cuttingly critical and may cause an authority to pause for thought.

8.5.3 Formal Statements

A formal statement by a protest group comes in many forms. These are important communications because they state the official position of the protesters and need to be carefully thought out and written. It is fairly certain that anything delivered in a formal statement will be twisted and used against a protest by the target authority. It therefore requires careful wording. Above all, there needs to be a strict control over all official and public communications from the protest group, especially in light of the widespread use of social media. An immense amount of damage can be caused by uncontrolled use of social media by protesters who are not authorised to speak on behalf of an organised group.

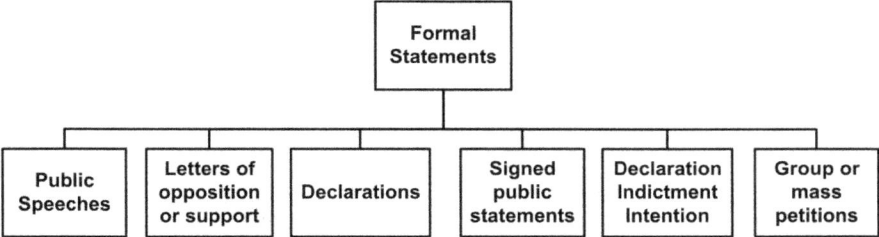

```
                        ┌──────────────┐
                        │    Formal    │
                        │  Statements  │
                        └──────────────┘
```

| Public Speeches | Letters of opposition or support | Declarations | Signed public statements | Declaration Indictment Intention | Group or mass petitions |

8.5.3.1 Public Speeches: Public speeches are made by appointed representatives of a protest movement and delivered to an audience of the general public. As with other formal statements, they seek to explain the position of the protesters and solicit public support for the protest campaign.

Considerations and risks: The content of a public speech should be carefully managed to ensure that it is consistent with a protest movement's objectives. The greatest risk of a public speech is that the crowd may be infiltrated with hecklers, paid by the target authority, who are determined to disrupt or ridicule the speaker. The best way of handling this is to suspend the speech until the disruption is past. It is better not to engage with a heckler.

Generally speaking, at public speeches, it is better to invite questions in advance so that proper answers can be formulated. Public speeches should be concise and finite rather than an open-ended discussion that can be manipulated by one's adversaries.

8.5.3.2 Letters of Opposition or Support: A protest group can make its views felt on a range of issues by means of letters of opposition or support. These can be delivered privately and simultaneously published or they can be conveyed in the form of an open letter. A protest group is not obliged to differ with every policy of an authority and occasional letters of support show that the protesters have a balanced position.

Considerations and risks: Letters of opposition or support constitute part of the public policy of a protest group, so they should be carefully controlled and written so that their contents cannot be twisted or misinterpreted by an adversary.

8.5.3.3 Declarations by Organisations and Institutions: A declaration by a protest group is an official communication where the group declares its belief or acceptance of one or more principles or actions. For instance, a protest group may declare that it believes in and supports the membership of the Palestinian authority in the International Criminal Court. The "declaration" is a statement of policy which originates in current affairs and which seeks to explain or clarify the group's position on a particular issue. Similarly, a group may declare that it accepts the principles of the European Charter of Human Rights. The declaration makes a broad statement of principle for the protest group.

Considerations and risks: As with all policy statements, a protest group needs to be circumspect and consistent when making declarations of any kind. These become part of the organisation's public policy base and should be carefully considered before being issued. It's better to say nothing than to rush out an ill-considered declaration.

8.5.3.4 Signed Public Statements: A signed public statement by a protest group is an official declaration issued by the group's organisers. A statement may concern the group itself, the group's management, its protest plans, a clarification, a report of an incident or a progress report. The statement is signed and can be used by members of the press in reporting on the protest group or it may be used in legal action by or against the protest group.

Considerations and risks: Signed statements need to be carefully phrased and should only be issued and signed by the executive organisers of a protest group. If the group has a legal advisor then they should be involved in checking such statements because they may have legal implications.

8.5.3.5 Declarations of Indictment and Intention: Declarations of indictment and intention are formal public statements which list specific grievances against an authority, and what specific actions the protest authors will take in response to those grievances.

These are useful documents in a protest because they help the organisers to tightly define the terms of reference of the protest and they help formulate the actions they intend to take. Obviously, the details of the intentions are not spelled out in such a document, but generic actions are mentioned.

For example, a statement of indictment might read: "We object to the draining of this unique marshland because it is an important wild bird sanctuary of international relevance" and the intention may read: "We intend to do anything within our power to obstruct the draining of this land by all physical, judicial and political means at our disposal, even if this means that we become guilty of minor misdemeanours. We do this because we feel that there is an overriding public interest at stake which [the authority] is ignoring".

Considerations and risks: This type of document is useful when the protest is an overt one. Obviously, such declarations would not be suitable in cases where actions are being taken covertly against an authority. In other words, such statements should only contain as much information as the organisers of the protest consider prudent and useful in terms of persuading both the public and the authority of the protest's motives and plans.

8.5.3.6 Group or Mass Petitions: Petitions are a fairly ancient means of garnering support for a protest action by gathering the signatures of those who support a written proposition. In modern times, e-petitions have become extremely popular and quite effective. These days, anyone can start a petition and even governments provide a platform for internet-based petitions in an attempt to appear to be interested in public opinion.

Petitions vary in scale from small, personal grievances with an authority to large-scale international human rights and environmental protests. Many of these petitions gather hundreds of thousands of signatures, sometimes even millions. They are hard to ignore by any authority and have proven useful in getting less liberal governments to act out of a sense of embarrassment.

One variant of mass petitions uses creative methods of petition delivery to heighten attention on the motives for the petition and increase public pressure. It's helpful to find creative ways to physically quantify the number of petition signatures. Images of a large number of well-labelled boxes being wheeled into a target's offices is a well-tried technique, but other tactics can be effective as well. For a petition asking the World Health Organisation to investigate and regulate factory farms, the international campaign organisation Avaaz set up 200 cardboard pigs - each representing 1,000 petition signers - in front of the WHO building in Geneva, providing the media with a visual hook on which to peg stories about factory farms and swine flu.

Greenpeace took a more extreme approach when delivering a petition against deepwater oil drilling in the Arctic. Greenpeace International sent its executive director to a controversial oil rig in the middle of nowhere, where he trespassed onto the rig to deliver the petition to the ship's captain - at which point he was arrested and subsequently held for four days. Between the unusual way it was delivered and the media coverage that resulted, the petition was difficult for the target to ignore. Having the Greenpeace director arrested just served to gain more publicity for the cause.

Considerations and risks: The text of a petition needs to be carefully constructed, so that it is sufficiently inclusive to large numbers of supporters, but also accurate and clear in its intent. For a petition to be successful it needs to be carried out in full view of the public. In the case of e-petitions this means that they need to be actively spread via social media. When designing a petition, leave enough time to gather signatures. Petitions often take some time to get momentum, so closing them too soon may mean important support is missed.

E-petitions have become rather ubiquitous in recent years. Many are excellent and driven by activists or just plain individuals with the highest of motives. However, some of the e-petitions which pop up have a fairly dubious origin and some are positively malicious. As for any petition, care has to be taken in what one signs. In some cases, it may also be more effective to send a personalised message to the person or authority to which the petition is being addressed. Petitions are easy to sign, but they shouldn't be used as a substitute for personal involvement and active protest.

8.5.4 Addressing Wider Audiences

Certain types of protest can work very well within a local context. Local planning problems or issues with local services are often best dealt with locally. However, some protests have wider implications and need to be publicised to a wider audience. There are various media methods available to help get a message to a wider audience.

Address Wider Audiences

- Slogans, caricatures symbols
- Leaflets, pamphlets
- Radio and television
- Media-Jacking
- Banners, posters
- Newspaper / Journals
- The Internet

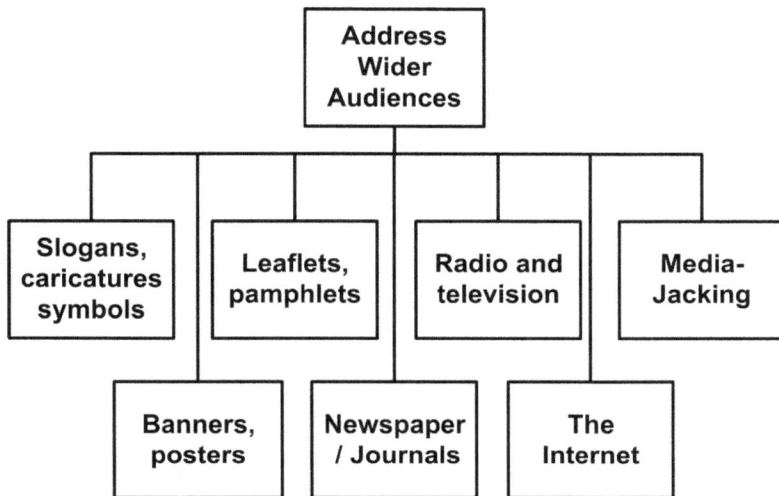

8.5.4.1 Slogans, Caricatures, and Symbols: One method of galvanizing a group of supporters is with the use of popular slogans, catchphrases, and easily identifiable symbols that communicate the protest's common message.

One example of such a symbol or caricature is the mask of the activist Anonymous Movement. The mask, said to represent the face of Guy Fawkes, is an instantly recognisable symbol, which immediately reminds sympathisers of one of the movement's ominous slogans: "We are Anonymous and we are Legion."

Considerations and risks: Having recognisable symbols and slogans helps reach a wider audience because it builds up a form of "brand recognition", so that whenever the symbol is seen in the press, on TV or the internet, the public instantly knows which organisation is referred to. Therefore the quality of the symbolism used is important because it will be associated for a long time with an organisation or protest movement. Thus, careful consideration needs to be given to these symbols and the "branding" of a protest movement.

8.5.4.2 Banners, Posters, and Displayed Communications: The use of physical banners, posters and other visual communications media are another important way of unifying and disseminating a protest message.

One popular contemporary action that is often used to draw attention to a target authority is a so-called "banner hang". Banner hangs can function as public service announcements by the protest group to alert the public of an injustice or a dangerous situation. They can be as low-tech and low-risk as several bed sheets with a protest message tied to road bridges. However, the banner hangs that really carry a serious media punch involve large pieces of cloth or netting deployed at great heights, often by experienced climbers. Greenpeace have become masters of this technique.

An interesting poster campaign took place in Britain in 2014 and 2015, when posters suddenly started appearing on London tubes and bus stops [Note 90] with thought-provoking statements such as "We caused the 2011 riots by shooting dead an unarmed civilian and then lying about it. And we got away with it." and "How can one even begin to speak about dignity in labour when one feels one's job should not exist?" and "It's as if there is someone out there making up pointless jobs just to keep us all working.", etc. The campaign was understood to be promoted by a UK anarchist group.

Considerations and risks: Sticking up posters may attract some minor legal risks, but in general none of these methods of communications carries much risk. The main issue is ensuring a consistency of message and a reasonable quality of production.

There are several design factors that should be considered when creating these protest media. Firstly, they should be consistent in their message. The messages should be short and clear. When possible, at least some of these banners and posters should be professionally produced so that they are clearly readable when broadcast or photographed. Other items used in a demonstration, such as mannequins or models for floats, can be homemade but they should be clear in what they represent. The impact of the message will be minimal if a passer-by has to stand and speculate about what a float may represent or what the crooked lettering on a banner actually says. It should be instantly obvious.

Dangerous banner-hangs need professional assistance. Banners can be hung from bridges, rooftops, railway sidings, public buildings and have even been suspended from tethered helium balloons. Safety is an important consideration as weather conditions can loosen banners and may cause accidents.

8.5.4.3 Leaflets, Pamphlets, and Books: Leafleting is the bread-and-butter of many campaigns. However, it is also very annoying and largely ineffective. Passers-by rarely read leaflets. So standard leafleting is really a waste of time. Despite this, modern campaigning groups have developed lots of ways of making leafleting much more effective. The basic principles are: Don't just hand out leaflets. Make it fun. Make it unusual. Make it memorable.

Some groups use theatre and costumes to hand out leaflets. In one example in the 1980s, activists opposed to U.S. military intervention in Central America dressed up as waiters and carried maps of Central America on serving trays, with little green plastic toy soldiers glued to the map. They would go up to people in the street and say: "Excuse me, sir, did you order this war?" When the "no" response invariably followed, they would present an itemized bill outlining the costs: "Well, you paid for it!" Even if the person they addressed didn't take the leaflet, they'd get the message.

Considerations and risks: Pushing leaflets on people who are not that interested just causes a littering problem and a waste of paper. Much better to target potentially interested members of the public or simply put your leaflets on a table (next to the place where you sign a petition perhaps) and let interested parties take a leaflet if they want one. Leaflet design needs to be carefully considered. Messages need to be short and clear and a leaflet should always suggest some practical action the reader can take and a means of joining the protest.

8.5.4.4 Newspapers and Journals: The conventional press still remains an important place to have one's opinions aired, even in the era of the internet. Many professional journals and quality newspapers are still bought and read and, of course, publication in the conventional media often means publication on their internet version as well.

The press is an important part of the constituency of a protest movement and it's vital to manage the press properly by ensuring that they remain fully informed of actions, protest developments and essential communications. Every protest movement should allocate one person (at least) to manage the press and forge personal relationships with appropriate correspondents. The scripting and generation of press releases should be considered a valuable activity in a protest campaign.

Considerations and risks: If certain elements of the press become irrevocably hostile to a protest campaign, it is unlikely that their position can be easily reversed. In this case it may be advantageous to focus on the more sympathetic elements of the press and that means restricting information to the antagonistic press, which then obliges them to request information from the press officer of a protest campaign. This can be used to make them "late reporters" of any developments and help the sympathetic members of the press to be "timely reporters" of such events.

8.5.4.5 Radio and Television: Visual and audio media are potent ways of delivering protest messages. They give the public the impression that a protest is significant and relevant and they provide a stage for the delivery of public messages and the display of protest symbols.

Considerations and risks: It is crucial to take some form of control over radio and television broadcasts of a protest event or interview in order to make sure that they provide a balanced and honest representation of the protest campaign. This is yet another reason to have a press officer in a protest campaign - someone who can ensure that the media have the latest press releases and speak only with properly authorised and fully-briefed members of the protest organisation.

These days it is also quite feasible for a protest group to have their own internet radio or TV station. The technology is highly available and either free or very cheap.

8.5.4.6 The Internet: As a form of protest, the internet opens a myriad of possibilities. However, in this section we will restrict ourselves to the use of the internet as a form of mass communication. There are a number of opportunities and the following are the most obvious and useful:

- Conventional websites
- Campaign blogs
- Social media
- Messaging systems
- Email campaigns
- YouTube
- Live web casting

Conventional websites: These are basically static websites that contain a profile of the protest campaign, its objectives, history, participants, plans, contact information, etc. It may contain press releases, a photo gallery, in-depth information about a protest subject and links to sites related to the protest and to other groups. These sites are designed to be low maintenance and not to host discussions or social interactions, although they may contain links to associated social media or blog sites, which are far more dynamic. There are a number of easy-to-use packages available which permit a layman to build a simple protest website.

Campaign blogs: A blog is a dynamic website which encourages the general public (or restricted groups of the public) to make comments about the protest campaign, and for the campaign to publish official news, documents, and photos / videos of protest actions. Blogs are easy to create and can be maintained by multiple "lay users" (make sure that users involved in maintenance understand that what they publish may be made public instantly). Blog contributions can also be configured to be "pre-moderated" by an administrator before they are posted to a public page. This helps to prevent unauthorised postings and abuse. Most blog systems are totally free to install and use.

Social media: There are a plethora of social media possibilities available to a protest campaign. At the time of writing Facebook and Twitter seem to be almost mandatory social media options. However, there are many more social media options. It's a given that fashions in social media are constantly shifting. A "must have" Twitter account today may be an unused irrelevance in two years time.

Social media interactions require careful control. All internet publications do. However, social media interactions tend to be instant and un-moderated, which means that anyone with the campaign's social media logins can instantly publish tweets or Facebook postings without prior approval. For this reason social media passwords need to be carefully controlled. In addition, it is quite easy for a malicious poster to place unwanted material on a Facebook page. This kind of activity needs to be monitored and nuisance contributors blocked.

In situations where rapid public group information needs to be disseminated, services such as Twitter can be useful to inform a large group of supporters and media about a particular event.

Messaging systems: There are many insecure messaging systems available, such as WhatsApp and Skype, which can be used to communicate non-sensitive information to campaign collaborators. However, confidential messaging systems which provide end-to-end encryption with a high degree of confidence can also be used. Many of these systems are still being rolled out at the time of publication (including new versions of WhatsApp with E2E encryption), but they need prior evaluation and peer testing before adoption.

Email campaigns and other communications: The internet provides an ideal and simple way to disseminate communications to large numbers of contacts by email. These communications can be highly professional and contain non-confidential information regarding a protest campaign.

For confidential communications by email, a campaign group will need to use a system of end-to-end (E2E) encryption, such as PGP. In end-to-end encryption systems there is no middle-man, no third party that knows anything about the encryption keys being used and thus the contents of emails remain completely secure, provided the devices at either end remain secure.

YouTube and similar video publication services allow videos to be rapidly published on the internet and the addresses of the videos disseminated to large numbers of interested viewers very quickly. YouTube videos can be uploaded and cross linked to websites, blogs and social media pages in just a few minutes at no cost.

Live webcasting: Webcasting is a form of instant broadcasting that uses various mobile devices (phone, tablet, etc.) to transmit instant video imagery to various internet based services, which are then accessible to the global public. This means that an incident taking place in New York can be viewed by internet users anywhere in the world almost instantaneously. Webcasts can be used for educational purposes as well as a means of instant reporting on an unfolding situation such as a demonstration. Various companies provide a service for individuals and groups to broadcast media directly and allocate a webpage where users can watch the streaming video.

Considerations and risks: Early in a protest campaign an IT specialist with internet experience should be appointed to look after the internet affairs of the organisation. Their first task will be to decide on a suitable name for an internet domain for the movement and to try and lease the name. Domain names should be kept very simple and demonstrative. As a minimum, a protest movement should try to lease a .com, a .org and a national version of a domain, such as myprotest.com, myprotest.org and myprotest.co.uk. Domains are cheap to lease. It is also important to find a hosting company to use to place internet material associated with these domains. There are plenty on the market and very reasonably priced. They need to be secure and neutral, so choose one that isn't based in the UK or US.

The person appointed to be responsible for the internet presence of the campaign should also be totally literate in installing and building static websites, blogs, managing social media connections and controlling security.

Having an internet presence in itself isn't enough to get your message out to the internet using public. Websites that aren't registered with the main search engines such as Google or Yahoo are similar to tiny radio stations, unknown to anyone but their owners, transmitting on an unknown frequency about an unknown subject and having no listeners at all. In order to become "known" it is important to carry out some basic so-called "search engine optimisation" (SEO), so that when users look for you in Google they find your websites, and, furthermore, when users search for your protest issues they also find your websites. Having an experienced internet technologist in your organisation can make the difference between your internet presences being found or being, in effect, invisible.

8.5.4.7 Media-Jacking: This is a technique which is designed to undermine the opposition's narrative by hijacking their media and other events, drawing attention to the protest group's arguments and capitalising on the target's media presence to use it on behalf of the protest. Media-jacking takes advantage of the fact that very often an authority or corporation has a far bigger media budget and media presence than a protest campaign.

There are several ways to design and execute a successful media-jacking. The first method is simply to commandeer the media event. One of the boldest examples of this occurred in 1991 during the first Gulf War, when an anti-AIDS organisation burst into a CBS TV studio during a live primetime news broadcast and took over the set, chanting "Fight AIDS, not Arabs."

More subtle means are also possible and a protest group may use an authority's media platform to tell their own story. In 2007, for example, Kleenex ran an expensive PR exercise where they interviewed people on the street for a commercial they were making, getting participants to cry and say: "I need a Kleenex." Greenpeace activists stealthily lined up to be interviewed, proclaiming that Kleenex was clear-cutting old growth forests to make their tissues. The protesters successfully shut down the shoot for the rest of the day, and a video of the action went viral on the internet.

Some forms of media-jacking provide an opportunity to gain control of a discussion from a biased authority by putting them on the spot in front of the media. This can have the effect of altering the public perception as to who the villain of the piece actually is. In an example that took place in 2006, activists with the Rainforest Action Network made fake press passes, put on suits and infiltrated the Los Angeles Auto Show. Rick Wagoner, the CEO of General Motors, was giving a keynote address about how "environmentally friendly" GM's cars are. The activists stepped on to the stage, and pretending to be officials at the show, they congratulated Wagoner, then told the audience that they were pleased to announce that GM was prepared to commit in writing to the promises he'd just made. They then unfurled a giant "green pledge" that they asked him to sign. He chose to refuse and by doing so triggered a press frenzy with over 700 media outlets running the story of GM's "Greenwashing exposed".

Considerations and risks: The media isn't a particularly level playing field when it comes to protest actions. Accurate and sympathetic media coverage is often based on having good relationships with journalists, so it is important that media-jacking actions don't alienate the very media professionals that cover the protest campaign.

8.5.5 Pressuring Individuals

Protests often come down to conflicts with stubborn, indifferent, stupid or ambitious individuals. The psychology of power is a complex subject, but suffice it to say that human beings often behave in an irrational way when they feel that their credibility or position is being threatened by a group of outsiders with an axe to grind. This may lead to a situation where a protest group feels that it is necessary to apply pressure to the individuals concerned, as distinct from addressing the faceless authority. Politicians and officials are the prime targets for such pressure.

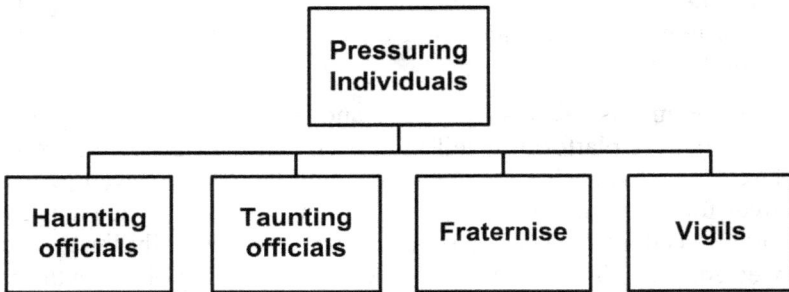

8.5.5.1 "Haunting" Officials: This is a method of harassing individual officials by placing them under continuous pressure to deliver information, political answers or administrative solutions regarding a particular protest issue. It requires a coordinated plan between several protest sympathisers to focus on key officials in a target authority. The method may take the form of ringing, emailing or physical visits to an official and may be carried out by one or more campaign sympathisers.

Public officials are required to be reasonably available to the public and this provides an opportunity to exercise some "administrative intimidation" to an official during working hours. Most officials will realise what is happening and try to refuse an appointment to a known agitator, in which case the strategy would be to send in the next campaigner to take up the "haunting".

Often disputes and protests arise because government officials are being officious and deliberately obstructive. They create administrative obstacles to a rational and peaceful solution and frequently do so to protect their own power. The balance of cost and benefit of their position for these officials can often be altered by a strategy of "haunting" them. At a certain moment their egotistic attachment to their position may be outweighed by the fact that their working life is becoming a total misery.

Considerations and risks: Government officials are trained to manage difficult and annoying public clients and for this reason it will be difficult to really get under the skin of a target official or group of officials. However, with good planning it can be done. Remember to leave the officials a way out of the harassment, so that they can retreat with "dignity" when they finally decide that it's easier to give in to the protest demands than to carry on the struggle.

8.5.5.2 Taunting Officials: This is the logical extension of "haunting" an official. It is the use of more derisory behaviour against one or more officials of an authority. It is sometimes called a "laugh in", though it may be more threatening than a simple taunt. It usually entails threats that officials will be reported to their employer, their union, or their professional body for incompetence, discrimination, or malpractice. It may also involve threats to their social status, especially in small communities.

The Escrache: In the Hispanic world the "Escrache" is the name given to a type of demonstration in which a group of activists go to the homes or workplaces of officials whom they want to condemn and publicly humiliate, in order to influence decision-makers and governments into a certain course of action. This term was born in Argentina in 1995 to protest the genocides of that country. It has since become widely used in Spain in recent years to protest on behalf of those being evicted from their homes because of inability to pay their mortgages. Bank officials and politicians have been confronted by hundreds of demonstrators standing in the gardens of their homes.

"Empty chair" protest: One interesting hybrid method to taunt an official or politician is the so-called "Empty Chair" protest. This works as follows: A protest group calls a public meeting or televised interview to discuss their grievances. They invite their own specialists and members of both sympathetic and unsympathetic political parties and government officials to participate. Naturally, the unsympathetic invitees are reluctant to participate for fear of suffering a humiliating defeat in a public debate. So they will try to wriggle out of participation.

At a certain moment, the protest organisers must accept that they cannot compel someone to attend their meeting or discussion. But there is one symbolic rebuke possible and that is to place an empty chair on the stage or in the studio with the appropriate name tag for each of the invitees that refused to participate.

The empty chairs send a powerful message to the audience that, though they were invited to debate the issues, these officials or politicians refused to do so. The audience will then draw its own conclusions as to whether they refused to discuss the issues out of cowardice or out of lack of conviction. Either way the protesters win.

Considerations and risks: These methods are highly personalised attacks on officials and need to be carefully considered before being used. Is a particular official really the correct target or is the official simply acting on the orders of a superior? Is there really a possibility for an official to alter the situation or is the official simply being blamed for a more endemic problem in the authority's system? If either is the case, then taunting an official is counterproductive and unfair. It will achieve nothing and will simply demonstrate an insensitive brutality. In this scenario it is much better to find the truly guilty party and taunt them.

8.5.5.3 Fraternisation: This is a form of subversion where individuals connected with an authority are targeted as being useful to a protest campaign and are deliberately cultivated as a source of information or insight into the authority. This process of deliberately befriending may take many forms and it is generally referred to as fraternisation. It may be done secretly or it may be done quite openly.

It is often useful to know what is happening in the "enemy camp" and the best way to do this is to have some good contacts on the inside of the authority that can keep protest campaign organisers informed.

Considerations and risks: Whoever is chosen as an inside source of information must be careful not to reveal their split allegiances. In some cases it may be better to completely disassociate the protest from the relationship with the insider. This provides more security because the authority will not realise that the insider is fraternising with members of the protest group.

8.5.5.4 Vigils: Vigils are largely symbolic assemblies, designed to show the strength of feeling of a protest campaign. In a religious sense they refer to a period of watchfulness and often imply staying awake overnight. Vigils in protests are often conducted with large-scale candlelight displays and sometimes are held in almost complete silence. However, protest vigils have also been conducted by single individuals. Vigils are often used to mourn the death of a public hero, to link a natural disaster or public tragedy to a political message or to protest the launch of a war.

Artistic vigils: A variant on a simple assembly, artistic vigils use imaginative clothing or formations to introduce a degree of thought-provoking symbolism and ritual into a vigil. For instance, the simple fact of women wearing black and gathering in silence on Fridays gave shape to the "Women in Black", a worldwide network of vigils. Begun by Israeli women during the first Intifada to protest the occupation of Palestine, it has since expanded across the globe and embraced broader anti-war and pro-justice themes, nonetheless maintaining its distinctive character.

Considerations and risks: The usual considerations of safety apply to large-scale vigils as to all other large gatherings. Vigils may last a long time, so organisers need to make sure that there are sufficient supplies to sustain a long demonstration and that the basic infrastructure is available to conduct the vigil safely. From a communications perspective it is important that the press are informed of the purpose of a vigil and are invited to witness the event.

Unfortunately, routine and self-righteousness can strip vigils of their power. In the American peace movement of the 1970s, '80s and '90s, the "candlelight vigil" - all too often a handful of dour people silently holding candles - became a standard, and fatally predictable, form of protest. This can be overcome by planning vigils to include some artistry in their delivery.

8.5.6 Assemblies, Processions, Marches and Art

This type of protest actions consists of active physical manifestations of protest designed specifically to be held in public and to demonstrate the motives and strength of feeling of a protest to both the public and the target authority and to allow for open communications with other members of a protest group.

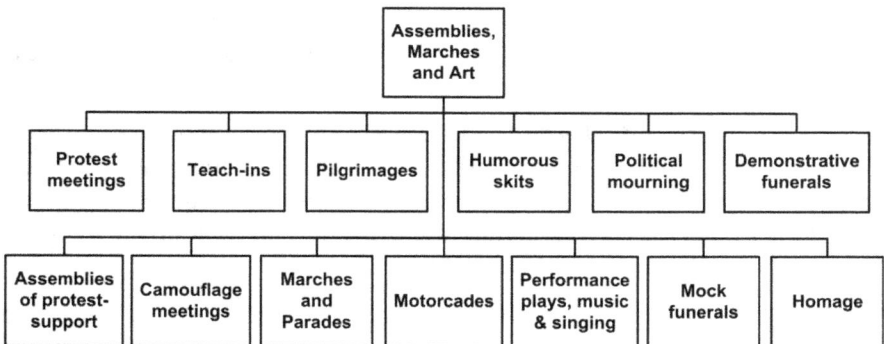

8.5.6.1 Assemblies of Protest or Support: Assemblies are gatherings of protesters or protest supporters who agree to meet in a pre-determined place. Assemblies are generally designed to communicate between protesters and supporters rather than as a manifestation to impress the public or the target authority. In many protest movements, such as the

Spanish 15M movement, an assembly is an open meeting of protesters who come together to discuss plans for their local branch of the protest movement. They then vote on proposals and plans for future acts of protest. In this context these assemblies are deliberately unstructured and each attendee has the same right to speak or make proposals as any other attendee. The only structure is that decisions may only be taken when there is a majority of support for a proposal.

Considerations and risks: The right to free assembly is part of the constitutions of many nations. However, there is always a caveat attached to these rights: this freedom is contingent on the good behaviour of an assembly. If an assembly becomes riotous, for instance, then the assembly becomes illegal in most countries. To avoid this excuse being used by an authority to break up an assembly, organisers need to insist that attendees behave in a disciplined way.

8.5.6.2 Protest Meetings: A protest meeting is a formal meeting of protest organisers and supporters to make and discuss plans and report on the progress of a campaign. Protest meetings are normally public events and members of the public are actively invited to join and participate in the protest campaign and the meeting.

Considerations and risks: Protest meetings can be hijacked by agents of an authority that are antagonistic to it. This is a risk for all forms of public meeting which is open to participation by all. Therefore, protest meetings need a structure and should follow a basic pre-agreed agenda. To allow for some flexibility the agenda can contain a section "any other business". Meeting organisers should enforce strict rules on subject matter and put limits on time spent on a subject, time taken by individual speakers and the right of reply from the protest organisation itself.

8.5.6.3 Camouflaged Meetings of Protest: In some repressive regimes, protest meetings are often forbidden. In these circumstances protest organisers have to meet under the cover of another innocent looking event. Sporting or other harmless meetings are often used to camouflage a protest meeting.

In Ireland, for instance, in the years before the Easter rising of 1916, the GAA, an Irish sporting organisation, was used to provide cover for meetings of Republicans at sporting events. The GAA was entirely infiltrated by members of the Irish Republican Brotherhood and despite this widespread subversion the British government remained largely oblivious to the uses to which the GAA was put by the mainstream Republican movement.

Considerations and risks: Clearly, in a political environment where protest meetings are banned, there are considerable risks in any form of protest meeting, even under the cover of a camouflage meeting of any kind. In the case of the Irish Republicans, they were quite careful to pick events in different parts of the country for their meetings so that it was almost impossible for potential infiltrators or informers to determine where high-ranking Republicans would meet next.

8.5.6.4 Teach-Ins: A teach-in is defined as "an extended meeting usually held on a college campus for lectures, debates, and discussions to raise awareness of or express an opinion on a social or political issue."

Teach-ins are somewhat different to protest meetings because they tend to be much larger, they have more speakers, and they are inclined to last significantly longer. The main objective of a teach-in is to provide as much information as possible on the topic of the protest. Opinions and discussions are encouraged with the goal that attendees develop their own opinions regarding the main protest issues. Teach-ins are often conducted in educational institutions. They have been popular since the 1960s and are again in use by the Occupy movement who hold teach-ins on the subject of capitalism and the problems of economic growth.

Considerations and risks: Teach-ins are normally held on private premises and are pre-arranged, with invitations sent to a selected guest list of potential sympathisers. Even though they encourage discussion, they still require a degree of structure in order to cover the subject matter which supports the protest without too many diversions.

Teach-ins should produce tangible results in the same way that traditional teaching or training events do, and these results should be measurable. Therefore, the syllabus and training course for a teach-in should be designed and prepared in just the same way as a formal training course and should include some means of evaluating the success of "the training". This might be a short written or verbal questionnaire for each participant.

8.5.6.5 Marches and Parades: These are both forms of mobile protest demonstrations that have a fixed starting point. Marches tend to have a fixed ending point, whereas parades do not. Both are designed to bring a protest to several different geographical points and pick up supporters en route. Marches and parades are good opportunities to deliver protest messages to the public and the press and to demonstrate to the authorities the strength of public feeling.

Where possible, marches and parades should be social events where the participants meet the public. Sometimes they can be light-hearted and even fun events and they are often themed and contain floats, theatrical components and music.

Flash mobs: An important modern variant on the mobile demonstration is the so-called "Flash Mob". A flash mob is an unrehearsed, spontaneous, contagious and dispersed mass demonstration. Flash mobs first emerged around 2003. The technique has since developed, with groups of people using email, blogs, text messages and Twitter to arrange to meet socially in a public place to demonstrate and socialise.

More recently, activists use flash mobs for organising spontaneous mass actions at short notice and they are now a powerful tactic for political protest, particularly under repressive conditions. For example, in the midst of a harsh crackdown on protests in Belarus in 2011, the dissidents, calling themselves "Revolution through the Social Network", began organising impromptu demonstrations, where protesters would simply gather in public spaces and clap their hands in unison. The result was the bewildering sight of secret police brutally arresting people for the simple act of clapping their hands: a powerful challenge to the legitimacy of an increasingly irrational regime.

In a hybrid use of the flash mob in Egypt, during the overthrow of President Hosni Mubarak, organisers called for protesters to gather (for safety) initially in alleys and other local "protected" spaces before moving into the streets in larger and larger numbers. The strategy worked as follows: starting small and away from the main protests made for a safe way to pool protesters together. It used an iterative approach to the psychology of "strength in numbers". As more people crowded the smaller streets, this gave rise to a sense of momentum and confidence. Starting in alleyways also localised the initiative. Neighbours were more likely to join the demonstration because they could see their friends or family out in the street.

Mobile communications technology has made the flash mob a reality. Flash mobs provide exceptional potential for dispersed, coordinated action and this potential has only just begun to be realized. Flash mobs are easy to organize, and resistant to both infiltration and pre-emption because of their friend-to-friend network topology. Thus, flash mobs are positioned to be the next popular tactic for protest movements. With flash mobs, activists have the potential to swarm target sites anywhere where necessary, with little chance of detection or coordinated prevention. Flash mobs are a classic example of an asymmetric strategy for civil rebellion because they connect lots of relatively powerless individuals into a coordinated mass capable of confronting much more powerful authorities, simply due to their speed of deployment, flexibility and better communications.

Treks: Another hybrid of the mobile demonstration is the trek. These are very long distance mobilisations designed to demonstrate the strength of feeling of a protest group. Stories of human resistance are full of walks, treks, sea voyages and even flights. Over the millennia, entire communities have packed up and voted with their feet, moving away from untenable situations on to more fertile lands. India's Salt March of 1932 is a well-known example of a mass, many-day trek. Gandhi conceived of this march as a living lesson for India, "creating a community, literally one step at a time", that both supported and embodied the idea of an independent India.

Many other treks have followed, usually with a commitment to demonstrate an ideal or alternative way of living. The 1986 US "Great Peace March for Global Nuclear Disarmament" flourished during its cross-continental trek, arriving in Washington, D.C., with 1,500 marchers and thousands more supporters. In the course of the 6000 km, the marchers not only educated and agitated for action on nuclear disarmament, but also built a mobile city.

Human banner: This is a way of organising a large group, at the beginning or end of a march or demonstration, to make a single, unified statement. In effect, the bodies of the participants are used to form either huge words or an image and, with good planning, these can produce works of aerial art, invisible from below but very impressive from above. If the press helicopters are hovering overhead you can use this technique to send a very clear message.

Considerations and risks: Most jurisdictions require that organised marches or parades are licensed events, so very often permission must be sought in advance from a local authority. Failure to have a licence may give rise to confrontation between police and marchers, which may or may not be in the interests of the protesters.

It is important to have good prior publicity for a protest parade. This will ensure that there are plenty of participants and that the public are fully aware of the event. Links between the event itself and the social media sites of the protest movement should be managed with live media being posted as the event progresses. Contacts with conventional press should be planned in advance so that the event gets the maximum coverage when the day comes.

Marches, parades and other demonstrations can quickly degenerate into violence, particularly when assaulted by police or counter demonstrations. It is very hard to choreograph such events and the only means to partially control them is the imposition of strict discipline.

Marches and parades need quite a lot of planning, and protest organisers should divide the work into various branches of responsibility such as: Legal and Permissions, Publicity and Press, Security and Discipline, Demonstration materials, Communications.

Long distance treks require enormous logistical planning and support.

8.5.6.6 Pilgrimages: A pilgrimage, despite its religious connotations, need not have a religious content. It may simply include a journey to a place which is revered for some reason, such as its connection with a person or an historical event.

Pilgrimages may also be political. For instance, every year large groups of Irish Republicans, including government ministers, visit Glasnevin Cemetery in Dublin to commemorate many of the Irish State's founding Republicans' graves. The traditional time to visit is at Easter to commemorate the 1916 Easter Rising against British occupation. The event is often marked by speeches and (sometimes) acts of defiance against continuing British involvement in Northern Ireland, such as the symbolic IRA salute to their dead with raised pistols shot over their graves. These types of pilgrimage provide a political respectability to a protest movement by creating a "tradition".

Considerations and risks: Pilgrimages provide an opportunity to link present politics with past events or persons. However, they also "chain" a protest movement to a place or person in a way which may not fit in with the contemporary objectives of the protesters.

Protest movements are about current issues and there is a risk that constant references to historical connections may taint a campaign and portray it as being a "left over" from a previous era, especially in the eyes of newer generations. Pilgrimages should therefore be used with some discretion.

8.5.6.7 Motorcades: In modern times motor vehicles have often been in the vanguard of protests, sometimes obstructing roads, and thus making critical areas impassable, or barricading protest areas for greater protection. During the fuel protests of 2000, in the UK, trucks were used to stop tankers from entering or leaving refineries, whilst in Tahrir Square in Cairo, demonstrators used burned-out vehicles to defend themselves against the brutality of the Egyptian military.

In Paris, in 2014, taxi drivers protested against competition by unlicensed cab drivers working for car-service companies such as the internet-based system "Uber". Drivers began causing serious disruptions around Paris' two main airports after parking their cars on motorways. The obstructions closed off two motorway exits and caused traffic delays that reached central Paris. Police forces were able to ease some of the congestion by forcing cab drivers to move their cars, but the next day drivers resumed their protest.

In other actions, motorcades have been used to deliberately cause congestion in large cities at rush-hour by driving very defensively or slowly. Motorcade actions cause enormous headaches for local police and disrupt business activities.

Considerations and risks: Obstructive behaviour may be a legal offence, but if the actions are carefully executed it will be very hard for the police to prove that a driver is part of a coordinated motorcade or go-slow action, provided that there is no dangerous driving involved.

8.5.6.8 Humorous Skits and Pranks: Sometimes the best way to draw attention to a protest issue is humour, whether in the form of skits, sketches or even slapstick humour. It can be obvious or deliberately coded, ironic, sarcastic or black. Humour can be a great unifying force and when used in political protest messages it is a powerful means of communication.

Methods of delivery include satirical magazines, cartoons, theatre, song, websites and social networking. Traditional working class folksongs in England have a long history of political irreverence. These often long and hilarious songs were theatrical pieces delivered with much jollity to full houses in theatres and are still an integral part of folk-culture of post-industrial England.

The writer Michael Olschimke, discussing the subject of political skits, suggested the following ideas:

- George Washington crossing the Delaware with a boatload of Revolutionary Patriots. In parody he replaces Washington with Bill Clinton crossing the Rio Grande with a boatload of American jobs, while he is signing the National Free Trade Agreement.

- Running a crutch up a flag pole, under the American Flag.

- Putting Lady Justice in a wheelchair with one side of her blindfold lifted up.

- Attaching a sling to the Statue of Liberty's arm.

The universality of humour and political satire as a response to dangerous or dire scenarios can be seen from Iraqi political comedians poking fun at the blood-thirsty ISIS movement to Saudi and Egyptian comics mocking their governments, whilst Palestinians make wise cracks about Israeli occupation and their own government's corruption.

Obviously, a lot of this type of satire and humour has to be aired on YouTube etc. because it's anathema for government-controlled national TV stations.

Considerations and risks: Political satire, most people would agree, is a healthy part of a democracy. Politicians are the most likely individuals to make themselves objects of derision, satire and abuse. Other forms of satire may also be quite reasonable. Social classes such as civil servants, the military, school teachers and unhelpful shop keepers have all been the bane of satire for centuries. Indeed, few of us have escaped being classified in one or more stereotypes open to a satirical comment.

There is a dangerously fine line though between satire and the realm of discrimination. Comments about a profession or a political party are one thing, but derisory or insulting comments about a racial group, a sexual orientation, a religion or a culture are quite different. In the rush to defend our own freedom of expression we do have to remember the rights of others to be free to believe, to live and to love as they wish, without our interference or criticism.

8.5.6.9 Performances of Plays, Music and Singing: Music and theatre can play a vital part in unifying a protest movement. Over the centuries there has been a succession of emblematic pieces of music and songs that symbolised important protests and revolutionary acts. The "International", "La Marseillaise", "No Pasarán" are just a few examples of such musical emblems. Amazingly, these songs still continue to be sung at protest demonstrations, decades (or centuries) after they were written. Despite the passage of time it seems that the basic struggles have remained the same and the songs associated with these struggles have retained their emotional appeal across generations. The use of communal singing is a powerful way of uniting a group in a common protest.

Considerations and risks: It is important to make the music fit the protest. A disagreement about a planning application probably doesn't need a rendering of "The International" and, in fact, probably requires no musical or theatrical component at all in order to be effective. On the other hand, when there is an escalation in a protest, the organisers should be ready to "add a soundtrack" to their protest if it is appropriate.

8.5.6.10 Political Mourning: Political mourning is an act of protest in which an unnecessary death or act of violence against an individual or group is used as an argument for political or social change.

The "Mothers of the Plaza de Mayo" are one of the best-known examples; others include the American Civil Rights movement, one of the most effective groups of political activists to organize protests around mourning. Both the deaths of Emmett Till (racial murder victim) and Martin Luther King (racial assassination), as well as police brutality against Rodney King, were used as an effective part of their strategy to advance their civil rights agendas. In Ireland the anniversary of the death of the Republican hunger striker Bobby Sands is still used as a date to remind Republicans of a greater struggle against English domination. More recently, the self-immolation of Mohamed Bouazizi on 17 December 2010 and the weeks of mourning which followed triggered the Tunisian revolution.

Associating the death(s) of a supporter(s) with a political protest creates a highly charged emotional atmosphere. It personalises a protest and it creates a direct link between an authority and the death of a protester. Often, this connection is made possible by the ineptitude of an authority and their mishandling of a dispute (as in the case of Bobby Sands) and it frequently signals the end of an authority's ability to control a protest, sometimes signifying their imminent defeat.

Considerations and risks: Controlling emotions in the event of a politically motivated death and mourning is very difficult. The death or abuse of someone at the hands of political adversaries can rapidly become highly emotive and may lead to public outrage and acts of retaliation. This is natural enough in many respects.

However, if the death of the victim is to become part of a protest action, these emotions need to be controlled. The positive aspects of the victim should be emphasised in a mourning protest. The reasons and injustice of their death are self-evident. To be effective, a protest should not degenerate into an excuse for abuse or revenge. The crime carries its own revenge and the protest should remain dignified. All the protest needs to do is to commemorate the facts. The rest of the protest plays out in the minds of the supporters and onlookers.

8.5.6.11 Mock Funerals: Funerals are emotive events and mock funerals are used to call to mind these emotions and associate them with the political issues which are the basis of a protest.

For example, a protest group in Dublin recently held a mock funeral when the government granted a licence for a contentious GM potato trial. The mock funeral was for the "Death of Good Food in Ireland", as the government decision signalled the end of GM-free farms in Ireland.

Mock funerals often involve a coffin (with an appropriate slogan) and mourners (dressed in appropriate black). The "funeral" often has a long cortège of supporters and walks slowly through a pre-determined route to a place where solemn speeches and a funeral homily may be made.

Considerations and risks: Mock funerals can be quite light-hearted, but always convey a serious message. They may attract large numbers of followers if properly advertised. As with other mobile demonstrations, they almost certainly need a licence from local authorities in big cities and the usual issues of security and discipline exist, as for all demonstrations. The press are generally quite fond of mock funerals because they enliven their reporting with something a bit unusual.

8.5.6.12 Demonstrative Funerals: A demonstrative funeral is a real funeral which is deliberately politicised to underline a protest message. If a person is killed during the course of a peaceful protest, or by the target of the protest, it can lead to a demonstrative funeral at which the victim becomes a martyr to the protest cause or attracts public sympathy for the cause.

During the "troubles" in Northern Ireland, many Republicans and ordinary members of the public were arrested and interned without charge for long periods. Many of them participated in hunger strikes and some died as a result of these protest actions. One of them was Bobby Sands, a protest leader and popular Republican. He was elected as an MP whilst in Long Kesh prison and led the Republican strikes there. He died in 1981 after 66 days without food. His death sent shock waves through the Republican community and his funeral was an event of huge proportions, with over 100,000 mourners following his funeral to the Republican burial plot in Belfast.

The death of Sands, the strength of public grief and the scale of his funeral triggered numerous international protests amongst sympathisers in France, Belgium, Russia, Portugal, Scandinavia, and the USA. For instance, in Russia, Pravda described his death as "another tragic page in the grim chronicle of oppression, discrimination, terror, and violence" in Ireland.

In Ireland itself the death and scale of sympathy and anger galvanised the Republican population against British occupation and converted an already violent civil insurgency into open civil war, which smoulders to the present day.

Considerations and risks: The example of Bobby Sands' death and funeral triggered a long period of rioting and violent revenge attacks in Ireland and on the British mainland. Political dialogue became impossible as a result of these escalations. The death and funeral of a much-loved victim at the hands of an oppressive regime creates an extremely emotional and dangerous environment and the line between protest and full-scale violent rebellion is quickly crossed as popular anger turns to calls for revenge.

8.5.6.13 Homage at Burial Places: Paying homage at a burial place is a means of reminding the world of an atrocity or other crime committed by an authority in the past and gives a protest group a strong, historical reason to continue their present struggle.

The act of homage provides a constant role in condemning an authority or reminding the public of the atrocities committed in the past. It has been employed for hundreds of years as a way of informing the current generation of past heroism. Homage may be paid to the victims of oppression, war, poverty or to those who struggled to relieve these evils. It may take place in a war cemetery, a concentration camp, or at the grave of a victim. All are sites of homage and represent powerful political symbols from the past that reinforce many on-going protest sentiments.

Considerations and risks: Homage to the dead is limited to the next one or two generations. Homage may mean little (emotionally) to any later generation.

It is a tragic fact that many of the younger members of the current generation have little emotional connection with the millions of deaths caused by the Nazi regime of 20th century Germany. It is understandable (though regrettable) that our children have no direct or even third party recollection or understanding of the awful atrocities committed just 75 years ago.

8.5.7 Withdrawal and Renunciation

Sometimes the most profound protest actions involve a refusal to participate: a public withdrawal from a public act. Such withdrawals can be deeply offensive to an authority, for instance when medals are refused or meetings are "blacked" by participants refusing to attend.

Renunciation is slightly different because it involves a protest group positively countering an authority or another protest group, as in the use of counterdemonstrations.

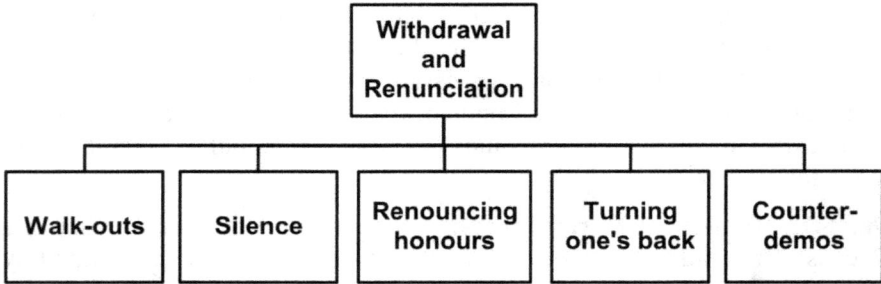

```
                    ┌─────────────────┐
                    │   Withdrawal    │
                    │      and        │
                    │  Renunciation   │
                    └─────────────────┘
```

Walk-outs	Silence	Renouncing honours	Turning one's back	Counter-demos

8.5.7.1 Walk-Outs: Walk-outs take place when a group of protesters leave a gathering or meeting, either one by one or en masse. The objective of a walk-out is to demonstrate that a significant group of participants dissent from the objectives of the meeting.

Walk-outs are designed to undermine the credibility of an authority by demonstrating that it has a strong and active opposition.

Considerations and risks: Walk-outs need to be well thought out. If one walks out on a meeting tonight and then joins it again tomorrow without any concessions, the original action is open to ridicule.

Walk-outs need to have tangible demands that everyone understands. Return is conditional upon these demands being met. Demanding too much may mean that a walk-out group is forced to concede. Thus, in general, reasonable demands should be made - at least in the first instance.

Walk-outs can be quite dramatic and should be filmed for release to the media or on the internet.

8.5.7.2 Silence: A silent demonstration can be one of the most profound acts of civil protest available to an activist group.

Silence is powerful and it's also versatile. It can signal disapproval and disagreement without being too disagreeable. At a time when people routinely use loud, caustic speech, angry voices and violent actions to project their point of view, silence can be an even louder statement. Without saying a word people can let others know exactly where they stand and what they stand for.

Few statements have been as powerful an indictment of injustice as the silent protester in Tiananmen Square in Beijing, standing his ground in the face of a phalanx of tanks. That protester said nothing, but the whole world got the message and was immensely moved by that act of silent defiance.

Considerations and risks: A protest group taking part in a silent demonstration needs to ensure that the reason for the silence is understood by the public. As in the silent anti-racist demonstrations of modern Germany or the muted scream demonstrations of modern Spain, the reasons for the silence must be effectively communicated to the public. Silent public demonstrations are only profound when the public knows why they are profound.

8.5.7.3 Renouncing Honours: Refusing an honour, such as a medal, is a very powerful act of defiance by one or more individuals that sends very strong signals to the public. It undermines the award giver and implies that it is a corrupt or dishonourable institution. It underlines the integrity of the person who is being offered the honour.

This is quite a common form of protest. In Britain, for instance, a land that wallows in the giving and taking of honours, by 2012 there was a list of 277 people who, over the years, had refused a CBE, OBE or knighthood. These included some fairly big names, such as Aldous Huxley, Lowry the artist, and sculptor Henry Moore, and, of course, John Lennon. Some other people forfeited their honours deliberately, such as Irish-born colonial officer Sir Roger Casement, convicted of treason for aiding those involved in Ireland's 1916 Easter Rising. He was executed and consequently lost the title "Sir".

Considerations and risks: There is not that much risk in renouncing an honour, except that you probably won't get invited to certain cocktail parties any more.

8.5.7.4 Turning One's Back: This is an old method, but still in use today. It is used by all kinds of protest groups, left and right. For example, in late 2014, the method was employed by the New York City police department as a protest against the death of two policemen. In the incident hundreds of police officers turned their backs on the New York mayor Bill de Blasio as he spoke during the funeral service for Rafael Ramos, one of two New York Police Department officers killed in an ambush shooting in Brooklyn. This protest action was used several times. At a hospital after the shooting, the police union's president, Patrick Lynch, and others, turned their backs on the mayor in a sign of disrespect.

The purpose of this symbolic protest is to demonstrate a great disrespect for an authority figure with the implicit threat that the authority will be ignored (or worse).

Considerations and risks: This is a powerful act of public disregard. Many authorities may be offended by this kind of action and seek revenge. In the example above, the NY police were fairly immune from revenge, but in other cases the protesters may not have so much influence and may be subject to persecution by an offended authority.

8.5.7.5 Counter-Demonstrations: A counter-demonstration has the purpose of deliberately countering another protest demonstration.

For example, in 2014 and 2015 there were a number of extreme right-wing demonstrations centred on stirring up anti-Muslim sentiment in Germany by a group called PEGIDA, which for a few months carried out routine mass demonstrations every Monday. There was also strong popular repugnance for these demonstrations and this led to many spontaneous counter-demonstrations. For instance, in Munich during the second Monday of January 2015 a demonstration group of several hundred right-wing PEGIDA demonstrators was confronted by more than 20,000 ordinary Munich citizens, angry at these right-wing demonstrators. The Munich citizen group (nonviolently) forced the right-wind demonstrators to abandon their protest and escorted them to trains to take them out of the centre of Munich.

Considerations and risks: Counter-demonstrations can turn violent as emotions are running high on both sides. They need to be especially well-organised and disciplined. In the example quoted above, any acts of violence by the counter-demonstrators would have damaged an honourable public cause.

8.6 Nonviolent Intervention

Intervention is different from non-cooperation or other forms of protest in that it calls for real physical action by the campaign participants rather than for simple protest.

Intervention may be a form of defence of the campaign or institution or, alternatively, intervention may be offensive as part of a strategy to move closer to the campaign's objectives.

Intervention is often more immediate and effective than non-cooperation or simple protest, but it is also harder to maintain and more taxing for the participants. Here we will examine various forms of nonviolent intervention:

Methods of Intervention

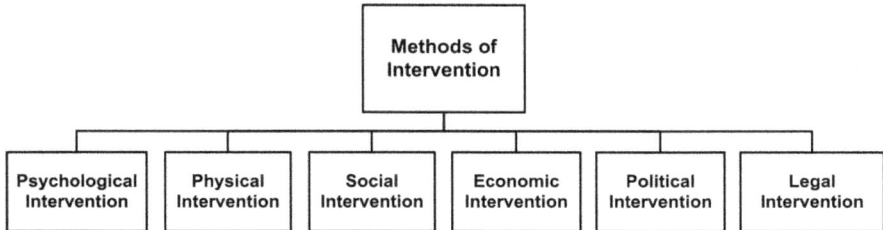

```
                    ┌──────────────────┐
                    │    Methods of    │
                    │   Intervention   │
                    └──────────────────┘
```

Psychological Intervention	Physical Intervention	Social Intervention	Economic Intervention	Political Intervention	Legal Intervention

8.6.1 Psychological Intervention

As the name implies, psychological intervention employs psychological methods to attract sympathetic attention to the demands of the protest campaign and to help pressurise an authority to accept protest campaign demands.

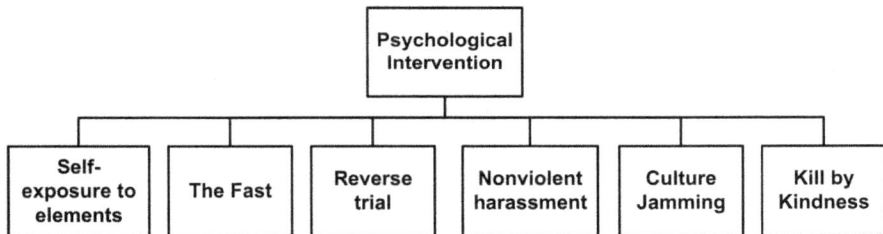

```
                    ┌──────────────────┐
                    │   Psychological  │
                    │   Intervention   │
                    └──────────────────┘
```

Self-exposure to elements	The Fast	Reverse trial	Nonviolent harassment	Culture Jamming	Kill by Kindness

8.6.1.1 Self-Exposure to the Elements: This is a form of physical protest where the participants endure long periods of physical exposure to the weather. It may be camping out in extremely cold or wet weather or refusing to leave a site in very hot conditions. It is somewhat akin to fasting because it attracts the attention and sympathy of onlookers and puts some responsibility for the welfare of the protesters in the hands of the authority.

Considerations and risks: The objective of this method is to gain sympathy, not to create a martyr. The personal risks of this method of protest may be considerable. Organisers need to be sure that the participants are physically very fit and the necessary support infrastructure should be very well organised. Provision of appropriate food, water and clothing are essential and a plan B is vital to rescue protesters and bring them to a place of safety if this method of protests goes wrong.

Historical and contemporary examples: During several protests in the UK in recent years, protesters have used this technique to demonstrate their strength of resolve to the authorities and public alike. The Greenham Common Women's Peace Camp was established in 1982 to protest the placing of nuclear cruise missiles at the Greenham base. The camp continued until 2000, occupied continuously, with numbers varying from as little as 30 to over 50,000 protesters at times in its history. During the 19 years of occupation living conditions in the scattered protest camps were extremely hard, with appalling weather conditions for months at a time, but the protesters refused to leave, even when exposed to extreme cold, snow, high winds and heavy rain.

In a similar vein, road protests of the last 30 years in Britain have involved protesters climbing into and living in trees threatened with felling by road builders. In more extreme cases they have protested by burying themselves in networks of underground tunnels on building sites and taking up residence in these cold, damp places for weeks at a time, simply to stop heavy machinery excavating these sites.

Such protest strategies gained considerable psychological sympathy for the protesters, as it was made abundantly clear how much they were willing to suffer and risk for their cause.

8.6.1.2 The Fast or Hunger Strike: The fast is an ancient way of registering a protest. Fasting is often used as a tool to make a political statement, to protest, or to heighten awareness of a cause.

A hunger strike (usually fasting in a group) is a method of nonviolent resistance in which participants fast as an act of political protest, hoping to attract public attention and provoke feelings of guilt in the authority and public, thus achieving their goal, such as a policy change.

Considerations and risks: The clear risk of fasting is that the participants may permanently damage their own health and maybe even lose their own lives in the protest.

Fasts need to be well publicised to be effective and the public should have a daily report on the condition of the participants to remind them of the issues at stake and how vital they are. Organisers of hunger strikes need to be prepared to abandon their actions if the lives of participants are at risk. A dead protester might be symbolically potent, but it is a tragic loss of life and rarely the best alternative for either the movement or the individual sympathisers.

Historical and contemporary examples: There have been numerous examples of protest campaigns using fasting and hunger strikes down the years. Ghandi was famous for his spiritual fasts, used both as a protest and also as a means of meditation.

In the West, political hunger strikes are generally a way of forcing a government to take note of a protest's demands and to get these demands out into the public domain and have them discussed. The intended effect of a fast or hunger strike is to create public sympathy for the hunger strikers.

The most prominent hunger strikers were in the Suffragette movements of the US and UK. Also the 1980s Irish Republican prisoners' hunger strikes, where many of the prisoners died as a result of their protest.

The most controversial contemporary hunger strikes are those that started in 2005 in Guantanamo Bay. The circumstances of these hunger strikes very much resemble those of the Irish Republican detainees in Northern Ireland mentioned above. The widespread Guantanamo Bay hunger strikes were started by prisoners protesting their innocence and illegal detention in the absence of any form of trial or other judicial process. These hunger strikes continue at the time of writing (2015), much to the embarrassment of the United States.

8.6.1.3 Reverse Trial: This is a technique where a defendant uses his trial to deliver not only a defence, but also takes the opportunity to accuse and deliver a case against his or her accusers.

In court the defendant can speak without the risk of accusations of defamation, he can make accusations which are placed on the public record and reveal confidential information against his accusers or third parties. Whilst such statements may have no bearing on his defence and may even damage it, the ability to speak freely in public provides a way of reversing a trial, so that, in effect, the defendant becomes the accuser.

A defendant may also induce one or more third parties to participate in the trial, either as witnesses or as so-called amicus curiae. These third parties can be examined by the defendant and can be induced to bring accusations into play, which can be aimed at demonstrating the malfeasance or misconduct of the prosecution.

Legal processes may restrict what can be admitted by a court as evidence. However, a defendant may be able to build a case against the accuser to be heard if he can demonstrate that his testimony is relevant to his own defence. For example, it could be argued that previous events, unconnected with the present case, demonstrate the accuser's historical lack of respect for the law, the environment or human rights. Whilst not directly relevant to the case, such evidence could be pivotal in undermining the respectability or credibility of the accuser.

In some cases a defendant may be able to argue that his actions were motivated by political or ethical considerations. This defence may provide a platform for a political statement, which can then include an attack on the bad conduct of the accuser.

Considerations and risks: The main risk with this strategy is that such evidence may be inadmissible. Therefore, very careful planning is required in the presentation of such testimony since it may also be damaging to the defendant's case. Using a trial as a means of presenting contradictory evidence needs to be carefully choreographed.

Historical and contemporary examples: The trial of Anne Hutchinson in 1637 is a well-known example where the defendant completely usurped the court and turned her case into a prosecution of her accusers. This lady had been accused of a variety of heretical offences, but primarily she was accused of undermining the religious establishment of Massachusetts.

She was an intelligent woman with great charisma and she was an eloquent speaker. She managed by a variety of linguistic and strategic traps to manipulate the court into giving her a platform to express her condemnation of the established church and its ministers and to promote her own vision of Christian faith and that of her own religious movement.

In the end, she was convicted anyway (the trial result was pre-determined) and she was banished, along with her many followers, from the colony of Massachusetts. However, her trial was widely followed and had the effect of undermining the Puritan stranglehold on the colony.

She received a posthumous pardon in 1987 from the Governor of Massachusetts and is now considered something of a feminist and free-speech hero.

8.6.1.4 Nonviolent Harassment: In the context of civil disobedience nonviolent harassment relates to collective action which disrupts and inconveniences an authority or the daily life of a target individual or group of individuals. The important caveat is that it is done peacefully, without any threat of violence.

Techniques may include the suspension of normal economic, professional or social activity aimed at a target by the simple closure or blockading of services, shops, places of work, banks, courts, post offices etc., together with a shutdown or obstruction of access to public services, schools, legal services, transport systems, electricity and fuel deliveries.

The absence of normal economic, legal and social interaction is quite disturbing to a target and causes those affected to reconsider the importance of the services they receive and the people that deliver them.

A typical example of nonviolent harassment occurs when strike-breaking workers are imported to replace workers that have taken industrial action against an abusive employer.

Very often the strike-breaking labour is more exploited than the original protesters. However, it is frequently necessary to exercise some form of nonviolent harassment to dissuade the strike-breakers from aiding the employer in breaking the strike.

Considerations and risks: Making life difficult by interrupting basic services is a form of harassment and should be considered carefully, both morally and legally. There are ethical justifications for this type of action, but every case should be carefully considered.

Those engaged in nonviolent harassment run the risk that their targets find alternatives. When services are withdrawn or disrupted, the obvious response for an authority is to look for alternative service providers. To avoid this, this type of action needs to be carried out across a wide spectrum of services, including specialised services, so that finding alternative providers is impractical.

Historical and contemporary examples: In January 2014, in an unprecedented action, criminal courts across England and Wales were severely disrupted when barristers and solicitors staged a mass walk-out in protest at government plans to slash legal aid fees by up to 30%.

It was the first time that barristers have withdrawn their labour, according to the Criminal Bar Association, and it was the first time that the two wings of the legal profession had taken co-ordinated, national action.

Thousands of barristers and solicitors working on publicly-funded cases refused to enter court for a half-day demonstration aimed at forcing the (Conservative) Justice Secretary into a last-minute rethink of proposals designed to save £220m a year.

Criminal barristers stated that the protest reflected mounting resentment over successive reductions in legal aid fees, which had already resulted in cuts of 40% for criminal cases since 1997. They warned that if the Ministry of Justice enforced the latest reduction it would lead to lower quality legal representation, miscarriages of justice and more criminals walking free from court.

This withdrawal action was later followed by another disruptive walk-out in March of 2014 and the boycotting of several high profile cases by barristers. This forced some defendants to manage their own defence, which resulted in the potential dismissal of their cases by the courts [Note 91].

8.6.1.5 Culture Jamming - Détournement: In a world where we face an onslaught of imagery connected with brands, nationality, advertising, news items and popular culture, we come to quickly associate an image with a concept.

We see a Union Jack and it conjures up a set of images and emotions associated with the nation it represents. We hear a particular pop tune and we instantly associate it with a time, a place, a group of people or a period. For most of us there are countless examples of cultural artefacts which trigger similar reactions. And this fact gives rise to an opportunity for a form of psychological disruption known as détournement or "culture jamming". In this technique, subversive and marginalized ideas can potentially be spread by expropriating artefacts drawn from popular media and "injecting" them with radical connotations.

The idea was popularized in the 1950s [Note 92] and the term "détournement" is borrowed from the French, and roughly translates to "overturning" or "derailment."

As a tactic, détournement appropriates and alters an existing media artefact, one that the intended audience is already familiar with, in order to give it a new, subversive meaning. In many cases, the intention is to criticize the appropriated artefact.

Détournement works because humans tend to be creatures of habit and often rely on imagery, familiarity and comfort as the final arbiters of "truth". Rational arguments and earnest appeals to morality may prove less effective than a carefully planned détournement that bypasses the audience's mental "filters" by mimicking familiar cultural symbols, and then "disrupting" them. Using national flags or other well-known nationalist or commercial imagery is a popular way of carrying out "cultural jamming".

Considerations and risks: As an act of psychological intervention, détournement requires the user to have some understanding of the most important signs and symbols of contemporary culture. The better you know a culture, the easier it is to alter, repurpose, or disrupt it.

To be successful, the media artefact chosen for détournement must be recognizable to its intended audience. Furthermore, the author of the détournement must be familiar with the subtleties of the artefact's original meaning in order to effectively create a new, critical meaning.

By itself, cultural jamming is unlikely to change anything. As a protest, it is funny but not really that fundamental. It should be remembered that the technique is only a single method of psychological intervention and not an end in itself. Détournement should be integrated into a larger campaign strategy.

Historical and contemporary examples: The neo-Situationist magazine Adbusters created an American flag bearing corporate logos instead of stars. The "stars and stripes" is so often used to quash dissent by equating America with liberty and progress. In this example the flag is altered to imply that corporations, not the people, rule America.

Another shockingly ironic example was of a pepper-spraying American cop springing up in the most unlikely contexts, such as in famous classic art works, pepper-spraying a copy of the US Declaration of Independence and characters in peaceful rustic settings.

8.6.1.6 Kill by Kindness: This is an action where protesters behave in such an exemplary way that it is hard for the authorities to deny their demands. For example, workers may work harder and longer than they are paid to do to bolster their case for better working conditions. The employers are placed in a difficult psychological position and may feel unable to refuse to negotiate with their workers. In civil disturbances, participants may exhibit acts of unprecedented kindness to their targets. Many examples of such behaviour have occurred over the years, such as making tea for the riot police etc. This strategy is often called "killing with kindness" because it neutralises the adversary, using kindness rather than an attack.

It's naïve to think that powerful authorities will change their ways just because of an appeal to their better nature or as a result of considerate gestures by a protester. However, in the world of nonviolent protest it is a central part of the philosophy to recognise the common humanity of both protesters and those in authority. The principle is that the more we humanise politics, the more likely we are to win over our adversaries in a nonviolent way. Thus, the bureaucrat who secretly agrees with the protest is more likely to quit, and lend his skills to "the revolution". The policeman who's been treated kindly by a bunch of demonstrators is much more likely to refuse an order to physically attack them. And with the general public witnessing the protest, they are also more likely to be moved to action themselves if they witness acts of kindness and humanity by the protesters.

Considerations and risks: There is the risk that an authority faced with highly motivated, cooperative staff or citizens may just ignore their demands and take advantage of their amiable behaviour. Therefore, those participating in such an action need to ensure that the authorities know that their good behaviour is conditional upon the goodwill of the authority and may be withdrawn at any time. The nonviolent component of a protest may have a time limit after which a protest may degenerate into an insurgency.

Historical and contemporary examples: One of the most emblematic examples occurred in October 1967, when anti-war marchers were confronted by 2500 Army National Guard troops forming a human barricade in front of the Pentagon. Demonstrators holding flowers placed some in the soldiers' rifle barrels. The action in itself changed nothing, but it inspired a generation of anti-war activists.

A more contemporary example occurred in 2012, when Alberto Casillas instantly became a national celebrity in Spain when he protected a group of protesters during an anti-austerity demonstration. The police were beating and attacking protesters violently, leading to some protesters and members of the public running into Casillas' café to escape the blows of police batons. When the police demanded that Casillas let them enter the café to detain the protesters, he stood against them at the door, and completely defenceless, he announced: "On my life, you will not enter! It will be a massacre." Casillas, an avowed supporter of the right-wing PP government party, said he thought the police behaviour towards the protesters was excessive, and even though he was a government supporter, he refused to let the police pass. The police were unwilling to forcibly enter Casillas' café and consequently left [Note 93].

8.6.2 Physical Intervention

Physical intervention is one way of attracting attention and pressurising an authority to accept protest campaign demands.

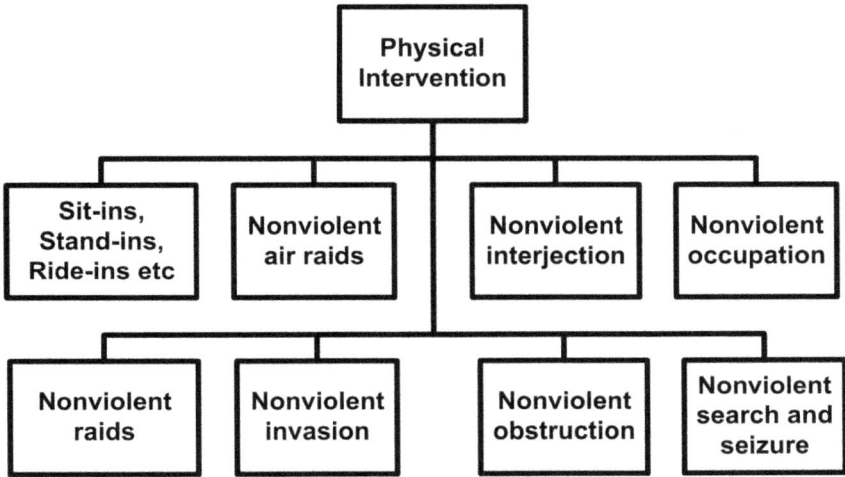

```
                          ┌──────────────────┐
                          │    Physical      │
                          │  Intervention    │
                          └──────────────────┘
```

Sit-ins, Stand-ins, Ride-ins etc	Nonviolent air raids	Nonviolent interjection	Nonviolent occupation

Nonviolent raids	Nonviolent invasion	Nonviolent obstruction	Nonviolent search and seizure

8.6.2.1 Sit-in, Stand-in, Ride-in, Wade-in, Pray-in: All of these methods have a similar role. They involve protesters gathering together to occupy a space or geographical zone, often against the wishes of the target authority, with the aim of attracting public attention to their protest demands.

A sit-in is an act where protesters seat themselves at a strategic location, often in a government or corporate office or in a busy street. They remain until they are removed, often by force, or are arrested, or until they feel that they have made their point. Sit-ins are generally quite a successful form of protest. They are disruptive and draw attention to the protest and its cause. They are effective in shutting down an area, a government building or a business. The forced removal of protesters, and sometimes the use of violence against them, often attracts the sympathy of the public, and helps the demonstrators get their message across. Sit-ins were very common and effective during the US Civil Rights protests of the 1960s.

A stand-in is another form of demonstration where participants stand together, sometimes in front of a government or corporate office building, to protest their cause. Stand-in protests are considered to be more aggressive than sit-ins. A sit-in is an attempt to deliberately attract attention with the hope of being forcibly removed. A stand-in is more of a challenge to the authority and carries the implication that the crowd is on its feet, mobilised and angry and should not be challenged by the authority, or else.....

A ride-in takes many forms. Protesters on bicycles may band together in large numbers to ride together through a city. Riders on horseback may ride together to make their protest demands heard. Motor bikers or car drivers may form protest convoys. Lorry drivers or farmers on tractors may cause disruption by forming large groups and driving through a busy area in a disruptive way. All of these actions are connected with gaining public attention for a protest's demands. These actions cause disruption and may cause significant economic damage as well.

A wade-in is a protest action where a group collectively enters a sea or a river together to highlight their demands. The first modern wade-ins took place in the USA in 1959 and in 1963, when hundreds of black civil rights demonstrators protested against the segregation of beaches in Mississippi by arriving en masse at the beach and wading into the water together. After many arrests and some violence from local white populations, the demonstrators won their demands for complete desegregation in 1968. This type of protest action is still used occasionally, notably when a protest action involves a sea or a river, such as in fishing protests.

A pray-in is a form of demonstration centred on the use of prayer as a means of making a protest. An example pray-in occurred in 2006, when a group of imams, Christian ministers and a Jewish rabbi staged a "pray-in" demonstration at Washington National Airport. They demanded an apology from US Airways for barring six Muslims from a Minneapolis to Phoenix flight the previous week. The religious leaders called for an end to racial profiling, saying it was unacceptable in America. Imam Omar Shahin, one of the six imams detained at the Minneapolis International Airport, said they had not done anything wrong or suspicious. The imams, who were returning from a religious conference, had prayed on their prayer rugs in the airport before the flight. After they boarded the flight, a passenger passed a note to a flight attendant. The men were then taken off the airplane, handcuffed and questioned [Note 94].

A nurse-in is a form of protest against public places that forbid mothers from breastfeeding their babies in public. In 2014, Claridges Hotel in London forbade a guest from feeding her baby in a public area. The story caused outrage when the ban was endorsed by the leader of the far right-wing UKIP party. In protest against the hotel's decision, the campaign group "Free to Feed" organised a "nurse-in" outside the hotel. The group described it as a peaceful demonstration in support of breastfeeding.

"Enough is enough. Claridges had ample time to apologise for their mistake and rectify the situation by changing their 'policy', which states that they allow nursing mothers 'as long as they are discreet'. Claridges seem to think that they are above the laws and legislation of this land," a statement on the group's website said [Note 95].

Considerations and risks: All of these actions may create an obstruction which carries the risk of legal action, including detention and/or eviction. Organisers must be prepared to support protesters in such legal cases, making sure that their lawsuits attract the maximum amount of press and political attention and that legal support is available in case prosecution ensues.

Historical and contemporary examples: In November 2014, as a response to the announcement that a Missouri police officer would not be indicted for the shooting dead of an unarmed black youth, demonstrators forced the shut down of at least three large shopping centres in Ferguson, as local residents took to the shops to protest against the Grand Jury's decision. Lying on the ground inside the malls in so-called "die-ins", the groups chanted: "Stop shopping and join the movement." As a result of the protest, the authorities were subsequently forced to close the shopping centres. This was quite a blow, especially on America's busiest pre-Christmas shopping day. Other stores in other parts of the country were similarly targeted with protesters lying down (as if dead). Stores in the Galleria Mall in Richmond Heights, a few miles south of Ferguson, lowered their security doors and locked entrances after the appearance of around 200 peaceful protesters shouting: "Black lives matter" and "Stop, don't shoot", whilst urging shoppers to quit the shopping centre in solidarity with their demonstration [Note 96]. Similar demonstrations spread to shopping centres in the United Kingdom [Note 97].

8.6.2.2 Nonviolent Raids: A nonviolent raid involves a peaceful, but forceful and surprise occupation or "raid" on an authority's premises. This might involve a large number of demonstrators or a single individual's action. It might be the planting of a banner in a spectacular display, a tactic much loved by Greenpeace, or it might be a demonstration of thousands entering the construction site of a nuclear power station to protest.

Considerations and risks: As with peaceful invasions and occupations, a short raid on an authority's premises carries the risk of arrest and detention by the authority. To be effective, a raid has to be fast and undetected. Greenpeace are masters of the "raid". They plan their raids very carefully and covertly. They make sure that they know the target site very well, rehearse their actions and then they act with military-style secrecy and perfect timing. Nonetheless, members of Greenpeace's raids are frequently arrested as a result of their efforts. Protest raid organisers need to be prepared for this and offer media coverage and appropriate political and legal support to the "raiders", should this happen.

Historical and contemporary examples: One of the more famous nonviolent raids occurred in 1930 in India, to protest against British rule and a British salt tax, when Mahatma Gandhi chose a nonviolent raid by hundreds of peaceful protesters (satyagrahis) at the Dharasana Salt works in Gujarat. Despite repeated attempts to enter the works, the demonstrators were brutally beaten and clubbed by British soldiers and police. Hundreds were arrested, but the ensuing publicity describing British brutality caused global condemnation.

A more contemporary example of the nonviolent raid took place in 1979. After the near meltdown of the Three Mile Island Nuclear Reactor in Pennsylvania, in March 1979, a protest movement against the opening of a nuclear power plant on Long Island, New York, began to attract attention and membership. In June of that year the movement (SHAD) hosted a rally and a march to the construction site of the nuclear plant. Organisers planned the event in conjunction with International Antinuclear Day. Approximately 15,000 protesters marched at the rally. Members of SHAD and dozens of local groups attended. After speeches and music, activists marched to the construction site. Some 600 protesters climbed the Shoreham fence and were arrested for trespassing. A smaller group of 20 destroyed the hinges on the main gate. The size of the raid sent a clear message to legislators, and the protests rumbled on for years. Finally, on February 28, 1989, New York governor Mario M. Cuomo agreed with the Suffolk County Legislature and announced that the Shoreham Nuclear Plant must close. The governor and LILCO (the constructors) signed an agreement to shut the plant. In 1992, Shoreham was fully dismantled, without ever generating any commercial electricity.

8.6.2.3 Nonviolent Air Raids: A nonviolent air raid involves the use of aircraft to carry out a protest or using some form of aviation to communicate with large numbers of supporters or the general public. The most common use of aircraft in a protest is in the dropping of leaflets on civil populations.

In modern times, drones are being used to gather information and photographs which are important to a protest. For example, drones and light aircraft have been successfully used to photograph environmental crimes and damage, such as the effects of illegal logging in Asia and Latin America and illegal bog-cutting in Ireland.

Other uses of aircraft in nonviolent protest include the deliberate violation of airspace to send a protest message or to force an authority to alter its plans by creating security alerts.

Considerations and risks: The use of aircraft is a complicated matter because of safety concerns. It should be carefully considered to ensure that there are no risks to public safety. In a volatile, emotionally charged situation, the use of aircraft may cause panic, either by protesters, the public, or members of an authority. This panic may give rise to unforeseen consequences such as stampedes, attacks on the aircraft or other violent and perhaps life-threatening reactions. It is essential to make sure that all concerned are aware of the nonviolent purpose of the aircraft in a protest action.

Historical and contemporary examples: One notorious use of an aircraft in a protest action took place on 28 May 1987, when Mathias Rust, a young German pilot, landed near Red Square in Moscow. Rust flew from Finland to Moscow, being tracked several times by the Soviet air force. Fortunately, despite his incursions into Soviet airspace, Soviet fighters never received permission to shoot him down, and during the flight he was even mistaken for a friendly aircraft. Finally, he landed his small aircraft right next to Moscow's Red Square near the Kremlin, much to the bewilderment of military guards and civilians alike. Rust claimed that he wanted to create an "imaginary bridge" to the East to reduce Cold War tensions. His flight through a supposedly impregnable air defence system shook the Soviet military and led to the dismissal of many senior officers. Thus, the incident both helped Mikhail Gorbachev implement his liberalising reforms by allowing him to dismiss numerous military officials opposed to him, whilst also reducing the prestige and image of invincibility of the Soviet military in the eyes of the Soviet people [Note 98].

8.6.2.4 Nonviolent Invasion: This is the entrance of a number of protesters into a forbidden area, such as a military zone. In recent decades, governments in the West have become increasingly sensitive about the public getting close to the seats of government, prime-minister's residences or similar high-profile government buildings. The excuse used for this defensive attitude is almost always security and prevention of terrorist attacks, though very likely the main reason is politicians' fear of an angry public confrontation. Thus they tend to hide themselves behind layers of "anti-terror" walls, gates, sentries and fences. Invading such a space is a dangerous, but powerful act of protest.

Considerations and risks: Entering restricted areas can be dangerous, but openly and in large numbers it can be done. These days even protesting in front of the British parliament is forbidden. Yes, even in the so-called "world's oldest democracy" the politicians are now frightened of their own people. This probably accounts for the aggressive tactics of London's police and their unprecedented recent purchase of several water cannons for crowd control. In such a climate the planning of nonviolent invasions needs to be carefully worked out. The organisers need to look at escape routes, points at which blockades and barricades should be erected, how an occupation is going to be supplied with food and drink, shelter, emergency medical facilities and sanitary facilities. Such mundane issues may make the difference between a successful and a failed invasion. There need to be contingency plans for attacks by police or military and there needs to be training for protesters in how to deal with crowd control measures such as tear gas, tasers, pepper spray, water canon, rubber bullets, etc. Maintaining discipline is also important to ensure that an authority is not given an excuse to use violent methods of dispersal. Organisers need to make sure that they have dedicated crews to film the entire protest, including any police violence, and ensure that the filmed material is uploaded onto the internet and sent to the press as soon as possible.

Historical and contemporary examples: There are many examples of this type of protest invasion. Military bases are a favourite target for such invasions, but there are also exclusion zones around sensitive activities, such as oil exploration sites, which are sometimes the target for an invasion by protesters trying to disrupt or stop the activity. Greenham Common US airbase in the UK was invaded on numerous occasions by anti-nuclear weapons protesters in the 1980s and 1990s. In various maritime protests, Greenpeace has used its ocean-going vessels to invade sensitive ocean oil prospecting sites to stop or delay oil exploration.

In 2004, the British Parliament was suspended after five protesters burst into the Commons chamber while MPs debated whether to ban hunting with dogs. Four of the men ran out from behind the speaker's chair and another wrestled past a doorkeeper from a different entrance. It later emerged that the intruders had probably been aided by a Commons pass holder. Police say they considered the invasion a "carefully planned operation". The Commons Speaker told MPs: "Eight protesters were let into the House of Commons, using a forged letter inviting them to a meeting in the Committee corridor. Once there, they were led into the small stairway to the north end of the corridor - probably by a pass holder who was clearly exceeding his or her authority." The men were bundled out of the chamber, which was then guarded by armed police. Outside

Parliament, police estimate there were between 8,000 and 20,000 protesters [Note 99]. The protest came only two days after a Fathers 4 Justice campaigner got onto the balcony of Buckingham Palace.

A completely legal, but very disruptive invasion comes every year in Spain when Spanish shepherds guide their flocks of 2,000 sheep through central Madrid's streets in defence of ancient grazing, droving and migration rights, which are increasingly threatened by urban sprawl and modern agricultural practices. In 2014, for instance, tourists and city-dwellers were surprised to see the capital's traffic halted to permit the huge flock to pass the city's most emblematic locations. The shepherds halted at the town hall, so that the chief herdsman could hand authorities 25 "maravedies" (copper coins first minted in the 11th century) as payment for the crossing. They then continued past central Puerta del Sol square and the Central Bank of Spain headquarters on their way to Retiro Park. Some Spanish herding routes have been used annually for over 800 years and Madrid sprawls across one dating back to 1372 [Note 100].

8.6.2.5 Nonviolent Interjection: This is a form of protest action where one or more participants block a person's access to their work or other activity or cause a disruption. It is not quite the same as an obstruction because it is relatively easy to remove or circumvent the person or persons making the interjection.

An example would be: standing in front of a vehicle and thus creating a risk that the person(s) would be driven over, unless the driver changes course. Another example would be to turn up uninvited at a meeting to make a protest statement.

It can be a particularly powerful symbolic protest action. The technique is frequently used to block access to a civil servant or other official to their place of work or a site they need to visit on official business or to interrupt an official meeting or other event.

Creative disruption: This form of nonviolent interjection is designed to expose and disrupt the public relations efforts of an authority during speeches, hearings, meetings, and fundraisers by means of visual displays, song, theatre, and humour.

Sometimes there is no option but to try to disrupt an event as a protest. Disruption can be an effective tactic, and has been used successfully by small groups of people, often with little advance notice or advance planning. However, disruptions can be more subtle and creative than a simple attempt to shut down a target. Indeed, sometimes a more oblique intervention that forces a response without actually preventing someone from speaking is more effective than just shouting someone down. For instance, when former House Speaker Nancy Pelosi held a rare town hall meeting in San Francisco in 2006, during the height of the wars in Iraq and Afghanistan, Code Pink demonstrators, angry that Pelosi was not pushing for a cut-off in war funding, waited until the question and answer session, then surrounded the stage with their "Stop Funding War" banners and stood there, silently, for the remainder of the meeting. The disruption was silent, but the message was loud and clear.

In a similar way, the creative use of a sign or banner can help a protest group avoid the accusation that they are attacking free speech because in effect they are simply adding an additional "layer" of speech, rather than denying anyone their right to speak. Protest songs can also be used in this way.

Theatre is another way to "disrupt without disrupting". For instance, when Jeane Kirkpatrick (Reagan's Ambassador to the UN) came to Berkeley in the 1980s, activists staged a mock death-squad kidnapping. "Soldiers" (students) in irregular fatigues marched down the main aisle of the hall where she was speaking, barking orders in Spanish and dragged off a few students (actors) kicking and screaming from the audience. Others then scattered leaflets detailing the U.S.'s and Kirkpatrick's support for El Salvador's death-squad government from the balcony onto the stunned audience.

Another interesting and illuminating interjection took place in early 2015, when a group of several protesters from the anti-war group Code Pink entered a US Senate Armed Services Committee meeting, waving signs and a pair of handcuffs and chanting: "Arrest Henry Kissinger for war crimes." The upheaval came during a committee hearing that also featured testimony from the former Secretaries of State Madeleine Albright and George P. Shultz, who were sitting at the witness table with Kissinger. As officers escorted the protesters out of the hearing room, John McCain, (the unsuccessful 2008 Republican presidential candidate and Vietnam veteran) growled: "Get out of here, you lowlife scum!" The protesters didn't succeed in arresting Kissinger, but many in the public and press found McCain's reaction to the protesters very illuminating and the disruption reminded many of the crimes against humanity committed by Kissinger during his bloody career.

Considerations and risks: In some jurisdictions, creating an obstacle to delay or disrupt a public servant may be construed as a criminal offence. Certainly in China, at the time of the Tiananmen Square protests, such behaviour was tantamount to suicide. In more liberal regimes, such "interjections" may be considered to be less serious offences, but may still be prosecuted as misdemeanours. Disrupting a public event may give rise to violent ejection and this may then be construed as heavy-handed authoritarian behaviour and used by the protesters to further justify their demands.

Historical and contemporary examples: One notable example of an intervention occurred during the demonstrations in Tiananmen Square in 1989. The response of the Chinese government to the demonstrations was to send tanks and armed soldiers to attack the demonstrators, resulting in an appalling massacre. In one act of extreme bravery, on June 5, 1989, a single protester stood in front of a column of tanks and they came to a standstill. This occurred on the morning after the Chinese military had effectively violently suppressed the Tiananmen Square protests. The protester became known as the Tank Man or Unknown Protester. The tanks manoeuvred to pass by the man, but he moved to continue to obstruct them. The incident was filmed and seen worldwide, despite China's attempts to suppress news of the Tiananmen massacre to the outside world. The incident of the solitary protester and the tanks has since become symbolic of the power of civil protest against the forces of a totalitarian state. For example, in April 1998, Time magazine included the "Unknown Rebel" in a feature titled "Time 100: The Most Important People of the Century".

8.6.2.6 Nonviolent Obstruction (Blockade): Nonviolent obstruction is a more extreme form of nonviolent interjection, where the objective of the protest is to actually physically obstruct one or more persons from passage. This might be the blockading of a building by large numbers of protesters, making entry to the building impossible. It may also involve the use of physical barricades, to make the movement of vehicles impossible. Barricades using fire are also used in some cases because they may deter even armoured vehicles from passing. Reinforced concrete barricades may prevent even tanks from entry to an area. At sea, obstructions can be created using fishing boats or other commercial vessels, or even placing lines of floating cable in the sea, which can make passage for other boats difficult or impossible. Other methods of blockade use vehicles or protesters chained together.

Blockades may serve one of three purposes:

- To shut something down, a coal mine, for instance.
- To protect something, for example a threatened forest or someone's home.

- To make a symbolic statement, such as surrounding a government building.

Considerations and risks: One of the great risks of a blockade action is if the action is being ignored by the authorities. This undermines the value of a blockade because the action fails to create a dialogue in which the protest demands can be stated and discussed. For this reason, blockades have to be quite aggressive and disruptive to be effective and this makes them a dangerous form of protest.

Symbolic blockades may involve the use of human beings rather than materials to create an obstruction. However, creating a physical obstruction inevitably means the construction of some form of physical barricade. In either case, manning any form of physical or symbolic barricade is one of the most risky of protest actions. People who man the barricades are literally in the front line against police or military brutality and, apart from physical violence, they also risk legal and moral denunciation. They may have to be equipped in preparation for being attacked with everything from water canon, tear-gas, rubber bullets to even live ammunition. For these reasons it is vital to ensure that whoever mans the front line barricades is well-trained and properly equipped and supported.

Organisers of such obstructions need to ensure that they can replenish these front line protesters with fresh personnel and that they can quickly relieve their lines, perhaps after a physical assault by police or military, and provide transport and medical attention to those that need it.

Other considerations that help to make a successful blockade are the following [Note 101]:

• **Good local information:** Before creating an obstruction, a protest group needs to have good local knowledge of the geography of the area. The obvious points of interest are the so-called "choke points". These are points where a target cannot walk, or drive around in order to pass.

• **Plan B:** Many demonstrations fail to impress because the organisers have neglected to make contingency plans if their blockade is broken. A well-planned blockade must have a plan B, where the protesters will redeploy to an alternative position to continue the protest if the original site is overrun by the authorities. The blockades should be quietly rehearsed by the key organisers in advance of the protest.

• **Plan for the aftermath:** The blockade itself is only a part of a protest. A lot of work will need to be carried out after a protest obstruction. There may be legal and political issues; there will certainly be press to manage, and a good protest organisation should have a well-prepared press strategy to explain the reasons for the blockade.

• **Knowing the limits:** The organisers of a protest obstruction need to understand their limits. Trying to hold on to a blockade at all costs is a foolish waste of energy. If a protest is being violently assaulted by an authority's police or other forces, then it is wise to abandon the blockade at a certain moment and re-form the demonstration somewhere else or on another occasion. A policy of "He who fights and runs away, lives to fight another day" is much more potent because it grinds down the authorities, wastes their resources and generates pro-protest sympathies. Also, it isn't a good strategy to exhaust the goodwill and spirit of a protest group in a single protest action and therefore organisers need to consider in advance at what point they should retrench.

Blockades can be dangerous actions and it is important to know when and how to withdraw a blockade. The golden rule is that if a blockade is to be abandoned, then everyone should abandon it. Someone leaving a railway line blockade may give a train driver the impression that the blockade is breaking up and that he should just keep driving. Such misunderstandings may be fatal.

• **Document everything:** Ensure that all preparations, the demonstration itself and the aftermath, are properly filmed and documented (times, places, people), so that the event can be publicised on the internet and elsewhere, and also in case there are legal complications. Any acts of unreasonable force by the authorities should be carefully filmed and chronologised.

• **Countermeasures to crowd control:** Make sure that all the latest countermeasures for crowd control weapons, such as tear gas, etc. are in place. For instance, one of the best and simplest preventions against tear gas is to use a few "scoop" squads with good gas masks and containers of water. When tear gas canisters arrive, send out the scoop squads to drop the canisters in the drums of water. This extinguishes their heater fuses and stops the tear gas being emitted. The best countermeasures for water cannon are to relocate. These are dangerous machines, but they are large and slow moving, so most protesters simply move their protest. Taser-proof clothing has also (almost) arrived and simple items of clothing, such as shirts that are impermeable to tasers are starting to be sold on the market. In the meantime, avoid such close contact with taser-equipped police. Ensure that front line demonstrators have the correct clothing, head protection and gas masks and some means of withstanding rubber bullet assaults. Look at the way the police are equipped to get an understanding of what the front line demonstrators will need.

Eviction blockade: A hybrid type of blockade is the eviction blockade. This is a strong show of physical resistance to an unjust eviction and is designed to force a moral confrontation (the right to housing) with a system that operates amorally (the banks or landlords).

Whilst eviction blockades don't always work, the negative publicity of breaking a community-supported eviction blockade tends to make local governments and banks more reticent to repeat violent evictions in the future. Effective eviction blockades create a dilemma for banks and local governments. If they call off the eviction, the family stays and the anti-eviction movement grows. If they go ahead with the eviction and break the blockade, they dramatically highlight fundamental injustices in the system, raise awareness of the movement and trigger consumer backlash against the financial institution involved. Governments try to absolve banks of the consumer backlash by creating so-called "toxic banks" to do the dirty work of eviction. These are banks where bad debts are concentrated and which do not operate in the retail banking arena, except to collect debts and evict debt defaulters.

Historical and contemporary examples: Eviction blockades are as old as evictions themselves, and, like evictions, they tend to surge in numbers in times of economic hardship. In the Great Depression in the USA, eviction blockades managed to help 77,000 families to keep their homes.

Modern examples of nonviolent obstruction are the eviction blockades used by the Spanish anti-eviction movement, known as the PAH. They operate in local cells, working with residents struggling to pay their mortgages. In the case of residents about to be evicted, the group organises demonstrations and blockades of homes to physically stop bank agents and police enforcing an eviction. In the 4 years up to October 2014 the group has stopped over 1100 evictions from being executed.

An interesting example of an eviction blockade took place in England, between mid 2014 and early 2015, when an elderly man, suffering from cancer, was to be evicted from his family home as a result of an administrative dispute with a now defunct British bank regarding disputed mortgage arrears. The amount involved was rather small, but nonetheless, the new owners of the bank decided to press the case and evict the man and his wife. After a YouTube appeal, a crowd of 300 strangers arrived to confront the bailiffs attempting to evict the couple from their home of 27 years. The bailiffs retreated. Six months later a second attempt to evict the man and his wife was met with a crowd of 500 strangers, blockading his house. The bailiffs were forced to abandon their plans to evict the homeowner, much to the satisfaction of the large crowd. The trigger for the support was a simple YouTube video which the man had made to try to explain his situation. It was clearly enough to muster a sizeable level of physical support to see off the bank's agents and bailiffs [Note 102].

A completely new type of blockade protest has recently developed in California, to block Google employees from commuting to their campus in Mountain View. Bay Area, and Oakland residents are angry that well-healed Google employees are pushing up their living costs. These well-paid new-comers, bussed to and from Google's offices, are altering the traditional left-wing and black artisan areas. Violent incidents against Google buses have already occurred and Google has responded by laying-on its own ferries for employees to cross the bay to get to work. It is unlikely that the local population of the area can withstand the gentrification that is taking place because of the presence of Google and other high tech corporations, but the effect of blind corporate wealth on this relatively poor area is proving to be divisive, and more blockades and social resistance seem inevitable [Note 103].

A maritime blockade protest took place in Spain in December 2014, when a protest by Spanish inshore fishermen, who have been refused access to their traditional fishing grounds by the Gibraltar government, used their vessels to disrupt the annual sea swimming competition by Gibraltar citizens in the disputed waters. The minor spat demonstrated that the loss of the fishing grounds would have repercussions on ordinary citizens [Note 104].

8.6.2.7 Nonviolent Occupation: This is an action where a group of protesters take and hold a public or private space in order to pressure a target authority. The occupation is often used to defend against a "development", to reclaim or squat on some property, or to assert sovereignty over the land (as in the case of indigenous people claiming their own land). Occupations are a popular tactic employed by social protest movements around the world, usually in conjunction with other actions, such as blockades, sit-ins, etc.

Large-scale occupations bring a level of solidarity that other protest actions may not be able to muster because they bring like-minded protesters together. They create a communal sense of purpose and they are good for protest moral. They also send a strong signal to the authorities that a peaceful protest has muscle and needs to be respected. We all know quite well that a large-scale occupation can rapidly turn from a good-natured, jovial, song-singing social event into a virulent, uncontrollably violent and destructive mob that no amount of police or military can contain. Any authority that doesn't believe this should revisit the documentary footage of armoured vehicles being thrown into the river Nile by hundreds of angry protesters being shot at with live ammunition [Note 134]. Hell hath no fury like an angry mob united.

The logic behind an occupation is that people reclaim buildings or space that they believe they are entitled to, thus highlighting the "theft" by the target authority. Most importantly, occupations undermine the target's position of authority because an occupation demonstrates that the authority is incapable of withstanding the force of citizen protest and is incapable of enforcing the status quo.

So, for instance, students may take over a university building, as happened in the US in the late 1960s, when African-American students occupied university buildings across the country. This led to the creation of many African-American studies departments. Similarly, workers may occupy a factory in which they work and environmentalists may defend land that they believe should be held in common and protected.

Occupations can also expose the arbitrary, unjust nature of private property, as in the case of homeless people squatting in empty offices owned by property speculators. These days, groups like La Via Campesina and the Landless Workers Movement (MST) actively help communities of peasants to occupy unused private land and reclaim it for their own common use.

In the environmental movement, tree-sits are an example of occupation techniques being used to defend forests from logging or developments, such as road-building projects. In the USA, groups like "Take Back the Land" apply this same principle to protest and stop foreclosures, defending housing as a human right by occupying threatened dwellings en masse. All across Europe, squatters movements have "taken back" speculatively abandoned buildings and turned them into homes and social centres again.

Occupations are also often used by indigenous groups to assert their hereditary rights to a piece of land. For instance, the occupation of Alcatraz Island in 1969, by "Indians of All Tribes" and the sixteen-month occupation by other Native Americans to defend the Minnehaha State Park from highway construction (which, they considered, would desecrate sacred land) in 1998, were just two such occupations of land by indigenous people. There have been many more.

Considerations and risks: Occupations are difficult to sustain indefinitely. Organisers need to have a plan which contains an exit strategy. Historically, occupations have tended to be spontaneous, but the long-lasting ones tend to be those that are well-planned.

The location chosen for an occupation site often determines its success. A number of considerations may affect the decision, such as the symbolic significance of an occupation site, the ability to disrupt the target authority, the capacity to publicise the occupation effectively in that location, the logistical difficulties of maintaining the action, public visibility and legal issues of ownership.

Occupations have a wide range of styles and formats, but all organisers focus on two important points:

- The logistics of maintaining a semi-permanent encampment, sit-in or rally, which requires food, shelter, defence from police raids, etc.

- The maintenance of a public pressure campaign that seeks to create a dilemma for the target authority. For example, the authority will be condemned if it clears the occupation, and condemned if it doesn't.

Another important consideration in deciding where to site an occupation is the objective of the occupation itself. In the case of a factory occupation, the idea may be to interrupt (or restart) production, so, clearly, the factory itself is the ideal location. In other cases, a park or other neutral space may be selected as a meeting place for a larger protest. This was the case in the large-scale protests in 2013-2014 in Taksim Gezi Park in Istanbul, Turkey. The park became a city centre rallying point for huge protests (ostensibly about protecting green spaces in the capital), which rapidly turned into wider discontent about the state of the country's secular traditions, democracy and the attitude of the president himself. In the USA, the Occupy Wall Street movement chose Zuccotti Park, close to Wall Street, from which to launch their tirades against the ills of unbridled capitalism. It was convenient to get to, spacious and close to the real target of the protest.

Historical and contemporary examples: Occupation as a protest method has a long history. The first recorded protest occupation was more than 3000 years ago, when ancient Egyptian tomb builders repeatedly occupied temples because King Ramses III failed to provide the workers with adequate provisions. In seventeenth-century England, the "Diggers" formed their agrarian community on common land which they squatted. Workers, soldiers and citizens established the Paris Commune in 1871 by squatting.

Today, and in recent years, we have seen widespread anti-capitalist occupations taking place, such as the occupation of the square in front of

St Paul's cathedral in London, the on-going Occupy movement's protests throughout the world, the colossal occupation of Cairo's Tahrir square and literally scores of similar examples of powerful large-scale occupations. The use of the technique seems to be growing in popularity.

8.6.2.8 Nonviolent Search and Seizure: The tactic of nonviolent search and seizure is based on the idea that any information that impacts on the general public, but is being hidden from them, should be "liberated". It is a form of protest intervention that involves showing up with a "citizens' search warrant" and attempting, nonviolently, to liberate the documents in question. In practice, the "liberation" of the documents may well be achieved by hacking into computer systems or theft of government or corporate databases.

Considerations and risks: Even though this tactic is unlikely to succeed immediately, the ensuing controversy (and possible arrests) can, nonetheless, eventually bring the secret documents to the public's attention. In several high-profile cases, the successful application of the tactic has created enough outcries for the target authority to be forced to make the documents public.

Historical and contemporary examples: Probably the most important modern cases of nonviolent search and seizure involved the Wikileaks revelations [Note 105] and the huge NSA leaks of Edward Snowden [Note 106]. Both WikiLeaks and Snowden found themselves in contact with highly privileged secret information that was definitely off-limits to citizens and yet directly concerned the public. WikiLeaks and Snowden took on the task to make this information completely public.

Apart from high profile cases, such as Wikileaks, the technique of "liberating" information is frequently used to expose all kinds of corporate and government malevolence. In modern times, there exist various legal routes by which information can be forced into the public domain. For example, requests under "Freedom of Information" legislation can be useful in obtaining and publishing information which would otherwise never be made public. And apart from these legal routes by which data can be liberated, there are always possibilities that information can be leaked by sympathetic officials.

Recently, some members of the press have engaged themselves in photographing documents in the hands of government officials and digitally enhancing them to deduce and publish their contents. The use of such cloak and dagger techniques is not the exclusive domain of government secret agents!

Other cases of search and seizure of incriminating documents have occurred with the names and details of clients being obscured such as Swiss (and other) bank account information copied and revealed to the press and tax authorities by bank employees protesting at tax evasion.

8.6.3 Social Intervention

Social intervention is the use of social actions to attract attention to the demands of a protest and to pressurise an authority to accept the protest campaign demands. The interventions centre on social activism rather than on any direct physical actions and are frequently focused on alternative social organisations, art, theatre, social gatherings, collective discussions and informal networks.

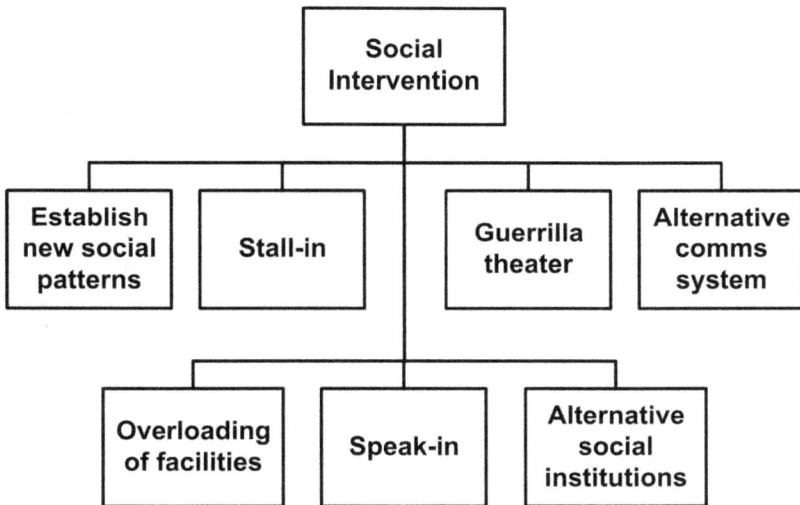

```
                    ┌──────────────┐
                    │    Social    │
                    │ Intervention │
                    └──────────────┘
```

Establish new social patterns | Stall-in | Guerrilla theater | Alternative comms system

Overloading of facilities | Speak-in | Alternative social institutions

8.6.3.1 Establishing New Social Patterns: This is also sometimes referred to as "prefigurative intervention", which is a way of demonstrating that there are better alternatives to the current system. Establishing alternative social patterns provide ways in which protest groups can make their protest demands and take real practical action at the same time.

It has long been common practice for a protest movement to establish alternative communities as part of the protest. For example, these may take the forms of temporary communes, squatter communities, protest camps, alternative food distribution, new forms of democratic "street" assemblies and all kinds of alternative social and sexual patterns of behaviour.

The establishment of new social patterns such as these has a powerful double effect. As part of an active protest or act of civil disobedience, the manifestation of alternative social orders provides a tangible demonstration to the members of a protest group and the public that alternatives to the status quo really do exist and that they can be successfully implemented. In addition, the practise of such alternative social patterns proves to the target authority that the demonstration is serious, practical, thought out and organised. Very often it makes the authority realise that they are at risk of being side-tracked into irrelevance by a group of demonstrators and their alternative systems.

Considerations and risks: There are sometimes legal risks in engaging in certain alternative social patterns of behaviour. Property laws in some countries forbid certain types of land occupation, for example. Public assemblies may be banned or need a license, and the use of public land and buildings may be restricted by governments to provide them with an excuse to use police or military force on a protest group. Good planning, the use of rapid "pop-up" actions and the employment of various means of distraction can circumvent even the best organised police or military controls.

Historical and contemporary examples: There have been (and there still are) many examples of alternative social patterns forming part of a protest movement. The Diggers of 17th century England formed whole agrarian communities on common land, employing a system of collaborative common labour to tend their crops and build their shelters. The blossoming of the 1960s counter-cultures of "flower-power", anti-war, free love and the hippie movement brought a whole period of unique social experimentation to post-war middle-class youth, along with an explosion in communal living, squatting, drug use and overt questioning of authority. By the time of the Paris student uprising of 1968, the use of counter-culture social alternatives was well established as part of the process of protest, with the Paris barricades and student-occupied parts of the city being run along communal, strongly anti-capitalist lines.

So potent was this period of post-war enlightenment that it still exerts a huge influence on protests to this day. The counter-culture alternatives established in this period continue to form a backdrop to more modern protests. The Occupy movement, 15M movement and many other Western protest groups that are in full swing in 2015 still apply the strongly democratic, all-inclusive and strongly communal approach to their protests and decision-making that were the hallmark of the 1960s social revolution. The availability of mobile internet technology has undoubtedly strengthened the sense of a communal network taking action together.

8.6.3.2 Overloading of Facilities (aka Paralysing): One method of social protest consists of the deliberate overload of social facilities. This involves the deliberate increase of demand for services far beyond the capacity of a department, business, or other institution to provide these services.

Overloading may be a short or long-term objective of a protest for various reasons. One obvious reason to apply this method is when a protest group wishes to demonstrate the inadequacy of a target authority, by demonstrating how easily its facilities can be overwhelmed.

Another reason to use this technique is when a protest group wishes to temporarily disable an authority's facilities. For example, a group may wish to make sure there is no police available in a certain area. They may do this by creating disturbances in other areas, to act as a distraction. This is rapidly becoming a popular technique in modern urban demonstrations because the distracting demonstrators have complete flexibility to form demonstrations and disappear again without any need to remain in place. It is also useful because only a small number of organisers need to know the real agenda, and this preserves the secrecy of the planning. The distracting protesters need know nothing of the real agenda, except what they need to know to maintain the distraction without being arrested. Police forces can also be overloaded by receiving a large number of hoax calls to emergencies which don't exist. The process of making hoax calls can even be automated to deliberately jam switch boards.

Other forms of facility overload concern systems such as state internet services, telephone exchanges, postal rooms, transport systems, roads and other infrastructure. In some cases it may be necessary to create infrastructure overloads in order to delay or block responses to a protest by the authorities.

Considerations and risks: Generally, it's difficult to prove that someone is wilfully overloading the facilities of an authority, providing that their use of the facilities is legal. An authority may suspect an overload attempt, but they probably cannot prove or avoid it. In some regimes, this suspicion may be enough for draconian methods to be employed to stop the abuse of the facilities, but in most cases there is little that can be done to combat a well-planned and executed facility overload.

Historical and contemporary examples: Modern methods of facility overload include the overload of technological facilities, such as email servers. During the NATO intervention in Kosovo, in 1999, activists objecting to the NATO involvement "email-bombed" NATO email addresses. In a similar way, in 1998, a part of the Tamil Tigers guerrilla group email-bombed Sri Lankan embassies around the world.

In a less technological vein, in 2009, anti-Obama protesters forced the closure of the switchboard of the University of Notre Dame, in protest at Obama being invited to the opening of the university. Huge numbers of protest calls meant that the switchboard was overwhelmed and the operators decided to close it down.

8.6.3.3 Stall-In: This is a form of protest action which deliberately attempts to cause an infrastructural failure, usually on an important access route. Often the participants operate in loosely connected groups, to avoid being detected by the authorities. They make their way in vehicles to pre-determined points and then simply stop or deliberately run out of fuel, in order to create large traffic jams and to cause inconvenience and embarrassment to the public authority, or to block access to police or military vehicles.

Considerations and risks: Deliberately causing a failure in a piece of public infrastructure is designed to attract public attention to an important issue or to assist in a larger protest by blocking access to infrastructure by the authorities. However, such acts may also attract public anger towards the organisers. The general public can be remarkably self-centred and often don't take kindly to being inconvenienced, whatever the ethical motivation for the action. This effect needs to be balanced against the need to bring the issue into the public domain, or the absolute need to jam up the infrastructure.

Sometimes, even a threat of such an action may be enough to have the desired effect, as we shall see in the example below.

Historical and contemporary examples: Louis E. Lomax first raised the notion of a World's Fair "stall-in" back in July 1963, during a speech at Queens College, New York. He called for 500 drivers to make their way to the fair in their cars and, by running out of fuel or simply stopping on the way there, create a traffic jam of historical proportions. This action was planned as part of the larger civil rights movement in the USA and was designed to interrupt access to the opening of the World's Fair.

Such was the backlash by the city authorities and the threat against protesters planning to participate in the action, that on the appointed day the area around the World's Fair was swarming with police and tow trucks, whilst police helicopters circled overhead. Protesters were publicly threatened with confiscation of their cars and the cancellation of their licence and insurance if they "stalled". In reality, the protesters secretly decided to cancel the protest and the huge police presence was confounded by having nothing to do. Not only did the protesters not show up, neither did most of the visitors to the World's Fair centre. Of the expected 250,000 attendees, only about 60,000 visitors turned out. In this respect, the demonstrators won a powerful protest victory, without a single act of disobedience [Note 107].

8.6.3.4 Speak-In (aka Heckling): This method involves a deliberate verbal interruption of a meeting, an interview, religious service or other gathering by activists wishing to express their protest message. Normally, the method remains a nonviolent intervention. Heckling is an ancient form of a "speak-in", during which a politician is continuously interrupted and verbally attacked by opponents wishing to impair his ability to deliver a message, to undermine his message or to silence him or her. It is not confined to informal political meetings and indeed, is normal practice in some of the world's longest established parliaments.

An important characteristic of "good quality" heckling is that it should be both focused and entertaining; ideally, it should be funny. Humorous heckling is much more effective that just hurling abuse. The heckler gets the sympathy of the audience and makes the target look silly. Good heckling is death by a thousand cuts, whereas shouting someone down is more akin to an attempt at crude assassination.

Considerations and risks: Deliberately interrupting the speech of another may be perceived as undemocratic and bullying, in some cases. However, there are ways of interjecting someone's speech, which are both light-hearted and devastatingly damaging to the credibility and message of the target. A really effective heckler needs to prepare his timing and interventions. For this it may be a good idea to get a press copy of a speech in advance, so as to work out appropriate and cutting heckles.

Historical and contemporary examples: There are an enormous number of examples of such protest actions everywhere in the world, ranking from clever and witty comments to large-scale interventions. For instance, in 2006, at the Royal College of Nursing conference, the British Health Secretary Patricia Hewitt was subjected to 50 minutes of catcalls, slow handclaps and derisive laughter, before being forced to abandon her speech to the union because delegates resisted all pleas to hear her out, in protest against government health policies [Note 108].

But, long before modern interventions like this, the politically vocal and radical flax workers of Dundee (their day job was "heckling" the flax fibres) refined the art of embarrassing politicians in the 19th century. Heckling can cut both ways. When the great 18th-century troublemaker John Wilkes was heckled by a man who cried: "Vote for you? I'd sooner vote for the Devil", Wilkes replied: "And what if your friend is not standing?" This latter is an example of good quality counter-heckling, as distinct from simply making a lot of noise, although shouting down an authority figure may be the only way to demonstrate the depth of feeling to the watching public in some cases and may be largely spontaneous.

One famous and witty heckler is Denis Skinner, the British MP who has been expelled from the House of Commons on several occasions for his disrespectful attacks on the Conservative party and British establishment. During Prime Minister's Questions on 25th April 2012, regarding the resignation of the special advisor to the Conservative Culture Secretary, Skinner retorted; "When posh boys are in trouble they always sack the servants", to much jollity from the opposition benches and even a few smiles from some conservatives [Note 109].

8.6.3.5 Guerrilla Theatre: This technique involves the use of spontaneous (or apparently spontaneous) acts of street theatre in unexpected venues as a means of communicating protest messages to the public. Very often these acts of theatre are short and shocking and often involve unsuspecting members of the public or sometimes actors, pretending to be members of the public.

In the early 1990s, Serbia became a centre for street guerrilla theatre (although it wasn't called that), as other forms of anti-war and anti-government protest were suppressed by the Milosevic regime. Indeed, for many, these street manifestations were the only form of political expression that was possible in that increasingly totalitarian, militaristic environment. It was in just such an atmosphere that another manifestation of the "Women in Black" protest became established [Note 110].

The theatre may include satirical sketches, comedy, music and audience interaction. The objective is to persuade the audience into considering the issue at hand and perhaps taking some personal action. Some acts of guerrilla theatre are deliberately designed to disrupt official events. In modern times, some theatre groups have started to specialise in this form of ad-hoc, surprise theatre. Any protest group considering this kind of intervention should probably make contact with one of these specialist theatre troupes.

Invisible theatre: This is a hybrid form of protest theatre that seeks to deliver important messages to onlookers, whilst the onlookers remain unaware that they are seeing a theatrical event. The types of issues addressed by invisible theatre include topics that people are often "too polite" to bring up, such as poverty, racism or homophobia.

Whilst invisible theatre seeks never to be recognized as theatre, it is performed in a public place. The goal is to make the intervention as realistic as possible, so that it provokes spontaneous responses from the public. The scene must be loud enough to be heard and noticed by people, but not so loud or conspicuous that it appears staged. Bystanders can and will engage with the scene as if it were real life, because for them it is real life. Invisible theatre can thus achieve things that most other theatre cannot, removing barriers between performer and spectator and creating very real situations, in which people can be obliged to rethink their assumptions and engage with sensitive issues they might otherwise avoid.

Invisible theatre might, for example, create a scene where a person from a racial minority seems to be suffering abuse in the street. Although all participants are actors staging the scene, the public don't know this and some members of the public will attempt to intervene, perhaps physically. Such a scenario could obviously become dangerous. Thus, invisible theatre carries with it significant ethical and safety considerations, which should be explored carefully before action is taken. Actors should rehearse a range of observer reactions, including aggression and abuse, and should be prepared for this. Having an escape plan or distress signal, and discussing ahead of time if or when to break character, is also advisable. Onlookers could also be pre-warned by the theatre group of an "unusual encounter", but not too prepared or else the technique has no value.

Image theatre: This is another form of theatre used in protests. It works by actors creating static imagery that conveys a protest message. For instance, a scene from Shell's oil spills in Nigeria may be depicted, to illustrate the impact on land and people. The theatre, once rehearsed, can be rapidly deployed outside buildings or be used to disrupt meetings (such as a Shell shareholder meeting).

Hoaxes: In the context of a protest, a hoax is designed to create a momentary illusion that exposes injustice through satirical exaggeration, or to demonstrate another reality to the one being pushed by an authority. Hoaxes are a form of theatre.

Hoaxes are also a way for activists to "buy" airtime that they can't afford. Instead of complaining that the press is set up to give voice to the interests of the powerful, the hoax puts the press bias to work on behalf of the protesters. Thus, by pretending to be a member of a powerful elite (politician or official) but telling a more interesting story, an activist can "commandeer the soapbox" and attract the press. When a hoax is revealed (usually within minutes or hours) an activist can then explain the reasons for the hoax to the public, taking advantage, of course, of any journalists present. It is generally best to reveal a hoax promptly. The ultimate goal is to spread more truth to more people, rather than perpetuating the hoax as long as possible.

In late 2014, during a period of anti-Islamic sentiment in Britain, a story appeared in the right-wing Daily Mail newspaper, which was headlined "Who is Britain's white jihadi youth?" The paper showed a photograph posted on Twitter of a white, Northern European teenager, allegedly by the name of "Jonathan Edwards", sitting between two armed jihadi fighters in front of an Isis flag, clasping a rifle. Shortly after this Daily Mail "exclusive", the Twitter scam was exposed as a hoax by its authors, much to its readers' disappointment and later derision of the newspaper by all concerned, including an anti-terrorist expert who had already warned that the photo was a complete fake. The hoax showed up the Daily Mail and its readers for what they really are - gullible, fairly ignorant xenophobes.

An even more audacious hoax targeted the British Prime Minister and the headquarters of the British Intelligence service, GCHQ, when a telephone caller to GCHQ managed to obtain the telephone number of the director of GCHQ. In an apparently separate incident, a caller rang David Cameron and pretended to be that same director of GCHQ and had a short conversation with the PM. Although the conversation was apparently cut short, it is understood that it represented a serious breach of security. No-one has been apprehended for the hoax calls, but Britain's intelligence services and the British Prime Minister's office suffered some embarrassment about how simply they had been infiltrated, despite their continuous diatribes about national security and the "war on terror".

Considerations and risks: Well-executed theatre is both entertaining and thought-provoking and causes little inconvenience to the public. It is therefore a generally harmless way of attracting public attention to an issue. Acts of guerrilla theatre are frequently filmed for distribution via various internet channels such as YouTube.

In terms of hoaxes, some parts of society don't appreciate the irony or reasoning behind a hoax. If these are the target audience, this method may not always be appropriate.

Historical and contemporary examples: The concept of guerrilla theatre has been around since at least 1965, when it was employed in San Francisco and its messages were targeted at capitalism and the Vietnam War.

Some less liberal authorities may object to it and arrest the participants, as they did with Pussy Riot in Russia, when the Russian Orthodox Church complained about their spontaneous street performances or as in the

Vatican in 2014, when a semi-clad protester pretended to steal the baby Jesus from the Vatican crib in St. Peter's Square [Note 111]. In the latter case, despite the fact that the action was a feminist protest action and pure theatre, the Vatican authorities locked up the woman involved and planned to try here. Obviously, not everyone has a sense of humour.

8.6.3.6 Alternative Social Institutions: The creation and use of alternative social institutions can propel a protest into a movement for direct intervention by providing alternative institutions to those of the target authority. This demonstrates the practicality of an alternative social order to that of the current authority and it provides a space for activists to take direct action to further their cause in a practical way.

Alternative social institutions can be created for literally any form or size of institution. They may be something as apparently insignificant as a local alternative system of food distribution to something as profound as an international alternative to a world religion. Indeed, the Reformation was a process which ultimately created a huge new alternative social institution - the reformed / Protestant Christian Church. At a more modest level, the entire cooperative movement was an attempt at creating a raft of alternative social and economic institutions to replace selfish money-grubbing capitalism.

In between these examples there are many opportunities for the creation of alternative social institutions. Here are some areas where alternative social institutions are often created as part of an alternative social vision: childcare, primary and secondary education, food production and distribution, land ownership, care for the aged, the organisation of medical care, energy production and distribution, house building, transportation, social security, raising group taxes and work sharing.

Considerations and risks: In most Western countries many centre or right-wing governments actually encourage private groups to partially "exit the system", but they draw the line when these groups wish to manage social responsibilities, such as law and order, health, education, raising taxes and social security. Clearly, authorities are happy to free themselves of certain costs, but they are unwilling to relinquish tax income or control of their populations. These limitations may bring conflicts between protesters and their alternative institutions and the forces of the state. Parents wishing to educate their own children may well find that this is illegal, and the state may ultimately seize children, who do not attend state-regulated schools, from their parents. The same goes for citizens operating their own security (police) services or private judiciary. This would certainly be considered illegal in most jurisdictions.

Historical and contemporary examples: Because of its particular constitutional make-up, the USA has a long history of left and right-wing libertarian protests producing all kinds of alternative social institutions, not all of them successful or progressive.

One old and traditional alternative social institution is the Amish community, which arrived in Pennsylvania in 1693. To this day, this large group of Swiss-German origin operates a largely separate state within a state, running its own schools, controlling its own lands and placing emphasis on hard work, family, their community and its rules. The use of modern equipment, electricity, television and cars is shunned. The community is exempted from social security related taxes and morally objects to the idea of receiving social security payments. Whilst the Amish are by no means a radical protest group, their philosophy and way of life is external to mainstream US capitalism and they passionately defend their right to live "aside" from the modern consumerism that surrounds them.

More modern manifestations of alternative social institutions include the upsurge in food cooperatives in poorer parts of Western cities, which began after the social revolutions of the 1960s. Examples exist in cities throughout Europe and the USA. Food cooperatives operate primarily to provide food to poor local residents, but also to act as central meeting points, cafés, places where employment can be found, goods exchanged, and help, medical and legal advice procured. They often also double as crèches for young mothers and provide important local social hubs. They generally work much more effectively than government-run community centres by providing support for the community by the community itself.

8.6.3.7 Alternative Communication System: Very often, effective communications systems are the preserve of authority. They have the resources to operate their own exclusive, secure communications networks. In the past these were largely unavailable to the general public. However, the advent of internet technology has made the use of websites, email, social networks, blogs and chat systems ubiquitous in most countries of the world.

Recent revelations that governments have started to harvest data from users has caused some alarm amongst the internet public and, as a response, there have been a large number of developments to provide additional protection to public internet users to ensure that their communications remain private.

The obvious examples of these alternate communications technologies include the use of email encryption, the use of end-to-end chat encryption and anonymity and the introduction of systems such as TOR, which allow a user to obfuscate their identity via a network of peer servers, so that they may access and use a website without their own identity being revealed.

Apart from the high-tech alternative communications systems, simple low-tech methods of communication have demonstrated that authorities can be frustrated by the simplest of mechanisms, such as a person to person conversation in a noisy environment. Many protest organisations have now taken to using old-fashioned trusted couriers to move information within their network rather than using the internet or telecoms systems.

Considerations and risks: Not all technological solutions are as safe as others when it comes to building alternative communications networks. There is always a risk that a user at one end of a communication may save a message in an insecure way and thus expose an organisation's communications to scrutiny. Hence organisations need to design and implement very strict alternate systems, which should not always rely on the same technology. If technological solutions are being used, these should integrate the strongest levels of encryption, both for communications and for storage of data. They should also incorporate strong virus protection and methods of so-called "burn-box" disposal of data, whereby disks can be absolutely deleted, destroyed or encrypted at short notice. No decent activist organisation can take itself seriously, unless it has a properly informed and qualified information technologist as part of its executive to look after technology and security.

Historical and contemporary examples: Over the years there has been a wealth of inventive means used to communicate with other members of a protest group. In North Korea, all kinds of data (including the latest Western movies) are smuggled around the country, using tiny pen drives or the even more tiny micro-SD cards. The huge advances in storage technology mean that something smaller than one's finger nail may now store the equivalent of 32,000 paperback books. It is easy to conceal and easy to dispose of.

Sophisticated email and instant messaging encryption systems provide end-to-end (E2E) encryption. These systems do not allow a third party to be involved in the encryption process, nor have access to encryption keys. This provides excellent security between two communicating parties, without the participation of service providers, etc.

Social networks are rather unsophisticated methods of communication and are relatively open. However, for mass movements of information about deployments of police, for example, they may serve their purpose and, of course, they serve an important role in publicising a fast moving protest action to the general public and the world's press.

Many internet services are relatively easy for an authority to interrupt and indeed, in areas with many mobile users, the protesters may actually cause failures in the availability of a mobile network themselves, simply by weight of their own numbers.

During the 2014 demonstrations in Hong Kong, many protesters suspected that the authorities were trying to shut down some cell networks in the city, so they began chatting using an app that doesn't require a central network connection. In the first day of the demonstrations up to 100,000 people downloaded the FireChat app. This service allows users to talk anonymously in chat rooms with groups of people nearby, and the connection works on Android and Apple via a Bluetooth or wi-fi connection. While around 33,000 people in Hong Kong were using the app simultaneously, it does carry some security risks and, at the time of writing, the app publishing company is busy trying to publish an encrypted version of the software.

Meanwhile, safer alternative communications applications, such as Serval Mesh and Commotion, have already been refined to improve security. These latter apps help to create a "mesh network" rather than a server-centric network. Phones communicate directly with other phones, without making any contact with the network operators' servers. In this way, users build up their own communications network, completely independent of the internet.

8.6.4 Economic Intervention

Economic intervention is the use of economic pressure and subversive economic actions to attract public attention to the demands of a protest and to compel an authority to accept the protest campaign's demands. These interventions centre on economic activism, aimed at undermining the property ownership and the economic activities of a target authority.

The main purpose of economic intervention is to undermine the economic probity and stability of an authority. This includes challenging and damaging the capital base and income of an authority.

Sometimes economic intervention includes demonstrating the possibility of alternative economic systems. In this case, economic intervention is not simply a protest action, but also a demonstration that there are viable alternative economic systems and that the status quo is often unfit for purpose, contrary to public interest and inefficient.

There are several types of economic interventions:

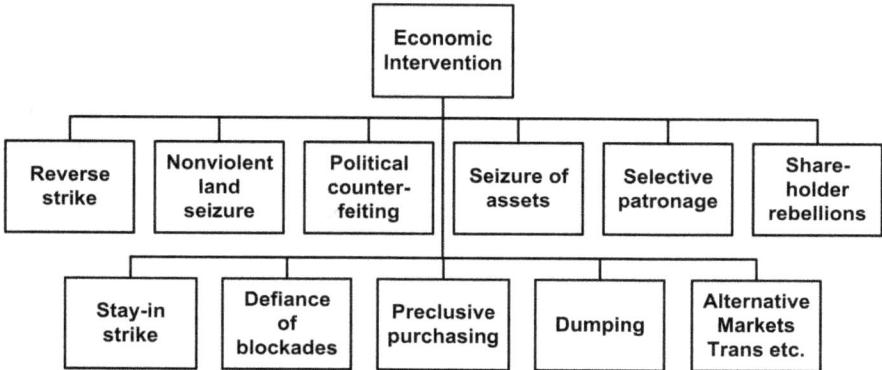

```
                          ┌──────────────┐
                          │   Economic   │
                          │ Intervention │
                          └──────────────┘
  ┌──────────┬───────────┬───────────┬───────────┬───────────┬───────────┐
┌────────┐ ┌──────────┐ ┌──────────┐ ┌─────────┐ ┌──────────┐ ┌──────────┐
│Reverse │ │Nonviolent│ │Political │ │Seizure  │ │Selective │ │Share-    │
│strike  │ │land      │ │counter-  │ │of       │ │patronage │ │holder    │
│        │ │seizure   │ │feiting   │ │assets   │ │          │ │rebellions│
└────────┘ └──────────┘ └──────────┘ └─────────┘ └──────────┘ └──────────┘
      ┌──────────┬───────────┬───────────┬───────────┐
   ┌────────┐ ┌──────────┐ ┌──────────┐ ┌─────────┐ ┌───────────┐
   │Stay-in │ │Defiance  │ │Preclusive│ │Dumping  │ │Alternative│
   │strike  │ │of        │ │purchasing│ │         │ │Markets    │
   │        │ │blockades │ │          │ │         │ │Trans etc. │
   └────────┘ └──────────┘ └──────────┘ └─────────┘ └───────────┘
```

8.6.4.1 Reverse Strike (Work-In): This is a rare form of economic intervention, where a group of workers refuses to stop working. In that sense, this form of action should not really be called a "strike".

One might wonder how this form of "intervention" exerts any form of pressure on a management. Well, consider a scenario where a company or government wishes to dismiss some employees because they argue that costs are too high or a department or company is making a loss. In such a case, employees may collectively decide to continue working on low (or no) wages simply to maintain the production or service until times improve.

There are several possible motivations for such an act of apparent altruism. Firstly, employees may not trust the reasoning of their employers and therefore use the "reverse strike" (work-in) as a means of removing the excuse of high costs or loss-making from the employer's argument. Secondly, employees may be protesting economic conditions that threaten their jobs, such as cheap imports, government cost cutting, the use of cheap labour, the export of jobs to low labour cost zones, etc. Finally, it may be that a group of workers have been vilified by their employers or another authority and they employ a "reverse strike" to publicly demonstrate their real will to work, their interest in their employer or the belief in the "common good". Occasionally, "reverse strikes" have been used during a factory closure by workers wishing to take control of their factory and working for nothing to maintain production long enough to negotiate a hand-over to a worker's cooperative.

A "reverse strike" differs from a "sit-in strike" or simple occupation because the strikers are intent on carrying out productive work rather than creating an obstruction or causing economic damage.

Considerations and risks: There are few risks associated with this kind of intervention, except that the participants may be working without payment, so this kind of action may have a limited lifespan. Generally, this form of intervention garners nothing but public sympathy and support. It would take a brave (unwise) employer to eject those willing to work for little or nothing, simply to save their jobs and sustain their employer's enterprise. Such gestures can trigger off strong emotions.

Historical and contemporary examples: Industrial history contains some notable examples of reverse strikes (work-ins). In the early 1970's, for example, the loss-making Upper Clyde Shipbuilders in the United Kingdom went into receivership, despite a full order book and forecasts for near-term profits. The Conservative government at the time refused to finance the short-term losses of the company and forced it into liquidation.

Rather than go on strike, which was the traditional form of industrial action, the union leadership decided to have a "work-in" and complete the orders that the shipyards had in place. In this way they dispelled the idea of the workers being 'work-shy' and also illustrated the long-term viability of the yards and the concept of the "right to work".

The work-in was led by a group of young shop stewards, all of whom were then members of the Communist Party of Great Britain. They wanted to ensure their members projected the best possible image of the yard workers, and insisted on tight discipline. The shipbuilders' tactics worked and public sympathy in the Glasgow area and beyond was soon firmly on the side of the workers.

In February 1972, the Conservative government relented and restructured the shipyards around two newly financed companies. This reverse strike is still perceived as an outstanding success because it engendered public support and removed the employers' and government's arguments about labour costs and workforce support for the company.

8.6.4.2 Stay-In Strike (aka Occupation): This is a strike action where a group of workers refuse to leave their workplace, but also (generally) refuse to work. A stay-in strike is designed for employees to take control of an authority's premises, their workplaces, and obstruct their employers from removing or replacing them. Sometimes, employees staging a stay-in strike may carry out basic maintenance and cleaning work to maintain a property, in order to avoid the accusation of trespass, economic sabotage or vandalism.

Stay-in strikes attract attention to a protest action, but, more importantly, they "jam-up" the employer's access to their property, their ability to use the property in a different way or hiring new employees. A "stay-in" strike effectively locks up capital by obstructing access to real estate.

Stay-in strikes are not limited to industrial workers. Students, professionals and even self-employed activists have protested using this form of action.

Considerations and risks: The laws of trespass vary widely. In some countries the case of an ex-employee occupying their old workplace may be construed as a criminal act, whereas in other jurisdictions such a protest may be tolerated as a legal act in a labour dispute.

Historical and contemporary examples: This is an old technique in the industrial world and there are many examples.

One notable and long-running example took place in 1973, when the workers at the Triumph Motorcycles factory at Meriden, West Midlands, UK, locked out the new owners following the announcement of their plan to close the factory.

The sit-in of the factory lasted over a year, until the British government intervened. The result was the formation of the Meriden Motorcycle Cooperative, which produced Triumphs until its closure ten years later in 1983.

8.6.4.3 Nonviolent Land Seizure: Control of land is a fundamental issue in human rights politics throughout the world and the seizure of land by peasants has been a constant theme for millennia in conflicts between hereditary land owners and the landless masses.

Thus, the seizure of land, or demands for various traditional land rights, rights of access, grazing, etc. is and always has been a hot subject. It is also a subject of dispute which often and very rapidly leads to violence.

Land seizure or the seizure of land rights (such as access) comes in many forms. In urban Western societies, protest groups may seize empty property in order to squat, or protest against homelessness or capitalist property speculation. Whilst the seizure of the properties may be entirely peaceful, the ejection of squatters is often fraught with physical violence, as the landlords exert their "rights" of possession.

At a less provocative level, urban activist groups have recently taken to quietly seizing unused "brown land" to create "community gardens", without the permission or knowledge of the landowners. When the owners want the land back, the temporary squatters simply relinquish the land without confrontation and move onto the next site. There seems to be a large stock of such brown land in most Western cities.

In other cases, conflicts arise over access to land. In the Western world there is a constant struggle between corporate or private landowners and the demands of landless citizens to have access to the countryside or other areas of cultural or natural heritage. Generally, these disputes and seizures centre on traditional "rights of way" across "private land" or access to common land and concepts such as the right to roam on private land.

More importantly, the struggle for land rights is most intense in those parts of the developing world that are targeted for agricultural or industrial development. These struggles often involve native populations fighting to hold onto their ancestral lands. Very often, these struggles involve corporate or private capitalist organisations, intent on dispossessing native people and "developing" their homelands, often for short-term gain. In these cases, the seizure of land by indigenous populations is often met with political and physical violence by its new "owners", often with the support of large multi-national corporations and the nodding acquiescence of Western governments or their clients. Conflicts between corporate interests and incumbent indigenous landowners are inevitable and frequently end in popular land seizures by the aggrieved locals.

Considerations and risks: Disputes based on ownership often become violent, and land ownership is probably the most contentious area of dispute. This is because land rights are so fundamental and such an emotive issue for many people. Therefore, seizing land, whilst still maintaining a nonviolent position, is a difficult proposition. In all likelihood, the party which is losing the land is going to react violently and, indeed, the laws which govern the ownership and title deeds to the land are often draconian and stacked in the favour of the perceived legal owner, against the landless claimant. Very often the real owner of the land (an indigenous group) has no formal title documents to that land.

In the case of land seizure by a protest group for the purpose of squatting, the owners of the land will certainly employ every trick (legal and otherwise) to regain possession of the property and this may well involve the use of physical violence against squatters.

Historical and contemporary examples: In many parts of Europe, up to the late Middle Ages, access to land depended largely upon a landless family's ability to farm it, under the "protection" of a feudal landlord. After some large economic catastrophes of the 14th century, land rights in Europe began to change, as landlords consolidated their property to maintain their control of the land. Almost immediately there were protest seizures of land by the landless and, indeed, the Peasant's Revolt of the late 14th century in England was an example of such a protest, which rapidly became a violent rebellion.

Despite the protest and land seizures by groups such as the Levellers and Diggers, by the 19th century there was little left of the vast tracts of common land which covered Europe just 300 years before. The Industrial Revolution completed the task of removing much of the peasantry from the land and driving them into the hovels and poverty of industrial cities in an act of "economic cleansing", which in some cases amounted to deliberate acts of genocide.

In modern times, the "land grabs" of the last centuries have continued and been completed. Sometimes these land grabs were driven by corporate greed for agricultural land or land for other primary industries, such as mining or commercial forestry. Sometimes they were (are) motivated by governments appropriating land for infrastructural projects to support such industries.

A recent and typical case of land seizure was by a dispossessed Amazonian tribe, in 2014. After years of waiting for the Brazilian government to sort out their land rights, some 13000 Munduruku Indians who live beside the Tapajós River in the heart of the Brazilian Amazon region, decided to take action. Besides temporarily occupying an office belonging to the Brazilian government's Indian agency, they started to demarcate the boundaries of their land. The Brazilian central government's preoccupation with hydroelectric power at the expense of Amazonian forest ecology and habitat is the primary reason for the tribe's current action to demarcate and "seize" their own land, in order to avoid it being flooded as part of yet another environmentally damaging hydroelectric scheme [Note 112].

8.6.4.4 Defiance of Blockades: A blockade is defined as an act or means of sealing off a place to prevent goods or people from entering or leaving. Blockades have long been used in military campaigns to force an enemy to surrender because of lack of food or supplies. In such cases a blockade is often referred to as a "siege". In non-military campaigns a blockade may selectively deny access to certain goods or people, to oblige an adversary to comply with a particular authority's wishes.

The defiance of a blockade is an effort by a protester or activist to make the blockade ineffective. It is usually a deliberate circumvention of a blockade to open up the movement of supplies of goods and access to blockaded populations or to demonstrate the inefficiency of the blockading authority.

Such blockade circumventions may be overt (such as airdrops of goods) or covert (such as smuggling). Blockades can also be made ineffective in other ways. For instance, if a blockaded population can demonstrate that the blockade is not having any detrimental effect on them, it ceases to be effective.

Considerations and risks: Blockades normally involve the use of some physical barriers and the threat of physical force. They also rely on the blockading authority's belief in their ability to prevail. Therefore, any strategy aimed at breaking a blockade will need to have to overcome one or all of these obstacles.

To secretly bypass a blockade requires a lot of ingenuity and a good understanding of how the blockade is maintained. Are there guards? If so, what are their routines? Are diversions useful and possible? Are there means of subverting the guards? Being caught in the act of smuggling may have serious legal consequences, since the smuggling may be construed as criminal, rather than politically motivated.

In an overt act of defying a blockade, activists must use either superior force or surprise to bypass the blockade. In this context "force" may also mean the power of public opinion. In this case, it is important that the activists make their plans and motives known very clearly and very publicly in advance, otherwise they run the risk of being branded as just more criminal smugglers.

Historical and contemporary examples: One allegorical tale of a siege being broken in a clever way took place during one of the Christian crusades to the Holy Lands. After a two year blockade of a large Arab walled city, the half-starved Christians surrounding the city were horrified when the Arabs holed up in the city began throwing food over the walls to them, in an apparent act of charity to the besieging Christians.

In despair, the Christian armies squabbled over the scraps of food, but then packed up and abandoned the siege, in disgust at being fed by those they were supposed to be besieging. What they didn't realise at the time was that the Arab occupiers inside the city walls were actually starving themselves and on the brink of surrender. The food supplies thrown over the wall to the invading Christian armies were in fact the last provisions left in the Arab city. A wise city governor, knowing the condition of the besieging Christian forces, correctly judged that the psychological effect on the Christians of receiving Arab charity would be so dispiriting that the Christians would leave the city and its people in desperation. He was right. This story illustrates the point that a blockade can be defied and broken, simply by making it appear not to be working.

A modern blockade which is often in the news is the blockade of the Gaza Strip by the Israeli military, which began in 2007. The Palestinians in Gaza have become adept at defying the blockade by digging smuggling tunnels into Egypt. Some tunnels have been constructed (apparently) to be large enough to allow the movement of large objects and many are equipped with electricity and communications equipment. Despite the constant attacks on their tunnels and their continuous destruction, the residents of Gaza continue to breach the blockade using such tunnels.

A more demonstrative attempt to break the Gaza blockade took place on 31 May 2010, when an aid convoy of six ships, known as the "Gaza Freedom Flotilla", arrived and attempted to run the blockade into Gaza. The ships were carrying humanitarian aid and construction materials. Before the flotilla's arrival, the vessels were violently attacked by the Israeli Navy and seized. The Israelis' use of live ammunition and the violence of their attack on unarmed volunteers in international waters led to the death of 9 volunteers and dozens of injured. Some of the dead volunteers had been shot in the back and Israel was condemned for using disproportionate force. Legal actions are currently pending against the Israeli government and individual members of the military for their role in the attack [Note 113].

Despite the Israeli attack on this aid convoy, 3 further attempts were made by groups of volunteers to break the blockade and, whilst all of these attempts failed, they again refocused world attention on the illegal blockade by Israel and the dreadful effects it has on the already wretched lives of those confined in the tiny Gaza enclave.

8.6.4.5 Politically Motivated Counterfeiting: This is an action where an activist group attacks a target authority by creating counterfeit versions of official currency, documents or other products. The objective of this act may be one of the following:

- to devalue the official documentation or currency issued by the target authority

- to damage the credibility or trustworthiness of a product or company

- to produce copies of useful documents (such as passports) to allow activists to circumvent or infiltrate a target authority

When we use the word "counterfeit", we most often think of counterfeit money. However, in the world of political protest there are much more interesting targets for counterfeiting than money. When the target authority is a government, the copying of legally useful documents, such as personal documents, driving licences, visas, passports, residence permits, travel permits and educational certifications may be much more important and valuable than cash. Think about political exiles fleeing the Soviet Union or Nazi Germany - they needed documents much more than they needed money.

The use of strategic counterfeits may also be designed to undermine confidence in an authority. These counterfeits may take the form of copies of government permissions, state issued guarantees, bonds and government issued certificates. Modern governments still rely heavily on document-based systems to identify people and, whilst generally all documents tend to have a computer record somewhere, routine use of documents such as birth certificates, passports or utility bills rarely sees them being thoroughly checked for authenticity. Non-government organisations will almost always tend to accept the authenticity of a document at face value, if it is a reasonably good resemblance. Anyway, non-government organisations don't usually have access to any means of verification.

For the sceptical reader, see how easy it is to obtain a US tax identification number from the US Internal Revenue Service. It can be done by post from a foreign country, or even by FAX, with the minimum amount of identification data or evidence. Put very simply, high quality government documents can be obtained just by using very low quality counterfeits from the world's most security-paranoid nation - the USA. As the Boston Globe reported in February 2014, the IRS is now "overwhelmed with identity theft and fraudulent tax refund claims". In this age of state surveillance and terabyte databases, organisations like the all-powerful IRS still work with many bits of paper, lots of human discretion and frequent human error.

In the corporate sphere, counterfeiting is often a purely criminal activity, designed to take advantage of high-value trade marks copied onto low-cost products. However, counterfeits of corporate certificates or shares, for instance, may also have potential to undermine confidence in a company or a regulatory system. A company which certifies its own products, for example, could be severely damaged if its certifications were discovered to be counterfeits. Apply such a scenario to a large-scale food producer or drinking water utility that tests and certifies its food products or drinking water against various health standards and one realises that undermining such certification has the potential to do significant economic damage.

In terms of protest movements, counterfeit activity tends to be concentrated around producing useful identity documents, though (for understandable reasons) there are no statistics available to indicate the level of counterfeit identity documents in existence, or their use by those engaged in civil disobedience.

One other interesting use of counterfeiting in a protest movement is the creation and dissemination of disinformation about protesters, their families, the protest group, plans for protest, the finances of a protest group, etc. The constant surveillance of protest groups by corporate or government intelligence agencies and police forces provide an excellent opportunity to mislead an authority by feeding it information designed to mislead. This might include fictitious CV's of non-existent or real members of the group, counterfeit bank statements, counterfeited meeting minutes or internal memos and counterfeit identity documents. The list of possibilities is endless. These can be paper documents or electronic documents. They can be fed to those spying on the protest group by "seeding" them in the office waste, sending them by unencrypted email, leaving them lying around the office, placing them in the filing cabinet marked "Strictly Confidential", etc. Using counterfeit documents in this way allows a protest group to define a completely synthetic narrative to give to the police or intelligence services about the protest group and its members.

Considerations and risks: Counterfeiting is considered a form of fraud in most countries because the law assumes that counterfeiting is done solely for economic gain. Unfortunately, a defence of moral obligation or political activism will probably not reduce the legal consequence of being caught in an act of counterfeit. In some extreme cases, counterfeit has been construed as treason and may even carry a death penalty. This has often been the case in times of war. Therefore, a major consideration in planning an act of counterfeiting must be that the person carrying out the counterfeit cannot be identified. Obviously, the quality of a counterfeit determines how convincing it will be.

Historical and contemporary examples: There are many historical examples where both governments and political activists have engaged in counterfeiting. In communist Russia after the revolution, Stalin had an active operation to counterfeit US dollars in order to raise hard currency.

The dollars were distributed through a Berlin bank and various US gangsters. During WWII, Nazis used skilled engravers, imprisoned in the concentration camps, to create high quality British sterling printing plates. The objective was the destruction of the British economy by undermining international confidence in sterling. In total the Nazis produced £134 million in forgeries, which was approximately 10% of all sterling in circulation at the time. Large amounts of sterling notes did enter circulation and large-scale recalls by the Bank of England took place in 1943. The United States' $100 note was (and perhaps still is) known to have been very exactly counterfeited by a Middle Eastern country or faction. The note is known as "super K". The U.S. General Accounting Office issued a report in February of 1996, mentioning the note, which it also refers to as the "Supernote" or the "Superbill".

8.6.4.6 Preclusive Purchasing: This is a method of inflicting economic damage on an adversary by the advance buying of goods, land or commodities in order to deprive the adversary of these commodities, or in order to drive up their price to the economic detriment of the adversary, or to block off a course of action by an authority.

The tactic is mostly used by governments in conflict with other governments, where the large-scale purchase or sale of commodities can damage the economy of an adversary. However, the strategy can also be used by protest groups; even small scale acts can have relatively profound effects.

Considerations and risks: Purchasing land or commodities may be an expensive exercise, especially if the goods or land purchased have no great long-term value. This creates some economic risk to a protest or activist group, but with some forward planning and a large group these risks can be minimised.

There are no legal obstacles to this kind of action in most jurisdictions but there is a chance that, in extreme cases, an authority may just seize control of land or commodities that it considers of "national importance", "for the public good".

Historical and contemporary examples: A fairly recent example of preclusive purchasing occurred in 2009, when Greenpeace began the preclusive purchasing of land that was being planned to be used as part of a new and contentious 3rd runway at Heathrow Airport, London. By buying parts of the land that would be needed for the airport expansion, Greenpeace was preparing for a long conflict with the government and developers. As a landowner, Greenpeace gained many negotiating privileges that it lacked as just another environmental NGO [Note 114].

8.6.4.7 Seizure of Assets: This concept is similar to the seizure of land by protesters, but is extended to other assets, such as buildings, vehicles, equipment and capital.

Protest groups may seize assets that they do not own or have any claim over for several reasons. The assets may be being used by an authority against the interests of protesters. For example, vehicles and equipment may be used to develop a disputed building site by felling trees, undertaking earthworks, etc.

In another scenario, assets may be unconnected with the obvious protest objectives, but are seized by protesters as a form of economic punishment for the authority's behaviour elsewhere. The assets may be held until an authority relents or may be disposed of to provide economic support to victims of the authority's behaviour. Alternatively, assets may be destroyed, but this action is properly referred to as "sabotage" rather than seizure.

Considerations and risks: There are considerable legal risks involved in seizing assets which do not belong to you. Even for political or moral reasons, such a seizure will be construed as theft by most courts in most jurisdictions, which will tend to favour the owners.

Governments of all shades routinely seize the assets of their citizens, even for relatively minor misdemeanours, such as failure to pay a local tax, but any concept of the citizenry seizing assets of a government or other authority as punishment for their crimes is held to be an unspeakable outrage.

The only way to mitigate the risks of legal action is to force an authority into negotiations. This can only be done by means of some form of political pressure, such as public anger, international condemnation, a threat of legal or other sanctions or a risk that the assets will be destroyed entirely and that further assets will be seized.

Historical and contemporary examples: In the Peasants Revolt of 14th century England, bands of armed peasants seized several royal palaces and a considerable amount of valuable goods and treasures belonging to the aristocracy and the king.

They used this booty to feed the nascent rebel army, but dumped much of the non-convertible treasures into the river, since their objectives were not short-term personal economic gain, but rather a protest at increased taxes.

In 2013, during one of a number of similar actions, native Canadian environmental protesters in Rexton, New Brunswick, confronted a fracking team in operation. The protesters confiscated the team's drilling equipment and trucks, and escorted its personnel off the exploration site. The protesters subsequently blocked access roads and effectively sealed off the area. Despite some assaults by police, the protesters were successful in stopping the fracking exploration. The protesters justified their action on the basis that confiscating the drilling equipment meant that there would be no drilling [Note 115].

In another example of the principle of asset seizure, in January 2015, villagers in Guangdong Province, China, protesting the construction of a coal-fired power station, seized an excavator and other construction equipment and demanded that the government release other protesting villagers. Despite the intervention of hundreds of police, the villagers of the area effectively controlled the construction site and most of the construction equipment on it and (at the time of writing) the protesters are close to forcing the government to agree to their demands.

8.6.4.8 Dumping: The dumping of commodities, as a means of inflicting economic pain or sending an economic message to the authorities, has become a popular strategy amongst hard-pressed farmers and fishermen in recent years, but it has been used for centuries by primary producers of many goods to defend their markets and recover their production costs.

Dumping involves the selling or donation of goods into an open market as a means of threatening a dominant competitor, such as a large producer. By dumping goods at low cost, a group of small producers can inflict economic damage on a large producer who is trying to control a market. It is a technique which seeks to effectively beat a dominant player at their own game.

In an agricultural context, the technique of "protest dumping" has been refined from the simple, one-off giving away or low cost sale of goods directly to the public. Today, farmers in many countries are again selling directly to the public, as a means of bypassing middlemen. This action is a form of protest dumping, which allows a farmer to inflict economic damage on dominant players in the food industry, whilst still maintaining a viable income.

Considerations and risks: The dumping of goods or commodities carries the risk of economic losses for the protest group involved. This risk can be obviated by working out alternative methods of distribution which have the same economic impact on the target, but no economic impact on the protest group.

For example, farmers markets and farm shops that sell directly to the public have proved a prime example of how producers can economically damage large food distributors, whilst maintaining their own farm incomes. At the same time, production surplus to sales can be distributed to the poor via voluntary organisations at zero or very low cost. This may provide little income for producers, but still has the effect of excluding the target organisations from this market. Even poor people are part of the market!

Historical and contemporary examples: An interesting variant of product dumping took place in the USA in 2013, when bartenders around the country took the unprecedented step of dumping Russian-made vodka in protest at new anti-gay laws in Russia. In the protest, barmen began pouring Russian vodka into the street and finding alternate non-Russian supplies.

See also the section "Small Farmers/Fishermen's Strike" for examples of primary food producers dumping food, sometimes onto the market and (unfortunately) sometimes onto the rubbish heap.

8.6.4.9 Selective Patronage: Selective patronage is the corollary of the concept of a boycott. A boycott focuses on a refusal to buy or deliver a particular product, or deal with a particular company, government or person. The objective of selective patronage involves acts which deliberately favour a defined group of providers, products or government over others. This strategy defines who should be patronised and who should not.

Generally speaking, those who are favoured with patronage are those sympathetic to the aims of the protest group. Those who are not patronised by the group have either no position or are averse to the protest's objectives.

The objective of selective patronage is to give economic benefits to those of like mind and to do economic damage to a protest's adversaries. Selective patronage campaigns are often combined with active boycott actions.

Considerations and risks: When making recommendations of who should be selected for patronage, it is important that the lists still provide for legitimate choices, otherwise there is a strong possibility that the recommendations will be labelled as simple cronyism. Another important consideration is that those excluded from a "preferred supplier" list have been excluded with very good reasons, which need to be documented in detail and made public. The whole exercise needs to be totally transparent and fair to be effective. Any hint at partiality will discredit this kind of action, for the general public as well as for other sympathisers.

Historical and contemporary examples: Campaigns of selective patronage were widely employed during the US civil rights movement in the 1960s. In one long running campaign, Baptist minister and activist Leon Sullivan managed to get black consumers to stop buying products from a bakery company called Tastykake because of their apparent discriminatory hiring policies. Consumers were urged to favour other suppliers. The loss of 20% of their customers obliged Tastykake to end the action by agreeing to meet the demands set by Sullivan and his colleagues. These demands included hiring African-Americans as drivers to deliver Tastykakes and African-Americans to work in office positions.

In recent years, several NGOs have focused on helping to relieve the plight of Palestinians in the occupied territories by helping them to export and market products grown or manufactured by Palestinian farmers or businesses. These products include olives, olive oil, locally made cosmetics, handcrafts and ceramics. Several internet shops now sell Palestinian-sourced products directly to the public [Note 116].

Another recent and interesting example of selective patronage is the emergence of products in the USA which are being labelled as "Guaranteed: Does NOT contain GMOs". The GM industry has spent many millions of dollars in the US in lobbying to ensure that food products with genetically modified ingredients are NOT labelled as "containing GM ingredients". In 2010, an initiative started to create a labelling system which guaranteed that a product did NOT contain GM ingredients. Sales of "No GM" labelled products rose dramatically from $0.5 billion in 2010, to $8.5 billion in 2014 [Note 118].

See also the section "Consumers' boycotts" for similar examples.

8.6.4.10 Alternative Markets: The use of alternative markets involves the deliberate avoidance of one market and the supply or patronage of another. As an act of economic protest, this can be employed both by suppliers and by consumers of a market. The objective is to inflict economic damage on markets that are unsympathetic to the protest objectives and to provide economic encouragement to markets that are sympathetic.

Considerations and risks: Generally, the use of alternative markets carries few risks, provided that they comply with local regulations. Alternative markets may require a degree of organisation and may initially not be viable. Specialist assistance may be required if alternative markets involve the sale of sensitive products, such as food.

Historical and contemporary examples: One of the fastest growing types of alternative market in the Western world is the "Farmers market". These markets attempt to bring local food produce from the farmers and producers directly to the consumer. In the last decade, the growth of such alternative markets has been attributed to rapidly declining food quality, continuous food scandals and an increased public awareness regarding food quality and health. The rate of growth of farmers markets in Europe and the USA has been exponential, with the number of markets in the USA having almost tripled between 2000 and 2013.

Another rapidly growing alternative market is the "Food Cooperative". These take various forms, but are essentially buying clubs, organised in a neighbourhood by a group of consumers. They get together to buy food in bulk at wholesale prices. Members of the cooperative then have a chance to buy this food at prices lower than those offered by conventional retailers. Often, food cooperatives may focus on buying organic, local and/or fair trade products.

8.6.4.11 Alternative Transportation Systems: The objective of alterative transportation systems is to create systems of transport for goods and people which do not rely on conventional methods of transport, such as air transport or the use of high energy road transport systems.

By using more independent and environmentally friendly transport systems, a group can isolate itself from both state-run and privately owned conventional transport systems. The primary motives for doing this are usually environmental. Transport is energy intensive and conventional systems of transport are very inefficient and often expensive. Alternative systems of transport may also include the use of conventional transport in an alternative way.

Considerations and risks: As an economic intervention, alternative transport systems are a relatively benign action, carrying little risk of failure or legal complications. Sharing transport with others may have some insurance implications that should be checked, for example in the case of a car-sharing scheme.

Historical and contemporary examples: Many environmental organisations have long been pressing for alternative public transport systems in cities, such as the free or low-cost use of bicycles for commuters and those making relatively short journeys within a city. Such systems have been widely and successfully adopted in many large cities, including London, and have demonstrated their ability to reduce congestion, pollution and costs for road maintenance [Note 117].

Other NGOs are concerned with the organisation of "car-pools", where several colleagues share one car rather than using one car each to get to work. Several car-pooling websites now exist, which allow users to find car-pools nearby or even to find and book low-cost lifts over long distances, even internationally.

The idea of long distance transport which is basically CO2 free has recently been pioneered by a group using a fleet of sailing ships to transport goods from Europe to the Americas and back again, using just wind power.

Other groups are concerned to reduce or eliminate the amount of transport involved in the goods we purchase and have created systems where a consumer can choose products that have low "food miles" ratings. This involves the use of product labelling to indicate how many miles of transport went into the manufacture of a particular product.

8.6.4.12 Alternative Economic Institutions: Economic institutions in this context refer to retail banks, insurance companies, merchant banks, investment banks and fund managers. Conventional economic institutions provide services to customers, but with their primary motivation being profits for their shareholders. Therefore, some conflict of interest exists in conventional economic institutions between the economic interests of the customers and the profit motives of the institution.

Alternative economic institutions are often driven by different motives to those of their conventional equivalents. Banks may be cooperatives, where all customers are also shareholders. This is the case with most credit unions. Specialist fund managers and investment banks may have an ethical motivation and only invest in certain types of industry where they are sure that there is no arms manufacture or tobacco production, for instance. Credit institutions may specialise in providing credit to the very poorest of a society, as is the case with the many "micro-credit" organisations which have sprung up in poorer parts of the developing world.

In recent years there has been a surge in the practice of "peer to peer lending" on the internet. In this alternative credit arrangement, individuals can raise funds for a project from other individuals, without dealing with a conventional bank. The investors can invest as little or as much as they wish and risk is reflected in the rate of return offered by the borrower. This system entirely bypasses the conventional banking industry and its regulations and controls.

Considerations and risks: Generally speaking, setting up any kind of public economic institution, such as a bank or fund manager, is a complicated business which, in most countries, is highly regulated. However, there are some exceptions to this, such as the establishment of a credit union. Savings clubs or investment clubs are informal or formal associations which are also often exempt from regulatory scrutiny. Cooperative organisations in some countries may also be allowed to extend credit to their members, without being formally identified as a credit institution. Private housing associations may also be able to provide credit to home buyers who are also members of the association. Providing insurance services is almost exclusively very highly regulated to ensure that insurers have the funding to cover their risk burden. However, some larger cooperative banks also provide insurance services.

Historical and contemporary examples: In the last 30 years there has been a rapid expansion in ethical funds and many conventional banks and fund managers now offer such investments.

Apart from these "ethical options" offered by high-street retail banks, there are now many banks offering a completely ethical alternative to the conventional banks. Triodos Bank is one such institution that provides an ethical portfolio of investment and banking services to its clients and has grown in just a few years to become a multi-billion Euro bank with a wide range of green and ethical investment options, including a micro-credit operation. It specialises in financing organic food production, renewable energy projects, sustainable industries and mortgages for low energy housing.

8.6.4.13 Shareholder Rebellions: A shareholder rebellion occurs when the shareholding owners of a company attempt to eject the management of the company or oppose the management's decisions. Shareholder rebellions may occur during shareholder meetings. Shareholders may also threaten to force down a company's share price by collaborating to sell many shares over a short period.

The objective of a shareholder rebellion is to force a decision or change of management of a company. The strategy is often used by activists seeking to force debate on a particular issue at shareholder meetings.

Whilst an NGO may be able to influence a company with public pressure etc., a company may also just choose to ignore them. A shareholder, on the other hand, has legal rights to be heard as a legitimate part-owner of a company. This fact can be very useful to a protest group in driving a discussion into a board meeting or shareholder meeting.

Since the 1980s, the concept of shareholder activism has become a standard strategy to pressure a company at their AGMs. In the early days, this might involve buying one share in a company and arriving to throw questions (or eggs) at the board of directors. Nowadays, shareholder activist organisations such as "Share Action" and "Sum of Us" have refined the protest methodology somewhat. Their members now attend corporate meetings armed with evidence of malpractice or unethical business activities. They have well-formulated questions and very often they hunt in packs, linking one question from one "shareholder activist" to those of others.

The strategy rarely gives rise to an instant result, but it puts CEOs and other executives under an increasingly penetrating and persistent spotlight. Cases such as the relationship between BT (British Telecom), the RAF and the control of US drones in a base in Djibouti forced an admission of a communications link, which had not previously been admitted by any of the governments involved, and the mercenary behaviour of BT in perpetrating an undeclared war in the zone.

Similar examples of a shareholder shining a spotlight on a company's management are equally illuminating when it's revealed how CEOs allow themselves multi-million pound pay rises, whilst making thousands of employees redundant.

Considerations and risks: Obviously, to stage any form of shareholder action, one needs to hold shares of the company in question in order to be invited to shareholder meetings. This is normally only possible in the case of public companies or cooperatives. However, acquiring such shares is a relatively easy matter that can be managed by any broker or bank. There are few risks involved. You can always sell your shares again after the action.

More to the point is whether a shareholder rebellion will be supported by other shareholders. Firstly, the objectives of the rebellion need to be clear. What is the desired outcome for the rebellion? A change of management? A change of corporate policy? A discussion?

After having decided on the objective, it is necessary to canvass support. Obviously, if there is no support for an issue, there is little point in trying to cause a shareholder rebellion, but the only way to know this is to canvass other shareholders and this is an important process.

Very often institutional investors will try very hard to appear to do the "right thing" in the public perception. Remember that such investors may be governments, pension funds, councils, etc. and may be prone to moral pressure. If an activist group planning a shareholder rebellion writes to some institutional investors (or even uses an open letter to them) requesting that they clarify their position on the issue at stake, it may well be that one may find more support for a rebellion than expected.

If there is significant support, then it is only a matter of calculating whether there is enough support to get a subject onto the agenda for discussion. It's important to note that in some jurisdictions the amount of participation a shareholder has depends on the level of shareholding they own, but most AGM agendas also leave time for "any other business".

Modern day shareholder activists have complained of two dispiriting aspects of the strategy and these are as follows:

• Investors tend to exhibit strong support for the status quo. Shareholders may noisily heckle a CEO, cheering the person who asks about his huge pay packet, but when it comes to it, many investors will vote for the pay packages the board demands, simply because they are inherently conservative.

• There are a lot of competing interests in a shareholder meeting. These range from serious questions about corporate governance and regulatory management by serious investors to earnest complaints from members of the public about someone in customer service who was rude to them on the phone These crank complaints discredit the honest campaigners that have real human rights grievances, for example.

Historical and contemporary examples: One notable example of a shareholder rebellion took place in 2008 at ExxonMobil, when the Rockefeller dynasty sponsored four shareholder resolutions demanding changes at Exxon to liberalise the company's stance on climate change.

Together with several other institutional investors, they demanded senior management changes, desiring the company to soften its line on climate change and the adoption of alternative energy. The company has long been involved in financing organisations promoting climate change denial. By 2009, the shareholder rebellion had forced some major changes in ExxonMobil management policy, including an agreement to a carbon tax.

In 2010, British Petroleum and Shell faced a shareholder revolt over their Canadian tar sands policy and, also in 2010, BP faced lawsuits from its shareholders over its poor management of safety prior to the disastrous explosion and oil spill at the Deepwater Horizon rig.

8.6.5 Political Intervention

Acts of political intervention seek to damage an authority by undermining its political authority and/or transferring political allegiances to another authority.

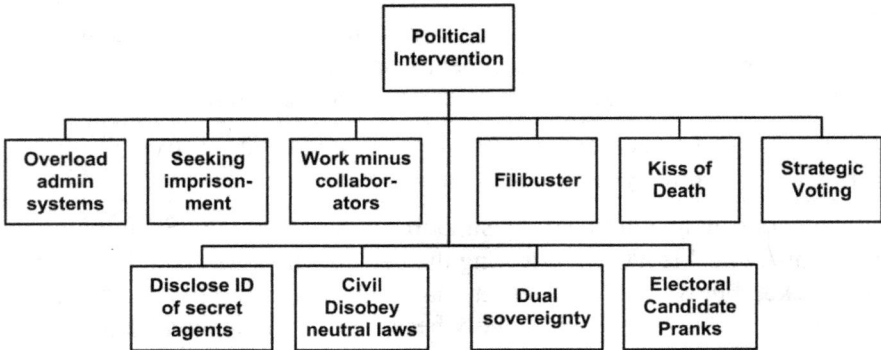

```
                        ┌──────────────┐
                        │  Political   │
                        │ Intervention │
                        └──────────────┘
```

| Overload admin systems | Seeking imprison-ment | Work minus collabor-ators | Filibuster | Kiss of Death | Strategic Voting |

| Disclose ID of secret agents | Civil Disobey neutral laws | Dual sovereignty | Electoral Candidate Pranks |

8.6.5.1 Overloading of Administrative Systems: This is an action which seeks to deliberately overload the administrative systems of an authority. In the case of a government, this may be a particular government department or a single process within that department.

The reasons for wishing to overload an administrative system are very diverse. It may be that a group wishes to temporarily distract an authority from its other responsibilities, or it may be an attempt to cause embarrassment to the authority, or to demonstrate to the authority or the public that the organisation is inefficient and prone to being overloaded. It may be that the intention is to force an authority to give a particular issue their complete attention.

Administrative overload doesn't imply complete administrative failure or a shutdown of an administrative process. It may mean that an administration just functions less efficiently than it should or becomes completely preoccupied with a single issue.

If causing a reduction in efficiency is the objective, often it is enough for a protest group to make an administrative system less responsive than normal. For example, slowing down a planning application may be enough for a protest group to buy time to gather more information or support for a more permanent end to a planned development. In this instance, a planning department could be easily overwhelmed by launching mass appeals against a particular planning application it has received.

In other examples, a police force could be inundated with huge numbers of trivial calls to attend minor or imaginary incidents or a company might be swamped by a wave of calls to a customer services, accounts or sales department. A customer wishing to draw attention to a particular problem can overload a corporate administrative system by complaining at many levels and to a range of regulatory and legal authorities as well as to the company's managements. This strategy effectively causes various levels of management to be obliged to evaluate a single complaint which is arriving on their desk from several different directions (See the example below).

Considerations and risks: Some cases of administrative overload may be illegal, such as wasting police time. However, with careful planning and coordination within a large protest group, administrative overload can be carried out with little or no legal implications.

Historical and contemporary examples: The use of administrative overload is in constant use by consumers, activist groups, tax payers and members of the electorate.

As an example we suggest a hypothetical case where a European telephone customer has received sub-standard service from their provider. After numerous calls and emails to Customer Services, it is clear that the provider is not going to rectify the problem any time soon. The customer then adopts a strategy of administrative overload. Firstly, the customer fully documents the incident, along with the chronology and their complaint. The next step is to discover the names, addresses and fax numbers of the company's entire board of directors. The aggrieved customer then sends a complaint to each director by registered post and by FAX. The customer now sends the same complaint to the National Telecoms regulator, several members of the national press, the European Directorate responsible for Telecoms Regulation and the national Consumer Ombudsperson. A copy is also sent to the Customer Services Manager of the Telecom's company by FAX and registered post. Within a short time the administration of the organisation will begin to contact the other parties to compare notes and, with a bit of luck, within a day all of the targets will be busy with little else but the customer's complaint. In this case, the customer's complaint is being sent not simply to the service provider, but also to national organisations that regulate and oversee the behaviour of the provider and to international authorities that oversee the overseers. The result is a climate of fear and paranoia which should quickly eclipse all routine complaints being handled by customer services. Meanwhile, company directors will be asking why they are being involved in such complaints and why isn't it being dealt with. That will bring further internal pressures to have the problem resolved. In this climate, problem resolution becomes the only means by which the administrative overload may be removed.

8.6.5.2 Disclosing Identities of Secret Agents: Disclosing the identities of secret agents is a modern form of political intervention. It is a way for individuals and the public to actively interfere in the process of government and to intervene in national issues without legal action.

This method of intervention may also serve the public interest and not just the narrow interests of a protest group. Secret or covert operations are by their nature intrusive to public interests, both politically and socially, especially in situations where an individual is covertly threatened or harassed by an agent of the state. In such cases, the most legally acceptable option for the victim is the disclosure of the identity of the participants.

The disclosure of agents' identities is effective at stalling actions by government, military, law enforcement and political entities because it undermines an authority's confidence in covert operations and the certainty that agents' identities will be concealed. It also raises moral questions about how a government deals with its own citizens.

Considerations and risks: Some people may see ethical obstacles in revealing the names of secret agents, since this may endanger their safety, but these arguments are actually rather spurious. Since the public is served by the agents of the government paid for by the taxpayer, then the disclosure of their identities is not unethical. Secret agents are not guaranteed the right to privacy, as their actions are sanctioned by our governments and are not private acts of an individual. Intelligence agents have no rights to special levels of privacy. However, whilst this may be true morally, in some jurisdictions (the USA), revealing the identity of a secret agent is considered a criminal offence. The intentional disclosure of the name of a "covered" operative is a crime under the U.S. Intelligence Identities Protection Act.

Historical and contemporary examples: In 2014, the Metropolitan police in the UK were obliged to pay £425,000 in compensation to a female political campaigner who was profoundly traumatised to discover that the father of her child was, in fact, an undercover police officer who had formed a relationship with her as part of his work, in a covert operation to infiltrate a peaceful environmental activist group in the late 1980s. In 2011, a group of activists unmasked the undercover agent and obliged him to make a full statement, admitting his role. A number of other undercover officers were also identified and, at the time of writing, the police are still resisting legal claims from more than 10 other women who say they have suffered emotional trauma after discovering that their one-time boyfriends were undercover officers [Note 119].

In July 2014, in an odd story, a US citizen, identified as a CIA officer, was expelled from Germany after he attempted to recruit two German citizens to pass information to him (one of the Germans was an intelligence officer). The spying attempt was a bizarre twist in the relationship between two countries that have been close allies for decades. Germany's chancellor Merkel appeared to be simultaneously trying to condemn the US' spying while salvaging the countries' ties, reportedly saying that spying on allies was a "waste of energy." The identity of the persons involved and how they were "outed" is not known.

8.6.5.3 Seeking Imprisonment: Seeking imprisonment is characterised by the purposeful attempt to become incarcerated by police by disobeying their orders in a peaceful and nonviolent manner.

Seeking imprisonment is an interesting and effective method of nonviolent protest and intervention because, when protesters actively seek incarceration, it takes away all of the power that police have in threatening incarceration by showing that the protesters are unafraid of being charged or imprisoned.

Because police are an extension of government, seeking imprisonment sends a similar message to government authorities, i.e. that the threat of imprisonment is ineffective. By actively seeking incarceration, protesters symbolically strip the government of the only power they have against their citizens.

Considerations and risks: Seeking imprisonment can be dangerous because police officers often become belligerent, especially when they are being ridiculed.

Historical and contemporary examples: The efficacy of this method is evident in the success of the movements that have used it in the past (and continue to do so to this day). Movements for women's rights, African-American civil rights and the struggle for Indian independence from Britain have all employed this tactic and all have been generally successful in achieving their demands.

The method of protest was especially prevalent during the Civil Rights Movement of the 1960s in the United States, when African-American people placed themselves in areas designated as "white only", knowing they would be arrested and beaten by police officers.

Seeking imprisonment also has become increasingly popular with the Occupy Wall Street protests, as protesters deliberately disobeyed police orders to not occupy certain properties, resulting in their arrest, beatings and other ill-treatment.

In modern times, the use of internet social networks and instant distribution of video media via YouTube etc. has added an extra edge to this strategy by having arrest incidents filmed and released to the media and public almost instantaneously.

8.6.5.4 Civil Disobedience of "Neutral" Laws: Some laws may be seen as morally repugnant to a protesting group. These laws are perceived to be so ethically obnoxious that a group may feel obliged to disobey them.

Aside from these "repugnant laws", there are also laws which are considered to be morally "neutral". These laws are usually concerned with routine administrative issues. These "neutral" laws may also be a target for disobedience.

The motives for disobeying such neutral laws are twofold. Firstly, it may be difficult to find any other obvious point of resistance to confront an authority about some other policy or behaviour. Therefore, a neutral law is selected and disobeyed as a deliberate, symbolic act of defiance and protest against the authority's disputed policy or behaviour. The method is also used to weaken a government during more advanced stages of its collapse, as was the case in pre-independence India, in the 1930s.

Considerations and risks: Disobeying a law may be a criminal act when committed by an individual, but it becomes a political or moral act when committed en masse. Thus, the strategy of disobeying "neutral" laws needs to be coordinated with a large group, so that authorities are either overwhelmed or so that amnesties can be negotiated or escalations threatened if governments attempt to impose penalties against participants. If 10 citizens refuse to pay a local tax, they will be prosecuted; if 5000 refuse, then it is much more likely that negotiations will ensue.

Historical and contemporary examples: Gandhi used this mechanism against the British colonial authorities in India and launched continuous campaigns of civil disobedience involving refusals to obey administrative laws concerning local taxes, levies and by-laws, amid wide-scale resignations from British-run civil service positions by Indian protesters.

8.6.5.5 Work-On Without Collaboration: This is a form of highly selective industrial action, where employees may continue to report for work, but withdraw cooperation and productive collaboration with their employers. The objective of the protest is to economically damage the employer without actually going on strike.

Considerations and risks: In most Western jurisdictions employee protection would probably ensure that such protesters could not be dismissed. However, in the US or other countries with poor employee rights, this form of non-collaboration would probably mean that the protesters would be sacked. The only possible salvation would be when the protests are organised by a large group; it would be harder to fire employees en masse.

8.6.5.6 Dual Sovereignty and Parallel Government: The concept of dual sovereignty and parallel government refers to the creation of an official or unofficial alternative political authority within an existing country.

When large sections of a society have been alienated from mainstream government for reasons such as ethnicity or profound political or religious differences, it sometimes happens that a parallel authority is created or allowed to exist to provide for the governance of the alienated group. The group, in effect, achieves a dual sovereignty by being citizens of the greater nation and also of their own ethnic, political or religious group.

Considerations and risks: Whilst this concept is by no means an ideal solution to the problem of colonisation, the use of parallel governments and dual sovereign nations may represent a short term and peaceful solution to the conflicts between rival groups within a country.

Historical and contemporary examples: There are numerous historical and modern examples of dual sovereignty. The obvious cases are the relationships of indigenous peoples of the USA, Alaska, Hawaii, New Zeeland, Australia and Canada to their national governments. These groups, after centuries of oppression and rebellion, have achieved some levels of autonomy and sovereignty in their own territories, whilst remaining citizens of the larger nation.

8.6.5.7 Filibuster: A filibuster is an action such as a prolonged speech that obstructs progress in a legislative assembly, while not technically contravening the required procedures. Filibusters can be used both within legislatures of all kinds, but also by the public in open public meetings with authorities.

Many people know about the U.S. Senate's procedural filibusters, in which a dissenting senator holds the floor to keep a vote from happening. The people's version, the public filibuster, is no different. When activists face hostile government agencies or hearings that exclude the public, this relatively low-risk tactic injects the public's voice into an otherwise closed-off process.

Considerations and risks: In the case of a public filibuster, the power of the filibuster depends on carrying out the action in a dignified manner, as well as choosing the appropriate topic and time. Calling such an action a "public filibuster" helps to lend legitimacy when the action is reported to the broader public.

Historical and contemporary examples: In 2007, a dozen members of Casino-Free Philadelphia decided to use the public filibuster at a Pennsylvania Gaming Control Board (PGCB) meeting. For two years, the PGCB had refused to let members of the public testify at so-called public hearings, but this time the protesters decided that the public was going to have its say. One at a time, members stood up and began testifying. Each one was told to be quiet by the chairwoman. A recess was quickly called and the members who had spoken were escorted out of the building by police and told they would not be allowed to return. When the board reconvened, the chairwoman warned the remaining members of the group not to interrupt. Naturally, one after another the members stood up and continued the filibuster. They spoke over the banging gavel of the distressed chairwoman and over the "official" testifiers, as they coolly tried to continue. Another recess was called, and then another, as the public filibuster continued. Finally, the PGCB shut down the entire meeting. The result: rather than risking another such engagement, the PGCB changed its policy to allow the public to actually speak at hearings.

8.6.5.8 Electoral Candidate Pranks: This is a type of protest action where someone stands as a candidate for election in order to deliver a protest message, rather than to actually achieve public office. One could say that this is a form of theatre, where the theatre set is actually the electoral system and the audience is the electorate. The technique can help to deliver a message, but it can also be used to spoil the chances of another candidate by undermining their credibility. It may also be used to ridicule the electoral system and the behaviour of the political classes in general.

This method works by taking advantage of the media attention focused on an electoral campaign. In some cases, where there is a contentious candidate, media attention can be quite intense. The protest candidate "piggy-backs" on this media attention, both to deliver the message and/or attack the other candidate in various ways (humour, irony, mimicry, derision, etc.).

Considerations and risks: One of the greatest risks of this technique is actually being elected if you really don't want to be.

Another problem may occur if there is a candidate running that you actually do support. In this case, a "theatre candidate" must take care to design a campaign in such a way that it enhances the favourite candidate, or at least doesn't interfere with him or her. Satire can upstage an ally to the point that it detracts from their campaign.

Humour is an important component in this technique. It's important to create a total persona, with all the necessary policies and manifestos worked out in advance. The preparation for this in itself can and should be a lot of fun, even though the objective may be deadly serious.

Historical and contemporary examples: An amusing example of this technique took place in the UK, in early 2015, when the comedian Al Murray decided to stand in the general elections in the same district as Nigel Farage, the notorious right-wing leader of UKIP. Al Murray stated in his party manifesto that Britain was now ready for a beer-swilling pub landlord to run the country and that he intended to "brick up the channel tunnel to stop immigrants coming to Britain", in comical references to Farage's constant preoccupation with immigration and the European Union. The comedian's manifesto contains a hilarious spoof of the right-wing ramblings of UKIP and Farage, sparking a great deal of mirth and jollity with the electorate, whilst subtly damaging the credibility of the real "beer-swilling" Farage. This prank caused some consternation within the ranks of UKIP. Their leader's sportingly tolerant smiles were quickly worn rather thin at the prospect of facing a hilarious mockery of his own bizarre policies played out by a competitor in a real-life general election campaign. Humour had the last laugh [Note 120] and UKIP was defeated in this town.

One case where electoral prank candidates did actually win and were actually elected to office was in Holland, in the late 1960s and early 1970s, when two similar anarchist groups, the Provos and the Kabouters (gnomes), won seats. Despite opposition from more traditional left-wing parties, they succeeded in conducting merciless comical and ironic attacks on conventional politicians and the police, and in the end deposed the mayor of Amsterdam and chief of police [Note 121]

8.6.5.9 Kiss of Death: This is a means of discrediting an authority, a company, a political party or a politician by declaring an affiliation or agreement with them on certain policies.

This technique works when, for example, an extreme right-wing political party expresses its agreement with a liberal party. The effect is that the liberal party is damaged by association with the admiring right-wing party in the eyes of the liberal supporters, even though the association is neither invited nor welcome. The beneficiary of this tactic is the right-wing party.

The damage done by such statements may be limited or it can be persistent. If a radical protest group continues to agree with the attitudes of a particular hard-line authority and this is repeated, then supporters of the authority become suspicious that they have "gone soft" or are "making deals". This may be far from the truth, but in the public psyche the damage is done, simply by association.

From the protester's point of view, all that is required to use this technique is to find issues where there is agreement, more or less, with an adversary and then to use every opportunity to express this agreement. Generally, there are a lot more issues that people agree on than issues that they disagree on, so this shouldn't be so difficult.

In the UK, when Tony Blair gave his undivided support to Ed Miliband, in early 2015, he effectively destroyed the chances of the Labour Party leader winning a majority in the 2015 elections. To be supported by Tony Blair is the ultimate political "kiss of death".

Considerations and risks: There are few risks involved for the protest group in using this strategy, provided that everyone in the group understands the underlying strategy and doesn't really believe that the protesters have "sold out". Indeed, the idea of sometimes agreeing with an adversary can be sold as the protest group being democratic, objective, "open-minded", "and willing to discuss differences".

8.6.5.10 Strategic Voting: This is the collective use of democratic elections to alter the outcome of an election by voting in a way which is not necessary a voter's real preference. The objective is to influence the overall result of an election rather than simply voting for a favourite candidate or option.

Strategic voting is just on the edge of civil disobedience because a voter is refusing to vote in a way which reflects their true opinion and therefore refusing to abide by the (informal) rules of democratic participation. Strategic voters instead vote to damage one political position and benefit another. This is voting in a way which is not the intended purpose of a civil democratic process, such as an election or referendum. Abstention is another form of strategic voting, as is voting for "none of the above". In some countries the latter is considered a legal vote, but in others it's regarded as a wasted or vandalised vote.

The vagaries of democratic systems sometimes mean that voting for one's favourite candidate may actually be a waste of a vote. The British ("first past the post") electoral system is a prime example of a system which favours larger parties over smaller ones. In other democracies, various hybrids of systems of proportional representation tend to create governments of coalitions rather than single party governments. Other systems set up minimum hurdles for any representation at all and some hybrids award "bonus" seats when a party achieves a certain level of support.

Understanding these systems provides a way for a group of electors to manipulate the outcome of an election by voting strategically. Perhaps they prefer party X, but fear that by voting for them, party Y will lose support, benefiting party Z by splitting the vote. In this case, a voter may prefer to vote for party Y, simply to block the worst option of party Z gaining an advantage.

Considerations and risks: There are no legal risks involved. These kinds of decisions are constantly made by electorates the world over. The greatest risk is to the democratic process, when large tracts of the population vote strategically instead of morally.

This kind of strategic voting behaviour tends to warp democracy and real choice. In fact, the correct action, when faced with an unrepresentative electoral system, should be to demand to change the electoral system to make it represent the truest views of the people. But electorates are conservative about democratic systems. For instance, the British electorate decided in 2011 to vote against the modernisation of the archaic and unfair British "first past the post" electoral regime and they rejected a form of proportional representation, which would have been far more democratic. It may take a generation before such a choice of democratic systems is offered to the British again. The incumbent members of Parliament will no doubt prefer to rely on the democratically dodgy "first past the post" system, in order that they can hold on to their seats in Parliament and their pensions.

8.6.6 Legal Intervention

Also referred to as "Impact litigation", these are acts of legal intervention which seek to use legal mechanisms to damage an authority by confounding or delaying its plans or by forcing it into expensive litigation.

Legal intervention may not, at first sight, appear to be a form of protest or intervention, but, in fact, legal intervention against a government is often seen (by an authority) as an act of outright aggression. Indeed, legal intervention can win victories that simply cannot be won in any other way.

In situations where demos, rallies, phone calls, letter-writing and logic hold no sway, a single, well-placed legal action can move mountains.

For instance, we have recently seen the European Court of Human Rights demanding that the British government reply to accusations made against their intelligence services. Their lawless, mass internet spying, without warrant or any form of judicial oversight, has been condemned as illegal. This court action provides a chance to cut through all the self-serving secrecy and scare-stories about terrorist bogeymen, and straight to the heart of the constitutional issue, namely the right that law-abiding citizens have the right to go about their daily lives unmolested, undocumented, and without being spied upon by the government.

Also consider the reaction to the application of the Palestinian Authority to join the International Criminal Court, at the end of 2014. Both the USA and Israel referred to the Palestinian application as if Palestine had launched a terror campaign, rather than agreeing to accept the judgements of the world's most important court of last resort! Thus, legal intervention may be construed as an act of disobedience, especially when an authority fears (as Israel does) that a court may expose it to proper legal scrutiny. However, legal action, by definition, is entirely within the law and it is therefore impossible to construe taking legal action as an "illegal" or unreasonable act of protest.

Legal intervention can be costly. Top lawyers don't come cheap, and a government has the power to drag out legal action for years, trying to bankrupt its opposition. However, some forms of legal action (taken by the European Commission on behalf of a complainant, for instance) are basically free of charge.

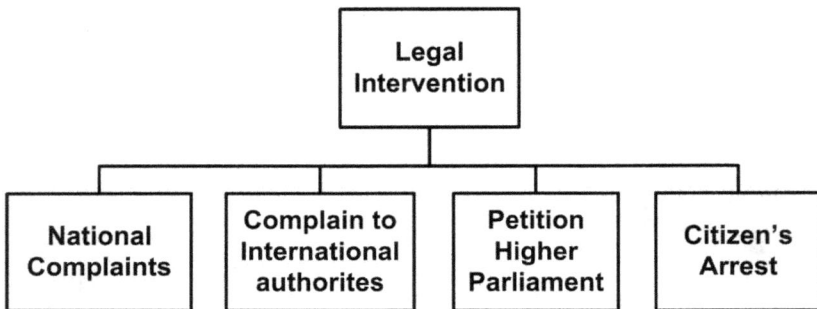

8.6.6.1 National Complaints: Depending on the jurisdiction, there is always a range of opportunities to formulate legal interventions against an authority.

Even in some of the world's least liberal regimes there are legal systems which can be used to challenge an authority in various ways. As a protest strategy this may not always provide a resolution to a conflict, but it often furnishes a means of delaying, publicising or defying an authority's actions, and is therefore sometimes useful.

A good example of this was an important case initiated in 2012 by a young woman, Cait Reilly, an unemployed geology graduate, who beat the UK Secretary for Work and Pensions in the British Supreme Court, where she was able to demonstrate the illegality of the so-called "workfare" schemes. These schemes obliged British unemployed to take unpaid, unskilled work with companies such as "Poundland" and "Tesco", with a threat that, if they refused the jobs offered, they would lose their very basic job-seekers allowance. The Supreme Court stopped short of ruling that the scheme represented a form of forced or slave labour, but it caused a major retreat by the Conservative government in its plans to force unemployed people to work for their pitiful unemployment allowance, rather than look for suitable employment.

Using national legislation in local courts: There are numerous possibilities to use national and local laws as a method to block or delay an authority. For instance, local laws may be used against a local authority. In Europe, for example, there are many planning regulations. This plethora of regulations can be applied against an authority. An illustration of this would be a local authority challenged to provide evidence that they have carried out or received an Environmental Impact Assessment for a new "development" project. We all assume that they did. But how often are these assessments properly made and how often are they challenged at a professional level? Very often planning applications fail to take account of zoning rules, environmental regulations, ancient access rights, the effects of a development on groundwater, traffic congestion, etc. These issues can be used to legally challenge a planning decision through local courts and systems of appeal. Even if the challenge fails, it will certainly cause a delay and can then often be escalated (in Europe to the European Commission and even the European Court of Justice, in some cases).

Judicial reviews: In many democratic nations it is also possible to escalate a legal conflict with an authority into a so-called judicial review. This allows a court to examine the legality of a decision made or action taken by a public body. It is a mechanism whereby a judge considers whether a public body has acted in accordance with its legal obligations and, if not, he can declare a decision taken by the authority to be invalid. The grounds for reversing an administrative decision by way of judicial review in the UK include: a/ illegality, b/ irrationality (unreasonableness) and c/ procedural impropriety.

In Britain, the use of judicial reviews is applicable to almost any government decision-making authority. The basic principles of public decision-making are:

• The decision-maker must have the authority to adjudicate. If such body has the authority to make the decision, it must not exceed the limits of its power.

• The citizen is entitled to a fair procedure in how the verdict is reached, the arbiter must not be biased and give a fair hearing to the plaintiff, who must be given an adequate opportunity to present his case. The petitioner must be informed of the matter and given a chance to comment on the material put forward by the authority.

• The decision-maker must comply with all legal requirements governing the findings and their origins. A decision cannot be arbitrary.

Normally, during the conduct of a judicial review or a legal action in the European courts, the disputed decision of an authority is suspended. Increasingly, government authorities are in favour of weakening the concept of judicial review because it provides citizens with a legal method of challenging them [Note 122].

Complaints to national regulators and ombudsmen: Another line of national legal intervention is the filing of a complaint with a regulator or ombudsman. Most Western countries deal with complaints from citizens via a number of state regulatory bodies (aka regulators). These organisations are designed to oversee and regulate the workings of various utilities, such as telecom companies, and the provision of certain government and utility services, such as water, energy, education, policing and healthcare.

Making a complaint to one of these organisations is relatively simple (they are designed to be sympathetic to public complaints) and they very often have a great deal of power, plus a direct line of communication to the managements of the organisations that they regulate. They are, therefore, a useful way to intervene when an authority is misbehaving. Sometimes even a threat of a complaint to a regulator is enough to get an authority to alter its behaviour.

Complaints to the police: In some cases it may be possible and useful to lodge a complaint regarding an authority with the police, if it can be demonstrated that an authority has broken the law, endangered life or property or is about to do so. In an earlier example we described how a citizen, campaigning to have potholes in roads around his home repaired, was completely ignored by his local authority, until he started to lodge formal written complaints (with photographic and written evidence) to the police as well. The police were then obliged to investigate the incidents with the council because of the potential hazard of traffic accidents. After some visits from the police, and fearing prosecution, the council began to act immediately when it was subsequently contacted by the campaigner with another "pothole complaint". They did so because they were aware that the campaigner would have lodged a parallel complaint with the local police.

Complaints to environmental "police": Some countries employ special police forces specifically to deal with environmental crimes or with the protection of wildlife or nature reserves. Some of these forces have quite substantial powers to act in order to stop or prevent an environmental crime, regardless of the perpetrator. In some cases, such a complaint may be an effective way of stopping or delaying an action by an authority. For example, if a rare species has been identified in an area ear-marked for development, a complaint to the environmental police can cause a suspension of work. For instance in Spain, the environmental police are part of the Guardia Civil (civil guard, a type of military police) but are trained specifically to deal with environmental crimes. They can take immediate actions (including making arrests) if they consider an environmental crime is being committed or is about to happen. In other countries there are other systems in place, such as wildlife or park rangers, environmental protection officers, etc. These may be civilians, but have the power to call in the police in cases where environmental crimes are suspected.

Aarhus Convention: One of the greatest obstacles to legal action by ordinary citizens is the cost of hiring lawyers and the consequences of losing a case if costs are awarded by a court against the complainant. This is one of the main reasons that ordinary citizens or small NGOs are reluctant to take legal actions, the so-called "chilling effect".

In some countries this problem has been alleviated, to some extent, on matters relating to the environment, if the country is a signatory of the UN Aarhus Convention. The convention came into force in 2001 and all EU countries have signed and ratified it. The Aarhus Convention grants the public rights regarding access to information and to justice, and public participation in government decision-making processes on matters concerning the local, national and trans-boundary environment. It focuses on interactions between the public and public authorities.

Aarhus has three main legal themes (or "pillars"):

• Access to information - public bodies should provide information and respond to requests for it.

• Public participation - the agreement sets out minimum requirements for public participation in various kinds of environmental decision-making.

• Access to justice - this means getting the right procedures in place so that no-one faces barriers to justice in environmental matters (e.g. not having to face excessive costs if a citizen takes a legal challenge).

This latter principle is designed to ensure that any member of the public has access to justice on environmental issues, without having to face excessive costs.

The implementation of the convention is still taking place and many countries are still not compliant with its principles (including the UK, for example). However, gradually, the principles are being enacted into legislation and argued in the courts and the implementation of reasonable costs for environmental legal actions is becoming a reality in many countries.

Freedom of environmental information regulations: One major obstacle for a small NGO or individual activist in the environmental field is access to information. Large authorities and corporations are often much better informed than a badly-funded NGO. Authorities can and do commission studies and reports, which are often kept private or are biased in their favour. Thus, an NGO is at some disadvantage when formulating a case. However, many countries have now implemented regulations governing access to information on environmental matters that somewhat redresses this knowledge imbalance.

For instance, the European Union has passed the European Council Directive 2003/4/CE on public access to environmental information (a spin-off from the Aarhus Convention), which is now law throughout the EU.

The main objective is found in regulation 4, which requires the relevant holder of environmental data (public authorities and many private companies) to engage proactively to make environmental information available for public inspection "by electronic means", which inevitably requires the data to be made publicly available online or via an electronic device in a public place. Recognising the reality of a wide diversity of information, the regulations allow alternative formats, but require that they be "easily accessible" to the public. The regulations set standards in terms of how quickly data must be made available (usually within 20 days after a request). Most countries do not charge for the data.

Sometimes even a request for data can be enough to trigger a reaction from an authority, but beware of the fact that public agencies very often try to make data as unusable as possible, to obfuscate anything dangerous to them. Therefore, be prepared to do some serious data processing when your data request is satisfied, in order to turn raw data into meaningful conclusions.

Considerations and risks: There are no legal risks inherent in any of these actions. Nonetheless, there are costs involved in some of these initiatives. Being very well prepared is important. Before taking legal action it is vital to have well-documented evidence - a surplus of evidence is better than risking evidence being deemed insufficient or being discredited. Stick to hard facts and exclude moral opinions when preparing legal actions. Legal cases are not about persuading the general public of a case, but rather about wining an action on strictly legal grounds.

8.6.6.2 Complaints to International Authorities and Courts: For various reasons protest groups, activists and NGOs often fail to persuade national courts or other national authorities that they have a case. Often national authorities conspire to ensure that there is no legal action possible against other parts of the government. They may ignore a complaint or erect obstacles to having the complaint heard properly or they may drag it into a long bureaucratic or political process from which it may never emerge.

In such cases it may be necessary to step outside the national legal system and address a complaint to an external authority above a national court. In the EU, that means recourse to various EU legal mechanisms. In other jurisdictions, legal escalation has different implications. In the USA, a citizen may be able to seek recourse in a federal court if they fail at state level. In other countries, it may well be that the next stage of authority is an agency of the United Nations, a much more fraught and uncertain route.

Here we will look at how the European system works and how it may be employed as a form of legal intervention against a national authority.

Appealing to the European judicial system: Escalating a national legal action in Europe is a relatively simple matter and, despite all the complaints one hears about "European interference" in national affairs, the

European citizen has the most powerful and accessible right of legal recourse of appeal against a decision of his own national judiciary or government of any citizen in the world today. Sadly, most European citizens are utterly unaware of how easy it is to access European justice and are completely ignorant of their rights as European citizens.

A serious drawback with the European legal process is its tardiness. Depending on how much the member state resists, a case may drag on for several years. However, a decision from the European Court of Justice is a powerful remedy and may carry huge fines and severe sanctions against a country that is found guilty. It's worth waiting for, but strategically it may be wise for an NGO to initiate European legal action at the early stages of a campaign, so that this slow legal process can proceed, whilst simultaneously continuing with other protest routes at the same time.

Complaints to the European Commission: If it becomes clear that a national government is failing to comply with the terms of a European Directive or a European Regulation, any European citizen has the right to make a complaint to the European Commission. A directive is a set of legal principles that need to be transposed into national laws by member states of the EU. A regulation is a legal act that becomes law throughout Europe simultaneously and is enforceable immediately. There are a lot of directives and regulations, and it's important for a protest group to inform themselves of these European laws.

In principle, it is normal to have exhausted all legal routes in a member state before resorting to the European Commission, but this is not always necessary. For example, if it is clear that a national government has failed to properly and legally implement an EU directive or regulation and there is a history of failure to do so, then it becomes clear that legal action in the member state would not yield a resolution. In such cases, the European Commission as the "Defender of the Directives" has a responsibility to evaluate whether or not a national government has implemented and is complying with a particular directive. Very often it is simple to demonstrate that a national government is negligent in its implementation just by virtue of overwhelming recent, historical and documentary evidence of breaches of the directive.

There are many EU directives on a whole range of subjects, from energy regulation to river water quality, and every year the body of legislation gets more complete. In general, EU legislation is highly sensible and liberal. The directives are easily accessible and, whilst the documents themselves are virtually unreadable for the layman, the EU provides a vast amount of helpful explanatory documents that are easy to read and understand. Indeed, the European Commission is specifically charged with making EU law accessible to the ordinary EU citizen. Making a complaint to the European Commission is free, as is any legal action which the Commission decides to take on the basis of a complaint. A complainant can choose to remain anonymous if there are any fears of reprisals from a member state's government.

Before making a complaint to the Commission, there are some basic tips that will help to streamline the process and to make the commission take the complaint seriously:

• If possible, determine which directives/regulations are being breached. This means doing some research. From this you should be able to determine which part of the EU Commission you need to address your complaint to. There are currently 33 "Directorate Generals", each with responsibility for a different area of legislation. For instance, you have the "DG for Humanitarian and Civil Protection" and there is a "DG for Environment". Check the EU website for a complete list.

• Look for alternative legal angles. For example, if you have a water pollution problem, you may also have risks to protected species of birdlife, protected species of plant, drinking water, or groundwater. The pollution may be in an EU-protected habitat. All these additional issues may also be the subject of EU directives and should be researched in advance.

• Ensure that you have good quality evidence, clearly, chronologically indexed. Throwing accusations around without good, undeniable proof will simply discredit a complaint. In the initial letter to the European Commission it is not necessary to furnish all information and evidence, but it may be useful to give a list of documented data and what it demonstrates.

A complaint to the European Commission can be made by anyone and you don't need a solicitor to do it. The commission will evaluate the complaint and if it sees some merit in it, the complainant will receive an acknowledgement and it will be allocated a case number.

The process then follows a fixed format with three stages:
- Formal notice
- Reasoned opinion
- Referral to the Court.

The first stage takes the form of a formal request for information to the government of the member state that is involved, in order to investigate the case; at this stage it remains confidential. At the reasoned opinion and referrals stages, the European Commission generally issues a press release, informing the public about the case and procedure. In exceptional cases of particular importance to citizens (for example, when it is clear that an offence has obviously been committed or where there have been a very large number of complaints), the Commission may decide to issue a press release even at the formal notice stage.

During the period of investigation, the European Commission will certainly contact the member state for clarification. At any stage after this, a member state may decide to attempt to comply with a directive (if there is non-compliance), and, in general, the Commission tries to give a member state an opportunity to correct a problem before further legal action. Also during this period, the commission will request more information from the complainant. At this point there is normally a deadline for resolution agreed between the Commission and member state. If this deadline passes without resolution, the Commission may decide to move the case to the stage of reasoned opinion.

Reasoned opinion is the process of evaluating whether a breach of directive has actually occurred. If the commission concludes that it has, then the member state must decide whether to negotiate a resolution or, if it refuses to accept that a breach has occurred, the member state may decide to take the risk of the case being taken to the European Court of Justice by the Commission. The decision of the European Court of Justice is final, so very often at this stage member states decide to negotiate a resolution with the Commission, rather than risk a decision going against them.

The European Court of Justice (ECJ): Following on from a complaint to the European Commission, when all else fails, the European Commission will refer a case to the European Court of Justice for adjudication. Generally speaking, the fact that the Commission refers the case to the court means that there is a very strong chance that the court will find in the favour of the complainant. The court sits in Luxembourg. Eventually, the court will make a decision and the member state is obliged to comply with this decision. Failure to comply will lead the Commission back to the court to request sanctions against a member state for continuing to fail to comply. The court may order lump sum fines and daily fines of eye-watering size for every day that a member state fails to comply with its orders.

None of the legal process costs the original complainant anything at all. Apart from providing evidence to the Commission to substantiate a complaint, the entire legal process is funded by the European Commission itself.

Petition EU Court of Auditors: The Court of Auditors is responsible for the independent oversight of EU finances. Its role is to improve EU financial management and report on the use of public funds. At first sight, this may seem an unlikely organisation to which a complaint against a national authority should be addressed. However, this very powerful agency is well-placed to investigate maladministration of European funds by an EU national government. So, for instance, if a member state has used EU funds for a project which is in breach of European law, the Court of Auditors will want to know why the funds were allocated and how these funds can be "clawed back".

Cases of suspected fraud in the use of EU funding are of interest to this agency. In cases where there appear to be breaches of EU law, and where EU funding is also involved, a complaint can and should be made to the Court of Auditors. An allegation to the Court of Auditors must be made directly to them (not via the European Commission, because the Court of Auditors are independent of all other EU institutions).

An investigation by the Court of Auditors adds additional pressure on an EU member state authority when the complaint is made in conjunction with a complaint to the European Commission. In this case, the member state faces both an imminent financial investigation alongside an ongoing legal probe. This strategy creates a "perfect storm" for any government that has something to hide in its dealings with the EU in terms of European law and the use of EU funds.

EU Ombudsman: So what can go wrong when dealing with the EU legal system? Generally, the European Commission is tasked with ensuring that EU directives are properly implemented by member states. This is their job and a fundamental role of the Commission. Therefore, they are keen to resolve implementation issues quickly and finally. However, if a complainant has any doubts about the behaviour of the Commission in the execution of its duty as "guardian of the treaties", then the EU Ombudsman is available to investigate the process and ensure that the citizen's complaint has been effectively handled by the Commission. The EU Ombudsman is probably the most important person in the European hierarchy. An accusation to the Ombudsman about the workings of any part of the EU administration is considered the "nuclear option" of complaints to Europe. The maladministration of any part of the European Union can be reported to the EU Ombudsman.

European Court of Human Rights (ECHR): This court was formed on the basis of the "European Convention of Human Rights" and it has 47 European "contracting" states that are subject to its judgements. It hears applications that a contracting state has breached one or more of the human rights provisions concerning the civil and political rights set out in the Convention.

An application to the court can be lodged by an individual, a group of individuals or one or more of the 47 contracting states. In order to fully understand how this court may be employed by an individual or NGO it is important to have a good understanding of the convention.

Generally speaking, all of the nations within the court's jurisdiction have (theoretically) incorporated all the provisions of the European Convention of Human Rights into their own national legislation. In Britain this implementation is the Human Rights Act (HRA) and every contracting nation has its own enacting legislation.

However, very often, promulgation has been somewhat half-hearted and there are cases where national legislation actually contradicts the terms of the Convention. In other cases, national legislation simply hasn't caught up with the Convention and sometimes national courts rule without proper reference to it.

In such cases where there is a clear contravention, it may be possible to apply to the European Court of Human Rights for a judgement. There are many conditions that need to be fulfilled in order to bring a case to the court, and local legal action should have been exhausted (or unavailable) before resorting to this (extremely busy) court.

Areas where the ECHR has been instrumental in the past in protecting human rights in Europe include the following landmark cases:

• **Privacy and private life:** In 2008, the Grand Chamber in Strasbourg heard the case of "S and Marper vs. UK". For four years, anyone arrested in England, Wales or Northern Ireland had a DNA sample taken and held in the National DNA Database. Even if charges were dropped or discontinued, the record remained. The court ruled that indiscriminate retention of fingerprints and DNA failed to balance public and private interests. It said there was "disproportionate interference" with the right to respect for private life and that this was unnecessary in a democratic society.

• **Education and children's rights:** The ECHR have been deployed to uphold the rights of children. Their rulings have meant compensation for minors who were abused, but ignored by social services, endorse the rights of children to express their religious faith, and supported families fleeing domestic violence.

In 2002, "Z and others vs. UK" examined social services' duty to protect children from torture. Z and her three siblings had suffered years of "horrific" neglect and abuse by their parents. Reports were ignored. The children were placed in emergency care five years after the first complaints. The court ruled that Article 3 of the ECHR - the prohibition of torture, inhuman and degrading treatment - had been breached. The UK had failed to protect the children from ill-treatment, and should have known of the extreme neglect. That no system was in place to compensate the children was also a breach of Article 13 of the ECHR - the right to an effective remedy.

• **Health:** Human rights laws have helped to trigger the right to access to life-saving drugs and have held hospitals to account when lapses in mental health treatment have resulted in suicide. In addition, they have given same-sex partners the equivalent rights and status as heterosexuals. In the UK, in the so-called "Mid Staffordshire" scandal, 100 claims were made in 2011, using the law implementing European human rights law into British law. These cases alleged that gross or degrading treatment of mostly elderly people at a hospital had caused or hastened their deaths.

In "Rabone vs Pennine", the UK Supreme Court heard in 2012 how Melanie Rabone suffered from depression and was admitted to hospital following a suicide attempt. She was assessed as a high risk, but was allowed home leave. She killed herself during the leave. In the legal case brought by Melanie's parents against the Pennine Care Foundation Trust, the court ruled that the trust had a duty under Article 2 of the UK Human Rights Act - the right to life. It should have taken steps to protect Melanie from the "real and immediate" risk of suicide. It failed in its assumed responsibility for an at-risk person.

• **Defence and foreign affairs:** Rights enshrined in the European Convention on Human Rights (ECHR) have been used to ensure that inquiries into civilian deaths in Iraq at the hands of British troops have been in-depth and independent. Article 2 of the ECHR - the right to life - was used to establish that any failure to properly equip British soldiers serving abroad would constitute a breach of their rights.

The case "Smith & Grady vs. UK", in 1999, dealt with the incident of two men in the UK military who were dismissed because of their homosexuality. It was MoD policy. A judicial review of the policy was unsuccessful and an appeal was refused. The two men's right to respect for their private lives and to be free from discrimination (Articles 8 and 14) was argued in the House of Lords. The court said that there had been "exceptional intrusion" into the men's private lives - and ruled that their rights had been violated.

• **Local government:** The British Human Rights Act has been used to stop councils from misusing closed-circuit TV (CCTV) surveillance, prevented local authorities from spying on parents believed to be subverting catchment-area rules for schools, and has been used against councils who have closed libraries and bypassed the rights of the disabled and the elderly.

The UK case of "Hillingdon Council vs Neary" involved a 21-year-old man with autism and severe learning disabilities who lived with his father. When his father became ill, the man was moved into a local authority "support unit". It was intended to be for a few weeks, until his father recovered. A year later, he was still being kept at the unit, against his father's wishes. Under Article 8 - respect for private and family life - the Court of Protection ruled, in 2011, that the removal of vulnerable adults from their relatives or carers could be justified only if the quality of care were better. Keeping the man away from his father for a year was judged to be in breach of his rights to family life. Article 5 of the UK Human Rights Act (the right to liberty and a quick decision by a court) was also ruled to have been violated.

The European Convention of Human Rights is a powerful legal instrument and provides for a great deal of legal leverage, at least for European citizens.

European small claims courts: The European small claims procedure applies to civil and commercial issues in cross-border litigation where the claim does not exceed €2000. It is a simplified claim process that has been available since 2009 in all EU Member States, except Denmark. It provides an easy and cheap method of making civil claims against entities in other EU countries. No lawyer is required to file a claim or defend a claim. It may be useful to harass and claim against an authority using an existing EU procedure.

International criminal court: This independent court is not part of the United Nations, but has a special relationship with the UN. It is unlikely that this court is relevant to most NGOs or activists, since it is normally only used by governments or when a case is referred to it by the United Nations. Also, the court deals exclusively with the judgement of political or military leaders accused of international crimes, such as genocide, war crimes and crimes against humanity. However, there is a possibility for individuals or NGOs to make submissions to this court via the so-called

"Pre-Trial Chamber". The court has the power to investigate any complaint when there is sufficient material evidence.

ILO: The international labour organisation: This UN Agency is responsible for establishing and monitoring standards used in the employment of human labour. The ILO has developed over 180 conventions, which have been adopted by its member states into their national legislation. These conventions relate to all aspects of working conditions. For instance, the ILO has conventions on discrimination, child labour, union rights, minimum wages, maritime labour, productivity and health and safety. To be able to make a complaint to the ILO it is important to understand the basic content of the ILO conventions.

Almost all members of the UN are also members of the International Labour Organisation. Although the ILO can and does register and publish complaints from individuals and NGOs against countries and organisations, it has no power to impose any form of sanction. However, there is an obligation on member states to rectify deviations from the ILO conventions to which they are signatories. Therefore, a complaint to the ILO can provide a useful and powerful lever to force an authority to act to enforce the rules agreed in ILO conventions. Anyone can make a complaint to the ILO and it should be properly backed up with good quality evidence. It carries no cost (apart from the time of the complainant).

The United Nations special rapporteurs: Although the UN has a responsibility for protecting human rights, in reality it has basically no facilities or mandate to punish countries or other entities that commit human rights abuses. However, it does have a strong investigative and reporting role via the so-called Special Rapporteur on Human Rights. This office can investigate individual complaints and conduct on-site studies of a potential human rights problem on the territory of any member state. Theoretically, the Special Rapporteur of the UN reports directly to the Secretary General of the UN. There are many themes covered by the special rapporteur and it's important to understand which themes are of interest to these offices. For instance, there are rapporteurs investigating issues relating to the "Right to Food", "Drinking Water", the "Right to Justice", "Environmental Rights", "Toxic Waste Movement", "Education", and "Cultural Rights", amongst others. Before contacting a rapporteur it's important to understand their particular speciality and to ensure that a case is properly documented and evidenced.

Considerations and risks: There is no legal risk in using any of these agencies as part of an attack on the behaviour of an authority. Clearly, reporting a country to the European Commission is not going to make the complainant very popular in that country, but legally the complainant is within his rights. Sometimes however, it may be wise for a complainant to remain anonymous, at least if there is a risk of the target authority resorting to "dirty tricks" against the complainant. It happens, and in some cases it is fatal.

8.6.6.3 Petition Higher Parliaments: Apart from the legal agencies of transnational organisations, such as the EU, there are other institutions which can be approached when seeking legal and political support against a national authority.

National parliaments: In most disputes with a national authority or a corporate authority, there will be some politicians who are sympathetic to the cause that is being championed. The majority of democratic countries provide an opportunity to raise a question in a national parliament and allow some time for both opposition and government members to ask questions of the government. This can be a very useful vehicle for forcing a government to face embarrassing questions publicly, and put them in a position where they are obliged to provide answers, again, in public. In Britain or Ireland this process is called "putting down a question" to the government. In order to do this, an activist or NGO has to formulate a brief and concise question and then find a sympathetic member of parliament to ask it at the next opportunity. Although answers may take some time in coming, they do carry some legal weight and certainly cannot be obvious lies. The phrasing of such questions is very important. The question should leave no room for fudging of answers.

Petition European parliament: The European Parliament provides a very interesting and powerful facility available to any citizen of Europe, which is the ability to petition the parliament in person. To quote from the European Parliament website:

"Any citizen of the European Union, or resident in a Member State, may, individually or in association with others, submit a petition to the European Parliament on a subject which comes within the European Union's fields of activity and which affects them directly. Any company, organisation or association with its headquarters in the European Union may also exercise this right of petition, which is guaranteed by the Treaty. A petition may take the form of a complaint or a request and may relate to issues of public or private interest. The petition may present an individual request, a complaint or observation concerning the application of EU law or an appeal to the European Parliament to adopt a position on a specific matter. Such petitions give the European Parliament the opportunity of calling attention to any infringement of a European citizen's rights by a Member State or local authorities or other institution."

This right represents an amazing way for any aggrieved citizen or protest group to take their case to the very highest political chamber in Europe. Although there is a healthy number of petitions passing through the parliament at any time, this particular European right is still largely unknown by the majority of EU citizens, who remain quite ignorant of their extensive rights under EU law.

As in any legal intervention, the first step in petitioning the European Parliament is to document the case, with particular reference to any infringement by a member state of any EU directive or regulation, and highlight any maladministration by any institutions of the EU. This can include delays, misuse of funds, failure to take infringement actions, etc. When a properly prepared case has been formulated (probably as part of a complaint to the European Commission) a petition to the European Parliament can be made.

This is a simple procedure, which is documented on the EU Parliament's website, but, effectively, it means writing to the Chairman of the Petitions Committee of the European Parliament in Brussels with a copy of your petition. The petition will then be registered and the petitioner will be notified when it is due to be heard. A petitioner may present the petition in person to the Parliament with the aid of all the usual gadgetry of overhead slideshows, video etc. Then there are opportunities for questions and clarifications from members of Parliament and the European Commission.

Additionally or alternatively, a petitioner can find an MEP to represent the petition on their behalf. Having some MEPs briefed on the content of a petition is useful to ensure that it gets the attention it deserves. Petitions that are judged admissible remain open for investigation and are reviewed at the next monthly Parliamentary meeting, as more information is available. The committee on petitions has wide powers that allow it to demand action on a petition by the Commission, to request more information from a member state, or to refer the petition to a specialised committee to investigate and to recommend actions to be taken.

A complaint to the European Commission, together with a petition to the European Parliament, is a perfect way to make sure that a complaint against a government of an EU member state is taken seriously and kept in the public eye.

Considerations and risks: There are no legal risks in raising any issue in any democratic parliament. There may be some small costs involved and, of course, the time required producing a properly documented and evidenced case.

Using questions or petitions to national or supra-national parliaments provides immense leverage against a national authority. It causes political embarrassment, maintains pressure on the authority and provides high quality media opportunities to publicise the complainant's case.

8.6.6.4 Citizen's Arrest: Many jurisdictions have a concept of a "citizen's arrest", whereby an ordinary member of the public, who is not acting as a sworn law-enforcement official, arrests another individual.

The rules vary widely from one country to another. In most countries the concept has been widely developed from ancient principles where citizens were encouraged to apprehend law-breakers and is based on concepts of citizen responsibility.

A citizen's arrest or an attempt at a citizen's arrest also makes a powerful protest gesture.

For example, in January 2014, Twiggy Garcia, a London bar worker, attempted to arrest Tony Blair for crimes against peace in Iraq. It was a brave effort to bring to justice a former prime minister, who many people regard as having got away with waging an illegal war.

This is the value of citizen's arrest's powers: in some jurisdictions they grant ordinary people the right to arrest the accused when the forces of law and order fail to do so. Often, the rich and powerful use their influence to evade justice. The right of citizen's arrest gives the poor and powerless the means to make sure they don't always get away with it. In Britain, the citizen's arrest statute dates back to medieval England and common law. Today it is enshrined in the "Police and Criminal Evidence Act 1984". Every citizen has the right to perform an arrest if they have evidence that a person has committed a crime. One of the great virtues of an attempted citizen's arrest is that, even if it doesn't succeed, it can help publicise an injustice. It's a dramatic way of raising awareness.

Considerations and risks: The use of force needs to be proportionate. There needs to be documented and reliable evidence against the detainee and the civil and human rights of the detainee must be fully respected. Attempts to arrest people without proper preparation can end in a fiasco, so it's important to have a fully developed plan for such an action.

8.7 Direct Action

Breaking away from the traditional definition of (Gene Sharp's) "Nonviolent Action", here we define a new category of civil rebellion, which we refer to as "Direct Action".

Direct action refers to certain types of civil rebellion which are distinguished from other forms of civil disobedience, protest or intervention because they involve and encourage deliberate acts of political (though not physical) violence. Whilst often associated with confrontation, direct action is essentially about power. Intelligent direct action assesses the power dynamics between authority and the citizen and attempts to shift power away from the elites and back to the masses.

As Frederick Douglass, the 19h century social reformer, said: "Power concedes nothing without a demand." Malcolm X elaborated the same principle: "Power never takes a step back, except in the face of more power." Thus, rather than hoping that our leaders will make changes reflecting popular opinion, a citizen protester can radically change the dynamics of power by means of the various forms of "Direct Action" available to us all.

The concept of "direct action" is not a new one. Some would argue that the Boston Tea Party was an example of "direct action" because it involved overt damage to property and an act of deliberate political violence. As an action, it actively attempted to intimidate and provoke the colonial authorities and throw down a challenge to British rule in America.

There have been many later examples of direct action; some sections of the anti-nuclear movement used acts of direct action, particularly during the 1980s. Groups opposing the introduction of cruise missiles into the United Kingdom employed tactics such as breaking into and occupying US air bases, as well as blocking roads to prevent the movement of military convoys and disrupt military projects. In the US, mass protests opposed nuclear energy, nuclear weapons, and the military in general, resulting in thousands of arrests. Many groups also set up semi-permanent "peace camps" outside air bases hosting nuclear weapons.

In modern times, Greenpeace have often pursued their objectives by means of various forms of direct action; for instance, by deliberately interfering with oil exploration vessels and by physical intervention in other environmentally dangerous projects. One of the best known and fearless protest groups applying direct action is Sea Shepherd. Since 1977, this smallish NGO has taken on the might of the Japanese whaling industry almost single-handedly. It was founded by Paul Watson after he split from Greenpeace because he felt that their position was not sufficiently confrontational. This NGO currently operates 3 vessels that aggressively and successfully interrupt Japanese whaling activities. Some governments (the US (FBI) for instance) consider Sea Shepherd to be "Eco Terrorists", largely because they are quite effective in their actions.

The techniques of direct action highlighted below refer to some of the most risky and dangerous forms of civil rebellion in existence.

Methods of Direct Action

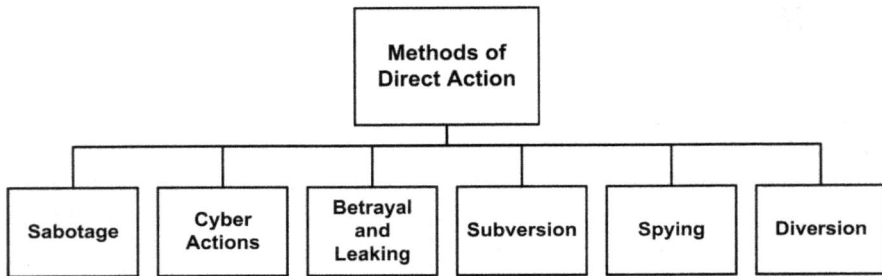

```
                        ┌─────────────────┐
                        │   Methods of    │
                        │  Direct Action  │
                        └─────────────────┘
```

| Sabotage | Cyber Actions | Betrayal and Leaking | Subversion | Spying | Diversion |

8.7.1 Sabotage

Sabotage is a deliberate act designed to weaken an authority or corporation by means of various acts of destruction, subversion, disruption or obstruction. Sabotage is a much more widespread activity in commercial circles than we would care to believe. It comes in all shapes and sizes, but ranges from stealing employees, documents and customers, to damaging computer systems or outright physical property damage. Generally, sabotage is defined by the fact that it is aimed at damage to non-human assets and is a nonviolent action.

Smaller organisations suffer much more acutely from sabotage attacks than their larger kin because they are unable to tolerate even small disruptions or losses as easily as very big targets. The greatest opportunity (and risk) of acts of sabotage are from employees that have a hidden agenda within an organisation.

```
                    ┌─────────────────┐
                    │                 │
                    │    Sabotage     │
                    │                 │
                    └─────────────────┘
        ┌───────────────┬───┴────┬───────────────┐
┌──────────────┐ ┌──────────────┐ ┌──────────────┐ ┌──────────────┐
│ Destruction of│ │  Sabotage by │ │  Sabotage by │ │  Sabotage by │
│   Property    │ │  Subversion  │ │  Disruption  │ │ Obstruction  │
└──────────────┘ └──────────────┘ └──────────────┘ └──────────────┘
```

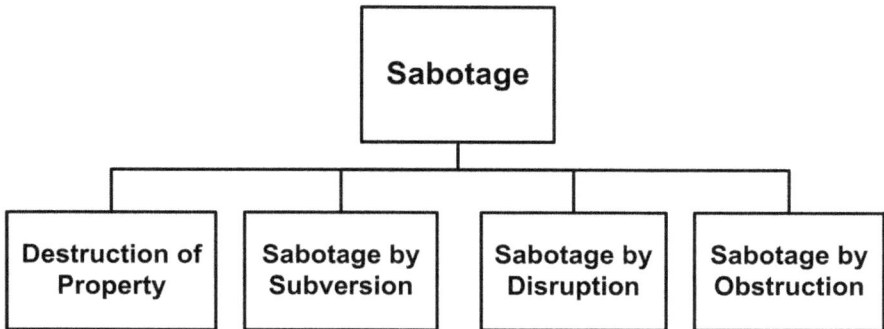

Ecotage: This is a hybrid form of sabotage, designed to help the cause of environmental protection in some way. It typically involves damaging organisations and equipment used in activities which are viewed as ecologically harmful. Examples of this include spiking heavy machinery with sugar in their fuel or disabling vehicles used by workers employed to damage an environmentally important site.

A large-scale example of ecotage took place in Britain, when hundreds of anti-cull saboteurs, angered by the culling of badgers, sabotaged the 2013 cull campaign by disrupting traps and digging up bait laid by gamekeepers and farmers, as well as disturbing the ground near badger setts and making noises at night so that the animals would be too scared to come out. The result of their sabotage was a very low rate of culling. Some scientists actually believe the campaign may have encouraged the dispersal of the badger population by frightening them enough to move to colonise new, quieter areas, where no badgers' colonies (or culls) existed.

8.7.1.1 Sabotage by Destruction of Property: This is the most obvious and popular form of sabotage. A protest group, in some circumstances, may be able to identify material assets owned by an authority or corporation that can be destroyed or damaged, thus weakening the authority by delaying or disrupting its plans or undermining its power.

In protests centred on land developments, roads or other infrastructural works, a protest group can simply target hardware being used as part of the work, such as earth moving machines, generators, pumps, diesel supplies, site accommodation, etc. In this case, sabotage of equipment or supplies probably won't stop a development, but it will cause a delay and some inconvenience.

In other forms of unwelcome developments, such as fracking exploration, a protest group can vandalise equipment, contaminate fuel supplies and generally degrade the operating environment for an exploration company, so that it becomes almost impossible to operate. It also then sends a signal to the corporation involved that future exploration and production costs will be inflated by the need for extraordinary levels of security and the need to replace equipment and materials which are sabotaged.

Considerations and risks: Most authorities and corporate organisations have a problem when someone deliberately damages or destroys their capital assets or supplies. Such acts are universally considered to be acts of vandalism or criminal damage, regardless of the moral imperatives of the perpetrator.

Sabotage by destruction of property is therefore an act that will certainly attract investigation and legal action. To avoid the consequences from such a reaction, a protest group needs to be highly organised, plan acts of sabotage properly and be properly equipped.

8.7.1.2 Sabotage by Subversion: Authorities can be critically undermined if it becomes clear that they have been overrun by infiltrators and that no part of an authority's organisation can be trusted. This happens when confidential information continuously leaks to the press or onto the internet, despite stringent attempts by an authority to maintain its secrecy.

The press, in recent years, has proven itself very adept at hacking the communications systems and securing the services of infiltrators in all strata of society. In particular, of course, the political classes have been a prime target. The level of insecurity has come to the point where British cabinet ministers are forbidden to bring mobile phones into cabinet meetings. Confidential documents must be covered at all times, in case they are photographed at high resolution by members of the press, and their contents published. Such paranoia reflects the fact that governments everywhere are quite compromised by infiltrators and whistleblowers within their own organisations and are surrounded by an antagonistic press corps, constantly on the lookout for scandals and other sensational stories.

Considerations and risks: Sabotaging an authority by subversive means carries some risks. In the examples above, members of the press have been prosecuted for hacking mobile phones and civil servants have been sacked and prosecuted for revealing confidential conversations and documents to the press. In some jurisdictions the consequences of being caught may even be fatal.

8.7.1.3 Sabotage by Disruption: There are many forms of disruption which may sabotage an authority. For instance, in anti-road protests in the UK over the last 20 years, activists have disrupted works by climbing into trees and refusing to leave. They tunnelled underground in areas about to be cleared for road building and refused to emerge. They stopped tree felling by putting nails into trees scheduled for felling, thwarting chainsaws. These acts of sabotage damaged almost nothing, but they did cause significant disruption to the plans of authorities; often buying time for the protesters to take alternative legal actions to stop a project or to await reinforcements.

Other forms of sabotage by disruption may include legal challenges to an authority's actions, such as temporary injunctions. Disruptions by the presence of the press can also be effective where an authority wishes to avoid being filmed in action.

Considerations and risks: Acts of physical disruption can be dangerous. In some countries, authorities would think nothing of killing a disruptive protester, as the following example demonstrates:

On 16 March 2003 in Gaza, a 23-year-old American peace activist, Rachel Corrie from Washington, USA, was murdered by an Israeli bulldozer driver. Rachel was a volunteer with the International Solidarity Movement and in Gaza opposing the bulldozing of a Palestinian home. Other foreigners who were with her said the driver of the bulldozer was aware that Rachel was there and continued to destroy the house. Initially he dropped sand and other heavy debris on her, and then the bulldozer pushed her to the ground, where he proceeded to drive the bulldozer over her body, fracturing both of her arms, legs and skull. She was transferred to hospital, where she later died.

This tragic story clearly illustrates that disruptive protesters need to exercise caution and be prepared to withdraw, if necessary. It is much better to make a strategic retreat and regroup later than to become just another victim of violent repression.

8.7.1.4 Sabotage by Obstruction: Overt demonstrations of physical obstruction, such as blockades, sit-ins, etc., can be used as a means of sabotaging an authority's plans. We have already described many methods of physical obstruction. Other forms of obstruction include the use of industrial action to trigger off obstructions by pickets. In recent demonstrations against fracking operators in both the USA and UK, demonstrators have managed successfully to completely sabotage the operator's plans by blockading roads with heavy machinery, tractors, etc. and second-locking access gates to drilling sites, so that operators couldn't enter their own sites.

Human obstructions may work in some environments and protesters chaining themselves to railway lines, entrances or machinery may cause some temporary obstructions.

In 2013, an unusual case of sabotage by obstruction occurred in New Jersey, when several lanes on an important road bridge were effectively closed by local officials, claiming the need for a traffic study. It transpired that the highly disruptive closure was, in fact, a form of political revenge for one political group's refusal to support another. What was most interesting about the action was the way in which local officials could cause political and infrastructural mayhem, simply by closing some lanes of a bridge for a few days. The political consequences of the huge ensuing traffic disruption were still playing out a year later.

Another interesting form of economic sabotage by occupation occurred in November 2013, when two council-owned houses were put up for auction in London and were expected to attract offers of around £3 million. The properties were being sold as "Vacant Possession", i.e. with no occupants. However, just as the auction was about to begin, a young woman stood up and told the room she had an announcement to make. "Excuse me. Sorry to interrupt," she began. "We are here to tell you that Lot No. 60 is a council house that is currently being occupied by community activists who don't want to see this property lost, because we believe that council housing is a public good and it shouldn't be being sold. If you want to buy it, you're buying it with 20 squatters." The protest announcement was designed to devalue the property, but it unfortunately failed. In fact, it did nothing to dampen the enthusiasm for the sale, and the buildings sold for £2.96m. The protest was one of a new wave of actions against, what the protesters consider, social cleansing of desirable parts of central London by property speculators, and the gross shortage of social housing for poorer tenants. The interruption of the house auction, together with the arrival of squatters (with much local support), created a new method to protest and publicise the increasing gentrification of various parts of the city.

Considerations and risks: Physical obstructions can be removed with time. Therefore, sabotage by obstruction should be seen primarily as a method of delay rather than the complete and final sabotage of an authority's plans. It should only be used when a protest group needs to "buy" time.

8.7.2 Cyber Actions

This is a set of methodologies also known as "Cyber activism" or "Internet activism". There are three basic groups/motivations for Cyber Activism:

• Internet freedom: There are many activists that see the internet as a key battleground for freedom of information, in the same way as press freedom. Their central issue is the freedom of internet use and they apply their technical skills to maintain and promote these freedoms.

• Protest users: There are an increasingly large and vibrant group of activists that use the internet to fight for other protest objectives. This group uses the internet as just one of several methods to conduct their campaigns. Virtually all serious protest groups are now represented on the internet and actively use so-called e-campaigning techniques.

• Hacktivists: A third group uses its technical knowledge to promote freedom of the internet, but also as a weapon to support other protest groups and to attack authoritarian regimes. The "Anonymous" group sometimes falls into this category. As a protest group, it has special interests in internet freedom and it expresses its support for internet freedom by using advanced technical actions against organisations that it considers to be repressive. However, it also throws its technical support behind actions which are unconnected to internet freedom.

With the rapid movement of large businesses away from conventional marketing and into the internet arena, the opportunities for conventional physical protests are becoming limited. These days many organisations only have an internet presence and this alters the paradigm used for moral confrontation and protest. In order to effectively protest against the immoral behaviour of internet-based companies, NGOs and protest groups must now adopt new strategies to confront and disrupt, or to focus attention on various ethical issues. There is a wide range of so-called "cyber-actions" available to do this.

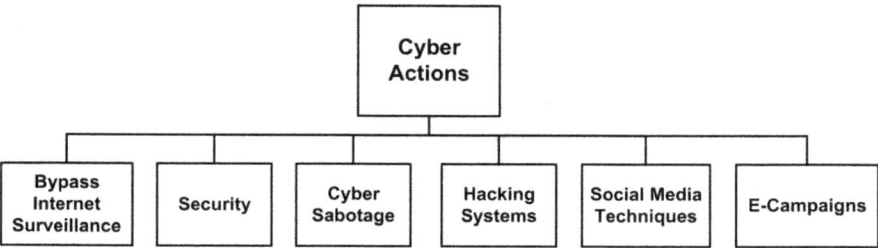

The internet is now so ubiquitous in all human activities, that it is almost inconceivable to organise any protest action without considering how the internet may be used to promote protest objectives. The internet brings new opportunities for communication and for a series of public challenges to authority. However, the internet also brings new threats to the security and privacy of a protest group.

8.7.2.1 Bypassing Internet Surveillance: Internet surveillance of various kinds is now a fact of life, both for individuals as for protest groups. Even before the intervention of government authorities, corporations spent large amounts of money on spying on activist groups that they see as a threat.

There are now many specialist companies (often staffed by ex police, intelligence agents or military personnel) that exist simply to "investigate" (spy) on protest groups. There is ample evidence to show that one of the areas of special interest is in internet surveillance of these groups [Note 123]. Together with the threat of government surveillance, there is a significant motivation for protest groups to take appropriate precautions to secure their internet presence against unwelcome interference or snooping. Avoiding this surveillance is now an important form of direct action and defiance of authoritarian control.

There are several factors that help to protect oneself or a protest group from state or corporate internet surveillance. One element is the public availability of very good encryption software which makes it practically impossible to circumvent properly implemented strong encryption in our internet communications. The second factor which limits internet surveillance is cost. One of the best defences against surveillance is to make it as difficult and expensive as possible by adding layers of security to everything we do when using an internet connection and by being rigorous in keeping our systems super clean. Properly disciplined computer use and security reduces opportunities for surveillance and makes it much harder (and more expensive) to spy on us. Finally, one important factor which works in the citizen's favour is the technical ignorance of many authorities. For some reason, many politicians have a very limited technical understanding of how the internet actually works and how its architecture is designed for resilience. This ignorance leads politicians to make rather stupid decisions, which are simple to circumvent as illustrated in the following example from Turkey.

During the Turkish demonstrations of June 2013, the Turkish government threatened to, and actually began to, restrict internet usage. The government's misunderstanding of the technical capacity of their young people became clear during one particular weekend, when the number of requests for VPN services in Turkey jumped tenfold. VPN services enable a user to effectively hide his internet activity. Thus, huge parts of the Turkish population responded to the government's spying and controls by simply bypassing them. Simultaneously, requests for encrypted email and instant messaging services leapt enormously [Note 124] for the same reasons.

The following techniques go some way towards building a secure internet or mobile environment which blocks unwelcome surveillance. This is a fast moving environment, with new privacy technology emerging on an almost daily basis. None of these techniques should be attempted without proper planning and research or without the assistance of an IT specialist. Keep an eye on new developments by looking at sites such as "HideMyAss" (http://wiki.hidemyass.com) to see up-to-date information on the latest techniques. Some of the following methods can also be used to bypass web censorship by governments, such as that of the Chinese, Iranian and Russian authorities.

• **User-anonymous networks:** TOR, I2P and various other user security networks make it possible for users to surf the internet anonymously, so that their activities and location cannot be discovered by government agencies, corporations, or by anyone else. These systems are mostly free, downloadable and usable on any mobile device or PC. In some cases, the software can be kept on a memory stick and used ad hoc on any PC. There are at least 10 similar systems available at the time of writing. The quality and security of these systems is constantly being upgraded and, before using any of these systems, it is important to check the current status (TOR has been occasionally compromised in the past, allegedly). These systems generally work by allowing a user to access a website, but with their own IP address not revealed to the web server. This is done (in the case of TOR) by encrypting and re-routing a request randomly through a huge global network of servers, so that when it arrives at the web server, the original IP address is unknown. These systems often allow secure chat, instant messaging as well as email and file-sharing and are often used for secure communications between journalists and sources such as whistleblowers. TOR has been used by Reporters without Borders, and, by 2013, TOR had around 4 million users, including bloggers, business executives, IT professionals and law enforcement officers as its key users. Needless to say that these systems are sometimes used by criminals, but then so are supermarkets!

• **Proxy servers:** A proxy server is a computer system (or an application) that acts as an intermediary for requests from other servers. A client user connects to a proxy server, making a request for some service, such as a file download, a server connection or a web page and the proxy server evaluates and passes on the request, returning its response to the client user. These days, most proxies are web proxies, designed to facilitate access to content on the web and provide anonymity.

There are several types of proxy servers, but one of the most interesting from a user or organisational security perspective is the "Open Proxy". An open proxy is a forwarding proxy server that is accessible by any internet user. There are many open proxies on the internet and many proxy servers are free to use. An anonymous open proxy allows users to conceal their IP address while browsing the web or using other internet services. Proxy servers are not extremely secure because there are a number of methods of 'tricking' the client into revealing himself, regardless of the proxy being used. However, a proxy server provides another layer of security and anonymity.

For organisations running websites on their own web servers, the use of a so-called "reverse proxy" is advisable to prevent certain types of operating system attacks on the web server itself. Again, it is just one extra layer of protection and does not protect against web application/service attacks.

• **VPN (Virtual Private Networks):** A virtual private network (VPN) allows connection to a private network across a public network, such as the internet. Thus, it allows an external computer or network-enabled device to send and receive data across shared or public networks as if it were directly connected to the private network. That means that the connected computer gets the benefit of all the resources and security of the private network. Communications are point to point and are encrypted. To prevent disclosure of private information, VPNs typically allow only authenticated remote access and make use of advanced encryption and authentication techniques.

VPNs are extremely useful for remote users to work securely on their own organisation's network as if they were physically connected to that network. It is important to choose a VPN service provider that can be trusted, uses 256bit encryption and doesn't log accesses to its network. There are many that fit this description and some which don't, so when selecting a VPN provider it's important to vet them, both technically and in terms of their security regime.

• **MAC spoofing:** Each network interface on your computer or any other networked device, such as a mobile phone or tablet, has a unique MAC address. These MAC addresses are assigned in the factory, but you can change, or "spoof", MAC addresses in the operating system software.

Why would you want to do this? Because they're unique, MAC addresses can be used to track you. When you walk around, your smart phone scans for nearby Wi-Fi networks and broadcasts its MAC address. A company named Renew London used rubbish bins in the city of London to track people's movements around the city, based on their MAC addresses.

Apple's iOS 8 will use a random MAC address each time it scans for nearby Wi-Fi networks, to prevent this sort of tracking. But if you want to be really free of the association between you and your devices (PC or mobile device), the MAC address needs to be changed (spoofed). The device can then not be associated with you. In Windows this is done using the Device Manager in the Control Panel. In Linux this is done with the Network Manager. In Mac OS this is done with an ifconfig statement. In android devices various apps are available that allow a device to be "rooted" (used as if you were a super user) and in this state the MAC address can also be altered.

• **E2E encrypted communications:** End-to-end encryption (E2EE) is a digital communications methodology. It provides uninterrupted protection of data between two communicating parties. It involves the encryption of data by an originating party to be readable only by the intended recipient, and for the receiving party to decrypt it with no involvement by any third party. The intention of end-to-end encryption is to prevent intermediaries, such as internet providers or application service providers, from being able to discover or tamper with the content of communications. End-to-end encryption generally includes protection of both confidentiality and integrity. Typical server-based communications systems do not include end-to-end encryption. These systems can only guarantee protection of communications between clients and servers, not between the communicating parties themselves. For this reason, an E2EE-based system is much more secure. There are many products now entering the market. Examples of end-to-end encryption include PGP for email [Note 125] and OTR for instant messaging. There are also E2EE systems for cloud storage, and voice telephone calls.

• **HTTPS Everywhere:** The use of browser add-ons can improve security by forcing the use of HTTP secure protocol. Hypertext Transfer Protocol Secure (HTTPS) is a communications protocol for secure communication over a computer network, with especially wide deployment on the internet. HTTPS adds the security capabilities of SSL/TLS to standard HTTP communications. The main motivation for HTTPS is to prevent external surveillance of a user's web activity. Any financial transactions made on the web will use HTTPS to ensure security, but actually all browsing should be carried out using HTTPS. This can be forced by using an appropriate browser add-on. There are many browser add-ons available which will enforce the use of HTTPS, such as "HTTPS Everywhere", for instance.

• **Air gaps:** Also called "sheep dip" machines. These are computers that have never been connected to the internet. A protest group could use such machines to work on, but in total isolation from the internet. When a file needs to be emailed or uploaded via the internet, then another internet-connected machine is used for this purpose. The process to do this securely is as follows: The file is first encrypted on the air gap machine, then placed on a memory stick and physically copied to the internet-connected machine. When receiving a file which has been transmitted via the internet, the process is reversed. Controlling the cleanliness of the memory stick is simple and it can be formatted daily and thoroughly deleted (using a file eraser). Maintaining air-gap machines which are never connected to the internet is a very sure way of ensuring that there is no surveillance of what is stored on these machines, even though it adds some inconvenience.

• **Surveillance jamming:** Most digital exchange and internet router manufacturers supplying internet service providers include facilities in their products for sniffing the content of telephone calls and plain text email and text messages at will. They euphemistically call these "legal interception" devices. In Ireland, for instance, the government has a company dedicated to building and deploying software to sniff this traffic and, using a range of complex algorithms, to automatically store copies of voice or mail traffic in which certain words are used. All of the world's large digital phone exchange manufacturers build these facilities and software onboard their exchange switching units. Clearly, the word "bomb" or "destroy" or "explosive" will be amongst the words being searched for by the "sniffer" algorithms, but there really isn't anything to stop a government using this commercially available software to track communications containing the vocabulary of protest, or particular names of people or places. The mechanism works by algorithmically "listening" to streams of subscriber traffic (voice or data) and as soon as a particular word occurs, the voice or data traffic is send as a file to be stored on a database with the associated meta-data of the source and destination. This continues until the transmission disconnects. The transmissions are then investigated manually.

The automated nature of these systems leaves them prone to attack by over-loading. Sending thousands or millions of emails out, seeded with key words, will cause the sniffer to store lots of meaningless records. The process of sending out large numbers of emails is simple to automate and its source and destination can be easily obfuscated using spoof IP addresses. All that is required is two email addresses and mail server software. There is some indication that groups are beginning to take this kind of jamming action, but there may well be an escalation of such acts of cyber sabotage against uninvited and illegal government surveillance.

Such counterattacks against intelligence agencies are being actively developed in response to the recent revelations by Snowden and others of extensive surveillance by NSA and GCHQ.

Internet censorship: The collapse of media freedom in Turkey in the last few years has taken its toll on journalists and on social media users. The government of prime minister Erdogan, accused of large-scale corruption, took various actions to restrict access to social media and the internet, in an attempt to stop the dissemination of these accusations and evidence.

The internet curbs were an attempt by Erdogan to stifle dissent. His orders gave the government's telecoms authority the power to block access to any website even without a court order. The only justification required was a suspicion that the content was deemed to infringe privacy or was offensive. Human Rights Watch stated that the restrictions raised concerns that a "defensive government is seeking to increase its power to silence critics and to arbitrarily limit politically damaging material online". The European Parliament's president at the time, Martin Schulz, called the laws a "step back in an already suffocating environment for media freedom".

This example of internet censorship illustrates why all forms of arbitrary, politically-motivated internet censorship are abhorrent and rather foolish. The workaround that Turkish tweeters used exploited a fundamental strength of the internet, obviously misunderstood by Erdogan's greying advisors. The internet is a network of networks, containing non-hierarchical routes that simply do not allow any one person to switch part of it off. This particular spat represented an important moment in the clash between the old elites and the new "connected" generation: a moment where a once-respected statesman (Erdogan) turned himself into a King Canute-like clown.

Other countries where internet censorship is rife, as we are constantly reminded by the Western press, include China and Iran. However, according to the OpenNet initiative, so-called pervasive censorship or interference at similar levels as China and Iran also exists in the USA, UK, Russia, India, Pakistan, the Persian Gulf nations, and parts of East Africa [Note 126].

Understanding the methods used to carry out internet censorship help us understand how these methods can be circumvented. The main methods of censorship used by governments are as follows:

• **Domain name system (DNS) filtering:** Here domain names are incorrectly resolved to return an incorrect IP address. This means that a web browser makes a request to the wrong IP address (web server). This censorship method can be circumvented by using an alternative, uncensored DNS server setting or entering the IP address of the website you want directly to the browser. This technique can also be bypassed by placing the domain name resolution in a local "hosts" file on your client PC (the "hosts" file is always referenced first when trying to convert a domain name into a real IP address.)

• **Internet Protocol (IP) address blocking:** IP addresses can be directly blocked by a service provider acting on the orders of a censoring government. This can be circumvented by using an unaffected proxy server to communicate with these IP addresses or by making a connection via a VPN service. However, proxies can also be blocked and there are moves afoot to block VPN traffic in some regimes (China and Iran). Nonetheless, external VPN services are constantly repositioning their products to bypass these systems of so-called "smart" internet censorship. For instance, the use of dynamic DNS services makes the blocking of a particular IP address a bit pointless because dynamic DNS bypasses the strict connection between a domain name and an IP address by allowing an IP address associated with a domain name to be dynamic.

• **Packet filtering:** This censorship method involves monitoring the contents of packets of data for particular keywords and then terminating a connection when they are found. This can be avoided using SSL encryption (https) or by reducing the MTU (maximum transmission unit) of a packet, so that keywords are harder to detect. The use of VPN services also bypasses packet filtering.

• **URL filtering:** This method of filtering scans URLs for keywords and refuses those which contain a pre-defined set of keywords. This is easily circumvented by using https, a VPN connection, or embedded escape characters in the URL. In the latter case, a real character is represented in a way which is meaningless to the filter but readable by the DNS server. These characters are often used in http requests.

• **Network disconnection:** This form of censorship involves the simple disconnection of internet services, routers and hardware. This action terminates one particular internet connection in the control of a censor, but is easily bypassed by using other connected networks, such as satellite internet connections, cross-border WiMax or cross-border mobile phone connections. Network disconnection (as practiced in Egypt by Mubarak) also has another side effect - it paralyses all business and internet-based government activity from export companies and banks to ministries and the military. A full network disconnection is akin to shooting off a leg because of an itch on your toe! This is perhaps why Mubarak had the internet reconnected after just 5 days - because the loss of business was seriously hurting his bank account and that of his generals.

• **Denial of service:** Governments block a website by trying to close it down using DoS attacks. This form of attack can only be maintained for a short time. Most attacked websites will quickly take evasive action against single source DoS attacks. Distributed DoS (DDoS) attacks from multiple sources are much harder to circumvent. Many websites will start up one or more mirror web sites to take over when a DDoS eventually takes down the original site. The censor then has to widen (and therefore weaken) his attack across a larger number of targets. Given that web servers are cheap and easy to replicate, it may well be possible to outgun a censor with lots of small web servers.

• **Portal censorship and search result removal:** This generally involves the removal of search results from a search engine. Certain countries forbid the transmission of certain material and insist that search engines remove links to those websites carrying such material from their search engine results. The bypass for this is to use another search engine or use the URL directly, once it is known.

• **Twitter blocking:** In recent years certain governments have sought to frustrate protest movements by blocking services like Twitter. The Turkish government did this in March 2014, to frustrate protest communications and the publication of corruption allegations against Turkey's Prime Minister Erdogan and his government. However, the protesters soon found ways around this blockade by: a/ using SMS to send tweets to their twitter page, b/ altering the 2 DNS settings on their devices, for instance, to use the Google or other DNS servers, and c/ finally set up their devices to use a VPN (virtual private network) instead of connecting directly to Twitter. In June 2014, as Turkish unrest grew, more than 120,000 people downloaded "Hotspot Shield", a free mobile app which provides a VPN service.

These young tech-savvy Turkish protesters clearly demonstrated that the traditional censorship mechanisms used by their authoritarian government no longer work in the face of the many technological methods of bypassing internet censorship.

Circumvention by satellite internet connection: Note that in all these cases of national censorship, an uncensored satellite internet service based in another country can always be used to bypass all forms of national filtering and censorship. The hardware and software are cheap and easy to install and, presumably, in countries like China and Iran, getting hold of the hardware should be simple enough. Once installed, satellite internet connections can be easily shared amongst a large community of users by using a fixed IP address or services such as DynDNS. VPN servers can also be set up and internet services re-established, at least for a group of users (depending on the bandwidth contracted). This method of connection is basically unbeatable, since the satellite dishes are reasonably small and look quite like TV dishes. Some even use satellites close to normal TV satellites, so they point in the appropriate direction as well.

Extreme circumvention of data censorship: Human ingenuity knows no boundaries. In Cuba, where internet connections for ordinary people are basically non-existent because of ancient infrastructure, a new "network" of data transmission has developed. It involves the downloading and copying of terabyte packages of internet pages onto portable hard disks. These are then copied and then recopied and sold to users once per week for a small sum of money. Thanks to the "Weekly Packet", Cubans can watch the latest movies as well as various television programs, including junk "telenovelas". In addition, they can read the latest editions of 500 magazines, including National Geographic, PC Weekly and the Economist, and play updated versions of various computer games. Unfortunately, the transmission is only in one direction, so the use of social media is not possible.

Considerations and risks: It is in everyone's interests to avoid internet surveillance. The same techniques used to spy on ordinary internet users are employed by governments, private corporations and criminal gangs. Protecting one's internet privacy from a criminal gang trying to defraud you requires many of the same counter-measures as those used to stop the prying eyes of your government's intelligence services. There are no risks involved in using any of the internet surveillance avoidance schemes above. In most cases, your service provider will not even know that you are using these techniques and, since they are all legal (and, indeed, often recommended techniques), there is no reason not to implement them as part of normal security measures.

8.7.2.2 Security: Many security concerns have tended to focus on internet security, especially since the revelations of Edward Snowden about the activities of the NSA and other intelligence gathering agencies. However, the internet is just one aspect of data security that a protest group needs to understand to stay safe from government or corporate surveillance. Having good IT security systems is also essential to modern protest organisations. Good IT security is tantamount to a snub to authoritarian governments, who would really prefer to monitor all communications between members of all protest NGOs, and all other computer activity as well, if they could.

Here are some other areas where a protest organisation should implement strong security:

• **Network security:** When a user connects to a network, they also connect to potentially millions of other machines across private networks and the internet. There are several security aspects that need to be considered when configuring a Local Area Network (LAN):

- Wireless networks should use encryption (WPA2-AES, for instance) to ensure wireless data is transmitted confidentially.

- Routers should have user id and password altered regularly.

- Change the default router SSID that is broadcast.

- Use MAC address filtering to exclude all but the devices that you own and use.

- Use a firewall (see below).

• **Securing your web browsers:** Since browsing is probably what users do most, it is worth taking browser security seriously. If you're unhappy that your click stream (the log of the sites you visit) is in effect public property as far as the security services are concerned, you might consider using freely available tools such as Tor Browser (or others). But to protect against the tracking of online behaviour, including through the use of cookies, a protest group should, at the very minimum, configure all browsers so that their security settings are appropriate. In Internet Explorer you may use the slider to set security settings at "highest", set the trusted sites settings, set cookie handling to "prompt" or even block all cookies, forbid the use of 3rd party browser extensions, etc. There are lots of published standards for these settings which change all the time and one should seek the most up-to-date advice for the best internet browser security [Note 127]. As mentioned, all browsers should always be configured to connect only to websites using the encrypted protocol https.

• **File encryption:** File encryption refers to a method by which data files are encrypted to protect them from unauthorised access when stored on servers, client PCs and mobile devices. Other forms of data encryption include full disk or disk partition encryption. Sensitive data stored on laptops, PCs, servers and mobile devices should always be stored in an encrypted form. There is a wealth of easy to use file encryption packages available, many of which are free and many of which provide effectively unbreakable encryption. These tools allow encrypted files and directories to sit side by side with unencrypted files on the same device and they make the whole process of encryption and decryption of files painless and almost transparent (except to request a key when opening, copying or moving a file). For Microsoft PCs, there is a built-in file encryption system as part of Windows and there are many 3rd party file encryption systems available in case you don't trust Microsoft.

• **Viruses, spyware and malware:** It goes without saying that the regular use of good quality 3rd party virus scans is essential to client user security. One area of special importance in a protest group's IT security refers to the early detection and disinfection of spyware and malware which may be used deliberately by an authority or corporate surveillance operation to gather information. Good quality spyware and malware removal software is essential to avoid and detect such infections. In fact, a good strategy is that one should use 2 or 3 different spyware and malware scanning software packages. Scanning of all PCs should be scheduled for at least once per day.

• **Private social networking:** Social networking for a protest group may be useful, but protest group organisers should simply delete their personal Facebook and Twitter accounts. These are just too easy to spy upon and hack. For the same reasons, protest organisers should never publish their name, date of birth, phone numbers or other personal details in connection with the protest group and, better still, in general, never at all.

• **Firewalls:** A firewall protects against connections to a network or a device via an open port. Firewalls reject requests for incoming and outgoing connections for all ports and applications, except those explicitly opened for normal communications by installed and firewall-registered software. Apart from pre-installed firewalls that come with a computer or mobile operating system, most routers also include a firewall. For extra security, it may be worth considering an additional 3rd party firewall, which may be either a hardware or software firewall.

• **Cloud services:** The message of the Snowden revelations to NGOs or protest groups is that they should avoid all cloud services (Dropbox, iCloud, Evernote, etc.) that are based in the US, the UK, France and other jurisdictions known to be tolerant of NSA spying. The working assumption should be that anything stored on such systems is potentially accessible by others. And if one must entrust data to them, then it is best to make sure it's encrypted.

• **Wireless networks:** Generally, keep Bluetooth on mobile devices switched off in any public location.

• **Search engine tracking:** All of the big search engines track your search history and build profiles of you in order (they say) to serve you personalised results, based on your search history. If you want to escape from this "filter bubble", you need to switch to a search engine that does not track your inquiries. The most obvious one at the time of writing is DuckDuckGo.

• **File storage and archiving:** An option that increasing numbers of users are exploring is running a private cloud service, using various safe software tools that provide Dropbox-like services, but on internet-connected drives that they own and control. And if protest group users carry around confidential data on a USB stick, make sure it's encrypted using something like TrueCrypt.

• **Location data:** Unless you want to be tracked geographically, it's best never to allow any application to have access to location data on any mobile device.

• **Good practice:** There are some basic things that internet-connected users should do to improve their security:

- Never open an attachment or click on a link in an email, unless you are COMPLETELY sure that the sender is trustworthy. Note that a lot of genuine looking emails may actually be spoof emails. If one accidentally opens a file or clicks on a link, isolate your PC at once and carry out a full virus and malware scan. When clear, reconnect and update your virus scanner, disconnect the PC again and then re-scan at the deepest level. Ideally, use a second uninfected PC to download the latest virus scanner updates, if necessary.

- Never, EVER give a password to anyone. No respectable organisation will EVER ask for a password, so anyone asking for a password is certainly motivated by criminal or authoritarian intentions.

• **Passwords:** Naïve passwords are still the main reason that systems get hacked. Using birthdays, names of spouses or kids, streets, schools or simple number sets is just stupid because professional crackers will try these at once. Use an obscure non-word, with at least one uppercase letter and a couple of numbers to keep snoopers out.

• **Security or password reset questions:** Really one of the most common methods of hacking an account. Anyone can probably find a user's first school, mother's maiden name or their best friend. If this is all that stands between them and getting control of an email or other account, then it's worth going to the registry of births or whatever to get this low-grade information. Therefore, if a user is obliged to answer standard questions, such as "first school" or "first pet" to set up an account, remember that the answer doesn't have to be true; it only has to be something you can remember.

• **Managing privileges:** Most PC users connect to their PC as an administrator. This is dangerous because most malware uses the privilege of the logged-in user. An administrator user can do anything and so, therefore, can a malware infection. It's worth creating a normal user for day-to-day use of a PC, with restricted privileges.

• **Free/open software licenses:** One important check against the NSA's war on security is transparency. In software published under free/open software licenses that can be independently audited, it is much harder to hide secret back doors. Thus, well-audited freeware (such as Firefox, for instance) is often preferable to many commercial alternatives (such as Google Chrome).

• **Deleting files:** By now, most people realise that when you delete a file from a PC, you actually don't delete the data. You simply tell the disk operating system that the file is gone, and so it stops appearing in lists of files. In reality though, the file data is still on the disk and can be very easily restored simply by telling the disk operating system that it is there again. To really get rid of a file in Windows there are various tools available ("Eraser" is one such tool and Windows provides the "sdelete" command line utility).

• **Email accounts - reset account contact email:** Keep at least one email account completely confidential and for use as an alternative contact email address for resetting critical accounts with banks, service providers, etc. Publicly known email accounts used by banks or important service providers can be hijacked, if known.

• **Smart phone security:** One of the most useful and most dangerous new facilities of the smart phone is geolocation. This enables the phone to know and use the handset's exact location for various useful facilities, like local weather forecasts or finding one's way around. It also creates a potentially huge security risk to a protest group. Thankfully, it can be switched off. However, there are a plethora of other security risks associated with smart phones. These include spyware that allows someone to listen in to and record calls, read texts, see photos and even watch their subjects via their phone's camera. Such invasive software is developing at an extraordinary pace and may be used for benign purposes (such as keeping an eye on an elderly relative or a small child, for instance). Frequently, it is used by authorities exhibiting control freak tendencies.

Considerations and risks: The intelligence services and criminal gangs of many countries will be quite upset if everyone was assiduous in implementing good network and client security. However, these security precautions are recommended by virtually everyone in the industry and there is no risk in implementing these countermeasures. The main risk is making everyone stick to good security practices.

A note about cryptography: One of the main technological advances that protect the individual from the state is the use of cryptography. Despite early attempts by governments to control the science and its resulting technologies, the creation of new software by talented activists liberated and democratised cryptography. It has now become standardised in all kinds of basic internet products, from web browsers to short message services.

Nonetheless, some technologies, notably those provided by larger US companies, are deliberately flawed to allow interception of traffic and decryption by intelligence services. In general, the best (safest) products tend to be non-commercial, highly peer-tested, non-US products. For instance, Cisco systems (a US company), one of the world's largest network router manufacturers, has admitted that its products were deliberately flawed to allow access by US intelligence services. For this reason, choosing encryption products carefully is of the utmost importance.

8.7.2.3 Cyber Sabotage: In some cases, protest groups have been known to engage in various forms of IT sabotage, taking advantage of the internet to gather information, undermine security, and damage IT systems belonging to authorities and corporate targets. There are a number of techniques of cyber sabotage, ranging from very primitive interventions, such as trolling, to very sophisticated attacks on very well-secured government databases. The range of possibilities continues to grow, but this section deals specifically with the common forms of sabotage in use at the time of writing.

• **IP spoofing:** The basic method used for moving data across the internet network and many internal computer networks relies on the so-called Internet Protocol ("IP"). Each packet of data using this protocol contains the numerical address of the source and destination of the packet. The source address is normally the address of the device that the packet was sent from (for example a router). By forging this header so it contains a different address, it is possible to make it appear that the packet was sent by a different machine (or router). The machine that receives these "spoofed" packets will send a response back to the forged source address. This, of course, means that this technique is mainly used when the spoofer doesn't care about actually seeing the response. IP spoofing is often used to mislead the receiver of the data about the sender. For this reason, IP spoofing is often part of a strategy of "denial of service" (DoS) attacks (see below), where a web server is saturated by requests and overwhelmed. Here IP spoofing is used to make the source of the attack difficult or impossible to trace and to force the initial target address to reply to the spoofed sender address, which is actually the real target of the DoS attack. This is done so that the victim of the DoS attack blames the wrong sender for the attack [Note 128]. It's a bit of a 3 card trick to the layman, but it's a favourite way of taking down a government or commercial website with very little risk of identifying the real perpetrator.

• **Denial of service (DoS):** A "denial of service" is a form of attack on a network or server with the intention of making the network or server unavailable to other users. These days, this almost always refers to attacks on services connected via the internet, mostly web servers. However, any publicly available server can be targeted, including servers used by government or corporate employees. A common method of attack involves saturating a target machine with external requests (such as requests for a webpage), so intensely that the server is unable to respond to legitimate traffic, or responds so slowly that it becomes effectively unavailable. Such attacks usually lead to a server overload at various levels.

There are various motivations for carrying out a denial of service attack. Some are simple vandalism, or even criminal attacks. However, increasingly, DOS attacks are being used as so-called "Internet Street Protest" against specific target authorities or corporate IT resources. For instance, in 2010 and 2011, when Mastercard and PayPal, under pressure from the US government, blocked the payment of legitimate donations to WikiLeaks, the best-known "hacktivist" group, "Anonymous", launched a DDoS attack against both sites in a programme of chaos it called "Operation Payback" [Note 129].

There are lots of hybrid forms of Denial of Service attacks, which we won't examine here in detail, but all rely on overloading the resources of a target server. Sometimes this is done using large numbers of "BOT" computers (client computers running software across the internet) which attack a pre-determined server and swamp it with requests. These bots are often innocent 3rd parties that have had a piece of malware installed on their machines, transforming them into a "BOT" to be used in a so called "Distributed Denial of Service" attack (because many bots are involved).

Some Denial of Service attacks use IP spoofing to pretend that requests are coming from another device. This can be used to force a legitimate service to send echo packets to the real target server (the spoofed sender IP address).

• **Trolling:** This is a fairly non-technical form of cyber-action, confined to the internet. There are many definitions of the term, but most people consider a "troll" in a negative sense. One definition runs as follows: "Trolling involves a person (or group) who sows discord by starting arguments or upsetting people, by posting inflammatory, extraneous, or off-topic messages in an online community (such as a newsgroup, forum, chat room, or blog) with the deliberate intent of provoking readers into an emotional response or of otherwise disrupting normal on-topic discussion."

Despite this negative definition, there are other forms of trolling. For example, where an agent provocateur takes to the internet and uses the same community resources such as blogs, comment boards, etc., but with the intention of injecting the views of a protest group and calling for action. For some, these views may also be considered objectionable "trolling", whilst for other members of the community these views may be entirely consistent with their own opinion.

Thus, a "troll" may or may not be objectionable (depending on one's views). However, there is one universal exception, the so-called "paid troll". These are persons paid by a pressure group of some kind, solely for the purposes of spreading disinformation, insults and generating dissent. This type of troll introduces nothing to a conversation, except venom. They tend to be in the pay of large lobby groups supporting contentious developments, such as GM, fracking, climate change denial, etc. The far right-wing is certainly the main source of paid trolls. Left-wing protest groups tend to have volunteers dedicated to spreading their message, but the right-wing tends to have to pay for its opinions to be spread. Sometimes a protest group may also need to keep a presence on a community site, to ensure that there is balance in the representations taking place. This could be construed as a form of "trolling", carried out by protest volunteers. The essential difference is that most anti-authoritarian protest groups seek to persuade those in a community by repeatedly presenting their views, rather than with threats or insults, and they are, generally, volunteers convinced of the correctness of a protest cause.

• **Doxxing:** This is short for "Dropping Docs". It is a technique that involves releasing personal information about someone onto the internet. This is information that could be embarrassing, personally revealing, or something that the victim would rather keep confidential. Doxxing uses existing data about an individual and pieces it together into a single file, which is then published on the internet.

This method may be very useful to a protest group when dealing with politicians, officials or executives. A typical doxxing attack may create a file with name, address, telephone number, family details, credit card and banking details, personal photographs, social security information, social media links and connections, YouTube links, etc., all gleaned from the internet (blogs, social networks, old cached websites, forums, etc.) and focused in a single place.

• **Internet slowdowns:** This new technique of protest involves causing a slowdown or complete break in internet services, affecting websites or email services, as a protest. In 2011, protesters against SOPA, the Stop Online Piracy Act, in companies large and small, demonstrated what might happen, were the SOPA to pass, by going "dark" for a day. This unprecedented act of protest was sufficient to trigger the end of SOPA legislation. Similar protests are being discussed as part of the campaign to protect net neutrality (the provision of equal services to all service provider customers). These slowdown protests were carried out with the cooperation of a lot of very large internet companies, also determined to preserve the freedom and equality of internet services for everyone.

Considerations and risks: Interfering with any computer system without the owner's permission is illegal in all Western jurisdictions and, indeed, in most developed countries. However, trolling is not and denial of service attacks are generally organised as totally anonymous protests. Many governments and corporations have engaged in DoS attacks against organisations in other countries and many employ trolls to attempt to control online discussions. These governments seem to feel that this behaviour is morally justified. Whether the same moral justifications can be made by a protest group engaged in some form of cyber sabotage against a government or corporation depends on the circumstances, but such actions do carry some risk of detection and legal sanctions against a protest group.

There is one legal school of thought that argues that DoS attacks are not illegal, but are simply an expression of freedom of speech or a demonstration, in the same way that protesters may stage a sit-in to occupy a physical space, or heckle a speaker on a stage. The argument goes that they use no form of malware or spyware and are thus not inherently malicious; that they cause no permanent damage to a system and do not penetrate any obvious form of security. The argument also continues that the target machines are indeed inviting public presence (in the case of publicly accessible websites this is certainly true) and, therefore, a DoS attack is similar to a large gathering in a public place and should legally be treated as such [Note 130].

Interestingly, "doxxing" is not necessarily illegal, but it can be far-reaching. It is an extreme action and should be reserved for those that really deserve it and certainly not used against ordinary people. It can lead to identity theft, harassment and stalking.

8.7.2.4 Hacking Systems: Hacking a system refers to an unauthorised user gaining access to a computer system for which they have no permission, deliberately using various methods to bypass the system's security. In general, this is a specialised task, normally undertaken only by those with an intimidate knowledge of a particular system environment. It is certainly not to be attempted at home! When hackers are employed to defend systems, this is often referred to as "Penetration testing". This is a euphemistic term for hacking with a defensive purpose.

There are many motivations for "hacking a system", ranging from childish curiosity, through principled intervention, to pure criminal intent. Here we are solely interested in the hacking of computer systems in a campaign of principled intervention as part of a greater protest. This is sometimes referred to as "hacktivism". An example of this occurred in January 2011, when an executive in the computer security firm HB Gary Federal claimed to have identified the leadership of the hacker collective "Anonymous". In response, the collective hacked the firm's email and other accounts, and released its files onto the internet. This created a rare opportunity to review the recent internal workings of an important private investigative firm and was a "shot across the bows" by Anonymous to anyone attempting to control their defence of internet freedom.

If one considers "hacking" an unauthorised intrusion into an authority's computer systems, one may find this morally repugnant. This is because we generally tend to hear about hacking attacks directed at some morally neutral business or government agency. However, imagine if we lived in a totalitarian regime, where a government spied on its citizens and persecuted those with opposing political attitudes, such as Stasi surveillance in former East Germany (and others closer to home). Would the hacking of such systems seem so objectionable in those circumstances? Such actions probably would not seem at all shocking to most of us in that scenario and, in fact, we may find them quite justified.

The primary reasons for a hacking attack are as follows:

- To obtain information from an authority's computer systems to aid a protest.

- To publish damaging confidential information stored on an authority's computer systems.

- To damage or destroy data on an authority's computer systems.

The methods used to gain unauthorised access to an authority's computer systems range from infiltration of their system management personnel and obtaining super-user logins and passwords, to exploiting subtle security weaknesses in an authority's computer system or network.

• **Website mirroring:** At the lowest end of this form of intrusion, an activist may wish to copy the contents of a website that is currently blocked for some users to an entirely different website. This is called "website mirroring" and is designed to stop authorities blocking access to a particular dataset on a certain website. This technique was used by WikiLeaks, when governments attempted to close down their main website; hundreds of copies of the original site were automatically spawned all over the world. Indeed, the controversial contents of the Wikileaks database were even made available as a torrent for peer-to-peer download by the general public.

• **Website intrusion and defacement:** This involves gaining access to a website or blog and making alterations to its contents. Defacement is generally meant as a kind of electronic graffiti, although recently it has been used as a means to spread messages in cyber protests. Access is usually gained by obtaining the ftp (file transfer protocol) username and password for the web server and then transferring in new pages with the same names as existing pages. Another access method is to gain administrator privileges to the underlying database used by a website, by "injecting" SQL commands into request strings when passing a legitimate request to a vulnerable website. This technique may be used to alter or drop user data in the database, for instance.

• **Website spoofing (phishing):** This is another method of gaining access to username and password data. Here the hacktivist has to create an identical copy of a legitimate website (easy to do by reverse engineering a website and then rebuilding it on another server). When the copy is running, all that is necessary is to persuade a user to connect to the website using the *almost* identical URL. Once there, the user will happily enter their user id and password and this then gives the hacker the information necessary to enter the real website in the role of that user. The spoofed website and redirection is disabled as soon as the information is obtained. A variation of this technique is referred to as "Spear phishing". This is an email spoofing fraud attempt that targets a specific organisation, seeking unauthorized access to confidential data. As with the email messages used in regular phishing expeditions, spear phishing messages appear to come from a trusted source and are very authentic in appearance.

• **Database access:** These days a lot of data is stored in structured databases, which provide distributed access to many users via the internet. Access to these databases is made through specific ports on a server, which allow a user to access a web-based interface, which in turn accesses a database server to retrieve data. There are many pieces of software available (called port scanners) which permit a hacker to detect which ports are open and deduce which ports are open for external users to access a database. Once access to the web-based software has been obtained, the next layer of access is database access. This is a great deal more difficult, since user names and passwords are well-protected on most SQL-based databases. However, it is amazing how often default system user id's and default passwords are not reset after a database is installed, thus providing possible entry points to a SQL-based database.

• **File server hacking:** This refers to a range of operating system vulnerabilities that permit access to networked file servers. File servers provide organisations with large volume shared file storage by multiple users. File servers have super-users and a super-user has privileges to read, delete, move or copy the contents of a file server (plus a lot more). File servers may contain any kind of data, ranging from trivial private data to confidential or even secret reports, minutes, or proposals being shared in an organisation.

• **Email server hacking:** Email servers are popular targets for hackers. Email services in large organisations tend to be placed on separate servers to those used to host a website, a database or a fileserver, etc. Most organisations have their email servers hosted by external service providers that can deliver good security. On the other hand, some organisations run their own email servers on their own hardware; a risky venture, as email servers may be hacked in order to read inbound and outbound emails, or even hijacked to deliver unauthorised and junk email as a proxy. Spoofing emails is simple and allows a hacker to send emails from an address which actually belongs to someone else and this, of course, can have some dramatic effects.

There are various ways to "harvest" valid email addresses from an email server by connecting to the server, using Telnet on port 25, and using SMTP system commands (VRFY and EXPN) to test for obvious email users, such as info or admin, or using standard usernames that we might know exist. Administrators tend to define users with a standard format for ease of administration. The most common format is as follows: *initials+surname, lowercase, all one word*, e.g. mjcoxall. There are several standard formats in use. This means that if you know one person's name and email address in an organisation and know the domain used by their email server (which is obvious from any email address for the organisation), then it is quite simple to guess the email address format being used and create several very good guesses at most employees' email addresses. This can then be tested by connecting to the server and verifying the address. From this point on, it is possible to spoof emails from this user. Of course, this opens up the possibility of so-called "spear phishing" attacks on other users, inside or outside an organisation, because spoof emails appear, to all intents and purposes, to be genuine and to come from a real and authoritative source.

If the email server is a UNIX system, a list of users is also easy to find and provides a starting point to find valid email server administrator addresses. With a user's password it is simple to connect to a POP server (incoming mail, usually port 110) and retrieve and read anyone's email (using the RETR command), without the user detecting that it has been read.

Another motivation for reading emails is to define and track "email chains" - the way that email users pass emails from one to another. This helps define the communications routes within a target organisation, such as a government authority.

• **Malware and spyware:** Malware is software used to gather information, gain access to a computer system or damage a computer system. Spyware is specifically used to pry on a user or organisation without their knowledge and to pass this information back to a spy. Within this group we have keylogger software that can capture keystrokes (including usernames and passwords) and transmit this information back to the perpetrator. Governments of all shades routinely use malware and spyware to carry out mass surveillance of their own populations (as revealed by Edward Snowden about the US National Security Agency). They also use malware to disrupt the systems of other governments. For instance, the use of Stuxnet against Iran by the USA and Israel. Such software is also used by (other) criminal organisations to perpetrate acts of fraud against individuals and commercial organisations. Both types of software can be delivered in several ways: via downloadable software from governments and companies, from CDs from certain companies (e.g. the Sony rootkit on some Sony CDs), embedded in pluggable devices such as memory sticks, "autorun" batch files, or via executable files on websites or at URLs transmitted to unsuspecting users by email. Once a piece of malware or spyware has infected a machine, it often spreads quickly across a network of similar machines and becomes quite difficult to detect and disinfect. Some forms of spyware and malware disable firewalls and anti-virus software, making detection and disinfection even more difficult. Some spyware and malware software is freely available on the internet and new software is constantly emerging and evolving.

• **Wi-Fi sniffing**: Products such as "Firesheep" sniff out and steal cookies (and the account and identity of the owner in the process) of popular web sites (like Facebook and Twitter) from the browsing sessions of other users on a Wi-Fi hotspot you're attached to. Firesheep is a Firefox extension, created to show how leaky the security of many popular web sites (like Facebook, Flickr, Amazon, Dropbox, Evernote, and more) is.

• **Voice phishing (aka vishing):** This is the technique whereby a hacker, pretending to be from an authority, phones an individual to obtain some information from them. This is a technique mostly employed by criminal gangs to defraud individuals of their money by asking for user names and passwords. It can and is also used by protest groups to obtain information about officials of an authority or corporation.

• **Other forms of hacking:** The use of biometric data has often been heralded by governments as the holy grail of identity protection. Finger prints, iris scans and facial recognition have often been bandied around as the ultimate technological solution to managing the identities of human beings by governments. Just to demonstrate that this hyperbole is nonsense, late in 2014, a German hacker used high resolution photographs to successfully recreate the fingerprints of Germany's Defence Minister. One of the photos he used was actually downloaded from a public government press office website! As the hacker pointed out: "Fingerprints might appear more secure than passwords. But if your password gets stolen, you can change it to a new one, but what happens when your fingerprint gets copied?" He quipped that politicians and officials would have to wear gloves in future (not much use with a touch screen). In a high profile stunt in 2013, the same hacker spoofed Apple's TouchID sensors within 24 hours of the release of the iPhone 5S. Using a smudge on the screen of an iPhone, he printed a dummy finger using wood glue and a graphene spray, which successfully unlocked a phone registered to someone else's thumb. The hacking demonstrations have highlighted a fundamental problem with biometric identification and security advisers are suggesting that biometric information should be accompanied by a password - thus making the biometric recognition technology somewhat redundant.

Considerations and risks: Many governments (including democratic Western governments) engage in all of the above activities covertly, always with the justification of "national security". However, most of the above activities are illegal in most developed nations.

A protest group may also be able to claim moral justification for some of these activities, but rarely will a government or corporation accept such a justification in a court of law. There are some serious risks here and the consequences of discovery may be many years of incarceration, or worse (in countries with capital punishment). Some government authorities may see these types of activity as being a threat to national security or as a form of "terrorism".

Note that in early 2015, Barrett Brown, a journalist and an alleged spokesman for the group "Anonymous", was sentenced to 5 years imprisonment as a result of his very tenuous connections with that group, for "hiding" evidence and threatening an FBI official. Clearly, anyone involved in collective "hacktivism" needs to maintain the highest levels of personal security from government authorities looking for a scapegoat for their own incompetence in the field of IT security.

8.7.2.5 Social Media and Communications: The rise in popularity of various social media and messaging applications in the last decade has been dramatic. There are now a plethora of social media platforms in use by hundreds of millions of users globally. In a similar way, the use of instant messaging has evolved from being just a teenage fad between friends to become an almost ubiquitous activity. Taken together with the huge escalation of mobile consumer technology, improved mobile bandwidth and the advent of the smart phone and reduction in costs, we now live in a world where we can have continuous instant interaction with our friends, family, colleagues and fellow protesters, anytime and almost anywhere.

This incredible increase in access to instant and mobile communications has, of course, impacted the way that people involved in a protest campaign communicate with each other and with the outside world. Once upon a time, a demonstration could come and go and, if there were no members of the press present, it would attract zero attention. Now, a demonstrator can film an entire demonstration, including acts of police brutality on his or her mobile phone and post it to YouTube within minutes. The protesters have thus taken control of their own news broadcasting in a truly unprecedented way.

With this new paradigm, news becomes almost instant and protesters' ability to communicate, organise and deploy has been immeasurably improved. Where once a meeting, march or demonstration had to be organised weeks in advance, with minimal chance of changing plans quickly and effectively, today "flash mobs" use social networks, email,

SMS, and instant messaging to organise demos at literally a few minutes notice.

Aside from access to these tools, the ability of those at the front line of a protest to use these tools has improved. Many of today's young demonstrators have hardly known a time when they didn't own a mobile device of some kind. Here we will examine just a few of the uses and benefits that this technology provides to a protest group:

• **Protest organisation, the web and social media:** It wasn't so long ago that the web was dominated by websites built by corporations, governments and large organisations. Although there were some technically adept groups creating websites, the process was awkward and time consuming. The advent of the "Blog" (weblog) changed all that. With just a little bit of persistence, anyone can now set up an attractive website based on a completely interactive blog, allowing for the delivery of an almost infinite number of web pages to the internet community. Most blogs can be deployed free of charge or placed on a group's own hosting service. Simultaneously, having a dedicated domain and hosting service has also got a great deal easier. For just a few euros a year, anyone can have access to website hosting and their own email server with their own dedicated domain name.

These two developments, taken together, democratised the web enormously. It was the equivalent of moving from a situation where we had, say, 4 TV stations broadcasting to the world to the potential scenario of everyone as a broadcaster.

The next step in this development was the use of the internet as a platform for social networking. Services such as Facebook allow users (or groups) to build an internet presence without any form of technical knowledge at all and to use this presence to connect with friends, colleagues or family in an almost limitless network. There are now several social networking services in operation and all permit the sharing of media, such as images, videos, sounds, etc., the sharing of files and the communication of personal and other news and gossip.

Of course, as is the case with any tool, social media services can be used for many purposes. Users may wish to publish baking recipes or they may wish to campaign for civil rights using a tool such as Facebook. These social networking tools are politically neutral (in theory, anyway) and there are few restrictions as to their use. They provide an excellent first step in delivering up-to-date information to members of a protest organisation and the general public. These sites can be maintained by several users simultaneously and can offer limited or open access to contributions from the public.

Blogs and social networking platforms have now become an essential place for a protest group to issue formal statements and provide visual and written evidence to support their grievances and demands. No self-respecting group can manage without a blog, as a minimum. It is one of the new public faces of a protest group.

• **Managing protest news:** For much of the modern world, the news is still delivered by mainstream media such as TV, radio and newspapers. However, in recent years, the advent of internet-connected mobile devices has meant that many consumers of news media employ PCs, laptops and mobile devices to read the news on the internet rather than buy a physical paper or sit down and wait for the news on the TV or radio.

In addition, the news media, conscious that they were being sidelined by the internet, have responded in two ways. Firstly, they have created highly useable, up-to-date news applications that can be accessed on mobile devices in order to maintain their market share as news providers. Secondly, most importantly, the mainstream media have also begun to monitor news events being posted on services such as YouTube, Netflix, etc. This second development is important because it is yet another means by which the broadcasting of news has become democratised. Anyone can post a video to YouTube and, if the story is newsworthy, it will rapidly receive a huge (viral!) audience and the attention of the mainstream media. Not to be outdone, once one media organisation runs a story found on the internet, the rest soon get into line and rebroadcast it. These days, much of what we read, watch or listen to from the big media organisations originates on the internet.

Another development which has also impacted the way events become "news" is the advent of message broadcasting services, such as Twitter. Twitter allows a user to build a network of "followers" who take an interest in the messages that the user sends out. These very short messages ("tweets") deliver a tight headline, but can be accompanied by links to other websites and media such as images. They can be targeted at specific twitter users or whole groups of users. In this process, an event can rapidly become "news" if it is perceived to be important by the other users that receive the original tweet and then proceed to "retweet" it to their own groups. Thus, within a few minutes a tweet can be propagated to vast numbers of participants in overlapping networks. Various software services monitor the progress of this propagation and mainstream news services collect this information and start to follow the story. In a sense, it democratises knowledge and opinion by means of ubiquitous sharing. It makes it easy to ignore opinions you find repugnant, whilst facilitating focus on opinions you find valuable.

For a protest organiser, these new tools and phenomena have become critically important when managing the media and every protest group needs to have a clear strategy about how and where information and news is placed on these various services. Timing, content and follow-up are the most important issues here. Posting and forgetting something is a waste of time. When posting news, it is important to trigger interest in it by sending out links to sympathisers and others. In this context, a protest group needs to have a media group (a group of sympathisers) in place to help to start the propagation of interest in a posting by passing on the links or tweets to their social networks.

- **Protest communications:** Prior to the internet and mobile communications, protest groups organised by having meetings, sending out fliers and planning actions weeks and months in advance. The entire process was cumbersome and inflexible. Changes of plan were virtually impossible. On the day, demonstrations or other protest actions were often frustrated by an authority knowing the plans in advance and blocking various protest actions because organisers were unable to communicate securely and instantly with their supporters to alter plans or change tactics.

The new technologies of the last two decades have changed all that. Communication between individuals and groups either publicly or confidentially is now instant and ubiquitous. Organisers, even at a distance, can monitor a protest action with live video feeds and information on police deployments or other problems and they can plan and organise alternate actions at a moment's notice. They can then relay these new plans to the protesters en masse or to individual local organisers almost instantly. For instance, attempts to "kettle" (contain) groups of demonstrators can be avoided simply by dissolving a concentration of protesters from one place and reassembling them in another. The police, having focused their attention on one site, are unable to redeploy rapidly and so end up policing an empty street or square, whilst the real demonstration is now suddenly surrounding a government building 2 km away.

Clearly, the authorities are aware of such protest tactics and have all kinds of methods at hand to block or intercept this kind of communication. Some authorities force mobile operators to block mobile signals in a certain area or compel them to "strangle" the mobile traffic (communications don't get in or out, as a user may be unable to connect to a mobile network). Other authorities may monitor voice and data communications to disconnect or prosecute participants at a later date. Nonetheless, protest communications have been vastly improved by recent mobile internet technology and, despite increased government surveillance, they really can't spy on everyone all the time.

• **Alternative communications:** Both the blocking and interception of communications can be avoided by protest organisers. As we will discover in the next section, "End-to- End" voice and data encryption systems are available for both mobile phone and other computer devices and these are effectively unbreakable by any authority. Some of these systems are actually free and are becoming the standard rather than the exception in internet and mobile communications. The market demand for strong encryption is a powerful force for good.

As for the blocking of communications, this is normally accomplished by an authority pressuring a telecoms provider. However, modern telephones embody the ability to communicate with other smart phones through their own internal Wi-Fi modems, without a user having any mobile coverage at all. Thus, huge informal, independent networks can be created using this technique. This was demonstrated in Hong Kong in late 2014, when the government effectively closed off the mobile phone networks, but the protesters continued to communicate via ad-hoc Wi-Fi networks spread across the city using the FireChat app.

Users of systems like FireChat know that there is nothing to stop the authorities joining the same network to monitor activity and it is recommended that people avoid real names. But this simple app is useful for information-sharing, though not for sharing secrets. Still, in a sense, that is exactly the point in a protest that set out to defend freedom of speech!

• **Security:** The issues of security on the internet have gravitated in recent years from fear of data being stolen by criminals to fear of data being intercepted by governments and other authorities. Security and privacy are now top considerations for many ordinary internet users, and even more so for those using the internet as a medium of protest.

Gladly, in the hectic world of the internet, for every problem there comes, quite quickly, a solution. The internet was designed to be resilient and, indeed, there are few actions by a government which don't already have countermeasures within a few weeks. When it comes to social media and protest communications, there are several important security issues:

• **Communications security:** Communications need to be secured using end-to-end encryption (preferably 256 byte encryption). That applies to mobile voice calls, instant messaging and all email. No important communications should take place without encryption. There is a lot of software available to implement this and the ideal situation is to reserve at least one email address dedicated to confidential communications and this must always be encrypted. Little by little instant messaging systems are also rolling out end-to-end encryption as standard. Voice encryption for mobile calls is readily available, as is software for encrypted Voice over IP (VoIP) calls.

In general, avoid public email systems such as gmail or hotmail. They are not secure. It is much better to have your own email server (in-house) or lease an email service as part of your domain hosting and implement a 3rd party end-to-end encryption regime on top of this. In general, avoid all service providers (of any kind) based in the USA. Also bear in mind that even with E2E encryption of email, the meta-data of an email is still unencrypted and may be quite revealing. This includes the origin and destination, time of sending of an email and this obviously cannot be encrypted if you want your email to actually arrive and get a reply.

• **Social media security:** Social media access and security needs to be carefully controlled. It is quite simple for an authority to hack a Facebook or Twitter account in order to post, alter and remove material from these accounts. Ideally, passwords should be altered every day by a system administrator according to a known algorithm that all contributors also know. This way there is a lower risk of a password "escaping" and falling into the wrong hands.

• **Security in general:** Password holders need to be strictly controlled by a system manager (custodian). Any changes in personnel (such as someone leaving the group) should immediately trigger a complete set of password changes across all the group's systems. That includes blog users and administrators, Facebook and Twitter users, Email, device and PC logins (including routers), instant messaging and VoIP logins. This kind of security is overkill, but it's better than being hacked by an unwelcome intruder. Remote access software should be strictly controlled, firewalls and virus, malware and spyware cleansing software checked, updated and run regularly (daily at least). A group should have a rehearsed plan of action if security is breached. This should include closing off of local area networks, and all mobile devices of the group and its organisers from connection to the internet, the implementation of a complete security audit of devices, including routers. This plan needs to have been prepared in advance and rehearsed.

8.7.2.6 E-Campaigning (Internet Activism): This is a whole range of activities that are based on using the internet to promote a protest movement's objectives, including the following:

- Networking with others to build a community.
- Fundraising to finance a protest.
- Lobbying sympathisers, those in authority or other influential persons.
- Organisation of the protest group and communication.

Internet activism takes advantage of techniques such as internet petitions, mass mailing, social networking, and short messaging to promote these objectives, together with conventional campaigning methods, such as public meetings, discussions, private planning meetings, talking to sympathisers individually and standing in the cold, asking for signatures or donations. Avaaz, one of the early internet campaigning groups routinely also runs traditional protest demonstrations outside government buildings, such as the British parliament. However, the internet is central to their strategy because it provides an excellent way of addressing large populations and building an organised community. In the case of Avaaz, this network of supporters can rapidly respond to a protest call, either with a petition signature, some finance, personal action, by lobbying or turning up at a physical demo.

Globally, there are now many groups that base their campaigns around the internet, such as Avaaz, Change.org, 38Degrees, 100Months etc., each with their own special approach: a central protest issue such as climate change or a geographical area where their protests are based. Avaaz is a multi-issue international campaign site that takes an interest in human rights, the environment and anti-war campaigns, with no geographical limits. Change.org has multiple national versions and focuses on both small personal rights protests right up to national and international campaigns.

These groups are all part of a growing global phenomenon, sometimes referred to as "clickactivism", which makes it very easy for sympathisers to contribute their name and support to a cause. Despite the doubts of their detractors, these internet campaign groups have in a short time managed to develop huge clout by delivering multi-million signature petitions to governments and are now taken very seriously by corporations and governments everywhere. They are capable of inflicting severe damage to the public image and confidence of a government or corporation that is foolish enough to ignore them and they have become very adept at leveraging new technology to power a campaign. The use of live streaming, on-site videos and imagery provides dramatic evidence to support their campaigns.

In parallel with these new e-campaigning groups, the more traditional protest NGOs have also started to adopt the same internet-based strategies as the "early adopters" such as Avaaz. Groups such as Greenpeace, Rainforest Network, Oxfam, the Open Rights Group and many other long-established campaigning NGOs have now firmly embedded e-campaigning at the centre of their protest activities.

Despite the euphoria of e-activism, many still recognise that making a lot of people click on "Sign now" hardly portents a social revolution. However, what it does do is to "consumerise" popular protest in a way which makes large corporations and governments very nervous. If millions of internet users are being persuaded to protest against, for instance, the environmental crimes of Shell or Nestlé, then clearly, this is going to trickle down to affect consumer sales, shareholder prices and the corporate bottom line. In this respect, this "automation of protest" is having exactly the right affect on these traditional targets - it is inducing fear and it is providing a powerful lever for change.

Here are some of the most obvious uses of internet campaigning:

• **Networking:** We use the internet for news, to make and maintain social contacts, and to share information, but it can also be a radical tool for connecting people around the world in the service of a common cause. That might mean signing a petition, but it can also involve taking real global action in our own towns and cities. At its best, a distributed action projects the power of the movement and gives activists a sense of being part of a greater whole. This is particularly useful when a movement is in its early days and membership is small or widely dispersed.

Creating social networks may need a combination of traditional networking and the use of social media to build networks of sympathetic people and organisations. Other groups may exchange links to and from their respective websites and blogs in order to help each other achieve more page views from new readers and help make their websites more available in search engines, such as Google. With time, a dedicated network of sympathisers can be established in this way and some of these internet sympathisers can be converted into real world activists.

• **Fundraising:** There are many fundraising options available on the internet. The most basic one is a PayPal donation button on a website or blog which allows users to make instant donations to a protest group. All that is needed is a verified PayPal account and the addition of the button and explanatory text. More targeted fundraising may involve the use of targeted emails or the sending of tweets to potential donors. Mass-mailing techniques can be used to personalise such appeals for donations and be addressed to vast numbers of potential sympathisers.

• **Lobbying:** Social Media platforms such as Facebook and Twitter are useful for static lobbying of supporters, authorities or politicians. However, one of the great innovations of our time is the online petition. These are now prolific and operate at all levels of protest, from a personal grievance with an authority right up to global environmental protests. The online petition platforms work by allowing a protest group to phrase a petition and then inviting subscribers to the petition to sign the petition electronically. When a target or time deadline is reached, the signatures are delivered electronically to the petitioners, who can then deliver them to the authority or person being petitioned. This is usually done with some fanfare and normally involves the delivery of the signatures on paper to heighten the impact.

• **Organisation of the protest group:** Rather than communicate organisational information to individual members of a protest group about developments, news, plans, people and progress, it is much more efficient and centralised to use a blog or website to deliver this information, in much the same way as a physical magazine would do (but without the cost or hassle). Thus, the internet is extremely helpful in establishing and maintaining a strong, well-connected organisation. Access to a website, social media site or blog can be restricted to members only, if necessary, as it acts as a central point for information and communication between organisers and sympathisers.

When it comes to using the internet to organise specific actions, there is a wealth of possibilities. Here are two typical actions that can be organised using the internet:

-   A day of action.
-   A call to action.

In a "day of action", a protest group places an announcement on all of its social networking and websites, calling upon its supporters to join the day of action in support of the protest. It might be a "no shopping day", "No Shell Petrol" day, but, whatever the cause, the group picks a day in the future and calls for all sympathisers to join with them in the day of action.

In a "call to action", a protest group tries to enlist new support for action on a particular issue from public and supporters. The call to action will include a discussion of the issue and what actions can and should be taken.

Websites, blogs and social media are perfect places for a call to action. The message should tell a story that the general public will easily understand, and it should motivate new volunteers. Depending on the situation, a call to action might include a demand to political leaders, or simply be an expression of grievances, like the call to occupy a site as part of a protest.

Considerations and risks: Using the internet as a tool of protest is fairly risk-free in democratic jurisdictions. The main drawback is the intelligence services constant attempts to infiltrate and spy on protest groups that they feel threatened by. The same cannot be said of jurisdictions such as Saudi Arabia or Iran, where social media are monitored and freedom of speech is just as restricted on the internet as it is in other media and where the consequences of an unguarded statement may give rise to acts of judicial violence. China, whilst reasonably tolerant of criticisms of the government, is believed to be particularly sensitive to any calls for action and an "army" of censors will remove any social media comments that smack of organised protest [Note 131].

8.7.3 Betrayal and Leaking

Betrayal is a breach of trust, breaking of a confidence or the deliberate breach of a contract between an individual or group and (in this case) an authority of some kind. Betrayal is the ultimate objective of all acts of infiltration. A group or individual that infiltrates an authority does so with the specific motivation of betraying the trust of the authority in some way.

There are many forms and motives for betrayal, with varying consequences. Treachery may range in magnitude from refusing to keep quiet about a personal scandal involving an official, right up to stealing and publishing corporate or government secrets which are capable of bankrupting a corporation or causing political instability. Fidelity is the opposite of betrayal and every one of us has, to some extent, a possibility to betray an authority or to be faithful to it. We may be loyal to our employers, the groups, parties or congregations we belong to, or we may, if circumstances demand it, betray them.

Disloyalty is one of the most powerful means of protest available because the betrayer may have an intimate knowledge of the inner workings and secrets of an authority and thus can deliver very damaging blows to them. Employee betrayal may be present for a long time before it is detected (if it ever is), so it has a huge potential to damage an authority.

"Leaking" is a form of betrayal and refers specifically to the release by an individual or group of confidential information owned by an authority in an act of betrayal. Leaking of information is carried out to damage an authority, inform another group or tell the general public of something confidential.

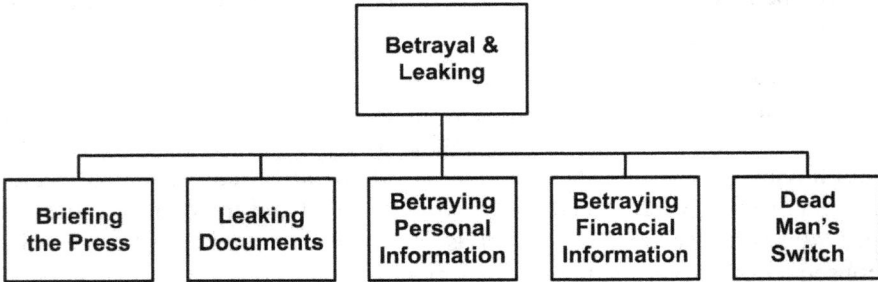

```
                    ┌──────────────┐
                    │ Betrayal &   │
                    │ Leaking      │
                    └──────────────┘
   ┌──────────┬──────────┬──────────┬──────────┬──────────┐
┌────────┐ ┌────────┐ ┌────────┐ ┌────────┐ ┌────────┐
│Briefing│ │Leaking │ │Betraying│ │Betraying│ │ Dead  │
│the Press│ │Documents│ │Personal │ │Financial│ │ Man's │
│        │ │        │ │Information│ │Information│ │Switch │
└────────┘ └────────┘ └────────┘ └────────┘ └────────┘
```

8.7.3.1 Briefing the Press: This is the act of providing the press with confidential information regarding an authority or other organisation. In the case of a campaign of direct action, the objective may be to cause damage of some kind to the authority or just to get some information out to the public. Briefing the press can be anonymous or it may be authored and signed by an individual or protest group. In modern times, it has become quite normal for the press to quote anonymously, in order to protect their sources. Indeed, a whole infrastructure now exists to allow informants to deliver information and evidence to the press without exposing themselves to retaliation from their targets. The press briefing can be accompanied by documentary evidence or it may be unsubstantiated.

Despite the power of the internet to inform the public, the traditional organs of the press are still immensely influential. Thus, briefing the press is still a very powerful form of leverage for a protest group. Even in countries where press freedom is restricted, the international press can exert significant pressure on a corporate or government authority. Obviously the traditional press tends to be taken more seriously and is perceived as being more independent than the web site of a protest group. The public perception is that any material that the mainstream press prints or broadcasts has been checked and verified to some extent.

Considerations and risks: There are risks involved in briefing the press and therefore it is sometimes wise to do this anonymously. The target of an attack from the press will often try to take revenge on the informant, whilst the press usually remains fairly untouchable, even in authoritarian regimes.

8.7.3.2 Leaking Secret Documents (Confidential Studies, Reports, and Meeting Minutes): The power of a leak which is well documented is immense, as both WikiLeaks and Edward Snowden found out. In both cases, the documentary evidence provided was so powerful and self-explanatory that very little commentary was required to convince the public of the depth of the underlying scandals that were being exposed. The effects of both incidents are still reverberating globally. Trust between citizens and governments was badly eroded by images of PowerPoint slides from the NSA blithely describing how they intended to spy on the internet activities of the entire US population by infecting millions of home computers with spyware. Such graphic revelations remain undeniable and extremely shocking.

There are many types of document which may be of interest to the public. These include copies of reports, emails, the minutes of meetings, telephone transcripts, logs of internet activity, logs of short message service activity, videos and image records and internal memos. Confidential diplomatic communications seem to be especially revealing.

Getting hold of such documents and disseminating them may be a great deal simpler than it first appears. We know now that even the most secure parts of US military and national intelligence services are effectively full of security holes. Bradley/Chelsea Manning taught us that with a vengeance. The widespread use of mobile devices and tiny high density storage devices, such as micro-SD drives, provides many opportunities to collect and smuggle documents from within a government authority or corporation. IT departments all over the world trust their most treasured data to the technologists who manage their systems (often external contractors), and the managers and executives of these organisations hardly understand the most basic principles of data security themselves. The level of trust they place in their IT departments is huge and most of the time they simply hope for the best.

Considerations and risks: Unless one can immediately and undeniably prove public interest, leaking of confidential documents is going to lead to legal revenge, as has been demonstrated in the way that Snowden, Manning and Assange have been treated by their respective governments and the USA. The best way to leak documents is to do so anonymously via the media or an organisation such as WikiLeaks.

8.7.3.3 Betraying Personal Information about Authority Members: The betrayal of personal information about an official or executive may have the effect of discrediting that person or even causing them to be removed from their post or forced to resign. The personal information may concern their behaviour in their professional capacity or in their private lives. It may concern social, sexual, political or financial behaviour and it may be associated with hard evidence or, perhaps, be purely circumstantial or hearsay. The word "allegedly" covers a myriad of legal obstacles when it comes to making unsubstantiated claims about someone in a target organisation.

Sometimes it becomes necessary to address an attack on an individual within a target authority. He may, for instance, represent a direct threat to a protest group or be an obstacle to reaching a resolution. He could even be the instigator of actions against which a protest group is campaigning. In such cases, the person(s) in question may need to be removed and this may be best achieved by discrediting them in the eyes of their peers or in the public eye. The technique also lends itself to the use of "guilt by association", where a person's good name can be damaged simply because of their previous associations with other discreditable individuals.

Considerations and risks: There is a risk that a protest group may be accused of blackmail or defamation, both of which have legal consequences, unless there is reliable evidence to prove claims against the target individual.

8.7.3.4 Betraying Financial Information about an Authority: Sensitive financial information or revelations about financial misconduct often prove damning to an authority or corporation. Revealing that a company has lost orders or is unprofitable may trigger a drop in its share price, an emergency shareholder meeting or the resignation of a senior executive. When a government department is shown to have grossly wasted taxpayer's money, the public often demands revenge in the form of someone senior losing their position. The key to these types of revelations is good documentary evidence, such as internal memos, emails, copies of financial projections, balance sheets, etc.

Considerations and risks: Some financial information may be confidential. Some government information may be covered by laws governing the secrecy of certain data, such as the "Official Secrets Act", forbidding disclosure. These regulations may trigger off legal sanctions against the betrayer, if the person's identity is revealed. For this reason, anonymity is preferable to an open disclosure. The press should be used as the conduit to get the information into the public domain.

8.7.3.5 Leaking Incriminating Information: Incriminating information about an authority or corporate organisation may cover a huge range of topics. It may concern poor corporate governance, neglected environmental responsibility, abuses of workers' rights, abuse of consumer rights and human rights. Many government agencies and companies are guilty of some or all of these offences and leaking evidence of their behaviour can be profoundly damaging to them, not only in the public eye, but also in terms of how they are trusted as a government or as employers, customers, suppliers or "corporate neighbours".

The leaking of incriminating information first means gathering evidence. This may be in the form of first hand testimony, photographic evidence, interview transcripts, independent specialist assessments (accountant's audits, laboratory reports, NGO assessments, for instance).

The next step is the creation of a "story board", which links the evidence into a plot that is coherent and simple to follow. The release of incriminating evidence needs to be managed carefully to avoid overloading the public. This is especially important when the evidence is complex. Complex inter-related evidence is best divided into several separate story threads to make each piece of evidence and conclusion understandable to the public. For example, if a company is guilty of environmental and human rights abuses, it may be better to split the evidence into two separate themes and, possibly, to release the incriminating evidence on different dates.

One of the problems of both the WikiLeaks and Snowden revelations was the sheer volume of evidence being released. The public were simply overwhelmed by the huge quantity of material and were somewhat numbed by the vastness of the revelations. We are still trying to take in and appreciate the implications of much of what was revealed in the last five years, so, clearly, the timing of a revelation is important to get the maximum effect from it. When the story is completed, properly cross-referenced and coherent, it is ready to be leaked to the press and to independent websites for publication. A copy can also be sent to the target organisation.

Considerations and risks: An organisation that has a properly formatted case of incriminating evidence against it leaked to the public, will seek to cover up, fudge and discredit the case. Then it will seek revenge on those that revealed the evidence and this is a risk. The case of Shell in the Niger delta is a case in point, where this company resorted to murder to cover up and suppress the evidence of its environmental and human rights abuses.

8.7.3.6 The Deadman's Switch: In some cases, an authority makes it an offence for a person or group to reveal that the authority has been spying on them or on their clients. Thus, we have learned that Google and Microsoft have been legally obliged to remain silent about the NSA's many requests for data on their clients. This ban on spying revelations creates a Kafkaesque form of authoritarian intervention in civil liberties.

In 2004, American librarians were distressed at the FBI's demands to examine their patrons' reading habits and use them to infer terrorist intent, and also at the FBI's gag orders preventing librarians from telling their patrons when the police had been spying. Jessamyn West, a radical librarian, conceived a brilliant countermeasure to the FBI gagging orders, which was to place a sign on the wall of her library, reading "THE FBI HAS NOT BEEN HERE (watch very closely for the removal of this sign)." She reasoned, if the law prohibited her from telling people that the FBI had been in, that wasn't the same as telling people that the FBI had not been there.

A similar action was recently used by the owner of WICKR, the secret instant messaging service for mobile devices, who noted in their transparency report that "Wickr has received zero secret orders from law enforcement and spy agencies. Watch closely for this notice to disappear."

Considerations and risks: There may yet be some legal reasons why this kind of statement may be rendered unlawful in some jurisdictions at some future time, although it will be a minefield to alter existing laws to make it illegal to tell the truth about what a government has NOT done.

8.7.4 Subversion of Authority

There are lots of definitions of the word "subversion". A reasonable one is: "actions designed to undermine the military, economic, psychological or political strength or morale of a governing authority."

Although this definition sounds quite destructive, in fact it describes what most of us do on a daily basis, as we constantly struggle to manage our relationship with, often faceless, authorities and sometimes absurd or unjust rules. Thus, the word "subversion" could describe the simple act of living with authority, bending their rules, dodging and weaving, just in order to get on with life in a pragmatic way. However, in this section, when we refer to subversion we are discussing the much more aggressive and organised methodology of undermining authority by a group of activists.

Some consider the use of subversion as alien in civil protests. The word carries connotations of sedition, treachery, secrecy, and illicit political action. However, these are precisely the strategies often employed by authorities against peaceful protest groups. Thus, per force, the use of subversion has now become an essential part of the armoury of every civil protest movement. Indeed, various forms of subversion have now evolved into part of the system of self-defence of any serious protest movement.

Undermining the credibility and strength of an authority often becomes an important objective of a civil rebellion or protest movement. The use of various subversive techniques is one of the most potent physically nonviolent methods of achieving protest objectives.

Subversion as a tool of political protest relies on a high degree of secrecy, good organisation and patience. Subversion is a labour and time-intensive investment that may yield very great benefits, but also carries a large personal and perhaps financial cost and some risks. Thus the use of subversion should probably only be undertaken in cases where protest campaigns are set to take a long-time (more than a year) and where conflicts with authorities are expected to become politically violent. Subversive techniques include the following:

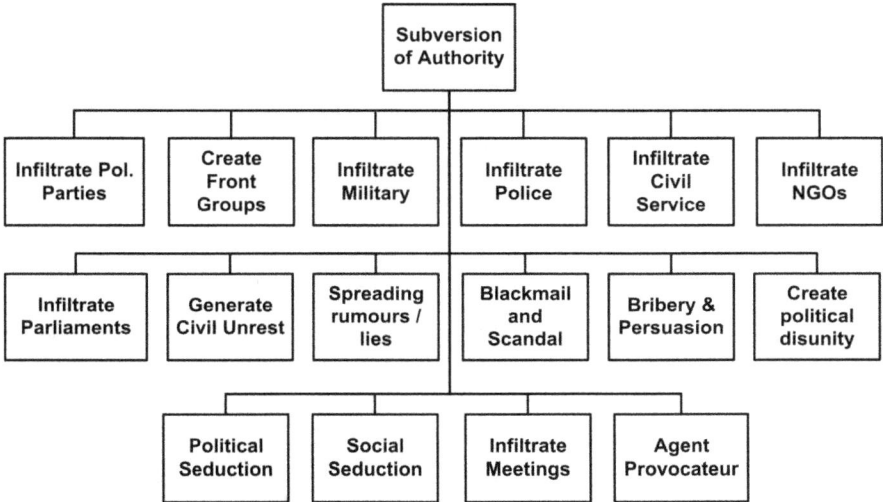

8.7.4.1 Infiltration of Political Parties: This involves joining a political party as an active member, attending meetings, taking on responsibilities and gaining access to party management, volunteering for administrative tasks. It also involves information gathering about party attitudes on various relevant issues: the behaviour and background of party officials, any hints of scandal or corruption, the financial position of the party, lists of local supporters and party members, etc. Infiltrating a political party to gather information may take some time before the infiltrator is sufficiently trusted to be a useful source of information. A political infiltrator may also act as an agent provocateur within a target political party and use their influence to push initiatives which benefit the protest group.

Considerations and risks: To rise to a position of trust in a political party is a slow process. Certainly in national politics it may take years. In local politics it may be a little easier, but then the quality of the information available to the infiltrator will be relatively poor. Because of time constraints it may be simpler to find someone who is sympathetic to the protest cause and already in an appropriate position of responsibility within the party, and see if they can be persuaded to spy on behalf of the protest group. Such an approach carries the risk that they will refuse and reveal the plot to the party, so this latter option needs to be carefully researched first.

8.7.4.2 Creation of Front Groups: A front group is an organisation that apparently represents one agenda, while in reality serving another (seemingly unconnected) party or interest, whose sponsorship is hidden or only occasionally mentioned.

Front groups are often used by political parties, governments and increasingly in retaliation by protest groups. The classic example of a front group is the "think tank". These are organisations established ostensibly to carry out research into a particular subject, but normally sponsored by sympathisers of the cause (party, government, protest group). Think tanks are often given grand names, such as "International Institute for Climate Studies". In reality, such sponsored think tanks compose and publish information and reports which are biased towards the opinions of their real sponsors. They are then referred to as "respectable, independent sources of data" to support their sponsors' arguments. The public often assume that such a grand sounding organisation must be credible. The "Global Climate Coalition", for example, didn't hide the fact that its funding came from oil and coal producers and car manufacturers. Nevertheless, its name alone was sufficiently misleading to be often confused with respectable organisations concerned with climate change, rather than being just a mouthpiece for a bunch of corporate environmental criminals. In this particular case, the front group was identified and forced out of existence by a public boycott of its corporate members.

These days, protest groups have also had to resort to creating front groups to counter their widespread use by governments and corporations. In a protest campaign, a small protest group confronted by multiple "expert" think tanks can find their voices drowned out. The general public, which is notoriously careless about checking facts and provenance, are easily fooled by the slick PR of corporate or government think tanks. In these circumstances, a protest group needs to level the playing field by creating its own front groups that are equally eloquent in delivering the arguments on behalf of the protest campaign [Note 132].

Astroturfing: This is the hybrid action where a front group masks their real sponsors to make it appear as though it originates from and is supported by grassroots participant(s). It is a practice intended to give the statements or front organisation more credibility by withholding information about their real financial or ideological connections. The term astroturfing is a derivation of Astroturf, artificial grass made to look like real grass. On the internet, astroturfers (aka trolls) mask their identity, and sometimes an individual operates with many personas to give the impression of widespread support for a particular client's agenda.

Considerations and risks: There are few risks involved in creating a front group, except that the links between the front group and the protest organisation may be somehow revealed. Even this may not be such a disaster, since it is deniable and, even if proven, it can be readily excused. Having several front groups is the best way to insure against this eventuality. If the first group is revealed as being partial to the protest group, it can be quietly abandoned and a second group can be called into play. Ideally, front groups should be registered in advance, so that they can boast of having been in existence "for more than 10 years", for example, to lend greater credibility.

8.7.4.3 Infiltration of the Military: Often members of the armed forces are sympathetic to political ambitions other than those of the authority they serve and they make themselves available as a source of information embedded within a branch of the military. Such affiliations between a protest group, civil rebellion and members of the military may last for years and provide high quality information on relevant military strategies, military deployments and the attitudes of the military towards a protest group and towards the government. Such infiltrations may also offer opportunities to recruit more members of the military to a protest cause.

An alternative use of infiltrated military staff includes their use in providing misleading information to their superiors. Incorrect intelligence information can be "fed" to the military, which may prove useful to a protest campaign in some circumstances.

Considerations and risks: Infiltrating a military unit for the express purpose of spying on them may well give rise to the accusation of undermining national security, which could carry some serious legal implications. This is best avoided by ensuring that such an accusation can never be proven. Communications between the infiltrator and protest group need to be narrowly limited to a very small group of "handlers" and must be very secure.

8.7.4.4 Infiltration of the Police: Police forces in many countries use infiltration of protest groups as a matter of course. What they often don't realise is the extent to which the police forces have been infiltrated by protest groups. A recent example is how the police and intelligence services on both sides of the border in Ireland had become thoroughly infiltrated by supporters of one or other cause in that country's insurgent struggle.

Policemen have political attitudes as well and very often the more educated members of the police have liberal attitudes and can be "turned" to support and provide insider information to a protest movement. As with military infiltration, there are lots of opportunities to obtain high-quality intelligence about police strategies, planned deployments, police intelligence operations and other information about individual officers, cases of corruption or malpractice and lists of other sympathetic officers. A well-placed police infiltrator can also be used to feed disinformation about the protest group to his colleagues.

The Police - a special case: Very often ordinary civilian police harbour the same sympathies as a protest group and it is important to harness this support where possible. For instance, in 2013, during the huge summer demonstrations held in Sofia, Bulgaria, tens of thousands of protesters took to the streets to vent their anger at the appointment of a dubious media magnate as the Chairman of the State Agency for National Security with no prior public discussion. This and some other very unpopular government diktats triggered large-scale demonstrations in front of the national parliament. What distinguished these demonstrations from others in other parts of Europe at the time was the behaviour of the police. Rather than baton-wielding aggressive riot police, the police response in Sofia was calm, sympathetic and cooperative. Indeed, it was fairly clear that many of the police felt just as indignant as the demonstrators. Both groups provided supplies of drinking water to each other to manage the high temperatures of a Bulgarian summer and the demonstrations were without any violent incident between police and demonstrators. This example of solidarity must certainly have sent a shiver down the spine of the new Chairman of the State Agency for National Security!

Considerations and risks: Infiltrating a police force would certainly be treated as a serious offence in most countries. Therefore, it is preferable to avoid being caught. Every precaution should be taken in communications between infiltrator and protest group. The safest type of police infiltrator would be the policeman that has actually been sent to infiltrate the protest group, if they can be identified and "turned".

8.7.4.5 Infiltration of the Organs of the State (Civil Service): The profile of a typical civil servant is as diverse as the profile of any member of the general public. Without a doubt, there will be members in any civil service who are both sympathetic to a protest cause and who occupy key positions in relevant government departments. Having sympathetic contacts in key positions in appropriate government agencies can be immensely useful in terms of gathering data about government plans, gathering embarrassing information, financial data or any hint of scandals or corruption, as well as feeding government agencies disinformation.

Considerations and risks: In most Western countries, civilian job contracts in the civil service forbid certain types of activity, including the involvement without permission from a department head in particular protest groups. Obviously, the removal or revelation of any document considered confidential would also be a sacking offence, and may even be a criminal offence, so great care is needed. The use of file encryption can reduce the risks and consequences of suspicion and detection.

8.7.4.6 Infiltration of Non-Government Organisations: Some NGOs may be unsympathetic to a protest movement's objectives and it may be necessary to infiltrate these organisations in order to understand their attitudes and intercept their communications and plans. Typical examples of the kind of NGO which may need to be infiltrated by, for example, an environmental protest group might include a local business association, a hunting club, a political lobbying group or right-wing protest groups.

Considerations and risks: NGOs have less power than government authorities to sanction an infiltrator. The main risk of being found out is expulsion from the NGO.

8.7.4.7 Infiltration of Parliamentary Membership: This is the process by which members of a protest group engage in local and national politics, which gives them access to local council, regional, national and federal parliamentary institutions.

Whilst acting in their capacity of elected representatives (for any party or as independents), the infiltrators' primary allegiance is to their protest group. They use their presence as members of parliament to channel privileged information to protest organisers. This may include information about the content of committee meetings, informal conversations, briefing to the press, executive meetings, etc.

These parliamentary infiltrators may also be able to influence other members of parliament to act in favour of the protest group and to use parliamentary procedure, such as the asking of questions, to promote the protest group's agenda.

Considerations and risks: The privileges enjoyed by parliamentary members in most jurisdictions mean that their membership of a protest group has few implications on their seat in an elected body. However, party affiliations may be undermined by revelations of a declared sympathy for a protest group, so it may be better not to reveal these sympathies too publicly.

8.7.4.8 Generating Civil Unrest through Boycotts, Demonstrations and Strikes: As agent provocateurs within other organisations, infiltrators can trigger antagonism towards a target authority and generate civil unrest by organising boycotts, protest demonstrations and strikes. For instance, an infiltrator in the civil service can use his or her position to agitate colleagues to take strike action against the authority for which they work. In a similar way, an infiltrator in an NGO or political party can push for that organisation to endorse a product or national boycott campaign.

Considerations and risks: In some countries deliberate incitement to boycott, take part in certain types of demonstration or organise strikes may be restricted or illegal.

8.7.4.9 Spreading Rumours and Lies: It's a sad reality that governments and corporations are quite capable of being totally unethical in their use of deceit and rumour mongering to discredit or destabilise their adversaries. Both are capable of compiling false or misleading "evidence" to discredit an activist or whistleblower. For this reason, a modern protest group has to be both capable of side-stepping such tactics and using the same tactics in retaliation against an authority, if necessary.

The creation and dissemination of rumours and lies is a low-cost form of manipulation. Virtually any message can be delivered in this way and the only way to avoid it is to be able to absolutely disprove an assertion publicly and instantly.

Even when disproved, a rumour or outright lie may still have a lasting effect. The principle of "no smoke without fire" may taint a target permanently. This works in both directions and protest groups must be alert to becoming targets of this particular "dirty trick" technique.

The types of content which are used to ferment damaging rumours and lies include the following - but the possibilities are endless:

- Fear mongering - revealing fearful future prospects.
- Scandal mongering - revealing past and present scandals.
- Allegations of financial corruption.
- Allegations of nepotism.
- Allegations of mismanagement or misgovernment.
- Allegations of current or past criminality.
- Allegations of incompetence.
- Allegations of abuse (human rights, civil rights, workers' rights, sexual, etc.).

The primary defence against this technique is to have an immaculately scandal-free organisation that is transparent and properly regulated. Alongside this, an organisation needs excellent press management machinery which can respond quickly and clearly to accusations. Ideally, an organisation should be fully prepared to manage these kinds of dirty tricks and have a set of standard responses developed in advance to deal with the eventuality. Scotching a rumour or disproving a lie gets much harder after the passage of time, so delays in responding to rumour-mongering must be avoided.

Considerations and risks: The internet provides an ideal channel for disseminating lies and rumours very effectively and also makes the origin of a rumour hard or impossible to identify, thus reducing the risk of detection.

8.7.4.10 Blackmail and Scandals: Governments and corporations are happy to use blackmail to persuade their adversaries to moderate or drop campaigns against them. Blackmail relies on one party being stronger than the other and, generally, authorities have a great deal more power than the average protest group. However, authorities and corporations can also be blackmailed by means of threats to reveal scandalous or damaging evidence about them.

Such was almost the case in late November 2010, when Julian Assange, of WikiLeaks, announced his intention to "take down" a top U.S. bank, which was not named, and reveal a corruption scandal within it. The Bank of America was said to be extremely concerned that it might be the subject of the WikiLeaks' upcoming revelations and the bank's share price dropped sharply during this period. In the end, the revelations were never made.

All governments and corporations have skeletons in their cupboards. A glance at some of the world's largest corporations reveals their shameful pasts as Nazi collaborators, gas chamber chemical manufacturers, suppliers of torture equipment and assistants in kidnapping, producers of toxic pharmaceuticals, deadly agricultural chemicals, contaminated food and a whole lot more. The ethics of many corporations has not radically changed with the passage of time. Governments also share in this wealth of corruption, depravity, cover-ups, illegality and immorality, both past and current.

Uncovering and building a case against an authority can provide a lot of leverage in persuading them to alter their behaviour to satisfy various protest demands. This could be referred to as blackmail.

A well-infiltrated authority will soon yield a useful set of potential scandals upon which a case can be built and documented. After documenting such a case, a protest group needs to offer to discuss the case with the authority's executives, at which point it can broach the subject of its demands in return for not revealing the information it has collected.

Considerations and risks: In some jurisdictions it is an offence to threaten a corporation in this way; however, the threat of revelation makes such a risk quite low. The cost of the revelations needs to be sufficiently high to force an authority to agree to the terms of the protest group's demands.

8.7.4.11 Bribery and Persuasion: The corollary of blackmail, with its implied threat of revelation, is the concept of bribery and persuasion. Here, a protest group can offer to give something in return for an authority accepting the protest demands. In "real world" negotiations it is often necessary to accept less than is demanded and a protest group may have to offer some form of cooperation to an authority in order to persuade them of their good will, or publicly demonstrate a compromise rather than a defeat.

This form of bribery may be made to a politician or official who may be trying to resolve a dispute in order to enhance their reputation or to save face.

Considerations and risks: The main risk here is that a protest group may be perceived as being weak and desperate to negotiate, if offering political bribes in order to win concessions.

8.7.4.12 Creating and Encouraging Political Disunity: Sometimes it's important to take advantage of existing conflicts between officials, or to create new enmities within an organisation, in order to weaken its authority. This can be achieved in a number of ways, but primarily by highlighting and exaggerating the differences between various competing cadres in a government or corporation.

All organisations contain conflicting groups that are engaged in local power struggles. These power dynamics can be used to reduce the overall solidarity and collaboration of a target authority. An agent provocateur or infiltrator can use their position to start and encourage disputes between competing groups. All that is required to engender division is a good understanding of the differences of opinion, political philosophy or background of the competing groups.

Considerations and risks: There are few risks involved in the encouragement of political disunity, provided that no-one realises that it is being encouraged by a 3rd party in order to achieve an alternative agenda.

8.7.4.13 Political Seduction: A member of a protest group with close associations with the personnel in a target authority may be capable of "turning" a politician, official or corporate employee, reversing their political position to be contrary to that of their employer. This process may be a lengthy one, involving all kinds of political and personal pressures and inducements.

In many ways, political seduction is much more effective than infiltration by outsiders. Someone who is already close to the seat of power is much more useful than some outsider who has to first gain an authority's trust.

Considerations and risks: Choosing an appropriate target for this strategy is the main problem here. It is necessary to find someone sufficiently high-ranking as to be useful, but also sufficiently open to persuasion as to be seduced into a change of political allegiance. The two characteristics do not often go together. However, a careful investigation of the background of a target official may reveal old alliances and sympathies that can be reignited to trigger off a political realignment.

8.7.4.14 Social Seduction: Very often social pressures can be brought to bear on individuals within an authority to persuade them to be sympathetic to a protest group's aspirations. An investigation into the private lives of officials, including their spouses, children, social activities, friends and extra-curricular interests, may help to gain leverage over them and persuade them to alter their position. The main lever for changing a target's political position to favour that of the protest group is peer pressure. For instance, if an individual is a member of a church or club and that church or club has adopted a policy of divestment from companies involved in Israel, it should be relatively easy to persuade the individual to adopt the same principles as their church or club.

There is a clear pressure on individual members to either conform or leave.

Considerations and risks: There are few risks involved in exerting peer pressure on "friends" to conform to a new political position or trying to influence other civilian groups (including the civil police) to take a sympathetic view of a protest campaign's concerns.

8.7.4.15 Infiltration of Public Meetings: Meetings held by protest groups are frequently infiltrated by agents of authority, such as the police or other paid agents, either to gather information or cause disruption. Of course, this infiltration can work both ways and protest groups may find it useful to infiltrate public or private meetings held by target authorities with the same goals in mind. Such infiltrations may have a wide audience, especially if they are reported on by the media or filmed and circulated on the internet.

Entering non-public meetings can be a great deal easier than one would think. Simply dress appropriately, carry some kind of briefcase, choose a badge if they are pre-printed or invent a name from a large organisation. Apologise for forgetting your business cards, take conference materials and proceed inside. Unless it's a super secure conference, you'll get inside with little problem.

There are many possible ways to disrupt a meeting. They include impersonation of a target authority's executives and the delivery of comical or satirical material to a waiting audience. This latter was the case of the "Yes Men" infiltration of Canada's main oil conference, in 2007. They were posing as Exxon and National Petroleum Council executives, explaining that the world was heading for imminent climate catastrophe, but that, whatever happened, they would guarantee the oil kept flowing, if necessary by converting the billions of dead people into petroleum! Other forms of disruption include so-called guerrilla musicals, staged in the middle of the meeting to interrupt speakers with satirical or comical songs.

Considerations and risks: If the infiltration of a meeting is designed to gather information, ensure that there are at least two infiltrators carrying out recordings from different locations, to avoid any possibility of ending up with a poor recording.

There is a strong risk of ejection if a protester or group starts to interrupt a meeting. If this is the intention, then it's important to make sure one member of the group is filming the whole interruption for later distribution.

8.7.4.16 Agent Provocateur: An agent provocateur is a person or group which infiltrates an organisation with the express intention of encouraging members of that organisation to behave in a way which damages the organisation. The technique is often used by authorities, such as the police or intelligence services, to infiltrate protest groups, but, of course, it can also be used by protest groups who infiltrate an authority.

The types of action an agent provocateur may encourage include the following:

• Making defamatory, incendiary, or ill-informed public statements that attracts criticism. Examples might include wild, insulting and easily disprovable accusations.

• Inducing unwise decisions by an authority based on disinformation provided by the agent provocateur. These imprudent decisions may cause an authority to break the law or fail to respect human and civil rights, thus attracting public disdain and possible legal action.

Considerations and risks: An agent provocateur relies on the existence of an unstable and fast moving environment, such as an open conflict or imminent threat, in order to operate. In a heated environment an authority may be persuaded to act improperly or foolishly. There are few risks involved in the role of agent provocateur because, after all, they only offer suggestions and encouragement. The actual actions are those of the authority, not of the agent provocateur.

8.7.5 Espionage and Intelligence Gathering

Espionage (spying) should be distinguished from intelligence gathering. Intelligence gathering may be carried out using publicly available data, whereas spying is by definition a covert action to obtain secret information from an authority, without permission.

Espionage against a government authority is, in most jurisdictions, an illegal act because it seeks to weaken authority. Nonetheless, certain information may give tremendous advantage to a group opposing an authority and, without doubt, espionage and intelligence gathering aimed at a target authority are an essential part of the activities of all protest groups.

```
                    ┌─────────────────┐
                    │  Espionage &    │
                    │  Intelligence   │
                    │   Gathering     │
                    └─────────────────┘
```

Intelligence Gathering	Commercial Espionage	Government Espionage	Counter-intelligence	Internal Security

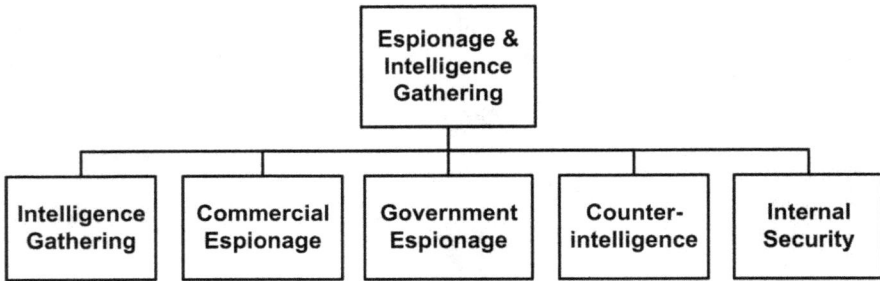

8.7.5.1 Intelligence Gathering: There is no doubt that what enables a protest movement most effective is a sound knowledge of their opposition. This kind of valuable intelligence is often publicly available. Here is a list of the information that can be gathered from public records and the press, and which can be immensely useful in understanding a target authority:

-   Personal and financial histories of executives, officials and politicians.
-   Known associates and friends of executives, officials and politicians.
-   Family members of executives, officials and politicians.
-   Business interests of executives, officials and politicians.
-   Press references to a target authority.
-   Infrastructure of a target authority.
-   Management hierarchy of a target authority.
-   Publications of a target authority.
-   Known communications of a target authority.
-   Legal actions of a target authority.

Considerations and risks: Intelligence gathering within the public domain carries little or no risks. The main problem for a small protest group is storing and correlating intelligence. Some effort should be spent on building database systems that allow the storage and interrogation of information about target organisations.

8.7.5.2 Commercial Espionage: Commercial espionage is the gathering of confidential information about a corporate organisation for use (in this case) by a protest campaign.

There are many methods by which commercial and confidential intelligence can be gathered. These include:

-   Physical and electronic surveillance.
-   Pilfering documents/used media, such as CDs, from waste bins.
-   Planting undercover operatives within a company's admin and IT departments.

- Spying on vehicle movements into and out of offices and tracking license plate numbers.
- Recording the movements and connections of executives and directors.
- Collecting phone records of company executives.
- Defining management structures.
- Recording academic and private records of key employees, directors, etc.
- Recording meeting agendas.
- Recording confidential meetings.
- Compiling phone and email contact lists.
- Collecting internal memos.
- Accruing internal planning documents (marketing, product, production, human resource).
- Collecting confidential legal correspondence.
- Accumulating banking and credit card information.
- Collecting confidential internal records, such as customer and supplier lists.
- Collecting detailed financial statements, bank transactions, etc.
- Compiling lists of staff members and their social security details.
- Gathering information on political connections and donations.

Considerations and risks: Corporate privacy laws may well make some of the above activities illegal, but since the intention would be to gather intelligence in a completely covert operation, the issue of privacy is largely irrelevant. However, the most problematic issue is the storage, sorting, correlation and retrieval of large amounts of intelligence data.

8.7.5.3 Government Espionage: This is the act of spying on government organisations and transmitting that information to a third party, in this case a protest group. This is the work of those who specifically infiltrate government agencies for the purpose of spying on them, or of those already working for a government agency and who decide to spy on behalf of a protest organisation.

When there is a conflict between a protest group and a government, normally there are just one or two government departments involved. For a protest group it is immensely useful to know the inner thoughts and plans of their adversaries in these government authorities. In general, this can only be achieved in a reasonable time by finding someone within the target organisation who is sympathetic to the cause and is willing to take the risk of spying for the group.

The kind of information which is useful to a protest group includes:

• How much information does the government already have about the protest group and where did they obtain it?

• Has the authority infiltrated the protest group? If so, by whom?

• Has the authority developed a strategy to deal with the protest? Will they consider negotiation or compromise?

• What are the short and medium term plans to attack the protest group?

• What are the authority's weaknesses regarding the protest campaign?

• Who in the authority is actually responsible and involved in planning responses to the protest? What are their family, business, political and social connections? What are their personal details (address, social status, background, etc.)?

• Someone infiltrating a government department will also need to collect documentary evidence of the actions of the department. This may be important in the event of an authority taking any extreme or illegal actions against a protest group. The kinds of documents which are useful are email addresses, emails, internal memos and meeting minutes.

Considerations and risks: Spying on your employer, especially if they happen to be a government department, carries the obvious risks of an illegal action. The person(s) chosen to get involved in this kind of activity need to be properly briefed and there needs to be excellent security, good organisation and a means of totally secure communication between the infiltrator and the protest group. Clearly, the infiltrator should have no obvious connections with the protest group or any of its organisers.

8.7.5.4 Counterintelligence (also referred to as Counterespionage): This is the process of protecting (in this case the protest group) against espionage by an authority. It refers specifically to all activities designed to stop an authority infiltrating or spying on a protest group. It doesn't refer to the management of internal security within the group. There are various strategies for protecting a group against the efforts of an authority to spy on it:

• **Collective counterintelligence:** Firstly, it is important to try to understand how the authority collects information about a protest group (phone taps, email interception, infiltration, intercepting physical post, bugging meetings, etc.). The protest group should nominate a security manager, responsible for continuously evaluating the group's security needs, as well as looking for and closing off security vulnerabilities.

• **Defensive counterintelligence:** Secondly, a protest group needs to develop methods and systems for thwarting the attempts of an authority to infiltrate them. This is the business of an internal security management and it may involve evaluating and implementing technological solutions to improve data and communications security, altering procedures to reduce risks of infiltration, and auditing and correcting security systems.

• **Offensive counterintelligence:** Finally, a protest group needs to take advantage of an authority's attempt to infiltrate them and it should use these attempts to feed disinformation to the authority .Alternatively, they should try to corrupt those attempting to infiltrate the group and persuade them to work for the group, whilst all the time appearing to seem loyal to their authority (become a so-called "double agent"). This is a great deal more complex than simply protecting a group from surveillance or espionage. To engage offensively in counterintelligence against an authority requires very good planning. For instance, to deliver disinformation to an authority, a protest group needs to develop a storyline which is credible and which achieves a particular strategic objective. A protest group may decide that it is useful to lull an authority into a false sense of victory and thus deliver a storyline which indicates that a protest group has decided to close down its operations in the near future. In such an event, an authority may also decide to lose its interest in the protest group.

Considerations and risks: Most protest groups fail to realise how devious and nervous most governments are. They naively assume that no respectable democratic government would ever stoop to trying to infiltrate a legitimate nonviolent protest group. How wrong they are! But, despite all the evidence to the contrary, there are still many ordinary citizen groups that are blissfully unaware of the level to which their organisations are infiltrated and spied upon. It is no exaggeration to say that a protest group should make its own security its first and highest priority.

8.7.5.5 Internal Security: Although a protest group's security is not in itself a method of civil disobedience, it could be argued that anything which frustrates an authority's attempts to control or spy is an act of defiance against the authority.

Basic security is vital for a protest group to defend itself against an authority. Perhaps in its early days a group might appear too irrelevant to be of interest to an authority, but with time, as a group becomes more effective, it comes to present a greater challenge to the authority's powers. At a certain moment an authority will start to take a more covert interest in a protest group, and at that moment the security of a protest campaign really does start to become an important issue. Authorities don't infiltrate and spy on protest organisations for fun. They do it with the clear intention of controlling, discrediting or destroying the protest group.

The first step for a protest group is to appoint a security manager, responsible for the following areas of internal security:

• **Evaluating the security needs of the group:** Evaluating potential vulnerabilities, necessary security technology, and developing formal security procedures for data and communications, good practice to maintain document and property security, and evaluation of systems of personnel security vetting. Designing a secure management structure, where confidential information is contained within a limited group.

• **Implementing and auditing security measures:** These actions include implementing procedures and technology for encrypted communications, encrypted storage, document disposal (shredding etc.), file destruction, personnel vetting, which involves checking the bona fides of new members or staff of the organising group, meeting security and physical counterintelligence measures.

• **Testing internal security:** This involves testing physical and communications security systems, auditing personnel, and ensuring conformity. There are several ways in which security can be practically tested. For instance, one might create a fake (but important) document and monitor to see if an authority has acquired it. A test of communications security might be to create a fake persona in the protest group and then communicate with a fake persona in another protest group. Monitor the reaction of the authority to see if the communication has been intercepted. In recent times there has been an upsurge in tools available to activists and journalists to identify surveillance spyware on their computers and mobile devices. Governments are increasingly using sophisticated technology that allows them to read activists and journalists' private emails, track their locations and remotely turn on their computer's camera or microphone to secretly record their activities. In a response to these risks, late in 2014, Amnesty International launched its own app called "Detekt", designed to alert activists to such intrusions, so they can take action [Note 133].

• **Planning infiltration and espionage of an authority's organisation:** A security manager may participate in the planning and execution of infiltration actions against an authority and the carrying out of acts of espionage.

External infiltration and espionage: It is very common for NGOs and protest groups to underestimate the risks to their security from external interests. Governments and corporations frequently use private intelligence companies to infiltrate protest groups [Note 123]. In the cases that are publicly known, many corporations have hired spies to obtain human intelligence, either directly or through intermediaries, using a false or misleading identity to infiltrate an organisation.

Often a spy poses as a volunteer or supporter, secretly harvesting information over a long period of time, or as a journalist, to gather a lot of information quickly. The spy may use recording devices to capture verbal communication near him. To obtain physical intelligence, such as documents, the most common technique appears to be what in the USA is referred to as "dumpster diving". This is the collection of rubbish (mostly paper, CDs, etc.) from waste bins on the protest group's property.

Corporations and governments also hire the services of experienced infiltrators, posing as volunteers, to survey a protest group's offices and to steal documents left unattended. Both offices and homes may be targeted for the gathering of physical intelligence.

Corporate spies may also plant bugs to obtain and transmit verbal communications; there is a wealth of different forms of electronic espionage available. The use of surveillance technologies has increased significantly in recent years. The "Coalition Against Unlawful Surveillance Exports", of which Amnesty International is a member, estimates that the industry is currently worth $5 billion (2014), so this is not spy fiction. Surveillance is big business. Some of the more common forms of electronic spying that occur are the following:

• **Vulnerability research.** An external spy may begin an electronic intelligence gathering effort by assessing the comparative vulnerabilities of a protest group's or NGO's computers, networks and electronic communications. Sometimes external agents may attempt to identify the times and dates when a subject is in the office or at home by using the pretence of being a commercial caller.

• **Computer hacking.** There are many different techniques available to professional spies who wish to hack a computer or network. Some of the more obvious ones may include vulnerability scanning (checking computers and networks for known security flaws, open ports, etc.), persistent software implants and creation of custom malware, password cracking, phishing (obtaining passwords by posing as a trustworthy entity), Trojan horses (establishing a back door into a computer or network that can be exploited later) and key loggers (recording of keystrokes on a computer for later retrieval).

• **Obtaining phone records.** This often involves the practice of creating a false pretext, or using a false identity or pretence to trick a telephone provider into releasing records of phone calls. Professional corporate spies may also breach online account administration tools that are made available to phone customers in order to collect telephone call details.

• **Wiretapping.** Professional corporate spies may tap phones in many ways, including implanting bugs in a handset or anywhere along a phone line, tapping outside phone connection boxes and using radio scanners.

• **Phone voicemail hacking.** Some phone voicemail systems can be easily hacked via web-based spoofing services which corporate spies can use to make their calls seem like they are coming from the voicemail that they are hacking into.

• **Theft of computers.** Computer data can be obtained by theft, especially of laptops and other mobile devices, such as tablets and smart phones.

Considerations and risks: Internal security is a huge, complex subject and a protest group should ensure they have the right person managing this task. There are companies that can advise on this, though they are sometimes the same companies used by governments and corporations to carry out spying on NGOs and protest groups. For a small group, the best option is to appoint someone from the founding group who is technically minded and willing to learn how to build and manage an effective security regime.

8.7.6 Diversion: This is a group of methods which are designed to divert and dissipate the energy and attention of an authority or other organisation during a protest action. Diversionary tactics may include forcing an authority to make corrections to its position, to justify its arguments, to defend its position, to deny wrong-doing, to defend against mock attacks and the deconstruction of its arguments or proposals.

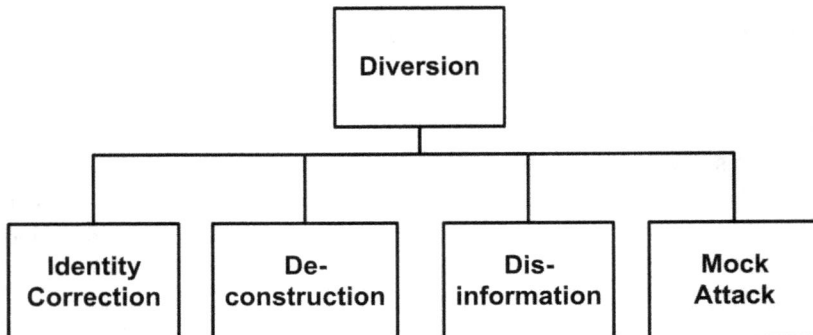

8.7.6.1 Identity Correction: This is a technique which seeks to publicly expose authorities or other organisations for what they really are. It is referred to as "identity correction" because the method attempts to correct the public perception of an authority.

A typical example would be a corporation which is actually utterly callous about human rights, workers' rights and the environment, but which spends huge amounts of money on PR to appear like a caring, environmentally sensitive, responsible company. Identity correction would seek to correct the corporation's image to reflect the truth.

The technique works by identifying and releasing a spoof statement of something that an authority actually could, but absolutely never would say.

For example, imagine a statement such as "the US Republican Party is committed to the elimination of child poverty within 5 years by cutting the US defence budget by 1%". Now, we all know that this statement is never going to be made because the Republican Party is not interested in child poverty, but rather is much more interested in guns and war. However, if this statement can be launched and attributed to a spokesperson for the Republican Party, they will then at some point have to contradict it. The contradiction will then reveal the true character of the Republican Party as being more interested in war than they are in child welfare.

In a real example, activists impersonating French officials announced that Haiti's debt - imposed when Haiti won independence from France, to compensate French slave-owners for their lost "property" - would at long last be forgiven. The statement was incorrect, of course, but the denials from France highlighted the despicable way that Haiti has been treated (and later punished) under French colonial rule.

Considerations and risks: The greatest difficulty with identity correction is persuading someone in the press that a spoof statement really does originate with the target authority or company. This requires some skill, to slip a statement onto the appropriate bit of the internet and get the press to run with it. The placing of statements on newspaper comment sites, political blogs, or on various social media sites sometimes does the trick. Alternatively, spoof websites for the authority in question can also be built and links distributed to make the statement look authentic.

8.7.6.2 Deconstruction: This is the technique whereby arguments, proposals or policies made by an authority, a corporation or other organisation, are publicly deconstructed in a very objective and complete way, so as to cause embarrassment to the authority and thus oblige them to restate their case, retract their case and/or shift position.

Some degree of deconstruction or doubt can be applied to most public statements in most contexts, but some statements or positions are less reliable than others. Governments frequently make uninformed statements in order to gain short-term political advantage. Politicians are notoriously ill-informed about much of what goes on in the real world. This makes them prone to accept and churn out their speech-writers' suggestions without question. The average politician works to deliver easy-to-digest news sound bites to achieve maximum news impact. This disinterest in nuance leaves many a political statement open to exercises in deconstruction.

To take an example, more than ten years ago we were assured that "within 18 months iris recognition would become the norm for biometric identification across the world, ranging from credit card verification, passport verification, national ID cards, computer logins to secure banking". Despite the howls of laughter from the IT world, politicians in many Western countries trotted out this (and other) mantras of biometric security. Ten years later, the widespread use of biometric iris data for identification is still as far away as ever (except in science fiction movies), bedevilled as it always was by technical hitches, poor accuracy, vast volumes of data, poor security and tremendous inconvenience. After years of political hype on iris scan identification, followed by lots of technical deconstruction, the technology has been quietly forgotten for mainstream identification purposes.

A similar case took place in 2015, when the British Prime Minister and Home Secretary both made statements in the House of Commons, promising that they would pass laws forbidding the use of encryption, so that intelligence services would have access to all communications on the internet, if necessary, in order to prevent terrorist communications. The deconstruction of this silly assertion followed within several minutes, when lots of IT engineers, E-commerce sites, such as Amazon, - and even the US President - pointed out that the entire global internet banking and e-commerce sector relied on exactly the type of encryption and security that the British government was proposing to forbid. The British government and Conservative party then went into a full reverse and buried the subject as quickly and quietly as it could, much to the amusement of the IT, E-Commerce and banking sector.

Considerations and risks: Deconstruction may be simple (as in the second example) or it may require quite a lot of work to completely and objectively dismantle an authority's statements. Subjects such as GM or shale gas fracking are complex and require a lot of multi-faceted arguments to deconstruct.

Very often the public ignores most of the scientific deconstruction and locks onto a single emotive reason to disbelieve or distrust an authority's original statements, such as "fracking has no negative effects on human health". In the case of fracking, a 10 second clip from a documentary, showing water, contaminated by methane, coming from a kitchen tap, and actually set alight by the home owner, did more to deconstruct the arguments for fracking than the 400 studies on environmental damage and risks to public health.

8.7.6.3 Disinformation: Disinformation is information which is inaccurate or false and is created and propagated deliberately. There are several reasons why a protest group may wish to deliberately create and spread false information:

• To discredit an authority (using the "mud sticks" principle). Sadly, the human race is bedevilled by the notion that there is no smoke without fire. In fact, creating smoke without fire is simple. Creating a set of allegations against a person or authority, however disprovable, eventually has the effect that some of the mud sticks.

• To manipulate the attitudes of an authority's supporters and the general public against the authority. The inherent distrust between the public and most authorities can be readily exploited by using disinformation that seems to confirm what the public already suspected. These might be suggestions of corruption, incompetence, cronyism, etc. Once launched, such rumours are difficult for an authority or official to quench.

• To cause embarrassment to an authority when documents or statements are proven to be untrue or false.

• To conflate truth and disinformation, so as to make an authority's statement conflicting and/or confusing. The public often pays little heed to the notion of cross-checking a source. A statement from an authority printed next to a rumour in a newspaper becomes intertwined in the public psyche. When the rumour is disproved, the public is left confused and perhaps disappointed. For instance, when the rumour of a new development, including a public medical centre, is disproved, it creates public confusion and disappointment.

• To censor an authority by combining large amounts of easily disprovable disinformation with a true statement, to such an extent that the authority's statements become valueless in the eyes of the public. When an authority spends a large part of its time denying rumours or unsubstantiated "leaks", the quality of the information coming from that authority is called into question. The public starts to ask, "is this real or is this just another rumour?"

Targets for disinformation may be an authority in the general sense or individual members of an authority, such as a minister or a government official. Other targets for disinformation may be a policy of an authority, a strategy, plan, report, investigation, inquiry or, indeed, any activity underwritten by an authority. All are suitable targets for campaigns of disinformation.

Disinformation works in one of two ways, depending on the objective of the campaign:

• **Believable disinformation:** This is disinformation designed to damage the opposition by undermining credibility and causing a scandal. This is a form of manipulation that requires a credible story, thus it's hard to prove that the disinformation is untrue. This allows for the disinformation to have a long-lasting and caustic effect on an authority.

• **Disprovable disinformation**: This is disinformation that is relatively easy to discredit. The objective here is to undermine the quality of an authority's statements. For this to happen, it must be relatively easy to show that a lot of the statements that appear to originate from the authority are nonsense.

Types of disinformation: There are two types of disinformation, non-malicious and malicious.

• **Non-malicious disinformation:** Not all disinformation is malicious in content, even though the motives for the disinformation are to attack the authority. For instance, one might "reveal" that the local council has proposed to finance a complete clean-up of some rubbish-strewn local beauty spot. This is completely untrue, of course. However, the local authority now has to deny this and in doing so, makes the statement that they are NOT going to take responsibility for cleaning this site. The initial statement is certainly not filled with malice, but the action causes embarrassment to the council by the very act of denying that it is true.

• **Malicious disinformation:** This is much more direct in its attack on an authority. For instance, a roads authority planning a new bypass may be planning a two-lane road. A protest group, seeking to stop the development, could suggest that the plans are being made with the contingency to expand the road into a six-lane motorway. This is completely untrue. However, the story is sufficiently shocking as to generate a backlash by the general public. Denials by the local authority are condemned as "cover-ups". The effect of this disinformation is corrosive and wears away at both the reputation and integrity of the authority and the desirability of their plans. This is particularly true when a piece of disinformation is hard to disprove (the "cover-up" scenario) and the conspiracy theorists spring into action.

Methods of dissemination: There are various ways in which disinformation can be disseminated; the press and internet being the main channels:

- Statements can be "leaked" to the press, purportedly coming from anonymous insiders in an authority.
- Press comment sites, political or local blogs can be used to introduce or spread disinformation.
- Social networking channels can be used to introduce a package of disinformation or to propagate the disinformation and give it credibility.

Considerations and risks: The use of disinformation is a powerful tool. It may also be unethical in some circumstances, depending on the severity of the case. The ethical question surrounding the use of disinformation fades into insignificance when used against a murderous totalitarian regime.

There are few risks involved in campaigns of disinformation. With a little care, it should be impossible for an authority to track the source of the disinformation.

Campaigns of disinformation need careful planning, with clear objectives. Over-doing releases of disinformation may jeopardise the effectiveness of a campaign. Sometimes, less may be more. Timing is also important. Each piece of disinformation has to have time to work fully and have the maximum effect on the authority. Crowding the public with disinformation may be counterproductive, create suspicions of malicious intent and may be a waste of effort, so careful choreography is essential.

8.7.6.4 Mock Attack: A mock attack is a distracting strategy used to waste the time and resources of an authority in dealing with an attack which never materialises. An attack may be a legal, political, media, or physical attack. A mock attack can be executed by a real protest organisation or by a mock protest organisation that does not really exist.

One objective of a mock attack is to alter the management imperatives of an authority in order to dissipate the authority's resources, focus and time. Mock attacks are sometimes used to test the response and preparedness of an authority in a way which provides a protest group with valuable information for a future real attack. Mock attacks can also be used to weaken the preparedness of an authority because an authority can never be sure when an attack is real or just another mock action, and may become complacent.

Mock attacks serve a protest group well because they are cheap to organise. They redress the imbalance of power between a small protest group and a large, well-financed authority. Mock attacks cause expense, distraction and annoyance to an authority and may make the authority look absurd in their over-reaction to a non-event. They cost a protest group virtually nothing.

Mock attacks can also be made by entirely imaginary "mock" protest groups. This strategy requires the creation of a protest group which does not actually exist, has no members, premises or organisers, but which may have a website or blog, etc. The communications of the mock group is controlled by an external handler, working for the real protest group. Mock groups can be used to make more radical mock attacks on an authority and, indeed, can be used to deliberately invite the attention of the police, intelligence services, anti-terrorist organisations, etc., if that serves the greater agenda. Leaking key data, such as addresses, plans and membership, about the mock protest group to security officials can be used to create some serious distractions, and, in combination with the strategy of malicious disinformation, can be used to direct security efforts at members of the authority itself and their families.

Simple examples of mock attacks can be announcements of public marches, assemblies or demonstrations to take place at a yet to be disclosed date ("members will be informed by their coordinators") in a certain location, followed by a deliberate confidential leak to the authority of the time and date. All that remains is to watch the authorities beef up their police and security machinery to control or stop the demonstration. Of course, one must ensure that their over-reaction is well documented and attended by the press, with the usual questions about waste of resources and tax-payers' money. Similar tactics can be used to have mock blockades, mock strikes, mock sit-ins, etc. The tactic of mockery is limitless.

In other forms of mock attack, a protest group can pretend to plan to stand a protest candidate in an election, or to make a complaint to a high or international court, to state that it has applied for an injunction against an authority or to claim to have criminal evidence against an authority or its officials. Many such mock attacks will trigger off defensive, time-wasting responses by an authority.

Considerations and risks: Mock attacks carry little risk for a protest group. Any accusation of not being serious can be rebuffed as a "change of plan" by the protesters. The disruption caused to an authority is purely the result of decisions by the authority and cannot be charged to the protest group, provided the protest group stays within the law. Fortunately, there are no jurisdictions where a protest group faces legal action for NOT carrying out some protest action.

Notes on Chapter 8

Note 1: 1997, May 12: Mother Jones "Boycott Shell now"; 2014, 38 Degrees: "Boycott Shell, Save the Arctic"; 1995 Greenpeace: "Shell reverses decision to dump the Brent Spar"

Note 2: 2010, November: Greenpeace "Help bluefin tuna before they go extinct", http://www.greenpeace.org/usa/en/news-and-blogs/campaign-blog/help-bluefin-tuna-before-they-go-extinct/blog/28210/

Note 3: Scarlett Johansson row has boosted Israeli settlement boycott, say activists (The Guardian, 6 February 2014) - http://www.theguardian.com/world/2014/feb/06/scarlett-johansson-israeli-settlement-boycott-activists

Note 4: 2009 Jerusalem Post: "British trade unions to boycott Israeli goods"

Note 5: Saturday 31 October 2009, Sussex Univ. "students at Sussex University vote to boycott Israeli goods". Indybay.

Note 6 Taylor, Jerome (30 June 2010). "Methodists launch boycott over West Bank" London: Independent.co.uk.

Note 7: Mozgovaya, Natasha (21 July 2010). "Food co-op in Rachel Corrie's hometown boycotts Israeli goods (Haaretz)".

Note 8: "Statement on Israeli settlements in the Occupied Palestinian Territory" (World Council of Churches, 2.09.2009)". Oikoumene.org

Note 9: Co-op boycotts exports from Israel's West Bank settlements (The Guardian, 29 April 2012).

Note 10: Dutch supermarkets ban settlement products (The Times of Israel, 22 July 2013).

Note 11: Presbyterians Vote to Divest Holdings to Pressure Israel (New York Times, 20 June 2014)

Note 12: Boycott news from issue 119 of Ethical Consumer July / August 2009, 'Shut Down H&K'

Note 13: 2014, January 30, BBC: "Scarlett Johansson quits Oxfam role over SodaStream row", http://www.bbc.com/news/world-us-canada-25958176

Note 14: 2014, 23rd Dec.: South China Morning Post print edition as "Non-cooperation is protesters' next gambit".

Note 15: Mon 25 Oct 2010, BBC Panorama: "The Great Housing Rip Off?"

Note 16: Jan 2015: The Journal.ie: "Thousands take part in anti-water charge protests across Ireland"

Note 17: Hickey, D.J.; Doherty, J.E. (2003): "A New Dictionary of Irish History from 1800." Gill & Macmillan, ISBN 0717125203

Note 18: Bailey, Brian J (1998). The Luddite Rebellion. NYU Press. ISBN 081471335-1

Note 19: Independent (London), 05/02/2015: Supermarket price war leads to 50% cut in dairy farmers.

Note 20: "Dock workers to boycott Israeli ship (Guardian Online, 3 February 2009)". Mg.co.za.

Note 21: "Sweden to launch weeklong boycott on Israeli ships" (Ynet News, 5 June 2010).

Note 22: "SOPA protests to shut down Web sites" The Washington Post January 17, 2012

Note 23: Sunday 21 July 2013, Helena Smith, Guardian "Greeks plan protests against Sunday trading"

Note 24: 1 April 2011, Occasional links & commentary on economics, culture and society: "No sympathy for the bankers", anticap.wordpress.com/2011/04/01/no-sympathy-for-the-bankers/

Note 25: Reuters, Tue Feb 18, 2014: "After depositor revolt, Thai Government Savings Bank scraps farm bank loan"

Note 26: Cooperman, Alan (29 September 2004). "Israel Divestiture Spurs Clash". The Washington Post.

Note 27: Le Soir, 7/4/2011: "Dexia Israël bientôt vendue"

Note 28: Kleinschmitt, Bernd (May 2, 2011). "Deutsche Bahn Withdraws from Project of New Railway Line from Tel Aviv to Jerusalem". European Jewish Post.

Note 29: Huffington Post, 27-06-2012: "Caterpillar Pulled From Socially Responsible Investment Indexes On Concern Over Israeli Use Of Bulldozers"

Note 30: Haaretz, Feb 01, 2014: "Denmark's largest bank blacklists Israel's Hapoalim over settlement construction"

Note 31: Haaretz, Jan 8, 2014: "Largest Dutch pension fund boycotts Israeli banks over settlement ties"

Note 32: 2014, 21st March, Guardian: "Student fees policy likely to cost more than the system it replaced", Shiv Malik.

Note 33: Marx, Karl "No Tax Payments!" Neue Rheinische Zeitung #145 (November 1848), Marxists.org

Note 34: Associated press, Dec 23, 2014: "Myanmar Villagers Remain in Standoff Over Mine"

Note 35: Irish Independent: "Garden means more than money as Helena (78) turns down £250,000"

Note 36: 01/02/2014, libcom.org: "Workplace organising guide specifically about employment in the UK"

Note 37: Thursday 04 October 2012, RTE News: "Wexford fishermen give away free monkfish after exceeding EU quota"

Note 38: November 06, 2014, Russia Today: "Protesting French farmers dump tons of manure at govt buildings"

Note 39: "Farmworkers' strike may be over - but everyone's a loser", Rebecca Davis, 23 January 2013

Note 40: Reuters, Thu Jul 11, 2013 "Greeks protest job cuts, unemployment hits new high"

Note 41: Reuters, Wed Nov 12, 2014: "U.S. nurses hold strikes, protests over Ebola measures"

Note 42: Bloomberg, November 26, 2014: "Five Ways to Measure Black Friday Strikes at Wal-Mart"

Note 43: Christian Science Monitor, March 10, 2004: "French science 'under attack'"

Note 44: The Globe and Mail, Sunday, Mar. 18 2012: "Air Canada seeks ruling on flurry of pilot sick calls"

Note 45: "International Covenant on Economic, Social and Cultural Rights", http://www.refworld.org/docid/3ae6b36c0.html

Note 46: Guardian, Seumas Milne, Friday 3 October 2014: "During the miners' strike, Thatcher's secret state was the real enemy within"

Note 47: The Business Journals, March 29, 2012: "Teamster Sanitation Workers Bring Republic Services Strike to Seattle"

Note 48: Guardian, Saturday 3 March 2012, Martin Dunne, "My job was replaced by a workfare placement" and Wednesday 22 February 2012: Polly Toynbee "Protest really does work - just look at Tesco and workfare"

Note 49: Guardian, 6 September 2014: "Italian air traffic controllers strike hits British flights"

Note 50: Daily Telegraph, 06 Aug 2012: "Spanish doctors and nurses protest over health care law for immigrants"

Note 51: Guardian, Thursday 22 May 2014: "Thailand army chief confirms military coup and suspends constitution"

Note 52: Tampa Bay Times: September 15, 2014: "Florida suspends a controversial exam as debate widens over school testing"

Note 53: Liverpool Echo, 28 April 2014: "Liverpool council boycotts the government's 'Help to Work' scheme"

Note 54: EurActiv.com, 19/05/2014: "Macedonian opposition boycotts Parliament over claims of election fraud"

Note 55: Reuters, Sat Nov 22, 2014:"Bahrain holds elections, Shi'ite opposition boycotts vote"

Note 56: Guardian, Monday 15 September 2014: "Israeli refuseniks will be treated as criminals, says defence minister"

Note 57: National Post, January 31, 2014: "'All we get is lip service': Thousands of furious veterans picket offices in battle with Julian Fantino"

Note 58: Guardian, Saturday 8 November 2014: "UK rights groups reject official inquiry into post-September 11 rendition"

Note 59: John Lang (May 4, 2000). "The day the Vietnam War came home". Scripps Howard News service.

Note 60: Todd Gitlin, The Sixties, New York: Bantam Books, 1987, p. 410

Note 61: Guardian, Thursday 21 June, 2012: "Doctors consider further strike action over pensions"

Note 62: Guardian, Wednesday 11 June 2014: "Taxi drivers in European capitals strike over Uber - as it happened"

Note 63: Wolfgang Rudig (1990). Anti-nuclear Movements: A World Survey of Opposition to Nuclear Energy, Longman, p. 135.

Note 64: Nathan Stoltzfus, Resistance of the Heart: Intermarriage and the Rosenstrasse Protest in Nazi Germany, Rutgers University Press (March 2001) ISBN 0-8135-2909-3

Note 65: Medic Wiki: "Pepper spray and tear gas" http://medic.wikia.com/wiki/Pepper_spray_and_tear_gas

Note 66: Spiegel Online, November 11, 2008: Anti-Nuclear Protest Reawakens: Nuclear Waste Reaches German Storage Site Amid Fierce Protests

Note 67: Hagan, John (2001). Northern Passage: American Vietnam War Resisters in Canada. Cambridge MA: Harvard University Press, pp. 77-78. ISBN 978-0-674-00471-9.

Note 68: Guardian, Wednesday 22 October 2014: "Nine injured as migrants rush Spanish border fence in North Africa"

Note 69: ABC News, Sep 2, 2014: "Lost in America: Visa Program Struggles to Track Missing Foreign Students"

Note 70: BBC News, 4 September 2014: "Issue of Calais migrants trying to reach the UK is not new"

Note 71: "Right to a sustainable energy future and community self-government ordinance, Sugar Hill, New Hampshire", http://www.sugarhillnh.org/app/attachments/084_Ordinance_exp_packet.pdf

Note 72: Guardian, 12 September 2014: "Israeli intelligence veterans' letter to Netanyahu and military chiefs - in full"

Note 73: Guardian, Tuesday 21 October 2014: "Lawyers urge peers to reject judicial review restrictions"

Note 74: BBC News, Friday, 26 March 2010: "Heathrow third runway opponents win court challenge"

Note 75: Boycott Workfare: Tescos: "Why would we pay you when we can pick up the phone and get more unemployed people who have to work for free?", http://www.boycottworkfare.org/

Note 76: Guardian, Friday 19 September 2014: "Plans to cut criminal legal aid in doubt after court ruling"

Note 77: Daily KOS Mon Oct 24, 2011 "Police REFUSE to arrest protesters"

Note 78: Independent, Sunday 11 January 2015: "Mutinous New York police turn a blind eye to petty crime in protest against Mayor Bill de Blasio"

Note 79: BBC News, 10 December 2013: "Yorkshire Regiment soldiers jailed for sit-in protest"

Note 80: The New York Times, Myre, Greg (21 April 2004). "Israeli Who Revealed Nuclear Secrets Is Freed".

Note 81: Guardian, Friday 10 October 2014: "This way to the Brexit: what would happen if Britain left the EU?"

Note 82: Deutsche Welle, 25.06.2013: "EU Expansion - EU warms to Serbia, Kosovo"

Note 83: Jerusalem Post, 02.08.2015: "FIFA threatens to expel Israel over restrictions on Palestinians".

Note 84: The Chester Chronicle, 11 July 2008: "North West Hunt Saboteurs Association posted a blacklist of country pubs on its website to put pressure on licensees",

Note 85: Time Magazine, Friday, Apr. 27, 1962: "The Archbishop Stands Firm.". Pages 45-46.

Note 86: The Atlantic, Nov 28 2014: "Protesting Black Friday for Michael Brown"

Note 87: The Times of Israel, August 20, 2013: "Roger Waters calls on musicians to boycott Israel"

Note 88: Birmingham Evening Mail (England), July 4, 2001: "Mayor's banquet hit by boycott"

Note 89: Huffington Post, 08/16/2012: "Pussy Riot Verdict Marks Putin's First Hundred Days"

Note 90: 2015 January 18, Guardian "Anarchy in the bus lane: how protesters quietly took over London's streets", www.theguardian.com/artanddesign/2015/jan/18/anarchist-posters-london-bus-tube-police-strike-magazine

Note 91: Guardian, Sunday 5 January 2014: "Barristers and solicitors walk out over cuts to legal aid fees"

Note 92: Guy Debord and the Situationists

Note 93: Business Insider, Sep. 26, 2012: "Why A Bar Owner Yelling At The Cops Is The Defining Image Of Spain's New Crisis"

Note 94: Washington Post, Monday, November 27, 2006: "Imams Stage Airport 'Pray-In' As Protest".

Note 95: Guardian, Tuesday 2 December 2014: "Claridge's hotel criticised after telling breastfeeding woman to cover up."

Note 96: The Blaze, Nov. 28, 2014: "Demonstrators Deploy Mass 'Die In' Tactics at Major U.S. Malls".

Note 97: Guardian, Wednesday 10 December 2014: "Hundreds stage 'die-in' protest in UK's Westfield mall over Eric Garner death"

Note 98: LeCompte, Tom (July 2005). "The Notorious Flight of Mathias Rust". Air & Space/Smithsonian (Washington, D.C.: Smithsonian Institution).

Note 99: BBC News, Wednesday, 15 September, 2004: "Pro-hunt protesters storm Commons"

Note 100: The Boston Globe and AP, November 03, 2014: "Herd of sheep takes over streets in Spain's capital"

Note 101: Adapted from the Ruckus Society's how-to guide, *A Tiny Blockades Book*:

Note 102: 26/01/2015, Huffington Post "Cancer-stricken Grandfather saved from bailiffs' eviction when crowd of 500 strangers surround his house" www.huffingtonpost.co.uk/2015/01/26/cancer-dad-tom-crawford-bailiffs-eviction-crowd-500_n_6545052.html

Note 103: Guardian, Tuesday 11 February 2014: "Oakland: the city that told Google to get lost"

Note 104: Guardian, Wednesday 21 August 2013: "Gibraltar: life under siege"

Note 105: New York Post. 29 November 2009: "WikiLeaks.org aims to expose lies, topple governments".

Note 106: The Washington Post, Peterson, Andrea. December 31, 2013: "Here's what we learned about the NSA's spying programs in 2013".

Note 107: The Harvard Crimson, April 21, 1964: "The Stall-In"

Note 108: BBC News, Wednesday, 26 April 2006: "Hewitt heckled by furious nurses"

Note 109: Guardian, Wednesday 25 April 2012: "PMQs and Jeremy Hunt's statement to the Commons: Politics live blog"

Note 110: Masaryk University, Czech Republic: Guerrilla Theater: Intersection of political activism and institutional performance (View on Serbia), ispo.fss.muni.cz/uploads/2download/mobsem2010/political_performance. pdf

Note 111: Russia Today, December 25, 2014: "Topless FEMEN activist 'kidnaps' Baby Jesus from Vatican nativity scene"

Note 112: Guardian, Monday 22 December 2014: "Amazonian tribe take initiative to protect their lands from dam project"

Note 113: Guardian, Monday 31 May 2010: "The Gaza Freedom flotilla"

Note 114: Guardian, Tuesday 13 January 2009: "Celebrities buy Heathrow land to delay third runway"

Note 115: CBC News, Oct 19, 2013: "Media vehicle seized by fracking protesters in Rexton"

Note 116: Examples include: Palestinian Solidarity Campaign http://www.palestinecampaign.org, Palestine Online Store http://palestineonlinestore.com/, Shop in Palestine http://www.shopinpalestine.com/

Note 117: Guardian, Wednesday 28 January 2015: "How Seville transformed itself into the cycling capital of southern Europe"

Note 118: Sources: SPINS, The Organic and Non-GMO Report, GM Watch, The Wall Street Journal, Non-GMO Project.

Note 119: Independent, Friday 24 October 2014: "£425,000 compensation payout for woman who unwittingly had baby with undercover police officer"

Note 120: Guardian, Wednesday 14 January 2015: "Last orders for Nigel Farage? Pub Landlord takes on Ukip"

Note 121: "Electoral Guerilla Theatre: Radical Ridicule and Social Movements". L. M. Bogad. New York: Routledge, 2005.

Note 122: Judicial Review, A quick and easy guide, Richard Stein, Leigh Day & Co Solicitors, London, www.leighday.co.uk/LeighDay/media/LeighDay/documents/JR-Quicky-and-Easy-Guide.pdf

Note 123: 2013 November 20, "Spooky Business: Corporate Espionage Against Non-profit Organisations", Gary Ruskin, www.corporatepolicy.org/spookybusiness.pdf

Note 124: 2013, June 4: Guardian: "Turkish protesters using encryption software to evade censors", www.theguardian.com/technology/2013/jun/04/turkish-protesters-encryption-software-evade-censors

Note 125: See "How to send and receive secure, encrypted emails in Thunderbird with PGP", www.katescomment.com/how-to-encrypt-email-pgp-thunderbird/

Note 126: Wikipedia: "Internet censorship and surveillance by country", OpenNet Initiative: "Summarized global Internet filtering data spreadsheet", 8 November 2011 and Reporters without Borders, "Enemies of the Internet", 2014.

Note 127: US-Cert: "Ten Ways to Improve the Security of a New Computer", https://www.us-cert.gov/home-and-business.

Note 128: 2003, March 11, IP Spoofing: An Introduction, Matthew Tanase.

Note 129: 2010, December 9th: Guardian: "WikiLeaks supporters disrupt Visa and MasterCard sites in 'Operation Payback'", www.theguardian.com/world/2010/dec/08/wikileaks-visa-mastercard-operation-payback

Note 130: 2010 December 9th. "Is Operation Payback A Crime...or just the modern equivalent of a sit-in?" www.techdirt.com

Note 131: Guardian, Saturday 14 February 2015: "The fascinating truth behind all those 'great firewall of China' headlines"

Note 132: The Centre for Media and Democracy (CMD): "Front Groups", http://www.sourcewatch.org/index.php/Front_groups

Note 133: Detekt is being launched by Amnesty in partnership with Digitale Gesellschaft, Electronic Frontier Foundation and Privacy International, Nov. 2014

Note 134: BBC News: 28 January 2011, "Egypt protests escalate in Cairo, Suez and other cities"

---o0o---

9. The Future of Civil Rebellion

9.1 Is Activism Dead?

There are many who claim that since the 1970's political activism has declined. We are told that today's students and teenagers are too comfortable, too selfish and too preoccupied by having fun and social networking to be engaged in real political activism. But the facts don't support this argument.

Let us take a look at internet activism, for instance, which is an arena where younger people feel comfortable to be politically active:

• There has been an explosion in the number of e-petition sites used to build petitions and collect signatures to support a huge variety of issues ranging from poor government services to climate change. In scale these petitions may be small local protests right up to large, global campaigns. E-petitions are so popular now that they have almost become an alternative form of referendum in some countries. They are often closely watched by governments and other authorities as a means of gauging the mood of the public. This is so much so that some governments (the UK for instance) are actually attempting to run their own e-petition websites to try to pre-empt these independent activist sites.

• There has been a huge makeover of activist organisations as they have moved from conventional protest to forming networks on the internet. Greenpeace is a case in point. It has transformed its communications using the internet to deliver news, find members, recruit supporters and to join in protests and organise physical actions. Many new activist organisations have also emerged and some have had a surprising degree of success. For instance, internet activist organisation Avaaz, founded in 2007 now boasts over 40 million members, has gathered over \$20 million dollars in donations from these members in just two years, from 2009 to 2011. It has fronted numerous online petitions and internet campaigns on a wide range of subjects, affecting human and civil rights, anti-corruption protests and the environment.

• The role played by social media in the Hong Kong protests, the Arab Spring movements, the recent Turkish demonstrations, the "Occupy movement", the Spanish, Greek and Portuguese political movements such as "15M" and the "Indignados" demonstrations, shows us that activism has modernised itself and is now firmly based around internet technology.

- The filming and internet broadcasting of acts of police murder and brutality in both Europe and the United States has shocked and angered millions. Again these documentaries are the work of individuals, transformed momentarily into activists, using the readily available communications and internet technology to get the truth out to the world.

These few examples serve to illustrate that activism is indeed alive and well, albeit now communicating and networking via the internet.

9.2 Apathy has Always Been With Us

Certainly there is still a largish group of selfish, politically and morally neutral "couch potatoes" in all societies. Such people know nothing of the world outside of their mediocre, self-centred lives and care less for the rest of the human race or the future of the planet. But these types of people have always been with us. Take a look at the attitudes of the general public in Britain in the early 20th century during the suffragette struggle to allow women to vote in elections. There was open antagonism to the suffragettes amongst the general public, which ranged right up to outright aggression, including amongst many ordinary women. This antagonism even led to acts of violence by members of the public against peacefully demonstrating suffragettes.

Until the world is ridded of fear, ignorance and apathy, alas, we will always have such asocial elements in all societies.

9.3 The Future of Civil Rebellion

Civil rebellion prospers when government fails. The more dysfunctional a regime, the more careless of the interests of its people, the more abusive of power, the more corrupt and the more self-interested a government, the more the anger of the people turns to acts of rebellion. When the speaking stops and the regime no longer listen, then the resistance begins. These are basic realities that are part of the political DNA of the human race and have not changed since the beginnings of civilisation. Fundamentally nothing has changed in the rules of engagement between authority and its subjects. All that changes is the quality, integrity and intelligence of our governments which, it appears, is largely a matter of chance.

Governments may be under the impression that they can buy off political disenchantment with jobs and a bit of money for the masses, and that this will somehow keep the lid on political rebellion. The Romans, in their famous "bread and circuses" policies, tried to use the same strategy to control the political ambitions of their people. Whilst having a temporary palliative effect, neither the free bread nor the Roman circuses could stop the decline and collapse of the empire. Excluding a population from participation in government is tantamount to declaring war on one's own citizens, and the outcome is always the same: the government eventually loses.

Some have argued that democratic societies are so well-developed today that no citizen need feel disenfranchised or excluded. In theory this should be true. In modern Western democracies there are theoretical checks and balances to control the excesses of government and allow communication between citizen and government. In reality, these democratic mechanisms are bypassed or circumvented by authoritarian politicians and officials that see such controls as an inconvenience rather than a constitutional right.

The impact of big money in democratic systems is totally corrupting. Political power no longer represents a way of serving society, but rather a way of serving oneself by looking after one's friends in the business community. Democratic government has now largely morphed into a way of facilitating capitalist ventures at the expense of the electorate. The electorate are valued now only as an indentured source of cheap labour or as gullible consumers of commodities they mostly don't want or need. Thus, whilst we may have our bread and circuses, the quality of our lives, the security of our future and that of our children, and our sense of belonging to a society has been ground under the heels of profiteering big business with the collaboration of political elites that don't even know we exist, except at election time. It's a sorry state of affairs.

It would be delightful to report that our political maturity had advanced to a point where we all felt part of our own self-government, where we felt listened to, where decisions were taken for the greater good and where universal human rights of the whole human family were paramount. But this is not the case, and we seem to be condemned to a roller coaster of dynastic swings between more liberal governments followed by various forms of authoritarian fascism. As long as this situation remains, there will always be a role for civil rebellion.

---oOo---

Glossary of Terms

Here we provide a glossary of relevant terms and some basic definitions related to civil disobedience:

Activist: An activist is a person who campaigns for some kind of social or political change. Someone who is actively involved in a protest or a political or social cause can be called an activist. Demonstrations, strikes, and sit-ins are all ways in which an activist works towards change. Someone who acts on what they believe is an activist.

Authority: Authority is the political power that derives from a social accord or convention, for example the laws or customs of a social group such as a state or an organisation, for instance a company. An authority has the power to give orders and make decisions; it has the power or right to direct or control someone or something. Orders are implemented by others through cooperation or obedience. An authority is the centre of control of state coercion via its military and police forces.

Authoritative: The word authoritative refers to the quality of leadership which enables the judgments, decisions, recommendations and orders of certain individuals and institutions to be accepted voluntarily or involuntarily, whether they are seen as prudent or wise or not.

Authoritarianism: Authoritarianism is rarely based on any ideology and authoritarian regimes are often driven by corruption, personal gain and the self-aggrandisement of a leader. In an authoritarian regime social and economic institutions exist that are not necessarily under governmental control. Bereft of ideology, authoritarianism lacks any moral high ground to control officials and has to rely on violence and bribery to maintain rule. Many authoritarian regimes descend into kleptocracy, tending to subvert the social contract by their vested interests and how they characterise behaviour of citizens and authority. For instance, when the regime is repressive and violent, this is "to preserve law and order". When the civil population attempts to defend itself, they are classed as "subversive and terrorist". Democracies can display authoritarian elements. See also totalitarianism for similarities. Authoritarianism differs from totalitarianism.

Barbarism: This is a characteristic of a cultural level more complex than primitive savagery, but less advanced than civilisation. It is marked by cruelty and lack of restraint. It is backward and lacks subtlety and humanity.

Capitalism: Capitalism is an economic system based on private ownership of wealth and the free and unfettered operation of trade markets. Capital is usually understood to be money that is put into a business, accumulated by a business, or used in some way to produce more money. In a capitalist economy, capital is owned by private individuals, as opposed to the state. Another important aspect of capitalism is the idea of a "free market," where, in capitalist theory, natural competition always leads to innovation and price controls. This market balance is a highly contested principle of capitalism.

Civic Abstention: These are acts by civilians of political non-cooperation with an authority.

Civic Action: These are nonviolent actions by civil society aimed at authority and conducted for political motives.

Civic Defiance: These are assertive acts of nonviolent protest, resistance or intervention, conducted for political purposes.

Civic Resistance: These are acts by civil society of nonviolent resistance with a political objective.

Civil Disobedience: This is a deliberate, peaceful violation of particular laws, decrees, regulations, ordinances, military or police orders. These are usually laws that are regarded as inherently immoral, unjust or tyrannical. Sometimes, laws of a morally neutral character may also be disobeyed as a symbol of opposition to wider policies of the government.

Civil Rebellion (peaceful): This is a group of actions by civilians against their government, which can range from peaceful civil disobedience through protest, civil intervention and direct action against an authority.

Civil War: A civil war is a conflict between groups within a single country. Most wars are fought between different countries. However, in a civil war a country becomes politically divided, and factions within the country battle each other for control of the country and domination of the other faction. Civil wars are much more divisive and painful than other conflicts, primarily because a country in a civil war is engaged in a highly self-destructive exercise with little to gain for either side.

Corruption (Political): Political corruption is the illegitimate use of power by government officials or politicians for private gain, in particular when an act is directly related to their official duties and involves trading in influence.

Coup d'état: A coup d'état is the violent overthrow or alteration of an existing government by a small group. A military coup is executed by a small group of military officers, controlling significant parts of the military, in order to seize control of government. Edward Luttwak, the military historian, defines the process of a coup as follows: "It consists of the infiltration of a small, but critical, segment of the state apparatus, which is then used to displace the government from its control of the remainder" [Note 1]. Bloodless coups are another variant of a coup, where the threat of violence is sufficient to dislodge an incumbent leadership. Coups tend to be fast and decisive changes of government. Slower moving or failed coups may drag a country into civil war.

Consensus: Consensus decision-making is a method by which a group makes decisions together. The group must be unanimous (or almost so, in some forms of consensus decision-making). The process of consensus decision-making seeks to find mutually agreeable solutions which everyone can agree upon, even if it isn't anyone's first choice. One important aspect of consensus decision-making is that, even if it demands compromise, it helps to build solidarity in a divergent group.

Conspiracy: A conspiracy is a secret agreement between two or more people to commit a disruptive, unlawful or harmful act. Conspirators "plot" together to carry out these acts.

Conspiracy theorists: These are people who believe that governments are operating with secret agendas invisible to the general public. Conspiracy theorists may or may not have evidence to substantiate their ideas.

Corporation: A corporation has a very particular legal meaning. It is a company that registers with a state government, so that in some senses it has the same rights and responsibilities as a physical person. Corporations must pay taxes and abide by laws. Being a separate entity, a corporation's failure does not result in its employees and managers being held responsible for its debts.

Democracy: Democracy is a form of government in which people choose leaders by voting. As an electoral method, democracy is an ancient system which has developed many variants over the centuries, using all manner of electoral systems in combination with many other forms of authority, such as monarchies, military juntas, and tribal systems. Democratic elections work on a simple principle that the majority rules. However, democratic systems in some jurisdictions have drifted far from the original ideals and the rules have become highly convoluted; sometimes using electoral colleges rather than simple popular votes. Democracies may also be restrictive in their electorates and only allow those of a certain age, status, sex or citizenship to participate. In modern democracies the system calls for the defence of the human rights of all citizens, active civilian participation in political life and the rule of law equally applied to all citizens. Democracy differs from consensus because democracy's method of decision-making does not demand consensus (a unanimous agreement), but rather a majority in favour of a motion, using some honest voting procedure.

Democratic Deficit: A "democratic deficit" happens when apparently democratic governments fall short of fulfilling the principles of democracy in their practices and where their democratic integrity is called into question.

Discrimination: Discrimination means making a distinction between two or more people or things for personal, emotional, political, moral, economic, aesthetic or social reasons. Usually, discrimination implies an unfair system that treats one group of people with less respect than another, giving rise to unfair treatment of people, based on race, religion, social class, gender, sexual orientation. Discrimination is often used by governments as a means of control.

Elite: In politics and sociology, elite refers to a small group of people who control a disproportionate amount of wealth or political power.

Ethics: Ethics may refer to the study of morality. To be ethical means to be following accepted rules of behaviour: to be morally right and good.

Fascism: Fascism is a political philosophy with totalitarian aspirations. Common definitions of fascism, especially when in power, have included its historical antagonism to socialism and liberalism. Fascism attracts its support primarily from the far-right. Fascism relies on repression of criticism or opposition, and exaltation of the state and/or religion above individual rights. Frequently, fascism centres on a leader cult. It is often based on a close relationship between business and government and control of the market place. Fascism relies philosophically on the exercise of power of the strong over the weak and concepts such as "survival of the fittest" as its moral basis.

Feudalism: This was a method of government and social system in medieval Europe, in which the nobility received land and capital from the Crown in exchange for military service. Vassals were in turn tenants of the nobles, while the peasants (serfs) were obliged to live on their lord's land and give him homage, labour, a share of the produce and occasional military service in exchange for military protection. Whilst feudalism was largely swept aside by the capitalist industrial revolution, many aspects of feudalism continue in Europe. This includes respect for unelected monarchies and a tolerance of landed gentries that give extraordinary land rights to elite families that were granted hundreds of years ago. Feudal attitudes towards the peasantry in these circles continue to this day.

Freedom of Speech: Freedom of speech is the political right to communicate one's opinions and ideas. Some types of speech are restricted in all jurisdictions (libel, obscenity etc.). In this context freedom of speech refers to the ability of citizens to express their political beliefs and their opinions about other political credos, and to comment on the behaviour and attitudes of politicians and government officials.

Insurgency: An insurgency is an armed rebellion against a state authority, with those taking part in the rebellion not recognized as belligerents, i.e. not members of an organised military. Not all rebellions are insurgencies. For instance, civil resistance / civil rebellion may be nonviolent and therefore not considered as an insurgency. All insurgencies contain some element of terrorism (the attempt to create an atmosphere of fear, generally for a political or ideological purpose).

Left-wing: This refers to political views that are usually progressive in nature; they look to the future, and aim to support those who cannot support themselves. People who are left-wing believe in equal distribution of wealth, universal social security, education and health care. They believe in equality, solidarity, the supremacy of human rights and the proper regulation of business, to protect the population whilst maximising and distributing the benefits of economic activity.

Maladministration: Maladministration is action by a government or its appointed officials resulting in some form of injustice. British law, for instance, defines maladministration as including the following acts by government or officials:

- Broken promises
- Delay
- Failure to follow procedures or the law
- Failure to investigate
- Failure to provide information
- Failure to reply
- Inadequate consultation
- Inadequate liaison
- Inadequate record-keeping
- Incorrect action or failure to take any action
- Misleading or inaccurate statements

Manipulation (political): Political manipulation is a form of deceptive social influence that aims to change the perception or behaviour of others. Political manipulation does not rely on discussion or persuasion, but seeks alterations in political attitude or affiliation by using a range of psychological tricks to alter the opinions of the victim. Most political parties engage in various forms of political manipulation. Methods of political manipulation include propaganda, deceit, agenda control, strategic voting, rhetorical manipulation, secrecy, historical manipulation and media manipulation.

Morality: Morality is the distinction between decisions, actions or intentions into those considered good or right and those considered bad or wrong. Morality is based on a body of standards or principles. This in turn is derived from a code of conduct based on a particular ideology, philosophy, cultural values or a religion. Moralities from very different origins often share common basic principles, even when codes of conduct vary quite significantly. Human moralities have many common threads. Thus, many principles of Christianity are shared by socialist morality, for example.

Oppression: Oppression is the exercise of authority or power in a cruel or unjust way. When oppression is used to target a particular group for political or ideological reasons, it is referred to as repression. In some societies oppression becomes systematic, using the police and military to apply the unjust use of coercion and violence to maintain control of a population.

Prejudice: In this context, prejudice refers to unreasonable feelings, opinions or attitudes of a hostile nature in relation to specific sexual orientation, ethnic, racial, gender, social, and religious groups. Prejudice implies prejudgment or the forming of an opinion before knowing the relevant facts of a case. The word is often used to refer to preconceived, usually unfavourable, judgements toward certain stereotyped groups by someone without recourse to much information about or contact with these groups. Prejudice is essentially a sentiment derived from ignorance. It is never derived from knowledge.

Protest(er): A protest is an objection to particular events, situations or policies. Protests can be expressed in words or deeds. Protests take many different forms: from individual statements to mass demonstrations. Sometimes, protesters organise a protest as a way of publicly expressing their opinions so as to influence public opinion or government policy, or both. Protesters sometimes undertake direct action in an attempt to bring about changes directly.

Repression (Political): Political repression is the persecution of an individual or group for political motives with a view to controlling or preventing them from taking part in the political life of a society. Repressive methods include surveillance abuse, police brutality, discrimination causing human rights violations, illegal imprisonment, citizen exile, stripping of citizen's rights, and violent acts of state terror, such as kidnapping, murder, torture, summary execution, forced disappearance and other extrajudicial punishments against dissidents, political activists, or the general population. Where political repression is sanctioned and organised by the state, it may legally constitute state terrorism, genocide, or a crime against humanity. Systemic and violent political repression is a typical feature of dictatorships, totalitarian states and similar regimes. Repressive activities have also been found within democratic regimes.

Revolution: A revolution is a fundamental change in power or organisational structures that takes place in a relatively short period of time. Revolutions may be political, social, technological or cultural. Political revolutions may occur because of a rebellion, a coup d'état, civil war, or a peaceful civil rebellion. Revolutions have occurred through human history. The results of a revolution include major changes in culture, economy, and/or socio-political institutions.

Right-wing: Right-wing beliefs value certain traditions that support old systems of capital distribution, survival of the fittest and economic freedom without regulation. They typically believe that business shouldn't be taxed or controlled and that government should have no role in social protection of the population. Right-wing followers tend to believe that they shouldn't have to contribute economically for someone else's education, social welfare or health services. Right-wing beliefs are centred on the supremacy of the individual rather than a sense of communal solidarity and a guarantee of universal human rights.

Riot: Generally, a riot can be defined as a noisy, potentially violent, public disorder caused by a group of persons in a public place. Riots are characterised by an organised or informal group lashing out in a violent public disturbance against authority, property or people. They often involve vandalism and the destruction of property. Riots occur as a reaction to specific grievances or a popular dissent. In the past, grievances have included poor working or living conditions, unfair taxation, economic austerity, oppression, conscription, conflicts between ethnic groups, political corruption, or legal frustration. Politically motivated riots tend to happen because people feel abused. They may precede more generalised revolutionary events, such as a full-scale insurgency. Riots often result from intractable authorities implementing draconian measures or refusing to negotiate with civilian protest groups. They can also happen as a result of protester frustration and can be taken as an early signal to authority that nonviolent protests are evolving into violent insurrection unless action is taken.

Ruling Classes: The phrase ruling class is a politically charged one since it implies that some classes rule and some do not. However, the sentiment is a reasonable one since the reality is that most parts of the world have their "ruling classes". A "ruling class" is the social class within a given society that decides upon and sets that society's political policy by mandating that there is only one such particular class in the given society, and they are that class. In some societies the ruling class is also the "upper class", which may be a group of aristocrats or businessmen who control the most material wealth and exert widespread influence over the other classes. The "ruling classes" choose to actively exercise power to shape the direction of a locality, a country, and/or the world. A society ruled solely by such an elite is referred to as an oligarchy.

Social Contract: In political philosophy, the phrase social contract refers to a political model, originating in the 17th and 18th century, that deals with the questions of the legitimacy of the authority of the state over the individual. The idea of a social contract is based on the concept that individuals have consented to surrender some of their freedoms and submit to the authority of the state (or to the decision of a majority of its people), in exchange for protection of their remaining rights. The idea of a social contract is riddled with problems. It implies that we have agreed to our part in the contract and have given active consent to be governed as we are. In fact, we find ourselves governed in a certain way simply because of an accident of birth and this has nothing to do with our consent to any social contract. Nonetheless, the model of a social contract can describe the relationship between authority and subject in terms of rights and responsibilities. A social contract implies a stable relationship between authority and subject, as distinct from a "social conflict" where the social contract has been breached.

Socialism: Socialism is a social and economic system based on social ownership of the means of production and the co-operative management of the economy. Socialism is predicated on democratic control in which everybody has the right to participate in the social decisions that affect their society. Economically, production under socialism is solely for use (not for profit or speculation). With the natural and technical resources of the world held communally and controlled democratically, the sole object of production is to meet human needs. This makes the concepts of buying, selling and money redundant. Instead, a socialist society offers all that is communally produced freely to all citizens, "each according to his needs". Central to the meaning of socialism is common ownership, which means that all the resources of the nation are effectively owned in common by the entire population.

Terrorism: There has been no officially recognised definition of terrorism thus far, but the Centre for European Security Studies proposed this definition: "Terrorism is defined as political violence in an asymmetrical conflict that is designed to induce terror and psychic fear (sometimes indiscriminate) through the violent victimisation and destruction of non-combatant targets (sometimes iconic symbols). Such acts are meant to send a message from an illicit clandestine organisation. The purpose of terrorism is to exploit the media in order to achieve maximum attainable publicity as an amplifying force multiplier in order to influence the targeted audience(s) in order to reach short- and midterm political goals and/or desired long-term end states. This definition avoids the concept of state terrorism, which is the terrorisation of a population by a government. The misuse of the word "terrorist" in recent years has led it to be used almost interchangeably with the word "dissenter" and it is casually applied to anyone who doesn't agree with a particular government.

Totalitarianism: Totalitarianism is a political system wherein the state holds complete authority over society and seeks to control all aspects of public and private life. It is the absolute domination of a state's citizens through the forceful imposition and maintenance of an ideologically-based political regime using armed violence. Totalitarian regimes are based on the complete subordination of the individual to the state and strict control of all coercive measures such as censorship and state terrorism. It is the political concept that the citizen should be totally subject to absolute state authority. Totalitarian leaders are often charismatic and regimes are often based on quasi moral concepts such as "saving the nation from its enemies". Totalitarian leaders may see their role as part of a longer dynasty of national saviours. Adolf Hitler and Stalin saw themselves in this light, despite their very different political views. Totalitarianism is inherently fascistic because it relies on the imposition of the power of the strong over the will of the weak, based on ideological supremacy using coercion and violence.

Vandalism: Vandalism is the deliberate destruction or spoiling of property. The term includes criminal damage such as graffiti and defacement directed towards any property without permission of the owner. It is often used specifically for acts of destruction against objects of artistic and architectural beauty. Politically, it extends from attacks on political symbols all the way to physical attacks on property, such as banks, shops, political offices, and government buildings.

---oOo---

Index

---oOo---

About the author and editor

Malcolm Coxall, the author, is a management consultant and systems analyst with more than 30 years experience. Starting with a career in industrial dispute arbitration for the International Labour Organisation, Malcolm later became a free-lance systems consultant, working in mainland Europe and the Middle East.

With experience working for many of the world's largest corporate and institutional players, as well as several government agencies Malcolm has acquired a ringside view of the human, organisational and management methodologies used by medium and large businesses in industries as diverse as banking, oil, defence, telecoms, manufacturing, mining, food, agriculture, aerospace, textiles and engineering.

Malcolm has published articles on political manipulation, sustainable agriculture, organic food production, forest biodiversity, environmental protection and environmental economics. Malcolm is the author of "Machiavellian Management - A Chief Executive's Guide" and of a series of textbooks dealing with relational database design ("Oracle Quick Guides"). He is active in European environmental politics and was the successful private complainant in the European Court of Justice in several cases of national breaches of European environmental law. He now lives in southern Spain from where he continues his consultancy work and writing, whilst managing the family's organic farm.

Guy Caswell, the editor, was born in Southampton, UK in 1955. He spent his formative years in Nigeria and worked in various jobs in England before leaving for Thailand in 1992, where he divides his time between teaching English in Bangkok and the family farm in the north-east of Thailand.

Guy graduated from Ramkhamhaeng University majoring in Thai language. As an English tutor, Guy claims to have the longest serving student in the world, a prominent Thai politician whom he has tutored in English continuously for 17 years. Guy's interests include politics, farming, playing guitar and Thai culture.

---oOo---